Societal Impacts on Information Systems Development and Applications

John Wang
Montclair State University, USA

Managing Director:	Lindsay Johnston
Senior Editorial Director:	Heather A. Probst
Book Production Manager:	Sean Woznicki
Development Manager:	Joel Gamon
Acquisitions Editor:	Erika Gallagher
Typesetter:	Jennifer Romanchak
Cover Design:	Nick Newcomer, Lisandro Gonzalez

Published in the United States of America by
Information Science Reference (an imprint of IGI Global)
701 E. Chocolate Avenue
Hershey PA 17033
Tel: 717-533-8845
Fax: 717-533-8661
E-mail: cust@igi-global.com
Web site: http://www.igi-global.com

Library of Congress Cataloging-in-Publication Data

Societal impacts of information systems development and applications / John Wang, editor.
    p. cm.
  Includes bibliographical references and index.
    ISBN 978-1-4666-0927-3 (hardcover) -- ISBN 978-1-4666-0928-0 (ebook) -- ISBN 978-1-4666-0929-7 (print & perpetual access) 1. Computers--Social aspects. 2. Computers and civilization. 3. Information technology--Social aspects. I. Wang, John, 1955-
  QA76.9.C66S628 2012
  303.48'34--dc23
                          2012000025

British Cataloguing in Publication Data
A Cataloguing in Publication record for this book is available from the British Library.

Table of Contents

Section 2
Systems and Management

Section 3
Modelling and Simulation

Section 4
Managing Databases of the Future

Section 5
Supporting Critical Decisions

Detailed Table of Contents

Section 1
Emerging Technologies and Economies

The Internet has changed the world in many ways. Online communications, financial and business-to-business transactions, electronic shopping, banking, and entertainment have become the norm in the digital age. The combined package of technologies that comprise the Internet—the information super-highway—have made all of this possible. The aging technological infrastructure that supports these webs of interconnected networks is being stressed to its performance limits. Recent advances in the backbone infrastructure that supports the Internet have helped alleviate some of these problems, but more challenges lie ahead for solving technology-related performance bottlenecks for many online applications, including high-definition interactive gaming. In this paper, the authors developed a technology assessment through multiple perspectives. While different components of the technology such as applications, protocols and network components are identified, other impact areas such as market and management are also evaluated. Elements of user behavior are evaluated within the market perspective. Evaluating technologies through these dimensions concurrently provides a balanced assessment among technical, economical, social and political factors.

Personal computers contribute significantly to the growing problem of electronic waste. Every computer, when finished with, must be stored, dumped, recycled, or somehow re-used. Most are dumped, at a huge cost to health and the environment, as their owners succumb to the desire to keep up with the ever-increasing power of new computers. Supercomputers and computer clusters provide more power than ordinary desktop and laptop computers, but they too are subject to rapid obsolescence. The authors have built a cluster of obsolete computers and have found that it easily outperforms a fairly standard new desktop computer. They explore how this approach can help to mitigate e-waste, and discuss the advantages and limitations of using such a system.

Development of the search engine as a major information and marketing channel resulted from innovative technologies that made it capable of presenting rapid, relevant responses to queries. To do this, the search engine compiles an index of web pages of information stored on the World Wide Web, ranks each page according to its incoming links, matches keywords in the query to those in its index, and returns what it determines are the most relevant pages to the searcher. Innovative and cost-effective ad placement algorithms have attracted advertisers to search engine websites and intensified the competitive dynamics among industry leaders. Their interacting software also continues to draw advertisers from traditional, mass marketing channels like television and newspapers to the online medium to cater to customers who have expressed an interest in their products and services.

The rapid development of Geographic Information System (GIS) and Global Position System (GPS) has attracted the attention of both business practitioners and academic researchers. GIS and GPS technologies, through providing optimized schedules, routings, and guidance, are especially important and helpful in transportation and logistics businesses. Though GIS and GPS technologies have been witnessed in many business sectors in developed countries, wide application of these technologies is still in its preliminary phase in companies in developing nations. In this paper, the authors present a study on the application of an integrated intelligent system that consists of GIS, GPS and related technologies to optimize logistic distribution of perishable products in urban environments. Through investigating GIS and GPS usage in a medium-sized logistics company in the unique settings of emerging economies, this paper addresses how these technologies enhance the management of businesses and analyze the interaction of GIS/GPS implementation and several key characteristics of the logistic distribution context by identifying major benefits, challenges, and limitations associated with the use of GIS and GPS.

This paper explores and extends the supply chain management strategy for food products effectively and efficiently through analysis of insights to linked partnerships within the supply chain due to the possibility of a global food crisis. The required solution is a collaboration of all parties in the supply chain since an effective supply chain management strategy (ESCMS) for food products is through proper insight between linked partnerships, including customer satisfaction through service quality, well-defined requirements and expectations, effective and clear communication, mutual relationship management, and close relationships from partnerships. ESCMS for food products must have the strategy of supply-to-stock and supply-to-order (efficient and responsive), effective collaboration within the supply chain, well-defined expectations and requirements, effective communication and information flow, mutual relationship management, and close relationships as partners. This insight of linked partnership throughout the supply chain would contribute by reducing and solving problems such as over supply, inconsistency of price (high and low), global food supply, and the conflict among partnerships, including an increase in the consistency of farmers' careers.

Section 2
Systems and Management

Chapter 6

The author's goal in this study is to investigate factors that impact the success of electronic government. The focus in this study is on several organizational and personal characteristics, including age, tenure, information system (IS) experiences, gender, education level, nationality, training in information system (IS), position, and experience in current job. The study is then applied to Kuwait, and electronic government success is measured using information system usage. The findings indicate that four out of the nine factors impact electronic government success. These four factors are age, IS experiences, education level, and training in IS. The author then examines several research and practical implications.

Chapter 7

DeLone & McLean's success model has been actively used since its first introduction in 1992. In this article, the authors extend this model to describe the success of knowledge sharing in an information system that included a part of the knowledge base of a private educational institute. As the supply of private education is increased, it is vital to be aware if the offered educational services support the use of the knowledge base and if the service is perceived satisfactory by the customers. In this descriptive qualitative case study, the authors discuss how the DeLone & McLean's information system success model can be used to assess educational services when apprenticeships form a salient part of teaching. This paper focuses on issues that interested the target organization.

Chapter 8

Essentialism and social constructionism theories have long explained the difficulties women experience as they aspire to higher managerial positions or enter science and technology fields. In the 1970s, the Women as Managers Scale (WAMS) sought to determine the extent to which males perceived females as being different from their social group. Given efforts to encourage women to consider IT careers and changes in public law and education that have occurred since the early 1970s, this study revisited the WAMS to compare current attitudes of young people toward women as managers. The results suggest that through the intangible individual differences of women, perspective, overtime, via training, by awareness, and with their greater participation in the workplace, there has been gradual improvement in the perception of women as managers by men in the science and technology fields.

Mindfulness is a whole state of being that is not usually linked with academic research in information systems. However if we take Denzin and Lincoln's (2000; 2003), first qualitative research phase, which is the consideration of the key role of the researcher in socially-situated research, it soon becomes evident that a mindful researcher (Fielden, 2005) is more likely to conduct quality research than one who is not. In this discussion paper the qualities of mindfulness (Fielden, 2005) are explored; Denzin and Lincoln's (2003) 5-stage qualitative research process is then mapped onto these multiple characteristics of mindfulness; and also onto a timeline for a typical qualitative research process in information systems. The paper concludes with suggestions on how to include mindful practices in research methods and supervision training in information systems, which is a contribution to the literature in this area.

Section 3
Modelling and Simulation

In this paper, a dynamic network DEA model is developed to evaluate the potential gains in final output from a merger of two firms. The two firms are allowed to have different production technologies or share a common technology. In a beginning period each firm uses period specific inputs to produce a final output and an intermediate output that becomes an input in the production of final outputs in a subsequent period. Firms that merge can use the intermediate input of one firm to produce final output for the other firm, leading to gains in final output for the two merged firms over what the firms could have produced individually. The method is applied to study Japanese cooperative Shinkin banks during 2003 to 2007. Mergers between banks in Nagasaki, Kagoshima, and Miyazaki prefectures tend to have the highest potential gains, while mergers between banks within Fukuoka prefecture and other prefectures and within Saga prefecture tend to have the smallest potential gains.

Heike Knörzer, Universität Hohenheim, Germany
Simone Graeff-Hönninger, Universität Hohenheim, Germany
Bettina U. Müller, Universität Hohenheim, Germany
Hans-Peter Piepho, Universität Hohenheim, Germany
Wilhelm Claupein, Universität Hohenheim, Germany

Interspecific competition between species influences their individual growth and performance. Neighborhood effects become especially important in intercropping systems, and modeling approaches could be a useful tool to simulate plant growth under different environmental conditions to help identify appropriate combinations of different crops while managing competition. This study gives an overview of different competition models and their underlying modeling approaches. To model intercropping in terms of neighbouring effects in the context of field boundary cultivation, a new model approach was developed and integrated into the DSSAT model. The results indicate the possibility of simulating general competition and beneficial effects due to different incoming solar radiation and soil temperature in a winter wheat/maize intercropping system. Considering more than the competition factors is important, that is, sunlight, due to changed solar radiation alone not explaining yield differences in all cases. For example, intercropped maize could compensate low radiation due to its high radiation use efficiency. Wheat benefited from the increased solar radiation, but even more from the increased soil temperature.

Asmeret Bier, Washington State University, USA

Thermal water quality trading markets give point source thermal polluters the option to comply with effluent restrictions by paying nearby landowners to plant shade trees. The shade trees cool the water, offsetting thermal pollution emitted by the point source. Thermal trading has the potential to create greater environmental benefits at a lower cost than traditional regulation, however; only one such program has been implemented to date in the United States. In this regard, a shift in potential stakeholders' perceptions of these markets could be useful in allowing the markets to spread. This paper explains why system dynamics modeling is a useful tool for creating such a shift in perception, and describes a method of teaching participants about thermal trading. The method begins with a classroom simulation exercise, uses lessons from that exercise to create a model of a thermal trading market, and uses that model to conduct policy design and uncertainty analyses.

Allyson M. Beall, Washington State University, USA
Andrew Ford, Washington State University, USA

Since the work of Tansley (1935) and others, many have embraced the concept that an ecosystem is a synergy of its parts. Numerous science-centric approaches have been developed to address ecosystem management, while also taking into account the needs of the public. Participatory environmental modeling using system dynamics is an effective process for facilitating the integration of ecosystem science and social concerns. This integration helps break barriers between disciplines while also identifying important feedbacks between traditionally segregated types of data. Using the art of facilitation and the science of model building, the methodology creates a common language that integrates various types of information into simulation models. This paper describes a diversity of case studies, that have used system dynamics to create platforms through which stakeholders can simultaneously explore their system, stressors to that system, potential tipping points, resilience, and prospective policies that address the environment, social concerns, and long-term sustainability.

Chapter 14

The Keys to the White House are an index-based prediction system that retrospectively account for the popular-vote winners of every US presidential election from 1860 to 1980 and prospectively forecast the winners of every presidential election from 1984 through 2008. The Keys demonstrate that American presidential elections do not turn on events of the campaign, but rather on the performance of the party controlling the White House. The Keys hold important lessons for politics in the United States and worldwide. A preliminary forecast based on the Keys indicates that President Obama is a likely winner in 2012, but also reveals the specific problems at home at abroad that could thwart his re-election.

Section 4
Managing Databases of the Future

Chapter 15

Advances in ecological science and increasing public environmental awareness have resulted in changes in the management of renewable natural resources. To achieve sustainable use of wildlife, managers need reliable data on populations, habitats, and the complexities of ecological interactions. The National Game Management Database (NGMD) was first mandated by the Hungarian Game Management and Hunting Law in 1996. In this paper, the authors summarize the origins, characteristics, development, and results leading to the final establishment of and uses for the NGMD. Goals of the NGMD are to store data on game populations and game management, provide input to spatial analyses and mapping, and to facilitate decision-making and planning efforts of game management administration. It contains information on the populations of game species, data from annual game management reports, trophy-scoring data, maximum allowed and minimum huntable population size, and maps and long-term game management plans for each GMU and the 24 game management regions. In Hungary, the NGMD was the first operating database in wildlife management and nature conservation providing full GIS capabilities, supporting geographical analyses.

Chapter 16

Healthcare IT and IS departments have the arduous task of managing the varied information sources into readily accessible, consistent and referential information views. Patient hospital workflows, from admission to discharge, provide a series of data streams for convergences into disparate systems. Protocols such as DICOM and HL7 exist for the purposes of exchanging information within the PACS and RIS information silos in the hospital enterprise. These protocols ensure data confidence for downstream systems, but are not designed to provide referential data cross system in the system-of-systems model. As data crosses the PACS and RIS information domains, data inconsistency is introduced. This paper explores the causes for data disparity and presents a referential data design for disparate systems through the implementation of an XML bus for data exchange and an RDF framework for data semantic.

Section 5
Supporting Critical Decisions

Land-use planning and environmental management often requires an implementation of both geo- spatial information analysis and value-driven criteria within the decision-making process. DECERNS (Decision Evaluation in Complex Risk Network Systems) is a web-based distributed decision support system for multi-criteria analysis of a wide range of spatially-explicit land management alternatives. It integrates mainly basic and some advanced GIS functions and implements several Multi-Criteria Decision Analysis (MCDA) methods and tools. DECERNS can also be integrated with a model server containing generic and site specific models for in-depth analysis of project and environmental risks as well as other decision criteria under consideration. This paper provides an overview of the modeling approaches as well as methods and tools used in DECERNS. Application of the DECERNS WebSDSS (Web-based Spatial Decision Support System) for a housing site selection case study is presented.

Chapter 18

An Agricultural Decision Support System for Optimal Land Use Regarding Groundwater
Vulnerability 274

Konstantinos Voudouris, Aristotle University, Greece
Maurizio Polemio, CNR-IRPI, Italy
Nerantzis Kazakis, Aristotle University, Greece
Angelo Sifaleras, University of Macedonia, Greece

The availability of quality water is a basic condition of socioeconomic development. The agriculture water demand can be damaged by contamination of groundwater resources. This paper proposes a tool to preserve groundwater quality by using groundwater vulnerability assessment methods and a decision support system (DSS). The mapping of intrinsic groundwater vulnerability was based on reliable methods, the DRASTIC and the SINTACS methods. A DSS was developed to assess the groundwater vulnerability and pollution risk due to agricultural activities and land use changes. The proposed DSS software package was designed using the Matlab language and efficiently performs tasks while incorporating new maps to cover new areas. The tool was tested at two study areas located in the Mediterranean that are dominated by different prevalent hydrogeological features, that is, the typical porous features of alluvial deposits in the Greek study area and the typical fissured and karstic features of limestones and dolostones in the Italian study area.

Chapter 19

Verification of a Rational Combination Approach for Agricultural Drought Assessment: A Case Study
Over Indo-Gangetic Plains in India 287

N. Subash, ICAR Research Complex for Eastern Region, India
H. S. Ram Mohan, Cochin University of Science and Technology, India

Agricultural Drought is characterized by a deficient supply of moisture, resulting either from sub-normal rainfall, erratic rainfall distribution, or higher water with respect to a crop. In spite of technological developments in providing improved crop varieties and better management practices, in India, agriculture has been considered a gamble due to higher spatial and temporal variability. The Rice-Wheat (RW) system is the major cropping system of the Indo-Gangetic Plains (IGP) in India and occupies 10 million hectares. In this paper, the authors have examined the possibility of rationally combining the rainfall anomaly index, a weather based index and an agriculture index based on the Crop Growth Simulation Model for a rice-wheat productivity assessment in selected sites of IGP in India. The district average yields of rice varied from 0.9 t/ha at Samastipur to 3.8 t/ha at Ludhiana. Rice yields decreased from the west to east IGP, and farmers in the western IGP harvested more rice-wheat than those in the eastern regions. The productivity gap showed that all the sites were produced only 50% of the potential in RW system productivity during the triennium ending period 2005. This paper may help researchers and planners to take appropriate measures for improving productivity.

Chapter 20

Hedonic pricing is an indirect valuation method that applies to heterogeneous goods investigating the relationship between the prices of tradable goods and their attributes. It can be used to measure the value of irrigation water through the estimation of the model that describes the relation between the market value of the land parcels and its characteristics. Because many of the land parcels included in a hedonic pricing model are spatial in nature, the conventional regression analysis fails to incorporate all the available information. Spatial regression models can achieve more efficient estimates because they are designed to deal with the spatial dependence of the data. In this paper, the authors present the results of an application of the hedonic pricing method on irrigation water valuation obtained using a software tool that is developed for the ArcGIS environment. This tool incorporates, in the GIS application, the estimation of two different spatial regression models, the spatial lag model and the spatial error model. It also has the option for different specifications of the spatial weights matrix, giving the researcher the opportunity to examine how it affects the overall performance of the model.

Preface

SOCIETAL IMPACTS ON INFORMATION SYSTEMS DEVELOPMENT AND APPLICATIONS

"Societal Impacts on Information Systems Development and Applications" belongs to *Advances in Information Systems and Social Change series* book project. There are five sections and 20 chapters in this book.

EMERGING TECHNOLOGIES AND ECONOMIES

Section one consists of five chapters. In Chapter 1, Ramin Neshati and Tugrul U. Daim present "Multidimensional Assessment of Emerging Technologies: Case of Next Generation Internet and Online Gaming Application." The origin of the Internet can be traced to the intercommunications of many computers over several networks. One of the first of these networks was the ARPAnet, developed by the Defense Advanced Research Projects Agency (DARPA). It was used by governments and universities and these institutions soon began to outgrow its capabilities. They realized the need for a network that would better support high-performance network applications. In response to these technology needs, the US government launched an initiative called Next Generation Internet (NGI), intended to examine performance and bandwidth bottlenecks. By the early 1990s the Internet had been embraced as the most desired medium of communications by government, research, and academic institutions, and more importantly, by a plethora of commercial and computing users worldwide.

With the more recent growth in the number of users, particularly as the populations of China and India migrated to online platforms, the issue of Internet performance reflected a new importance and urgency. Furthermore, new high-definition content on the Web meant that the amount of information being placed on the networks was also growing exponentially. The Internet, in its present form, cannot scale to meet the number and nature of performance demands already placed on it, to say nothing of a new generation of more complex interactions. The increasing demand for content-rich media, for example high-definition entertainment—from downloadable movies to interactive games and other such content—is straining current network capacities, resulting in poor user experiences. These and emerging new applications will demand much higher bandwidth and performance than is available today. Some of these applications include real-time interactive gaming, collaborative grid computing and so on. New technologies and architectures are needed to scale the existing uses to a broader community of users worldwide, and to facilitate new, sophisticated applications that require expansive computation with fast real-time response.

This chapter explores three focus areas: applications, protocols, and network components. The diffusion of Internet technologies follows the characteristics of a central diffusion system. In such a system, national governments and technical subject-matter experts hold sway in technology definition, adoption, and replacement decisions. Although there are many counter examples where technologies diffuse in an ad-hoc manner without any central authority or control, by-and-large, the technologies that pertain to the backbone of the Internet infrastructure (such as routing and switching) follow the centralized model. The sources of technological innovation in such a system stem from formal research and development projects with the direction of the diffusion being top-down, from experts to the masses. The needs of end-users, and in the context of the online gaming community, are generally met as innovations become available and cannot be ameliorated through regional or local technology solutions. Online gamers are at the mercy of Internet administrators and technical subject-matter experts for viable roadmaps of technologies to solve their performance and bandwidth bottlenecks. These conditions are currently defining this digital landscape and are anticipated to remain in the foreseeable future.

In Chapter 2, Timothy M. Lynar, Simon, Ric D. Herbert, and William J. Chivers urge "Clustering Obsolete Computers to Reduce E-Waste." Information Systems almost invariably involve the use of electronic equipment, and thus contribute to the growing problem of electronic waste. Computer hardware just a few years old is discarded, put into indefinite storage, or sent to developing countries for scrapping in a manner that is hazardous both to the environment and to the health of the people employed in the scrapping process. Lynar *et al.* have devised a novel approach to mitigating this problem. Computing-intensive applications tend to be carried out on either a supercomputer or a cluster of ordinary desktop computers. Many institutions and organisations opt for a cluster because the cost of a supercomputer is prohibitive; unfortunately, a cluster requires significantly more hardware than a supercomputer, so its environmental cost is far higher at both ends of its life cycle: manufacturing and disposal. Lynar and his colleagues have built a cluster using obsolete computers destined for the scrapheap, thereby reducing the introduction of new machines.

This research shows that this cluster outperforms a standard new desktop computer, and they conclude that it can be expanded to perform as well as a smaller cluster of new computers. The computers in their cluster will eventually become scrap, but prolonging their life in this way offers a slight reduction in the number of new computers that must be manufactured, and so helps to diminish the very real problem of electronic waste. Furthermore, as the computers in the cluster reach the end of this second life and become truly unusable, they can be replaced with newer scrap computers, allowing the cluster to continue indefinitely without ever requiring the manufacture of a single computer. In addition to the environmental benefits that follow from their use of obsolete computers, there are financial benefits as well: in using donated waste hardware and open source software, they have constructed their cluster for the cost of no more than a few days of labour. Lynar and his colleagues do not suggest that everyone contemplating the purchase of new computer should instead build a cluster of old computers; but they do encourage others to follow their example either when planning intensive computation or when building a cluster for educational use.

Chapter 3, entitled "The Search Engine as an Internet Service Channel," was written by Leslie S. Hiraoka. In July 2009, search engines responded to 113 billion queries by presenting ranked, hyperlinked sources of information that resided on the WWW. This represented a 41% increase in search usage that began when the WWW's system and software were released in 1992. With the exponential expansion of the Web, considerable expertise was needed for locating, retrieving, and indexing the text and data on the WWW that enabled the search engine to respond quickly with relevant sources of information to users of its service. Because of the vast amount of information in their indexes, search providers use various algorithms to present information that is relevant and fits the needs of the information seeker. If they fail in this effort, the user can easily transfer her search to another provider. Feedback is consequently immediate and to hold on to customers, search engines are under considerable pressure to make their service is differentiated and easy to use with rapid response times which ultimately yield useful information to the users.

When search results are presented, they are often accompanied by advertisements that are related to the topic being searched, making the search process more of an interactive marketing experience. Such ads are the principal source of income for the search companies and they compete for advertisers by assisting in the design of ads which are placed close to search results for viewing by users who had expressed an interest in a particular ad's product or service. Online ad revenues for Google, the leading U.S. and world's engine, reached $23 billion in 2009 and because the market is expanding, the competition among the providers for innovative retrieval, search presentation, and ad placement software has intensified. Furthermore, competition from social networking firms like Facebook has emerged as their revenues are also strongly tied to online ads. The search competition is also going global with the emergence of Baidu.com as the largest search provider in China, the nation with the largest Internet usage.

The growth of the global Internet and accompanying World Wide Web paralleled the globalization of business with the rise of the emerging markets known collectively as the BRIC's that stands for Brazil, Russia, India, and China. The offshore outsourcing of work and jobs as well as direct foreign investments abroad were, subsequently, made by multinational firms from mature economies like the United States as well as western European countries. These events became a major concern of policy makers in Washington, D.C. In contrast, the analysis and findings in this chapter clearly indicate that U.S. high-tech firms and start-ups are maintaining and in many cases strengthening their lead in Information Technology and related fields like software development, networking, and digital, mobile devices. For example, Google's developments of its PageRank, AdWords, and AdSense programs have become defining outcomes of R&D efforts in Silicon Valley. Such results are analysed in the author's book, *Underwriting the Internet: How technical advances, financial engineering, and entrepreneurial genius are building the information highway,* which was published in 2005 and provided the basis for not only this chapter but its sequel "The evolution of indigenous search engines in emerging and advanced economies" which takes the global competition in search to foreign countries, especially China. Google's efforts there encountered considerable obstacles from the government and it closed its Beijing search operations. The U.S. government responded with the Internet Freedom speech of Secretary of State Hillary Clinton, which elevated the commercial competition to a bilateral governmental level with both the United States and China clearly articulating their very strong concerns and interests in this critical IT field.

In Chapter 4, "GIS and GPS Applications in Emerging Economies: Observation and Analysis of a Chinese Logistics Firm," Bin Zhou, Jeffrey Hsu, and Yawei Wang address an important yet less focused research area: applications of Geographic Information System (GIS) and Global Position System (GPS) in emerging economies. The rapid increase in the development of GIS and GPS in recent years has attracted the attention of both business practitioners and academic researchers. GIS and GPS technologies, through providing optimized schedules, routings, and guidance, are especially important and helpful in transportation and logistics businesses. Though GIS and GPS technologies have been witnessed and used in many business sectors in developed countries, wide application of these technologies is still in its preliminary phase in companies in developing nations and there is little existing research on such topics. To fill the void of this interesting and important area, the authors presented an in-depth study on the current GIS and GPS applications in logistics companies in China.

Through a case study, they investigated implementation issues associated with GIS and GPS technologies from both technological and organizational perspectives. Impressively, the study contributed rich information about GIS/GPS usage and provided valuable findings that facilitate a deeper understanding of the benefits of GIS and GPS technologies in logistic operations. In addition, the authors provide analysis as to why these benefits exist. This study highlights the potential of GIS and GPS related technologies for enhancing operating efficiency and productivity, improving communications and relationship building, and facilitating collaboration and strategic planning of a firm. Further, major challenges and limitations that the firm has to face while implementing GIS and GPS technologies in its daily logistic operation were identified and discussed. These challenges and limitations are comprised of some key characteristics that are common to small and medium-sized firms in developing countries. For instance, the study pointed out that accuracy issues, lack of technological maintenance, and updates for existing GIS and GPS software continue to plague the development and competitiveness of these technologies in developing markets. Moreover, insufficient support from related organizations, and isolation of the GIS database from other key functions, such as customer service, are also contributing factors that hinder the effective application of these technologies. The authors also provided several critical managerial insights based upon their findings. For example, they concluded that effective connectivity between GIS databases and other key functions are important and that necessary links and external support from related organizations should be established. Finally, the authors assert that GIS and GPS technologies should be encouraged in all business areas within the firm.

"Effective Supply Chain Management Strategy for Food Products: An Insight to Linked Partnerships" is the last chapter of section one. Witaya Krajaysri explores supply chain management strategy for food products through the analysis of partnership linkages from the context of a possible global food crisis. The required solution in today's global food marketplace should include collaboration between all parties within the supply chain. Since an effective supply chain management strategy (ESCMS) for food products results, in part, from effective partnerships, including customer satisfaction, effective and transparent communication And relationship management. ESCMS for food products should possess, as part of its core strategy, the capacity for supply-to-stock and supply-to-order responsiveness, effective collaboration within the supply chain, well-defined expectations and requirements, and consistent information flow, the focus of relationship management as a function of the supply chain can address critical issues such as oversupply, price-point divergence, storage, distribution and inputs.

SYSTEMS AND MANAGEMENT

Section two involves four chapters. In Chapter 6, Helaiel Almutairi identifies "Factors Impacting the Success of Electronic Government: A Micro Level and a Back Office View." In this chapter, Almutairi examines the emergent global phenomenon known as electronic government. More specifically, he investigates factors impacting the success of electronic government activities. The importance of this topic results, in part, from the huge public resources invested in electronic government projects and, as noted in the chapter from the high failure rate of electronic projects developing countries. In a world where public entities, governments, regulatory agencies, NGOs, et cetera are increasing their influence over broad spheres of governance, possessing the capacity and infrastructure to enhance managerial and decision making capacities of these entities can potentially result in much needed transparency and effectiveness.

Almuntairi's contribution to this issue emerges most clearly in his recognition of the long-term potential of more effective governance as a result of electronic government projects. In part this requires an understanding of some of the antecedent factors that impact the efficacy of electronic government projects. In addressing this issue, Almuntairi recants the value of adopting a more holistic view. Factors and interrelationships within a public policy/governance context may be identifiable.

Toward this end, Almutairi conducted a comprehensive review of two bodies of literature; one related to e-gov success and the other related Information System success factors. The fragmentation of both literatures has led the author to develop a categorization sigma using existing Information System models. In doing so, the Almutairi has visibly contributed to enhancing the logical order and the robustness of the literature related to e-gov success and in identifying future areas for research.

The author focused his efforts in developing success factors that are related to e-gov back office operations, considered a new trend in egov literature. This literature defines e-gov as a fundamental re-design of internal work processes and as part of the broader reconsideration as to how work is conducted within governments. In this context, Almutairi proposes a model for e-gov success that includes including content management system that captures critical characteristics such as: age, tenure, Information System experience, gender, educational level, nationality, training in Information System, position, and experience in current job. Contrary to most studies in the e-gov success literature, the author focuses mainly on factors related to the back office activities. The model was applied to Kuwaiti e-gov project and Information System usage was used as a measure for e-gov success. Almutairi found that four of the proposed nine factors directly impacted their e-gov success. These factors include: age, Information System experiences, education level, and training in Information System. Almutairi, then, examined several research and practical implications. This chapter represents a great place to begin understanding the long-term potential electronic governance activities.

In Chapter 7, Raija Halonen, Heli Thomander, and Elisa Laukkanen establish "DeLone & McLean IS Success Model in Evaluating Knowledge Transfer in a Virtual Learning Environment." Dr. Raija Halonen and her co-authors introduced an interesting study in which they applied the well-known IS success model developed by McLean and DeLone to assess Information Systems in a private educational enterprise. In their study, they analysed the success of knowledge sharing in a virtual learning environment, not unlike environments that are increasingly utilized as primary platforms for educational transfer. Contrary to the main usage of the McLean and DeLone IS success model, the authors utilised the model as a descriptive tool.

The empirical research material was collected in a mid-size private academy where the role of its virtual learning environment was significant. The usability and success of the virtual environment was crucial for the academy. However, due to the distance teaching protocols, it was challenging to receive significant response from the students. Previous studies have affirmed the easy of collecting data from students in a face to face environment in contrast to synchronous or asynchronous modalities. In addition to the descriptive use of the IS success model, the study emphasised the importance of apprenticeships in teaching. In apprenticeships, the students must express their explicit as well as their tacit knowledge.

Halonen and her co-authors were able to describe how knowledge was transferred with the help of the virtual learning environment. Their results have been thoroughly reviewed among researchers from around the world. In addition to verifying the usability of the learning environment, their study also revealed some of the challenges to improving the integration between a virtual learning environments and critical emergent research streams on learning transfer.

In Chapter 8, Gary Hackbarth, Kevin E. Dow, Hongmei Wang, and W. Roy Johnson analyse "Changing Attitudes toward Women IT Managers." This is an interesting chapter that addresses whether attitudes toward women as managers have changed over time? The authors surveyed U.S. business students who were soon to graduate and found, perhaps surprisingly, that men's attitudes had improved whereas women's attitudes toward women managers had remained relatively unchanged since the WAMS instrument was originally used in 1975. Further, they found in a review of previous surveys that men's views toward women as managers had been improving over time though important cultural distinctions were evident when the survey was used in other countries. This comprehensive review of all WAMs studies provided a historical context in which to judge their results and raises several possibilities for future research.

The authors began this chapter with the intent to learn more about why women are not staying in the Information Technology (IT) and Information Systems (IS) fields long enough to be promoted to senior leadership positions. They chose existing survey instrument that had been validated and used as a measurement tool reflecting several decades of research. As a result of evolving societal mores, wide swings as to perceptions of traditional gender roles and the emergence of many senior executive women in companies from Xeroz, HP, and IBM, it's difficult to reconcile the many inconsistencies reflected in the data on this important issues. This chapter represents a great starting point on these and similar questions.

The authors also brought to light some of the issues pertaining to using the same instrument over several decades. Statistically, it is desirable to use exactly the same instrument to measure the same things – yet over long periods of time, the meaning of words, translation of words into different languages, situation analysis, cultural perceptions, et cetera, may change thus affecting the construct validity of the instrument. For instance, the survey instrument seeks opinion data about women's issues including pregnancy, biological differences, etc. However, after 30+ years of data collection utilizing these same instruments, one can anticipate potentially biased results. This raises the question of whether or not survey instruments should be rewritten to reflect current perceptions, rephrased for different cultures, and whether or not valid statistical comparisons may even be made among such instruments.

In Chapter 9, Kay Fielden focuses on "Re-Conceptualising Research: A Mindful Process for Qualitative Research in Information Systems." In this thoughtful discussion on mindful practices that should be adopted by qualitative researchers in Information Systems, Professor Fielden explores many dimensions of mindfulness that is derived from diverse disciplines including anthropology, ethics, behavioural science, sociology, social science, and psychology. These dimensions of mindfulness include: a knowledge and practice in exploring the inner self, how relationships are formed and maintained with others in a mindful manner, understanding the interplay between intuition and rationality, the importance of empathy, mental flexibility, and the ability to understand multiple points of view, as one prepares to conduct qualitative research. A novel approach taken in this chapter is its aim to map mindfulness qualities required at different research phases. This is further categorised into pragmatics, process, and philosophy. As qualitative research progresses, mindfulness qualities can also be mapped onto a timeline from research inception, research process, and finally, research publication.

Professor Fielden's multidisciplinary background in mathematics, computer science, and social ecology, as well as her interests in spirituality, have allowed her to broaden her focus in this discussion on adopting a novel approach to training IS researchers in the growing field of applied computing of applied computing. The debate from Professor Fielden is rigorously argued, well-informed, and supported by a broad-based and interdisciplinary literature. Debates on the role and nature of qualitative research have a legitimate place in Information Systems as evidenced by Michael Myer's excellent work on Qualitative Research in ISWorld. This chapter reflects, in part, a philosophical debate designed to investigate the many facets of mindfulness and then to place these within the researcher's capacities as outlined by Denzin and Lincoln in their summation of the five phases of qualitative research. IS researchers, practitioners, and teachers will all benefit from this by developing a deeper understanding of mindful practices in qualitative research.

MODELLING AND SIMULATION

Section three entails five chapters. In Chapter 10, Rolf Färe, Hirofumi Fukuyama, and William L. Weber highlight "A Mergers and Acquisitions Index in Data Envelopment Analysis: An Application to Japanese Shinkin Banks in Kyushu." Merger and acquisition (M&A) activities between firms can be economically valuable when the managerial inefficiencies of one firm can be reduced by another firm's managers, or when there are scale, scope, quality, or product mix inefficiencies and complementarity that can be leveraged. Researchers have examined the timing of M&A activities in response to macroeconomic dynamics and changes in government regulatory and tax regimes and found that M&A activities are often concentrated in post-deregulatory periods. Many papers in the financial and accounting literature have examined the ex post outcomes of mergers and acquisitions by surveying managers about whether the merger or acquisition helped meet long-term goals or by examining excess stock returns. In contrast to the ex post literature on M&A outcomes, the authors develop an ex ante index of the potential gains from a merger or acquisition between two firms. Their approach utilizes DEA (data envelopment analysis) to construct a production technology in which firms use various inputs to produce a final output and an intermediate output. The intermediate output produced in one period can be used to produce final outputs in a subsequent period. The authors assume that if an M&A occurs, the intermediate outputs can be reallocated between the two firms and used to produce final outputs in the subsequent period. A potential M&A is deemed efficient if the sum of two firms' final outputs increases in response to a reallocation of the intermediate output.

The authors use their method to examine potential mergers between Japanese Shinkin banks whose primary objective is to provide loans to small and medium sized businesses within the prefecture. Shinkin banks use deposits, physical capital, and labour to produce an intermediate output of securities investments and a final output of loans. Securities acquired in one period can be sold in a future period with the proceeds used to finance loans. Their estimates indicate that intra-prefecture mergers between banks in Fukuoka would yield the smallest gain in final outputs, while mergers between banks in Nagasaki would yield the largest gains. For inter-prefecture mergers, the largest potential gains are for banks in Nagasaki and Kagoshima, and in general, for banks in Kagoshima and the other six prefectures on Kyushu Island. The authors' method provides important information on the potential value of M&A activities and can be generalized to evaluate, for instance, gains from school consolidation, or to help determine the optimal degree of centralization among governments.

In Chapter 11, Heike Knörzer, Simone Graeff-Hönninger, Bettina U. Müller, Hans-Peter Piepho, and Wilhelm Claupein demonstrate "A Modelling Approach to Simulate Effects of Intercropping and Interspecific Competition in Arable Crops." Interspecific competition influences individual growth and performance. Neighbourhood effects become especially important in intercropping systems, and modelling approaches could be a useful tool to simulate plant growth under different environmental conditions. Among other benefits, they can help identify appropriate combinations of different crops while managing competition. This study gives an overview of different competition models and their underlying modelling approaches. To model intercropping in terms of neighbouring effects in the context of field boundary cultivation, a new approach was developed and integrated into the DSSAT model. The results indicate the possibility of simulating general competition and beneficial effects due to different incoming solar radiation and soil temperatures in a winter wheat/maize intercropping system. Considering factors other than the competitive ones are important. For example, sunlight, due to changing solar radiation does not explain yield differences in all cases. In such instances, intercropped maize could compensate for low radiation due to its high radiation use efficiency. In addition, wheat benefited from the increased solar radiation, but even more from the increased soil temperature.

In Chapter 12, Asmeret Bier shows "A System Dynamics Approach to Changing Perceptions about Thermal Water Quality Trading Markets." Thermal water quality trading markets give point source thermal polluters the option to comply with effluent restrictions by paying nearby landowners to plant shade trees. The shade trees cool the water, offsetting thermal pollution emitted by the point source. Thermal trading has the potential to create greater environmental benefits at a lower cost than traditional regulation, however; only one such program has been implemented to date in the United States. In this regard, a shift in potential stakeholders' perceptions of these markets could be useful in allowing the markets to spread. This chapter explains why systems dynamics modelling is a useful tool for creating such a shift in perception. Moreover, it describes a method of teaching participants about thermal trading. The method begins with a classroom simulation exercise, uses lessons from that exercise to create a model of a thermal trading market, and uses that model to conduct policy design and uncertainty analyses.

In Chapter 13, Allyson M. Beall and Andrew Ford contribute "Reports from the Field: Assessing the Art and Science of Participatory Environmental Modelling." For natural resource users and managers, the integration of adaptive management, sustainability, social concerns, and science is challenging. Moreover, when including varying social norms and scientific uncertainty, even the identification of "the problem" can be difficult. Beall and Ford describe participatory modelling case studies that utilize system dynamics in such a way that biophysical information is made both transparent and relative to interested stakeholders. The interests of those stakeholders may be integrated into potential biophysical responses to social needs so that policy options may be tested. The authors use their unique comparative framework to describe a diversity of case studies ranging from water resource management and adaptations to climate change, to endangered species management and agriculture. They have further contributed to the literature by designing and utilizing continuums to compare, among other things, the social history of the stakeholders in each case study, the perceived complexity of the "actual" problem each case study describes, and the availability of scientific data. This comparative framework and description of participatory modelling and facilitation techniques offers a unique look into the options available to practitioners to adapt and customize both process and model to specific situations. Further, by countering many Scholars' hesitancy to model highly uncertain systems the authors help us understand the importance of modelling ill-structured and highly uncertain systems.

For stakeholders interested in utilizing participatory modelling, the authors describe how the discovery process of participatory model building and the potential to test simulated management options in advance of field-testing. Such a process enables interested parties to clarify "the problem," analyse potential biophysical and social responses, all while simultaneously embracing the inherent uncertainty that comes with natural resource management. Perhaps most importantly, the authors describe how participatory environmental modelling helps interested parties better understand the system as a synergistic whole that operates over both time and space with internal feedback, inherent or emergent tipping points, and a resilience that is distinctive to that system.

In Chapter 14, Allan J. Lichtman delivers "The Keys to the White House: A Preliminary Forecast for 2012." This chapter presented a new vision of how American presidential elections work and a new means for forecasting presidential election results. It was based on the Keys to the White House, a historically-based prediction system that retrospectively accounted for the popular-vote winners of every American presidential election from 1860 to 1980 and prospectively forecast well ahead of time the popular-vote winners of all presidential elections from 1984 to 2008.

The Keys give specificity to the theory that presidential election results turn primarily on the performance of the party controlling the White House. The model demonstrates that governing (as opposed to campaigning) counts in American presidential elections. If the nation fares well during the term of the incumbent party, that party wins another four years in office; otherwise, the challenging party prevails. According to this approach, cynicism on the part of the American polity means that the voting public pays little attention to politicians' behaviors during an election. Unlike nearly all other predictive models, the Keys rely on an index rather than a regression-based method of forecasting. The Keys consist of 13 true-false questions that gauge the performance and strength of the incumbent presidential party. When five or fewer keys are false the party holding the White House wins another term in office, otherwise the challenging party prevails. At the time of the original paper's publication (January 2010), the Keys indicated President Obama is a likely winner in 2012, but they also revealed the specific problems that could thwart his re-election.

Unlike traditional models, the index method does not require specification in advance of an election of the numerical relationship between the presidential vote and particular explanatory variables. It includes a much wider array of predictor variables than regression models. It combines both mathematical and judgmental indicators to obtain a more realistic assessment of the factors that determine presidential outcomes. The Keys model also utilizes no polling data. The Keys hold lessons for politics in the United States and worldwide. It appears that political leaders need not move to the ideological center. As demonstrated by presidents such as Franklin Roosevelt and Ronald Reagan, a strong ideology can guide policy initiatives that keep in line the keys needed to retain the White House. Given that campaigns do not decide elections, the model also indicates that candidates should abandon conventional politics and develop the themes, issues and grassroots support needed for effective governance. Beyond the United States, as democracy inevitably spreads across the globe, world leaders should take heed that those who serve their people well will likely succeed politically in free and fair elections.

MANAGING DATABASES OF THE FUTURE

Section four comprises two chapters. In Chapter 15, Sándor Csányi, Róbert Lehoczki, and Krisztina Sonkoly review "National Game Management Database of Hungary." Advances in ecological science and increased public environmental awareness have resulted in changes in the management of renewable natural resources. To achieve sustainable use of wildlife, managers need reliable, accessible, and well-designed data on populations, habitats, and the complexities of ecological interactions. The National Game Management Database (NGMD) was first mandated by the Hungarian Game Management and Hunting Law in 1996. In this chapter the authors summarize the origins, characteristics, development, and results leading to the final establishment of and uses for the NGMD. Goals of the NGMD are to store data on game populations and game management in a way that can be used for multiple analytical procedures, provide input to spatial analyses and mapping, and facilitate decision-making and planning efforts at various levels of game management administration. The NGMD was developed on personal computers using commercial software, including the database format and software used for spatial data management and analysis (GIS). The NGMD designed and developed regularly updated special computer programs for data input and statistical output (descriptive statistics for various scales).

The NGMD is primarily based on data provided by the 24 game management regions of Hungary with nearly 1390 game management units (GMU). It contains information on the populations of game species, data from annual game management plans and reports, trophy-scoring data, maximum allowed, and minimum huntable population size. This information also includes digital maps for each GMU and the 24 game management regions, and the long-term game management plans of the GMUs and the 24 game management regions. This information on game populations and management provides an approach to analyse trends of game populations in relation to harvest and/or environmental changes. During the last one and a half decades, the NGMD has facilitated the decision-making and planning efforts at various levels of game management administration. Through the implementation of the 3-level game management regions and the partitioning of the 24 game management regions we can solve real world problems. The ability to balance a scientific approach with practical requirements seems to be an essential element for successful conservation of biodiversity and wise use of renewable natural resources like wildlife populations. The NGMD's compatibility with other data collected from various researches, forestry and agriculture, for example, is an important strength. This connectivity facilitates a broadening of the applicability of wildlife population and management data. In Hungary, the NGMD was the first operating database in wildlife management and nature conservation providing full GIS capabilities, supporting geographical analyses.

In Chapter 16, Larbi Esmahi and Elarbi Badidi address "Managing Demographic Data Inconsistencies in Healthcare Information Systems." This is one of the major problems facing current healthcare systems, which consists of insuring interoperability between different components of the system and managing data inconsistencies. The chapter starts with a review of the architecture and operational situation for many of existing healthcare systems. The review reveals that patient hospital workflows, from admission to discharge, provide a series of data streams for convergences into disparate systems. Protocols such as DICOM and HL7 exist for the purposes of exchanging information within the PACS and RIS information silos in the hospital enterprise. These protocols ensure data confidence for downstream systems, but are not designed to provide referential data cross system in the system-of-systems model. As data crosses the PACS and RIS information domains, data inconsistency is introduced. In fact, the framework used to manage the patient hospital workflow is usually implemented as a collection of subsystems with standalone data silos. This creates problems of data redundancy and inaccuracy, and it confuses the authoritative provisioning of data with referential copies.

A critical analysis of this situation leads the authors to the identification of the main causes for data disparity in these systems. A scenario based approach is used in the chapter for describing the causes of data inconsistencies, where a data flow example is used to explain each inconsistency problem. In order to remediate to some of these causes, some solutions have been proposed in previous studies. However, most of the solutions focus on using message oriented systems where one or more protocols are proposed for processing the exchanged messages. The authors utilize a very simple and elegant approach by considering the use of XML and Semantic Web technology.

One of the major contributions of this work is the proposition of a referential data design that can be integrated into existing systems. This solution insures both the management of interconnection between data silos and the exchange and transfer of different types of patients' data. The referential design is implemented in two layers. The first layers consist of an XML bus that convert data and serves as pipe for data exchange between disparate systems. The second layer consists of a metadata structure that is added to the XML bus in order to provide referential data cross systems. This second layer is meant to represent relationships between data within a system friendly format. The metadata layer is implemented as a Resource Definition Framework (RDF) for semantic data.

SUPPORTING CRITICAL DECISIONS

Section five entails four chapters. Chapter 17, entitled "Multi-Criteria Spatial Decision Support System DECERNS: Application to Land Use Planning," was written by B. Yatsalo, V. Didenko, A. Tkachuk, G. Gritsyuk, O. Mirzeabasov, V. Slipenkaya, A. Babutski, I. Pichugina, T. Sullivan, and I. Linkov. Land-use planning and environmental management often requires an implementation of both geospatial information analysis and value-driven criteria within the decision-making process. DECERNS (Decision Evaluation in Complex Risk Network Systems) is a web-based distributed decision support system for multicriteria analysis of a wide range of spatially-explicit land management alternatives. It integrates mainly basic and some advanced GIS functions and implements several Multi-Criteria Decision Analysis (MCDA) methods and tools. DECERNS can also be integrated with a model server containing generic and site specific models for in-depth analysis of project and environmental risks as well as other decision criteria under consideration. This chapter provides an overview of the modelling approaches as well as methods and tools used in DECERNS. Applications of the DECERNS WebSDSS (Web-based Spatial Decision Support System) for a housing site selection case study are presented.

In Chapter 18, Konstantinos Voudouris, Maurizio Polemio, Nerantzis Kazakis, and Angelo Sifaleras present "An Agricultural Decision Support System for Optimal Land Use Regarding Groundwater Vulnerability." Groundwater is the main source for drinking and irrigation use for several countries, such as those in the Mediterranean region and numerous coastal areas around the world. A crucial goal for any country relying on groundwater for sustainability is to preserve its availability and quality. The authors describe in this chapter the main methods for groundwater vulnerability assessment considering typical porous aquifers on the alluvial or coastal plains and the peculiarities of rocky aquifers. Furthermore, they also present additional methods for assessing groundwater risks and hazards in the case of agricultural activities. The concept of groundwater vulnerability is based on the assumption that the physical environment may provide a certain degree of protection for groundwater against human activities. In other words, vulnerability represents the degree of weakness of one aquifer system to pollution. From an operational point of view, the chapter also describes some interesting case studies of relevant farming areas located in southern Italy and northern Greece.

There has been growing interest over the last decade for Decision Support Systems (DSS) regarding natural resources management. In this chapter, the authors contributed to the literature by presenting a computer-based system to support decision making regarding groundwater resource management. They presented a reliable tool for managing the effects of agricultural or anthropogenic activities on groundwater quality while pursuing sustainable growth. The proposed software package has been designed using the Matlab language. More precisely, the proposed DSS software package makes use of all the programming capabilities that are offered from Matlab. Moreover, the proposed DSS software is a user-friendly application for both the novice user (e.g., a student) and an operations research scientist alike. A plethora of other Matlab-based DSSs have also been developed as tools for the teaching of Operations Research, Optimization Theory, and Decision Making in general.

An important feature of the proposed DSS is the fact that new maps can be incorporated in order to cover new geographical areas. The user may be advised about which area to select with respect to the level of the vulnerability on the map. Furthermore, the DSS is able to visually inform the user about other potential suitable areas in the map. Finally, the proposed DSS could be easily joined to other packages (e.g., irrigation type, crop type, type of fertilizers, water consumption) to create a more comprehensive tool in order to define land allocation and protection zoning.

In Chapter 19, N. Subash and H. S. Ram Mohan stress "Verification of a Rational Combination Approach for Agricultural Drought Assessment: A Case Study over Indo-Gangetic Plains in India." Agricultural drought is characterized by a deficient supply of moisture, resulting either from sub-normal rainfall, erratic rainfall distribution, or higher water with respect to a crop. In spite of technological developments in providing improved crop varieties and better management practices, Indian agriculture has been considered a gamble due to higher spatial and temporal variability. The Rice-Wheat (RW) system is the major cropping system of the Indo-Gangetic Plains (IGP) in India and occupies 10 million hectares. In this chapter, the authors have examined the possibility of rationally combining the rainfall anomaly index, a weather based index and an agriculture index based on the Crop Growth Simulation Model for a rice-wheat productivity assessment in selected sites of IGP in India. The district average yields of rice varied from 0.9 t/ha at Samastipur to 3.8 t/ha at Ludhiana. Rice yields decreased from the west to east IGP, and farmers in the western IGP harvested more rice-wheat than those in the eastern regions. The productivity gap showed that all the sites produced only 50% of the potential in RW system productivity during the triennium ending period 2005. This chapter may help researchers and planners to take appropriate measures for improving productivity.

In Chapter 20, Zisis Mallios explores "Irrigation Water Valuation Using Spatial Hedonic Models in GIS Environment." The author deals with the problem of the unsustainable use of water resources, and in particular the use of water in agriculture. Irrigated agriculture consumes by far most of the water worldwide. M modern trends in the management of water resources propose to address water as an economic good thereby seek to introduce more efficient water prices. Moreover, environmentalists seek an efficient water allocation system and the author presents an application of the hedonic pricing method, conducted in a typical rural area of northern Greece, in an effort to obtain an estimate of the value of irrigation water. Hedonic pricing is an indirect valuation method that applies to heterogeneous tradable goods by investigating the relationship between the prices of those goods and their attributes. In the case of irrigation water, its value results through the estimation of the hedonic pricing model that describes the relation between the market value of the cultivated land parcels and its characteristics.

In this particular application of the hedonic pricing method, the author describes how a very common problem in applications of this method, the issue of spatial auto correlation of the data, is addressed using two well-known spatial autoregressive models. In this instance, the author focuses on the spatial lag and the spatial error model. He also describes how the assessment of the spatial regression models has been incorporated in the environment of geographical Information Systems, highlighting the advantages of the combination of these two tools (Spatial regression and GIS).

The author also focuses on an important element of the spatial regression models, the spatial weights matrix. The spatial weights matrix defines the neighborhood set of each observation and how much each of the neighbors affects others. He investigates how different specifications of the spatial weights matrix affect the overall performance of the spatial lag and the spatial error model. More specifically, he examines if all the neighbors affect in the same way the price of each observation or if this price depends on the distance of each of the neighbors. The main conclusions arising from this examination is the importance of testing different specifications of the spatial weights matrix among other tests performed in the modeling procedure. This is necessary in order to find the suitable specification to the sample data used in the model estimation. Finally, there is the need to further investigate the specification of the spatial weights matrix and propose different specifications that can lead to more efficient parameter estimates.

John Wang
Montclair State University, USA

E. LaBrent Chrite
Montclair State University, USA

Section 1
Emerging Technologies and Economies

Chapter 1
Multidimensional Assessment of Emerging Technologies:
Case of Next Generation Internet and Online Gaming Application

Ramin Neshati
Intel Corporation, USA

Tugrul U. Daim
Portland State University, USA

ABSTRACT

The Internet has changed the world in many ways. Online communications, financial and business-to-business transactions, electronic shopping, banking, and entertainment have become the norm in the digital age. The combined package of technologies that comprise the Internet—the information superhighway—have made all of this possible. The aging technological infrastructure that supports these webs of interconnected networks is being stressed to its performance limits. Recent advances in the backbone infrastructure that supports the Internet have helped alleviate some of these problems, but more challenges lie ahead for solving technology-related performance bottlenecks for many online applications, including high-definition interactive gaming. In this paper, the authors developed a technology assessment through multiple perspectives. While different components of the technology such as applications, protocols and network components are identified, other impact areas such as market and management are also evaluated. Elements of user behavior are evaluated within the market perspective. Evaluating technologies through these dimensions concurrently provides a balanced assessment among technical, economical, social and political factors.

INTRODUCTION

The genesis of the Internet can be traced to the intercommunication of many computers over several networks. A computer network is comprised of a set of nodes and links to connect them to provide the data transport infrastructure. The basic building blocks are routers, switches and circuits. One of the first of these networks was the ARPAnet, developed by the Defense Advanced Research Projects Agency (DARPA). It was used by governments and universities and these

DOI: 10.4018/978-1-4666-0927-3.ch001

institutions soon began to outgrow its limitations. They realized the need for a network that would better support high-performance network applications. In response to these technology needs, the US government launched an initiative called Next Generation Internet (NGI), intended to examine performance and bandwidth bottlenecks. In response to the goals outlined in the High-Performance Computing Act (HPCA) of 1991, the Office of Technology Assessment (OTA) of the United States Congress published a series of reports that provides an assessment on technology and research requisites, and highlights some of the issues that need to be addressed in order to scale the Internet for high-speed, high-bandwidth applications in various deployment scenarios (US Congress, 1993). Many of the recommendations of these reports have been studied and implemented in government-funded research networks with the expectation that the industry would adopt and diffuse these technological advancements. Indeed, many of the OTA recommendations have been developed, deployed and diffused in recent years. The OTA goals were largely met except for terabit per second networking.

By the early 1990s the Internet had been embraced as the most desired medium of communications not only by government, research and academic institutions but more importantly by a plethora of commercial and computing users worldwide. With the more recent growth in the number of users, particularly as the populations of China and India come online, the issue of Internet performance takes on added importance and urgency. Furthermore, new high-definition content on the web means that the amount of information being placed on the networks is also growing exponentially. The Internet, in its present form, cannot scale to meet the number and nature of performance demands already placed on it, to say nothing of a new generation of more complex interactions. The increasing demand for content-rich media, for example high-definition entertainment—from downloadable movies to

interactive games and other such content—is straining network performance, resulting in poor user experience. These and emerging new applications will demand much higher bandwidth and performance than is available today. Some of these applications include real-time interactive gaming, collaborative grid computing, and so on. New technologies and architectures are needed to scale the existing uses to a broader community of users worldwide, and to facilitate new, sophisticated applications that require expansive computation with fast real-time response. All computer networks deploy a variety of technology architectures. For the purposes of this paper, we will anchor on the ISO/OSI seven-layer architecture as a reference point for the three areas of interest highlighted by the OTA report (US Congress, 1993). Figures 1 and 2 in Appendix A depict the ISO/OSI architecture model. In this model, data flows from one system to another through a series of layers. At each layer, the data is encapsulated with protocol and control semantics until it reaches the transmission medium where it is digitally routed to its destination through the network. At the destination, the control information and protocol semantics are removed as the data moves up the protocol stack before it reaches the intended application. As mentioned, numerous technologies come into play in computer networks such as the Internet, and this paper will elaborate on only a few of these technologies. The OTA report identified three areas of focus for the Internet as follows: Applications, Protocols, and Network Components

For purposes of technology assessment and evaluation, we will map the OTA focus areas of applications, protocols and network components to the Application, Transport/Network and Data Link layers of the ISO/OSI model, respectively (for further clarity, these layers appear in the TCP technology stack as shown in Figure 3 in Appendix A). At the Application layer, the technology object of concern is data, and in the context of this paper the issue is the amount of data and whether there are adequate technologies in place to manage the data for optimal transmission from the origination point to its destination. We will examine data compression technologies and in particular the MPEG-4 compression standard. At the Transport/Network layer, the technology object of concern are protocols and data transmission semantics, and in the context of this paper the issue is whether recent technology acquisitions and diffusions will be sufficient to accommodate the necessary bandwidth performance requirements of our intended application—online gaming. Here, we will review the partial deployment of the IPv6 routing standard. Finally, at the Data Link layer, the technology object of concern are data relay algorithms, and in the context of this paper the issue is whether future improvements in gigabit ATM switching fabrics and architectures will sustain the backbone of the Internet for massive bandwidth and performance scaling. The interconnected networks of Internet Service Providers (ISPs) compose the largest part of the Internet infrastructure and switches are a fundamental part of this infrastructure because they speed up data transportation. There are many different types of switches and networks. ATM is an important, and highly competitive, technology both for long distance telecommunication and for local-area networks (Inouye et al., 1996).

As has been mentioned the application of interest, in evaluating and assessing the technologies that are needed for its support, is high-definition, interactive online gaming. This is a growing area of interest for Internet users across the globe and one that may place a lot of strain on the performance of the web. For example, in a recent press release, Sun Microsystems announced 'Project Darkstar' as an 'important technology foundation in the exploding multiplayer online game marketplace.' In effect, Sun has launched the high-performance infrastructure and enterprise-grade server solutions for the open source development of gaming applications. According to Sun's management, game developers will be given Java-based programming interfaces for increased productivity,

Application Programming Interfaces (APIs) to facilitate integration of third party extensions, and enhancements for scalability, robust performance, and fault-tolerant operations. The source code for Project Darkstar will be made available under a General-Purpose License (GPL) to ease technology adoption[1]. Online gaming refers to games that are played over a computer network like the Internet. Modern online games have complex graphics and virtual worlds populated by many players simultaneously. Many online games have associated online communities, making them a form of social activity beyond single player games. Some examples of online games include: World Of Warcraft, Final Fantasy XI and Lineage II. Massively multiplayer online games are capable of supporting hundreds or thousands of players simultaneously and are played on the Internet. These games can enable players to cooperate and compete with each other on a massive scale (Douglas et al., 2005). Networked interactions across time and space generate massive amounts of data that must be carried across the Internet. The amount and type of data and the number of network users are the essence of the Internet performance problem being discussed in this paper. In considering the end-to-end scenario depicted in Figure 5 in Appendix A, several performance pinch points emerge. These bottlenecks directly impact the issue of bandwidth and performance scaling to meet the challenges of high-definition interactive gaming. In the not-too-distant future, we should expect a new crop of compelling high-definition games which users across the world will use for entertainment and other purposes. What medium will transport the massive amounts of data generated by these games? The Internet, of course! What can be done to anticipate such performance-hungry applications? What technologies are needed and should be in place to anticipate and accommodate the vast demands on network bandwidth and performance? We shall address these and related questions in this paper.

LITERATURE REVIEW

In recent years much research has been dedicated to finding new and innovative ways to scale the Internet for high-speed and high-bandwidth applications. The problem here is to confine the plethora of available research. For example, many advances have been made in developing Quality of Service (QoS) technologies, network traffic conditioning, intelligent components and so on (Smith & Weingarten, 1997; Miras, 2002; Apigian et al., 2006; Sevcik, 2006) . Network research is an iterative process of 'spiral design' that requires continuous feedback and improvement. The network drives the application and the application drives the network (Smith & Weingarten, 1997). Research on the NGI initiative revealed that the Internet will not be capable of supporting mission-critical applications such as national security, economic competitiveness and social agendas such as education, health care and so on (US Congress, 1993)[2]. With respect to raw performance, Apigian et al. (2006) studied Internet performance and usability by surveying 257 IT managers, and crafted 'different strategic profiles and their desired performance levels' with the implication that the scaled up performance needs of some user profiles will vastly outstrip current capabilities. Sevcik (2006), a leading authority on Internet traffic, performance and technology, believes that the '20-fold increase in demand over a decade is double the 10-fold improvement in overall Internet performance…'. The most prevalent research taxonomy about the Internet includes service quality for time-sensitive applications, traffic conditioning for congestion management, and dynamic, variable performance scaling. One of the stated goals of the NGI is the transmission of the entire contents of the Encyclopedia Britannica in less than a second (Smith & Weingarten, 1997). This goal has yet to be met. Additional research on QoS centers on the effects of network latency and delay on the overall quality of immersive audio-visual applications. In one

study, researchers found interactive video to be especially susceptible to bandwidth availability on demand (Miras, 2002).

The current literature on IPv6 adoptions points to the fact that many domestic and foreign companies have incorporated or are steadily incorporating IPv6 capabilities into their hardware and software products. Estimates suggest that about one-third of desktop computers currently deployed in the United States are IPv6-capable (Johnson et al., 2003). Foreign governments see a swift transition to IPv6 as a way to gain a competitive advantage in the equipment and applications markets. This, in turn, has raised concerns about the pace of IPv6 deployment within the United States and whether a lag in deployment jeopardizes the competitiveness of domestic firms in cutting-edge IT markets or, worse, has adverse security implications (Deering & Hinden, 1998). When ATM was developed in the early 1990s, it was considered to be the perfect multimedia transport and the beginning of a new era in networking because of its ability to provide high quality of service from end to end. ATM switch market declined more than 6% during 2003 and an additional 3% during 2004 mostly due to cost and challenges from incumbent technologies. Regardless of these challenges, the ATM switch remains an essential component in the ability of network service providers to offer frame relay and ATM services. The ATM switch will continue as a key part of most large networks, but it is unlikely to be a growth market for network equipment providers. International Data Corp. (IDC, Framingham) predicts that the increasing importance of data traffic in the public network and the limitations of current router-based technology bode well for frame relay and asynchronous transfer mode. Frame relay, and especially ATM, is well positioned to take advantage of an increasing demand for rapidly growing and bandwidth-efficient data networks. Viewed as an innovation when first introduced, frame relay service is now a trusted and widely accepted Wide Area Network (WAN) technology.

Another factor shaping the ATM market is figuring out how to better support the exploding amount of traffic generated by the continuing growth of the Internet [3]. With the problem clearly articulated and supported by a survey of the relevant literature in the field, we now turn our attention to the methodology to be used in evaluating the technologies in question.

METHODOLOGY

Benson and Sage (1993) have proposed a triple-gateway model for evaluating emerging technologies. This model postulates that a technology must pass through market, management and technical gateways before it can become commercially or socially worthwhile. These gateways act as filters in identifying technology acquisition and deployment issues. Market gateway includes the following elements: new uses, user skepticism, requirements for behavior adjustment, competitive technologies, unpredictable technological development and legal barriers. Management gateway includes the following elements: risk taking and factors of production. Technology gateway includes the following elements: innovativeness of technology, number of constituent technologies, manufacturing difficulties and institutional changes (Benson & Sage, 1993). In the market gateway we identify the usefulness of a proposed technology. User requirements, competitive landscape, potential disruptive technologies and legal and environmental issues are qualitatively analyzed. In the management gateway we analyze risk and risk mitigation in the context of the relevant organizations. In the technology gateway we probe into the level of innovation, complexity of the technology, manufacturability and institutional change. We shall deploy the Benson and Sage triple-gateway technology evaluation methodology in analyzing the technologies under discussion using Table 1:

Using opinion data from five experts, we are able to quantify and assign weights to each of the three gateways in this model to indicate their relative importance to each other. The factors within each gateway are assigned uniform ratios as percentages of the gateway weights. This data is shown in Tables A5 and A6 in Appendix A and in the technology evaluation section below. The uniform distribution of the gateway weights among the factors within each category is deemed to a reasonable approximation for purposes of quantitative analysis in this paper. A variable assignment of weights to each factor will not substantially change the outcome of the technology evaluation and assessment. Further, a simple five point ordinal assessment scale is used to gauge the impact of bandwidth and performance on overall user experience in online gaming applications using the following qualitative definitions:

Table 1. Weights for gateways and factors

Gateways	Factors	Weight	Grade
Market (0.18)			
	New uses	3%	1-5
	User skepticism	3%	1-5
	Behavior adjustment	3%	1-5
	Competition	3%	1-5
	Unpredictable technology	3%	1-5
	Legal barriers	3%	1-5
Management (0.51)			
	Risk	25%	1-5
	Production	26%	1-5
Technology (0.31)			
	Innovativeness	8%	1-5
	Constituent technologies	8%	1-5
	Manufacturing difficulty	8%	1-5
	Institutional changes	7%	1-5
		100%	

5: Excellent
4: Good/Acceptable
3: Fair/Needs-improvement
2: Poor/Annoying
1: Unacceptable

Sixteen technology managers from three local companies in the Portland, Oregon metropolitan area who expressed moderate to high knowledge in online gaming applications graded the above factors on the five-point scale. Refer to Table A6 in Appendix A for details of the grading data. The averages of these grades are used in the technology evaluation section below. A grade when multiplied by the corresponding weight yields an assessment score for the factor under consideration. A score of 4 or higher is deemed by the author as necessary for a positive user experience with lower scores requiring improvement to positively impact user experience.

Other methodologies were considered and rejected for the analysis in this paper. For instance, Karsak and Ahiska (2005) have defined a common weight multi-criteria decision-making (MCDM) methodology that provides discriminating power for technology selection. This methodology evaluates decision-making in view of multiple ordinal outputs given a single exact input parameter. This model seeks to optimize deviations from a known efficiency point of reference. This methodology is not suitable for the analysis in this paper since the problems highlighted here are inclined towards technology replacement and diffusion and have less to do with pure technology selection. Braglia and Petroni (1999) have put forward the data envelopment analysis (DEA) methodology. This model takes into account the cost and benefit perspectives by measuring the relative efficiency of linear programming problems. This approach increases the discriminatory power of the standard DEA, but it is not germane to our concern since DEA is mostly aimed at optimizing efficiency in manufacturing and related fields and has less to do with technology evaluation and selection.

The triple gateway model defined by Benson and Sage is the most applicable methodology for the technology assessment at hand.

ANALYSIS

The analysis contained in this paper is comprised of technology gap analysis and technology evaluation and selection analysis.

Gap Analysis

In defining the existing technology gaps, we have identified the current capabilities and future desired capabilities. The gap between the current and the future desired states are depicted in Figure 4 in Appendix A (Miras, 2002). From this diagram, it can be seen that the current end-user networking speeds of 2-10Mbps must be scaled to 1.5Gbps and higher in order to support immersive, high-definition applications such as online interactive gaming. Using the Linstone perspectives model, we can further analyze these gaps along technical, organizational and personal dimensions (Linstone, 1999).

- **Technical:** In the technical dimension, technology standards must exist in order to enable the seamless and compatible scaling of the bandwidth and performance of the Internet to enable high-definition and content-rich media such as will be required by future online gaming applications. Further, the integrated hardware and software systems to facilitate our target applications must be functional and available. Lastly, the end-to-end operation of the online gaming application must be reliable, scalable and upgradeable to such a degree that it can be deployed anytime and anywhere. These technical gaps manifest themselves in the network in the form of protocol inefficiencies, and system latencies. What can be done to mitigate such gaps? We shall discuss that in the following section.

- **Organizational:** In the organizational dimension, there are a few gaps to note. The OTA report noted that funding for government-sponsored research networks was limited and that future research would need to be funded by the industry (US Congress, 1993). Will there be sufficient funding to explore the high-performance and high-bandwidth needs of online gaming applications? What governmental or non-governmental standards bodies will be needed to maintain and promote the development of these standards? The ad-hoc nature of industry support for online gaming, such as the example of the Sun Microsystems announcement mentioned in the introductory section of this paper[4], points to the fact that each company is interested in promoting its own technology base as the standard (e.g., Java programming APIs) and that the development community can expect to face and reconcile between multiple such standards and interfaces.

- **Personal:** In the personal dimension, user experience, learning curve, cost and affordability of technology acquisition, ease of access, and choice of available or alternative technologies are significant in determining the gaps. For the avid gamers, the learning curve gap is quickly bridged through the community benefits of, and association with like-minded gamers. Similarly, the gaps in technology affordability and acquisition can be mitigated given compelling reasons and benefits for the avid user. However, the user experience gap is in question. Will the performance and bandwidth necessary to create a positive user experience exist in the Internet of tomorrow? This is one of the key questions we highlight in this paper.

2.1.1 Technology Needs

T	Internet technologies to address performance scaling for online games
O	Standards bodies to define architectures to facilitate technology diffusion
P	Adequate bandwidth to provide rich user experience for online games

2.1.2 Technology Capabilities

T	Compression technology to minimize the amount of data transmission. Network routing technology to optimize and reduce network latencies. Switching technology to ensure intelligent gigabit networking
O	Structure and influence to expedite adoption of needed technologies
P	Experienced and avid online game enthusiasts across the Internet

2.2 Technology Analysis

Technologies that pertain to data compression, network routing and packet switching will be analyzed in this section.

Requirements and Candidate Technologies

The bandwidth requirements of audio and video are very different. Compressed audio can be transmitted under 1KB per second. In contrast, uncompressed audio will require 200KB per second. Compressed video will require anywhere between 10-20MB per second, depending on the screen dimension and resolution, while high-definition video will require 5-10Gb per second (Smith & Weingarten, 1997). According to researchers at the Argonne National Laboratory, the bandwidth needs of immersive applications (such as real-time gaming, simulations, rendering, etc) are several

GB per second and growing (Childers, 2000). The technology requirements for our three focus areas are as follows:

- **Applications: MPEG-4:** MPEG-4 is a suite of standards which has many different parts, where each part standardizes audio, video, file formats and other entities. MPEG-4 provides standard data compression capable of enabling good multi-media quality at substantially lower bit rates than previous standards without the added design complexity. For example, typical bandwidth requirements for MPEG-4 encoded video is approximately 4Mb per second while the same for broadcast-quality high-definition content using MPEG-2 is roughly 20Mb per second, a 1:5 ratio (Miras, 2002). The same video stream, in raw uncompressed format would require nearly 2Gb per second bandwidth. MPEG-4 is flexible and applicable to a variety of usages in various networks and systems, including low and high bit rates, as well as low and high resolution content (Burroughs & Lattrell, 1998). Table 1 in Appendix A (Burroughs & Lattrell, 1998) depicts the various compression technologies and their capabilities. As can be seen from this table, MPEG-4 is the only viable data compression standard that can facilitate high-bandwidth (gigabit and above) applications.
- **Protocols: IPv6:** The Internet Protocol (IP) is an international communications standard that is essential to the operation of both the public Internet and many private networks. IP provides a standardized envelope that carries addressing, routing, and message-handling information, thereby enabling a message to be transmitted from its source to its final destination over the various interconnected networks that comprise the Internet. The current generation

of IP, version 4 (IPv4), has been in use for more than 20 years and has supported the Internet's rapid growth during that time. With the transformation of the Internet in the 1990s from a research network to a commercialized network, concerns were raised about the ability of IPv4 to accommodate anticipated increasing demand for Internet addresses. In 1993, the Internet Engineering Task Force (IETF) began a design and standardization process to develop a next generation Internet Protocol that would address, among other issues, the predicted exhaustion of available IPv4 addresses. The resulting set of standards, collectively known as IP version 6 (IPv6), was developed and finally emerged in 1998 (Marsan, 2000).

The benefits of IPv6 over IPv4 are many and are itemized below (as well as in Table A1 in Appendix A)[5]:

- Increased address space
- Improving address allocation
- Facilitating end-to-end services and applications
- Simplified mobility
- Improved quality of service (QoS)
- Reduced network administration costs
- Increased overall network efficiency
- The costs of stakeholder adoption of IPv6 are spread across the following (Stoneman, 2001):
- End Users
- Hardware and software vendors
- Internet service providers (ISPs)

Finally, the factors influencing the cost of adoption among the various user groups are (National Telecommunications and Information Administration, 2004):

- The type of Internet use or type of service being offered by each organization
- The transition mechanism(s) that the organization intends to implement (e.g., tunneling, dual-stack, translation, or a combination)
- The organization-specific infrastructure comprised of servers, routers, firewalls, billing systems, and standard and customized network-enabled software applications
- The level of security required during the transition and
- The timing of the transition

Network Components: ATM

Asynchronous Transfer Mode (ATM) is the technology of choice for the Broadband Integrated Services Digital Network (B-ISDN). ATM transports a wide variety of services in a seamless manner. Because switching is not part of the ATM standards, vendors use a wide variety of techniques to build their switches. The aim of ATM switch design is to increase speed, capacity and overall performance. ATM switching differs from conventional switching because of the high-speed interfaces (50 Mbps to 2.4 Gbps) to the switch, with switching rates up to 80 Gbps in the backplane. In addition, the statistical capability of the ATM streams passing through the ATM switching systems places additional demands on the switch (Robertazzi, 2003). ATM networks are fundamentally connection-oriented, which means that a virtual channel (VC) must be set up across the ATM network prior to any data transfer. A virtual path (VP) is a bundle of virtual channels, all of which are switched transparently across the ATM network based on the common VPI (refer to Figures 5-7 in appendix A). ATM switching is deployed in high-speed interconnects. Interest in using native ATM for carrying live video and audio has increased recently. In these environments, low latency and very high quality

of service are required to handle audio and video streams (Robertazzi, 2003). To sum up, ATM is a network technology that supports real-time voice and video as well as data both local and wide area networks (LANs & WANs). The topology uses switches that establish a logical circuit from end to end, which guarantees quality of service (QoS). However, unlike telephone switches that dedicate circuits end to end, unused bandwidth in ATM's logical circuits can be appropriated when needed. For example, idle bandwidth in a videoconference circuit can be used to transfer data.[6] From the above analysis, the candidate technologies of interest in this paper have been identified as MPEG-4 for data compression, IPv6 for network routing and ATM switching.

Evaluation

The triple-gateway method explained in the Methodology section above will be used to evaluate the candidate technologies of choice. The technology evaluation is shown below.

RESULTS

The global scope of the Internet means that both domestic private investment and the standards infrastructure supporting the Internet must evolve in a timely manner. That evolution will be complex as there are multiple industries involved in the delivery of Internet infrastructure. The Internet is migrating to the new technologies we have assessed. This diffusion will take some time to complete. Therefore, a number of trends and potential barriers must be continually monitored and assessed. For example, major portions of the Internet infrastructure hardware and software markets appear to be IPv6 capable already, and over the next four or five years the vast majority of network hardware, operating systems, and network-enabled software packages (e.g., databases, email) will be sold with IPv6 capabilities. This capability is not actually turned on, however. In the next few years, users will begin to enable this capability in operating systems, or they will purchase operating systems with IPv6 on by default. In fact, the majority of Linux-based operating systems are IPv6 enabled today, and Windows Vista is IPv6 enabled by default. As operating systems become enabled and early adopters provide use experiences, respondents predict that users will start to enable routers, followed finally by applications. More generally, emerging and future peer-to-peer Internet applications will exhibit an iterative relationship with the supporting infrastructure. That is, the availability of a higher capacity and more efficient standards infrastructure leverages private-sector innovation, which, in turn, increases the use of and demand for improvements in the supporting infrastructure.

The results in the Evaluation section above shows the application of the Bensen and Page triple-gateway methodology to our three technologies. These technologies conveniently map to the three focus areas highlighted in the OTA report (applications, network protocols and network components) (US Congress, 1993). From the weighted importance of the model's various factors in the three gateways, it can be deduced that compression technologies are important to the provision of acceptable user experience in the context of the high-definition, online interactive gaming. ATM switching technology is needed as well but there is considerable risk in its broad diffusion due to compelling incumbent technologies, thereby giving rise to volume production approval risks.

One method to evaluate and assess these technologies is to consider a combination of scenarios with the MPEG-4, IPv6 and ATM technologies. To do this, we define three scenarios as follows:

- Scenario A: MPEG-4 and Ipv6 and not ATM
- Scenario B: MPEG-4 and not Ipv6 and ATM

- Scenario C: not MPEG-4 and Ipv6 and ATM

We shall qualitatively analyze and discuss these three scenarios below along the Linstone perspectives model:

From an analysis of these technologies along the TOP perspectives, it is clear that ATM switch diffusion will continue to be challenged by cheaper incumbent technologies such as gigabit Ethernet alternatives. IPv6 adoption, although subject to time, is on a roll and will soon replace the incumbent technology for all the benefits discussed above. While MPEG-4 compression provides a 5-fold improvement in previous data compression technologies, and provides multi-data type flexibility, there are several follow-on technologies that are at various stages of definition and maturity and will provide even greater compression ratio and other benefits than MPEG-4. Technology availability is not a major issue. Standards proliferation and diffusion and overall user experience and cost of adoption will continue to be matters of concern in the future.

CONCLUSION AND LIMITATIONS

This paper delved into three focus areas outlined in the Advanced Network Technology assessment of the OTA: applications, protocols and network components. The findings of the technology assessment and evaluations in this paper centered on the various technologies that comprise the OTA focus areas. In particular, the roles of MPEG4 compression, IPv6 routing and ATM switching technologies were assessed and evaluated vis-à-vis their impact on bandwidth and performance for high-definition, interactive online gaming applications. Some of these technologies are at various stages of diffusion and have replaced incumbent technologies.

The diffusion of Internet technologies follows the characteristics of a central diffusion system

Table 4.MPEG-4

Gateways	Factors	Weight	Grade	Score
Market				
	New uses: high as it can be applied to multiple data types	3%	4.38	0.131
	User skepticism: low as the benefits delivered are compelling	3%	4.50	0.135
	Behavior adjustment: none as the algorithms are embedded and do not interface with the user	3%	4.63	0.138
	Competition: moderate as there are other standards in development	3%	3.69	0.165
	Unpredictable technology: low uncertainty	3%	3.63	0.108
	Legal barriers: low as the technology is freely licensed	3%	4.38	0.131
Management				
	Risk: low risk of commercialization	25%	4.81	1.202
	Production: low risk of materials and capital; technology is available	26%	4.23	1.099
Technology				
	Innovativeness: moderate since other improvements are coming	8%	3.50	0.280
	Constituent technologies: many offshoot technologies being defined	8%	3.44	0.275
	Manufacturing difficulty: low	8%	4.06	0.324
	Institutional changes: none	7%	4.56	0.319
		100%		**4.307**

Table 5. IPv6

Gateways	Factors	Weight	Grade	Score
Market				
	New uses: rapid growth in the number of mobile and portable devices that connect to the Internet	3%	4.38	0.131
	User skepticism: low as it speeds up data transfer on the Internet	3%	4.81	0.144
	Behavior adjustment: none as hardware and software are acquired through routine upgrade	3%	4.88	0.146
	Competition: low as this is a regulated environment	3%	4.69	0.140
	Unpredictable technology: low uncertainty	3%	4.19	0.125
	Legal barriers: minimal as adoption is on strong upward curve	3%	4.31	0.129
Management				
	Risk: low as the entire value chain has agreed on the standard	25%	3.75	0.937
	Production: manageable as capital and materials are being diverted to technology ramp	26%	3.19	0.829
Technology				
	Innovativeness: high as it removes significant barriers to performance	8%	4.06	0.324
	Constituent technologies: vary from hardware to software and links	8%	2.88	0.230
	Manufacturing difficulty: low	8%	3.81	0.304
	Institutional changes: moderate as the technology ramp continues	7%	3.25	0.227
		100%		**3.666**

Table 6. ATM

Gateways	Factors	Weight	Grade	Score
Market				
	New uses: moderate	3%	3.06	0.091
	User skepticism: difficult as there are inaccurate user perceptions	3%	2.31	0.069
	Behavior adjustment: none	3%	4.38	0.131
	Competition: entrenched alternative	3%	2.88	0.086
	Unpredictable technology: low	3%	3.88	0.116
	Legal barriers: none	3%	4.00	0.120
Management				
	Risk: moderate to high	25%	3.00	0.750
	Production: both capital and materials available	26%	3.75	0.975
Technology				
	Innovativeness: high	8%	4.38	0.350
	Constituent technologies: variable	8%	3.56	0.284
	Manufacturing difficulty: none	8%	4.31	0.344
	Institutional changes: high risk	7%	2.81	0.196
		100%		3.512

as defined by Rogers. In such a system, national governments and technical subject-matter experts hold sway in technology definition, adoption and replacement decisions. Although there are many counter examples where technologies diffuse in an ad-hoc manner without any central authority or control, by-and-large the technologies that pertain to the backbone of the Internet infrastructure (such

Table 7.

		A (not ATM)	B (not IPv6)	C (not MPEG-4)
T		ATM switches don't provide an ideal environment for connectionless network protocols such as IPv4, IPv6. This shortcoming in the LAN area has opened the way for Gigabit Ethernet switches, which use a familiar technology.	IPv4 cannot accommodate anticipated increasing demand for Internet addresses. IPv6 offers opportunities for wireless sensor networks and peer-to-peer communications, not possible with IPv4. Lack of traffic conditioning.	Lower data compression ratio means more bulk data transfer, which in turn could lead to more network latency and data loss. MPEG-2 or other variants not capable of providing rich media compression resulting in sub-optimal use of available bandwidth.
O		Standards for interconnecting existing networks to an ATM backbone need to be developed and proliferated.	Concerns about the pace and lag of US deployment of IPv6 will jeopardize competitiveness of US firms in leading-edge IT markets. US competitiveness impacts national security.	Standards development organizations may throttle new architectures and algorithms if adoption rate does not ramp up.
P		ATM switching rates exceed 80Gbps. Enhanced QoS features enable smooth transmission of multimedia content. Lack of ATM switching will affect the end-user experience.	Lack of QoS capabilities will impact end-end user experience.	Lost data or low performance will negatively impact gaming experience.

as routing and switching) follow the centralized model. The sources of technological innovation in such a system stem from formal research and development projects with the direction of the diffusion being top-down, from experts to the masses. The needs of end-users and in our context the online gaming community, are generally met as innovations become available and cannot be ameliorated through regional or local technology solutions. Online gamers are at the mercy of Internet administrators and technical subject-matter experts for viable roadmaps of technologies to solve their performance and bandwidth bottlenecks, both now and into the foreseeable future.

This paper has several limitations. Our main objective was to evaluate on line gaming as an emerging technology. We were able to identify the main constructs; however there is need for further analysis. Secondarily we tried to operationalize the theory of multiple perspectives. In this case we were able to introduce a framework which again needs further improvements. The scales used in this paper had limitations as well. We used a standard 1-5 scale with uniform explanations. Further research would need to identify custom explanations for each criterion. Also there is no measure of dispersion associated with the analysis. Standard deviation is important in understanding the variation of the data. Inclusion of additional experts and assessing dispersion will also enhance this study

REFERENCES

Apigian, C. H., Ragu-Nathan, B. S., & Ragu-Nathan, T. S. (2006). Strategic profiles and internet performance: an empirical investigation into the development of a strategic internet system. *Information & Management, 43*(4), 455–468. doi:doi:10.1016/j.im.2005.11.003

Benson, B., & Sage, A. (1993). Emerging technology-evaluation methodology: with application to micro-electromechanical systems. *IEEE Transactions on Engineering Management, 40*(2), 114–123. doi:doi:10.1109/17.277403

Braglia, M., & Petroni, A. (1999). Evaluating and selectng investments in industrial robots. *International Journal of Production Research, 37*(18), 4157–4178. doi:doi:10.1080/002075499189718

Burroughs, S. H., & Lattrell, T. R. (1998). Data compression technology in ASIC cores. *Journal of Research and Development (Srinagar), 42*(6), 725–732.

Childers, L. (2000). Access grid: immersive group-to-group collaborative visualization. *Argonne National Laboratory*. Retrieved from http://www.fp.mcs.anl.gov/fl/publications-electronic-files/ag-immersive-821.pdf

Deering, S., & Hinden, R. (1998). *Internet protocol, version 6 (ipv6) specification*. Retrieved from http://www.ietf.org/rfc/rfc2460.txt

Douglas, S., Tanin, E., Harwood, A., & Karunasekera, S. (2005). Enabling massively multi-player online gaming applications on a p2p architecture. In *Proceedings of the International Conference on Information and Automation*, Colombo, Sri Lanka (7-12).

Inouye, L., Moser, L. E., & Melliar-Smith, P. M. (1996). QuickRing ATM switches. In *Proceedings of the Annual Conference on Emerging Technologies and Applications in Communications, (etaCOM)* (32-35).

Johnson, D., Perkins, C., & Arkko, J. (2003). *Mobility support in IPv6*. Retrieved from http://users.piuha.net/jarkko/publications/mipv6/drafts/mobilev6.html

Karsak, E. E., & Ahiska, S. S. (2005). Practical common weight multi-criteria decision-making approach with an improved discriminating power for technology selection. *International Journal of Production Research, 43*(8), 1537–1554. doi: doi:10.1080/13528160412331326478

Linstone, H. A. (1999). *Decision making for technology executives: Using multiple perspectives to improve performance.* Boston, MA: Artech House.

Marsan, C. (2000). Stanford move rekindles 'net address debate. *Network World Fusion.* Retrieved from http://www.nwfusion.com/news/2000/0124ipv4.html

Miras, D. (2002). *A survey of network qos needs of advanced internet applications.* London: University College.

National Telecommunications and Information Administration. (2004). *Technical and economic assessment of internet protocol version 6 (IPv6).* Retrieved from http://www.ntia.doc.gov/ntiahome/ntiageneral/ipv6/draft/discussion-draftv13_07162004.pdf

Robertazzi, T. G. (1993). *Performance evaluation of high speed switching fabrics and networks: ATM, broadband ISDN, and MAN technology.* New York: IEEE Press.

Sevcik, P. (2006). Application demands outrun internet improvements. *Business Communications Review, 36*(1).

Smith, J. E., & Weingarten, F. W. (1997). *Research challenges for the next generation internet.* Wasthington, DC: Computing Research Association.

Stoneman, P. (2001). *The economics of technological diffusion.* Malden, MA: Blackwell Publishing.

U.S. Congress. (1993). *Advanced network technology background paper* (OTA-BP-TCT-101).

ENDNOTES

[1] http://research.sun.com/spotlight/2007/2007-08-30_darkstar.html

[2] http://www.cel.sfsu.edu/institute/

[3] http://www.pcmag.com/encyclopedia_term/0,2542,t=ATM&i=38115,00.asp; http://blogs.zdnet.com/ITFacts/?p=5489; http://entmag.com/news/article.asp?EditorialsID=1779

[4] http://research.sun.com/spotlight/2007/2007-08-30_darkstar.html

[5] www.ietf.org/html.charters/ipv6-charter.html

[6] http://www.cs.purdue.edu/homes/fahmy/cis788.08Q/atmswitch.html; http://www.cisco.com/univercd/cc/td/doc/cisintwk/ito_doc/atm.htm; http://gnrt.terena.org/content.php?section_id=139

APPENDIX A: TABLES AND FIGURES

Figure 1. The ISO/OSI 7-layer model (Source: US Congress, 1993)

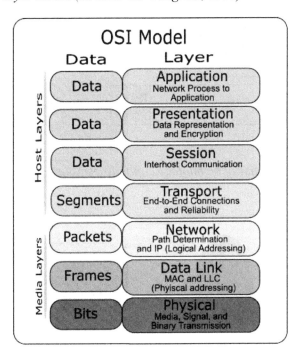

Figure 2. The ISO/OSI 7-layer model (Source: US Congress, 1993)

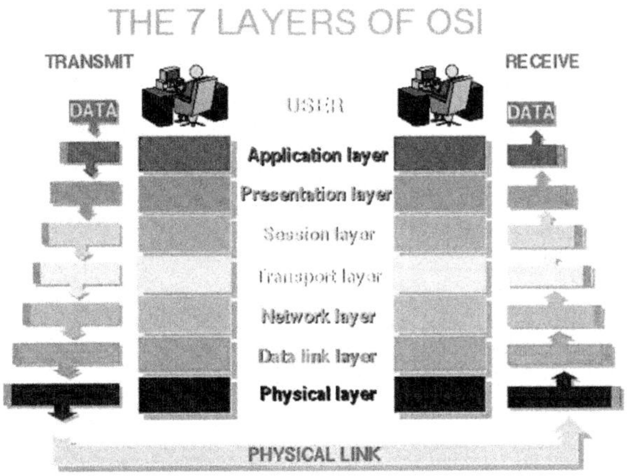

Figure 3. The TCP technology stack as mapped against the OSI model (Source: US Congress, 1993)

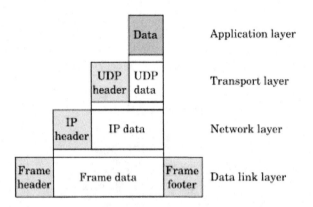

Figure 4. Current and desired states of technology capabilities(Source: Douglas et al., 2005)

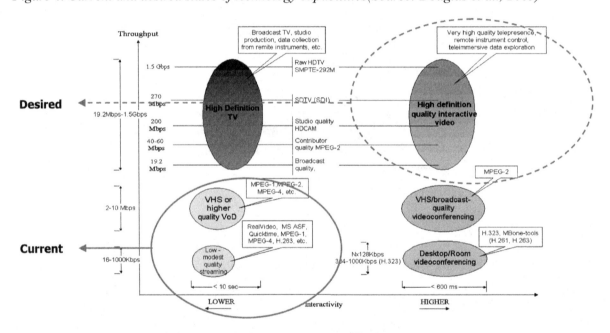

Figure 5. ATM switching network (Source: Robertazzi, 2003)

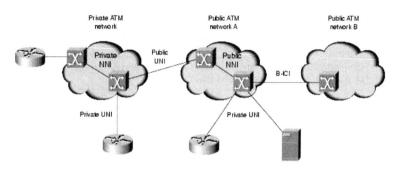

Figure 6. ATM switching as mapped to the OSI model (Source: Robertazzi, 2003)

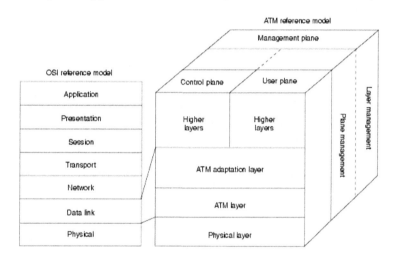

Figure 7. ATM virtual channels (Source: Robertazzi, 2003)

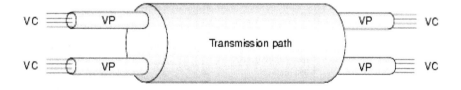

Table A1. Comparison of various compression technologies

Format	VCD	SVCD	DVD	HDDVD HDTV (WMVHD)	AVI DivX XviD WMV	MOV Quick-Time	RM Real-Media	AVI DV
Resolution NTSC/ PAL	352x240 352x288	480x480 480x576	720x480² 720x576²	1920x1080² 1280x720²	640x480²	640x480²	320x240²	720x480 720x576
Video Compression	MPEG1	MPEG2	MPEG2, MPEG1	MPEG2 (WMV-MPEG4)	MPEG4	Sorenson, Cinepak, MPEG4 ...	RM	DV
Video bitrate	1150kbps	~2000kbps	~5000kbps	~20Mbps (~8Mbps)	~1000kbps	~1000kbps	~350kbps	25Mbps
Audio Compression	MP1	MP1	MP1, MP2, AC3, DTS, PCM	MP1, MP2, AC3, DTS, PCM	MP3, WMA, OGG, AAC, AC3	QDesign Music, MP3 ...	RM	DV
Audio bitrate	224kbps	~224kbps	~448kbps	~448kbps	~128kbps	~128kbps	~64kbps	~1500kbps
Size/min	10 MB/ min	10-20 MB/ min	30-70 MB/ min	~150MB/min (~60MB/min)	4-10 MB/ min	4-20 MB/ min	2-5 MB/ min	216MB/min
Min/74min CD	74min	35-60min	10-20min	~4min (~10min)	60-180min	30-180 min	120-300 min	3min
Hours/DVD	N/A	N/A	1-2hrs (2-5hrs[a])	~30min (~1hrs)	7-18hrs	3-18hrs	14-35hrs	20min
Hours/DualLayer DVD	N/A	N/A	2-4hrs (5-9hrs[a])	~55min (~2hrs)	13-30hrs	6-30hrs	25-65hrs	37min
DVD Player Compatibility	Great	Good	Excellent	None	Few	None	None	None
Computer CPU Usage	Low	High	Very High	Super high	Very High	High	Low	High
Quality	Good	Great*	Excellent*	Superb*	Great*	Great*	Decent*	Excellent

Table A2. Benefits of IPv6

Benefits	Magnitude of Potential Benefits	Timing Issues	Likelihood of Occurence	Key Factors in Realizing Benefits of IPv6
Increased address space	Large	No near-term shortage in U.S.	Medium/High	Removal of NATs; growth in number of end-to-end and other applications
Simplified mobility	Large	New applications will likely flow from Asian test markets	Medium/High	Growth/demand for new applications
Reduced network administration costs	Modest	Cost may increase during transition	Medium (in the long term)	Removal of NATs
Improved overall network efficiency	Modest	Efficiency may not improve until after large scale transition	Low	Removal of NATs
Improved QoS capabilities	Modest/Small	Few benefits in the near future	Low	Ongoing standardization and subsequent implementation of QoS "flow label" field

Table A3. Cost of adoption of IPv6

Stake-holders	Relative Cost	Transition Cost Breakdown			Timing Issues	Key Factors in Bearing Costs
		Hard-Ware (HW)	Soft-ware (SW)	Labor		
Hardware Vendors	Low	10%	10%	80%	Currently most are providing IPv6 capabilities	Rolling in IPv6 as standard R&D expense; international interest and future profits incentives investments
Software Vendors	Low / Medium	10%	10%	80%	Currently some are providing IPv6 capabilities	Interoperability issues could increase costs
Internet Users (large)	Medium	10%	20%	70%	Very few currently using IPv6; HW and SW will become capable as routine upgrade; enabling cost should decrease over time	Users will wait for significantly lower enablement costs or (more probably) a killer application requiring IPv6 for end-to-end functionality before enabling
Internet Users (small)	Low	30%	40%	30%	Availability and adoption schedules	With little money to spare, these users must see a clear return on investment (ROI)
Internet Service Providers (ISPs)	High	15%	15%	70%	Very few offering IPv6 service; no demand currently; very high cost currently to upgrade major capabilities	ISPs see low or nonexistent ROI, high costs, and high risk

Table A4. Relative cost of IPv6 by stakeholders

Item	Hardware, Software, Service Providers	ISPs	Enterprise Users	
Hardware				
Replace interfacing cards	H		M	
Replace routing/forwarding engine(s)	M	M		
Replace chassis (if line cards will not fit)		M	M	
Replace firewall		M	M	
Software				
Upgrade network monitoring/management software		H	H	
Upgrade operating system		M	H	
Upgrade applications				

continued on following page

Table A4. Continued

Item	Hardware, Software, Service Providers	ISPs	Enterprise Users	
• Servers (Web, DNS, file transfer protocol (FTP), mail, music, video. etc.)			L	
• Enterprise resource planning software (e.g., PeopleSoft, Oracle, SAP, etc.)			H	
• Other organization-specific, network-enabled applications			H	
Labor				
R & D	M	L		
Train networking/IT employees	H	H	H	
Design IPv6 transition strategy and a network vision	M	H	M/H	
Implement transition:				
• Install and configure any new hardware	L	H	H	
• Configure transition technique (e.g., tunneling, dual-stack, NAT-port address translation	M	M	M	
• Upgrade software (see Software section above)		L/M	L/M	
• Extensive test before "going live" with IPv6 services		H	H	
Maintain new system		M/H	M/H	
Other				
IPv6 address blocks			L	
Lost employee productivity				
Security intrusions		H	H	
Foreign activities		M	M	
Interoperability issues		M/H	M/H	

Table A5. Expert opinion on the relative importance of the three gateways

Pair-wise comparison of choices (100 point spread)					
<u>Choices</u>					
S1 = Market Gateway					
S2 = Management Gateway					
S3 = Technology Gateway					
Expert #1					
S1	**S2**	**S1**	**S3**	**S2**	**S3**
30	70	40	60	70	30
Expert #2					
S1	**S2**	**S1**	**S3**	**S2**	**S3**
20	80	50	50	60	40
Expert #3					
S1	**S2**	**S1**	**S3**	**S2**	**S3**
40	60	30	70	50	50
Expert #4					
S1	**S2**	**S1**	**S3**	**S2**	**S3**
20	80	20	80	70	30
Expert #5					
S1	**S2**	**S1**	**S3**	**S2**	**S3**
30	70	30	70	70	30

Table A6. Result of pair-wise comparison using the PCM tool

	Market	**Management**	**Technology**
Mean	0.18	0.51	0.31
Std Dev	0.04	0.08	0.07

Table A7. Survey results for grading gateway factors on a 5-point scale for MPEG-4, IPv6 and ATM technologies, respectively

MPEG-4	Factors	Survey Results	Average
Market			
	New uses	5,4,5,5,4,3,5,5,4,5,4,5,3,4,4,5	4.38
	User skepticism	4,4,5,4,5,4,5,4,5,5,5,5,4,4,4,5	4.50
	Behavior adjustment	5,5,5,5,4,5,5,5,4,5,5,4,4,3,5,5	4.63
	Competition	4,3,4,4,4,3,4,5,4,3,3,3,4,3,4,4	3.69
	Unpredictable technology	3,4,3,4,5,4,3,4,3,3,3,4,4,4,3,4	3.63
	Legal barriers	4,5,4,3,4,5,5,5,4,5,4,5,4,4,4,5	4.38

continued on following page

Table A7. Continued

MPEG-4	Factors	Survey Results	Average
Management			
	Risk	5,5,5,5,4,5,5,5,4,5,5,5,5,4,5,5	4.81
	Production	5,5,4,4,4,4,4,4,5,4,4,4,5,4,4	4.23
Technology			
	Innovativeness	3,4,3,3,3,4,3,4,4,4,3,4,3,4,4,3	3.50
	Constituent technologies	4,4,4,3,4,3,3,3,3,3,4,3,3,4,3,4	3.44
	Manufacturing difficulty	5,5,4,4,4,4,4,4,5,4,3,3,3,4,5,4	4.06
	Institutional changes	5,5,4,5,5,5,5,4,4,5,3,4,5,5,4,5	4.56
IPv6	**Factors**	**Survey Results**	**Average**
Market			
	New uses	3,4,4,5,5,5,5,5,5,4,4,5,5,4,3,4	4.38
	User skepticism	5,4,5,5,5,5,5,5,4,5,5,5,4,5,5,5	4.81
	Behavior adjustment	5,5,5,5,5,5,5,5,5,5,4,4,5,5,5,5	4.88
	Competition	4,5,5,5,5,5,4,4,5,5,5,5,4,4,5,5	4.69
	Unpredictable technology	5,4,4,5,4,4,4,5,4,3,4,4,4,4,5,4	4.19
	Legal barriers	4,5,5,5,4,5,4,4,3,4,4,4,5,5,5,3	4.31
Management			
	Risk	3,3,4,4,4,3,3,4,4,4,4,5,4,4,4,3	3.75
	Production	3,3,4,3,3,3,3,3,4,3,3,4,3,2,3,3,4	3.19
Technology			
	Innovativeness	5,5,4,4,4,4,4,4,5,4,4,3,4,4,3,4	4.06
	Constituent technologies	3,3,3,2,3,3,3,2,3,3,3,4,3,3,2,3	2.88
	Manufacturing difficulty	4,4,4,4,5,4,4,3,4,4,3,3,4,4,4,3	3.81
	Institutional changes	4,3,4,4,4,3,3,3,3,4,3,2,2,3,3,3	3.25
ATM	**Factors**	**Survey Results**	**Average**
Market			
	New uses	2,3,2,3,3,3,2,3,4,4,4,3,3,4,3,3	3.06
	User skepticism	2,2,3,3,2,2,2,2,2,3,2,2,2,3,3,2	2.31
	Behavior adjustment	4,4,4,4,5,5,4,4,5,5,4,5,5,4,3	4.38
	Competition	3,3,2,3,3,4,3,3,2,3,3,4,3,3,2,2	2.88
	Unpredictable technology	4,4,4,3,4,4,5,5,5,4,4,3,4,3,3,3	3.88
	Legal barriers	4,3,4,5,5,5,4,4,3,3,4,4,5,4,4,3	4.00
Management			
	Risk	3,3,3,2,3,3,3,4,4,3,4,3,3,2,3,2	3.00
	Production	3,4,3,3,3,4,4,4,4,3,4,5,5,4,3,4	3.75

MPEG-4	Factors	Survey Results	Average
Technology			
	Innovativeness	5,4,4,5,5,4,4,4,5,4,4,5,4,5,4,4	4.38
	Constituent technologies	3,4,3,4,3,4,3,4,4,4,3,4,3,4,4,3	3.56
	Manufacturing difficulty	4,4,4,4,5,4,4,4,5,5,5,4,4,4,5,4	4.31
	Institutional changes	3,4,3,3,2,2,2,3,3,4,3,3,3,2,2,3	2.81

Chapter 2
Clustering Obsolete Computers to Reduce E-Waste

Timothy M. Lynar
University of Newcastle, Australia

Simon
University of Newcastle, Australia

Ric D. Herbert
University of Newcastle, Australia

William J. Chivers
University of Newcastle, Australia

ABSTRACT

Personal computers contribute significantly to the growing problem of electronic waste. Every computer, when finished with, must be stored, dumped, recycled, or somehow re-used. Most are dumped, at a huge cost to health and the environment, as their owners succumb to the desire to keep up with the ever-increasing power of new computers. Supercomputers and computer clusters provide more power than ordinary desktop and laptop computers, but they too are subject to rapid obsolescence. The authors have built a cluster of obsolete computers and have found that it easily outperforms a fairly standard new desktop computer. They explore how this approach can help to mitigate e-waste, and discuss the advantages and limitations of using such a system.

INTRODUCTION

Electronic waste (e-waste) or waste electrical and electronic equipment (WEEE) is a vast and burgeoning problem in today's society, and personal computers contribute significantly to this problem. Every computer, when finished with, must be stored, dumped, recycled, or somehow re-used. Most are dumped, at a huge cost to health and the environment, as their owners succumb to the desire to keep up with the ever-increasing power of new computers. Supercomputers and computer clusters provide even more power than ordinary desktop and laptop computers, but they too are subject to rapid obsolescence. This paper examines how clusters of obsolete computers can help to mitigate e-waste.

DOI: 10.4018/978-1-4666-0927-3.ch002

We propose the following hypotheses:

1. The lives of obsolete computers can be usefully prolonged by building them into a computing cluster.
2. A cluster of obsolete computers can perform at least as well as a new computer.
3. A large enough cluster of obsolete computers can perform comparably to a smaller cluster of new computers.

After discussing the problem of e-waste and the purpose of computing clusters, we explain the reasons for building a cluster from obsolete rather than new computers. We then report on the cluster we have built, on its performance, and on its advantages and limitations.

The novelty of this research is that it is proposing a new method of e-waste management. We are proposing to re-use old desktop machines for the purpose of mitigating the creation of new clusters. We are proposing that this be an ongoing process, with newer waste computers continually replacing older redundant machines.

E-WASTE

E-waste is a recent term referring to electronic goods that have been discarded or have entered a period of disuse. E-waste can include many items such as televisions, electronic audio equipment, white goods, mobile phones, and computer systems (ABS, 2006; Terazono et al., 2006). However, the definition and assessment of e-waste differ across organisations and countries. Terazono et al. (2006) observe that "there is no standard definition of e-waste, and the methods used to estimate e-waste generation are not compatible among countries".

The component of e-waste that we address here is computers, particularly personal computers constructed out of ordinary commodity parts.

Why is E-Waste a Problem?

E-waste is increasingly becoming an issue for both developing and developed nations. E-waste has become an issue in Australia and the rest of the world, for a number of reasons including the large and growing quantity of e-waste, the methods of disposal and deconstruction of e-waste, the quantities of non-renewable resources in e-waste, the potential environmental and health effects of incorrect disposal of e-waste, and the potential for damage to the reputations of companies and countries.

There is already a large and growing quantity of e-waste in Australia and throughout the world. An Australian Bureau of Statistics report notes that e-waste is a rapidly growing source of waste in Australia, and little of it is currently recycled. "E-waste is one of the fastest growing waste types. Very little of the increasing amount of e-waste generated in Australia is being recycled, with most of it ending up in landfill" (ABS, 2006).

The Australian Bureau of Statistics found in 2006 that Australians purchase 2.4 million personal computers each year (ABS, 2006). Presumably almost as many computers are made obsolete each year, and this is a growing problem: "It is estimated that there are currently around nine million computers, five million printers and two million scanners in households and businesses across Australia... E-waste in Australia is growing at over three times the rate of general municipal waste" (ABS, 2006).

There are numerous metals and chemicals used in the production of electronic goods, some of which can cause serious health and environmental consequences. E-waste, and particularly computer waste, is both valuable and hazardous. Personal computers contain a large variety of materials including toxic and valuable metals: "A typical PC consists of 23 percent plastic, 32 percent ferrous metals, 18 percent nonferrous metals, and 12 percent electronic boards (gold, palladium, silver, and platinum)" (Krikke, 2008). The toxic constituents include heavy metals such as lead, mercury, arsenic, and cadmium, and also chemicals such as brominated flame retardants (Terazono et al., 2006). The valuable materials in e-waste can be difficult to extract, and the methods of disposal or recycling can dictate the environmental and health effects that the waste will have. It is these effects that appear to be one of the primary concerns relating to electronic waste.

Disposal Methods

Four basic methods are employed for dealing with e-waste: reuse the item, recycle the item, dump the item, or store the item.

Landfill and storage are the two main methods employed in Australia. Australia has a significant number of computers disposed of every year. According to ABS (2006), "it has been estimated that in 2006 there will be around 1.6 million computers disposed of in landfill, 1.8 million put in storage (in addition to the 5.3 million already gathering dust in garages and other storage areas) and 0.5 million recycled in Australia alone".

Recycling of e-waste can take many forms. At the low technology end of the spectrum, people are employed to remove components manually and sort parts into piles of like materials based on the observation of a part's properties. At the high technology end, computers are first shredded into uniform-sized pieces then sorted in machines (Krikke, 2008). Some machines use magnets, x-rays, or alternating electrical currents to separate metals, while others sort plastics based on their density (Krikke, 2008).

However, much e-waste is exported each year to developing nations, and ends up in the unofficial recycling industry where low technology methods of recycling and deconstruction are generally used (Li et al., 2006).

Many individuals who believe that their e-waste is being recycled may find that it has been exported to another country for processing, even though its export and import are illegal in many nations. Cairns (2005) observes that "A substantial quantity of the equipment returned for recycling, more than half by some estimates, may actually be exported for disposal in other countries where environmental and occupational health protections are weak and landfills are not properly controlled".

Li et al. (2006) posit three economic reasons for developed countries to export e-waste to developing countries such as China: the lower cost of recycling waste, lower labour costs, and larger demand for the secondary materials that can be recovered from the waste. There is a growing demand for natural resources in China, and some of the metals that can be recovered from the e-waste are valuable (Tong, 2004). Indeed, it is estimated that despite their low quantity, precious metals make up some 80% of the value of recycled computers (Streicher-Porte et al., 2005).

Many developing nations import e-waste. In some, such as China, its importation is illegal (Li et al., 2006), but it still takes place under different names. E-waste is often transformed into 'metal scrap', which is then sold overseas for further processing. In Korea, "crushed e-waste is categorized as scrap that is needed to be recycled overseas. This e-waste is exported under the name of mixed metal scrap" (Terazono et al., 2006). This method of exporting e-waste appears common in many nations. "The US exports more than $1 billion of scrap to China annually" (Krikke, 2008). However, it cannot be determined what quantity of this scrap metal is a result of e-waste.

Even without importation, China has e-waste problems of its own. In 2003 China domestically consumed 30.7 million new personal computers, and it is estimated that by 2010 China will have over 70 million obsolete personal computers (Li et al., 2006).

Due to tradition and cultural differences the Chinese people are unlikely to dispose of e-waste in landfill: "According to the traditional economical custom, Chinese seldom discharge their used electrical and electronic products, even if these products are out of date or broken" (Li et al., 2006). Instead they either store them or recycle them.

Guiyu, in Guangdong Province, southern China, has a concentration of unofficial electronics recycling programs, typically using very basic methods. The recycling methods and the waste products appear to be causing significant damage to the environment and the health of the workers. Guiyu is famous for its "primitive techniques used in extracting metals from used products, such as open burning of e-wastes" (Terazono et al., 2006). There has been a significant amount of media attention to the issue of e-waste because of Guiyu. It appears that the Chinese government has now taken steps towards cleaning up the unofficial recycling industry in China, through the creation of recycling parks and the introduction of new laws (Li et al., 2006).

The export of e-waste is not limited to Asia. There is a growing trend to export e-waste to Africa, where its disposal is typically different from that in Asia (Schmidt, 2006).

In Africa there is generally little or no attempt to recover materials from the e-waste, so it is often piled up and burnt. It would appear that a proportion of the waste is resold or used for refurbishing. Many of the waste items may have come in as legitimate donations, while others may have been purchased, with the cost being paid for by the transportation of useless components whose disposal is costly in the west, such as CRT displays (Schmidt, 2006).

The Basel convention is an international agreement that prohibits the international movement of certain hazardous wastes; e-waste is included under Annex VIII List A of the convention (Basel, 1989). The preamble of the convention document makes it clear that the intention of the prohibition is due to the potential negative effects of certain waste products on the environment and on human health. As of 2006 the Basel convention had been signed by 168 countries (ABS, 2006). However, this does not appear to have stopped the movement of e-waste from developed countries to developing countries.

CLUSTERS FOR HIGH PERFORMANCE COMPUTING

Research institutions routinely utilise high performance computing equipment to run experiments and to train and teach students.

Historically, processor-intensive applications such as computer modelling have employed supercomputers, but this high performance is costly. While supercomputers yield the highest performance feasible, they also have the highest cost of any system (Schneck, 1990).

A cheaper alternative is promised by clustering, which offers the computing power of a supercomputer at a far lower price (Sterling et al., 1999). A cluster is a group of stand-alone computing elements that usually reside in the same location. Clusters comprise independent and self-supporting computing systems networked together to provide a means of interaction that can be utilised in the completion of common tasks (Sterling et al., 1999). A cluster works by distributing the processing load of an application among its stand-alone computing elements, which can be anything from powerful servers to humble personal computers, or a combination (Sterling et al., 1999). For this reason it is feasible to develop a cluster for a fraction of the cost of a supercomputer.

Clusters are typically used to run research applications or other applications that require substantial computation. Clusters are not designed as a desktop replacement but as a substitute for a supercomputer or other high-performance computing resource.

Clusters have been used for many such tasks; in prior research we have used clusters for the computation of computationally intensive agent-based models (Lynar et al., 2009). Other researchers have utilised clusters for a variety of computational tasks including mapping (Hangrove et al., 2001).

For a cluster to operate, an application must be programmed in a way that allows it to be distributed among the nodes of the cluster. When the application is executed on the cluster, each node simultaneously processes its own part of the application. This is known as distributed parallel computing.

We intend to use our e-waste cluster for educational activities and for data mining. Data mining is an ideal task, as the records can be divided evenly amongst the nodes in the cluster and only minimal data needs to be transferred between the nodes, allowing for substantial scalability.

Modern computing power, parallel programming, and clustering techniques allow for the creation of high performance computing environments at a relatively low cost. However, this small cost is still too high for many institutions. Further, from an e-waste point of view, it typically adds to the problem, as there will generally be more hardware in a cluster than in a supercomputer.

A CLUSTER OF OBSOLETE COMPUTERS

Streicher-Porte et al. (2005) traced the entire life cycle of the personal computer in Delhi, from production through sale and consumption, reuse and refurbishment, to the material recovery in the mainly informal recycling industry. The study revealed that prolonging the life span of a personal computer creates value by means of refurbishing and upgrading activities, and slows down the flow rate of the whole system. It concluded that life-prolongation is one of the simplest ways of preventing an uncontrolled increase in environmentally hazardous emissions by the recycling sector (Streicher-Porte et al., 2005).

While refurbished computers can be a boon to people who have no alternative, they are not so appealing to institutions in the developed world, where the ever-increasing power and capability of new computers are harder to resist.

This is where cluster computing can contribute to the solution. Clusters can be created out of disused personal computers. Many personal computers that would otherwise be recycled, dumped, or stored indefinitely can be given a second life as nodes in a cluster of reused commodity workstations. If a cluster of reused workstations can fulfil needs that would otherwise require a cluster of new computers, those new computers would never enter the supply chain, thus reducing the inevitable consequent e-waste.

The process of constructing a cluster of reused computers would not be without its costs. The computers would still need to be set up as a cluster, and would still consume electricity, possibly more than a comparable cluster of new computers. Furthermore, the nodes in the cluster would still eventually need disposal. However, if they were replaced on a rolling basis by newer obsolete computers, the cluster would be continually upgraded at no additional cost to the environment. With these upgrades the cluster would benefit from the same new technological advantages in performance and power consumption as would new computers.

In addition, the construction of clusters from e-waste saves money. An e-waste cluster can be created at little or no cost, as the computers are generally available at no cost at all.

There has been some previous work on the construction of clusters out of donated hardware, and the results were positive (Hangrove et al., 2001). However, there are a number of limitations to using e-waste computer systems for high performance computing environments, and these limitations need to be explored to understand the full cost of utilising e-waste as a substitute for new computers in a cluster.

First, the computers used in the cluster do not execute applications as fast as newer computers, so more of them are needed to create a comparable resource. Second, the need for more computers means that the power consumption will be greater. And third, the equipment is nearing or even beyond the end of its designed life-span and is therefore more susceptible to hardware faults.

IMPLEMENTING AN E-WASTE CLUSTER

To test our hypotheses we have created a cluster from hardware that would otherwise have joined the e-waste stream. The cluster was constructed entirely from donated obsolete computers, network switch, and cables. The only cost associated with the creation of the cluster was the time spent setting it up and sorting through the e-waste to identify suitable equipment, a task that took one person three days. We do not believe that it would have taken any less time to set up a similar cluster with new hardware.

Hardware

This project has so far received 56 computers. Despite their age and obsolescence, only 12 had some form of hardware fault, and seven of those were easily fixed. Three of the faults were related to the floppy disc drive and three to the hard disc drive, which, as moving components, are most susceptible to error. Neither of these components was required for use in the cluster, so the faulty items were simply removed. Reliability of the other components of the e-waste computers did not appear to be an issue.

The cluster used for this paper consists of eight computing nodes, all of which are standard commodity desktop computers between four and a half and six years old. All computers contain old 100MBs network interface cards, and we have connected them with a 100MBs switch. The processors are single-core Pentium 4s, with clock speeds of 2.4 or 2.66 GHz.

Table 1 lists the cluster nodes, along with a new computer that was used for comparisons.

The computers in the cluster are computers that have been disused and discarded from our university, and are a cross-section of the computers received for the project. The new computer was the most recent computer available to the authors for examination. This computer was not e-waste at the time of writing and would appear to be representative of average mid-range new computers of the time.

Software

Like the hardware, all software used in the creation of this cluster was obtained at no cost. The OpenMPI implementation of the Message Passing Interface (MPI) was used to enable the execution of parallel applications on the GNU Debian operating system (Debian, 2007). The operating system was created with the Debian live project (Baumann, 2008) so that it could be booted and run without interacting with the hard disc drives of any computers in the cluster. This operating

Table 1. The cluster nodes and the new computer

Node name	Processor	Memory
Computer 1	Pentium 4 2.4GHz	256 MB
Computer 2	Pentium 4 2.4GHz	256 MB
Computer 3	Pentium 4 2.4GHz	256 MB
Computer 4	Pentium 4 2.4GHz	256 MB
Computer 5	Pentium 4 2.4GHz	256 MB
Computer 6	Pentium 4 2.4GHz	256 MB
Computer 7	Pentium 4 2.66GHz	512 MB
Computer 8	Pentium 4 2.66GHz	512 MB
New computer	Athlon 64X2 2.8GHz	1024 MB

system was loaded from a CD-ROM during boot of the first node, and subsequent nodes were booted from the same CD-ROM across the network.

This approach makes it simple to reconfigure the cluster as required. With all nodes connected to the network switch, each node but the first must have its BIOS settings adjusted to boot from the network. The node is then turned on, whereupon it boots from the network and automatically becomes part of the cluster. Thus the size of the cluster is determined simply by how many nodes are booted in this way.

PERFORMANCE OF THE CLUSTER

We have tested our cluster with a standard benchmark, to assess its computing power, speed, and electrical power efficiency.

Computing Power

To measure the computational performance of the cluster we executed a common linear algebra algorithm on both the 8-node cluster and the new computer. A synthetic benchmark, High Performance Linpack (HPL), was used on the cluster and on the new computer. The HPL benchmark is a parallel benchmark that runs over MPI and uses the single process multiple data (SPMD) model of parallel computing (Wang et al., 2004). The HPL benchmark is widely used and recognised, and is the benchmark that is used in compiling the Top500 supercomputer list (Top500, 2007).

In configuring the benchmark, the following parameters were altered from the default. PxQ, the number of process rows and columns, was set to 1x2 for the new computer, as it has a dual processor, and 2x4 for the grid, as it has eight processors. NB, the granularity of block size, was set to 100. N, the dimension of the matrix and thus a measure of problem size, was increased in increments of 1000 until memory was exhausted.

The HPL results indicate that the cluster performed at a maximum of 6.32 Gflops and the new computer performed at a maximum of 2.235 Gflops.

Given that the computers used in the cluster are up to six years old, this is a promising result. It should be noted that the problem size (N) for the cluster was significantly larger than for the new computer, which would not be able to process such a large problem without resorting to the use of swap space. The new computer was able to handle values of N up to 10,000, while the cluster handled N up to 13,000.

Speed

The HPL benchmark may not accurately measure the performance of a cluster of heterogeneous hardware (Wang et al., 2004). It may underestimate the performance of such a cluster, as the problem size is limited by the computer with the least amount of available RAM (Loreto et al., 2005). For this reason a second test was conducted to compare the cluster and the new computer on the same problem.

For this test the benchmark was set with the same problem size, N, of 3000, which is the default. PxQ was set to 4x4, dividing the problem up so that each node would have to process at least two sets of data. This test was designed to determine how quickly the cluster and the new computer would compute the same SPMD application. The Linux *time* command was used to measure the time each system took to execute the same application.

The test was executed 10 times on the cluster and 10 times on the new computer. As shown in Figure 1, the cluster consistently outpaced the new computer, which performed the task in an average time of 190 seconds as compared with 156 seconds for the cluster. A one-way Analysis of Variance (ANOVA) was used to compare the execution times, and showed the difference to be significant, with p<0.001.

Power Consumption

Power consumption measurements were taken for each node of the grid and for the new computer under similar environmental conditions, both while the computers were idle and while they were executing a computationally intensive benchmark. Not surprisingly, the cluster consumed significantly more power than the new computer.

When the systems were idle, the cluster consumed 468W of power while the new computer used 80W. When computing the performance benchmark, the cluster consumed 537W and the new computer 92W. Figure 2 shows the comparison.

The power efficiency of a system is calculated by dividing its measured power consumption by its measured performance (Adams & Brom, 2008). For the cluster, with 537W and 6.32 Gflops, this gives an efficiency of 85 W/Gflops. For the new computer, with 92W and 2.235 Gflops, the

efficiency is 41 W/Gflops. So while the cluster has significantly more computing power than the new computer, its higher consumption of electrical power should be considered when deciding whether an e-waste cluster is an acceptable use of resources.

Cost Efficiency

Adams and Brom (2008) define a system's cost efficiency as its price/performance ratio, and assert that at $94.10 their cluster is the first Beowulf cluster to break the $100/Gflops barrier. By the same measure of capital cost, our new computer cost about $1,000/Gflops, while our cluster cost $0/Gflops, and can therefore lay claim to being the first Beowulf cluster to reach the $0/Gflops barrier.

While it is hard to put a monetary value on the environmental cost of disposal, again the cluster costs nothing because it is built from components that were already destined for disposal.

Figure 1. Time taken to execute benchmark

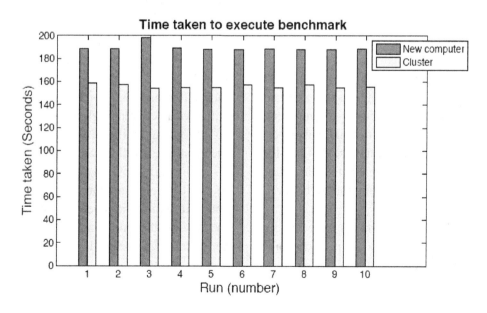

Figure 2. power consumption (in Watts) of the cluster and the new computer

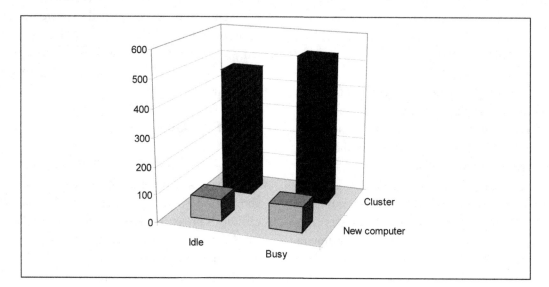

CONCLUSION AND FUTURE WORK

In response to our first and second hypotheses, we have shown that we can prolong the lives of obsolete computers by combining them in a cluster, where for computing-intensive operations they outperform a standard new computer. Of course we are not suggesting that users replace their personal computers with clusters. Rather, we are suggesting that a cluster of reused computers can provide a greater computational ability than a standalone workstation and as such would be a reasonable resource for computationally intensive tasks, for which a conventional cluster might otherwise be used. At the very least, we have shown that in circumstances that call for a cluster of computers, it is feasible and indeed easy to build that cluster from computers that were otherwise destined for the growing stream of e-waste. For teaching uses, therefore, a cluster such as this should be more than adequate.

Our third hypothesis was that a large enough cluster of obsolete computers can perform comparably to a smaller cluster of new computers.

Our exploration demonstrates that the size of the cluster can be increased very easily, bringing about a corresponding increase in computing power. Essentially, we believe that we can increase the power of the cluster almost indefinitely by increasing its number of nodes. Therefore we have the means to emulate a cluster of new computers, and indeed a supercomputer, simply by saving enough old personal computers from the scrapheap. Furthermore, our cluster can be continually upgraded as newer computers are scrapped, so it will experience a growth in power that is in step with that of new computers. Even though there is a trend to make newer computers more environmentally friendly, their disposal will still have a very real impact on the environment, so prolonging their lives by building them into the cluster will still reduce that impact.

We intend to build a significantly bigger cluster, to use it for computational modelling tasks of a sort that require massive computing power, and to seek out other computationally intensive tasks for which it can be used. We shall do this in the knowledge that we are, in a small way, contributing to a solution to the e-waste problem.

ACKNOWLEDGMENT

The authors acknowledge the Editor-in-Chief of the journal, Professor John Wang, and the anonymous reviewers for their indispensable input, which has significantly improved the paper.

REFERENCES

ABS. (2006). *Australia's environment: Issues and trends 2006*. Cat. no. 4613.0, Australian Bureau of Statistics, Canberra.

Adams, J. C., & Brom, T. H. (2008). Microwulf: A Beowulf cluster for every desk. In *SIGCSE '08: Proceedings of the 39th Technical Symposium on Computer Science Education* (pp. 121-125).

Basel (1989). *Basel Convention on the control of transboundary movements of hazardous wastes and their disposal*. United Nations Environment Programme (UNEP). Retrieved May 4, 2008, from www.basel.int/text/con-e-rev.pdf

Baumann, D. (2008). *Debian live: Live Debian systems*. Retrieved July 19, 2008, from debian-live. alioth.debian.org

Cairns, C. N. (2005). E-waste and the consumer: Improving options to reduce, reuse and recycle. In *Proceedings of the 2005 IEEE International Symposium on Electronics and the Environment* (pp. 237-242).

Debian (2007). *Debian – The universal operating system. software in the public interest*. Retrieved May 28, 2007, from www.debian.org

Hangrove, W., Hoffman, F., Sterling, T., & Kay, C. (2001). The do-it-yourself supercomputer. *Scientific American, 285*(2), 72–80.

Krikke, J. (2008). Recycling e-waste: the sky is the limit. *IT Professional, 10*(1), 50–55. doi:10.1109/MITP.2008.16

Li, J., Tian, B., Liu, T., Liu, H., Wen, X., & Honda, S. (2006). Status quo of e-waste management in mainland China. *Journal of Material Cycles and Waste Management, 8*(1), 13–20. doi:10.1007/s10163-005-0144-3

Loreto, D., Nordlander, E., & Oliner, A. (2005). *Benchmarking a large-scale heterogeneous cluster*. Retrieved 20 June 2008, from beowulf.lcs. mit.edu/ 18.337-2005/projects/top500writeup.pdf

Lynar, T., Herbert, H., & Chivers, W. (2009). Implementing an agent based auction on a cluster of reused workstations. *International Journal of Computer Applications in Technology, 34*(4), 230–234. doi:10.1504/IJCAT.2009.024071

Schmidt, C. W. (2006). Unfair trade e-waste in Africa. *Environmental Health Perspectives, 114*(4), A232–A235.

Schneck, P. B. (1990). Supercomputers. *Annual Review of Computer Science, 4*, 13–36. doi:10.1146/annurev.cs.04.060190.000305

Sterling, T., Salmon, J., Becker, D., & Savarese, D. F. (1999). *How to build a Beowulf*. London, MA: MIT Press

Streicher-Porte, M., Widmer, R., Jain, A., Bader, H.-P., Scheidegger, R., & Kytzia, S. (2005). Key drivers of the e-waste recycling system: assessing and modeling e-waste processing in the informal sector in Delhi. *Environmental Impact Assessment Review, 25*, 472–291. doi:10.1016/j.eiar.2005.04.004

Terazono, A., Murakami, S., Abe, N., Inanc, B., Moriguchi, Y., & Sakai, S.-I. (2006). Current status and research on E-waste issues in Asia. *Journal of Material Cycles and Waste Management, 8*(1), 1–12. doi:10.1007/s10163-005-0147-0

Top500 (2007). *Top500 supercomputing sites.* Retrieved 20 June 2008, from www.top500.org

Tong, X. (2004). Global mandate, national policies, and local responses: scale conflicts in China's management of imported e-waste. In *Proceedings of the 2004 IEEE International Symposium on Electronics and the Environment* (pp. 204-207).

Wang, P., Turner, G., Lauer, D., Allen, M., Simms, S., Hart, D., et al. (2004). Linpack performance on a geographically distributed Linux cluster. In *Proceedings of the 18th International Parallel and Distributed Processing Symposium* (pp. 245-250).

This work was previously published in International Journal of Information Systems and Social Change, Volume 1, Issue 1, edited by John Wang, pp. 1-10, copyright 2010 by IGI Publishing (an imprint of IGI Global).

Chapter 3
The Search Engine as an Internet Service Channel

Leslie S. Hiraoka
Kean University, USA

ABSTRACT

Development of the search engine as a major information and marketing channel resulted from innovative technologies that made it capable of presenting rapid, relevant responses to queries. To do this, the search engine compiles an index of web pages of information stored on the World Wide Web, ranks each page according to its incoming links, matches keywords in the query to those in its index, and returns what it determines are the most relevant pages to the searcher. Innovative and cost-effective ad placement algorithms have attracted advertisers to search engine websites and intensified the competitive dynamics among industry leaders. Their interacting software also continues to draw advertisers from traditional, mass marketing channels like television and newspapers to the online medium to cater to customers who have expressed an interest in their products and services.

INTRODUCTION

In July 2009, search engines responded to 113 billion queries, presenting requested information in the form of text on web pages, images, and other files that resided on the World Wide Web (WWW). This represented a 41% increase in search usage that began when the WWW's system and software were released in 1992. With the public expansion of the web, considerable expertise was needed for locating information and navigating it required services that catalogued its contents on directories, portals, and indexes. Search engines retrieve text and other data on the web and then index the information enabling them to respond quickly to queries from users of their service. Because of the vast amount of information in their indexes, search providers use various algorithms and formulas in an attempt to present results that are relevant and fit the needs of the information seeker. If it provides results that are specious or useless, the user can easily transfer the search to another provider. Feedback from users

DOI: 10.4018/978-1-4666-0927-3.ch003

is consequently immediate and to hold on to their customers, search engines are under considerable pressure to make their services easy to use with rapid response times that provide useful information links (Mostafa, 2005; Williams et al., 2008).

When search results are presented, they are often accompanied by advertisements which are related to the topic being searched, making the search process an interactive marketing channel for services and products. These ads are the principal source of income for these companies and they compete for advertisers by assisting in the designing of ads which are then placed close to search results for viewing by users who expressed an interest in a particular ad's service or product. Online ad revenues for leading U.S. search engines ranged from $2.8 billion to $11.7 billion in 2007 and because the market is expanding, the competition among search engines for innovative search and ad placement software has intensified (Nocera, 2008).

By detailing the competitive dynamics of the search service industry, this study will focus on how innovative technology and entrepreneurship gained market share for the leading search channels – Google, Yahoo, and Microsoft – and gave rise to online advertising revenue. The growth of the industry will be placed in the context of the development of the Internet and WWW as an information, communications, and marketing medium, followed by the technological advances in search services. The underwriting of the search business by capital markets and by raising ad revenues is detailed followed by an examination of the competitive dynamics of the industry. Concluding remarks are then made.

INDUSTRIAL FRAMEWORK

The Personal Computer (PC)

The commercial success of the IBM PC, first sold in 1981, marked a major shift in the industry by downsizing the computer and its cost and making it available for individual use at home and at work. Technological advances in user-friendly software and powerful micro-processing semiconductor chips also made the PC efficient in creating files, documents, and databases and its use spread rapidly among professionals, office workers, and students who had relied on the typewriter. Microsoft became the main beneficiary of this transition even though it did not develop but instead purchased the technology for the operating system (OS) software that IBM leased for its PC. In the partnership, Microsoft's management, unlike its counterpart at IBM, understood that software controlled the computer, and the PC with applications programs like word processing would commercially supplant the bigger mainframe machine. The mainframe was also a stand-alone machine that did not share its processing power with other computers. This changed with the spread of the desktop computer especially at research and development (R&D) firms where work on technical projects was conducted simultaneously by engineering teams. Such efforts could be accelerated if the machines were networked allowing information and work to be shared among members of the team. To advance the time-sharing of computing power, Sun Microsystems introduced the first networked work station – a more powerful PC – in 1982 adding to the flexibility and utility of desktop computers (Southwick, 1999). These attributes resulted in a major shift of marketing power from hardware manufacturers of large computers like IBM and DEC to software developers like Microsoft and assemblers of PCs like Compaq which acquired DEC and its Alta Vista search engine in 1998 (Steinmuller, 1996).

Commercial Use of the Internet

The PC was also instrumental in transforming the Arpanet – the secure, communications network of the U.S. Department of Defense (DOD) – into a publicly-used medium. It was established as a "survivable communications network" connecting military installations and command centers that could withstand a nuclear attack and launch retaliatory strikes. It also linked DOD-funded research centers and facilitated the time-sharing of computer resources which could then be used at other sites. Another major application was the digital transmission of messages or email (Abate, 1999).

As individual ownership and processing power of the PC grew, hackers began to threaten the security of the Arpanet and compelled the DOD to replace it with a more secure network. In 1987 the Arpanet became a public network that was renamed the Internet and operated by the National Science Foundation, a government agency. In 1991 the U.S. Congress authorized use of the Internet as a commercial medium and marketing channel for private enterprise. The measure extended to linked websites on the WWW since they resided on server computers that comprised part of the Internet's hardware (Shipley & Fish, 1996).

For accessing information, Tim Berners-Lee, creator of the WWW, developed an addressing format that identified the server where desired information was stored. These became known as uniform resource locators that begin with the familiar http://www, followed by the specific server and file's name. In addition, Berners-Lee created a browser that could request the transmission of an information file back to the user's computer (Berners-Lee, 1999). His, browser, however, was difficult to use, prompting Netscape and Microsoft to begin the commercial development of their own browsers which became the Netscape Navigator and Microsoft Internet Explorer (IE). This competition was underwritten by capital markets such as New York's Wall Street which was becoming aware of the remarkable strides made by high-tech firms in using the Internet as a communication, information, and e-commerce channel. A user-friendly browser was seen as a major development for navigating the Internet and

creating business opportunities in merchandising, subscription services, and advertising (Clark, 1999). As such, the browser battle was watched intently not only by the stock market but by founders of Yahoo and Google who were developing their own tools for ordering and navigating the web: an online directory in the case of Yahoo and a search engine in the case of Google.

In the battle, Microsoft handily defeated the much smaller Netscape with the former's financial and technical resources derived from its monopolist position in PC operating systems (OS) playing a decisive role. The Netscape Navigator 1.0 browser shipped in 1994, a year ahead of the IE, but the latter was bundled into Microsoft's Windows 95 OS. IE was now imbedded in almost every new PC using Windows 95 and buyers had no need to obtain the Netscape browser. By 1998, IE had more users than Navigator resulting in a downturn in Netscape's earnings and its acquisition by AOL, the leading Internet service provider. In retrospect, Microsoft's IE brought visitors to its MSN website, but it failed to direct them to potential services such as online transactions of stocks and bonds and content (news, weather forecasts, sports scores, etc.) that made the Internet experience meaningful. And as the number of websites multiplied, it was Yahoo and Google, startup companies at Stanford University, which established more competitive franchises for navigating and finding information on the WWW. Moreover, in 2004, the open-source, free web browser – Mozilla Firefox – was launched to challenge IE (Krishnamurthy, 2009).

Dot-Com Era

Yahoo's guide to the web was introduced in 1994 to direct Internet 'surfers' to sites its founders had determined were interesting. The number of sites grew quickly as dot-com firms used them to introduce their high-tech products and services. Yahoo subsequently reorganized its heavily-trafficked guide into a directory listing of TV programs, sports, finance, movies and other categories and used banner ads to cover software development and computer costs. In the Internet's early days, most users, especially those new to the web, just wanted to view what was available on the WWW as opposed to making a stock transaction or conducting intensive research on a particular topic. In response to increasing demand, Yahoo added a search engine to its directory but the underlying function was performed by a third party such as Alta Vista or Inktomi. As explained by Yahoo's first chief executive officer (CEO): "Search as a stand-alone service was very capital intensive – so much capital and bandwidth. The economics had not yet emerged to justify the investment" (Battelle, 2005, p. 63). Instead, Yahoo concentrated on satisfying users of its directory by providing links to other websites containing related information and by recommending interesting items, events, products, and services on its home page.

Yahoo's free service continued to attract monthly visitors which increased from 6 million in 1994 to 40 million in September 1999 and reached a record 180 million in December 2000. The visitor growth accompanied the dot-com boom in Internet startup companies which were being supplied operating funds from venture capitalists and Wall Street investors. The startups, in turn, developed hundreds of new Internet-related services and advertised them on the WWW. Yahoo's directory became a primary way of finding information about the new listings and its homepage became a portal or first site that users turned to for guiding them in cyberspace. The growing traffic prompted Yahoo to add its own "surprisingly deep and varied collection of content and services that ranged from financial information and services, to customizable TV listings, maps, on-line phone books, email, chat rooms and more" (Mossberg, 1998, p. B1).

Nevertheless, Yahoo's directory was distinct from being a search engine. Interested users clicked on a category and were given web pages that Yahoo had determined would be of interest to the user. A search engine, in contrast, receives specific queries containing keywords from users which are then presented links to information that was retrieved and indexed by the search engine. More specificity and familiarity with the topic are thus required in using it while a directory can be simply scanned to see if there was anything of interest. In the early 1990s, Internet surfers generally used Yahoo's directory. Many quickly realized, however, that the web had become a vast storehouse of knowledge which could be searched for in-depth information, and used to make online purchases and sales. To accommodate these users, Netscape entered into an arrangement with five major search engines: Yahoo, Magellan, Lycos, Infoseek, and Excite. Each served as Netscape's search engine on a rotational basis and was paid $5 million. Since it did not have a search function at the time, Yahoo relied on Inktomi to create the search index it used on Netscape's and its own home page (Wikipedia, Web search engine, 2008).

Yahoo's user-friendly search engine and directory also attracted advertising revenue with third-quarter revenue rising from $16 million in 1997, to $61 million in 1998, to $152 million in 1999, to $296 million in 2000. For the full year 2000, ad revenue was over $1 billion compared to revenue of about $7 million in 1996, the year the company's stock began trading on the Nasdaq stock market (Hansell, 2001). Neither the lack of revenue nor a loss for the prior year failed to dent its initial public offering (IPO) with its offering price of $13 a share rising to a high on the first day of trading of $43 a share and close at $33. The sale of 2.6 million shares brought a $33.8 million capital infusion to the young, dot-com company and continued the boom in hugely successful IPOs begun by Netscape in August 1995 (Lewis, 1996). Unlike Netscape, however, Yahoo's stock price would rise throughout the late 1990s and then fall in the Wall Street crash that began in March 2000 to end the dot-com boom. And while Netscape was taken over by AOL, Yahoo acquired its own search technology by buying Inktomi and Overture Services which itself had acquired AlltheWeb and Alta Vista search engines. These acquisitions, moreover, were made at rock-bottom prices because of the stock market's crash.

Prior to the acquisitions, Yahoo rose to the top of the search engine market using the technology of others. The number of searchers using Yahoo climbed from 14.8 million in August 1997 to 26 million in August 1998 and to 33 million in August 1999. These numbers were nearly twice as much as for its closest competitor Infoseek with Lycos, Excite, and Alta Vista trailing. "Yahoo had maintained its lead by continuing to innovate, that is, by providing a superior product. The results also suggest that consumers are primarily interested in search engines that provide relevant hits" (Gandal, 2001, p. 1116). Technological innovation, relevant information, and advertising revenue consequently became important competitive advantages which Google considered in developing its search engine. Microsoft also entered the business as MSN Search but unlike Google which developed its own index, MSN used Inktomi as its search provider.

INNOVATIVE TECHNOLOGIES

Lawrence and Giles (1999) found that search engines are increasingly falling behind in their efforts to index the web. "The publicly indexable World Wide Web now contains about 800 million pages, encompassing about 6 terabytes of text data on about 3 million servers" (p. 107). Index coverage with respect to the web's size was estimated to be 16% for the leading search provider, Northern Light, followed by ten others including Alta Vista at 15.5%, Microsoft at 8.5%, Google at 7.8%, and Yahoo at 7.4%. Furthermore, search engines were taking longer to index new or modified web pages and encountered greater costs in indexing and processing search queries. Consequently, "there are diminishing returns to indexing all of the web, because most queries

made to the search engines can be satisfied with a relatively small data base" (Lawrence & Giles, 1999, p. 109).

As a late entrant, Google was handicapped by a number of factors, including:

1. Lack of brand-name recognition in information technology which Alta Vista, Yahoo, and Microsoft had from their established franchises in search, directory-portal navigation of the WWW, and PC software, respectively.
2. Absence of Internet traffic that could be directed to use an onsite search engine.
3. A smaller index from which to draw its response to queries.
4. Lack of an online advertising method for generating revenue.
5. Operating losses from the time of its incorporation in 1998 to 2000.
6. The impending Wall Street crash that delayed its IPO and capital infusion from the sale of securities on capital markets until August 2004.
7. The demise of dot-com startups that had become major Internet advertisers.

Development of PageRank

A principal disadvantage for early search engines occurred in the way they presented relevant and, frequently, irrelevant responses to a general query. If a query of 'internet,' for example, was submitted, the search engine would have the problem of inferring what type of information about the Internet should be returned to the searcher. In addition, which of the pages retrieved from the index should be presented at the top of the results' page with the understanding that a searcher would click on one or two top-ranked links to see if they yielded relevant information. If they did, more results would probably be clicked on. If not, the search engine would be abandoned and the process probably continued on another engine. In such a competitive environment, Google focused solely on developing a search function instead of becoming a portal, browser, or directory. It could then make the following specific commitments to its users:

1. To provide the most relevant, objective, and useful search results with no payment accepted for including or highly ranking a result.
2. To provide the most relevant and useful advertising that would not distract or be an annoyance to the searcher.
3. To keep improving its technology to provide the user with a meaningful search experience.
4. To provide its services to everyone in the world (Prospectus, 2004, p. 70).

The commitment to produce relevant results was made after Google's cofounders, Larry Page and Sergey Brin, realized that leading providers in the late 1990s frequently returned results that were irrelevant to the user. Furthermore, the processing time for retrieving and presenting results was too long with both problems exacerbated by the rapidly expanding WWW. The former had become a problem because search technology at the time attempted to infer what the searcher was seeking by matching terms in the query with terms indexed by the search engine. After finding a set of matching web pages, the engine then ranked each page according to which were expected to be the most relevant and returned the ranked set to the user. The leap in inferential judgment is where the search process faltered especially in returning results to a one-term query as ambiguous and open-ended as 'internet.' As text-matching engines returned more irrelevant than relevant results, searchers turned to Netscape's browser and Yahoo's directory in an effort to find what they were seeking. This was the norm, until Page and Brin developed a technique that was interactive and responded to specific queries with a ranked list of hyperlinks to relevant sources of information (Brin & Page, 1998).

The algorithm would become known as PageRank with the name trademarked by their new company, Google. PageRank's process patent which expires in 2017 was assigned to Stanford University where the research was done to develop the tool by Page and Brin as part of their graduate work in computer science (Battelle, 2005). Stanford agreed to exclusively license its use to the company until 2011, after which it can be licensed to other enterprises. Google will then have perpetual but non-exclusive licensing rights to the patent (Prospectus, 2004, p. 80).

Combining Ranking Techniques

PageRank relies on the uniquely democratic nature of the web by using its vast link structure as an indicator of an individual page's value (Wikipedia, PageRank, 2008).

PageRank treats a link from web page A to web page B as a 'vote,' by page A, in favor of page B. The PageRank of a page is the sum of the PageRank of the pages that link to it. The PageRank of a web page also depends on the importance (or PageRank) of the other web pages casting the votes. Votes cast by important web pages with high PageRank weigh more heavily and are more influential in deciding the PageRank of pages on the web (Prospectus, 2004, p. 78).

The above extract explains how PageRank determines a 'popularity' score for a given web page in the search engine's index. This score is derived from the number of incoming links and the 'importance' of those pages, as indicated by their PageRank, which are sending out the links. The importance of an out linking page is, in turn, increased by its own incoming links and reduced by the number of links that it sends out (Carr, 2008; Langville & Meyer, 2006, pp. 30-32). The analogy can be made to a popular person receiving a large number of telephone calls and making few outgoing calls. This contrasts with a person who is neither popular nor important who receives few calls and has to make outgoing calls in order to communicate with others.

Because search engines are mainly used to get information on events and personalities who are 'in the news,' the popularity or importance of a web site can be used as a surrogate measure for how relevant the page would be to the person doing the search. Enumerating attributes such as popularity or importance also allows the search engine to calculate the PageRank for each indexed document before the query is initiated, making the technique query independent. This enables a faster response time for presenting search results. To further refine its ranking model, Google combined it with the query-dependent, text-matching techniques that were used by earlier search algorithms. Google's "text-based scoring techniques [however, did] far more than count the number of times a search term appears on a web page. For example, [its] technology determines the proximity of individual search terms to each other on a given web page, and prioritizes results that have search terms near each other" (Prospectus, 2004, p. 78).

The PageRank of a particular document is consequently based, in part, on the number of incoming links from pages that have their own PageRankings. These factors are combined with a text-matching technique and other parameters to yield the document's PageRank. While PageRank is at the heart of Google's search software, its determination is kept confidential to prevent external manipulation of search rankings that could do irreparable damage to the integrity and public's confidence in its search results. On May 27, 2003, the U.S. Western District Court of Oklahoma concluded that Google's right to keep its internally developed PageRanks confidential was "entitled to full constitutional protection" and dismissed the lawsuit seeking the release of their proprietary source code (Langville & Meyer, 2006, pp. 28, 52-55).

As the court case indicates, interest in gaming the ranking system grew after Google's search engine — launched in 1998 — yielded more relevant results than earlier providers. This also

resulted in the greater use of search engines with Google conducting 250 million searches per day while Overture Services and Inktomi did 167 million and 80 million, respectively. Usage rates, furthermore, were expected to increase by 20% per year forcing Google:

To spend substantial amounts to purchase or lease data centers and equipment and to upgrade [its] technology and network infra-structure to handle increased traffic on [its] web sites and to roll out new products and services. If [it did] not implement this expansion successfully, this could damage [its] reputation and lead [it] to lose current and potential users, advertisers, and Google Network members [third parties that generate revenue for Google by using its ad placement program on their web-sites] (Prospectus, 2004, p. 14).

Its late entrance also resulted in the company placing seventh in index size among 11 major full-text search engines: "While having a larger index of web pages accessed does not necessarily make one search engine better than another, it does mean the 'bigger' search engine has a better opportunity to return a longer list of relevant results. As a result, search engines are constantly battling for the title of 'The World's Largest Index'" (Langville & Meyer, 2006, p. 20). The index battle accelerated after Google took the lead in 2000 (with an index of 0.5 billion pages) over Inktomi, Alta Vista, and AlltheWeb. AlltheWeb went ahead in 2002 with an index of 2 billion pages. The lead was retaken by Google when it increased its index to 3 billion pages and subsequently to 8.1 billion pages in November 2004.

Together with its ranking technology, growing index, and publicity surrounding its successful IPO, Google became the largest search engine with a 37% share of the industry followed by Yahoo with 27%. The latter, meanwhile, purchased Inktomi in 2002 and Overture Services in 2003 which had acquired AlltheWeb and Alta Vista. The technology from these firms were combined into Yahoo!Search which was launched in 2004.

During the interim period, Yahoo used Google to power its search services and terminated the arrangement when its engine became available. At the same time, Microsoft developed its own search engine which it launched in 2005. In July 2009, the U.S. industry was still led by Google with 76.7 billion monthly searches conducted for a 67.5% worldwide industry share, followed by Yahoo with 8.9 billion searches and a 7.8%% share, and Microsoft with 3.32 billion searches.

UNDERWRITING COMMERCIAL SEARCH

The three companies were adversely affected by the dot-com implosion in 2000, but to different degrees. Microsoft could fall back on its billion-dollar franchise in PC software, but its online search business was overshadowed by the rise of Google. The latter's development of AdSense and AdWords programs for securing advertising revenue rapidly occurred after its new PageRank technology attracted funds from angel investors and a $25 million investment from venture capital firms. In return, several investors received seats on Google's board and were instrumental in recruiting an experienced manager to be chief executive officer (CEO) of the startup. He would lead the firm through its successful IPO in 2004.

Downturn in Online Advertising

Yahoo was the most adversely impacted by the $7 trillion meltdown in equity markets just as it was building its own search capabilities. Moribund stock and bond markets could no longer be used to raise capital through the sale of securities. In addition, its stock price which had reached a record high of $237.50 a share on January 3, 2000, nosedived to $8.02 a share in 2002 following a steep downturn in advertising. Its dot-com ads fell from $459.1 million in 2000 to $97.4 million in 2001 as startup firms which were some of its

biggest advertisers went out of business. Many were small companies with little if any operating earnings to cover their advertising expenses. They, instead, had been using capital raised by selling equity to venture capitalists and institutional investors on Wall Street. The falloff in dot-com ads was also impacted by the downturn in advertising that Yahoo received from traditional corporate advertisers like auto and electronics manufacturers, as explained below:

The problem is that five years of experience shows very limited value for the sort of ad that Yahoo and other sites sell most — the ubiquitous rectangular banner. Those banners, as it seems, are not as entertaining as TV, not as informative as print, and not as personal as direct mail (Hansell, 2001, pp. 1, 14).

The implosion struck Yahoo in the first quarter of 2001, with revenues falling 21% and losses for the year reaching $92.8 million. The company was forced to dismiss 12% of its workforce including its CEO and implement a new business plan to cover the lost revenue. It started charging for information and services on its websites because they were too costly to be given away. Plans to build its own search engine were accelerated and a hostile takeover of HotJobs.com, the leading online job listing agency, began. HotJobs was an attractive acquisition because its income came from charging employers monthly listing fees as set forth in yearlong contracts. Gross margins of the agency approached 90%. Even with the grim financial news, however, use of the Internet kept growing exponentially and Yahoo benefited from this with an 86% increase in online transactions in the 2001 Christmas selling season. This was unexpected since the terrorist attack on New York's World Trade Center had sent the U.S. economy into recession. The event, however, failed to deter and even encouraged consumers to buy online, use a credit card to cover the transaction, and have the merchandise delivered to their homes (Hiraoka, 2005).

Yahoo also opened franchises in Asia where Internet traffic was expanding at a faster rate than in the United States. It formed Yahoo Japan in 1996 with the Softbank Corporation and because of the joint venture's success, went on to invest in auction site Gmarket of South Korea and the Alibaba Group of China which controls Alibaba. com, an online business-to-business marketplace. During the U.S. recession, Yahoo Japan reported a 152% rise in profits and 130% revenue increase even as its U.S. parent's ad revenues were declining sharply. The difference arose because Japan never had a dot-com boom and Yahoo Japan never received much ad revenue from Internet startup firms. Instead, its revenue base was built on ads from traditional sources such as restaurants, retailers, and services like travel agencies. Profits were then employed to make Yahoo's search engine a leader in the Japanese market even as Google was becoming the dominant provider in the United States (Tanikawa, 2001).

AdWords and AdSense

Google established its AdWords program which placed relevant, query-related, non-intrusive text ads next to search results to finance the development and maintenance of its search engine. The software program enabled queries seeking information about a product like digital cameras to receive both links to information about the item as well as ads from sellers of the product. If a searcher showed interest in a particular ad by clicking on an ad, the advertiser would pay Google at the prearranged click price. AdWords was an improvement over banner ads because it:

1. Presented potentially-useful ads to the searcher who had already expressed an interest in the product or service.
2. Targeted the ads to an interested audience in contrast to banner or TV ads that were mass

marketed to viewers who were, for the most part, not interested in them.
3. Was a cost-effective marketing program affordable to even small advertisers which paid from pennies per click up to $5.00 per click for the ad placement.
4. Included the ad's popularity as measured by the number of times it was clicked to set the payment rate, as explained below.
5. Offered a discount that "automatically lowered the amount advertisers actually pay to the minimum needed to maintain their ad position," again aiding small advertisers (Prospectus, 2004, p. 78).

An example of how the company conducted its auction to set the payment per click can be illustrated with three bidders seeking to place ads in a top position close to the highest-ranked page result. Bids from the three are $1.00 per click from the first bidder, $0.60 per click from the second, and $0.50 per click from the third bidder with the lowest price per click set by Google at $0.05. At the close of bidding, the click rate for the best ad position is set at $0.61 which goes to the highest bidder and is a penny more than the second-highest bid. The payment rate for the second bidder is $0.51, a penny more than what was bid by the third bidder. The third or lowest bidder pays the minimum rate of $0.05 per click. The position of the ads is subject to change if, for example, the ad for the third bidder is clicked on more times than the ad of the second bidder. Google would then elevate the ad from the third bidder and downgrade the ad position of the second bidder. The shift is justified accordingly:

If an ad does not attract user clicks, it moves to a less prominent position on the page, even if the advertiser offers to pay a high amount. This prevents advertisers with irrelevant ads from 'squatting' in top positions to gain exposure. Conversely, more relevant, well-targeted ads that are clicked on frequently move up in ranking, with no need for advertisers to increase their bids. Because we are paid only when users click on ads, the AdWords ranking system aligns our interests with those of our advertisers and our users (Prospectus, 2004, p. 78).

In addition to the above user-friendly features, advertisers can create their text-based ads and have them online within 15 minutes. The sign-up process which cost $5.00 in 2004 includes the bidding for favorable ad positions and specifying of keywords in the query that initiates the placement of a particular ad. Consequently, each advertiser will know what its payment-per-click rate was before the ad was displayed and can even arrange to set daily spending limits that placed a cap on advertising expenditures. This allowed the marketer to ensure that revenues from the ads covered their costs. Similar to other online transactions, the sign-up cost could be paid with a credit card (Prospectus, 2004, p. 76).

In 2003, Google launched its AdSense program that placed related ads on non-Google web pages that contained information about a product or service. With AdSense, vendors of a product like digital cameras could have their ads placed on websites created by third-party publishers that contained information about the camera. The publishers who created these sites would register, at no cost, to have relevant ads displayed on their sites thereby becoming Google Network members. Members would then share the ad proceeds with Google whenever an ad on their site was clicked. AdSense, as a result, extended Google's advertising program beyond search to publishers of websites like newspapers, magazines, books which sought to increase revenue by having relevant ads placed on their sites (Battelle, 2005).

Google's IPO

The above programs in ad placement and page ranking allowed Google to become profitable, starting in 2001, when it reported net income of

nearly $7 million. Growing search traffic increased income to $105.6 million in 2003 and together with the bottoming of U.S. equity markets in the same year, prompted the company to schedule the initial public offering (IPO) of its common shares for August 18, 2004. Proceeds from the sale of 14,142,135 shares exceeded $1.1 billion at the offering price of $85 a share and the shares began trading on the Nasdaq National Market. Strong demand from investors caused the stock price to rise and encouraged more investors to buy it. The successful IPO enabled Google to raise capital on Wall Street by selling its securities. The consequences were a boon to the startup company which was competing against the much larger companies, Microsoft and Yahoo, which had formidable brand-name recognition, strong balance sheets that could underwrite R&D projects and marketing campaigns, and heavy Internet traffic on their websites. Indeed, business analysts compared Google to the browser firm Netscape which was crushed when Microsoft launched its competing IE browser. And as in the case with Netscape, Yahoo and Microsoft became intent on duplicating the innovations made by Google to advance their commercial interests in the search engine market.

COMPETITIVE DYNAMICS IN THE SEARCH MARKET

Rising Stock Price

Figure 1 shows how Google's stock performed on Wall Street.

Following its opening trading day in August 2004, the stock reached $240 a share before dropping to $160 a share at the end of 2004. It then climbed strongly in 2005, reaching $500 a share in 2006. The rocketing price caused a sensation on Wall Street and placed Google's competitive position on a par with its bigger rivals. It also brought more traffic to Google's search engine than any marketing campaign could have done to attract advertising revenue. There were times when adverse news caused its stock price to drop as at the end of 2004 and the beginning of 2006. But the continuing rise in net income from $399 million in 2004 to $4.2 billion in 2007 kept its stock price on an upward trajectory.

Channel Transitions

Google, even before its IPO, had become a leader of search in a number of ways:

1. It built the largest index for use in replying to queries.
2. While Microsoft and Yahoo were using third-party providers, Google developed its own search capabilities.
3. Using its page-ranking innovation, it passed Yahoo in 2002 to become the industry leader (see Figure 2).

4. It had become a profitable enterprise even in the midst of the dot-com stock market crash and U.S. recession.
5. The income allowed Google to increase its high-tech employment base from 300 employees in 2001 to 1,400 employees in 2003 (Malone, 2004).
6. The increased technical and financial resources aided in the development and deployment of its AdWords and AdSense programs, and they helped Google become the leader of online ad sales when it passed Yahoo in 2005 (see Figure 3).

Competitive Reactions

Although Yahoo lost its lead in search in 2003, the year brought other, more favorable transitions. Online advertising, following declines for the three preceding years, turned around and registered a 20% gain. Still the leader in online advertising, Yahoo reported that its revenues surged by 84%

Figure 1. Google stock price ($ per share)

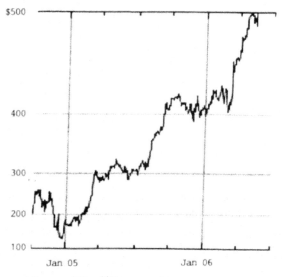

Source: http://finance.yahoo.com

Figure 2. Share of search market

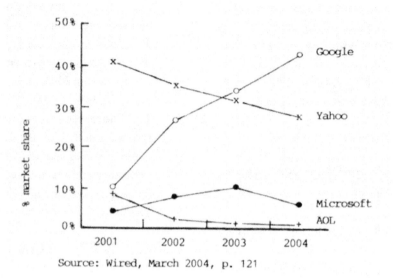

Source: Wired, March 2004, p. 121

Figure 3. Online ad sales as % of U.S. total

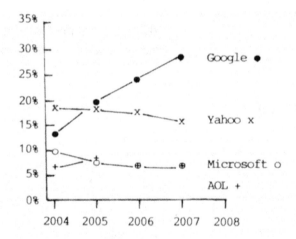

Source: Wall Street Journal, 11 April 2008, p. B7

and the inflow financed the launch of its own search service. It did this by buying Inktomi and Overture Services for $2 billion and combined them with its resources into a new search engine which was called Yahoo!Search. The development not only led to the ending of its reliance on Google's search engine, but it brought in-house Overture's pay-per-click advertising technique that was the basis for Google's highly lucrative AdWords program. Google was subsequently sued by Overture Services for patent infringement in April 2002 when the latter was still an independent company. A settlement was reached in 2004 when Yahoo was issued 2.7 million shares of common stock in Google and received perpetual licensing rights to the patent (Wikipedia, AdWords, 2008).

Microsoft also came out with its search engine in November 2004 but, nevertheless, retained Yahoo's search service. "To the surprise of some analysts, Microsoft plans to continue using Yahoo's Overture advertising-placement service" (Markoff, 2004, p. C1). Two reasons that explain why Microsoft continued the relationship include:

1. With the ascendance of Google, Microsoft began losing some of its best employees to the new search leader.
2. Microsoft made a $44 billion takeover bid for Yahoo in February 2008 in an effort to upgrade its search capability.

With a flat stock price, Microsoft's management came under increasing pressure from its shareholders to increase its 4% worldwide share of search and its 7% share of U.S. online advertising. In its September 26, 2005 cover story, *Business Week* cited four organizational developments that could account for the less than stellar performance:

1. Innovation stagnation caused by the company's concentration of its resources on its existing software products and not pursuing promising but risky new areas like search.
2. Slow product development in both existing and new areas because of top management's indecisiveness about acquiring the technology or developing it in-house. The company, for example, attempted to acquire Overture Services but lost in the bidding to Yahoo. It then made a hostile bid for Yahoo.
3. Bureaucratic red tape that replaced decision-making with endless paper-shuffling and rounds of meetings which are endemic to large organizations.

4. Sagging morale prompting its best employees to leave (Greene, 2005).

Like almost all its competitors, Microsoft made China's huge emerging market a priority growth area (Xing et al., 2009; Yang et al., 2005). The effort, however, was thwarted by the organizational difficulties listed above resulting in its 20 product-development centers in China competing with and hiring employees away from each other.

Microsoft's Hostile Bid

In 2006, Microsoft began negotiations to acquire Yahoo and failing to reach agreement, made a hostile $44.6 billion bid to acquire the smaller company over the objections of the latter's CEO and board. The gulf separating the companies can be ascribed to the different eras that gave rise to each enterprise with Microsoft becoming a software powerhouse in the PC era and Yahoo building its reputation as a directory-portal service used for navigating the web. Moreover, the co-founders of Yahoo like their counterparts at Google were graduate students at Stanford University where their respective companies were formed. Their current headquarters, moreover, are close to each other in Silicon Valley while Microsoft is based in the state of Washington. Yahoo has also upgraded its search engine by acquiring companies and retaining their key employees which as discussed, has become a problem at Microsoft. The situation can become acute because if Microsoft is successful in its takeover of Yahoo, it will then confront the task of folding Yahoo's 14,300 work force into its 80,000 employee base. There is a distinct possibility that key people will relocate to nearby Google. If such an exodus occurs, Microsoft will be acquiring a corporate shell that has been abandoned by Yahoo's employees who hold the knowledge to its search technology. Because of such risks, Microsoft's determination to take over Yahoo wavered in the ensuing months while Yahoo's CEO and board maintained their resolve not to be taken over. It then abandoned its proxy fight to have its slate of directors replace Yahoo's existing board members. As to how Microsoft will "compete with Google's ever-widening lead in search and advertising as the computer world shifts from desktop products to online software and services supported by ads" remains in limbo even as technological change makes the search channel more productive and useful (Helft & Sorkin, 2008, p. A1).

CONCLUSION

This case study examines the technological innovations in search engines that made them one of the most used service channels on the Internet. Presenting relevant results to search queries was a major problem for early search engines that was, in part, overcome by using the web's linkages to determine if an indexed website would be a useful source of information. Earlier algorithms matched keywords in the query with those in the index and when combined with the new technique based on links, produced superior search results. Industry data indicate that customer satisfaction increased when the hybrid technique became available making Google, where the innovation occurred, a leading search provider.

Because of its large number of search users, Google took the lead in U.S. online ad revenues related to search results thus becoming not only a major channel for finding information but a heavily used marketing channel. The latter arose from its placement of relevant ads next to appropriate search results which made it superior to the mass marketing of TV ads to largely disinterested viewers.

Its climb from obscure startup to high-tech frontrunner can be ascribed to its late entrance

in the business which made it necessary to offer a better service. Two of its foremost competitors had already established worldwide franchises, but not in search, forcing them to commit resources to the other areas. The larger organizations also suffered from the absence of a clear strategic search plan. The ongoing competition, however, means that no firm has a lock on being a leader of these important service channels and a new startup with innovative technology, entrepreneurial genius, and financial acumen can emerge to produce a major paradigm shift.

ACKNOWLEDGMENT

Research assistance provided by Kaichun Wang in the preparation of Figures 1, 2, and 3 is gratefully acknowledged. Travel support was received from Kean University to attend the 2009 Hawaii International Conference on Business where a preliminary version of this paper was presented.

REFERENCES

Abate, J. (1999). *Inventing the Internet* (chapters 1-2). Cambridge, MA: MIT Press.

Battelle, J. (2005). *The search: How Google and its rivals rewrote the rules of business and transformed our culture* (pp. 75-76, 152). New York: Portfolio.

Berners-Lee, T. (1999). *Weaving the web*. San Francisco, CA: Harper.

Brin, S., & Page, L. (1998). The anatomy of a large-scale hypertextual web search engine. *Computer Networks, 30,* 107–117.

Carr, N. (2008). *The big switch: Rewiring the world, from Edison to Google* (p. 219). New York: W.W. Norton & Company.

Clark, J. (1999). *Netscape time.* New York: St. Martin's Press.

Gandal, N. (2001). The dynamics of competition in the internet search engine market. *International Journal of Industrial Organization, 19,* 1103–1117. doi:10.1016/S0167-7187(01)00065-0

Greene, J. (2005, September 26). Troubling exits at Microsoft. *Business Week,* 98-108.

Hansell, S. (2001, March 11). Red face for the Internet's blue chip. *New York Times,* Section 3, pp. 1, 14.

Helft, M., & Sorkin, A. R. (2008, February 2). Eyes on Google, Microsoft bids $44 billion for Yahoo. *New York Times,* A1.

Hiraoka, L. S. (2005). *Underwriting the Internet: How technical advances, financial Engineering, and entrepreneurial genius are building the information highway* (pp. 96–97). Armonk, NY: M.E. Sharpe.

Krishnamurthy, S. (2009). Case: Mozilla vs. Godzilla − The launch of the Mozilla Firefox browser. *Journal of Interactive Marketing, 23*(3), 259–271. doi:10.1016/j.intmar.2009.04.008

Langville, A. N., & Meyer, C. D. (2006). *Google's PageRank and beyond: The science of search engine rankings.* Princeton, NJ: Princeton University Press.

Lawrence, S., & Giles, C. L. (1999). Accessibility of information on the web. *Nature, 200,* 107–109. doi:10.1038/21987

Lewis, P. H. (1996, April 13). Yahoo gets big welcome on Wall Street. *New York Times,* 33-34.

Malone, M. S. (2004, March). Surviving IPO fever. *Wired,* 115.

Markoff, J. (2004, November 10). Microsoft unveils its Internet search engine, quietly. *New York Times,* C1.

Mossberg, W. S. (1998, March 19). Yahoo! challenges AOL as a portal to World Wide Web. *Wall Street Journal,* B1.

Mostafa, J. (2005). Seeking better web searches. *Scientific American, 292*(2), 67–73. doi:10.1038/scientificamerican0205-66

Nocera, J. (2008, February 2). A giant bid that shows how tired the giant is. *New York Times,* C1.

Prospectus. (2004, August 18). *Of initial public offering for Google's common stock filed with Securities Exchange Commission.* Retrieved September 8, 2009, from http://www.sec.gov/Archives/edgar/data/1288776/000119312504073639/ds1.htm

Shipley, C., & Fish, M. (1996). *How the World Wide Web works.* Emeryville, CA: Ziff-Davis Press.

Southwick, K. (1999). *High noon: The inside story of Scott McNealy and the rise of Sun Microsystems* (Chapter 1). New York: John Wiley & Sons.

Steinmuller, W. (1996). The U.S. software industry: An analysis and interpretive history. In D. Mowery (Ed.), *The international computer software industry: A comparative study of industry evolution and structure* (pp. 24-52). New York: Oxford University Press.

Tanikawa, M. (2001, March 11). A cautious sibling waits to see what works. *New York Times,* Section 3, p. 14.

Wikipedia. (2008). *AdWords.*

Wikipedia. (2008). *PageRank.*

Wikipedia. (2008). *Web search engine.*

Williams, K. C., Hernandez, E. H., Petrosky, A. R., & Page, R. A. (2008). Fine-Tuning useful e-commerce practices. *Journal of Technology Research, 1,* 1-19. Retrieved from www.aabri.com

Xing, R., Zhang, Y., Wang, Z., & Xia, J. (2009). Broadband challenge facing global competitiveness. *International Journal of Society Systems Science, 1*(3), 293-305.

Yang, D., Ghauri, P., & Sonmez, M. (2005). Competitive analysis of the software industry in China. *International Journal of Technology Management, 29*(1-2), 64–91. doi:10.1504/IJTM.2005.006005

Chapter 4
GIS and GPS Applications in Emerging Economies:
Observation and Analysis of a Chinese Logistics Firm

Bin Zhou
Kean University, USA

Jeffrey Hsu
Fairleigh Dickinson University, USA

Yawei Wang
Montclair State University, USA

ABSTRACT

The rapid development of Geographic Information System (GIS) and Global Position System (GPS) has attracted the attention of both business practitioners and academic researchers. GIS and GPS technologies, through providing optimized schedules, routings, and guidance, are especially important and helpful in transportation and logistics businesses. Though GIS and GPS technologies have been witnessed in many business sectors in developed countries, wide application of these technologies is still in its preliminary phase in companies in developing nations. In this paper, the authors present a study on the application of an integrated intelligent system that consists of GIS, GPS and related technologies to optimize logistic distribution of perishable products in urban environments. Through investigating GIS and GPS usage in a medium-sized logistics company in the unique settings of emerging economies, this paper addresses how these technologies enhance the management of businesses and analyze the interaction of GIS/GPS implementation and several key characteristics of the logistic distribution context by identifying major benefits, challenges, and limitations associated with the use of GIS and GPS.

INTRODUCTION

Logistics management has been an area that attracts the attention of both academic researchers and business practitioners for decades. Logistics and transportation are significant concerns in supply chain management since they play key roles in the physical movement of raw materials, semi-finished and finished products in a system that consists of a variety of entities such as suppliers, manufacturers, distributors, and customers. Logistics costs usually account for a quite significant share of the total costs for a firm. Both fixed and

DOI: 10.4018/978-1-4666-0927-3.ch004

variable costs, such as the cost of vehicles, labor costs of drivers and dispatchers, cost of fuel, can be found in the logistic distribution process. Hence, one of the biggest challenges in the management of logistic distribution is how to efficiently move the required goods from one entity to another while effectively have these costs under control.

In recent years, the advancement of Information Technology (IT) has substantially facilitated business decision making in countless ways. In particular, the introduction and application of Geographic Information Systems (GIS) and Global Position Systems (GPS) in the past decades provide diversified benefits to both commercial and individual users. The research and development of GIS and GPS technologies can be traced back to the 1970s (Parkinson, 1996), when the NAV-STAR Global Positioning System was designed and launched by a small group of military officers and civilians. The plan was to develop a new navigation system that would utilize radio-ranging measurements from a constellation of satellites. Later, wide application of these new technologies was first found in military, where they are used as effective data collection and planning tools, then in a wide-range of civil/commercial situations, such as emergency management (Derekenaris, Garofalakis, Makris, Prentzas, Sioutas, & Tsakalidis, 2001), vehicle delivery and routing (Keenan, 1998), urban and forest planning (Sui, 1998), as well as construction and material management (Li, Kong, Pang, Shi, & Yu, 2003).

Among a variety of commercial applications of GIS and GPS technologies, vehicle delivery and routing become vitally important in modern logistics and supply chain management. High costs in the distribution process perplex logistics managers and they become even more critical to the survival and success of every business given that demands for fossil-based energy continue to grow and expectations from customers continue to rise.

The control of logistics costs is especially difficult when considering that goods in the shipment are perishable and specialized equipments/handling are necessary and required (Butler, Herlihy, & Keenan, 2005). Problems can arise from both the storage and delivery operations since perishable products are usually expected to be stored and delivered within a particular time frame, and therefore the resulted costs are much higher.

On the other hand, even though the implementation of GIS and GPS technologies has been seen in many business sectors, due to the newness of the commercialization of these technologies, academic research on these issues has a relatively short history. Indeed, current research on the development and usage of GIS and GPS technologies is limited to practices in developed nations and many problems are largely unexplored. In particular, very few studies have investigated issues such as: a) what are the roles played by GIS, GPS and related technologies in logistics companies in developing countries; b) what are the major benefits and challenges generated by using these technologies for transportation and distribution of perishable goods; c) what lessons and insights can be learned from the process to improve logistics management. In this research, we aim to address these issues and present a case study of a Chinese company who focuses on distributing perishable products to its customers.

This paper is our first attempt and is a preliminary step towards answering the aforementioned questions. Based upon existing literature on GIS/GPS practice and theories, as well as our own observations and interviews with business practitioners, we investigate the interaction of GIS/GPS implementation and several key characteristics of the logistic distribution context and attempt to identify the benefits, challenges, and limitations associated with using of GIS and GPS in the unique settings of emerging economies.

Our research findings demonstrate how the usage of these technologies helps to facilitate the effective and efficient management of the distribution of perishable goods. We discuss challenges encountered by firms in developing nations and compare these issues with those faced by companies in developed countries. For instance, compared to firms in the United States and the western European countries, logistics companies in China have to deal with more obstacles such as sparse digital mapping resources, inadequate technological supports, and expensive maintenance and update costs. Companies normally cannot afford to have the most recent software and equipments, which can cause considerable problems during the implementation process. Moreover, unlike firms in developed nations, many companies in emerging economies do not have effective management information systems such as the enterprise resource planning (ERP) system. Hence, communication and information sharing are difficult to achieve. We also aim to provide important managerial insights for logistics managers for reaping the benefits and overcoming the challenges.

The remainder of the paper is structured as follows. In Section 2, we present a brief review of related literature on GIS and GPS technologies and their applications. In Section 3, a case study of a Chinese logistics company is introduced and discussed. Section 4 integrates the case study's results and the findings of previous research, reveals important issues in the implementation process, and elaborates major benefits and challenges stemming from GIS and GPS usage in such situations. Valuable insights for managing GIS and GPS usage in companies in emerging economies are also provided. Lastly in Section 5, the paper concludes with a discussion of the study in terms of contributions and limitations.

LITERATURE REVIEW

In recent years, the exponential growth of logistics service along with the fast development of web-based electronic business, for instance, business-to-business (B2B) and business-to-customer (B2C) has greatly accelerated the civilian usage of GIS and GPS related technologies. Increased demands for high-quality, Just-in-Time (JIT) service also pose considerable challenges to logistics companies and force them to seek new alternative means to operate more effectively.

While GIS serves as a computer-based intelligent system that integrates data collection, storage, and analysis, GPS along with General Packet Radio Service (GPRS) technologies can be used to collect and transmit important real-time data to GIS for further manipulation. Altogether, the integrated system can perform complicated analytical functions and then present the results visually as digital maps, tables, and graphs, allowing decision-makers to virtually see the issues before them and then select the best course of action. In fact, GIS and GPS based technologies can be applied and found in a wide-range of practices, ranging from parcel/product delivery, hazardous material transportation, to ambulance and fire truck dispatching.

Some research particularly focuses on the usage of GIS and GPS in vehicle monitoring and routing. Zito, D'este, and Taylor (1995) explored the application of GPS technologies for constructing intelligent vehicle-highway systems. They discussed the use of GPS for obtaining information with respect to the position, speed, as well as travel direction of vehicles. Hafberg (1995) studied the concepts and techniques to combine GIS, GPS, and other digital communication technologies to locate the position and velocity of vehicles, and emphasized the importance of the connection with the central monitoring system.

Derekenaris et al. (2001) investigated a system that integrates GIS and GPS technologies for the effective management of ambulances and emergency incident handling. Their paper discussed GIS and GPS assisted operations for the handling of emergency incidents as well as routing of ambulances to the incident sites and to the closest appropriate hospitals.

Similar problems are analyzed in the practice of home delivery business. Weigel and Cao (1999) studied the application of GIS and OR techniques in the problems of technician-dispatching and home-delivery of Sears. Similarly, Jung, Lee, and Chun (2006) studied the implementation of GIS and related technologies in parcel delivery service. In particular, the system consists of three sub-systems: a) pickup and delivery sequence planning system; b) pick up and delivery monitoring system; and c) PDA execution system. With the integration of GIS, GPS and wireless PDA equipments, the system is successful in improving the effective management of parcel pickup and delivery operations.

Another stream of research investigates the integration and interaction of GIS/GPS and Decision Support Systems (DSS). Keenan (1996) discussed the advancement of PC-based working environment and its contribution to the wide application of GIS in mapping and routing related problems where GIS serves as a generator for developing a routing DSS. Imielinski and Navas (1999) described the technical development of GPS and its important usage for geographic data collection. Their research studied the problem of global positioning system based addressing, vehicle routing, and resource discovery.

In addition, the problem of logistic handling of perishable products also attracts the interests of researchers. Basnet, Foulds, and Igbaria (1996) discussed a microcomputer-based decision support system, the Fleetmanager system, for milk collection in New Zealand. Butler et al. (2005) investigated using GIS based information technology and DSS for the management of milk collection in Ireland. In particular, they presented a case study of a dairy company that collects milk from about 800 farms. The dairy uses a DSS to contain and maintain relevant data on all of the farms. Their paper addressed how GIS and DSS allow a scheduler to interact with optimization algorithms to plan milk collection routes, as well as using automatic data capture devices and database systems to provide effective management of milk collection operations for the dairy. Additional

important literature on GIS and DSS application and integration includes, for instance, Franklin (1992), Crossland, Wyne, and Perkins (1995), Frank (2000), Laurini (2000), Tanzi (2000), and the references cited therein.

In summary, research on GIS and GPS technologies has explored many different business sectors. However, limited work has been done on the problem of GIS/GPS-assisted logistic distribution of perishable goods. Moreover, situations and challenges of GIS and GPS application in logistics firms in emerging economies are left largely untouched by most of the research in the past. Hence, in this paper, we aim to address these issues and focus on revealing valuable findings and providing important insights with respect to the interaction of GIS/GPS and other essential functions of a firm.

RESEARCH METHODOLOGY

In this section, we describe in detail the methodology employed in this research. A case study that consists of interviews and observations was conducted in a medium- sized logistics company, Company J, which provides third-party transportation/logistics as well as warehousing service to customers in Beijing, China. In particular, we explore issues and try to answer major questions including, the relation of GIS and GPS usage and the performance of a firm; primary benefits stemmed from and major challenges and problems encountered in the implementation and operating process; and what lessons and insights can be generated from the study.

As a preliminary step of a larger project, this case study reveals important findings and generates valuable insights. Based on these results, questionnaires are being developed for later larger-scale research study that focuses on exploring the application of impacts of GIS and GPS usage in multiple related industries. We address these issues and provide insights through conducting in-depth analysis. In addition, since broad industrial application of GIS and GPS related technologies is still in its emerging stage, especially in developing countries, and academic research in this area is still at a preliminary phase where no theoretical base has been established, case study method suits the purpose of this research.

Research Participants

Company J, based in Beijing China, is a medium-sized logistics company with about 200 employees. The company's primary business is to offer logistics and warehousing service to varied customers in the city of Beijing. The company owns more than 150 trucks and vans which are kept in four major locations.

This study selects and focuses on a newly-established department that provides delivery service of perishable products such as seafood, frozen meat, and prepared food, by using 20 refrigerated trucks. The company has its own facility to store these perishable products. Due to the special characteristics of perishable goods and highly-strict requirements from customers, the company started a pilot program and equipped and implemented both GIS and GPS technologies and equipments for advanced monitoring and controlling of fleet and services for more than half a year.

Interviews were conducted with both dispatchers and truck drivers in the new department. In particular, two control center dispatchers, with an average of five years of industry experience, and ten drivers, with an average of seven years of industry experience, were interviewed. Out of the two dispatchers, one interviewee has seven months experience with GPS and GIS related technologies while the other has more than a year of experience.

In addition, out of the ten drivers, six interviewees have considerable experiences (more than two years) of using GPS and GIS related technologies in both domestic and international companies, while other interviewees have rela-

tively fewer experience (less than one year). Since the interviewees come from different skill levels with mixed work experience, their opinions add to more complete understandings of the research questions of this study from varied perspectives.

Moreover, the company, along with the group of interviewees included in our study, bears some key characteristics, such as relatively short history of GIS/GPS usage, diverse experiences in employees, limited locations, and smaller-scale operations, of typical small and medium-sized logistics companies in emerging markets, which make them suitable targets in this research study.

Research Procedure

Both telephone and face-to-face interviews were included in the research to gather important data and information. In particular, telephone interviews were conducted for driver participants while face-to-face interviews were conducted for both center dispatchers and drivers on the site of the company. Telephone interviews were used in the case study because they provided more flexibility, since drivers normally work outside the company during a regular work day.

On the other hand, face-to-face interviews at the company's location provided researchers with the opportunities to experience their daily operations and logistic procedures. Specifically, a half-day observation at the dispatching center of the company was conducted. During the on-site observation, special attention was paid to the work flow, work environment, and how the center and drivers communicated with each other. Each interview lasted approximately 20 minutes and all interviews were scheduled and finished within a week. Notes were taken during the interviews and these notes were further reviewed and analyzed in later stages of the research.

Since this research focuses on a relatively new area and aims to provide initial, first-hand knowledge on the application of GIS related technologies in emerging economies, research questions used are open-ended. These questions cover a variety of issues on GIS and GPS usage as well as collaboration concerns in logistics firms. For instance, a typical question asked at the beginning of the interview is "how do you describe the impact of using GIS and GPS technologies on your job?" The opening question is very general but is served as a good start that leads to detailed follow-up questions to investigate the practices and incidents that contribute valuable and rich information to this case study.

The focus of this case study is to answer "how" and "why" questions with respect to GIS and GPS usage and their impact. Once the interviews were finished, we utilized an "explanation-building" (Baxter & Jack, 2008) method to analyze the results. Yin (2002) states that "explanation-building" is an iterative process used in case studies by building an explanation about the case and identifying a set of causal links. It is an important analytic technique that consists of series of iterations.

Based on this method, first, answers of the total twelve participants were randomly separated into six groups, with each group consists of two different individual results. Secondly, detailed review and analysis of the first group of answers was conducted by the researchers, who took notes and formed a list of hypotheses related to the research questions of interest. General hypotheses resulted from the analysis include, for instance, "GIS and GPS usage can help to improve real-time monitor and control of fleet", "use of these new technologies helps to reduce lead time and costs for the company", "employee trainings are necessary for using the software and equipments", "technological supports and updates are important to maintain the advantages brought by GIS/GPS", etc.

Thirdly, interview results of the second group were reviewed, where special attention was paid to confirming or rejecting the initial hypotheses. Moreover, in light of the answers from the second group, we revised the original list of hypotheses. Lastly, in the fourth step, the iterative process was

continued by analyzing the answers from the third group of answers corresponding to the revised list of hypotheses. This procedure was followed until all the interview answers were investigated. We finished the analysis by comparing all the findings and formalized a final list of hypotheses and concluded the entire study.

Research Findings

In this section, major findings of this case study are presented. In particular, in section 4.1, an overview of the GIS and GPS application in Company J is provided. We address issues such as where and how these new technologies are used. Section 4.2 discusses four major benefits brought by using new GIS and GPS systems, including: *reducing operating lead time*, *facilitating the management of vehicles and personnel*, *enhancing demand and supply management*, and *assisting strategic planning*. Section 4.3 analyzes some challenges and limitations found during the implementation process, including: *accuracy and update of GIS and GPS, separation of customer service and GIS/ GPS*, and *lack of related supports for incidents management*. Lastly, in section 4.4, we discuss some managerial insights and possible solutions to the problems.

Overview of GIS and GPS Application

In Company J the entire delivery procedure starts with the receipt of customers' orders. These orders are then scheduled based upon expected delivery date, time, and location. Next, schedules along with orders' information are sent to drivers who then load the products on the trucks from warehouses. Finally, products are delivered to customers. While order receiving and delivery scheduling are conducted at the dispatching center where customer and order related database is kept and managed in computer terminals, the delivery of goods is the last step of the operating process.

Stringent requirements of perishable products and high expectations from customers lead to higher costs for the company. Moreover, delivery is the critical contacting point where the service quality is experienced and the company aims to monitor and evaluate. Hence, it is natural and very important for the company to enhance the effective control of its delivery operations for competitive and sustainable advantage.

The intelligent system currently used in Company J has three key components, which includes geographical information system (GIS), global positioning system (GPS), and wireless communication system. These new technologies were applied and expected to improve three major areas: a) develop optimized delivery schedules; b) provide real-time tracking and fleet management capabilities; and c) reduce manual operations.

While the GIS and related software are installed in the computer workstations in the control (dispatching) center, both GPS receivers and GPRS-based mobile terminals are equipped in each truck. These systems and hardware were all purchased from and installed by an outside vender in Beijing.

GPS is used intensively in the daily delivery operations. As observed in the field study, the primary roles of the GPS receiver are to send and receive satellite signals, demonstrate planned delivery routes and projected delivery time, illustrate customers' locations and neighborhood, and transfer real-time data with respect to vehicles' condition, e.g., travel time, speed, and direction. Company J strongly promotes GPS usage and requires that each driver must turn on the GPS receiver once the vehicle is on the road.

In addition, it was observed that each driver (truck) is provided with a GPRS-based communication mobile terminal (e.g., handheld PDA). While the GPS receiver serves as the media to transmit data for better real-time monitoring of the fleet, the GPRS mobile terminal is used to achieve products-related information exchange between drivers and the dispatching center. This includes, for instance, customers' data, products/ order information, delivery confirmation, as well as future schedules. In fact, GPS and GPRS devices, coupled with mobile phones, are the three primary tools used by the drivers to communicate not only with the dispatching center but among the drivers as well. During the interview, many drivers described the mobile devices as "simple", "flexible", and "fast", and stated that these mobile devices considerably facilitate their operations and greatly enhance productivity.

Lastly, the GIS software packages are installed in the computer workstations in the dispatching center. The GIS software offers a rich set of functions and tools that help to promote the management of logistics service. For instance, as we observed in the control center, with simple operations, the system can provide complete knowledge including digital maps, truck information, real-time monitoring and tracking, customers and products data, as well as delivery/route planning. We present in Figure 1 a simple illustration of the GIS/GPS architecture in Company J.

In general, the GIS, GPS, and GPRS-based mobile communication technologies are extensively used in the delivery of perishable goods and the manger describes the system as "part of the company" and "cannot work without it". Moreover, the management has established a set of policies to regulate and standardize the usage of these new technologies. Daily operations are frequently monitored to ensure procedure is complied and policies are followed. In what follows, we will discuss the benefits as well as challenges associated with effective GIS and GPS usage in Company J.

Benefits of GIS and GPS Usage

We now provide a detailed discussion about the primary benefits stemmed from the implementation and application of GIS and GPS technologies in the company.

Figure 1. Illustration of the architecture of the GIS, GPS, and GPRS systems used in Company J

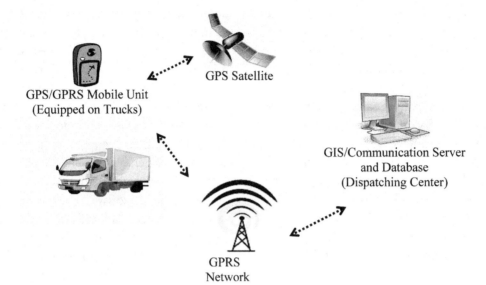

Reducing Operating Lead Time

As a distributor of perishable products, how to reduce lead time is one of the top concerns of Company J. Due to the special characteristics of the products, specific delivery time windows are required by customers. If the products are delivered outside these time windows, customers have the right to refuse to accept either partial or all of the orders, which result in significant loss for Company J. In addition, majority of the customers (e.g., supermarkets and restaurants) are located in downtown Beijing area, where traffic condition is extremely busy and highly unpredictable. Under these circumstances, the company faces substantial challenges: it must maintain sufficient inventories, trucks and personnel to fulfill demands; it also must manage to deliver these products in a timely and cost-effective manner.

Before the implementation of GIS and GPS technologies, a typical delivery of products involves at least four major steps: a) driver picks up customer/order information from the dispatching center; b) products are loaded on the truck from the warehouse; c) driver delivers products to customers' sites; and d) driver returns to the company with delivery confirmation and picks up next shipments.

As one driver pointed out in the interview, "delivery schedules were really difficult primarily due to demand uncertainty, (customers') requirement, and traffic condition. Sometimes, the traffic was really bad and when we returned to the center, it was too late to make the next shipment." In the past, a driver normally made no more than three deliveries per day. Large time gaps between schedules, created to buffer unexpected situations, were very common. Another driver explained, "our job was dependent upon the schedules. But once on the road, we were alone and the communication (between us and the center) was very difficult. When problems occurred, we had to stop and waited for the instructions from the center. This waiting time could last from an hour to half a day".

Significant improvement is realized by using GIS and GPS which reduce the operating and delivery lead time for the company in two ways. First, the new system helps to optimize delivery schedules. As witnessed by the researcher in the field study, the GIS system sorts and determines shipments based on customers' locations, route and truck information, as well as each driver's delivery regions. Dispatchers can easily generate shipping schedules, delivery routes, and projected delivery times for all vehicles. Second, new technologies help to improve information exchange and shorten communication time. Through mobile GPS and GPRS devices installed on trucks, dispatchers and drivers are able to send and receive important information such as delivery confirmation messages and new orders within seconds.

With the assistance of the new system, operating lead time is considerably shortened. As one dispatcher commented, "sending and receiving information are much faster and easier than before (using GIS/GPS), which greatly improve efficiency and accuracy." Unnecessary time-consuming manual operations are eliminated. To comply and coordinate with the new intelligent system, the company has implemented and required employees to follow a new operating procedure, which was consolidated from the original four steps to an easy two-step process: a) order/customer information is sent to the driver

and products are loaded on the truck; b) delivery messages are sent back to the center and next order/customer information is received. Based on the records of the company, each truck load normally consists of three deliveries. With the help of these new technologies, drivers now can make each delivery much faster and then return to warehouses to pickup products for more deliveries, which was almost impossible in the past. Now, during a regularly working day, the number of deliveries per truck is almost doubled from three shipments to five to six shipments. In Figure 2, we compare the operating procedure before and after the usage of GIS and GPS related technologies in Company J.

Facilitating the Management of Vehicles and Personnel

Effective management and monitoring of vehicles and personnel is a big challenge faced by Company J. As in many small and medium-sized firms in developing countries, due to budget constraints, the company did not have any formal communica-

Figure 2. Comparison of delivery operation before and after GIS/GPS usage in Company J

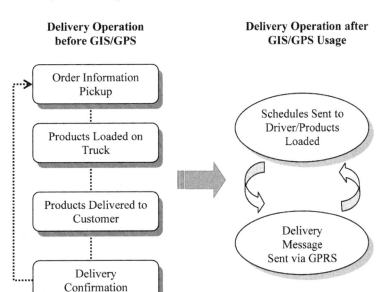

tion systems and equipments in the past. Mobile phones were the only device used between the drivers and dispatchers and they were normally used only when emergent situations occurred. The lack of real-time monitoring and communication hurts the effective management of vehicles and personnel. One dispatcher described this issue as follows: "(the center) could not control the vehicles on the road. We did not know where they were and how they were. When there was an emergency, drivers relied on their own judgment and took actions. In fact, they rather informed us after the incidence was solved."

GIS and GPS related technologies used in the company fundamentally resolve these issues from several aspects. First, the system provides many "real-time" tools and functions. Every vehicle is assigned a unique code and the control center can monitor and obtain a variety of information with respect to any specific vehicle and driver. In particular, useful functions and information such as exact real-time position and movement of each vehicle, delivery routes, zoom in/out, historical data of the vehicle and driver, and future schedules are all available and can be shown on the digital map in the control center. Dispatchers described the benefits, "Knowing the location of a truck and driver on the map helps us to monitor and improve the delivery service, prepare for unexpected events, and make better schedules."

Second, the use of GIS and GPS enhances the utilization of existing vehicles and personnel, improves Just-In-Time service, and reduces energy consumption per delivery. In particular, through generating optimized delivery schedules and routes, the system helps to improve efficiency and productivity. Drivers can easily avoid existing and potential traffic jams with the help of GIS and GPS guidance. For instance, based on the records of the control center, utilization of truck load (TL) capacity is jumped from 66% to 95% and the number of deliveries per truck is doubled.

Lastly, the new system also helps the company improve incidents management. Using GIS/GPS for incident management is not uncommon in many sectors, for instance, ambulance tracking and route guidance, police or fire fleet management, and dangerous goods transportation. However, these applications in developing countries are relatively new and related supports are quite limited due to both low technologies and high costs. The major benefit provided by the GIS/GPS system is the road safety function. When an unexpected event such as traffic accident or robbery occurs, alarm function of the GPS can help the driver to send emergency signals to the control center within seconds. Moreover, the system can also record and retrieve all related historical information during the period of time before the events happened.

These functions provide important evidence for possible insurance claims, customer complains, and police/fire reports. As one dispatcher commented, "The emergency alarm system works very well. Our system immediately reflects any incident on the digital map which allows me to inform the management, the customers, and make alternative schedules in a timely manner."

Moreover, we found an additional advantage brought by the application. A number of interviewees in the study stated that it helps to improve the working relationship among employees and increase team spirit in the company. For instance, as one driver described, "We know that we are part of the team. There are always people back in the dispatching center and on the road that we can count on whenever something happens."

Enhancing Demand and Supply Management

Distribution of perishable products requires particularly high levels of collaboration and coordination among varied functions. Tasks are interdependent and have close ties with each other and any problem in one specific area may cause unexpected and irreversible negative impacts on the entire operations of the company. In Company J, the application of GIS/GPS technologies helps to achieve better control in two particular areas: demand and supply management.

First, GIS provides rich tools and options with respect to customer and demand related management. Employees can conduct a variety of data mining and analysis that would never be accomplished in the past. These new tools include, for instance, store and maintain list of customers and their geographic locations, store and update customers' order information, search any particular customer or region of interest, search specific orders based on customers' name, regions, or time frames, and obtain historical shipping data. All these results can be retrieved and visually demonstrated on the computer screens. In addition, one can also conduct statistical and spatial analysis on existing customer density, sales density, and current distribution operations. Compared to the original customer and demand management if any, the GIS-assisted operation is in general an effortless process which greatly improves efficiency and effectiveness in this area.

Second, GIS also provides important support of supply management for Company J. Based upon optimized delivery schedules, improved utilization of vehicles and personnel, as well as enhanced customer/order management provided by the new system, one can make more accurate demand forecast and thus procurement of the products. For instance, one interviewee particularly mentioned that: "In the past, at the end of every month, having either a good amount of unsold products or stock out was considered 'normal'. The company used to buy less each time but with more frequencies to solve this issue, it didn't help." Indeed, GIS and GPS serve as a central point for maintaining efficient and effective supply and demand management. Dispatchers commented the benefits and revealed that: "After using (GIS and GPS), both the order quantities and frequencies are stabilized and the purchasing costs are reduced."

Assisting Strategic Planning

Another benefit generated by the usage of GIS and GPS technologies is that it helps the company's long-term strategic planning.

The new system enhances warehouse location and capacity planning for Company J. As described by the dispatchers during the interview, the company is using the GIS database to analyze demand information and geographic locations of clusters of customers in any particular district, which assists strategic planning issues such as opening new warehouses or closing existing ones in certain districts as demands change. Moreover, management uses this system to plan and control the capacities of current warehouses. For instance, the system demonstrates any warehouse that is approaching its limits or all warehouses whose products are below a given level. Key decisions such as increase or decrease capacities are made based upon these analyses.

Second, management uses historical data in the intelligent system to discover areas of potential new customers. One dispatcher gave an example of how GIS helped in this aspect: "We used the (GIS and GPS) system to collect information of our delivery networks and customers, which is then used to produce necessary maps of current operations. We then explore these data and graphs to locate possible new customers in these districts. This is definitely a valuable tool to have which enables us to develop new customers and businesses". As mentioned by the interviewee, the company is also planning to use GPS/GIS to further extend their operations to other related third party logistics (3PL) service.

Challenges and Limitations

The aforementioned major benefits generated by using GPS/GIS in Company J greatly help to reduce unnecessary costs and wastes, improve productivity, and enhance its service abilities. On the other hand, however, we also find some critical issues during the implementation process. We now provide a detailed discussion of these challenges and limitations.

Accuracy and Update of GIS and GPS

The use of GPS in vehicles to provide navigation is one of many functions that benefit the company, particularly the drivers. The availability of both accurate and prompt navigational guidance is the key to shorten travel time and reduce stress when the road and traffic condition vary or the driver is unfamiliar with the delivery neighborhood. To sustain these advantages, data installed in both the GPS and GIS terminal requires necessary and regular updates to keep up with real-world geographic changes such as construction of new roads or buildings.

Unfortunately, two factors make these updates difficult to be realized. First, GIS and GPS technologies in China are still in their preliminary phase in terms of both development and distribution. As in most developing nations, digital mapping data has been scarce and historically quite expensive to obtain. Indeed, limited geographic data and resources as well as inadequate technological supports contribute to the poor maintenance of GPS and GIS. Quality of guidance and real-time tracking is not guaranteed which can cause unexpected troubles to the company. In addition, due to costs concerns as in many small firms in emerging economies, the company could not afford to equip the most advanced systems. Some random and objective sources of errors such as the canyoning effect in urban areas from high-rise buildings in Beijing (Mintsis, Basbas, Papaioannou, Taxiltaris, & Tziavos, 2004) also contribute to the accuracy problem of the GPS devices.

Several interviewees commented on the issue of digital map and accuracy problems and gave some typical examples, which include: a) areas that the GPS cannot provide detailed geographic plots; b) newly-constructed roads or bridges were not shown on the map; and c) wrong directions. Like many fast growing cities in emerging economies, Beijing has experienced rapid development in the past decade. It is imperative to maintain and update GPS and GIS related systems regularly, since new roads, bridges, and buildings emerge almost every day. Under such a circumstance, how to update the GPS/GIS data in an effective and efficient way is a big challenge to many small and medium-sized firms including Company J.

Separation of Customer Service and GIS/GPS

GIS and GPS technologies establish an effective link between the control center and vehicles through real-time information exchange, conveniently transferring data such as order and delivery messages within the company. However, these advantages cannot be enjoyed by the customers. During the interview, the lack of information sharing between company J and its customers is a prominent issue brought by many employees. In particular, due to financial and personnel constraints, the company does not have any formal order tracking service available, such as online tracking, to their customers.

To inquire order and shipping information, customers have to call the company's dispatching center, which is not only inconvenient but generates additional responsibilities to the dispatchers. One interviewed dispatcher commented: "We do not have an independent customer service department. The only way that a customer can find out the condition of their shipment is to contact our control center. The volume of calls (from the customers) can be quite daunting sometimes which can considerably disrupt our regular jobs, since we just have only two dispatchers to manage our system during the day."

The separation of vehicle/product data provided by the GIS/GPS technology and customer service not only brings additional challenges to the normal operations of the control center but hurts the service ability of the company in general. To solve these issues, the company plans to establish a new webpage that will be linked with the existing vehicle and products database to provide full information to customers. Customers will have the access to frequently up-dated information with respect to any specific product, shipment, and delivery to their interests. However, how to effectively design and develop the information sharing mechanism and protocol between costumers and Company J so as to take full advantage of GIS and GPS technologies remain the next major challenge to the company.

Lack of Related Supports for Incidents Management

Effective use of GIS and GPS technologies for incidents handling requires necessary supports from other related organizations such police, fire departments, and hospitals. Whenever emergent incidents occur, advanced GIS and GPS provide users with multiple functions and options to inform concerning parties and messages can be sent simultaneously within seconds. However, in our study we found that these supports are either very limited in the system used by Company J.

As described by the interviewees, in the event of emergent incidents, for example traffic accidents, drivers via GPS alarm function report the situation back to the company who then contact police department for assistance through telephone. The GPS alarm is connected with the GIS in the dispatching center and it benefits the company very much in the form of "real-time" monitoring of the fleet and provides better controls. However, it is worth mentioning that there is no effective automatic communicating system exists between the dispatching center and other organizations, e.g., police and fire departments. Interviewees said that the lack of necessary outside supports for incidents management creates unavoidable difficulties for deliver timely and effective solutions to incident-involved drivers and trucks.

For example, one dispatcher mentioned that she received the alarm message and immediately talked to the driver during the first couple of minutes of the accident. She then contacted the police and fire departments and reported the incident. However, it took traffic police over half an hour to arrive at the accident site. Drivers also complained about the slow response after the alarm was sent. They mentioned that the alarm is helpful for letting the company know about the incidents but it generally took too long for help to come. Even though we did not have explanations from the interviewees for why it took such a long time, we believe the waiting time can be shortened if the alarm can be sent directly to traffic police department to ensure timely responses.

Solving this problem is not an easy task for the company, since the process involves broader collaborations and supports from different organizations. In particular, although the use of GIS and GPS technologies has experienced dramatic increase in the past several years in Beijing, business applications are relatively isolated and exclusive to the users themselves. As in other growing economies, due to various financial and technological constraints, necessary supporting infrastructures are either missing or still in the planning phase, which make the solutions difficult to achieve in a short period of time and thus cannot satisfy the immediate needs from the society. However, despite these difficulties, these problems must be handled and resolved so as to maintain a sustainable business development for companies in developing countries.

DISCUSSION

Based on our research findings, we now provide some important insights and guidelines for logistics managers regarding the use of GIS and GPS technologies.

Firstly, effective connection between GIS database and other key functions should be established. Though a common technology used in many logistics firm in developed countries, enterprise resource planning (ERP) system is still rare in companies in emerging economies. Management should set up common platforms where appropriate software need to be implemented and linked with key functions, such as procurement, marketing, and accounting/finance, of the company. Technical support should be given to integrate GIS with other corporate software to facilitate information sharing. For instance, GIS could be integrated with corporate warehouse and customer database so one can import/export information of any interested order and customers when needed. Independent customer service department should also be established where web-based customer inquiry interface should be managed and updated. As mentioned, an increasing number of research papers has been done on the integration of GIS and Decision Support Systems (DSS) and demonstrated the advantages of such situations. Logistics managers should be aware of such integration technologies and implement them whenever appropriate.

Secondly, necessary links and external supports from related organizations should be set up. Though a complicated and time-consuming process, a comprehensive and complete GIS-based intelligent system should be developed which should incorporate both internal functional departments and external supporting organizations such as police, fire departments, hospitals, and insurance companies. Such a system will not only benefit the company itself but related organizations in terms of improved communication and coordination, data and information sharing, and quick support and response. For instance, whenever accidents occurs, the GIS/GPS based system would automatically inform the company's control center, customers, police and fire departments, where corresponding actions would be taken. To achieve this, intelligent systems are required to be equipped in each of these concerned organizations and attention should be paid to system and structural compatibility among varied organizations where effective protocol such as each party's rights and responsibilities should be included and clarified. We wanted to point out that the development of these effective external supports is beyond the power of any single firm and it cannot be done without governmental assistance and support, especially in developing nations.

Thirdly, GIS and GPS technologies should be encouraged to use in all business areas. The pilot program is a preliminary test which has quite satisfactory results but not without problems. Management should develop a strategic plan and implement GIS and GPS related technologies to all other business areas in addition to the perishable food department. To reach this goal, necessary hardware and software should be equipped and trainings should be provided to involved employees to secure their abilities to use and take advantage of these new technologies. In particular, trainings need to be designed to enhance both technological skills and collaboration capabilities among varied functional areas.

CONCLUSION

This paper explored GIS and GPS usage in a medium-sized logistics company in China. We investigated the implementation issues of GIS and GPS technologies from both technological and organizational perspectives. The study confirmed the potential of GIS and GPS related technologies for enhancing operating efficiency and productivity, improving communication and relationship building, and facilitating collaboration and strategic planning of a firm. Using "explanation-building" method, we provided answers to important research questions such as "how these new technologies are used in the logistics company?" and "why they are important?"

The case study presented rich information that facilitates deeper understanding about the benefits of GIS and GPS technologies in logistic operations and provided analysis of why these benefits exist. For instance, optimized delivery schedules and routes are made possible by the GIS and GPS systems, real-time monitoring and data transfer are obtained between dispatchers and drivers, and better demand and supply management are achieved. These advantages and benefits are guaranteed by both new technologies and coordination within the company itself. For example, the company provided sufficient technological and personnel support to maintain the normal operations of the intelligent system, which significantly eliminates redundant manual operations. Moreover, the GIS and GPS adoption in Company J follows a "top-down" approach where the management strongly encourages the use of the new system to ensure maximized utility and optimized results.

We also identified and discussed major challenges and limitations that the firm has to face while implementing these technologies. These challenges and limitations bare some key characteristics and reflect some common issues of small and medium-sized firms in emerging economies, where businesses have experienced rapid growth but their technology and infrastructure are still less-developed. These challenges include, for instance, lack of maintenance and updates for existing GIS and GPS software, insufficient supports from related organizations, accuracy issues, and isolation of GIS database from other key functions such as customer service.

Compared to firms in the United States and the western European countries, logistics companies in China have to deal with major obstacles such as sparse digital mapping resources, inadequate technological supports, and expensive maintenance and update costs. Moreover, due to financial constraints, companies normally cannot afford to have the most recent software and equipments. These challenges can cause considerable problems during the implementation process. Moreover, unlike firms in developed nations, many companies in emerging economies do not have effective management information systems such as the ERP system. Hence, communication and information sharing are limited and difficult to achieve. Integration of GIS and other important database such as warehouse and customer data should be established to obtain company-wide control. Lastly, it is also worth pointing out that more problems and limitations may emerge in companies that operate in even smaller or less developed cities, where infrastructures are far from advanced and general business environment is considered to be less favorable. For instance, geographic data is simply hard to locate in many small cities where addresses and postal codes are either not standardized or incomplete.

We also wanted to point out that the results of this study should be interpreted cautiously, since it was conducted within a single organization and with a limited number of subjects. The generalability of its findings needs to be validated and it would be meaningful to test these findings with more data and organizations. Successful implementations of integrated GIS/GPS systems require various kinds of supports from both within and beyond a single firm, which include appropriate strategic planning, organizational and functional structures, and development of information technology. To this end, we plan to conduct future research that contains extensive surveys and interviews in varied organizations on GIS and GPS usage to obtain more generalized outcomes and insights. Another interesting extension of our current research is to conduct comparative studies on GIS application and its impact on firms in developing and developed nations. To this end, continued larger-scale research is planned to address these issues and to explore broad-range of business sectors in the United States and China.

ACKNOWLEDGMENT

We want to thank the Editor-in-Chief John Wang and the anonymous referees for their valuable inputs that help to improve the paper.

REFERENCES

Basnet, C., Foulds, L., & Igbaria, M. (1996). Fleet manager: A microcomputer-based decision support system for vehicle routing. *Decision Support Systems, 16,* 195–207. doi:10.1016/0167-9236(95)00010-0

Baxter, P., & Jack, S. (2008). Qualitative case study methodology: Study design and implementation for novice researchers. *Qualitative Report, 13,* 544–559.

Butler, M., Herlihy, P., & Keenan, P. (2005). Integrating information technology and operational research in the management of milk collection. *Journal of Food Engineering, 70,* 341–349. doi:10.1016/j.jfoodeng.2004.02.046

Crossland, M., Wyne, B., & Perkins, W. (1995). Spatial decision support systems: An overview of technology and a test of efficacy. *Decision Support Systems, 14,* 219–235. doi:10.1016/0167-9236(94)00018-N

Derekenaris, G., Garofalakis, J., Makris, C., Prentzas, J., Sioutas, S., & Tsakalidis, A. (2001). Integrating GIS, GPS and GSM technologies for the effective management of ambulances. *Computers, Environment and Urban Systems, 25,* 267–278. doi:10.1016/S0198-9715(00)00025-9

Frank, W., Thill, J., & Batta, R. (2000). Spatial decision support system for hazardous material truck routing. *Transportation Research Part C, Emerging Technologies, 8,* 337–359. doi:10.1016/S0968-090X(00)00007-3

Franklin, C. (1992). An introduction to geographic information systems: Linking maps to databases. *Database, 15,* 12–21.

Hafberg, G. (1995). Integration of geographic information systems and navigation systems for moving (dynamic) objects like vehicles and ships. In *Proceedings of ESRI User Conference* (pp. 272-274).

Imielinski, T., & Navas, J. (1999). GPS based geographic addressing, routing, and resource discovery. *Communications of the ACM, 42,* 86–92. doi:10.1145/299157.299176

Jung, H., Lee, K., & Chun, W. (2006). Integration of GIS, GPS, and optimization technologies for the effective control of parcel delivery service. *Computers & Industrial Engineering, 51,* 154–162. doi:10.1016/j.cie.2006.07.007

Keenan, P. (1996). *Using a GIS as a DSS generator. Perspectives on DSS.* Mytilene, Greece: University of the Aegean.

Keenan, P. (1998). Spatial decision support systems for vehicle routing. *Decision Support Systems, 22,* 65–71. doi:10.1016/S0167-9236(97)00054-7

Laurini, R. (2000). A short introduction to TeleGeo Processing and TeleGeo Monitoring. In *Proceedings of the Second International Symposium on Telegeoprocessing* (pp. 10-12).

Li, H., Kong, C. W., Pang, Y. C., Shi, W. Z., & Yu, L. (2003). Internet-based geographical information systems for e-commerce application in construction and material procurement. *Journal of Construction Engineering and Management, 129,* 689–697. doi:10.1061/(ASCE)0733-9364(2003)129:6(689)

Mintsis, G., Basbas, S., Papaioannou, P., Taxiltaris, C., & Tziavos, I. (2004). Applications of GPS technology in the land transportation system. *European Journal of Operational Research, 152,* 399–409. doi:10.1016/S0377-2217(03)00032-8

Parkinson, B. (1996). *Global Positioning System: Theory and applications* (*Vol. 1*). Washington, DC: American Institute of Aeronautics and Astronautics, Inc.

Sui, D. (1998). GIS-based urban modeling: Practices, problems, and prospects. *International Journal of Geographical Information Science, 12*, 651–671. doi:10.1080/136588198241581

Tanzi, T. (2000). Principles and practices in TeleGeomatics. In *Proceedings of the Second International Symposium on Telegeoprocessing* (pp. 10-12).

Weigel, D., & Cao, B. (1999). Applying GIS and OR techniques to solve Sears technician-dispatching and home-delivery problems. *Interfaces, 29*, 112–130. doi:10.1287/inte.29.1.112

Yin, R. (2002). *Case study research*. Thousand Oaks, CA: Sage Publications.

Zito, R., D'este, G., & Taylor, M. (1995). Global positioning systems in the time domain: How useful a tool for intelligent vehicle-highway systems? *Transportation Research Part C, Emerging Technologies, 3*, 193–209. doi:10.1016/0968-090X(95)00006-5

This work was previously published in International Journal of Information Systems and Social Change, Volume 1, Issue 3, edited by John Wang, pp. 45-61, copyright 2010 by IGI Publishing (an imprint of IGI Global).

Chapter 5

Effective Supply Chain Management Strategy for Food Products:
An Insight to Linked Partnerships

Witaya Krajaysri
Mae Fah Luang University, Thailand

ABSTRACT

This paper explores and extends the supply chain management strategy for food products effectively and efficiently through analysis of insights to linked partnerships within the supply chain due to the possibility of a global food crisis. The required solution is a collaboration of all parties in the supply chain since an effective supply chain management strategy (ESCMS) for food products is through proper insight between linked partnerships, including customer satisfaction through service quality, well-defined requirements and expectations, effective and clear communication, mutual relationship management, and close relationships from partnerships. ESCMS for food products must have the strategy of supply-to-stock and supply-to-order (efficient and responsive), effective collaboration within the supply chain, well-defined expectations and requirements, effective communication and information flow, mutual relationship management, and close relationships as partners. This insight of linked partnership throughout the supply chain would contribute by reducing and solving problems such as over supply, inconsistency of price (high and low), global food supply, and the conflict among partnerships, including an increase in the consistency of farmers' careers.

INTRODUCTION

Everyone agrees that the world's population will exceed 8 billion people by 2025 and mostly in developing countries (Eicher & Staatz, 1998). With population growth, and income growth, even modest income growth in developing countries by 2025, the demand for food consumption will be increased. This will cause a food shortage crisis at that time, if effective and efficient management and preparation steps are not implemented. Meanwhile, we have so worry about the population growth for more than 8 billion in 2025. There is an indication of an impending food crisis occurring

DOI: 10.4018/978-1-4666-0927-3.ch005

based on signals from 2008 of uncertain price and supplies of rice.

Rising food prices and dwindling global stocks have put many governments in developing Asia and the Pacific under enormous pressure to put food on the table of the most vulnerable and poor in their countries. Over a billion people in the region are seriously affected by the food price surge, as food expenditure accounts for 60% of the average total expenditure basket. Food and energy together account for more than 75% of total spending of the poor in the region. In addition, underinvestment in agriculture has led to stagnating food-grain yields and slow development of high- yielding and pest-resistant varieties. Incentives for farmers have been distorted by interventionist policies, and change in land-use patterns in developing economies has led to loss in agricultural land. Higher disposable incomes in rapidly developing Asian economies and a shift to greater meat-based protein consumption have led to greater demand for food and feed grains in the region (Kuroda, 2008).

Furthermore, Vietnam and India, the major rice exporting countries, have reduced their exports of rice to global markets in order to preserve and ensure domestic consumption (Khor, 2008). Moreover, looking at the supply-demand dynamics, the era of cheap food is over. And this has serious implications for developing Asia. High food prices will undermine the gains in poverty reduction in Asia and make it difficult to attain the Millennium Development Goals of halving extreme poverty by 2015. The situation is serious, and governments have responded with subsidies, imposed price controls and caps on exports to offer immediate short-term relief. While the domestic imperatives to do so are understandable, we feel these measures are likely to be counterproductive and prolong vitality (Kuroda, 2008).

The rice price in Thailand which is the world's biggest rice exporter still stays high (Reuters, 2009). It is responsive to the severity of the food

crisis and the need for prompt action, the World Bank Group set up the Global Food Crisis Response Program (GFRP) in May 2008 to provide immediate relief to countries hard hit by food high prices. Most of them are so worried about the crisis and need to have the security (World Bank Online, 2009). Soaring prices have been blamed on lower agricultural production, weather shocks, more meat consumption, and shifts to biofuel crops as follows. 1) Wheat prices are up 120%. 2) Rice prices are up 75%.and 3) Poor families spending up to 80% of their budget on food (World Bank online, 2008). The incomes from rising the price are not equal the poor reduction (Ivanic & Martin, 2008). In many poor countries, the recent increase in prices of staple food raise the real incomes of those selling food, many of whom are relatively poor.

According to Kevin Cleaver, Director Agriculture and Rural Development, World Bank have said that "About 60% of the extra food to meet the increasing demand will come from irrigated agriculture. At the same time, we face the challenges of increasing farmer incomes, reducing rural poverty and protecting the environment, all from an increasingly constrained water resources base (World Bank Online, 2006). Furthermore, In the World Bank's new report "Reengaging in Agricultural Water Management: Challenges and Options" indicated that by the year 2030 food demand will double as world population increases by an additional two billion people. The increase in food demand will come mostly from developing countries (The World Bank, 2006).

A continuous rapid rising in price and reduced stock of the global rice supply, has caused food riots in many countries, including some in Asia. Policy makers are scrambling to know the causes and find solutions (Khor, 2008). Therefore, it is important to study and find out the solution of the food crisis from uncertain price and stock by understanding demand and supply within the supply chain. The purpose of this study is to explore and extend supply chain management strategy effectively and efficiently through insight of linked partnerships for food products. The expected result must come from the insight of linked partnerships for effective supply chain management strategy of food products should be and how it should be applied.

The first goal of this paper, is to explain the strategy of effective supply chain management for food products and collaborative strategy such as customer satisfaction; so it must consider an understanding of service quality requirements and expectations, effective and clear communication between affected groups, mutual relationship management and, close relationship in partnerships. Secondly, effective supply chain management strategy (ESCMS) for food products through insight of linked partnership has been combined and built as a conceptual model for resolution of food crisis. Finally, the concept has been analyzed and discussed for contribution and the limitation of the application to solve the problem through the whole supply chain network.

LITERATURE REVIEW

Effective Supply Chain Management Strategy (ESCMS) of Food Products

A supply chain however must also be dynamic in the sense of change over time, that change can come either through adaptation to a changing environment or productive initiatives to gain competitive advantage. This includes the possibility to meet unrecognized customers needs or apply the new technology (Skjott-Larsen et al., 2007).

Supply chain is defined by the council of Logistics Management as "the process of planning, implementing and controlling the efficient, cost effective flow of materials, in-process inventory, finished goods and related information from the point of origin to the point of consumption for

the purpose of conforming to customer requirements. However, a company or organization's supply chain is not limited to delivering goods to the end-consumers (Roy, 2003). Additionally, supply chain can be defined as set of firms that pass material forward. Several independent firms are involved in manufacturing a product and placing it in the hands of the end user in a supply chain – raw material and component producers, product assemblers, wholesalers, retail merchants and transportation companies are all members of the supply chain (LaLonde & Masters, 1994). Supply chain also defined as the alignment of firms that brings products or service to market (Chandra & Grabis, 2007; Lambert et al., 1998; Mentzer et al., 2001).

General Food Supply Chain

Food supply chain may be defined more closely due to the specific nature of the product. Agriculture forms the raw material base, with primary production supplying the processing industries, where the product reaches its final form. Distribution of the food product includes variety of middlemen that take care of wholesale, retail and catering functions (Eastham et al., 2001). Packaging and transport industries also have a significant role in the food supply chain in getting the right type of product to the consumer at the right place and time (Lorentz, 2006). The general agribusiness supply chain is shown in Figure 1.

Supply chain management (SCM) has the key objectives to provide best value to customer by measuring, planning and managing all the links of chain. In any business or operation, a manager has to find a balance between two conflicting objectives of demand and supply from operations. The voice of customer is articulated as customer service which is the primary objective of supply chain management. Supply chain would start from the customers demand and return or reverse to the point of origin. If we can solve the cause of

Figure 1. General food supply chain

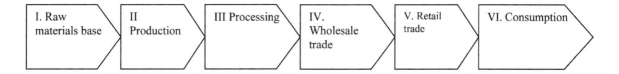

supply chain failure from the lack of understanding customers demand, then we should be able to solve the food problem. To approach the design of supply chain of the organization, it must have both efficient and responsive supply chain (Basu & Wright, 2008; Ling, 2007).

Supply Chain Strategy of Food Products

The responsive supply chain (supply to order) is aimed to react quickly to market demand. This supply chain model is best suits the environment in which demand predictability is low, forecasting error is high, product life cycle is short, new product introductions are frequent, and product variety is high. It should be applied with the food products that become the perishable. Meanwhile, an efficient supply chain (supply to stock) is aimed to coordinate the material flow and services to minimize inventory and maximize the efficiency of the manufacturers and service providers in the chain. This supply chain model fit the environment in which demands are highly predictable, forecasting error is low, product life cycle is long, new products introductions are infrequent, product variety is minimum production lead time is long and order fulfillment lead-time is short. This design will match competitive priority emphasizing on low cost operations and on-time delivery. The efficient supply chain also includes line flows, large volume production, and low capacity cushion (Ling, 2007; Balou, 2008). To manage supply chain for food product effectively, it should be applied both efficient and responsive supply chain.

The supply chain of food products should be clearly understood since from the supply of food products until the final demand or from farm to the table. The flow of information and physical goods from both customers and suppliers to the business or the conversion centre (e.g., a factory or a warehouse or an office) is termed as inbound logistics. Likewise, the flow of information or goods and services from the conversion centre to the customer constitute outbound logistics. To put it simply inbound logistics relate to demand and procurement (buyers, customers or users) while outbound logistics relate to supply and service (suppliers, seller, or providers) (Basu & Wright, 2008). Supply chain management of food products will be the management of upstream and downstream relationships between suppliers and customers to deliver superior customer value at less cost to the supply chain as a whole or mixed outbound and inbound logistics or collaboration within supply chains (Christopher, 1992) (See Figure 2).

Collaboration within Supply Chains

The supply chain of foods products has started from farmers as the suppliers passed the logistics process through the factory and/ or mills (inbound logistics), delivered to the warehouse or distribution center, then moved to supermarket or market, finally sent to the end customers or consumers (Figure 2). The movement of food products within supply chain really needs to have effective coordination or collaboration as the partnership with good understanding to each others. Due to it is

Figure 2. Supply Chain Strategy of foods Products

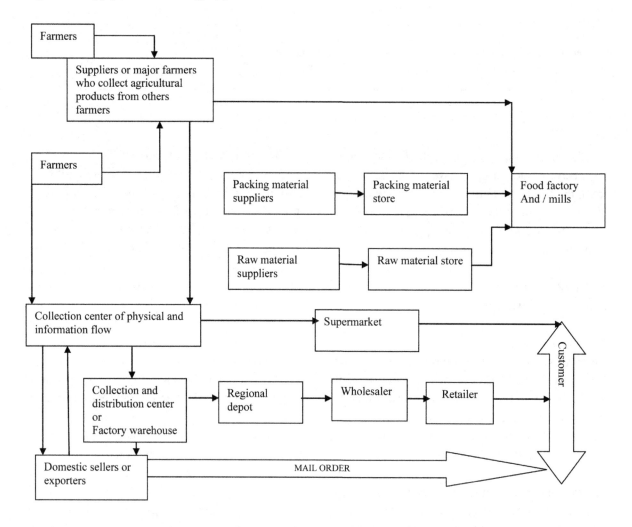

quite long chain between the points of origin to the point of consumption. As demand and supply management can help manage the supply chain of food products effectively. Demand management can be done through collaboration within supply chain (Ling, 2007). The supply chain can be effective and efficient network between the linked partnership for satisfying customer needs at appropriate prices with a variety of goods and services at a given level of cost, agility, and risk. It is modularity and the commitments to enhance collaborations that can be guarantee such effectiveness and efficiency (Chan & Lee, 2005).

Collaborative commerce is a good milestone, which make product development and daily operations more effective and efficient by using a Website. It has been defined as the use of a business-to-business exchange to facilitate the flow of information rather than to process transactions (Bechek & Brea, 2001). It integrates the company's core business processes within the supply chain, including its customers (Gossain, 2002). It is the accumulation of effective and flexible collaborations with appropriate partners that leads to higher competitiveness in the market. This process is called supply chain synthesis (Tompkins, 2000). It is holistic, continuous improvement process of ensuring customer satisfaction through the commitment to the supply chain. To ensure the customer satisfaction it must consider understanding the service quality, well defined requirements and expectations, effective and clear communication between each others, mutual relationship management and, close relationship as partnership.

Service Quality of Linked Partnership

Service quality stems from a comparison of what customers feel a seller should offer (i.e., their expectations) with the seller's actual service performance (Gronroos, 1982; Lehtinen & Lehtinen, 1982; Lewis & Booms, 1983; Sasser et al., 1978). Therefore, the notion that service quality is a function of the expectations-performance gap was reinforced by a broad-based exploratory study (Parasuraman et al., 1985). The gaps between customers' expectations and the perceptions of service providers' performance from the gaps model of Zeithaml and Bitner (1996) are shown in Table 1.

Well-Defined Requirements and Expectations

Every party within supply chain needs to clarify role, responsibilities as well as expectations and requirements of each other's (Razzaque & Zheng, 1998). Several authors have well-defined requirements, procedures and systems: the success of a partnership depends on having a clear definition up-front of delivery service levels, material flows, inventory control, order management, and others (Bagchi & Virum, 1998; Dauherty et al., 1996; Lieb & Randall, 1996). It is very necessary for every party in supply chain know real needs of other linked partnership by checking and asking. Reading (2002, p. 165) suggested that the effective service starts with a product or service that meets a real customer's needs, therefore, you

Table 1. Gap models of service quality

Gap 1	Difference between **consumer expectations and management's perceptions** of consumer expectations(Not knowing what customers expect)
Gap 2	Difference between management **perceptions of consumer expectations** and service quality specifications(The wrong service quality standards-management may not be willing or able to put the systems in place to match or exceed customers' expectations)
Gap 3	Difference between **service quality specifications and the service actually delivered** (he service performance gap-when employees are unable and/or unwilling to perform the service at the desired level)
Gap 4	Difference between **service quality and what is communicated about the service to consumers** (when promises do not match delivery)
Gap 5	Difference between **consumers expectations** and **perceptions** (when actual services delivered do not meet customers' expectations)

Source: Adapted from Zeithaml et al. (1996)

must ensure your product or service genuinely meets that need.

Effective and Clear Communication

Communication between suppliers and customers must be effective and clear (Razzaque & Sheng, 1998). This is essential for coordination of supply chain (Andel, 1994; Bowman, 1995; McKeon, 1991; Trunick, 1989). Close coordination would help to reduce any communication errors between suppliers and customers. Inaccurate and misleading information can create many problems and present obstacles to the proposed changes that could result in a very dissatisfied workforce. This can be solved by developing and implementing an aggressive communication plan (Zhu et al., 2001). Effective communication and coordination would help to create teamwork efficiency that would result in a satisfactory service outcome.

Mutual Relationship Management

Success of supply chain management also depends on the relationship of the suppliers and customers based on mutual trust and faith (Bradley, 1994; Martha & Krampel, 1996; Richardson, 1997; Sheehan, 1989). This does not imply that control measures are redundant; firms should mandate the period for reporting by the service providers (Razzaque & Sheng, 1998; Richardson, 1990).

It is essential for the company to manage the mutual relationship with both customers and supplier to have insight between the linked partnerships. The alliances of the customers and supplier should aim to build mutual trust and a continuous commitment in order to make the alliance successfully understood by both sides (Martha & Krampel, 1996; Richardson, 1997). It will help to obtain good coordination and exchange useful information that will result in an appropriate and the most effective outcome.

Close Relationship as Partnership

A close working relationship between all linked parties within supply chain is considered crucial for the success of the partnership; the success of supply chain management also depends on a customer-supplier or user- provider relationship based on mutual trust and faith (Bradley, 1994; Sheehan, 1989). The success criteria needed to establish sustainable partnerships in the area of contract logistics are the various relationships between the people involved (Razzaque & Sheng, 1998). Bradley (1993) also divided successful partnerships into two categories as those in which both sides have made substantial financial investments and those where the relationship has developed and expanded over a long time. According to Gooley (1994), successful partnerships generally follow five principles:

1.   Concentrate business with relatively few partners. By doing so, the buyer gets better pricing and better service.
2.   Carry out joint improvement efforts with partners-identify the operation and service areas that need improvement.

3.   Institute a formal system for measuring partners' performance-helps to verify provider's compliance with the service contract's terms and to help identify problems.
4.   Employ a two-way feedback system. Partnerships thrive on communication that allows both parties to discuss problems and decide on plans of action.
5.   Let partner performance determine routing choices and rate level.

A partnership between firms demands a high level of understanding by firms of their own business as well as the business of their counterparts (Richardson, 1993). Buying firms are able to achieve superior customer service by working closely with partners to improve the logistics process. Together they could offer faster deliveries and more accurate information. Successful business performance will be achieved by structuring the business to meet customers' expectations. Strong and productive partnerships between buyers and suppliers are important for effective supply chain management. Such partnerships should be based on mutual understanding, which can be hampered by a perception gap between the supply chains partners with respect to what are the critical factors for a successful buyer-supplier relationship (Kim et al., 1999).

Therefore, the all players within the chain must understand the demand and supply of each other's very well. Every player within the supply chain must help reduce gap of service quality. They must not ignore to promote mutual relationships among themselves. If there are not understanding occur, every members must ask each others as service quality concepts which mentioned above. It will help create the insight among linked members or partnerships within supply chain.

The effective supply chain strategy (ESCMS) and collaboration management including understanding customers and suppliers as the partnership can be combined and rebuilt as the conceptual model in Figure 3.

Figure 3. Conceptual Model of Effective supply chain management strategy (ESCMS) of food products through insight of linked partnership

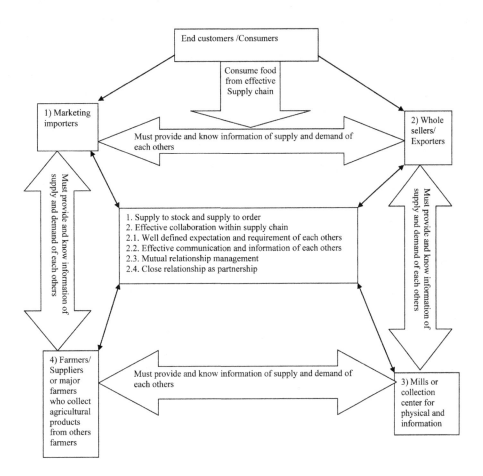

ESCMS FOR FOOD PRODUCTS THROUGH AN INSIGHT OF LINKED PARTNERSHIP

After reviewing the existing literature which has been collected from supply strategy both supply to stock and supply to order including customer satisfaction through service quality, well defined requirements and expectations, effective and clear communication between each others, mutual relationship management and, close relationship as partnership. The study can summarize the concept of effective supply chain management

strategy **(ESCMS)** for food products through insight between linked partnerships as follows:

1. Supply to stock and supply to order strategy,
2. Effective collaboration within supply chain,
    ◦ Well defined expectation and requirement of each other,
    ◦ Effective communication and information to each other,
    ◦ Mutual relationship management and,
    ◦ Close relationship as partnership. (Figure 3)

Supply to stock and supply to order- the upstream in supply chain since farmer, mill and, food industrial factory must consider applying the supply chain strategy both supply to stock (efficient supply chain) and responsive supply chain (supply to order). Due to they must have both customer service quality and cost management. They cannot ignore the customer and consumer which are important for them.

Effective collaboration within supply chain- all members in the supply chain are important to manage supply chain effectively and efficiently. Both sides of supply chain must manage mutual relationship and treat each other as the partnership not just the customer or supplier. The upstream or supplier side must understand expectation of the downstream very well. Meanwhile, the downstream or customer must know what the suppliers have. Finally, both upstream and downstream must have effective communication and share information to each other. They have to be able to communicate to each other effectively by having the good information of other sides such as from EDI (Electronic data Interchange), single window, internet or other computer application system.

ANALYSIS AND IMPLICATION

The study wants to find the practical determinants and strategy to reduce and solve the problem of global food crisis within supply chain. Moreover, the concepts of effective supply chain management strategy for food products through the insight of linked partnerships might have both a contribution and limitation in the applicable method.

CONTRIBUTION

Since supply chain management can be mentioned as a whole process of business administration, the movement of products especially food from the point of origin to point of consumption within

supply chain must rely on the network or partnership. The upstream and downstream cannot function alone. Once, the supply chain has been managed effectively and efficiently through insight of linked partnership, it should contribute in the following ways.

Reduce the Problem of Over Supply

If the food suppliers can understand the demand forecast of the downstream side, they should be able to produce, supply and, provide the right quantity. According to the mission of logistics or supply chain management is "to get the right goods or services to the right place, at the right time, and in the desired condition at the lowest cost and highest return on investment".

Reduce the Problem of Inconsistent Price

Once, the food suppliers or upstream can apply the supply strategy both supply to stock (efficient supply chain) and supply to order (responsive supply chain), and, they understand the requirement of linked downstream. They can reduce unnecessary cost from the movement; because every movement or flow of product is cost effective, since the food products are more sensitive to management than other industrial products.

Increase the Consistent Career for Farmers

Most farms are in developing areas, they do not have contribution from their government, resulting in a lack of advanced technology, knowledge and management. Most of them must depend on the seasonal rain and the price determination of a middle man. Several researches about farmers in developing countries in Asia found that most of them have a lot of debt. If they know the future from demand forecasting, it should contribute to making their career more consistent and stable.

Reduce the Problem of Global Food Supply

To solve the global food crisis, an integrated strategy must be implemented worldwide. Due to globalization resources and problems can flow to each other easily. For example, when there is a financial crisis in the United States of America, it impacts the rest of world. Similarly, swine flu that occurred first in Mexico has spread to Europe and Asia quickly. As every country has more interaction in any activity, especially as people buy and eat food from other countries. Therefore, to solve the global food crisis an effective supply chain methodology must be implemented throughout the world with well understood linked partnerships.

Reduce the Conflict among Partnership

If every part of supply chain, both upstream and downstream can understand each other well, it will help promote a good relationship. That is to reduce the conflict from others and make them happy and successful. Successful business performance will be achieved by structuring the business to meet customers' expectations and requirements. Strong and productive partnerships between buyers or customers and suppliers are important for effective supply chain management.

LIMITATION

On the other hand, to manage supply chain of food products effectively and efficiently through the insight of linked partnerships have several limitations. First there are several parties involved; it is difficult to manage the relationship to each other effectively and efficiently. Second, many food product suppliers come from Asian countries which are still poor and lack advanced technology, management and knowledge. They might not be able to apply the concepts effectively and efficiently, as they have to have advanced technology to support effective communication and information for demand forecast, since information systems are very important in logistics and supply chain management. Also, most of the food suppliers are in developing countries in Asia and still have political and social conflicts that seriously hamper cooperation or collaboration in a partnership. This can be a serious obstacle in developing a strategic partnership within the supply chain.

CONCLUSION AND FURTHER STUDY

As supply chain started from the customers demand, every part of the supply chain must be able to responds to those demands place upon it. The principles of an effective supply chain management strategy for food products through insight of linked partnerships should be an effective concept that responds to the customers' demands. The concept would be comprised of the following:

1. Supply to stock and supply to order (efficient and responsive) strategy,
2. Effective collaboration within supply chain,
    - Well defined expectation and requirement of each other,
    - Effective communication and information to each other (share information),
    - Mutual relationship management and,
    - Close relationship as partnership.

This study can contribute to reduction of problems in the following areas:

1. Over supply,
2. Inconsistency of price both high and low,
3. Global food supply, and
4. The conflict among partnership.

Figure 4. Apply the concepts of effective supply chain management strategy (ESCMS) for food products

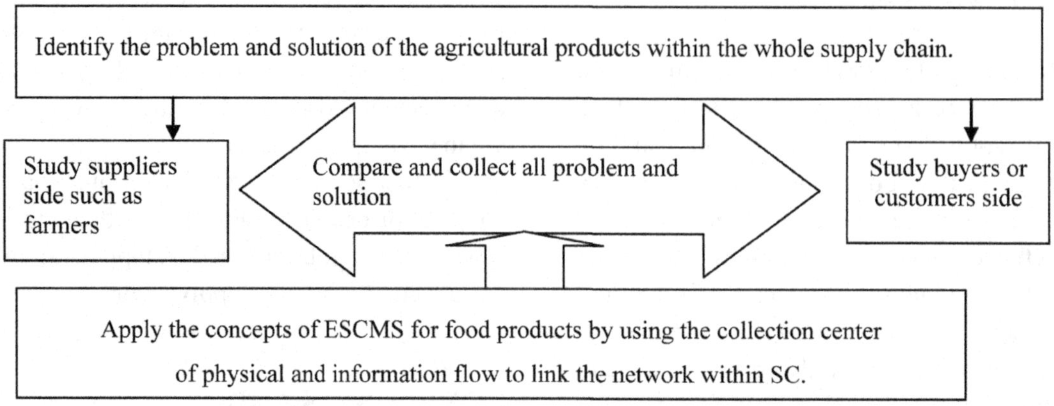

In addition, it also helps describe a methodology for improving the consistency of farmers' careers. On the other hand, the study also has some limitations of applying the concepts because of the difficulty to manage relationships among linked partnerships or members. The lack of advanced technology in some developing areas might also be an obstacle to applying these concepts.

FURTHER STUDY

This study defines the concepts of effective supply chain management strategy for food products through insights of linked partnerships. The objective is to reduce the problems of global food crisis such as rice price, inefficient supply and demand of food products. Most of the rice or food suppliers are in developing countries in Asia which consists of poor framers with a lack of advanced technology, management and knowledge. They might not have sufficient important information systems to manage demand forecast within the supply chain. In addition, Thailand which is the biggest rice exporter in the world has the problem of poor farmers, with significant debt trying to grow rice. They have to borrow money to do

agriculture, but the rate of return on investment is lower than the interest rate. Therefore, a further study should research the topic of "supply chain management strategy of food products from postharvest to marketing in Thailand through insights of linked partnerships". The research will apply the model of physical and information flow which have to develop collection center for physical and information. Figure 4 shows the applied research of this concept.

REFERENCES

Andel, T. (1994). Seal your victory through logistics communication. *Transportation & Distribution*, 88-94.

Bagchi, P. K., & Virum, H. (1998). Logistics alliances: trends and prospects in integrated Europe. *Journal of Business Logistics*, *19*(1), 191–213.

Balou, R. (2008). Supply chain/ logistics strategy. *Business Logistics/Supply Chain Management*. Upper Saddle River, NJ: Pearson.

Basu, R., & Wright, J. N. (2008). The role of supply chain as a value driver. *Total Supply Chain*. Maryland Heights, MO: Elsevier.

Bechek, B., & Brea, C. (2001). Deciphering collaborative commerce. *International Journal of Business Strategy, 3*(4), 36–38. doi:10.1108/eb040157

Bowman, R. J. (1995). A high wire act. *Distribution,* 78-81.

Bradley, P. (1993). Third party logistics: DuPont takes the plunge. *Purchasing,* 33-7.

Chan, C. K., & Lee, H. W. J. (2005). Understanding and managing the intrinsic dynamics of supply chains. In *Successful Strategies in Supply Chain Management* (p. 174). Hershey, PA: IGI Global.

Chandra, C., & Grabis, J. (2007). Knowledge management as the basis of crosscutting problem-solving approaches. In *Supply Chain Configuration: Concepts, Solutions, and Applications* (p. 130). New York: Springer.

Christopher, M. (1999). Logistics and supply chain management: strategies for reducing cost and improving service. *International Journal of Logistics, 2*(1).

Daugherty, P. J., Atank, T. P., & Rogers, D. S. (1996). Third-party logistics providers: purchasers' perceptions. *International Journal of Purchasing and Materials Managements, 32*(2), 23–29.

Eastham, J. F., Sharples, L., & Ball, S. D. (2001). *The catering and food retails industries: contextual insights. Food Supply Chain Management: Issues for the Hospitality and Retail Sectors* (pp. 3–21). Oxford, UK: Butterworth & Heineman.

Eicher, C. K., & Staatz, M. J. (1998). *International agricultural development.* Baltimore: Johns Hopkins University Press.

Gooley, T. B. (1994). Partnership can make the customer-service difference. *Traffic Management, 42*(5).

Gossain, S. (2002). Craking the collaboration code. *The Journal of Business Strategy, 23*(6), 20–25. doi:10.1108/eb040282

Grönroos, C. (1984). A service quality model and its marketing implications. *European Journal of Marketing, 18*(4), 36. doi:10.1108/EUM0000000004784

Ivanic, M., & Martin, W. (2008). Implications of higher global food prices for poverty in low-income countries. *World Bank Policy Research Working Paper, 4594.*

Khor, M. (2008). Global crisis as food price soar: global trend. *Third World Network.* Retrieved from http://www.twnside.org.sg/title2/gtrends/gtrends201.htm

Kim, B., Park, K., & Kim, T. (1999). The perception gap among buyers and suppliers in the semiconductor industry. *Supply Chain Managements: An International Journal, 4*(5), 231–241. doi:10.1108/13598549910294920

Kurada, H. (2008). Solving Asia's food crisis. *Today's Wall Street Journal Asia.* Retrieved from http://online.wsj.com /public/article print/SB120994263541666093.html

Lalonde, B., & Masters, J. (1994). Emerging logistics strategies - blueprints for the next Century. *International Journal of Physical Distribution & Logistics Management, 24*(7), 35–47. doi:10.1108/09600039410070975

Lambert, D. M., Stock, J. R., & Ellram, L. M. (1998). *Fundamentals of Logistics Management* (p. 130). Boston: Irwin.

Lehtinen, U., & Lehtinen, J. R. (1982). *Service quality: a study of quality dimensions.* Finland: Unpublished Research Report, Service of Management Group, OY.

Lewis, R. C., & Booms, B. H. (1983). *The marketing aspects of service quality. Emerging Perspectives in Services Marketing* (pp. 99–107). Chicago: American Marketing Association.

Lieb, R. C., & Randall, H. Y. (1996). A comparison of the use of third–party logistics services by large American manufacturers. *Journal of Business Logistics, 17*(1), 305–320.

Ling, L. (2007). Demand management: customer order forecast. In *Supply Chain Management: Concept, Techniques and Practices Enhancing Value Through Collaboration* (p. 117). Hackensack, NJ: World Scientific Publishing.

Lorentz, H. (2006). *Food supply chains in Ukraine and Kazakhstan.* Turku School of Economics, Electronic Publications of Pan European Institute. Retrieved from http://www.tse.fi/pei/pub

Martha, J., & Krampel, W. (1996). Start relationship on the right foot. *Transportation & Distribution, 73*(3), 75–76.

McKeon, J. E. (1991). Outsourcing begins in-house. *Transportation & Distribution,* 25-8.

Mentzer, J. T., DeWitt, W., Keebler, J. S., Min, S., Nix, N. W., Smith, C. D., & Zacharia, Z. G. (2001). Defining supply chain management. *Journal of Business Logistics, 22*(2), 125.

Parasuraman, A., Zeithaml, V. A., & Berry, L. L. (1985). A conceptual model of service quality and its implications for future research. *Journal of Marketing, 49*, 41–50. doi:10.2307/1251430

Razzaque, M. A., & Sheng, C. C. (1998). Outsourcing of logistics functions: a literature survey. *International Journal of Physical Distribution & Logistics Management, 28*, 2.

Reading, C. (2002). Synthesizing the strategy. In *Strategic Business Planning: A Dynamic System for Improving Performance & Competitive Advantage* n (2nd ed.). London: Kogan Page Limited.

Reuters. (2009, March 13). Thai rice prices to stay high. *The Rice Problem.* Retrieved from http://www.inquirer.net/specialfeatures/riceproblem/view.php?db=1&article=20090313-193988

Richardson, H. L. (1990). Explore outsourcing. *Transportation & Distribution,* 17-20.

Richardson, H. L. (1997). Contract time: switch partners or keep dancing? *Transportation & Distribution, 38*(7), 47–52.

Roy, A. (2003, January). How efficient is your reverse supply chain? *Effective Executive,* 52-55.

Sasser, W. E. Jr, Olsen, P. R., & Wyckoff, D. D. (1978). *Management of Service Operations: Text and Cases.* Boston: Allyn and Bacon.

Sheehan, W. G. (1989). Contract warehousing: the evolution of an industry. *Journal of Business Logistics, 10*(1), 31–49.

Skjott-Larsen, T., Schary, P. B., Mikkola, J. H., & Kotzab, H. (2007). Introduction to the supply chain. In *Managing the Global Supply Chain* (3rd ed.). Frederiksberg, Denmark: Copenhagen Business School Press.

The World Bank. (2006). *Reengaging in agricultural water management: challenges and options.* Washington, DC: World Bank. Retrieved from www.worldbank.org

Tompkins, J. A. (2000). *No boundaries.* Raleigh, NC: Tompkins Press.

Trunick, P. A. (1989). Outsourcing: a single source for many talents. *Transportation & Distribution,* 20-23.

World Bank Online. (2006, March 18). *A global food crisis can be averted.* Washington, DC: World Bank. Retrieved from www.worldbank.org/

World Bank Online. (2008). *Speech of world bank managing director at the US-Arab economic forum*. Washington, DC: World Bank. Retrieved from http://web.worldbank.org/

World Bank Online. (2009). *Food crisis - what the world bank is doing*. Washington, DC: World Bank. Retrieved from http://www.worldbank.org/html/extdr/foodprices

Zeithaml, V. A., & Bitner, M. J. (1996). Customer expectations of service. In *Services Marketing*. New York: McGraw-Hill.

Zhu, Z., Hsu, K., & Lillie, J. (2001). Outsourcing a strategic move: The process and the ingredients for success. *Management Decision*, *39*(5), 373–378. doi:10.1108/EUM0000000005473

This work was previously published in International Journal of Information Systems and Social Change, Volume 1, Issue 3, edited by John Wang, pp. 62-74, copyright 2010 by IGI Publishing (an imprint of IGI Global).

Section 2
Systems and Management

Chapter 6

Factors Impacting the Success of Electronic Government:
A Micro Level and a Back Office View

Helaiel Almutairi
Kuwait University, Kuwait

ABSTRACT

The author's goal in this study is to investigate factors that impact the success of electronic government. The focus in this study is on several organizational and personal characteristics, including age, tenure, information system (IS) experiences, gender, education level, nationality, training in information system (IS), position, and experience in current job. The study is then applied to Kuwait, and electronic government success is measured using information system usage. The findings indicate that four out of the nine factors impact electronic government success. These four factors are age, IS experiences, education level, and training in IS. The author then examines several research and practical implications.

INTRODUCTION

Egovernment is not just about putting forms and services online. It provides the opportunity to rethink how the government provides services and links them in a way that is tailored to the user's needs. Burns and Robines (2003: 26)

The above definition of electronic government (egov) clearly indicates that egov represents a great opportunity for governments to enhance their operational transparency, which is an im-

portant issue, especially given the current economic downturn and increasing public pressure for internal accountability (Davison et al., 2005). The root of the egov phenomena springs from the increasing role of information system (IS) plays in public organizations. Nowadays, IS is considered an important enabler of efficiency and effectiveness in many aspects of public organizations such as customer service, creating new products and services, and improving decision making (Almutairi, 2008; Cater-Steel, 2009). This vital role of IS is mainly due to the great enhancement

DOI: 10.4018/978-1-4666-0927-3.ch006

in the abilities of these systems which caused a paradigm shift in the practice and management of these systems (Conger, 2009).

Egov has become, therefore, a must for any nation that aims for better government (Gupta & Jana, 2003). This essential role that egov could play in national governance has made egov a global phenomenon that is attracting the attention of politicians and ordinary citizens (Grand & Chau, 2006) which triggered countries around the world to invest massive public resources in order to establish egov projects (Petricek et al., 2006).

The great interest in egov has been echoed in the research area through the emergence of a new line of research that mainly focus on issues related to egov. Studies in this line of research could be classified into three broad areas: egov development and evaluation, egov adoption and implementation, and the impact of egov on citizens and businesses (Srivastava & Teo, 2007). However, there are still vast research areas that need to be explored in this line of research (Bannister, 2007). One of such area is that related to factors impacting egov success.

The importance of egov success factors springs from the high failure rate of egov project implementation in developing countries, which is 85% (Heeks, 2003). The high failure rate needs to be decreased by understanding and controlling factors that impact egov success. Reviewing egov literature to find studies on this issue, however, revealed a serous shortage.

Based on the preceding discussion, this study attempts to enhance the knowledge about factors influencing egov success. Jansen (2005) argued:

Rather than regarding e-government as a separate research area, one should see it as a vast area of variety of empirical studies, in which, one should apply existing scientific knowledge, theories and methodologies from as well IS research as from e.g. organizational studies, political sciences, etc. (p.2)

Following the above suggestion, empirical studies found in both egov literature and information system (IS) literature are used to pinpoint a set of factors that are investigated in this study.

LITERATURE REVIEW

Several researchers have investigated factors that could influence the success and failure of egov. Table 1 presents a sample of these studies. Studies in Table 1 provide a good indication of the growing interest in looking for egov success factors, the variety of success measures and factors used in these studies, and the variety of success factors found significant in these studies.

However, studies in Table 1 also presents a challenge to anyone interested in finding a gap in literature that dealt with egov success factors. A major source of this challenge is the variety of egov success factors used in these studies which put, in the forefront, the issue of putting order in these studies in the form of categorizing them into specific categories which would facilitate, then, the identification of gaps and shortcomings.

In the context of this study, this categorization was provided by positioning egov success factors, which are found significant in studies in Table 1, in an egov evaluation model. To shade more light on this effort, the discussion moves to another line of research in egov literature that is egov evaluation literature.

Egov evaluation literature is closely related to egov success factors literature. Egov success factors literature is the other side of the coin of egov evaluation literature. In the egov evaluation literature, when pinpointing to egov aspects that need to be taken into account in the egov evaluation and how each aspect should be measured, these egov aspects become egov success factors when discussed in egov success factors literature.

Therefore, egov models developed in the egov evaluation literature can be used to assist

Table 1. Summary of studies investigated egov success factors

Study	Country	Measure of success	Factors investigated	Factors found significant
Al-Mashari (2007)	Canada, the USA, the UK, Dubai Government, the Republic of Singapore, and Malaysia	ranking of egovernment in international studies, such as a United Nations report regarding e-government and the Accenture report	start-up initiative, EG systems and implementation approaches., EG projects, EG developments, and evaluation..	clear objectives/vision, full support of management, designing a framework that connects all organizations together, focusing on human efforts and providing services, improvement of organizational procedures and employees, and providing enough financial resources.
Shi (2002)	United States	a combination of user satisfaction and perceived benefits for egov	transformational leadership, strategic planning, size and complexity of the website	Transformational leadership and strategic planning
Luna-Reyes et al. (2008)	Mexico	several items such as cost reduction, effective polices and programs, productivity, and IT infrastructure	institutional arrangements, organizational forms and characteristics of information technologies	All factors were significant.
Joia (2007)	Brazil	Not stated	Training, organizational culture, and security	All factors were significant.
Sahu and Gupta (2007)	India	Focused on intention to use egov	effort expectancy, performance expectancy, facilitating conditions, perceived strength of control, social influence, anxiety, top management support, and voluntariness of use	All factors were significant ; expect for voluntariness of use
Vonk et al. (2007)	Dutch	Diffusion of geographic information system	Organizational (e.g. attitude of management, implementation support by organization, organizational culture) and human factors (e.g. attitude of employees, awareness of potentials).	All factors were significant and at the top of these factor were attitude of management, social organization of users, and awareness of potential.

in pinpointing and categorizing egov success factors. This categorization, in turn, would help in determining whether there is a gap in egov success factors literature.

In this study, among the available egov theoretical models in egov evaluation literature (e.g., Gupta & Jana, 2003; Kunstelj & Vintar, 2004; Halaris et al., 2007), the one developed by Halaris et al. (2007) is used to assist in the categorization of the previously discussed egov success factors. The decision to use the Halaris et al. (2007) model is due to the model's simplicity and comprehensiveness. The Halaris et al. (2007) model consists of the following four layers: (1) a back office process performance layer that includes factors mainly found in quality models for traditional

government services; (2) a site technical performance layer that includes factors of the technical performance of the site such as site reliability and security; (3) a site quality layer that includes factors of site usability and interface; and (4) an overall customer satisfaction layer that includes the overall level of quality perceived by the user measured against the user's expectations.

Truing to the egov success factors in Table 1, it is noticeable, the diversity in these factors that can be categorized according to the layers in the model developed by Halaris et al. (2007).

The first layer in the Halaris et al. (2007) model may include the following success factors: creating clear objectives/vision, having the full support of the highest levels of authority, designing a framework that connects all organizations together, focusing on human efforts and providing services, improvement of organizational procedures and employees, and providing enough financial resources (Al-Mashari, 2007); transformational leadership (Shi, 2002); cost reduction, effective polices and programs (Luna-Reyes et al., 2008); process reform (Ray & Mukherjee, 2007); training, organizational culture (Joia, 2007); the attitude of management, the social organization of users, and an awareness of potential (Vonk et al., 2007); effort expectancy, performance expectancy, facilitating conditions, perceived strength of control, social influence, anxiety, and top management support (Sahu & Gupta, 2007).

The second layer in the Halaris et al. (2007) model may include the following success factors: IT infrastructure (Ray & Mukherjee, 2007; Luna-Reyes et al., 2008); and security (Joia, 2007).

The third layer in the Halaris et al. (2007) model may include the following success factors: size and complexity of the website (Shi, 2002).

The fourth layer in the Halaris et al. (2007) model may include the following success factors: citizen participation (Luna-Reyes et al., 2008); and people's evaluation of the system (Ray & Mukherjee, 2007).

The previous categorization of success factors indicates a focus on success factors related to the first layer (back office process performance layer) in the Halaris et al. (2007) model.

This focus mirrors what exist in the general egov literature. Recent studies in egov literature have called for a shift from the focus on technical aspects of egov, or what is called "front desk", to the internal organizational process, or what is called "back office" (e.g., Burns & Robines, 2003; Gupta & Jana, 2003; Kunstelj & Vintar, 2004; West, 2004; Davison et al., 2005).

In the egov literature, there are two views of egov. The first view (front office) defines egov as providing electronic services via the internet to customers (Kunstelj & Vintar, 2004) while the

second, new, view (back office) defines egov by looking beyond providing electronic services to issues related to redesigning internal process and rethinking how work is conducted in government (Burns & Robines, 2003). The second view bases its argument on propositions such as egov benefits realization needs significant internal process redesign (Davison et al., 2005) and development of e-government demands a holistic strategic approach that includes the entire public administration (Kunstelj & Vintar, 2004). Of course, these two views have impacted how egov is evaluated in the form of developing measures that evaluate front office and back office. Recently in the egov literature, several researchers have attempted to combine the two types of measures (back and front) into a comprehensive model; one of which is Halaris et al. (2007) model that is used in this study to categorize egov success factors.

After establishing a categorization of the egov success factors and positioning all studies in Table 1 within this category, the next step is to evaluate the current status of egov success factors literature to pinpoint gaps and weakness.

To accomplish this step, there is a need, further, to look at another similar, but well developed, literature to the egov success factors literature for the purpose of comparing between the two literatures in term of factors included, for example. Doing so is in agreement with Jansen (2005) suggestion of not viewing egov as a separate research area and that existing scientific knowledge from other fields should be applied to egov.

Herein, the discussion turns to the information system (IS) literature. In this literature there are several factors that have been investigated and found to have an impact on information system success. These factors include: user training, computer experience, end user support, and management (Igbaria et al., 1995); computer skill, IS experience, technical backing, and IS support, (Ndubisi & Jantan, 2003); staff seniority (tenure), level of education, and age (Burton-Jones

& Hubona, 2005); organizations support and IS experience (Anakwe et al., 1999); and education, training, organizational support, and anxiety (Al-Gahtani, 2004).

A research question emerges from the preceding discussion: are there other factors that impact the success of egov aside from the one already investigated in the few studies available in egov success factors literature?

Answering this research question would enrich egov success factors literature by uncovering more factors that influence the success of egov which, in turn, would lead to ensuring the success of the egov project by taking into consideration these success factors and to save public resources by preventing the failure of egov project.

In this study, the impact of age, tenure, IS experiences, gender, education level, nationality, training in IS, position, and experience in current job on the success of egov are investigated. These factors are categorized into two groups: organizational (IS training, tenure, IS experiences, position, and experience in current job) and personal (gender, age, education level, and nationality). Figure 1 illustrates the study's model and the following two hypotheses are tested:

H1: Organizational factors have an impact on egov success in Kuwait.
H2: Personal factors have an impact on egov success in Kuwait.

Figure 1. The study's model

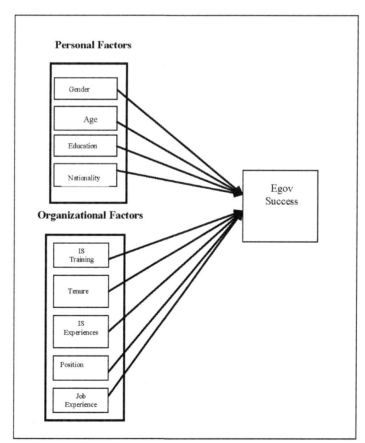

RESEARCH METHODOLOGY

Sampling

Using a simple random method, a sample is taken from the eighteen Kuwaiti ministries and from employees who used information systems in these ministries. The random method used consists of two steps. First, Identification of the employees who used information systems is done through a visit to the human resource departments in the ministries. Second, each employee is a signed a number and then the study's sample is randomly chosen. Using this random method, all employees have a chance to be chosen in the sample.

Collection of data is mainly done with a questionnaire instrument. The questionnaire is divided into two sections. Section one consisted of questions measuring IS usage, which is the variable used to measure egov success and is discussed in more detail latter. The second section consisted of questions concerning the independent variables which are age, tenure, IS experiences, gender, education level, nationality, training in IS, position, and experience in current job.

During the period of this egov project in Kuwait (2002-2007), the questionnaire was administrated yearly for six consecutive years, using the same methodology each time. The repetition of the same data collection methodology was to eliminate any variations that could threaten the validity and reliability of the collected data. A total of two thousands usable questionnaires were collected which were used as the input for the data analysis.

Measurement

Egov success: There is no agreement in the egov literature on a unified measure for egov success. Approaches regarding this point, however, can be summarized into two general views. The first view uses as a measure for success front office indicators such as site maintenance, site navigation, site content, links, contacting the organization, and

page structure (Holliday & Yep, 2005). A new view, on the other hand, uses indicators that are related to the back office such as cost reduction and productivity (Luna-Reyes et al., 2008). The second view is based on a strongly emerging line of research in egov literature that is support by both theoretical and empirical studies (e.g., Westholm & Aichholzer, 2003; Kunstelj & Vintar, 2004; West, 2004). Furthermore, within this new line of research, there are several studies that argue that information system usage is an indictor of the success of egov in influencing the back office (e.g., Graafland & Ettedgui, 2002; Lee-Kelley & Kolsaker, 2004).

Consequently, in this study, information system usage is used as indicative of egov success. This choice is further enhanced by the usage of this variable by several researchers in the general information system usage in as indictor of information system success (e.g., Davis, 1989; Straub et al., 1995).

The Igbaria et al. (1989) measure is used as a gauge of information system usage (ISU). Using this measure, ISU is assessed in four categories: daily use of IS, the average use of IS in the respondent's job, the extent of IS use in administrative applications and the number of IS packages used. There are twenty items (dimensions) in the measure and all items are based on a six-point Likert scale. The first item examined, the average IS use during a single working day, has responses that range from "no use" to "more than 3 hours." The second item examined, the frequency of IS use, has answers ranging from "no use" to "a few times a day." The extent of IS usage in administrative functions is examined through its use in eight tasks (historical referencing, looking for trends in historical references, finding problems/alternatives, planning, budgeting, communicating with others, controlling and guiding activities, and making decisions). Survey responses range from "no use" to "very high use." The number of IS packages used is examined by measuring the use of ten common software types, such as spreadsheets, word processing, data management packages, modeling systems, statistical systems, graphical packages, making diagrams, programming/advance programming, and communication packages. Answers ranged from "no use" to "very high use." The methods of measurement employed have been previously tested by other researchers and found to be valid and reliable (e.g., Anakwe et al., 1999).

The measure was subjected to a multi-step process to check for validity and reliability. First, the questionnaire was submitted to a panel of four professors who worked at Kuwait University to check whether items in the questionnaire measure what they should and whether they suit the Kuwaiti business environment. Minor changes related to the questions format were suggested by the panel such as the space between the questions and the size of the font. All these changes were taken into consideration in the questionnaire's final version.

Second, a pilot study was conducted to check whether items in the questionnaire were understandable and clear. The study covered fifty employees from two Kuwaiti ministries. The findings of the pilot study indicated that all questions and concepts were clear and understandable.

Cronbach's alpha (an internal consistency technique) was used to measure the reliability of each measure. A cutoff of 0.70 is considered the minimum acceptable level of reliability (Nunnally, 1967). This cutoff is adopted in this study. The Cronbach's alpha for the measure was (0.92). Thus, this measure exceeded the cutoff accepted in this study.

As it is unknown whether the four ISU dimensions are equally or unequally used by the respondents, factor analysis is used to determine the weight of each ISU dimension. Table 2 presents the findings from this analysis.

It is clear from Table 2 that the normal average should not be used because the four dimensions are not equally used. Thus, and based on the weight values in Table 2, the weighted average is used

in this study and is calculated using the following formula:

$$X_2 + 0.267*X_3 + 0.094*X_4 + 0.082*X_1 \; 0.557*$$

Figure 2 and Table 3 present the statistics for the weighted average. The weighted average use of information systems in the Kuwaiti ministries is 2.51 and the standard deviation is 1.00. For the purpose of simplicity, this weighted average number is transformed to the nearest whole number, which was 3. To get a deeper understanding of the use pattern within the users of information system, these users were divided into two groups: group (0) uses IS => 3(=>60%); and group (1) uses IS < 3 (<60%). Logically, the second group (uses IS < 3) represents a concern for anyone who is responsible for the egov project and its success. Thus, data analysis focuses on this group. Of course, the two groups represent two faces of the same coin. This step, the division of the two use groups, is also a must due to the logistic regression statistical technique used in this study.

The nine independent variables (age, tenure, IS experiences, gender, education level, nationality, training in IS, position, and experience in current job): These variables are measured using nominal or ordinal measures. Gender and nationality are measured using nominal measures, while the other independent variables (age, education, service the public sector, service in the current organization, experiences in the use of IS, training in the use of IS, and position in the organization)

Table 2. Relative importance (weight) of each ISU dimensions

Weight	Dimensions (X)
0.557	USE SW (X_1)
0.267	THE AVERAGE USE OF IS (X_2)
0.094	IS use in work (X_3)
0.082	USE APL (X_4)
1.000	Total

Figure 2. Histogram of the weighted average distribution compare with normal curve

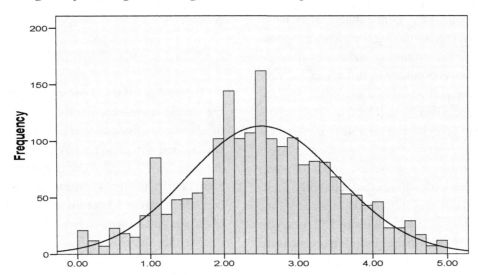

are measured using ordinal measures. These nine independent variables represent characteristics (organizational/personal), so they do not represent a measure of a dimension or an attitude. Thus, there is no reliability and validity for these variables.

Data Analysis and Results

As stated above, the data analysis is conducted using logistic regression (LR) with the statistical software SPSS (version 17.0). Similar to linear regression, LR is considered useful for situations in which you want to be able to predict the presence or absence of a characteristic or outcome based on values of a set of predictor variables. Different from linear regression, however, LR is suited to models where the dependent variable is dichotomous, such as the dependent variable in this study. Based on LR, regression coefficients can be used to estimate odds ratios for each of the independent variables in the model. Several researchers (e.g., Hair et al., 1998; Claudia & Claudio, 2006) recommend using LR as it is less affected by variance covariance inequalities across group, is able to handle categorical variables easily, and offers case-wise diagnostic measures for examining residuals. For these reasons, LR is used in this study.

Also used in this study is a stepwise logistic regression analysis, which determines the directional influence of each independent variable and within group (Ind.V) on the dependent variable. Further, binary logistic regression analysis is used because the dependent variable in this study is binary. A '0' for the dependent variable states that the average of IS usage >=60%, and a '1' states that the average of IS usage <60% among nine independent variables (factors): Gender, Age, Education, Nationality, Service the public sector, Service in the current organization, Experiences in the use of IS, Training in the use of IS, and Position in the organization.

Table 3. Descriptive statistic of the weighted average

N Valid	2000
Mean	2.5126
Std. Deviation	1.00775
Minimum	0.00
Maximum	5.00

Overall, a significant Wald Statistic for the regression coefficient B as the determinant of model entry (SIG Wald>0.05), an exponential form of the regression coefficient Exp(B) (odds ratio) represents the ratio-change in the odds of the event of interest for a one-unit change in the predictor. A sufficient Nagelkerke (1991) Pseudo-R2 as Goodness-of-Fit indicator and a positive discriminating power are required to support the hypothesis (factors affecting the weighted average of IS usage) (Claudia & Claudio, 2006). Following is a discussion of the data analysis findings.

Table 4 presents the results of LR. This table is divided into two parts: measures of goodness of fit and classification result. Regarding the first part, the results show that the model is fit with a $\chi2 = 61.1$ and significant of p=0.000. Regarding the second part, the discriminating power of the binary logistic regression model is confirmed by a model prediction rate of 69.3% for the weighted average of IS usage. After assessing the overall fit of the regression model, the analysis turns to the next step, which is assessing the impact of the independent variables on the dependent variable.

Table 5 shows the findings from assessing the impact of the independent variables on the dependent variable. Furthermore, Table 5 shows that impact of each subcategory/group of the independent variables on the dependent variable, which is one of the major advantages of using logistic regression. The results of LR show in Table 5 that only four variables with a significant Wald Statistic are included in the regression model. These variables are experiences in the use of IS, education, training in the use of IS and age, the significance of the Wald Statistic (SIG Wald>0.05) on the weighted IS usage. The Nagelkerke Pseudo-R2 has a value of 0.043 for the weighted average of IS usage, indicating an acceptable quality of the regression function.

We can use the model to estimate the usage probability of any individual. For example, for an individual who is between 20 and 29 years old, has institutional education, has between 1 to 5 years of experience in the use of IS and no train-

Table 4. Measurement of goodness of fit LR model and classification results

Classification Results				
Measure			Value	
-2LL			2406.8	
χ^2			61.6	
Degree of freedom			16	
SIG.			0.000	
Nagelkerke R^2			0.043	
Goodness of Fit				
Observed		Predicted		
		USE <60%		
			N	Y
USE <60%	N		19 3.1%	596 96.9%
	Y		19 1.2%	1366 98.9%
Overall Percentage 69.3%				

ing in the use of IS, the logit=0.928. To get the probability IS usage for this individual, we have used this formula [1/ (Exp (-0.928) +1)]. The result that he probably will use IS <60% is 0.7166. Thus, the probability that he will use IS >= 60% is 0.2834. Table 6 shows the probability of estimated IS usage for each significance independent variable with groups.

DISCUSSION

The purpose of this paper is to investigate factors that influence egov success as measured by information system usage (ISU). This study focuses on several organizational and personal factors: age, tenure, IS experiences, gender, education level, nationality, training in IS, position, and experience in current job. Figure 3 illustrates factors found significant in this study. The study found, however, that education level, age, experience in IS, and training in IS are the only statistically significant factors influencing egov success (information system usage). Following is a discussion of the study's findings.

Table 5. The parameter estimates summarizes the effect of each significance independent variable with groups

Variables	B	S.E.	Wald	df	Sig.	Exp(B)
Age			9.390	4	.052	
Less than 20 years	-1.146	.613	3.496	1	.062	.318
Between 20 and 29 years	-.245	.314	.609	1	.435	.783
Between 30 and 39 years	.030	.314	.009	1	.923	1.031
Between 40 and 49 years	-.103	.335	.095	1	.758	.902
Bigger than 49 years	.000					1.000
Education			18.685	4	.001	
Less than high school	.196	.474	.170	1	.680	1.216
High school	.503	.470	1.147	1	.284	1.653
Institutions	.204	.452	.203	1	.652	1.226
BS	-.154	.450	.117	1	.733	.857
Master	.000					1.000
Experiences in the use of IS			25.870	4	.000	
Less than one year	.938	.191	24.226	1	.000	2.555
Between 1 to 5 years	.515	.176	8.535	1	.003	1.673
Between 6 to 10 years	.387	.177	4.747	1	.029	1.472
Between 11 to 15 years	.407	.198	4.223	1	.040	1.503
Between 16 to 20 years	.000					1.000
Training in the use of IS			13.790	4	.008	
None	-.025	.157	.026	1	.873	.975
Less than 7 days	-.226	.157	2.062	1	.151	.798
7 and less than 30 days	-.277	.139	3.954	1	.047	.758
30 and less than 90 days	-.665	.200	11.061	1	.001	.514
90 and less than 180 days	.000					1.000
Constant	.479	.525	.831	1	.362	1.614

***The parameters associated with the last category (Reference) of each factor are redundant given the intercept term.

The study's findings indicate that users who could contribute to the establishment of a successful egov project have certain organizational and personal characteristics. These characteristics are being less than 29 years old, having a bachelor degree, having six or more years of experience in IS, and have thirty or more days of training in the use of IS. Regarding the other side of the coin, which is users who could contribute to making an egov project unsuccessful, the study's findings indicate that they are 30 or older, have an institution (community college) level education or less, have less than six years of experience in IS, and have less than 30 days of training in the use of IS.

The significant influences of education level, age, experience in IS, and training on information system usage on egov success found in this study is consistent with the few studies in egov literature that indicate the important role these factors play in egov success. In these other studies, success is measured by none information system usage

Table 6. Estimated probability IS usage of each significance independent variables with groups

Variables	Classification	use < 60%	use >= 60%
Age	Less than 20 years	.53333	.46667
	Between 20 and 29 years	.68712	.31288
	Between 30 and 39 years	.71274	.28726
	Between 40 and 49 years	.66204	.33796
	Bigger than 49 years	.67925	.32075
Education	Less than high school	.70745	.29255
	High school	.76587	.23413
	Institutions	.71223	.28777
	BS	.63960	.36040
	Master	.66667	.33333
Experiences in the use of IS	Less than one year	.77458	.22542
	Between 1 to 5 years	.68652	.31348
	Between 6 to 10 years	.67230	.32770
	Between 11 to 15 years	.68872	.31128
	Between 16 to 20 years	.60000	.40000
Training in the use of IS	None	.72569	.27431
	Less than 7 days	.69030	.30970
	7 and less than 30 days	.67480	.32520
	30 and less than 90 days	.56693	.43307
	90 and less than 180 days	.70675	.29325
Total		.69250	.30750

variables (e.g., Shi, 2002; Al-Mashari, 2007; Luna-Reyes et al., 2008) or by the information system usage variable or variables that are related to ISU (Joia, 2007; Vonk et al., 2007; Sahu & Gupta, 2007).

The study's findings are consistent with the bundle of studies in the general information system literature that provide evidence for the vital role these factors (education level, age, experience in IS, and training) play in impacting information system usage (e.g., Igbaria et al., 1998; Anakwe et al., 1999; Ndubisi & Jantan, 2003; Al-Gahtani, 2004; Burton-Jones & Hubona, 2005). For example, Ndubisi and Jantan (2003) found a relationship between computer skill (IS experience) and technical backing (IS support) on one side and IS usage. The researchers stated,

"The importance of computing skill and technical backing in determining IS usage in SMF is stricking" (p. 447).

Furthermore, the study's findings are consistent with the prominent theories in IS literature that attempt to explain how innovations are adopted and spread such as diffusion theory (Rogers, 1962). According to this theory, innovators and early adopters of innovations are usually young, well educated, and with higher incomes than later adopters and laggards. The present results show that the young and/or highly educated are more likely to be users of the system than their older and/or less educated counterparts.

Looking deeper at the factors that this study finds to be significant (education level, age, and experience in IS, and training), one could argue that

Figure 3. Factors found significant in the study

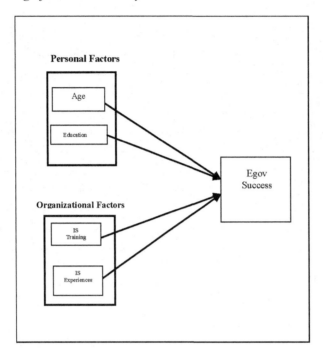

they reflect two dimensions of knowledge about information system or egov: "what" and "how". The "what" dimension reflects the theoretical side of IS or egov knowledge which could include aspects such as understanding the benefits gained from egov. The "how" aspect, on the other hand, reflects the practical side of IS or egov knowledge such as knowing how to operate and use computer and applications software.

In IS literature, two concepts that are very close to the "what" and "how", and which have been extensively investigated and are found to be related to information system usage, are perceived usefulness (PU) and perceived ease of use (PEOU). PU is very close to the "what", while PEOU is close to the "how". Several researchers have found these two concepts to be related to ISU (e.g., Igbaria et al., 1995; Al-Gahtani, 2001; Burton-Jones & Hubona, 2005). Of course, in the context of egov literature, the impact of these concepts has still not been comprehensively investigated. However, the empirical evidence

from the IS literature clearly indicates that there is a high probability that the "what" and "how" play a major role in the success of egov when measured by information system usage. A possible explanation for how the "what" and "how" impact egov success, measured by ISU, could be found using the concept of expectation gap (Taylor & Todd, 1995), which is the gap between the user's expectations and the real or actual abilities of the information system or egov. Taylor and Todd (1995) have pointed out how inexperienced users might have an expectation gap due to their unrealistic expectations about the IS system, which negatively affects their perception and usage of the IS system. The researchers argue that there is a need to close the expectation gap by setting realistic expectations through communicating to the inexpert user, "the facilitating and constraining factors that may limits systems usage as well as the benefits of the system, ensuring that both are adequately taken into account" (p. 570). Thus, the "what" and "how" play an important role in closing the expectation gap.

In addition, factors found to be significant in this study (education level, age, and experience in IS, and training) raise very important questions about the role that top management could play in the successful implementation of egov. In the IS literature, the role of top management in the successful implementation is well studied and empirically supported (e.g., Igbaria, 1990; Igbaria et al., 1998). For example, Igbaria et al. (1998) finds a support for the relationship between training and management support and ISU which leads the researchers to conclude, "this emphasizes the need to coordinate top management blessings with the efforts of staff to provide training and education programs. Adequate training provided internally or externally will help the user to make full use of computers" (p. 118). Further, Igbaria (1990) states, "Management support and IC support are considered to be influential in helping end-users build a computing infrastructure by developing a wider selection of software tools potentially useful in the future, and in applying computer technology to support a wider variety of business tasks" (p. 147). Thus, in the context of egov literature, there is a need to investigate the role of top management in egov success.

Implications for Research and Practice

The study's findings have several implications for research and practice. For practice, undertaking the responsibility and participation in vital projects such as egov is always the task of the brave due to the numerous factors that must be taken into consideration in order to make the project successful. This study, however, has pinpointed to several factors that, when taken into consideration, could assist in the success of information system usage within the egov project.

First, employees' experiences in information need to be increased before and during the launch of an egov project. This could be done in several ways, such as making information system courses an integrated and essential part of all educational curriculums in all educational stages. An employee would then be subjected to information systems even before becoming an employee. In this case, the employee would have at least twelve years of experience before he enters the employment phase of his life. On the other hand, the IS experience of current employees could be increased by restructuring their work so it completely depends on IS, as well as designing carrier plans that allow these employees to take organizational positions that depend on IS. This will enhance the IS experience of organizational members in a short time-span.

Second, to increase the chance of successful egov, employees should have, at least, a university degree. In order to hire such employees, management may do two things. First, changes can be made to human resources and recruitment procedures so that only applicants with at least a university degree are hired. Second, the educational level of current employees can be enhanced and raised by giving these employees the opportunity to advance their education level. Increasing the number of scholarships and offering on-line degree are examples of how management could increase the education level of organizational members.

Third, training plays an important role in exposing employees to new methods, and new versions of old methods, with which they are not familiar. Employees with such training would make the full use of IS and be more productive in their work. To realize successful egov, managers need to increase IS training opportunities for their employees either through in-house or out-of-house training.

Fourth, young people are extensive users of information systems in their day-to-day tasks. They are closer to entering, or have already entered, the digital world. With a project that relies heavily on new technology, such as an egov project that has creating "E" in all aspects of a country as a goal, the most suitable people to be included in such projects are the ones that are most technologically oriented. Thus, young people need to be attracted by management to their egov project.

The study's findings also have several implications for research. First, as discussed above, the factors found significant in this study (education level, age, experience in IS, and training) reflect two dimensions of knowledge about information systems or egov: "what" and "how". There is a possibility that there are intermediate concepts between the four factors found to be significant in this study and egov success as measured by information system usage. Future researchers may attempt to include other concepts that could be used as a proxy to the "what" and "how" such as perceived ease of use (PEOU) and perceived usefulness (PU) and position them between the four factors and ISU.

Second, there could be an inside interaction between the four factors. For example, when an employee scores high in IS experience, educational level, and period of IS training but he is old in terms of age, what would his IS usage be? Unfortunately, the inside interactions between the four factors are not taken into consideration in this study. In the future, researchers are advised to investigate these types of interactions and their impact on ISU.

Third, the focus in this study is on factors impacting the back office of egov. The front office of egov, such as the web side of egov, is not taken into consideration in this study. Researchers are strongly urged to further investigate factors impacting the success of both the back and front offices of egov and the inside interactions between all these factors. Creating a model that illustrates these factors and their impacts would certainly advance our knowledge in this area and would be highly appreciated by researchers in the field.

CONCLUSION

The goal of this paper is to uncover factors that could impact electronic government success. This issue, uncovering key success factors, is vital nowadays due to the great attention egov receives and the huge public resources invested in egov projects around the world. In this study, the focus is on nine organizational and personal factors which are: age, tenure, IS experiences, gender, education level, nationality, training in IS, position, and experience in current job. Egov success is measured using information system usage. The study indicates that only four factors (education level, age, experience in IS, and training) have a statistically significant impact on egov success as measured by information system usage.

Finally, success in any project cannot be completely guaranteed for many reasons. In organization theory, concepts such as bounded rationality and complex violent external environments could be one reason for the inability to guarantee success. However, we have learned from the literature that institutionalization of change plays an important role in the success of change, which could be done and is due to the creation and design of a new form of an organization that is based on new change elements (Tolbert et al., 2008). Gradually these new change elements become the "ways to do business," replacing old form of organizations. Consequently, electronic government success is a goal that is not easy to accomplish without making a national plan that covers all aspects of society. Which factors to include in this plan is a major responsibility for research to uncover. Future researchers are urged to continue uncovering factors that could impact electronic government success.

REFERENCES

Al-Gahtani, S. S. (2001). The applicability of the TAM model outside North America: an empirical test in the United Kingdom. *Information Resources Management Journal, 14*(3), 37–46.

Al-Gahtani, S. S. (2004). Computer technology acceptance success factors in Saudi Arabia: an exploratory study. *Journal of Global Information Technology Management, 7*(1), 5–30.

Al-Mashari, M. (2007). A benchmarking study of experiences with electronic government. *Benchmarking: An International Journal, 14*(2), 172–185. doi:10.1108/14635770710740378

Almutairi, H. (2008). Information system usage and national culture: evidence from the public service sector. *International Journal of Society Systems Science, 1*(2), 151–175. doi:10.1504/IJSSS.2008.021917

Anakwe, U. P., Anandaeajan, M., & Igbaria, M. (1999). Information technology usage in dynamic in Nigeria: An empirical study. *Journal of Global Information Management, 7*(2), 13–21.

Bannister, F. (2007). The curse of the benchmark: an assessment of the validity and value of e-government comparisons. *International Review of Administrative Sciences, 74*, 71–188.

Burn, J., & Robins, G. (2003). Moving towards egovernment: A case study of organizational change processes. *Logistics Information Management, 16*(1), 25–35. doi:10.1108/09576050310453714

Burton-Jones, A., & Hubona, G. S. (2005). Individual differences usage behavior: revisiting a technology acceptance model assumption. *The Data Base for Advances in Information Systems, 36*(2), 58–76.

Cater-Steel, A. (2009). IT service departments struggle to adopt a service-oriented philosophy. *International Journal of Information Systems in the Service Sector, 1*(2), 69–77.

Conger, S. (2009). Information technology service management and opportunities for information systems curricula. *International Journal of Information Systems in the Service Sector, 1*(2), 58–68.

Davis, F. D. (1989). Perceived usefulness, perceived ease of use, and user acceptance. *Management Information Systems Quarterly, 13*(3), 319–339. doi:10.2307/249008

Davison, R. M., Wagner, C., & Ma, L. C. K. (2005). From government to e-government. a transition model. *Information Technology & People, 18*(3), 280–299. doi:10.1108/09593840510615888

Graafland, I., & Ettedgui, E. (2002). Benchmarking e-government in Europe and the US. *Statistical Indicators Benchmarking the Information Society.* Retrieved September 14, 2008 from http://www.sibis-eu.org/

Grand, G., & Chau, D. (2006). Developing a generic framework for e-government. In H. Gorden & F. Tan (Eds.), *Advance topic in global information management* (Vol. 5 pp. 72-76). Hershey, PA: IGI Global

Gupta, M. P., & Jana, D. (2003). E-government evaluation: a framework and case study. *Government Information Quarterly, 20*(4), 365–387. doi:10.1016/j.giq.2003.08.002

Hair, J. F., Tatham, R., Anderson, R., & Black, W. (1998). *Multivariate data analysis.* Upper Saddle River, NJ: Prentice Hall.

Halaris, C., Magoutas, B., Papadomichelaki, X., & Mentzas, G. (2007). Classification and synthesis of quality approaches in E-government services. *Internet Research, 17*(4), 378–401. doi:10.1108/10662240710828058

Heeks, R. (2003). *Success and failure rates of e-government in developing/transitional countries: overview* (Tech. Rep.). Manchester, UK: University of Manchester, E-government for development, institute for development policy and management.

Holliday, I., & Yep, R. (2005). E-government in China. *Public Administration and Development, 25*, 239–249. doi:10.1002/pad.361

Igbaria, M. (1990). End-user computing effectiveness: a structural equation model. *Omega, 18*(6), 637–652. doi:10.1016/0305-0483(90)90055-E

Igbaria, M., Guimaraes, T., & Davis, G. (1995). Testing the determinants of microcomputer usage via a structural equation model. *Journal of Management Information Systems, 11*(4), 87–114.

Igbaria, M., Pavri, F. N., & Huff, S. L. (1989). Microcomputer application: an empirical look at usage. *Information & Management, 16*(4), 187–196. doi:10.1016/0378-7206(89)90036-0

Igbaria, M., Zinatelli, N., & Cavaye, A. L. M. (1998). Analysis of information technology success in small firms in New Zealand. *International Journal of Information Management, 18*(2), 103–119. doi:10.1016/S0268-4012(97)00053-4

Jansen, A. (2005, November 21-23). Assessing E-government progress-why and what. In B. Tessem, J. Iden & G. E. Christensen (Eds.), *Proceedings of the fra norsk konferanse for Organisasjonevs bruk av IT (Nokobit)*, Bergen, Norway.

Joia, L. A. (2007). A heuristic model to implement government-to-government project. *International Journal of Electronic Government, 3*(1), 1–18.

Kunstelj, M., & Vintar, M. (2004). Evaluating the progress of E-government development: a critical analysis. *Information Polity, 9*, 131–148.

Lee-Kelley, L., & Kolsaker, A. (2004). E-government: the 'fit' between supply assumptions and usage drivers. *Electronic Government, 1*(2), 130–140. doi:10.1504/EG.2004.005173

Loebbecke, C., & Huyskens, C. (2006). What drives netsourcing decisions? An empirical analysis. *European Journal of Information Systems, 15*, 415–423. doi:10.1057/palgrave.ejis.3000621

Luna-Reyes, L., Gil-Garcia, J. R., & Estrada-Marropuin, M. (2008). The impact of institutions on interorganizational IT projects in the Mexican federal government. *International Journal of Electronic Government, 4*(2), 27–42.

Ndubisi, N. O., & Jantan, M. (2003). Evaluating IS usage in Malaysian small and medium-sized firms using the technology acceptance model. *Logistics Information Management, 16*(6), 440–450. doi:10.1108/09576050310503411

Nunnally, J. (1967). *Psychometric theory*. New York: McGraw-Hill.

Petricek, P., Escher, T., & Margetts, H. (n.d.). The web structure of E-government -developing a methodology for quantitative evaluation. In Proceedings of the *The International World Wide Web Conference Committee (IW3C2)*. Retrieved on August 29, 2008 from http://www.iw3c2.org/

Ray, S., & Mukherjee, A. (2007). Development of a framework towards successful implementation of e-governance initiatives in health sector in India. *International Journal of Health Care Quality Assurance, 20*(6), 464–483. doi:10.1108/09526860710819413

Rogers, E. M. (1962). *Diffusion of innovation*. New York: Free Press.

Sahu, G. P., & Gupta, M. P. (2007). Uses' acceptance of E-government: a study of Indian central excise. *International Journal of Electronic Government Research, 3*(3), 1–21.

Shi, W. (2002). The contribution of organizational factors in the success of electronic government commerce. *International Journal of Public Administration, 25*(5), 629–657. doi:10.1081/PAD-120003293

Srivastava, S. C., & Teo, T. H. (2007). E-Government payoffs: evidence from cross-country data. *Journal of Global Information Management, 15*(4), 20–40.

Straub, D., Limayem, M., & Karahanna-Evaristo, E. (1995). Measuring system usage: implication for IS theory testing. *Management Science, 41*(8), 1328–1342. doi:10.1287/mnsc.41.8.1328

Taylor, S., & Todd, P. (1995). Assessing IT usage: the role of prior experience. *Management Information Systems Quarterly, 19*(4), 561–571. doi:10.2307/249633

Tolbert, C. J., Mossberger, K., & McNeal, R. (2008). Institutions, policy innovation, and e-government in the American states. *Public Administration Review, 68*(3), 549–563. doi:10.1111/j.1540-6210.2008.00890.x

Vonk, G., Geertman, S., & Schot, P. (2007). New technologies in old hierarchies: the diffusion of geo-information technologies in Dutch public organizations. *Public Administration Review, 67*(4), 745–756. doi:10.1111/j.1540-6210.2007.00757.x

West, D. (2004). E-Government and the transformation of service delivery and citizen Attitudes. *Public Administration Review, 64*(1), 15–27. doi:10.1111/j.1540-6210.2004.00343.x

Westholm, H., & Aichholzer, G. (2003). Prima Strategic Guideline 1: eAdministration. *PRISMA Project and Information Society Technology*. Retrieved on May 25, 2008 from http://www.eivc.org/uni/Uploads/admin/SG1administration.pdf.

This work was previously published in International Journal of Information Systems and Social Change, Volume 1, Issue 2, edited by John Wang, pp. 19-35, copyright 2010 by IGI Publishing (an imprint of IGI Global).

Chapter 7

DeLone & McLean IS Success Model in Evaluating Knowledge Transfer in a Virtual Learning Environment

Raija Halonen
National University of Ireland, Galway, Ireland & University of Oulu, Finland

Heli Thomander
University of Oulu, Finland

Elisa Laukkanen
University of Oulu, Finland

ABSTRACT

DeLone & McLean's success model has been actively used since its first introduction in 1992. In this article, the authors extend this model to describe the success of knowledge sharing in an information system that included a part of the knowledge base of a private educational institute. As the supply of private education is increased, it is vital to be aware if the offered educational services support the use of the knowledge base and if the service is perceived satisfactory by the customers. In this descriptive qualitative case study, the authors discuss how the DeLone & McLean's information system success model can be used to assess educational services when apprenticeships form a salient part of teaching. This paper focuses on issues that interested the target organization.

INTRODUCTION

This paper highlights the need to assess information systems that form the base business idea in private educational enterprises. Even if it is challenging to evaluate the quality of educational systems due to the versatility of available criteria (Wang et al., 2009), we add into the discussion of assessing education by introducing a descriptive qualitative case study where education with a virtual learning environment was seen as a service by a private organization. The service

DOI: 10.4018/978-1-4666-0927-3.ch007

was offered to adult students who were seen as customers of the organization. As the competition between education providers was increasing, it was essential to evaluate the services that were offered in the field. To describe the service, we used the success model originally developed by DeLone and McLean (1992) and later modified and assessed by several researchers (e.g., DeLone & McLean, 2003; Holsapple & Lee-Post, 2006; Lin, 2007; Wang et al., 2007; Petter et al., 2008).

In virtual learning environments the participants typically communicate with other participants (Piccoli et al., 2001). There are electronic services where the product is not a physical ware or digital information product – instead, the services concentrate on producing pure service (Tiwana & Ramesh, 2001). Therefore, it is reasonable to assess the interaction between the participants as an important element of the service. In this paper the focus is limited to describe how knowledge sharing was perceived in the virtual environment. In the vocational schooling where the accepted apprenticeship formed the central part of the degree, the role of tacit knowing was emphasized.

In this paper knowledge is understood as hierarchical concepts of data, information and knowledge. Besides concepts, knowledge is seen as a state of mind, object, process, prerequisite of accessing information, and in our paper, especially skills. We also look at knowledge as classified into tacit and explicit knowledge and note its cultural, functional, embedded, individual, social and pragmatic nature (Alavi & Leidner, 2001; Blackler, 1995; Choo, 1998; Nonaka, 1994.)

We acknowledged the ambiguous nature of knowledge and we aimed to find out how knowledge is introduced in the literature. As our empirical material was collected from a private educational organization, we also looked knowledge as a key property of the organization (Becerra-Fernandez & Sabherval, 2001; Nissen, 2002). Among other means, the property was accessed with the help of a virtual learning environment and that set requirements to the information system. However,

as the information system was seen as a service, its value and usefulness was to be assessed.

The research approach was qualitative and interpretive (Walsham, 1995, 2006) and we converged the research problem with the help of a case study (Stake, 2000; Yin, 2003). Before introducing the case, we take a look at prior literature focusing on knowledge management, knowledge transfer and virtual learning environment. We emphasize the role of interaction and service as the case represents a core product of a private organization.

PRIOR LITERATURE

In this section we discuss the key concepts in our study. First, the nature of knowledge management and knowledge transfer is discussed. Then, virtual learning environment is presented emphasising its service nature. Finally, we introduce the DeLone & McLean success model and how it is used in prior studies related to virtual learning.

Knowledge Management and Knowledge Transfer

Knowledge can be found in several contexts such as relationships between people, processes, organizational memories and products. Therefore, it is important to understand its nature and value, not to forget its maintenance and transfer in its contexts. Before knowledge can be re-used, it must be stored and transferred for instance in organizational memory. Furthermore, to acquire organizational memory it necessitates that knowledge is acquired and used in the organization. All storages – man-made databases, online data sources, emails – are explicit knowledge which is created from tacit knowledge. The storages are not useful to other people if the storages are not connected well to the tacit knowledge of the user. (Huysman et al., 1994; Walsham, 2001.)

Nonaka and Takeuchi (1995) defined the creation of tacit and explicit knowledge being affected by processes of socialisation, externalisation, combination and internalisation. According to the definition, socialisation is about sharing experiences. New tacit information is created by shared experience in social interaction. Tacit knowledge, such as mental models and technical skills, can be achieved by spending time in a joint environment by observing, imitating and practising. In externalisation tacit knowledge is expressed by concepts and tacit knowledge is made explicit to be shared with others who can use it as a base for new knowledge. Dialog is a good tool to transfer knowledge to others. Interaction between individuals is used when solving conflicts between tacit knowledge and surrounding context or between several people (Nonaka & Takeuchi, 1995; Nonaka & Toyama, 2003.)

To be created, knowledge requires appropriate circumstances. Nonaka and Konno (1998) use the concept of *ba* to describe a shared space to enable knowledge creation in organizations. In their conception, *ba* is kind of a platform that includes four types of *ba*, namely originating *ba*, interacting *ba*, cyber or virtual *ba* and exercising *ba*. *Ba* is kind of a mechanism to promote interaction to be used in knowledge creation and knowledge transfer. The mechanisms are seen as a physical space such as a meeting room or a virtual space such as email or even as a mental space such as shared feelings and concepts.

In organizations, knowledge is stored and organised in organizational memory, where knowledge is again retrieved to be used (e.g., Alavi & Leidner, 2001). Thus, knowledge is a part of organizational memory. With the development and widespread availability of advanced information technologies, information systems have become an essential part of this memory. Acquiring organizational memory and using it includes its acquisition and use. Organizational memory and knowledge management are related with each other and they influence organizational efficacy.

Organizational efficacy is measured by finding out how efficiently the organization performs the critical activities that produce the product sold by the organization. (Huysman et al., 1994; Jennex & Olfman, 2002; Stein & Zwass, 1995; Walsh & Ungson, 1991.)

Knowledge is found and shared with the help of interaction between actors. Individual interaction can influence organizational or team-based knowledge base either positively or negatively. Conducive communication reveals all available knowledge and it may enable the actors in the group to easily accept what is pertinent, relevant or useful in the current situation. Correspondingly, disruptive communication may discourage actors in the group to see the need to find additional information or the need to change available information into appropriate mode (Propp, 1999.)

Virtual Learning Environment as a Service

Web-based learning is defined as studying and learning using Internet (Wang et al., 2007) whereas virtual learning environment is understood as a computer-based environment that often is relatively open system. In addition, in a virtual learning environment interaction between participants is significant. Similar to computer-based learning, a virtual learning environment enables a student to use learning material independently, to study subjects in different order and to use convenient material. With the help of interaction a virtual learning environment extends the learning process from individual learning experience to more communal direction. Web-based learning can also be seen as a process where study material is delivered to students with the help of Internet, intranet or extranet, as audio or visual recordings, as satellite broadcastings, with the help of interactive television or as CD-recordings. Especially, in a virtual learning environment a student can communicate with other students and teachers. (Piccoli et al., 2001; Holsapple & Lee-Post, 2006.)

E-service is web-based service where interaction between customers and service providers takes place partly or totally in Internet. Customers may also receive the service using Internet directly at their homes. (Rust & Kannan, 2003; Surjadjaja et al., 2003.) As concepts, there are differences between e-service and web-service. Web-service is often seen as software or applications available in Internet and the concept is used when referring to technique whereas the concept of e-service is used either in the meaning of Internet-based versions of legacy services or as a synonym to web-services. E-services are often called as Internet-services or web-based services, too (Baida et al., 2004.)

Furthermore, e-services may be classified according to their business character in three groups: Firstly, e-service can be a part of a process related to selling a concrete ware. Secondly, e-service may concentrate on producing products that are in digital mode, such as software. Thirdly, there are e-services where the product is not a concrete ware nor a digital information product but pure service. Real-time interaction provided by Messenger is a good example of pure services. Thus, e-services can be classified in physical, digital and pure services (Tiwana & Ramesh, 2001.)

Chiu et al. (2005) approached virtual learning as a service and they introduce a concept of e-learning service. Virtual learning can be enabled in serveral synchronic or asynchronic techniques. Synchronic web-based learning includes real-time interaction between students and teachers while asynchronic web-based learning reminds individual studying but includes non-real-time interaction with teachers for example with the help of emails and discussion boards (Chiu et al., 2005.)

In all, one can conclude that virtual learning is defined in serveral ways and it may be realised by using real-time or non-real-time techniques. It also includes tecniques such as Internet but also interaction without Internet.

DeLone & McLean IS Success Model

In their well-known success model for information systems (in this paper called D&M1992) DeLone and McLean aimed to present influential factors and their relationships. The measure classes in D&M1992 include several known measures and only relevant measures should be chosen in each research case. Since its introduction, the model has been applied and modified in hundreds of studies which proves that a general approach is needed to measure the success. DeLone and McLean modified their model later and instead of five factors ('system quality', 'information quality', 'use', 'user satisfaction' and 'individual impact') that influence 'organizational impact' the new model (in this paper called D&M2003) includes six factors that influence 'net benefits'. (DeLone & McLean, 1992; DeLone & McLean, 2003; Petter et al., 2008.) The developed model included 'service quality' as a new factor, 'individual impact' was removed, and 'intention to use' was added related to 'use'. In addition, 'net benefits' replaced 'organizational impact' as an output of the measure.

DeLone and McLean applied D&M2003 also in measuring e-commerce success. They note how the measures in the six dimensions of the models are chosen to fit e-commerce and include measures such as download time, relevancy, overall support, easiness in navigation, time saving (DeLone & McLean, 2004).

Holsapple and Lee-Post (2006) extended the evaluation to concern the total process of web-based learning and its total quality. They used both D&M1992 and D&M2003 but they note that especially D&M2003 appeared useful because it had already been developed to serve in assessing Internet-based systems. In their model Holsapple and Lee-Post emphasise the processual nature of evaluation and they included in their model as an approach the development of the web-based learning system and its phases (Holsapple & Lee-Post, 2006.) Wang et al. (2007) explored the use of D&M2003 in assessing success of web-based learning systems from the organizational approach. They also modified the model to be used from the learner's point of view.

Lin (2007) used D&M2003 focusing on factors that influence successful use of web-base system ('online learning system'). Lin studied how system quality, information quality and service quality influence use via user satisfaction and intention to use.

In all, one can conclude that the success models developed by DeLone and McLean (1992, 2003) have been used in the context of virtual learning. However, the studies have focused on separate courses or information systems instead of long-term learning.

Methodology

This study was a qualitative case study (Stake, 2000; Yin, 2003). Eisenhardt (1989) delineates case study as a research strategy that focuses on understanding the dynamics present within single settings. Eisenhardt also supposes that case study research has important strengths like novelty, testability and empirical validity which arise from the close linkage with empirical evidence. While the study was a qualitative case study, we completed it with quantitative figures that helped us to get a deeper conception about the empirical material. This approach is in line with the instructions of Brannen (2005) who delineates the use of mixed research methods by adopting a research strategy with more than one type of research method. Brannen concludes that mixed methods research also means working with different types of data. Furthermore, as limitations of one research perspective can be addressed by using an additional research perspective (Kaplan & Duchon, 1988), in our study the total sample was 25 and the quantita-

tive figures acted as descriptive additions in our qualitative study. We also applied "experiential" research methodology introduced by Grant et al. (2001) that highlights the need to understand the backgrounds of the phenomena under study. Indeed, experiential research methodology involves both academics and practitioners who share their perspective in the research project. This approach was essential in our study especially due to the role of apprenticeship in the research focus.

The empirical material was collected with a questionnaire that was addressed to a carefully chosen group. Ideally, the questionnaire was addressed to students of basic or vocational examinations in computing or information systems and an essential requirement was that the virtual learning environment was used in the teaching. Four courses were still ongoing and one was ended before the questionnaire was available. Only students who had visited the virtual learning environment in the past 1.5 months were chosen to the respondent group and finally the target group consisted of 64 students. The questionnaire included 29 closed questions and 3 open questions and the used arguments based mainly on questions by Holsapple and Lee-Post (2006) and Wang et al. (2007). Only relevant questions and measures were included as advised by McLean and DeLone (1992, 2003). 25 responses were received and 52% of them represented long-term studies while only 6 replies (24%) represented pure apprenticeship studies. Altogether 11 students replied that they had participated in apprenticeships and 14 students had no experience of finished apprenticeships so far. As the final number or received responses was 25, the use of quantitative research methods was not adequate. Indeed, the study was descriptive in nature.

While the closed questions based on the frameworks used by Holsapple and Lee-Post (2006) and Wang et al. (2007), the answers were interpreted in the framework (Figure 1) correspondingly. The open responses were interpreted and themes (see Silverman, 2000) were searched in them. As the focus of the study was to describe knowledge transfer in the environment, we articulated only the questions that were related to the focus. From the 32 questions 8 questions addressed apprenticeship. As the interaction took place in the virtual learning environment, also the experiences about the environment were analyzed. In addition, responses to questions "What else would you like to have?" and "What has been most difficult?" were interpreted in this study.

Empirical Illustrations

The case organization was a private education institution that offered different schooling including basic, further and supplementary vocational education, apprenticeship programs, labor policy education programs, and courses designed to meet individual requirements. In 2007 there were 13000 students of who most were working adults who studied for vocational degrees. Typical schooling included contact learning, distant learning and learning in work. In certain programs, the degree was passed with apprenticeships in individual tasks.

In the beginning of 2008 the institution decided to take actions to evaluate its services as a private provider of vocational education. Therefore, a development project was initiated. The project focused on developing web-based teaching and it aimed to diversify and increase the offering of web-based studies. The current research was to contribute the development project. As the virtual learning environment was one of the core services provided by the organization we wanted to find out how the service was perceived by its users. In the assessment we used the success model introduced by DeLone and McLean (2003). In Figure 1 we described the evaluation model that was used in our study. The measures were classified accord-

Figure 1. Modified evaluation model

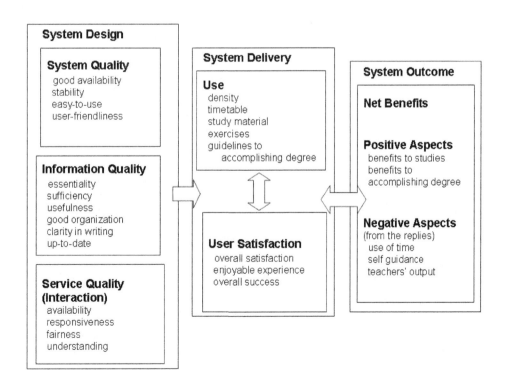

ing to the framework described by Holsapple and Lee-Post (2006). Holsapple and Lee-Post define system design with three components, namely system quality, information quality and service quality (see Figure 1). Next the findings are introduced according to the factors.

System Quality

In our study, System Quality was related to the learning platform Moodle that was mainly perceived stable and available. Even if the technology as such was not a core issue in our study, Moodle was needed to share knowledge about apprenticeships and studies. Two respondents out of 25 disagreed while the others agreed that Moodle operated without blames.

Information Quality

Regarding to apprenticeships, information quality was measured with an argument "Instructions about apprenticeships guide me in making the degree." Out of the respondents, 16 students perceived that they had gained from the virtual

learning environment. Seven students did not agree or disagree and one student disagreed. As 14 students had so far no experiences of finished apprenticeships, the result was interpreted positive. When asked about getting relevance information, nobody disagreed strongly. One student disagreed and the others agreed or strongly agreed. Likewise, the other questions about information quality revealed that information was experienced useful, well organized, clearly written and up-to-date. Thus, information quality was evaluated positive.

Service Quality

In the context of sharing knowledge about apprenticeship, service quality was about interaction between teachers and students. Students were asked if they received answers to their questions in the virtual learning environment. The responses revealed that the students were mainly satisfied with their teachers' responses (Figure 2).

Concerning the perceived satisfaction on the interaction, nobody was totally dissatisfied but the other evaluations were dispersed (Figure 3).

Figure 2. Experienced teachers' responses

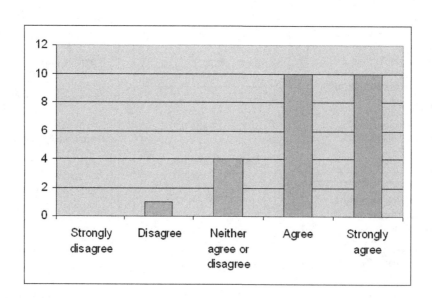

System Delivery

In the modified framework (Figure 1), system delivery consisted of Use and User Satisfaction. The questions were about instructions concerning degrees and using the virtual learning environment. One student used the environment once a month and another even fewer. 17 students used the environment several times a week and six students once a week.

Again, one student informed not using the virtual learning environment when seeking information about apprenticeships (Figure 4). However, only 11 students out of the 25 respondents had given apprenticeships at the time. Thus, the responses reveal that the students used the system to find out information about giving apprenticeships already before it was topical. Likewise, the students responded positively when asked about using patterns of apprenticeships in their plans. 16 students strongly agreed, 5 students agreed and 2 students did not agree or disagree.

In the study, User Satisfaction was about opinions of using the virtual learning environment. The attitudes were positive as 19 students strong-ly agreed and the rest agreed when asked if they were satisfied about having the virtual learning environment in use. Those 11 having returned their apprenticeships were asked additionally if the environment made it easier to return material concerning their apprenticeship. The satisfaction was obvious as 6 students strongly agreed, 1 student agreed and 4 students did not agree nor disagree. An interesting finding came with the other question addressed to those 11 students who had given their apprenticeships: "With the environment, I get valuable information from the reviewers before the evaluation discussion." Only 2 students strongly agreed, 1 student agreed and 8 students neither agreed nor disagreed.

System Outcome

According to the model by Holsapple and Lee-Post (2006), system outcome consists of positive and negative aspects. In our study, positive aspects were explored with measures such as improved learning, increased possibilities to study and saving time. The students expressed that the content and use in studies were beneficial (Figure 5).

Figure 3. Experienced interaction between teachers and students

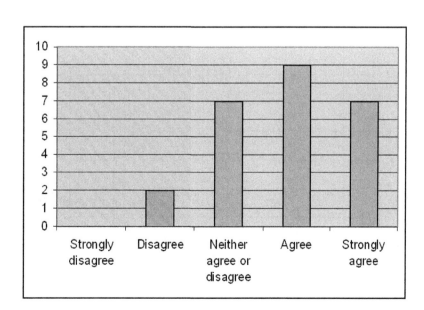

Figure 4. Use of environment when seeking information about apprenticeships

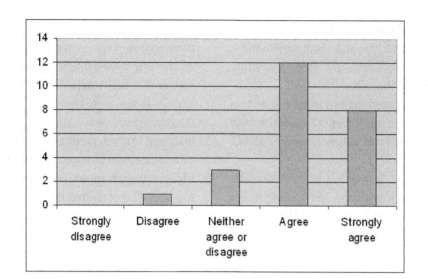

In addition, positive aspects were revealed with measures concerning user satisfaction such as using the virtual learning environment and perceived usefulness of the environment.

The negative aspects were not addressed in the questionnaire but they were interpreted from the responses. The responses to the open question

"What was most difficult" revealed for example that *"The most difficult problems were tied with spending time ..."* and *"It was difficult to find self-discipline to carry out the studies."* A significant negative aspect was interpreted from the responses to the question if reviewers' feedback benefited evaluating discussions. Even if the number of

Figure 5. Usefulness of virtual learning environment in studies

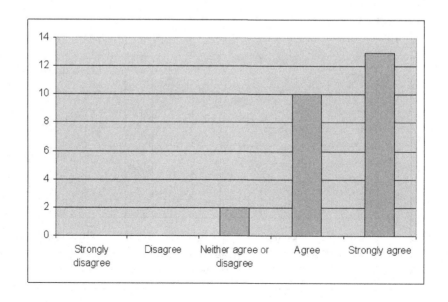

having returned their apprenticeship was small, the result was negative as three students were satisfied but the rest neither agreed nor disagreed.

To find out the experiences on apprenticeships of the students the questionnaire included questions related directly to the apprenticeships such as: "What kind of support related with studies and apprenticeships would you like to get in the virtual learning environment?"

The responses revealed:

I would like to get more extensive description on how the apprenticeship must be done and carry out. It is really difficult to discover anything if you haven't seen how the others have done and understood it.

A demo about the apprenticeship already in the beginning of the studies could help the student. It would be nice to see a "ready" apprenticeship folder ...

I desire virtual apprenticeship models ... maybe even extracts as a dialog from an apprenticeship session ...

These extracts showed how abstractly the students perceived the apprenticeships. They wanted to have some "concrete" description about apprenticeships shown by their peer students. However, one student announced to be satisfied:

I've received valuable information concerning e.g. building my apprenticeship folder etc. Thanks!

As the aim of the study was to benefit the development efforts of the organization, the questionnaire included a question to let the respondents express their wishes. The wishes were about getting more material into the virtual learning environment, and having more exercises and patterns how to answer them.

DISCUSSION AND CONCLUDING WORDS

This qualitative and descriptive study aimed to find out how students experienced knowledge transfer when a virtual learning environment was the main platform for communication and interaction. The findings are described with the help of the success model developed by McLean and DeLone (2003). Instead of measuring the success factors with quantitative methods, the model was used as a descriptive tool. With this study, we wanted to add to the discussion about assessing learning environments, and instead of paying attention to time spent in school or the number of students in the class (Wang et al., 2009), we focused on a virtual learning environment. As knowledge is a diversified concept (Alavi & Leidner, 2001; Nonaka & Takeuchi, 1995), we tried to find out if it was successfully transferred in a virtual learning environment that formed shared space (c.f. *ba*) to enable knowledge creation and transfer (Nonaka & Konno, 1998). In the target organization, knowledge transfer was an essential part of the schooling where apprenticeship was a central issue. The teachers had to be able to transfer knowledge related to the many professions that the students desired to get degree in.

The problem was how to show one's ability that could not be written down or was difficult to articulate. As the individual tasks differed, there was no explicit apprenticeship. Instead, every one of them differed from earlier ones and it aroused several questions from the students. Further, as the students were adults and already participating in the working life, they pursued at professional qualification and competence.

The knowledge was partly saved in the virtual learning environment; partly it was tacit in the possession of the teachers. Correspondingly, the students had to be able to show their ability and transfer knowledge when they had to give evidence of their expertise; and then, knowledge was possessed by them.

As an environment desired for interaction between students and teachers (Piccoli et al., 2001; Chiu et al., 2005), the virtual learning environment was a place for social interaction that enabled tacit knowledge to be created (Nonaka & Takeuchi, 1995; Nonaka & Toyama, 2003). With the help of the virtual learning environment the knowledge was to be created and shared between members in the environment and to be used by them when they entered the environment with their individual knowledge, as Propp (1999) describes. The empirical material showed that knowledge transfer was not found easy by the students. For instance, somebody wanted to have *"more extensive description on how the apprenticeship must be done"*.

From the organization's point of view, it was important to get the knowledge stored in the organizational database to be used later (Huysman et al., 1994; Jennex & Olfman, 2002). When the virtual learning environment was used, the written text was stored in the database. This was not experienced easy as can be drawn from the poor output to the argument of getting valuable information from the reviewers before the evaluation discussion. Only one student was satisfied with teachers' input.

In our research we studied a virtual learning environment as an enabler of transferring knowledge. The evaluation was made by the success model originally introduced by McLean and DeLone (2003). Among other IS evaluations, D&M2003 has been in use in several evaluations concerning virtual learning (Holsapple & Lee-Post, 2006; Linn, 2007; Wang et al., 2007). Therefore it was a natural choice in our study. While most studies of computer systems are based on measuring quantitative outcomes (Kaplan & Duchon, 1988), our study was a descriptive qualitative study that was supported by quantitative approach. However, at the same time the small sample size suggests further studies with more extensive number of respondents.

In this paper, we discussed only the issues and measures related to knowledge that was in close connection with apprenticeships in the organization. In so doing, we also showed that D&M2003 is usable also in evaluations that are difficult to put in explicit form. In our research we evaluated how knowledge was transferred between students and teachers in a case where both teachers and students had to be able to save and transfer knowledge.

We asked students how they perceived the environment especially associated with apprenticeships and we got elucidating responses. As apprenticeship was a central part of the degree, students told that they really looked for information concerning apprenticeships from the virtual learning environment. They also used the offered models of apprenticeships when designing their ones. The responses also revealed that the students desired more explicit information about apprenticeships.

Finally, it would be interesting to enquire teachers' responses on the same issues, namely how they perceived the use of the virtual learning environment in their challenging work with students who perform studies especially emphasizing apprenticeships.

ACKNOWLEDGMENT

First, the students are warmly acknowledged. Second, the authors are grateful for the constructive comments of the anonymous reviewers. The earlier version of this article was published in Sprouts Working Papers on Information Systems.

REFERENCES

Alavi, M., & Leidner, D. E. (2001). Review: Knowledge management and knowledge management systems: Conceptual foundations and research issues. *Management Information Systems Quarterly*, 25(1), 107–136. doi:10.2307/3250961

Baida, Z., Gordijn, J., & Omelayenko, B. (2004). A shared service terminology for online service provisioning. *ACM, 15*(1), 1–10.

Becerra-Fernandez, I., & Sabherval, R. (2001). Organizational knowledge management: A contingency perspective. *Journal of Management Information Systems, 18*(1), 23–55.

Blackler, F. (1995). Knowledge, knowledge work and organizations: An overview and interpretation. In C. W. Choo, N. Bontis (Eds.), *The Strategic Management of Intellectual Capital and Organizational Knowledge*. New York: Oxford University Press.

Brannen, J. (2005). Mixing methods: The entry of qualitative and quantitative approaches into the research process. *International Journal of Social Research Methodology, 8*(3), 173–184. doi:10.1080/13645570500154642

Choo, C. W. (1998). *The knowing organization: How organizations use information to construct meaning, create knowledge, and make decisions.* New York: Oxford University Press.

DeLone, W. H., & McLean, E. R. (1992). Information systems success: The quest for the dependent variable. *Information Systems Research, 3*(1), 60–95. doi:10.1287/isre.3.1.60

DeLone, W. H., & McLean, E. R. (2003). The DeLone and McLean model of information systems success: A ten-year update. *Journal of Management Information Systems, 19*(4), 9–30.

DeLone, W. H., & McLean, E. R. (2004). Measuring e-commerce success: applying the DeLone & McLean information systems success model. *International Journal of Electronic Commerce, 9*(4), 9–30.

Eisenhardt, K. M. (1989). Building theories from case study research. *Academy of Management Review, 14*(4), 532–550. doi:10.2307/258557

Eisenhardt, K. M., & Graebner, M. E. (2007). Theory building from cases: Opportunities and challenges. *Academy of Management Journal, 50*(1), 25–32.

Grant, K., Gilmore, A., Carson, D., Laney, R., & Pickett, B. (2001). "Experiential" research methodology: an integrated academic-practitioner "team" approach. *Qualitative Market Research: An International Journal, 4*(2), 66–74. doi:10.1108/13522750110388563

Holsapple, C. W., & Lee-Post, A. (2006). Defining, assessing, and promoting e-learning success: An information systems perspective. *Decision Sciences Journal of Innovative Education, 4*(1), 67–85.

Huysman, M. H., Fisher, S. J., & Heng, M. S. (1994). An organizational learning perspective on information systems planning. *The Journal of Strategic Information Systems, 3*, 165–177. doi:10.1016/0963-8687(94)90024-8

Järvinen, R., & Lehtinen, U. (2004). Services, e-services and e-service innovations – combination of theoretical and practical knowledge. *Frontiers of e-Business Research,* 78-89.

Jennex, M. E., & Olfman, L. (2002). Organizational memory / knowledge effects on productivity, a longitudinal study. In *Proceedings of the 35th Annual Hawaii International Conference on System Sciences, USA* (pp. 1029-1038).

Kaplan, B., & Duchon, D. (1988). Combining qualitative and quantitative methods in information systems research: A case study. *Management Information Systems Quarterly, 12*(4), 571–586. doi:10.2307/249133

Lin, H.-F. (2007). Measuring online learning systems success: Applying the updated DeLone and McLean model. *Cyberpsychology & Behavior, 10*(6), 817–820. doi:10.1089/cpb.2007.9948

Nissen, M. E. (2002). An extended model of knowledge-flow dynamics. *Communications of the Association for Information Systems, 8,* 251–266.

Nonaka, I. (1994). A dynamic theory of organizational knowledge creation. *Organization Science, 5,* 14–37. doi:10.1287/orsc.5.1.14

Nonaka, I., & Konno, N. (1998). The concept of *"Ba":* Building foundation for knowledge creation. *California Management Review, 40,* 40–54.

Nonaka, I., & Takeuchi, H. (1995). *The knowledge-creating company – How Japanese companies created the dynamics of innovation.* Oxford, UK: Oxford University Press.

Nonaka, I., & Toyama, R. (2003). The knowledge-creating theory revisited: knowledge creation as a synthesizing process. *Knowledge Management Research & Practice, 1,* 2–10. doi:10.1057/palgrave.kmrp.8500001

Petter, S., DeLone, W., & McLean, E. (2008). Measuring information systems success: models, dimensions, measures, and interrelationships. *European Journal of Information Systems, 17,* 236–263. doi:10.1057/ejis.2008.15

Piccoli, G., Ahmad, R., & Ives, B. (2001). Web-based virtual learning environments: a research framework and a preliminary assessment of effectiveness in basic IT skills training. *Management Information Systems Quarterly, 25*(4), 401–426. doi:10.2307/3250989

Propp, K. M. (1999). Collective information processing in groups. In L. R. Frey, D. S. Gouran, & M. C. Poole (Eds.), *The handbook of group communication theory & research* (pp. 225-250). Thousand Oaks, CA: Sage Publications.

Rust, R. T., & Kannan, P. K. (2003). E-service: A new paradigm for business in the electronic environment. *Communications of the ACM, 46*(6), 36–42. doi:10.1145/777313.777336

Silverman, D. (2000). Analyzing talk and text. In N. K. Denzin & Y. S. Lincoln (Eds.), *Handbook of qualitative research.* Thousand Oaks, CA: Sage Publications, Inc.

Stake, R. E. (2000). Case studies. In N. K. Denzin & Y. S. Lincoln (Eds.), *Handbook of Qualitative Research* (pp. 435-454). Thousand Oaks, CA: Sage Publications Inc.

Stein, E. W., & Zwass, V. (1995). Actualizing organizational memory with information systems. *Information Systems Research, 6*(2), 85–117. doi:10.1287/isre.6.2.85

Tiwana, A., & Ramesh, B. (2001). E-services: Problems, opportunities, and digital platforms. In *Proceedings of the 34th Hawaii International Conference on Systems Sciences* (pp. 1-8).

Walsh, J. P., & Ungson, G. R. (1991). Organizational memory. *Academy of Management Review, 16*(1), 57–91. doi:10.2307/258607

Walsham, G. (1995). Interpretive case studies in IS research: nature and method. *European Journal of Information Systems, 4,* 74–81. doi:10.1057/ejis.1995.9

Walsham, G. (2001). Knowledge management: The benefits and limitations of computer systems. *European Management Journal, 19*(6), 599–608. doi:10.1016/S0263-2373(01)00085-8

Walsham, G. (2006). Doing interpretive research. *European Journal of Information Systems*, *15*(3), 320–330. doi:10.1057/palgrave.ejis.3000589

Wang, J., Xia, J., Hollister, K., & Wang, Y. (2009). Comparative analysis of international education systems. *International Journal of Information Systems in the Service Sector*, *1*(1), 1–14.

Wang, Y.-S., Wang, H.-Y., & Shee, D. Y. (2007). Measuring e-learning systems success in an organizational context: Scale development and validation. *Computers in Human Behavior*, *23*(4), 1792–1808. doi:10.1016/j.chb.2005.10.006

Yin, R. K. (2003). *Case study research: Design and methods* (3rd ed.). London: Sage Publications.

This work was previously published in International Journal of Information Systems and Social Change, Volume 1, Issue 2, edited by John Wang, pp. 36-48, copyright 2010 by IGI Publishing (an imprint of IGI Global).

Chapter 8
Changing Attitudes toward Women IT Managers

Gary Hackbarth
Northern Kentucky University, USA

Kevin E. Dow
University of Alaska Anchorage, USA

Hongmei Wang
Northern Kentucky University, USA

W. Roy Johnson
Iowa State University, USA

ABSTRACT

Essentialism and social constructionism theories have long explained the difficulties women experience as they aspire to higher managerial positions or enter science and technology fields. In the 1970s, the Women as Managers Scale (WAMS) sought to determine the extent to which males perceived females as being different from their social group. Given efforts to encourage women to consider IT careers and changes in public law and education that have occurred since the early 1970s, this study revisited the WAMS to compare current attitudes of young people toward women as managers. The results suggest that through the intangible individual differences of women, perspective, overtime, via training, by awareness, and with their greater participation in the workplace, there has been gradual improvement in the perception of women as managers by men in the science and technology fields.

INTRODUCTION

The positive contributions of female Information Technology (IT) workers is well documented, but concern has been raised in recent years about the decline in numbers of women both in industry and in educational programs leading to IT in-

dustry positions. Several explanations have been proposed to explain the decline of women within the IT workforce. Either essentialism or social constructionism theories have long explained the challenges women experience as they aspire to higher managerial positions or entrance into the science and technology fields (Trauth, 2002).

DOI: 10.4018/978-1-4666-0927-3.ch008

Essentialists assert that there are fundamentally different group-based male and female bio-psychological natures at odds with each other. Further, social constructionists suggest a social shaping that argues for positions and job types defined as masculine and outside the female domain.

An emerging view suggests that socio-cultural factors influenced by individual differences may affect a women's choice of career in the IT workplace (Trauth, Quesenberry, & Huang, 2008). Trauth argues for an individual differences perspective on gender and technology that moves away from the group level of analysis to focus on women as individuals (Trauth, 2002; Trauth, Quesenberry, & Huang, 2008). This view suggests that each woman has individual (both tangible and intangible) attributes that allow her to succeed or fail on her own. Tangible attributes like strength and intelligence can be measured while intangible attributes like work ethic and inter-personal skills are harder to quantify. It is our contention that over time, these intangible attributes, with training, awareness, and with greater participation of women in the work place have gradually improved how men view women in the IT workforce.

Given efforts to encourage women to consider IT careers, changes in public law and education initiatives that encourage women to consider the IT workforce as a career occurring since the early 1970s, essentialism or the social constructionism perspectives may only be part of the story of the decline in numbers of women in the IT workforce. We revisited the Women as Managers Scale (WAMS) as a benchmark measure to compare current attitudes of young people toward women as managers in response to the decline in the number of young women willing to acquire the education and training necessary to enter and to ascend the ranks of management for successful IT/IS careers. The 1970s Women as Managers Scale (WAMS) sought to assess how males perceived females as different from their social group (Peters, Terborg, & Taynor, 1974; Taynor & Deaux, 1973; Terborg & Ilgen, 1975). Thus, our research question is:

"Have the attitudes of young men and women toward women as managers changed since the early 1970s?"

First, the research background for the Women as Managers Scale (WAMS) will be reviewed from the prospective of previous developmental methodologies, then the results, and finally limitations to the study. Moreover, our research findings will be juxtaposed with previous results followed by a discussion of women as manager's trends and some possible directions for future research.

THE DECLINE OF WOMEN IN THE IT WORKFORCE

Over the past thirty years, the United States (U.S.) business environment has experienced tremendous political, social, and economic upheaval often directed toward improved managerial opportunities for women. In the U.S., women have entered all facets of the labor market and are currently about half of the workforce. It can be argued that women have already attained business career parity, including commensurate compensation, for managerial and professional positions in many fields. The leadership of the United States has been mirrored to a lesser extent by Japan and other developing countries but success is seen as tapering off (Owen & Portillo, 2003). In particular, data from the late 1990s shows that general gains in employment opportunities did not extend to similar increases in the number of women holding IT/IS managerial positions. By 2000, American women comprised 47 percent of the total workforce; while only 29 percent of workers in IT/IS were women.

Moreover, many American women in IT/IS experienced lower overall salaries struggling with the incompatibility between career orientation and assigned job tasks (Igbaria, Parasuraman, & Greenhaus, 1997). Of note, 18 percent of men working in IT/IS occupations earned more than $70,000 annually, but only 8 percent of the women earned this sum. Moreover, the U.S. Small Business Administration has suggested that women are an unseen and unheard presence in the technology industry even though they are educated, willing, and experienced.

From the IT user side, women have become a potent force in the information economy. By the end of 2000, 52 percent of online shoppers were women and were a majority of total Internet users. However, there seems to be an incongruity in the workplace. Although, there are increasing numbers of women using the Internet commiserate with tremendous job opportunities existing in the information economy, the number of women entering the IT field appears to be shrinking. Yet, in contrast to female managers in IT/IS with women outside the field, women working in full-time positions earned a median income of $38,000, 60 percent higher than women working outside the IT/IS industry. Nevertheless, a recent government report stated that women in IT/IS continue to be both underpaid and underrepresented. Given the growth and wide use of IT/IS by women, pay, authority, and opportunity parity between men and women in IT/IS occupations should be the norm; but it appears not to be so.

These trends suggest that women are not progressing in or toward the IT field. Other observers suggest that females are not being encouraged as much as males in school; they lack female mentors, the support of other women, and a strong job market with higher starting salaries (McGrath & Cohoon, 2001). Interestingly, 18 percent of girls believe that they could hack into their schools computers.

Currently, the number of high-level female managers remains low. Women comprise approximately 10 percent of senior managers in Fortune 500 companies (Kaminski & Reilly, 2004; Swartz, 2008). Furthermore, the prospect of increasing these numbers seems unlikely, particularly as the number of women selecting IT/IS as a career comes from a pool of female IT graduates that varies between 14-20 percent of all students in IT degree

courses (Hellens, Nielsen, & Trauth, 2001; Trauth, Quesenberry, & Morgan, 2004) Historically, by 2000, women were only 29 percent of the technology workforce compared to 40 percent in 1986 (Nielsen, Hellens, Beekhuyzen, & Trauth, 2003). Explanations vary from the unpredictable nature of computing to social conditions that channel men and women into disciplines and careers labeled appropriate for their gender (Hellens, Nielsen, & Trauth, 2001; Kaminski & Reilly, 2004). In response to these trends, numerous strategies have been implemented, including university *curricula* designed to counter false perceptions of computing and to overcome perceptions of stereotypical career paths, developmental mathematical and computing programs for women, and the formation of numerous IT support groups (Clayton & Lynch, 2002; Teague, 2002).

THE WOMEN AS MANAGERS SCALE (WAMS)

Rapid political, social, and economic changes over the past 30 years have brought more women into managerial positions. Although there have been problems with women breaking the proverbial glass ceiling (The failure of women to move into senor executive circles in any large numbers), it is generally believed that women and men are better learning to relate (Billard, 1992). Terborg et al. (1977) assumed that male managers would perceive a threat from programs promoting the advancement of female managers and that this would result in stereotypic outcomes for all respondents. Terborg et al. (1977) expected stereotypical male managers to deny women opportunities because of bio-psychological differences or that the jobs were deemed to be masculine. But, they found no evidence of this even as the sampled organizations were actively hiring and promoting women.

Over time, women-specific issues have become less problematic through education, administrative and legal remedies to pregnancies, family issues, and the understanding of unique female medical conditions. For example, tele-working has become a viable alternative for working mothers (Perez, Carnicer, & Martnez, 2002). Importantly, recent studies have suggested fewer and fewer differences between male and female managers giving some weight to the individual differences perspective on gender (Trauth, 2002; Trauth, Quesenberry, & Huang, 2008). Nonetheless, group differences between men and women on factors such as stress and job burnout continue to be investigated by contemporary researchers.

Many gender and sex discrimination studies focus on sex role stereotypes to explain why women are not advancing into management ranks in the private sector. IT/IS researchers have examined the differences and similarities in human capital variables (Measurable attributes such as Length of Service, Educational Attainment, and Job Certifications.) for male and female IT/IS workers and how these differences affect job outcomes (Igbaria & Greenhaus, 1992; Igbaria, Parasuraman, & Greenhaus, 1997). Women entering IT/IS fields are often employed at lower levels, make less money, and eventually have greater intent to leave than their male counterparts (Baroudi & Igbaria, 1994). These results suggest that stereotypical attitudes still exist and that they describe actual differences that influence the recruitment, retention, and advancement of women in IT jobs.

In this context, we sought to measure changes over time in worker attitudes toward women in management positions using the Women as Managers Scale (WAMS). WAMS, as shown in Appendix A, was developed in the early 1970s to measure stereotypical attitudes of men and women in business settings (Peters, Terborg, & Taynor, 1974; Taynor & Deaux, 1973; Terborg & Ilgen, 1975; Terborg, Peters, Ilgen, & Smith, 1977). Originally designed as a diagnostic tool for industry, the WAMS is a management tool given periodically to workers to evaluate education and training programs. The WAMS measures attitudes toward women in business situations to detect po-

tentially discriminatory behavior toward women. Such an evaluation instrument helps define and understand barriers inhibiting the successful integration of women into managerial positions. More specifically, WAMS was developed to demonstrate that barriers to women do exist and to serve as a standardized instrument that could provide a reasonable profile of employees' attitudes on this issue. Thus, in conjunction with diagnostics designed to improve employee attitudes toward women, the WAMS could serve as "before" and "after" measures to assess the effectiveness of employee training programs.

Table 1 summarizes previous WAMS studies and their primary findings. Previous WAMS studies consistently found that women scored better than men on summary scores (c.f., Cohen & Leavengood, 1978; Dobbins, Cardy, & Truxillo, 1988; Owen & Todor, 1993; Peters, Terborg, & Taynor, 1974; Terborg & Ilgen, 1975; Terborg, Peters, Ilgen, & Smith, 1977). Moreover, this relationship has also held true for international studies on Indian, Chinese, Nigerian, and Chilean students (Cordano, Scherer, & Owen, 2002). Summary scores simply add the individual score from each question based on a 7-point Likert scale. Previous research results further suggest that age, marital status, or organizational characteristics do not contribute appreciably toward predicting WAMS attitudes (Terborg, Peters, Ilgen, & Smith, 1977).

GENDER IDENTITY

The legislative, economic, and social changes occurring since the inception of the WAMS instrument have positively changed both male and female attitudes towards working women. One aim of our study was to determine if negative perceptions of women as mangers still exist, given our era of political correctness, and whether perceptions of social identity have changed over the three decades since the WAMS instrument was developed. The decline in females entering

Table 1. Summary of previous studies using WAMS

Study	Sample Group	N	Male Mean (STD)	Female Mean (STD)	Major Findings
Peters, Terborg, and Taynor (1974)	Undergraduate students	USA (345 male, 196 Female)	Male 109.15 (19.03)	Female 132.27 (13.83)	Gender had the largest impact on differences in WAMS scores.
Terborg and Ilgen (1975)	Undergraduate students Admin personnel	USA(18 male, 7 Female)	No published WAMS Scores	No published WAMS Scores	Females offered lower starting salaries; Females often assigned routine tasks more frequently than changing ones
Terborg, Peters, Ilgen, and Smith (1977)	Full-time employees of a international distributing company	USA (180 male, 100 female)	Male 102.11	Female 119.38	Women with a formal education score higher on the WAMS. Age and martial status do not appreciably affect attitudes.
Garland and Price (1977)	Undergraduate Business students	USA (123 males)	Male Success 104.58 (22.98) Male Failure 105.02 (15.24)		WAMS Scores affected by gender but not by descriptions of success or failure. WAMS positively related to ability and effort in success condition and negatively related to ability in failure condition.
Cohen and Leavengood (1978)	Undergraduate students	USA (78 males)	Male 109.91 (19.34)		WAMS scores supported the notion that sex role stereotypical attitudes and discretionary behavior are different. The study questioned the predictability of the WAMS.
Stevens and DeNisi (1980)	Undergraduate Business students	USA (143 male, 83 female)	Male 109.23	Female 131.65	Replicated the WAMS results of Garland and Price (1977) finding that females scored higher than males.
Crino, White, and DeSanctis (1981)	Business students University managerial personnel	USA (654 male, 350 female) USA (200 male, 396 female)	Male 103.10 Male Managers 111.26	Female 129.65 Female Managers 128.36	WAMS may be measure that is more reliable for students than managers and for males than for females both within and cross groups. WAMS may have reliability and dimensionality problems.
Garland, Hale, and Burnson (1982)	Large Human Services Agency	USA (52 male, 58 female)	Male employees 116.77	Female Employees 129.43	Gender had the largest impact on differences in WAMS scores. No other demographic variables had a significant impact.
Ilgen and Moore (1983)	Not applicable	Not applicable	No published WAMS Scores	No published WAMS Scores	This paper countered a previous paper (Crino et al. 1981) that suggested the possibility of differential subgroup reliability and dimensionality problem for the WAMS.

continued on following page

Table 1. Continued

Study	Sample Group	N	Male Mean (STD)	Female Mean (STD)	Major Findings
Crino, White, and Looney (1985)	Not applicable	Not applicable	No published WAMS Scores	No published WAMS Scores	This is a rebuttal paper countering the assertions presented in the Ilgen and Moore (1983) paper.
Dobbins, Cardy, and Truxillo (1988)	Undergraduate students	USA (51 male, 52 Female)	120.4(16.8) Compiled Score	120.4(16.8) Compiled Score	Female rates of performance were evaluated less accurately by raters with traditional stereotypes of women and higher by raters with non-traditional stereotypes of women.
Gulhati (1990)	Mid-level Indian managers in health, education and social organizations	India (56 male, 117 female)	Indian Managers 105.75	Indian Managers 116.3	Largest differences in WAMS scores occurred between men and women in comparison to differences in age, education, job level and job sector
Owen and Todor (1993)	Undergraduate Students and HR management professionals	USA (119 male, 118 female) USA (114 male, 170 female)	Male 78.61 HR Professionals 127.65	Female 79.89 HR Professionals 133.9	Men in both groups held stronger negative attitudes toward women as mangers than did the women.
Tomkiewicz and Adeyemi-Bello (1995)	Current and recent Nigerian college students and American business school graduates	Nigeria (43 male, 27 female) USA (40 male, 34 female)	Nigerian Male:88.1 Male USA 103.1	Nigerian Female: 108.2 Female USA 115.2	Nigerian males are more negative toward women as managers when compared to Nigerian women, American males and American females.
Cordano, Scherer, and Owen (2001)	Undergraduate Business Students	USA (95 male, 99 female) Chile (144 male, 74 female,)	No published WAMS Scores	No published WAMS Scores	Gender explains three times more variance than culture in the WAMS scores.
Cordano, Owen, Scherer, and Munoz (2002)	Undergraduate Business Students	USA (95 male, 99 female) Chile (144 male, 74 female,)	No published WAMS Scores	No published WAMS Scores	Found two similar factors labeled Abilities and Acceptance in both cultures.

IT/IS can perhaps be traced to a "backlash" attitude among American males and females that has emerged as a late reaction to the last decade of "political correctness" and diversity initiatives from governmental agencies and special-interest groups (Owen & Todor, 1993).

Social Identity Theory (SIT) suggests that people classify themselves and others into social categories, such as organizational membership, job type, gender, and age (Ashforth & Mael, 1989). Social classifications allow us to define others as well as ourselves within a social environment. Our personal identity encompasses idiosyncratic characteristics like body attributes, abilities, psychological traits, and personal interests, whereas social identity encompasses salient group classifications of the people around us. For instance, initiatives concerned with getting women into IT management positions might emphasize skill acquisition to counter perceptions that women are not technologically minded. However, as new models of masculinity emerge, males may be acquiring the flexibility and the organizational and communication skills deemed innate to women (Hellens, Nielsen, & Trauth, 2001).

This perspective suggests that gender identity is a two-dimensional construct with masculine traits comprising one dimension and female traits the other (Palan, 2001). Furthermore, gender is a cultural definition, differing from the definition of sex, and reflects behavior appropriate to sexes in a given society at a given time. Interestingly, when WAMS was developed, early gender identity research hypothesized a single bipolar dimension with masculine and feminine traits at opposite ends of a spectrum. Gender identity was believed correlated with biological sex and constrained by societal stereotypes. As these stereotypes changed, development of a two-dimensional gender identity model emerged in which masculine and feminine traits coexisted in varying degrees as two orthogonal dimensions within a single individual (Palan, 2001), so at least some stereotypical myths of gender identity may have been debunked. Thus, we state Proposition 1 in the null.

Proposition 1: Gender Identity Roles have not changed in the past 30 years.

The development of the WAMS focused on two main content areas reflecting the essentialism and social constructionism points of view concerning males. These were (1) general descriptive traits and behaviors of managers, i.e., leadership, decision making, assertiveness, and competitiveness, and (2) female-specific stereotypes thought to represent barriers to the successful integration of

women into managerial positions. The traditional male stereotype sees males as more independent, objective, competitive, logical, skilled in business, and able to make decisions more easily than women. Female stereotypes suggest that women are more gentle, sensitive, tactful, dependent, passive, and illogical.

GENDER ATTITUDES

The WAMS is a 21-item attitude scale (Appendix A) designed to elicit an individual's degree of stereotypical behavior toward women as managers (Peters, Terborg, & Taynor, 1974). Experimentally, these 21 items came from a principle component analysis using an orthogonal rotation that accounted for 48 percent of the variance and resulted in three interpretable factors. The first factor, "General Acceptance of Females as Managers," represented the first ten items and accounted for 20 percent of the variance. Factor two, "Feminine Barriers," includes items 11 thru 15, which explained 13 percent of the variance. The third factor, "Manager's Descriptive Traits," consisted of the final six items and accounted for 15 percent of the variance. The scale was developed, tested, and evaluated by surveying undergraduate students enrolled in business programs of several large Midwestern and Southern universities (Peters, Terborg, & Taynor, 1974). A nonstudent sample of 180 male and 100 female full-time employees of an international distributing company also validated the scale (Terborg, Peters, Ilgen, & Smith, 1977).

Thus, the WAMS incorporated sufficient generalizability applicable to many managerial situations while retaining psychometric soundness (the applicable design, administration, and interpretation of quantitative tests) as well as construct validity. Our next set of propositions considers today's perceptions and attitudes towards women as managers in the context of the three factors from the original WAMS study. Essentially, this set of propositions states that there are no differences between the perceptions of men and women on each of the three interpretable factors. The following propositions are stated in the null.

Proposition 2: There is no difference between the attitudes of men and women in the general acceptance of females as managers.

Proposition 3: There is no difference between the attitudes of men and women with respect to female barriers.

Proposition 4: There is no difference between the attitudes of men and women in managerial descriptive traits.

RESEARCH DESIGN AND DATA COLLECTION PROCEDURE

Our sample consists of 162 male and 94 female undergraduate business students from a large Midwest university who represent future trainees and employees in the disciplines of Management Information System (MIS) (30 percent) and General Management (70 percent) fields, such as Human Resource Management and Industrial Relations. Our sample ethnicity consisted of 83 percent Caucasian, 1 percent Asian, 1 percent Black, and 14 percent Hispanic subjects who responded to the WAMS instrument as part of a volitional course component used for research in upper division business school classes. The ages of the male subjects ranged from 20-38 years with an average age of 23 and a standard deviation of 2.97 years. The ages of the female subjects ranged from 19-35 years with an average of 22 years and a standard deviation of 2.66 years.

Twenty-one WAMS items were assessed via seven-point Likert scales ranging from strongly disagree, a one, to strongly agree, a seven. Scores were summed together across all 21 items rather than a standard deviation being calculated for each item in order to be consistent with previous studies. Higher summed scores represent a more positive attitude toward women as managers. Previous studies used a summary score for comparisons between groups. We have chosen the same analysis method for our results to have generalizable meaning.

Subjects completed the survey instrument voluntarily with no course penalty for non-participation. The surveys were reviewed for completeness by the researchers when the surveys were turned in, with any corrections or additions to the survey being made at that time by the subject. No names or identifying marks were indicated on the survey instrument to assure the respondents of their anonymity.

RESULTS AND DATA ANALYSIS

The WAMS scores (summed across all 21 items) ranged from a low of 64 to a high of 146. The mean summed score of women was 132.9 with a standard deviation of 8.93. The mean summed score of men was 117.2 with a standard deviation of 18.92. This difference is statistically significant at $p < 0.01$. Interestingly, we found a statistically significant, $p < 0.01$, difference on each WAMS item between men and women.

We tested Proposition 1 through a comparative examination of the mean responses of men and women from the Peters et al. (1974) study. As presented in Figure 1, both responses from men and women improved across the two studies. Further examination reveals that the summed responses for attitude of female students toward women as managers did not change since the Peters et al. (1974) study ($t = 0.52$, $df = 192$, p was not significant); the summed responses of men significantly improved over the same period ($t = 5.7$, $df = 338$, $p < 0.001$).

We investigated Propositions 2, 3, and 4 by summing responses for both male and female students over each of the three factors to provide additional insights into time-related changes concerning contemporary perceptions and attitudes toward women as manager constructs. Specifically, both women ($t = 3.88$, $df = 192$, $p < 0.002$) and men ($t = 6.90$, $df = 338$, $p < 0.001$) have realized significant improvements on the general acceptance of females as managers factor.

Similar results were obtained for the manager descriptive traits factor, men ($t = 3.37$, $df = 192$, $p < 0.001$) and women ($t = 6.75$, $df = 338$, $p < 0.001$), respectively. However, the results for feminine barriers factor exhibited a different pattern. Women displayed a marked decrease in their attitudes and perceptions ($t = 13.81$, $df = 192$, $p < 0.001$), whereas men showed no statistically significant change ($t = 0.35$, $df = 338$, p was not significant). These results indicate that men have shown overall improvement in their attitudes and perceptions of women as managers whereas women have not.

Table 2 contains the interpretable factor correlation matrix and alpha reliability coefficients. These parameters exceed the minimum values suggested by Nunnally and evidence of an acceptable level of internal consistency (Nunnally & Bernstein, 1994). Following Peters et al. (1974), additional

data analysis used Principle Component Analysis (PCA). Once again, a contemporary PCA assessment of the WAMS factor structure yielded three interpretable factors, which together accounted for approximately 56 percent of the variance (48 percent in original study). Separately, factor one comprised 40 percent (20 percent), factor two 9 percent (13 percent), and factor three 7 percent (15 percent) of the variance, respectively. In plotting each of these factors against one another, we found a number of influential points divided between men and women. Even with these points removed, the results were structurally identical to the presented results further supporting the view that gender identity is a two-dimensional construct made up of masculine and feminine traits.

Based on the content of items loading at or above the salient value (i.e., using the highest loading in those instances where items cross-loaded), the extracted factors were labeled identically as those in Peters et al. (1974). However, seven of the 21 WAMS items had very significant cross loadings on other factors (viz., items 4, 5, 8, 9, 10, 15, and 16). The significant level of these

Figure 1. Descriptive statistics: WAMS means and standard deviations

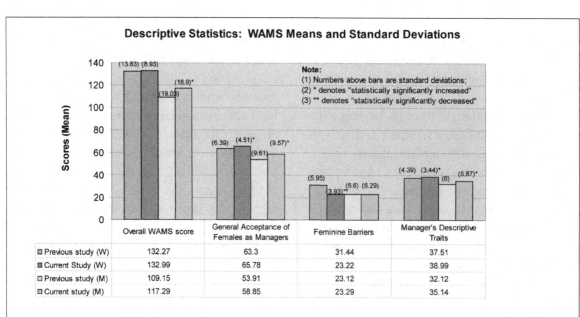

Table 2. Inter-correlations, Means, Standard Deviations (SD), and Internal Consistency of Study Constructs (n=254)

	MEAN (STD DEV)	FACTOR 1	FACTOR 2	FACTOR 3
FACTOR 1	6.14 (0.87)	0.89		
FACTOR 2	5.12 (1.26)	0.63	0.69	
FACTOR 3	6.09 (0.90)	0.74	0.56	0.84

Notes: All intercorrelations are significant at $p<0.01$ Coefficient α can be found on the diagonal

cross-loadings suggests that several WAMS items no longer currently "tap" relevant values or outlooks. For instance, item 15 (see Appendix A) refers to "women staying at home." Since the early 1970s, tele-working has become a viable alternative work option for both men and women (Perez et al., 2002). Additionally, item 16, which is to women's mathematical and mechanical skills, may be influenced by the increased emphasis on mathematics and computing programs now available to women (Clayton & Lynch, 2002). Business students would know this and might interpret these questions differently from a pre-PC generation of students. Further, the individual differences perspective proposed by Trauth, Quesenberry, and Huang (2008) suggests that these questions might reflect individual choices rather than essentialism or social constructionism explanations.

A two-step approach further evaluated Propositions 2, 3, and 4. Rather than using the summed scales for further testing, a multivariate approach considered the degree of inter-item correlation across each of three WAMS factors. The first step computed the Mahalanobis distance metric for each of the three factors for both men and for women (Doty & Glick, 1994). A multivariate measure of the separation of a data set from a predefined point in multidimensional space (the ideal profile) satisfies the need to use a Euclidian distance measure to test a typology. Moreover, this measure, the Mahalanobis distance, retains the complex, interrelated nature of all items used to measure WAMS. This metric provides a holistic fit by considering the inter-item correlation between responses for each of the interpretable factors compared to the implied ideal response set for each of the interpretable factors. The defined ideal response on each item is a Likert Scale "7" (or a "1" for the reverse-scaled items) anchored by Strongly Disagree and Strongly Agree. As the adherence to the theoretically ideal profile increases, Mahalanobis' distance gets smaller. Therefore, lower scores on WAMS using this methodology mean more favorable scores. Table 3 contains the Mahalanobis distance metric descriptive statistics.

The second step ran a series of statistical tests on the women's and the men's Mahalanobis distance metrics for each interpretable factor. Specifically, women and men significantly differed on the general acceptance of females as managers factor ($t = 3.25$, $df = 252$, $p < 0.001$) and on manager descriptive traits ($t = 2.73$, $df = 252$, $p < 0.003$). These results indicate that men and women still reflect different attitudes and perceptions of women as managers. However, the gap between the attitudes of men and women appears to be closing. Effect sizes were computed for each of the three factors using the methodology outlined by Rosenthal (1995).

COMPARISON WITH PREVIOUS STUDIES

Consistent with recent studies, we found that men and women differ significantly on the WAMS (Gulhati, 1990; Owen & Todor, 1993). Impor-

Table 3. Mahalanobis distance for each WAMS item by gender

Panel A: Desirability of women in managerial roles						
GENDER	N	MEAN	STD DEV	EFFECT SIZE	MINIMUM	MAXIMUM
Women	94	2.95	1.33	0.0989	1.00	8.64
Men	160	3.69	2.30		1.00	12.09
Panel B: Perceived ambition of women						
GENDER	N	MEAN	STD DEV	EFFECT SIZE	MINIMUM	MAXIMUM
Women	94	3.16	1.01	0.0347	1.19	6.77
Men	160	3.40	1.40		1.19	7.82
Panel C: Perceptions of femininity as a hindrance						
GENDER	N	MEAN	STD DEV	EFFECT SIZE	MINIMUM	MAXIMUM
Women	94	2.17	1.34	0.0960	0.36	9.03
Men	160	2.71	1.79		0.36	8.50

tantly, men's attitudes toward women as managers appeared to have improved significantly since the original study. As shown in Figure 1, the summed scores for males were statistically higher than those found in previous studies. Training and education may have had an effect in countering longstanding gender stereotypes. Additional support comes from comparing past evaluations of men and women in industry, as shown in Table 1. The same increasing trend is evident across both students and industry.

Peters et al. (1974) identified three separate factors but chose to use the WAMS as a single scale. We also found three interpretable factors but with seven of the items cross-loading on other factors. Interestingly, the Peters et al. (1974) study found possible problems with differential subgroup reliability and dimensionality for the WAMS, whereas others refuted that claim (Crino, White, & DeSanctis, 1981; Ilgen & Moore, 1983), affirming the original findings of reliability and dimensionality for the scale. More recently, Cordano et al. (2002) showed that the dimensionality of WAMS includes two factor labeled "Abilities" and "Acceptance" for both U.S. and Chilean students. Similarly, Crino et al. found that the

WAMS instrument was more reliable for males than females.

Recent advances in Item Response Theory (IRT) suggests the continuous building of item question banks, regularly evaluating items to improve the quality of item test banks, and selecting different item subsets depending on the purpose at hand. This approach is important when working with important constructs developed 30 years ago if a researcher may not be sure or wishes to modify/enhance the original question set by including additional items to tap current reflections of the underlying construct that were not anticipated by the original developers (Singh, 2004). Our findings also suggest the revising of the WAMS instrument based on high cross loadings and the possibility that several WAMS items may no longer measure appropriate factors (Cohen & Leavengood, 1978). The individual differences perspective (Trauth, Quesenberry, & Huang, 2008) would suggest a different theoretical perspective upon which to base a revision of the instrument. Furthermore, in our view, a 21-item instrument is long and somewhat difficult to use, particularly if one wanted to use the WAMS as either a dependent or independent variable as part of a larger model.

CONTRIBUTIONS TO
THE LITERATURE

This study found that the WAMS was still valid in predicting male and female attitudes towards managers. We found that male's attitudes toward women as managers seem to have improved over the years. It is important to note that even though male attitudes would have appeared to have improved, women's participation in the IT/IS and science fields is still declining or at least static. An individual differences perspective may help explain this seemingly paradoxical situation.

In explaining these results, we give more credence to Trauth's emerging individual differences theory (Trauth, 2002; Trauth, Quesenberry, & Huang, 2008; Trauth, Quesenberry, & Morgan, 2004) that suggests a greater impact of individual differences and socio-cultural influences in affecting a women's decision to enter the IS/IT field. We believe that males with strong anti-female attitudes still exist (as some of our outliers would suggest), but given the general improvement in male summary attitudinal scores, there should be greater improvement in the numbers of women entering the IS/IT field then the popular press indicates. There seems to be more going on than just stereotypical male attitudes affecting a women's decision to enter the IT/IS workforce. Our results are intended to further an ongoing research stream suggesting the lack of female participation in the IS/IT, science, and engineering fields is more complex than previously thought and that the remedies to solve this problem need to be more encompassing as well.

LIMITATIONS

Our study did not include an industry sample or seek to re-validate the scale against other cultures. Peters et al. (1974) similarly did not use business students which makes comparisons between studies easier but fails to address the attitudinal

changes that might be compared in the workforces of two different eras. Similar longitudinal studies comparing industry workers across cultures would be useful in developing a more comprehensive instrument as well as considering a revision to the WAMS instrument consistent with an individual differences perspective.

FUTURE RESEARCH

Used repeatedly, WAMS measures changes in attitudes of men and women towards women as mangers overtime. While we looked at this comparison over a 30-year period, we did not directly compare the same student sample group. Future studies could look at students or business people after a training treatment and then be measured again to determine the veracity of WAMS to measurement changes in women as manager attitudes. Future studies should use larger sample sizes so that Structural Equation Modeling (SEM) techniques can be used to refine the WAMS scale. SEM is an appropriate technique for determining cause-and-effect relationships. Thus, a more rigorous examination of women as manager's attitudes affecting salary, promotions, stress, burnout, and other factors might be examined under a more critical eye.

Given our results, further study in the various interventions that have been enacted and proposed to create opportunities and encouragements for women to enter the IS/IT fields would be interesting.

CONCLUSION

We found that men have increased their acceptance of woman as managers over the last three decades. Other studies suggest similar progress in closing the gender gap. Researchers conducting a meta-analysis of raw wage differentials between men and women over the last four decades found the differential fell from 65 percent to only 30 percent due to better labor market endowment of females which came about because of better education, training and work attachment (Weichselbaumer & Winter-Ebmer, 2005). Clearly, societal, educational, and political attention on gender equality and diversity issues seem to be incorporated into our decision making. Further, beginning in the 1960's, women have gradually over taken men in college graduation rates with the associated benefits of increased personal earnings, higher family standard of living and a higher probability of avoiding income deprivation (Diprete & Buchman, 2006). Gender gaps in competitiveness in the Unites States have sharply decreased since 1972 when women held just 18 percent of administrative positions until 2002, when the number of these positions increased to 46 percent (Porterfield & Kleiner, 2005). Today, there is agreement that the closing of the gender gap is an indication of economic growth and human development.

As we noted in previous WAMS studies in the international context, men showed a greater tolerance for women as managers. Hossain and Tisdell (2005) found the status of women in Bangladesh improved through education and increased participation in policy making bodies. Instruments like the WAMS are one useful tool to measure progress and target areas for improvement in managerial settings.

We would all like to see practical decisions about job placement, promotions, etc. made because of individual ability rather than because of gender. But, it is often difficult to show discrimination (Weichselbaumer, 2004). The literature shows that differences within males and within females on ability variables are far greater than the differences between the means of the sexes. There are also many contradictions relative to gender differences. In addition, results are often confounded by unconscious bias, the actual task used and over generalization from one sample to a population (Weichselbaumer & Winter-Ebmer, 2005).

Given all the above, there is still inherent value in the WAMS. The WAMS captures multiple constructs and demonstrably shows positive progress in the male acceptance of women managers. There was shift toward a stronger perception in the desirability of women in managerial roles across both genders and a de-emphasis of the stereotyped traits of perceived ambition of women and perception of feminity as hindrances. This would suggest societal education and training programs are working. However, our results also suggest that the WAMS can be improved by revising questions, removing questions, possibly adding questions, or rewording questions that target gender-identity concepts in the context of the individual differences perspective. The root concepts captured within the theoretical and stereotyped questions upon which WAMS was based still exist but can be better grounded in newer theory to make the scale more useful then it currently is. WAMS is not perfect but it does address dimensions of gender inequality not served by other instruments and thus offers additional insights into managerial selection and leadership assignment processes.

REFERENCES

Ashforth, B. E., & Mael, F. (1989). Social identity theory and the organization. *Academy of Management Review, 14*(1), 20–39. doi:10.2307/258189

Baroudi, J. J., & Igbaria, M. (1994). An examination of gender effects on career success of information systems employees. *Journal of Management Information Systems, 11*(3), 181–201.

Billard, M. (1992). Do women make better managers? *Working Woman, 17*(3), 68–71, 106–107.

Clayton, D., & Lynch, T. (2002). Ten years of strategies to increase participation of women in computing programs: The central Queensland University experience: 1999-2001. *SIGCSE Bulletin, 34*(2), 89–93. doi:10.1145/543812.543838

Cohen, S. L., & Leavengood, S. (1978). The utility of the WAMS: Shouldn't it relate to discriminatory behavior. *Academy of Management Journal, 21*(4), 742–748. doi:10.2307/255716

Cordano, M., Scherer, R. F., & Owen, C. L. (2002). Attitudes toward women as managers: Sex versus culture. *Women in Management Review, 17*(2), 51–60. doi:10.1108/09649420210421754

Crino, M. D., White, M. C., & DeSanctis, G. L. (1981). A comment on the dimensionality and reliability of the women as managers scale (WAMS). *Academy of Management Journal, 24*(4), 866. doi:10.2307/256183

Diprete, T. A., & Buchman, C. (2006). Gender-specific trends in the value of education and the emerging gender gap in completion. *Demography, 43*(2), 1–24. doi:10.1353/dem.2006.0003

Dobbins, G. H., Cardy, R. L., & Truxillo, D. M. (1988). The effects of purpose of appraisal and individual differences in stereotypes of women on sex differences in performance ratings: A laboratory and field study. *The Journal of Applied Psychology, 73*(3), 551–558. doi:10.1037/0021-9010.73.3.551

Doty, D. H., & Glick, W. H. (1994). Typologies as a unique form of theory building: Toward improved understanding and modeling. *Academy of Management Review, 19*(2), 230–251. doi:10.2307/258704

Gulhati, K. (1990). Attitudes toward women managers: Comparison of attitudes of male and female managers in India. *Economic and Political Weekly, 2*(1), 17–24.

Hellens, L. A. V., Nielsen, S. H., & Trauth, E. M. (2001). *Breaking and entering the male domain: Women in the IT industry.* Paper presented at the 2001 ACM SIGCPR Conference on Computer Personnel Research, San Diego, CA.

Hossain, M. A., & Tisdell, C. A. (2005). Closing the gender gap in Bangladesh: Inequality in education, employment and earnings. *International Journal of Social Economics, 32*(4), 439–453. doi:10.1108/03068290510591281

Igbaria, M., & Greenhaus, J. H. (1992). Determinants of MIS employees' turnover intentions: A structural equation model. *Communications of the ACM, 35*(2), 34–49. doi:10.1145/129630.129631

Igbaria, M., Parasuraman, S., & Greenhaus, J. H. (1997). Status report on women and men in the IT workplace. *Information Systems Management, 14*(3), 44–53. doi:10.1080/10580539708907059

Ilgen, D. R., & Moore, C. F. (1983). When reason fails: A comment on the reliability and dimensionality of the WAMS. *Academy of Management Journal, 26*(3), 535. doi:10.2307/256265

Kaminski, J. A. M., & Reilly, A. H. (2004). Career development of women in information technology. *SAM Advanced Management Journal, 69*(4), 20–30.

McGrath, J., & Cohoon, J. M. (2001). Toward improving female retention in the computer science mMajor. *Communications of the ACM, 44*(5), 109–114.

Nielsen, S. H., Hellens, L. A. v., Beekhuyzen, J., & Trauth, E. M. (2003). *Women talking about IT work: Duality or dualism?* Paper presented at the SIGMIS Conference, Philadelphia, PA.

Nunnally, J. C., & Bernstein, I. H. (1994). *Psychometric Theory* (3rd ed.). New York: McGraw-Hill.

Owen, B. M., & Portillo, J. E. (2003). *Legal reform, externalities and economic development: measuring the impact of legal aid on poor women in Ecuador.* SSRN Working Paper Series.

Owen, C. L., & Todor, W. D. (1993, March-April). Attitudes toward women as managers: Still the same. *Business Horizons*, 12–16. doi:10.1016/S0007-6813(05)80032-1

Palan, K. M. (2001). Gender identity in consumer behavior research: A literature review and research agenda. *Academy of Marketing Science Review*, *10*, 1–24.

Perez, M. P., Carnicer, M. P. L., & Martnez, A. (2002). Differential effects of gender on perceptions of teleworking by human resources managers. *Women in Management Review*, *17*(6), 262–275. doi:10.1108/09649420210441914

Peters, L. H., Terborg, J. R., & Taynor, J. (1974). Women as managers scale (WAMS): A measure of attitudes toward women in management positions. *A Catalog of Selected Documents in Psychology*, *4*(27).

Porterfield, J., & Kleiner, B. H. (2005). A new era: Women and leadership. *Equal Opportunities International*, *24*(5-6), 49–56. doi:10.1108/02610150510788150

Rosenthal, P. (1995). Gender differences in managers' attributions for successful work performance. *Women in Management Review*, *10*(6), 26. doi:10.1108/09649429510096006

Singh, J. (2004). Tackling measurement problems with item response theory: Principles, characteristics, and assessment, with an illustrative example. *Journal of Business Research*, *57*, 184–208. doi:10.1016/S0148-2963(01)00302-2

Taynor, J., & Deaux, K. (1973). When women are more deserving than men: Equity, attribution, and perceived sex differences. *Journal of Personality and Social Psychology*, *23*(5), 360–367. doi:10.1037/h0035118

Teague, J. (2002). Women in computing: What brings them to it, what keeps them in it? *SIGCSE Bulletin*, *34*(2), 147–158. doi:10.1145/543812.543849

Terborg, J. R., & Ilgen, D. R. (1975). A theoretical approach to sex discrimination in traditionally masculine occupations. *Organizational Behavior and Human Performance*, *13*, 352–376. doi:10.1016/0030-5073(75)90056-2

Terborg, J. R., Peters, L. H., Ilgen, D. R., & Smith, F. (1977). Organizational and personal correlates of attitudes toward women as mangers. *Academy of Management Journal*, *20*(1), 89–100. doi:10.2307/255464

Trauth, E. M. (2002). Odd girl out: An individual differences perspective on women in the IT profession. *Information Technology & People*, *15*(2), 98–118. doi:10.1108/09593840210430552

Trauth, E. M., Quesenberry, J. L., & Huang, H. (2008). A multicultural analysis of factors influencing career choice for women in the information technology workforce. *Journal of Global Information Management*, *16*(4), 1–23.

Trauth, E. M., Quesenberry, J. L., & Morgan, A. J. (2004). *Understanding the under representation of women in IT: Toward a theory of individual differences*. Paper presented at the SIGMIS'04, Tucson, AZ.

Weichselbaumer, D. (2004). Is it Sex or Personality? The impact of sex stereotypes on discrimination in applicant selection. *Eastern Economic Journal*, *30*(2), 159–186.

Weichselbaumer, D., & Winter-Ebmer, R. (2005). A meta-analysis of the international gender wage gap. *Journal of Economic Surveys*, *19*(7), 459–512.

APPENDIX A: THE WOMAN AS MANAGERS SCALE (WAMS)

1. It is less desirable for woman than men to have a job that requires responsibility.
2. Women have the objectivity required to evaluate business situations properly.
3. Challenging work is more important to men than it is to women.
4. Men and women should be given equal opportunity for participation in management training programs.
5. Women have the capability to acquire the necessary skills to be successful managers.
6. On the average, women managers are less capable of contributing to an organization's overall goals than are men.
7. It is not acceptable for women to assume leadership roles as often as men.
8. The business community should someday accept women in key managerial positions.
9. Society should regard work by female mangers as valuable as work by male managers.
10. It is acceptable for women to compete with men for top executive positions.
11. The possibility of pregnancy does not make women less desirable employees than men.
12. Women should no more allow their emotions to influence their managerial behavior than would men.
13. Problems associated with menstruation should not make women less desirable than men as employees.
14. To be a successful executive, a woman does not have to sacrifice some of her femininity.
15. On the average, a woman who stays at home all the time with her children is a better mother than a woman who works outside the home at least half time.
16. Women are less capable of learning mathematical and mechanical skills than are men.
17. Women are not ambitious enough to be successful in the business world.
18. Women cannot be assertive in the business situations that demand it.
19. Women possess the self-confidence required of a good leader.
20. Women are not competitive enough to be successful in the business world.
21. Women cannot be aggressive in business situations that demand it.
    Note: Items 1, 3, 6, 7, 15, 16, 17, 18, 20, and 21 should be reversed scored so that a high scale score is associated with a favorable attitude toward women as managers.

This work was previously published in International Journal of Information Systems and Social Change, Volume 1, Issue 3, edited by John Wang, pp. 28-44, copyright 2010 by IGI Publishing (an imprint of IGI Global).

Chapter 9

Re–Conceptualising Research:
A Mindful Process for Qualitative Research in Information Systems

Kay Fielden
Unitec Institute of Technology, New Zealand

ABSTRACT

Mindfulness is a whole state of being that is not usually linked with academic research in information systems. However if we take Denzin and Lincoln's (2000; 2003), first qualitative research phase, which is the consideration of the key role of the researcher in socially-situated research, it soon becomes evident that a mindful researcher (Fielden, 2005) is more likely to conduct quality research than one who is not. In this discussion paper the qualities of mindfulness (Fielden, 2005) are explored; Denzin and Lincoln's (2003) 5-stage qualitative research process is then mapped onto these multiple characteristics of mindfulness; and also onto a timeline for a typical qualitative research process in information systems. The paper concludes with suggestions on how to include mindful practices in research methods and supervision training in information systems, which is a contribution to the literature in this area.

INTRODUCTION

In this discussion paper, the concept of mindfulness is explored with respect to qualitative research in information systems. The main premise of this discussion is that mindfulness is an essential characteristic for a qualitative researcher in information systems. The concepts explored derive from diverse bodies of knowledge that include psychology (Brown & Langer, 1990; Langer,

2000, Kerr 2008), spirituality (Goodenough & Woodruff, 2001; Herold, 2005; Lau, 2007; Zukav, 1989), ethics (Anderson, Reardon, & Sanzogni 2001), sociology (Wheatley, 2005; Snowdon, 2002; Braud & Anderson, 1998; Waddock, 2001), knowledge management (Bellinger, Castro & Mills, 2004; Butler 2001; Day, 2005; McKenna, Rooney, & Liesch, 2006; Jashapara, 2005) and systems thinking (Ackoff, 1999; Checkland, 1984; Churchman, 1968; Flood, 1990; Jackson, 2003; Midgley, 2000). These bodies of knowledge, in general, exist outside of the bounds of scientific

DOI: 10.4018/978-1-4666-0927-3.ch009

knowledge. In this paper, these bodies of knowledge are considered in exploring mindfulness as a means of capturing a deeper meaning of the whole person as the main instrument of qualitative research.

The order of the paper is: the characteristics of mindfulness are described (Fielden, 2005); a typical qualitative research process is defined (Denzin & Lincoln, 2000; 2003); mindful qualities are then mapped onto Denzin and Lincoln's 5-stage research process as well as a typical research project timeline. Implications arising from these mappings for educating qualitative researchers in information systems are also explored. Finally, directions for future reflection and application of mindfulness and limitations of the views presented in this paper are presented.

MINDFULNESS

Mindfulness evokes the image of flexible and alert awareness (Weick & Sutcliff, 2006). Mindfulness is a counterfoil to mental rigidity. While concentration focuses attention, mindfulness determines on what the attention will be focused (Figure 1). Mindfulness also detects when attention strays (Kerr, 2008). Mindfulness is an act of neutral observation, where awareness of distractions occurs. This is followed by refocusing as distractions occur. Mindfulness usually requires immersion in the process at hand for a state of meta-awareness to emerge. Meta-awareness is being aware of what is happening as participation occurs (Fielden, 2005).

Mindful practices abound in most spiritual traditions (Lau, 2007), and for those people who regard the world as a rational, mechanistic domain, these traditions, and therefore the development of mindfulness largely go unattended. Spiritual practices, such as meditation, hone the mind to become aware of multiple ways of being, or as Reason (2002) suggests 'knowing the unknown".

Figure 1 shows the multi-faceted nature of mindfulness. In the top left quadrant, qualities of mindfulness related to cognitive maturity are shown: meta-awareness and presencing (Scharmer, 2007). Characteristics of mindfulness that can be trained by meditative practices (Herold, 2005) are shown in the next two columns: immersion, refocussing, un-distractedness and focus of awareness. Personal qualities of intuition, respect, reverence, integrity, non-judgement, courage and humaneness (Seeley & Reason, 2008; Wheatley, 2006) are shown in the top right quadrant. Elements of mindfulness acquired through spiritual practices (Lau, 2007): discernment, discrimination, spiritual awareness, integration of heart and intellect, and appreciation and understanding are shown in the middle right sector of Figure 1. Holistic properties of mindfulness are shown in the bottom left quadrant of Figure 1: evolutionary process (Scharmer, 2007), likelihood of chaos (Jackson, 2003), and state of mind and practice (Reason & Bradbury, 2001). Qualities of mindfulness that relate to knowledge of the self are shown at the bottom of the next two columns (Fielden, 2005): mindfulness and the self, multiple layers of self, transformation of the self, and understanding multiple points of view. Intellectual characteristics of mindfulness: mental flexibility, socially-situated mindfulness, awareness of novel distinctions and transformation of others are shown in the bottom right quadrant. In Figure 1, mindful qualities are also related to Denzin and Lincoln's (2003) five research phases.

Part of a researcher's toolkit is a well-developed intellect that notices novel distinctions (Figure 1). While (Brown & Langer, 1990) suggest that mindfulness and intellect share an emphasis on the importance of cognitive flexibility, intelligence, they suggest, looks for an optimal fit between individuals and their environment (Weick & Sutcliff, 2006). Mindfulness theory, on the other hand emphasises that individuals may define their relation to the environment in several ways. This ability to notice novel distinctions is a key require-

Figure 1. Research phases (RP) and mindfulness (Note 1: Denzin and Lincoln's (2000; 2003) Research Phases Note 2: Fielden's (2005) mindful dimensions)

Meta-awareness **RP5**	Immersion **All RPs** **RP4 mostly**	Re-focusing – knows when mind strays Needed to move out of chaotic thought **RP4-5**	Intuition -little understood in IS research - may be used without awareness **RP4-5**	Respect, Integrity, Reverence Personal research requirement **RP4**
Presencing Particularly **RP4**	Un-distracted Particularly as views of others are sought **RP4**	Determines focus of awareness **RP4-5** - this may change during **RP4-5**	Non-judgmental – free from bias Hard to be in this state -all academics required to make judgments **RP4-5**	Courage Humaneness Personal research requirement **RP4**
		Mindfulness	Discernment & Discrimination **RP4-5** (particularly)	Spiritual Awareness **RP4** Personal research requirement
Evolutionary Process **RP3-5**	Maybe chaotic at times **RP1-5** Particularly before & during immersion (**RP1-3 & initially RP4**)	Listening to Self **RP4-5**	Heart & Intellect Core requirement for sensitive data collection **RP4**	Appreciation & understanding Personal research requirement **RP4**
State of Mind & Practice **RP5** (Moves from situated within academia to immersion in case – linked to meta-awareness in **RP5**)	Mindfulness & the Self **RP1-5**	Multiple layers of self **RP1-5** May emerge at anytime **RP1-5**	Mental flexibility **RP1-5**	Socially situated Data collection – practical Others theoretical **RP1-4**
	Transformation of Self **RP1-5** May emerge at anytime during the whole **RP** – usually as a result of immersion	Understanding Multiple points of view Required for gathering rich data **RP1-5**	Notices novel distinctions The essence of research **RP1-5**	Transformation of others Should not be part of qualitative research May emerge from changes brought about through qualitative research

ment in identifying new research opportunities. Mental flexibility (Kerr, 2008) is also required to view existing situations, data, or analysed results from different points of view either theoretically or practically. Understanding multiple points of view is a necessary requirement for gathering the rich data needed particularly for qualitative research.

In regarding mindfulness as both a state of mind and a practice, one can start to envision mindfulness as an integrated whole. Essential qualities of mindfulness understood by multiple religious traditions (Lau, 2007), including Buddhism, Confucianism, Hinduism, and the ancient Greeks, are mindfulness as the path; mindfulness as observation free from bias, need, and prejudice; and mindfulness as immersion - a deep understanding of self and the beings of others. The mindful researcher develops a greater self-awareness, understands the rational, emotional, spiritual, and psychological self in the process of knowing and in relationship to known facts. As awareness of multiple layers of self emerge, so maturity within and across self-layers emerges. The mindful self is aware of mindfulness as an evolutionary process. The mindful self also knows and is aware of the likelihood of chaos, especially in initial research phases (Figure 1).

Langer (1989) and Brown and Langer (2000) in developing a theory of mindfulness suggested that in a mindful state the self implicitly recognises that there may be no optimal perspective or view on a particular situation and therefore, the self does not seek to select a single response, but rather considers available alternatives.

Zukav (1989) believes that intuition is 'the voice of the soul' (p83). Without intuition researchers do not have access to whole systems that emerge, nor do they have the mechanisms that enable deep and powerful contact with the divine. Mindful researchers are more likely to embrace the spiritual dimensions of mindfulness: humaneness, courage, respect, integrity and reverence. These mindful dimensions do not appear

to be included in research training curriculum in information systems.

Non-judgment is a paradoxical mental state for an information systems researcher, although non-judgement is implied in grounded theory (Glasser & Strauss, 1967) where the researcher is instructed to wait until the theory emerges from the data. Non-judgement is also implied when any form of systemic thinking is utilised as a research tool. Emergence is considered as a core systems property in gaining new information about the system as a whole (Checkland, 1984).

Immersion is an assumed state for most researchers. It is assumed that immersion in the data will automatically occur. Being aware and mindful of what immersion is adds to a researcher's toolkit. Awareness of changed states of consciousness, mental focussing, the nature and impact of distractions on immersion and the importance of chaotic thought processes that precede immersion are all mindful skills that can be learned. These learned processes do not normally form part of an information systems research methods course. Initial states of confusion are identified by Wheatley (2001b) as characteristic of mindful engagement. She also suggests that listening, rather than engaging in our own inner dialog in our heads, is a necessary precursor to mindful engagement and immersion (Wheatley, 2001a). Wheatley states that if we do not listen to self, others, and our surroundings, we cannot be present in our social interactions.

Practises that include: training in listening to the self and inner dialogue so these can be distinguished from listening to others, particularly when data is being collected; familiarisation with inner chaos – a common state during the early stages of a research project; a growing awareness of evolutionary conceptual maturity as research progresses; an understanding of multiple points of view; and an acknowledgment of the many layers that make up the self; are all important mindful qualities for information systems researchers.

Qualitative research in information systems predominantly occurs within some societal domain. Becoming aware of the social situation and the ways in which the researcher interacts within this social situation are desirable. In many ways an information systems researcher is a guest in these private spaces, as an observer or as a data gatherer. A mindful researcher enters such a domain with a greater awareness of culture, protocols, practices and procedures and in turn is enriched by the research experience.

Fine-tuning discernment and discrimination occurs as the mindful intellect matures. Heart and intellect can and do operate together in an integrated manner for greater appreciation and understanding of socially-situated knowing. The mindful intellect notices and acts upon novel distinctions with greater flexibility, more assurance and in less time. The socially situated self is transformed by mindful interactions with others. Mindful interactions have an empowering effect on all those within the social situation.

Reason and Bradbury (2001) suggest that socially situated knowledge is a characteristic of knowledge and Butler (2001) identifies contexts of practice that include both social settings and the minds of the knowers. Langer (2000) limits her studies in cognitive psychology to the simple act of drawing novel distinctions in the domain of rational thought. She suggests that drawing novel distinctions can lead to a heightened state of involvement and wakefulness or of being present.

Meta-awareness and presencing can be classified as mindful dimensions only achieved with some degree of cognitive maturity. Both require awareness of what is happening while it is happening. Both require a detached self to notice and learn from the process being experienced. It appears that meta-awareness and presencing belong at a higher cognitive level (but not necessarily high spiritual, emotional, or psychological levels). This is achieved through mindful practice and training.

Meta-awareness is achieved most frequently in both Eastern and Western spiritual traditions through meditation and/or prayer. Meta-awareness is achieved by designers, artists, and innovators by immersion in a particular creative act so that flow

(Csikszentmihalyi, 1979) is experienced. Meta-awareness is a skill seldom taught, learned, or practiced in Western spirituality. Meta-awareness is an essential cognitively mature characteristic of mindfulness.

Scharmer (2000; 2007) describes presencing as "learning from the future as it emerges" rather than from reflecting on past experiences (p. 18). Presencing, therefore, is the embodiment of foresight when applied to research practices. Presencing is also a necessary quality of mindfulness, related to but different from meta-awareness. Meta-awareness is being aware of what is happening as it happens, while presencing is the ability to learn from the future as it emerges. Both meta-awareness and presencing are situated on the same timeline continuum and, as well, on similar levels of conceptual abstraction as sense-making models of the world are formed in interpreting research findings (Figure 2).

Beachboard (2002) suggests that "multiple methods [of research] informed by differing ontological and epistemological perspectives are not desirable but necessary in achieving research rigor and relevance within the information systems community" (p. 1662). Butler (2001) argues for a constructivist viewpoint in making sense of knowledge gained from research: one that considers knowledge as being both "situated and distributed" in "contexts of practice" (p. 1464). He also argues that knowledge "originates in the minds of knowers." In Table 1, philosophical foundations are mapped through Denzin and Lincoln's five research phases.

These mindful concepts derive from diverse bodies of knowledge that include psychology (Brown & Langer, 1990; Langer, 2000, Kerr 2008), spirituality (Goodenough & Woodruff, 2001; Herold, 2005; Lau, 2007; Zukav, 1989), ethics (Anderson, Reardon, & Sanzogni 2001), sociology (Wheatley, 2005; Snowdon, 2002; Braud & Anderson, 1998; Waddock, 2001), knowledge

Figure 2. Mindfulness qualities and the research process

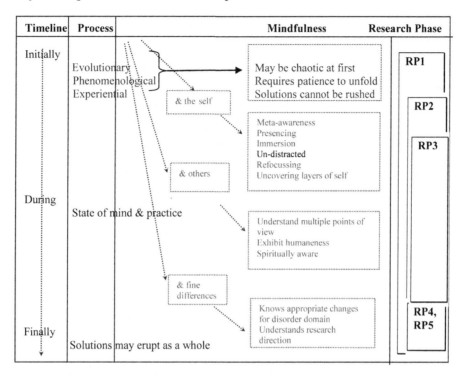

management (Bellinger, Castro & Mills, 2004; Butler 2001; Day,2005; McKenna, Rooney, & Liesch, 2006; Jashapara, 2005) and systems thinking (Ackoff, 1999; Checkland, 1984; Churchman, 1968; Flood, 1990; Jackson,2003; Midgley, 2000). These bodies of knowledge, in general, exist outside of the bounds of scientific knowledge. In this paper, these bodies of knowledge are considered in exploring mindfulness as a means of capturing a deeper meaning of the whole person as the main instrument of qualitative research in information systems.

RESEARCH PROCESS

Most qualitative information systems research is situated within a specific time and place in an organisation. In the first research phase an information systems researcher is usually situated within academia, and 'knows the self' as an academic researcher (Table 1). Research rules, proposal

approvals and ethical considerations all form part of the research process in the academic domain. Philosophically, academic research is usually grounded in a recognised body of theory; and builds on the research of others. The information systems researcher therefore has little knowledge of the situated self in the world the application domain. When we consider that qualitative research in information systems has borrowed notions from many different discipline areas. Myers (1994) suggests that qualitative research is underpinned by three main philosophical assumptions: positivist research, interpretive research and critical research. Myers (1994) also suggests that positivists generally assume an objective that reality that can be described by measurable properties that are independent of the researcher and any measuring devices.

In interpretive research, reality is believed to socially-constructed through language, consciousness and shared meanings. Hermeneutics and phenomenology underpin interpretive research

Table 1. Pragmatics, process & philosophy/research phase

RESEARCH PHASE	PRAGMATICS	PROCESS	PHILOSOPHY
RP1Researcher Academic researcher view, subjective self in the process	Little historical or political view of research context in business How to enter business domains	Multiple roles Proposal approval Power and control issues	May have academic philosophical knowledge e.g. systems theory, appreciative systems . . .
RP2Theory Situated within philosophical foundations			Theory resides within this domain
RP3 Strategy Situated within academia, about research context (practice)	Suitable theory may not be practical	Ethical dilemmas, proposal approval	Research strategy situated within academia
RP4 Data Collection Pragmatics – informed by philosophy and formal process	May have emergent results Cultural issues may arise May have communication dilemmas What is not said or is not permitted to be said	Ethical dilemmas at data collection Language of data collection tools may be academic Distorted results	
RP5 Interpretation about research context embedded in theoretical language	Reporting & interpreting emergent results Reporting language Missed data not reported or analyzed	What to report – political correctness What is not reported What is accepted as legitimate research Acceptance of emergent results	Results embedded in philosophical, academic interpretation

(Boland, 1985). Meaning is gained from interpretive results through attempting to understand phenomena via the meanings that people assign to them (Walsham 1993, p. 4-5). Interpretive research does not predefine dependent and independent variables, but focuses on the full complexity of human sense making as the situation emerges (Kaplan & Maxwell, 1994).

Critical research assumes that social reality is historically constituted and is focussed on understanding the forces at play in considering opposing arguments, and aims to find emancipatory solutions.

Regardless of underpinning philosophical considerations for the type of qualitative research being conducted, there are defined research phases as highlighted by Denzin and Lincoln (2003) and an information systems researcher in research phase one will consciously or unconsciously be embedded within one of three main philosophical foundations. Pragmatically, there is usually little historical or political understanding of the research in the full context of the business research problem being investigated. As an academic, the information systems researcher has multiple roles and is usually embedded in an academic research culture with power and control issues with respect to funding, ethical approval and researcher status.

Mindful qualities that are most valuable to a qualitative researcher in research phase one include immersion, in which the researcher immerses him/herself in the current project. This may be a chaotic process as multiple layers of the self are revealed in the research process. This is turn requires mental flexibility.

Research phase two is conducted entirely within academia where theoretical paradigms and perspectives are explored and is the domain in which mindful qualities are most easily applied as the researcher is within her/his own 'comfort zone'. Fielden and Joyce (2008) in considering the theoretical positioning of academics writing on academic matters discovered that only 17/219 contributing authors embedded themselves in any interpretive theory in positioning their research in the chosen domain. Immersion, chaotic moments, and mental flexibility are required in exploring the multiple points of view presented. Finding the gaps in the literature requires the researcher to notice distinctions and gaps in a particular domain. It is important to note at this stage that the information systems researcher is much more likely to be working only within an intellectual, rational mindset. The humane qualities required in interacting with others are not likely to be present.

Research phase three is the traditional starting point for most information systems research – setting research strategies and this takes place within academia (Table 1). Theoretical ethical dilemmas are resolved, proposals approved and boundary setting for potentially unknown situations take place. Research phase three provides many situations in which chaotic thought processes occur as planning for the unknown takes place. In research phase three, mindfulness has the opportunity to deepen to encompass research as an evolutionary process and the mental flexibility required to deal with novel situations. The reflective researcher will also be noticing changes in the self as immersion takes place. Ethical dilemmas require the researcher to consider the way in which he/she interacts with participants in socially-situated research, gaining a deeper understanding of multiple points of view.

In research phase four data is collected and analysed and it is here that the information systems researcher moves from the sheltered world of academia into the less familiar research application domain. It is in Research phase four that many mindful characteristics (Figure 1) are required as socially-situated and empathetic knowing is activated. It is likely that the more mindful the researcher the richer the data gathered. Whilst the mental models underpinning Research phase four is grounded in academic theory and philosophy. This does not necessarily mean that the information systems researcher is equipped to gather data in a mindful manner. In research phase four, mental, spiritual and humane agility may be required within the social situation presenting. Immersion, refocussing, intuition, respect integrity, reverence, presencing, being focussed, practising non-judgement and discernment may all be mindful qualities required. Listening to the whole self – intellect, heart and spirit is required to exhibit the mindful qualities of appreciation and understanding, respect, reverence, appreciation and understanding.

The final stage of the research process is, once again situated within academia. Research results are embedded in the underlying theory and philosophical approaches and written in academic language. Pragmatically, issues surrounding the interpretation of data are underpinned by the mindful maturity of the researcher. Mindful maturity occurs as the researcher integrates the mindful qualities of all aspects of being in researching in social situations.

It can be seen from Table 1 that it is in the second research phase that philosophical foundations of information systems are explored. The information systems researcher brings to the research process a particular philosophical perspective gained through research experience and training. In this phase, the information systems researcher is most likely to be engaged intellectually. It is in research phase four that mindful maturity is most required, as the information systems researcher moves into social situations to gather data from participants.

Regardless of whether qualitative information systems research is positivist, interpretive, or critical there is little influence from socially-constructed application domains when exploring philosophical frameworks. It therefore seems inevitable that little or no theoretical understanding of information systems research crosses into these domains (Table 1).

When mindful qualities are applied to the timeline for a typical research project (Figure 2) it can be seen that if the researcher practices mental flexibility and mindful awareness, different mindful qualities are required depending in which research phase the research is situated. Initially an awareness and familiarity with chaotic thought processes become a valuable skill that in turn aids a researcher's understanding of the research domain. During the research process a deeper understanding of immersion and self experiences are beneficial. During social interaction within the research domain an understanding of multiple points of view and an awareness and practise of humaneness enrich both the participants and the researcher experientially. When research data is analysed and reported (Research phases 4-5), the mindful qualities that differentiate the fine differences required to recommend changes are required.

A mindful approach to the research process adds a 'whole being' dimensions to the practice of qualitative research in information systems. Not only does the researcher need to engage the intellect in the research process, the engagement of the emotional and the spiritual dimensions of being are engaged as the research involves participants in an ethically sound, culturally aware manner. A deepening of understanding about what it means to be a qualitative information systems researcher is more likely to occur in adopting a mindful approach.

RECOMMENDATIONS AND CONCLUSION

Information systems researchers who have become mindful practitioners are more likely to produce quality research findings that benefit both participants and academia. In order to produce mindful researchers it is recommended that mindful practices be included within information systems research methods classes. It is also recommended that postgraduate supervisors be trained in mind-

ful practices so that they can support and develop their students as mindful researchers. The author is experienced in IS research methods instruction, systems thinking knowledge and practice, and spiritual practices who is also a trained mediator. The combination of these attributes has given rise to this discussion paper. Mindful practices have become the norm for the author.

A suggested plan to train mindful information systems researchers is to:

1. Increase the awareness of mindfulness by introducing practices and skills into research training curriculum. One way to do this is to role-play ethically challenging situations in research training. Another way to increase the awareness of mindfulness is with increased participation in academic research approval processes, thereby becoming exposed to a wider range of ethical dilemmas;

2. Train postgraduate supervisors and educators in both mindful practices and how to teach mindful practices. This is a very difficult thing to achieve when faculty members are trained only in rationalist, positivist approaches. When many of our information systems researchers have been trained to perform positivist, objective research, mindful qualities are not likely to part of the trainer's tool kit. This is perhaps the hardest of all requirements. Many information systems educators have been trained in positivist research techniques that require engagement of the intellect alone. It requires a major mindset shift to include mindful practices like immersion, meditation, reflexivity and awareness of the self in the process;

3. Include awareness of multiple points of view in research training curriculum. One suggesting is to include an introduction to systems thinking, complexity theory and chaos theory (as the author has done in her postgraduate research methods class). Many systems thinkers and practitioners (Checkland, 1984;

Jackson, 2003; Flood, 2000; Midgely, 2000; Churchman, 1968 von Bertalanffy, 1976; Ackoff, 1999) provide sound theory and practice in systems thinking approaches to researching multiple points of view; and

4. Role model mindful practices in teaching and supervision. This can be achieved through dealing with uncertainty and chaos, mediated solutions, self-responsibility, respect for others and acting with integrity. A recent comment from a postgraduate supervision student was "I feel valued and at the same time highly motivated after a meeting with you". This comment illustrates the importance of mindful practice as described above.

It is evident therefore that to become a mindful information systems researcher requires more than the standard research methods training in which the steps of various research methods are learned and applied. How does a researcher learn to refocus the mind, not become distracted or practice non-judgement? These are skills of a zen master, a spiritual guru or a priest. Why should a qualitative researcher acquire such skills? On the other hand, if a qualitative researcher does become acquainted with 'self in the process', and develops a heightened sense of awareness of the effect that he/she has on others as research progresses, then the more likely it is that other qualities such as immersion and focussing will occur. This in turn should lead to higher quality research reports and outcomes fed back into the application area as opposed to research that just produces academic articles. Perhaps including meditative practices within a researcher's training would be a good idea. If, however postgraduate supervisors do not practise mindfulness then these qualities developed in student researchers may not be recognised and therefore are not likely to be developed any further.

Quality research reports in the academic domain may be evaluated according to the rigorous way in which research was conducted. What if these rigorous results were gleaned from data gathered by insensitive interviews, poorly facilitated focus groups with a lack of awareness of the effect the researcher was having on the participants?

In this paper, the concept of mindfulness has been applied to a typical qualitative research process (Denzin & Lincoln, 2003). If indeed, we are to become better information systems researchers it seems a sensible approach to address ways in which the research process can be improved. One limitation (and a potential benefit) of this paper is that it has raised more questions than answers. It is in the questioning and the reflection on own practices that we develop as mindful practitioners and researchers. Implementing the changes suggested in the plan above would guide future research in this area.

REFERENCES

Ackoff, R. L. (1999). On learning and the systems that facilitate it. *Reflections*, *1*(1), 14–24. doi:10.1162/152417399570250

Anderson, P., Reardon, M., & Sanzogni, L. (2001). Ethical dimensions of knowledge management. *AMCIS2001* (pp. 2058-2062).

Beachboard, J. C. (2002). Rigor, relevance and research paradigms: A journey from practitioner to neophyte researcher. *AMCIS2002* (pp. 1660-1666).

Bellinger, G., Castro, D., & Mills, A. (2004). *Data, information, knowledge, and wisdom.* available at: www.systems-thinking.org/dikw/dikw.htm, accessed February 14 2009.

Boland, R. (1978). The process and product of system design. *Management Science*, *28*(9), 887–898. doi:10.1287/mnsc.24.9.887

Braud, W., & Anderson, J. (1998). *Transpersonal research methods for the Social Sciences: Honoring human experience*. USA: Sage Pub.

Brown, J., & Langer, E. (1990). Mindfulness and intelligence: A comparison. *Educational Psychologist, 25*(3/4), 305–320. doi:10.1207/s15326985ep2503&4_9

Butler, T. (2001). Making sense of knowledge: A constructivist viewpoint. *AMCIS2001* (pp. 1462-1466).

Checkland, P. (1984). *Systems thinking, systems practice.* Great Britain: John Wiley & Sons Ltd.

Churchman, C. W. (1968). *The systems approach.* New York: Laurel.

Courtney, J. F., Croasdell, D. T., & Paradice, D. B. (1998). Inquiring organizations. *Australian Journal of Information Systems, 6*(1), 75–91.

Csikszentmihalyi, M. (1979). The flow experience. In G. Davidson (Ed.), *Consciousness: Brain and states of awareness and mysticism* (pp. 63-67). Simon & Schuster.

Day, R. E. (2005). Clearing up "implicit knowledge": implications for knowledge management, information science, psychology, and social epistemology. *Journal of the American Society for Information Science and Technology, 56*(6), 630–635. doi:10.1002/asi.20153

Denzin, N. K., & Lincoln, Y. S. (Eds.). (2000). *The handbook of qualitative research* (2nd ed.). Thousand Oaks, California: Sage Pub.

Denzin, N. K., & Lincoln, Y. S. (Eds.). (2003). *The landscape of qualitative research: Theories and issues* (2nd ed.). Thousand Oaks, California: Sage Pub.

Fielden, K. (2005). Chapter 11: Mindfulness: An essential quality of integrated wisdom. In J. Courtney, J. D. Haynes & D. Paradice (Eds.), *Inquiring Organizations: Moving from Knowledge Management to Wisdom* (pp. 211-228). Hershey, USA: Idea Group Inc.

Fielden, K., & Joyce, D. (2008). An analysis of published research on academic integrity. *International Journal of Information Integrity, 4*(2), 4–24.

Flood, R. L. (1990). Liberating systems theory: Toward critical systems thinking. *Human Relations, 43*(1), 49–75. doi:10.1177/001872679004300104

Gan, Y., & Zhu, Z. (2007). A learning framework for knowledge building and collective wisdom advancement in virtual learning communities. *Educational Technology & Society, 10*(1), 206–226.

Glasser, B., & Strauss, A. (1967). *A discovery of grounded theory.* Chicago: Aldine.

Goodenough, U., & Woodruff, P. (2001). Mindful virtue, mindful reverence. *Zygon, 36*(4), 585–595. doi:10.1111/0591-2385.00386

Haynes, J. (2001). Inquiring organizations and tacit knowledge. *AMCIS2001* (pp. 1544-1547).

Herold, K. (2005). *A Buddhist model for the informational person.* Paper presented at the second Asian Pacific Computing and Philosophy Conference, Bangkok.

Jackson, M. C. (2003). *Systems thinking: creative holism for managers.* Chichester Hoboken, N.J. Wiley.

Jashapara, A. (2005). The emerging discourse of knowledge management: a new dawn for information science research. *Journal of Information Science, 31*(2), 136–148. doi:10.1177/0165551505051057

Kaplan, B., & Maxwell, J. A. (1994). Qualitative research methods for evaluating Computer Information Systems. In J.G. Anderson, C.E. Aydin, & S.J. Jay (Eds.), *Evaluating Health Care Information Systems: Methods and Applications* (pp. 45-68)., Thousand Oaks, CA: Sage.

Kerr, M. (2008). *Sense of self among mindfulness teachers.* Bangor University, Bangor, UK.

Kurtz, C. F., & Snowden, D. J. (2003). The New dynamics of strategy: sense-making in a complex-complicated world. *IBM Systems Journal*, 1–23.

Langer, E. J. (2000). Mindful learning. *Current Issues in Psychological Science, 9*(6), 220–223. doi:10.1111/1467-8721.00099

Lau, N. S. E. (2007). *Cultivation of mindfulness: Spirituality in education.* Paper presented at the Conference on Making Sense of Spirituality, United Kingdom.

McKenna, B., Rooney, D., & Liesch, P. W. (2006). Beyond knowledge to wisdom in international business strategy. *Prometheus, 24*(3), 283–300. doi:10.1080/08109020600877576

Midgley, G. (2000). *Systemic intervention: Philosophy, methodology, and practice.* New York: Kluwer Academic/Plenum Publishers.

Myers, M. D. (1994). Quality in qualitative research in Information Systems. In *Proceedings of the 5th Australasian Conference on Information Systems* (pp. 763-766).

Reason, P., & Bradbury, H. (Eds.). (2001). *Handbook of action research: Participative inquiry and practice.* Thousand Oaks, CA: Sage.

Reason, P., & Bradbury, H. E. (2005). Living as part of the whole: the implications of participation. *Journal of Curriculum and Pedagogy, 2*(2), 35–41.

Rowley, J., & Slack, F. (2009). Conceptions of wisdom. *Journal of Information Science, 35*(1), 110–119. doi:10.1177/0165551508092269

Scharmer, C. O. (2000, May 25-26). Presencing: Learning from the future as it emerges: On the tacit dimension of learning revolutionary change. In *Conference on Knowledge and Intuition,* Helsinki, Finland.

Scharmer, C. O. (2007, May 2). *Theory U: Leading from the future as it emerges* (1st ed.). SoL, the Society for Organizational Learning.

Seeley, C., & Reason, P. (2008). Expressions of energy: An epistemology of presentational knowing. In P. Liamputtong & J. Rumbold (Eds.), *Knowing Differently: Arts-based and collaborative research methods.* New York: Nova Science Publishers.

Snowden, D. J. (2002). Complex acts of knowing: Paradox and descriptive self-awareness. *Special Edition Journal of Knowledge Management, 6*(2), 1–13.

von Bertalanffy, L. (1976). *General system theory: Foundations, development, applications.* New York: Braziller.

Waddock, S. (2001). Integrity and mindfulness: Foundations of corporate citizenship. In J. Andriof & M. McIntosh (Eds.), *Perspectives on Corporate Citizenship.* Sheffield, UK: Greenleaf Publishing.

Walsham, G. (1995). Interpretive case studies in IS research: nature and method. *European Journal of Information Systems,* (4): 74–81. doi:10.1057/ejis.1995.9

Weick, K., & Sutcliffe, K. (2006). Mindfulness and the quality of organizational attention. *Organization Science, 17*(4), 514–524. doi:10.1287/orsc.1060.0196

Wheatley, M. (2001a). *Listening.* Berkana Institute Writings. Retrieved September 26, 2004, from http://www.berkana.org/resources/listening.hmtl.

Wheatley, M. (2001b). *Partnering with confusion and uncertainty.* Shambala Sun. Retrieved September 22, 2008 from http://www.margaretwheatley.com/articles/partneringwithconfusion.html.

Wheatley, M. (2005). *Leadership and the new science: Discovering order in a chaotic world* (3rd ed.). Berrett-Koehler Publishers, Inc.

Zukav, G. (1989). *The seat of the soul.* New York: Simon and Schuster Inc.

This work was previously published in International Journal of Information Systems and Social Change, Volume 1, Issue 1, edited by John Wang, pp. 44-55, copyright 2010 by IGI Publishing (an imprint of IGI Global).

Section 3
Modelling and Simulation

Chapter 10
A Mergers and Acquisitions Index in Data Envelopment Analysis:
An Application to Japanese Shinkin Banks in Kyushu

Rolf Färe
Oregon State University, USA

Hirofumi Fukuyama
Fukuoka University, Japan

William L. Weber
Southeast Missouri State University, USA

ABSTRACT

In this paper, a dynamic network DEA model is developed to evaluate the potential gains in final output from a merger of two firms. The two firms are allowed to have different production technologies or share a common technology. In a beginning period each firm uses period specific inputs to produce a final output and an intermediate output that becomes an input in the production of final outputs in a subsequent period. Firms that merge can use the intermediate input of one firm to produce final output for the other firm, leading to gains in final output for the two merged firms over what the firms could have produced individually. The method is applied to study Japanese cooperative Shinkin banks during 2003 to 2007. Mergers between banks in Nagasaki, Kagoshima, and Miyazaki prefectures tend to have the highest potential gains, while mergers between banks within Fukuoka prefecture and other prefectures and within Saga prefecture tend to have the smallest potential gains.

INTRODUCTION

In the two decades since the collapse of the Japanese real estate and stock market bubbles, financial markets and institutions have undergone deregulation along with an unprecedented wave of mergers and acquisitions. However, the financial service industry is still subject to many regulations, including risk-based capital regulations and service provider regulations. (Saunders & Cornett, 2008) In particular, regional banks and cooperative Japanese Shinkin banks (credit

DOI: 10.4018/978-1-4666-0927-3.ch010

associations) are still restricted by law to provide financing to small and medium sized businesses and members in a particular geographic region, usually the prefecture. From 1968 to 2006, the number of Shinkin banks decreased from 520 to 292 as a consequence of mergers, acquisitions, and bankruptcies that were part of the new competitive environment. Still, the small size of Shinkin banks relative to regional banks, national banks, and international banks suggests that further efficiency gains might be realized by mergers and acquisitions. In order to assess potential and/or actual efficiency gains from mergers and acquisitions, we need a suitable method.

The purpose of this paper is to develop a DEA (data envelopment analysis) mergers-acquisitions model which can gauge gains in outputs or efficiency from mergers and acquisitions. We construct such a model by extending Färe and Grosskopf's (1996) dynamic DEA model. Earlier work in this area measured the benefits of diversified versus specialized firms and included research by Baumol, Panzar, and Willig (1982), Färe (1986), Färe and Primont (1988), and Färe, Grosskopf, and Lovell (1994). The major feature of our model is that it allows resources to be reallocated among firms over time, so that larger joint quantities of final output or higher efficiency might be realized through two firms combining resources and jointly optimizing their outputs.

As an illustration of our method we use data on Japanese Shinkin banks. Shinkin banks are cooperative credit associations whose primary objective is to provide loans to small and medium sized firms in a specific region, usually the prefecture. As with most banks, the timing of the loans they make is discretionary. Some banks might find that regional economic conditions are such that they and their customers would be better served if loans are delayed for one or more periods. While deposit funds can be combined with labor and capital and transformed into loans, the amount of suitable loans will generally not equal raised funds. Although the neoclassical model would

suggest that interest rates change so as to reach equilibrium, the cooperative nature of Shinkin banks suggests that non-price rationing might also take place. Moreover, numerous studies, beginning with Stiglitiz and Weiss (1981) found that adverse selection among borrowers might cause banks to ration credit, rather than raise interest rates during periods when the lending environment becomes more risky. Because of the potential for non-price rationing, we allow Shinkin banks to save deposits by also investing in securities. Such securities can be sold in future periods with the proceeds used to finance loans above the amounts that would normally be feasible from deposits raised in a one period production model. Thus, we treat securities investments as an intermediate output in one period that can be used, along with deposits, labor, and capital to finance loans in a future period. In addition, our model allows resources from two firms in different regions to be combined so that jointly produced final outputs might potentially increase.

A GENERAL PRODUCTION TECHNOLOGY

We denote A and B as index sets of Regions A and B. Let $a \in A$ be a firm in Region A and $b \in B$ a firm in Region B. Let K_A and K_B represent the number of firms producing in region A and region B. These firms are assumed to maximize final outputs over two periods, t and $t+1$. Let $\mathbf{x}_a^\tau$ and $\mathbf{y}_a^\tau$ denote vectors of N inputs and M outputs for firm $a \in A$ at times $\tau = t, t+1$. We distinguish between final output $^f y_a^t \left(\tau = t, t+1; a \in A \right)$ and intermediate output $^i y_a^t \left(\tau = t, t+1; a \in A \right)$. Intermediate outputs are produced in one period, t, and used as an input to produce final outputs in the next period, $t+1$. We would like to examine effects of mergers and acquisitions by a DEA model in which an acquirer (decision maker) can decide the amount of intermediate outputs (inputs) by maximizing the sum of final outputs over time. The production process is based on Shephard's (1953, 1970) production theory and Färe and Grosskopf's (1996) dynamic production model. The underlying technology for the firm $a \in A$, which locates in Region A, is defined by the firm a-output possibility set for time t (see Equation 1).

This set consists of the feasible summed amounts of final output and intermediate output (input), represented by $\left({}^f y_a^t + {}^i y_a^t \right)$, which can be produced from a fixed level of $(\mathbf{x}_a^t, {}^i y_a^{t-1})$. The firm a-output possibility set for time t+1 is obtained as shown in Equation 2, where ${}^i \hat{y}_a^t$ is the intermediate input chosen by the firm in the previous period. We assume that the intermediate output ${}^i y_a^t$ is the same as the intermediate input ${}^i \hat{y}_a^t$ when the firm does not cooperate or merge with another firm. However, in our mergers-acquisitions analysis, we allow the intermediate inputs (outputs) of two firms to be combined, so that we

can estimate any potential output gains[1]. In a similar fashion, we define output possibility sets for firm $b \in B$ as Equations 3 and 4.

Using that notation, we define the two-period joint output possibility set between Region A and Region B as

$$
\mathbf{P}\left(\mathbf{x}_a^t + \mathbf{x}_b^t, \mathbf{x}_a^{t+1} + \mathbf{x}_b^{t+1}, {}^i y_a^{t-1} + {}^i y_b^{t-1}\right)
$$

$$
= \left\{ \begin{array}{l} \left(\left({}^f y_a^t + {}^i y_a^t, {}^i \hat{y}_a^t, {}^f y_a^{t+1} + {}^i y_a^{t+1} \right), \right. \\ \left. \left({}^f y_b^t + {}^i y_b^t, {}^i \hat{y}_b^t, {}^f y_b^{t+1} + {}^i y_b^{t+1} \right) \right) \end{array} \left| \begin{array}{l} \left({}^f y_a^t + {}^i \hat{y}_a^t \right) \in P_A^t(\mathbf{x}_a^t, {}^i y_a^{t-1}) \\ \left({}^f y_a^{t+1} + {}^i y_a^{t+1} \right) \in P_A^t(\mathbf{x}_a^{t+1}, {}^i \hat{y}_a^t) \\ \left({}^f y_b^t + {}^i \hat{y}_b^t \right) \in P_B^t\left(\mathbf{x}_b^t, {}^i y_b^{t-1}\right) \\ \left({}^f y_b^{t+1} + {}^i y_b^{t+1} \right) \in P_B^t\left(\mathbf{x}_b^{t+1}, {}^i \hat{y}_b^t\right) \\ {}^i y_a^t + {}^i y_b^t = {}^i \hat{y}_a^t + {}^i \hat{y}_b^t \end{array} \right. \right\}
$$

$$(5)$$

where the equality restriction

$$
{}^i y_a^t + {}^i y_b^t = {}^i \hat{y}_a^t + {}^i \hat{y}_b^t \tag{6}
$$

allows for a reallocation of intermediate outputs (inputs) between firms, but the sum of intermedi-

Equation 1.

$$
P_A^t\left(\mathbf{x}_a^t, {}^i y_a^{t-1}\right) = \left\{ \left({}^f y_a^t + {}^i y_a^t \right) \,\middle|\, \left(\mathbf{x}_a^t, {}^i y_a^{t-1}, {}^f y_a^t + {}^i y_a^t\right) \in \Re_+^{N+1+1} \text{ is feasible in Region } A \right\} \tag{1}
$$

Equation 2.

$$
P_A^{t+1}\left(\mathbf{x}_a^{t+1}, {}^i \hat{y}_a^t\right) = \left\{ \left({}^f y_a^{t+1} + {}^i y_a^{t+1} \right) \,\middle|\, \left(\mathbf{x}_a^{t+1}, {}^i \hat{y}_a^t, {}^f y_a^{t+1} + {}^i y_a^{t+1}\right) \in \Re_+^{N+1+1} \text{ is feasible in Region } A \right\} \tag{2}
$$

Equation 3.

$$
P_B^t\left(\mathbf{x}_b^t, {}^i y_b^{t-1}\right) = \left\{ \left({}^f y_b^t + {}^i y_b^t \right) \,\middle|\, \left(\mathbf{x}_b^t, y_b^{t-1}, {}^f y_b^t + {}^i y_b^t\right) \in \Re_+^{N+1+1} \text{ is feasible in Region } B \right\} \tag{3}
$$

Equation 4.

$$
P_B^{t+1}\left(\mathbf{x}_b^{t+1}, {}^i \hat{y}_b^t\right) = \left\{ \left({}^f y_b^{t+1} + {}^i y_b^{t+1} \right) \,\middle|\, \left(\mathbf{x}_b^{t+1}, {}^i \hat{y}_b^t, {}^f y_b^{t+1} + {}^i y_b^{t+1}\right) \in \Re_+^{N+1+1} \text{ is feasible in Region } B \right\} \tag{4}
$$

ate outputs must equal the sum of intermediate inputs. Figure 1 is a pictorial representation of the two-period joint output possibility set (5).

A MERGERS AND ACQUISITIONS INDEX

A Two-Period Maximal Joint Final Output Model

To develop the mergers and acquisitions (M&A) index we consider the case where a single final output is produced. Multiple final outputs can be handled in our framework by using a variant of Farrell distance functions maximized over several periods. Assuming a single output, we develop the two-period maximal joint final output model. This model takes the form shown in Equation 7.

In (7) we allow for the reallocation of intermediate output and input between firms $a \in A$ and $b \in B$. That is, the choice variable ${}^{i}y_{k}^{t}$ need not be equal to the choice variable ${}^{i}\hat{y}_{k}^{t}$ for $k = a, b$. The objective function,

$$f_{a+b}\left(\mathbf{x}_{a}^{t}, \mathbf{x}_{a}^{t+1}, {}^{i}y_{a}^{t-1}, \mathbf{x}_{b}^{t}, \mathbf{x}_{b}^{t+1}, {}^{i}y_{b}^{t-1}\right),$$

shows the sum of maximal final outputs when firms $a \in A$ and $b \in B$ merge and reallocate intermediate inputs between the firms.

A DEA Implementation and a Mergers and Acquisitions Index

In order to make the model practical, we employ a non-parametric DEA (data envelopment analysis) specification. At time t the firm a-output possibility set is constructed as:

Figure 1. A pictorial representation of the network model

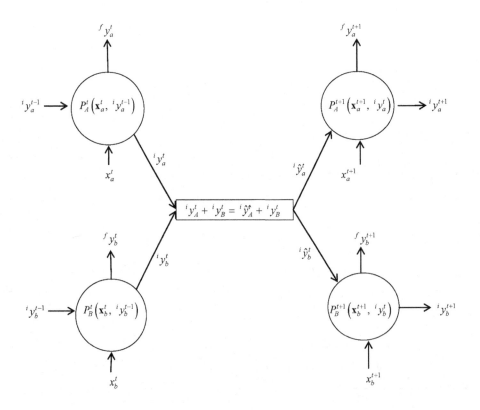

Equation 7.

$$
f_{a+b}\left(\mathbf{x}_a^t, \mathbf{x}_a^{t+1}, {}^iy_a^{t-1}, \mathbf{x}_b^t, \mathbf{x}_b^{t+1}, {}^iy_b^{t-1}\right) = \max_{{}^iy_a^t, {}^iy_b^t, {}^i\hat{y}_a^t, {}^i\hat{y}_b^t}\left\{ {}^fy_a^t + {}^fy_a^{t+1} + {}^fy_b^t + {}^fy_b^{t+1} \right|
$$

$$
\left. \begin{pmatrix} \left({}^fy_a^t + {}^i\hat{y}_a^t, \ {}^i\hat{y}_a^t, \ {}^fy_a^{t+1} + {}^iy_a^{t+1}\right), \\ \left({}^fy_b^t + {}^iy_b^t, \ {}^i\hat{y}_b^t, \ {}^fy_b^{t+1} + {}^iy_b^{t+1}\right) \end{pmatrix} \in \mathbf{P}\left(\mathbf{x}_a^t + \mathbf{x}_b^t, \ \mathbf{x}_a^{t+1} + \mathbf{x}_b^{t+1}, \ {}^iy_a^{t-1} + {}^iy_b^{t-1}\right) \right\}
$$

$$
= \max_{{}^iy_a^t, {}^iy_b^t, {}^i\hat{y}_a^t, {}^i\hat{y}_b^t}\left[{}^fy_a^t + {}^fy_a^{t+1} + {}^fy_b^t + {}^fy_b^{t+1} \ \left| \ \begin{matrix} \left({}^fy_a^t + {}^i\hat{y}_a^t\right) \in P_A^t(\mathbf{x}_a^t, {}^iy_a^{t-1}) \\ \left({}^fy_a^{t+1} + {}^iy_a^{t+1}\right) \in P_A^t(\mathbf{x}_a^{t+1}, {}^i\hat{y}_a^t) \\ \left({}^fy_b^t + {}^i\hat{y}_b^t\right) \in P_B^t\left(\mathbf{x}_b^t, {}^iy_b^{t-1}\right) \\ \left({}^fy_b^{t+1} + {}^iy_b^{t+1}\right) \in P_B^t\left(\mathbf{x}_b^{t+1}, {}^i\hat{y}_b^t\right) \\ {}^iy_a^t + {}^iy_b^t = {}^i\hat{y}_a^t + {}^i\hat{y}_b^t \end{matrix} \right. \right].
$$

(7)

$$
P_A^t\left(\mathbf{x}_a^t, {}^iy_a^{t-1}\right) = \left\{ \left({}^fy_a^t, {}^i\hat{y}_a^t\right) \ \left| \ \begin{matrix} {}^fy_a^t + {}^i\hat{y}_a^t \leq \sum_{a'=1}^{K_A} z_{a'}^t \left({}^fy_{a'}^t + {}^i\hat{y}_{a'}^t\right) \\ \sum_{a'=1}^{K_A} z_k^t \, x_{nk}^t \leq x_{na}^t, \quad (n=1,...,N) \\ \sum_{a'=1}^{K_A} z_{a'}^t \, {}^iy_{a'}^{t-1} \leq {}^iy_a^{t-1} \\ z_{a'}^t \geq 0 \quad (a'=1,...,K_A), \\ {}^iy_a^{t-1} \geq 0, \ {}^fy_a^t \geq 0, \ {}^i\hat{y}_a^t \geq 0 \end{matrix} \right. \right\}
$$

(8)

$$
P_A^{t+1}\left(\mathbf{x}_a^{t+1}, {}^i\hat{y}_a^t, {}^iy_a^{t+1}\right) = \left\{ \left({}^fy_a^{t+1} + {}^iy_a^{t+1}\right) \ \left| \ \begin{matrix} {}^fy_a^{t+1} + {}^iy_a^{t+1} \leq \sum_{a'=1}^{K_A} z_{a'}^t \left({}^fy_{a'}^t + {}^i\hat{y}_{a'}^t\right) \\ \sum_{a'=1}^{K_A} z_{a'}^{t+1} \, x_{na}^{t+1} \leq x_{na}^{t+1} \quad (n=1,...,N) \\ \sum_{a'=1}^{K_A} z_{a'}^{t+1} \, {}^i\hat{y}_{a'}^t \leq {}^i\hat{y}_a^t \\ z_{a'}^{t+1} \geq 0 \quad (a'=1,...,K_A), \\ {}^i\hat{y}_a^t \geq 0, \ {}^fy_a^{t+1} \geq 0, \ {}^iy_a^{t+1} \geq 0. \end{matrix} \right. \right\}
$$

(9)

where the z_k^t's are intensity (structural) variables that form linear combinations[2] of observed inputs, final and intermediate outputs at time t, and intermediate output at time t-1. The production possibility set for firm $a \in A$ depends on the observed inputs and outputs of all $a' = 1, ..., K_A$ firms in region A. Similarly, the production possibility set for the same firm in period t+1 depends on the observed inputs in period t+1, chosen intermediate outputs in period t, and final output chosen by all $a' = 1, ..., K_A$ firms in region A.

For firm $b \in B$, we can construct output possibility sets similar to $P_A^t\left(\mathbf{x}_a^t, {}^iy_a^{t-1}\right)$ in (8) and $P_A^{t+1}\left(\mathbf{x}_a^{t+1}, {}^i\hat{y}_a^t\right)$ in (9) and label them as $P_B^t\left(\mathbf{x}_b^t, {}^iy_b^{t-1}\right)$ and $P_B^{t+1}\left(\mathbf{x}_b^{t+1}, {}^i\hat{y}_b^t\right)$.

Now let us construct a measure of final outputs that can be used to examine the impact of mergers and acquisitions. To do so, construct the maximal final output for firm $\alpha \in A$ as

$$
f_a\left(\mathbf{x}_a^t, \mathbf{x}_a^{t+1}, {}^iy_a^{t-1}, {}^i\hat{y}_a^t, {}^iy_a^{t+1}\right)
$$

$$
= \max_{{}^i\hat{y}_a^t, {}^fy_a^t}\left[{}^fy_a^t + {}^fy_a^{t+1} \ \left| \ \begin{matrix} \left({}^fy_a^t + {}^i\hat{y}_a^t\right) \in P_A^t(\mathbf{x}_a^t, {}^iy_a^{t-1}) \\ \left({}^fy_a^{t+1} + {}^iy_a^{t+1}\right) \in P_A^t\left(\mathbf{x}_a^{t+1}, {}^i\hat{y}_a^t, {}^iy_a^{t+1}\right) \\ {}^iy_a^{t-1} = {}^iy_a^{t-1}, \\ {}^iy_\alpha^t = {}^i\hat{y}_a^t, \\ {}^iy_a^{t+1} = {}^iy_a^{t+1} \end{matrix} \right. \right]
$$

(10)

In (10), we assume that $^i y_a^t = {}^i \hat{y}_a^t$ since we assume that firm $a \in A$ tries to maximize its own final output without considerations of any other firms. Therefore, the observed intermediate output at time t and intermediate input at time $t+1$ are the same for firm $a \in A$. It should be noted that the restriction $^i y_a^{t-1} = {}^i y_a^{t-1}$ in (10) is the initial condition and the restriction $^i y_a^{t+1} = {}^i y_a^{t+1}$ is the end condition. Hence, we treat them as exogenously given. These transversality conditions are employed because they are a natural choice given the absence of widely accepted alternatives, even though the choice would affect the final outcome. Similar to (10), we can construct the maximal final output for $b \in B$ as

$$
f_b \left(\mathbf{x}_b^t, \mathbf{x}_b^{t+1}, {}^i y_b^{t-1}, {}^i \hat{y}_b^t, {}^i y_b^{t+1} \right)
$$

$$
= \max_{{}^i y_b^t, {}^f y_b^t} \left\{ {}^f y_b^t + {}^f y_b^{t+1} \left| \begin{array}{l} \left({}^f y_b^t + {}^i \hat{y}_b^t \right) \in P_B^t(\mathbf{x}_b^t, {}^i y_b^{t-1}) \\ \left({}^f y_b^{t+1} + {}^i y_b^{t+1} \right) \in P_B^t \left(\mathbf{x}_b^{t+1}, {}^i \hat{y}_b^t, {}^i y_b^{t+1} \right) \\ {}^i y_b^{t-1} = {}^i y_b^{t-1}, \\ {}^i y_b^t = {}^i \hat{y}_b^t, \\ {}^i y_b^{t+1} = {}^i y_b^{t+1} \end{array} \right. \right\}
$$

$$
\tag{11}
$$

Utilizing the reallocation constraint (6) as well as formulations (10) and (11), we obtain the maximal joint final output measure as

$$
f_{a+b} \left(\mathbf{x}_a^t, \mathbf{x}_a^{t+1}, {}^i y_a^{t-1}, \mathbf{x}_b^t, \mathbf{x}_b^{t+1}, {}^i y_b^{t-1} \right)
$$

$$
= \max_{{}^i y_a^t + {}^i y_b^t, {}^f y_a^t + {}^f y_b^t} \left\{ {}^f y_a^t + {}^f y_a^{t+1} + {}^f y_b^t + {}^f y_b^{t+1} \left| \begin{array}{l} \left({}^f y_a^t + {}^i \hat{y}_a^t \right) \in P_A^t(\mathbf{x}_a^t, {}^i y_a^{t-1}) \\ \left({}^f y_a^{t+1} + {}^i y_a^{t+1} \right) \in P_A^t(\mathbf{x}_a^{t+1}, {}^i \hat{y}_a^t) \\ \left({}^f y_b^t + {}^i \hat{y}_b^t \right) \in P_B^t \left(\mathbf{x}_b^t, {}^i y_b^{t-1} \right) \\ \left({}^f y_f^{t+1} + {}^i y_b^{t+1} \right) \in P_B^t \left(\mathbf{x}_b^{t+1}, {}^i \hat{y}_b^t \right) \\ {}^i y_a^t + {}^i y_b^t = {}^i \hat{y}_a^t + {}^i \hat{y}_b^t \\ {}^i y_a^{t-1} = {}^i y_a^{t-1} \\ {}^i y_b^{t-1} = {}^i y_b^{t-1} \\ {}^i y_a^{t+1} = {}^i y_a^{t+1} \\ {}^i y_b^{t+1} = {}^i y_b^{t+1} \end{array} \right. \right\}
$$

$$
\tag{12}
$$

Equation (10) shows that the objective is the maximal final outputs of merging firms $a \in A$ and $b \in B$. Comparing

$$
f_{a+b} \left(\mathbf{x}_a^t, \mathbf{x}_a^{t+1}, {}^i y_a^{t-1}, \mathbf{x}_b^t, \mathbf{x}_b^{t+1}, {}^i y_b^{t-1} \right)
$$

with the sum of (10) and (11), we obtain the DEA based mergers and acquisitions index (M&A) as

$$
M \& A = \frac{f_{a+b} \left(\mathbf{x}_a^t, \mathbf{x}_a^{t+1}, {}^i y_a^{t-1}, \mathbf{x}_b^t, \mathbf{x}_b^{t+1}, {}^i y_b^{t-1} \right)}{f_a \left(\mathbf{x}_a^t, \mathbf{x}_a^{t+1}, {}^i y_a^{t-1} \right) + f_b \left(\mathbf{x}_b^t, \mathbf{x}_b^{t+1}, {}^i y_b^{t-1} \right)}
$$

where the M&A takes values greater than or equal to one. If the M&A is equal to one, then a merger or acquisition does not increase final outputs. If it is greater than one, then the merger will increase final outputs. See Table 1 for the complete DEA specification of our model.

AN ILLUSTRATION: APPLICATION TO JAPANESE CREDIT ASSOCIATIONS

As an illustration of our method we use data on 29 Japanese cooperative Shinkin banks (credit associations) that operated during 2003 to 2007. Shinkin banks raise deposits from members and then provide financial services for small and medium-size firms within a geographic area (usually prefecture) and are organized on a membership basis under the Credit Association Law of 1951. Although lending is confined to the members in the region, Shinkin banks can accept deposits from nonmembers. Tatewaki (1991) and the Shinkin Central Bank's homepage provide a more detailed account of Shinkin banks. (http://www.shinkin-central-bank.jp/index_e.html)

The bank efficiency literature has identified several methods for defining bank outputs and inputs. In the asset approach of Sealey and Lindley (1977), loans and securities on the asset side of the balance sheet serve as outputs which are produced from various kinds of deposits located on the liability side of the balance sheet. In the user cost approach of Hancock (1985), outputs include those assets or liabilities that generate

Table 1. Optimization problems in DEA

$$f_a\left(\mathbf{x}_a^t,\ \mathbf{x}_a^{t+1},\ {}^iy_a^{t-1},\ {}^i\hat{y}_a^t,\ {}^iy_a^{t+1}\right) = \max_{{}^fy_a^t,\ {}^i\hat{y}_a^t}\ {}^fy_a^t + {}^fy_a^{t+1}\ \text{subject to:}$$

$${}^fy_a^t + {}^iy_a^t \le \sum_{a'=1}^{K_A} z_{a'}^t\left({}^fy_{a'}^t + {}^iy_{a'}^t\right),\quad {}^fy_a^{t+1} + {}^iy_a^{t+1} \le \sum_{a'=1}^{K_A} z_{a'}^t\left({}^fy_{a'}^t + {}^iy_{a'}^t\right),$$

$$\sum_{a'=1}^{K_A} z_{a'}^t\ x_{na'}^t \le x_{na}^t \quad \left(n=1,...,N\right),\quad \sum_{a'=1}^{K_A} z_{a'}^{t+1}\ x_{na'}^{t+1} \le x_{na}^{t+1}\ \left(n=1,...,N\right),$$

$$\sum_{a'=1}^{K_A} z_{a'}^t\ {}^iy_{a'}^{t-1} \le {}^iy_a^{t-1},\quad \sum_{a'=1}^{K_A} z_k^{t+1}\ {}^iy_{a'}^t \le {}^i\hat{y}_a^t,$$

$${}^iy_a^{t-1} = {}^iy_a^{t-1},\qquad {}^i\hat{y}_a^t = {}^iy_a^t,\qquad {}^iy_a^{t+1} = {}^iy_a^{t+1}$$

$$z_{a'}^t \ge 0\ \left(a'=1,...,K_A\right),\quad z_{a'}^{t+1} \ge 0\ \left(a'=1,...,K_A\right)$$

$${}^iy_a^{t-1} \ge 0,\ {}^fy_a^t \ge 0,\quad {}^iy_a^t = {}^i\hat{y}_a^t \ge 0,\ {}^fy_a^{t+1} \ge 0,\quad {}^iy_a^{t+1} \ge 0$$

$$f_{a+b}\left(\mathbf{x}_a^t,\ \mathbf{x}_a^{t+1},\ {}^iy_a^{t-1},\ \mathbf{x}_b^t,\ \mathbf{x}_b^{t+1},\ {}^iy_b^{t-1}\right) = \max_{{}^fy_a^t + {}^fy_b^t,\ {}^i\hat{y}_a^t + {}^i\hat{y}_b^t}\ {}^fy_a^t + {}^fy_a^{t+1} + {}^fy_b^t + {}^fy_b^{t+1}\ \text{subject to:}$$

$${}^fy_a^t + {}^i\hat{y}_a^t \le \sum_{a'=1}^{K_A} z_{a'}^{t,A}\left({}^fy_{a'}^t + {}^iy_{a'}^t\right),\quad {}^fy_a^{t+1} + {}^iy_a^{t+1} \le \sum_{a'=1}^{K_A} z_{a'}^{t,A}\left({}^fy_{a'}^t + {}^iy_{a'}^t\right),$$

$$\sum_{a'=1}^{K_A} z_{a'}^{t,A}\ x_{na'}^t \le x_{na}^t \quad \left(n=1,...,N\right),\quad \sum_{a'=1}^{K_A} z_{a'}^{t+1,A}\ x_{na'}^{t+1} \le x_{na}^{t+1}\ \left(n=1,...,N\right),$$

$$\sum_{a'=1}^{K_A} z_{a'}^{t,A}\ {}^iy_{a'}^{t-1} \le {}^iy_a^{t-1},\quad \sum_{a'=1}^{K_A} z_k^{t+1,A}\ {}^iy_{a'}^t \le {}^i\hat{y}_a^t,$$

$${}^iy_a^{t-1} = {}^iy_a^{t-1},\qquad {}^iy_a^{t+1} = {}^iy_a^{t+1}$$

$$z_{a'}^{t,A} \ge 0\ \left(a'=1,...,K_A\right),\quad z_{a'}^{t+1,A} \ge 0\ \left(a'=1,...,K_A\right)$$

$${}^iy_a^{t-1} \ge 0,\ {}^fy_a^t \ge 0,\quad {}^iy_a^t \ge 0,\ {}^fy_a^{t+1} \ge 0,\quad {}^iy_a^{t+1} \ge 0,$$

$${}^fy_b^t + {}^i\hat{y}_b^t \le \sum_{b'=1}^{K_B} z_b^{t,B}\left({}^fy_{b'}^t + {}^iy_{b'}^t\right),\quad {}^fy_b^{t+1} + {}^iy_b^{t+1} \le \sum_{b'=1}^{K_B} z_{b'}^{t,B}\left({}^fy_{b'}^t + {}^iy_{b'}^t\right)$$

$$\sum_{b'=1}^{K_B} z_{b'}^{t,B}\ x_{nb'}^t \le x_{nb}^t \quad \left(n=1,...,N\right),\quad \sum_{b'=1}^{K_B} z_{b'}^{t+1,B}\ x_{nb'}^{t+1} \le x_{nb}^{t+1}\ \left(n=1,...,N\right),$$

$$\sum_{b'=1}^{K_B} z_k^t\ {}^iy_{b'}^{t-1} \le {}^iy_b^{t-1},\quad \sum_{b'=1}^{K_B} z_{b'}^{t+1}\ {}^iy_{b'}^t \le {}^i\hat{y}_b^t,$$

$${}^iy_b^{t-1} = {}^iy_b^{t-1} \ge 0,\qquad {}^iy_b^t \ge 0,\qquad {}^iy_b^{t+1} = {}^iy_b^{t+1} \ge 0,$$

$$z_{b'}^{t,B} \ge 0\ \left(b'=1,...,K_B\right),\quad z_{b'}^{t+1,B} \ge 0\ \left(b'=1,...,K_B\right)$$

$${}^fy_b^t \ge 0,\qquad {}^fy_b^{t+1} \ge 0,$$

revenues and inputs are those assets or liabilities that generate costs. Berger and Humphrey (1992) provide a review of these approaches. Glass, McKillop, and Morikawa (1988) conclude that estimates of cost efficiency for Japanese banks are not strongly dependent on how bank outputs and inputs are measured.

We assume that Shinkin banks produce two outputs using three inputs. The outputs are the value of loans (y_1) and the value of securities investments (y_2). We use y_1 as final output and y_2 as the intermediate investment output. The loan output, y_1, provides services to member firms and thus it is used as the final output. We perceive y_2 as an intermediate investment output. We model Shinkin bank managers as pursuing their primary mission of making loans to enhance members' welfare. In some periods, bank managers might have more deposits and other raised funds than welfare enhancing lending opportunities. In these instances, the Shinkin bank manager can produce securities investments that can be liquidated in a future period and transformed into loans. Since both loans and securities are denominated in yen, they can be added as required in our model.

The three variable inputs are labor (x_1), physical capital of tangible and intangible fixed assets (x_2), and raised funds (x_3). Labor equals the number of full-time workers. Physical capital (x_2) equals the asset value of tangible and intangible fixed assets, and x_3 is the sum of total deposits and premiums, negotiable certificates of deposit and borrowed money, commercial paper, total exchange-credits, and other liabilities. Deposits, rather than raised funds are used as the third input in Fukuyama's (1996) Shinkin bank study. The current study uses raised funds, following Fukuyama and Weber's (2008a) banking study. In the bank intermediation framework, Shinkin banks which use fewer deposits and more non-deposit funds to produce service outputs of loans and securities, would be more productive than Shinkin banks that produce the same amounts of loans and securities with the use of more deposits and fewer non-deposit

funds. Hence, we employ raised funds so as to avoid this potential bias.

We focus on Shinkin banks on Kyushu Island, which is the third-largest island and most southwesterly of the four main islands of Japan, with an area of 35,640 km². Kyushu consists of seven prefectures: Fukuoka, Kagoshima, Kumamoto, Miyazaki, Nagasaki, Oita and Saga. Kyushu Island has a population of 13 million and the largest city is Fukuoka with 1.4 million people. Kyushu's population and gross domestic product are approximately those of the Netherlands. Although Kyushu Island is not a political jurisdiction at present, the area might become one if Japan adopts a federal system[3] by abolishing prefectures.

In the face of declining fertility and increased life expectancy, the population in the Kyushu area has been aging rapidly. Kyushu Island has been called "Car Island" due to the large number of automobile manufacturing plants of Nissan, Toyota, and Dihatsu. The recent worldwide economic slump stemming from the US subprime loan problems has had an effect on the real economy and it is likely that the region will undergo a restructuring of its major industries, including the financial sector.

Researchers such as Fukuyama (1996), Satake and Tsutsui (2002), Miyakoshi and Tsukuda (2004), Harimaya (2004), and Fukuyama and Weber (2008b) have estimated and found evidence of scale inefficiency and technical inefficiency for regional banks in Japan. In the near future, merger and acquisition activity is expected to increase among banks as regulators and bank managers seek ways to improve performance. Therefore, it is timely to study the potential efficiency gains from merger and acquisition of local financial institutions in Kyushu.

Recent research by Hosono, Sakai, and Tsuru (2007) examined the causes and consequences of merger and acquisition activities among Japanese Shinkin banks during the 1990 to 2002 period. These researchers compare the five year period before and after a merger by constructing

Table 2. Descriptive statistics

	mean	std dev	max	min
asset	162377.2	139646.8	633373	36008
equity	8623.5	7923.4	43013	1034
$^f y$ =loans	91923.5	78510.1	344563	19359
$^i y$ =securities	28806	34570.9	178152	3077
x_1=labor	221.6	177.7	815	57
x_2=capital	3190.8	2896.3	11548	439
x_3=raised funds	148936.3	128313.4	593779	33588

hypothetical pro forma balance sheets of target and acquired Shinkin banks for the 97 mergers and acquisitions that took place among Shinkin banks. Actual mergers only occur among banks within the same prefecture. They find that larger Shinkin banks are more likely to acquire smaller and slower growing Shinkin banks. In addition, they argue that their research findings do not support the efficient markets hypothesis where efficient banks acquire inefficient banks and the acquisition subsequently helps to improve the health of the inefficient bank. Instead, they argue that M&A activity is consistent with a desire among banks to become "too big to fail" or because of government attempts to stabilize local banking systems in order to maintain a commitment to small business lending. In contrast to the work of Hosono et al. (2007) our method allows the potential gains from mergers and acquisitions to be estimated ex ante, rather than be inferred from an ex post examination of balance sheet and income statement data.

Table 2 reports descriptive statistics of input and output data and assets and equity capital. Total Shinkin bank assets average 162,377 million yen and equity averages 8,623 million yen. Shinkin banks employ an average of 221 workers, have physical capital of premises and other fixed assets of 3,191 million yen and raised funds averaging 148,936 million yen. These inputs are used to generate the intermediate output of securities

investments that average 28,806 million yen, which is then used in a subsequent period along with raised funds to generate final loan output which averages 91,923 million yen.

Although we developed our M&A index so that each bank can face a different technology, our empirical work assumes that each bank in the Kyushu region has access to the same financial technology, i.e., A=B. This assumption is also employed because we have only two Shinkin banks in Nagasaki and Oita prefecture, and only three banks in Kagoshima. In general, one needs more firm observations than the sum of the number of inputs and the number of outputs to construct a meaningful DEA technology. Therefore, we construct the M&A index relative to the Kyushu technology.

Table 3 lists the Shinkin banks on Kyushu Island and the prefecture to which they belong. Joint final outputs are obtained by pair-wise comparisons between banks. In our Kyushu sample there are 29 banks and hence there are $406 = (29 \times 29 - 29) / 2$ M&A index values. We estimate the M&A index for three periods: 2003 to 2005, 2004 to 2006, and 2005 to 2007. Table 4 lists the average estimates for the M&A index for banks in each of the seven prefectures. In the first row of Table 4, we evaluate mergers between banks in Fukuoka prefecture and the other six prefectures. The nine banks in Fukuoka prefecture can be merged with each other in

Table 3. List of Shinkin banks used in this study

Bank Name	Prefecture
OOITA SHINKIN BANK	Oita
OITA MIRAI SHINKIN BANK	Oita
KAGOSHIMA SOGO SHINKIN BANK	Kagoshima
AMAMI OSHIMA SHINYO KINKO	Kagoshima
KAGOSHIMA SHINKIN BANK	Kagoshima
AMAKUSA SHINKIN BANK	Kumamoto
KUMAMOTO SHINKIN BANK	Kumamoto
KUMAMOTO DAI-ICHI SHINKIN BANK	Kumamoto
KUMAMOTO CHUO SHINKIN BANK	Kumamoto
KISHIMA SHINKINBANK	Saga
IMARI SHINKIN BANK	Saga
KARATSU SHINKIN BANK	Saga
SAGA SHINKIN BANK	Saga
TACHIBANA SHINYO KINKO	Nagasaki
NISHIKYUSHU SHINKIN BANK	Nagasaki
IIZUKA SHINKIN BANK	Fukuoka
ONGA SHINKIN BANK	Fukuoka
OKAWA SHINKIN BANK	Fukuoka
OMUTA YANAGAWA SHINKIN BANK	Fukuoka
FUKUOKA HIBIKI SHINKIN BANK	Fukuoka
TAGAWA SHINKIN BANK	Fukuoka
CHIKUGO SHINKIN	Fukuoka
HITA SHINYO KINKO	Fukuoka
FUKUOKA SHINKIN BANK	Fukuoka
TAKANABE SHINKIN BANK	Miyazaki
NANGO SHINKIN BANK	Miyazaki
NOBEOKA SHINKIN BANK	Miyazaki
MIYAZAKI SHINYO KINKO	Miyazaki
MIYAKONOJO SHINKIN BANK	Miyazaki

$36 = (9 \times 9 - 9)/2$ different ways. The mean value of the M&A index for banks in Fukuoka prefecture is 1.09 for the period 2003 to 2005. This index value means that on average, a merger between two Shinkin banks, both residing in Fukuoka, would result in an approximately 9% gain in final outputs during 2003 to 2005. There are three banks in Kagoshima prefecture and 27 alternative M&A combinations of those three

banks with the nine banks in Fukuoka prefecture. On average, the gain in final loan outputs in 2003 to 2005 averaged 30% for those mergers. The remainder of the first row (Fukuoka) gives the potential merger gains of Fukuoka banks with banks in the other prefectures. Mergers between banks in Fukuoka and Saga prefectures would yield the smallest potential gains in final outputs, while mergers between banks in Fukuoka and Kagoshima would yield the largest potential gains in final loan outputs.

The remainder of Table 4 gives the mean index values for the other possible M&A combinations within and between prefectures during the 2003 to 2005 period. The largest intra-prefecture gains are for bank mergers in Nagasaki, followed by Miyazaki and Kagoshima. The smallest potential gains from intra-prefecture mergers are within Fukuoka and Saga. For mergers between Shinkin banks in two different prefectures the largest gains are for those banks in Miyazaki and Nagasaki. The smallest gains from inter-prefecture bank mergers are for banks in Fukuoka and the other six prefectures on Kyushu Island.

Tables 5 and 6 report the estimates of the M&A index for the periods 2004 to 2006 and 2005 to 2007. In the 2004-2006 period, the smallest potential gains from intra-prefecture mergers are for banks in Kumamoto and Saga, while the largest gains from intra-prefecture mergers are for banks in Nagasaki and Kagoshima. For inter-prefecture mergers, the greatest potential gains would be between banks in Kagoshima and banks in any of the other six prefectures. The smallest inter-prefecture merger gains are between banks in Fukuoka and Saga prefectures. For the 2005 to 2007 period the smallest gains from intra-prefecture bank mergers are in Fukuoka (8% gain), followed by Kumamoto (9% gain), and Saga (12% gain). The largest potential intra prefecture gains would be for banks in Nagasaki (49% gain) followed by Kagoshima (44% gain). For inter-prefecture mergers, the smallest potential gains are for banks in Fukuoka and Saga and for banks in Fukuoka and

Table 4. Estimates of gains from mergers and acquisitions, 2003-2005

		Fukuoka	Kagoshima	Kumamoto	Miyazaki	Nagasaki	Oita	Saga
Fukuoka 9 banks	# of cases	$\frac{9 \times 9 - 9}{2} = 36$	9×3=27	9×4=36	9×5=45	9×2=18	9×2=18	9×4=36
	mean	1.091	1.299	1.101	1.190	1.245	1.214	1.077
	max	1.279	1.446	1.222	1.441	1.434	1.321	1.306
	min	1.006	1.051	1.024	1.031	1.063	1.068	1.001
	std dev	0.064	0.104	0.050	0.105	0.109	0.069	0.072
Kagoshima 3 banks	# of cases		$\frac{3 \times 3 - 3}{2} = 3,$	3×4=12	3×5=15	3×2=6	3×2=6	3×4=12
	mean		1.441	1.311	1.447	1.466	1.385	1.369
	max		1.474	1.405	1.544	1.514	1.420	1.461
	min		1.416	1.161	1.345	1.421	1.356	1.246
	std dev		0.030	0.070	0.051	0.036	0.026	0.066
Kumamoto 4 banks	# of cases			$\frac{4 \times 4 - 4}{2} = 6$	4×5=20	4×2=8	4×2=8	4×4=16
	mean			1.135	1.225	1.271	1.241	1.225
	max			1.184	1.319	1.337	1.294	1.743
	min			1.099	1.126	1.187	1.169	1.058
	std dev			0.033	0.056	0.058	0.041	0.193
Miyazaki 5 banks	# of cases				$\frac{5 \times 5 - 5}{2} = 10$	5×2=10	5×2=10	5×4=20
	mean				1.454	1.488	1.351	1.295
	max				1.578	1.598	1.381	1.504
	min				1.325	1.369	1.300	1.177
	std dev				0.099	0.071	0.026	0.088
Nagasaki 2 banks	# of cases					$\frac{2 \times 2 - 2}{2} = 1$	2×2=4	2×4=8
	mean					1.507	1.379	1.358
	max					1.507	1.386	1.480
	min					1.507	1.375	1.302
	std dev					-	0.005	0.068

continued on following page

Table 4. Continued

Oita 2 banks	# of cases						$\frac{2\times2-2}{2}=1$	$2\times4=8$
	mean						1.326	1.279
	max						1.326	1.341
	min						1.326	1.224
	std dev						-	0.040
Saga 4 banks	# of cases							$\frac{4\times4-4}{2}=6$
	mean							1.130
	max							1.217
	min							1.017
	std dev							0.080

Table 5. Estimates of gains from mergers and acquisitions, 2004-2006

		Fukuoka	Kagoshima	Kumamoto	Miyazaki	Nagasaki	Oita	Saga
Fukuoka 9 banks	# of cases	$\frac{9\times9-9}{2}=36$	$9\times3=27$	$9\times4=36$	$9\times5=45$	$9\times2=18$	$9\times2=18$	$9\times4=36$
	mean	1.10196	1.29956	1.06869	1.20846	1.25647	1.19068	1.07680
	max	1.30519	1.44146	1.16592	1.40459	1.42326	1.28113	1.30649
	min	1.01658	1.05460	1.00800	1.03146	1.06185	1.05858	1.00050
	std dev	0.06378	0.09990	0.04271	0.10394	0.10817	0.05985	0.07233
Kagoshima 3 banks	# of cases		$\frac{3\times3-3}{2}=3,$	$3\times4=12$	$3\times5=15$	$3\times2=6$	$3\times2=6$	$3\times4=12$
	mean		1.44420	1.28296	1.45462	1.46900	1.36203	1.36000
	max		1.47169	1.37687	1.50716	1.50827	1.39634	1.44079
	min		1.42435	1.12031	1.41028	1.43015	1.32428	1.22683
	std dev		0.02458	0.07919	0.03247	0.03201	0.03024	0.06400
Kumamoto 4 banks	# of cases			$\frac{4\times4-4}{2}=6$	$4\times5=20$	$4\times2=8$	$4\times2=8$	$4\times4=16$
	mean			1.07325	1.18423	1.22804	1.18454	1.16002
	max			1.12745	1.27711	1.30369	1.23670	1.59346
	min			1.03548	1.07545	1.13503	1.11260	1.01275
	std dev			0.03420	0.06209	0.06350	0.04313	0.17368

continued on following page

Table 5. Continued

Miyazaki 5 banks	# of cases				$\frac{5\times5-5}{2}=10$	5×2=10	5×2=10	5×4=20
	mean				1.17176	1.33277	1.26630	1.15220
	max				1.22783	1.38914	1.33439	1.26745
	min				1.12348	1.25106	1.19161	1.05901
	std dev				0.03521	0.05549	0.05242	0.05318
Nagasaki 2 banks	# of cases					$\frac{2\times2-2}{2}=1$	2×2=4	2×4=8
	mean					1.50725	1.34370	1.33782
	max					1.50725	1.35272	1.42270
	min					1.50725	1.33631	1.25196
	std dev					-	0.00701	0.06369
Oita 2 banks	# of cases						$\frac{2\times2-2}{2}=1$	2×4=8
	mean						1.27550	1.22887
	max						1.27550	1.28443
	min						1.27550	1.17605
	std dev						-	0.03728
Saga 4 banks	# of cases							$\frac{4\times4-4}{2}=6$
	mean							1.07324
	max							1.16614
	min							1.01533
	std dev							0.08127

Table 6. Estimates of gains from mergers and acquisitions, 2005-2007

		Fukuoka	Kagoshima	Kumamoto	Miyazaki	Nagasaki	Oita	Saga
Fukuoka 9 banks	# of cases	36	27	36	45	18	18	36
	mean	1.08709	1.29795	1.10151	1.12126	1.25799	1.21838	1.09897
	max	1.27493	1.45286	1.28218	1.26638	1.44153	1.35027	1.29199
	min	1.00390	1.04992	1.00439	1.01709	1.05995	1.05690	1.00240
	std dev	0.06101	0.10273	0.07765	0.06160	0.11051	0.07875	0.06753
Kagoshima 3 banks	# of cases		3	12	15	6	6	12
	mean		1.43870	1.28760	1.35253	1.45599	1.37695	1.35866
	max		1.46300	1.39445	1.43452	1.48210	1.41830	1.44518
	min		1.41565	1.10020	1.22619	1.42628	1.30612	1.23056
	std dev		0.02370	0.09227	0.06290	0.02388	0.03869	0.06671

continued on following page

Table 6. Continued

Kumamoto 4 banks	# of cases			6	20	8	8	16
	mean			1.09110	1.12459	1.23790	1.21428	1.19063
	max			1.19414	1.23249	1.32938	1.31012	1.63024
	min			1.02311	1.03100	1.12123	1.10246	1.00520
	std dev			0.06008	0.06525	0.08941	0.07312	0.19145
Miyazaki 5 banks	# of cases				10	10	10	20
	mean				1.17176	1.33277	1.26630	1.15220
	max				1.22783	1.38914	1.33439	1.26745
	min				1.12348	1.25106	1.19161	1.05901
	std dev				0.03521	0.05549	0.05242	0.05318
Nagasaki 2 banks	# of cases					1	4	8
	mean					1.49398	1.36599	1.34125
	max					1.49398	1.39165	1.42107
	min					1.49398	1.33641	1.28249
	std dev					-	0.02976	0.05276
Oita 2 banks	# of cases						1	8
	mean						1.31974	1.26491
	max						1.31974	1.34676
	min						1.31974	1.18373
	std dev						-	0.05888
Saga 4 banks	# of cases							6
	mean							1.12275
	max							1.19225
	min							1.04068
	std dev							0.06001

Kumamoto. The largest potential inter-prefecture merger gains are for mergers between banks in Kagoshima and Nagasaki.

CONCLUSION

In this paper we have constructed a mergers and acquisitions index in a DEA framework. In our approach, firms use inputs in one period to produce final outputs and an intermediate output. The intermediate output from the previous period then becomes an input in the production of final outputs in the following period. To examine the potential gains from mergers and acquisitions we assume that when two firms merge, the intermediate outputs produced by one firm can be transferred to the other firm to be used as an intermediate input in the production of final outputs in the subsequent period. Thus, the sum of final output produced by the two merged firms can increase as intermediate outputs/inputs are reallocated.

We apply our method to the study of Japanese cooperative Shinkin banks. These banks have a primary objective of providing loan services to small and medium sized businesses within the prefecture. Loan services are generated by combing raised funds, physical capital, and labor. The intermediate output is securities investments, which can be sold in a subsequent period with the proceeds used to finance loans. Our estimates indicate that intra-prefecture mergers between banks in Fukuoka would yield the smallest gains, while mergers between banks in Nagasaki would yield the largest gains. Between two prefectures, the largest potential merger gains are for banks in Nagasaki and Kagoshima, and in general, for banks in Kagoshima and the other six prefectures on Kyushu Island.

Our method of evaluating mergers can be extended to analyze merger gains when firms produce multiple intermediate outputs that become inputs in future periods and are used to produce multiple final outputs. Here, a reasonable approach would use Shephard distance functions or the directional distance function. In addition, the production period could be lengthened so that intermediate outputs can be saved for a number of periods until used in the production of final outputs and mergers between three or more firms could be evaluated. Finally, extensions of our method can be applied to the public sector where various agencies often have overlapping goals that might be better co-ordinated through a single agency. For instance, Jackson, Illsley, Curry, and Rapaport (2008) present evidence that existing regional planning entities in northern British Columbia suffer from a lack of an integrated planning process in regard to sustainable development in formerly resource based communities. Combining resources from these disparate planning entities might result in enhanced economic and amenity values. Lozano and Guttierez (2008) show that indicators such as life expectancy, adult literacy, school enrolment, and GDP, when evaluated using DEA methods are highly correlated with the United Nation's Human Development Index. Since separate government agencies seek to enhance those indicators, merg-

ing the resources of those agencies might result in higher levels of human development.

ACKNOWLEDGMENT

This research is partially supported by the Grants-in-aid for scientific research, fundamental research (B) 19310098, the Japan Society for the Promotion of Science.

REFERENCES

Baumol, W. J., Panzar, J. C., & Willig, R. D. (1982). *Contestable markets and the theory of industry structure*. New York: Harcourt Brace Jovanovich.

Berger, A. N., & Humphrey, D. (1992). Measurement of efficiency issues in commercial banking, in Z. Griliches (Ed.), *Output measurement in the service sector* (pp. 245-278). Chicago: The University of Chicago Press.

Charnes, A., Cooper, W. W., & Rhodes, E. (1978). Measuring the efficiency of decision making units'. *European Journal of Operational Research*, 2, 429–444. doi:10.1016/0377-2217(78)90138-8

Cooper, W. W., Seiford, L., & Tone, K. (2006). *Introduction to data envelopment analysis and its uses with DEA-solver software and references*. New York: Springer Publishers.

Färe, R. (1988). Addition and Efficiency. *The Quarterly Journal of Economics*, *101*(4), 861–866. doi:10.2307/1884181

Färe, R., & Grosskopf, S. (1996) *Intertemporal production frontiers: with dynamic DEA*. Norwell, MA: Kluwer Academic Publishers.

Färe, R., Grosskopf, S., & Lovell, C. A. K. (1994). *Production frontiers*. Cambridge, UK: Cambridge University Press.

Färe, R., & Primont, D. (1988). Efficiency Measures for Multiplant Firms with Limited Data. In W. Eichorn (Ed.), *Measurement in economics: Theory and applications of economic indices*. Heidelberg, Germany: Physica-Verlag.

Farrell, M. J. (1957). The measurement of productive efficiency. *Journal of the Royal Statistical Society* (Series A120), 253-261.

Fukuyama, H. (1996). Returns to scale and efficiency of credit associations in Japan. *Japan and the World Economy, 8*, 259–277. doi:10.1016/0922-1425(96)00041-2

Fukuyama, H., & Weber, W. L. (2008a). Japanese banking inefficiency and shadow pricing. *Mathematical and Computer Modelling, 48*, 1854–1867. doi:10.1016/j.mcm.2008.03.004

Fukuyama, H., & Weber, W. L. (2008b). Estimating inefficiency, technological change and shadow prices of problem loans for regional banks and shinkin banks in Japan. *The Open Management Journal, 1*, 1–11. doi:10.2174/1874948800801010001

Hancock, D. (1985). The financial firm: Production with monetary and non-monetary goods. *The Journal of Political Economy, 93*, 859–880. doi:10.1086/261339

Harimaya, K. (2004). Measuring the efficiency in Japanese credit cooperatives. *Review of Monetary and Financial Studies, 21*, 92–111.

Hosono, K., Sakai, K., & Tsuru, K. (2007). *Consolidation of banks in Japan: Causes and consequences* (Tech. Rep. 07-E-059). Research Institute of Economy, Trade, and Industry, RIETI.

Jackson, T., Illsley, B., Curry, J., & Rapaport, E. (2008). Amenity migration and sustainable development in remote resource-based communities: Lessons from northern British Columbia. *International Journal of Society Systems Science, 1*(1), 26–46. doi:10.1504/IJSSS.2008.020044

Lozano, S., & Gutierrez, E. (2008). Data envelopment analysis of the human development index. *International Journal of Society Systems Science, 1*(2), 132–150. doi:10.1504/IJSSS.2008.021916

Miyakoshi, T., & Tsukuda, Y. (2004). Regional disparities in Japanese banking performance. *Review of Urban and Regional Development Studies, 16*, 74–89. doi:10.1111/j.1467-940X.2004.00081.x

Satake, M., & Tsutsui, Y. (2002). Why is Kyoto a haven of shinkin banks? Analysis based on the efficient structure hypothesis. In T. Yuno (Ed.), *Regional finance: A case of Kyoto*. Tokyo: Nippon Hyoron Sha.

Saunders, A., & Cornett, M. M. (2008) *Financial institutions management: A risk management approach*. New York: McGraw-Hill/Irwin.

Sealey, C., & Lindley, J. T. (1977). Inputs, outputs and a theory of production and cost at depository financial institutions. *The Journal of Finance, 33*, 1251–1266. doi:10.2307/2326527

Shephard, R. W. (1953). *Cost and production functions*. NJ: Princeton University Press.

Shephard, R. W. (1970). *Theory of cost and production functions*. NJ: Princeton University Press.

Stiglitiz, J., & Weiss, A. (1981). Credit rationing in markets with imperfect information. *The American Economic Review, 82*(3), 393–410.

Tatewaki, K. (1991). *Banking and finance in Japan: An introduction to the Tokyo market*. London: Routledge.

ENDNOTES

[1]   This will be discussed when we introduce the mergers and acquisitions index.

[2]   While the current paper assumes constant returns to scale, variable returns to scale can be modeled by imposing the linear convexity restriction $\sum_{a'=1}^{K_A} z_{a'}^t = 1$.

[3]   Japan has recently been discussing the restructuring of Japan's prefecture system into a federalist nation system (similar to the USA's federal system).

This work was previously published in International Journal of Information Systems and Social Change, Volume 1, Issue 2, edited by John Wang, pp. 1-28, copyright 2010 by IGI Publishing (an imprint of IGI Global).

Chapter 11
A Modeling Approach to Simulate Effects of Intercropping and Interspecific Competition in Arable Crops

Heike Knörzer
Universität Hohenheim, Germany

Simone Graeff-Hönninger
Universität Hohenheim, Germany

Bettina U. Müller
Universität Hohenheim, Germany

Hans-Peter Piepho
Universität Hohenheim, Germany

Wilhelm Claupein
Universität Hohenheim, Germany

ABSTRACT

Interspecific competition between species influences their individual growth and performance. Neighborhood effects become especially important in intercropping systems, and modeling approaches could be a useful tool to simulate plant growth under different environmental conditions to help identify appropriate combinations of different crops while managing competition. This study gives an overview of different competition models and their underlying modeling approaches. To model intercropping in terms of neighbouring effects in the context of field boundary cultivation, a new model approach was developed and integrated into the DSSAT model. The results indicate the possibility of simulating general competition and beneficial effects due to different incoming solar radiation and soil temperature in a winter wheat/maize intercropping system. Considering more than the competition factors is important, that is, sunlight, due to changed solar radiation alone not explaining yield differences in all cases. For example, intercropped maize could compensate low radiation due to its high radiation use efficiency. Wheat benefited from the increased solar radiation, but even more from the increased soil temperature.

DOI: 10.4018/978-1-4666-0927-3.ch011

INTRODUCTION

Intercropping, defined as growing two or more crops simultaneously on the same field (Federer, 1993), is widespread all over the world. Especially in smallholder farming like in Africa (e.g., Malawi: 80 – 90% of soybean cultivation), India (17% of arable land) or China (25% of arable land), intercropping is a common cropping system. In times of climate change, rising food prices, shortage of arable land and food in third world countries and countries with a rapidly increasing population, adjusted traditional cropping systems become more and more important. Farmers tend to utilize every square centimetre of available arable land for production and for diversification of their families diet. Besides, there is a so-called unconscious intercropping: Because fields and farm size are very small (0.1 – 2 ha), the sum of field borders can be considered as intercropping in a larger scale (Figure 1).

Competition results not only in a survival of the fittest, but also in an optimal use of ecological niches. Agriculture can utilize interspecific competition in order to adjust cropping systems. Some attempts have been made to investigate and im-

prove the various forms of intercropping. An increasing number of these research efforts, especially during the 1990's, were done by modeling studies in order to simulate interspecific competition. Most models dealing with interspecific competition are common crop grow or crop/weed models extended with a submodel or additional algorithms. In most cases, modeling a cereal-cereal interaction, the crops of choice are a cereal-legume mixture as on one hand, this crop combination is a common and widespread intercropping system due to the advantages of nitrogen supply by the legume and on the other hand, these species are already included in most crop growth models.

Nevertheless, intercropping has always been considered as a secluded cropping system within one field so far. But in African and Asian countries, where intercropping is widespread, the system can be extended to a much larger scale: common on-field intercropping goes along with small field size on average, low mechanization level and hence, small field boundary distances. For example in China, where the average farm size is around 0.1 ha, small fields alternate as stripes with different crops grown on it and turn-

Figure 1. In China, the average field size is very small and fields alternate as stripes with different crops grown on it, turning field boundaries into a kind of unconscious intercropping at a larger scale (A, B). For illustration, field boundaries are marked with white lines (A) and field length and width are between 5 to 20 m.

A)

B)

ing field boundaries into a kind of unconscious intercropping at a larger scale. To simulate not the secluded intercropping system explicitly, but the field boundaries could turn modeling of a single cropping system into modeling of more regional considered cropping patterns.

Competition for light seems to be the most palpable, both, for measurements in the field and for submodeling. However, intercropping cannot be considered solely as a change in available solar radiation within a dominant and understorey canopy, as it influences also soil properties like temperature and moisture, root distribution, microclimate conditions like wind speed and humidity, pests and diseases and nutrient availability for the plants standing next to each other. The possibilities to model intercropping are various: modified weather and climate-, soil-, growth factors and plant health-indices are imaginable. But as data collection in the field is difficult in intercropping systems, modelers often restrict modeling of intercropping to competition for solar radiation (Ball & Shaffer, 1993; Baumann et al., 2002; Lowenberg-DeBoer et al., 1991; Wiles & Wilkerson, 1991). Even there, weekly plant samples and data collection or samples in more frequent intervals are necessary. However, most models simulate the effect of intercropping using a similar model approach for simulating e.g., competition for solar radiation (see subsection 'background').

The development of a general competition algorithm to be introduced as a submodel in existing crop models might be a chance to promote the intercropping research turning from evaluating and validating to adjusting cropping systems or to develop appropriate and improved intercropping systems. Nevertheless, research still strives for finding such a general algorithm. In addition, introducing a generalized submodel is not easy to handle all over the various models and needs sometimes a reprogramming of the model. After all, it would be a competition submodel for solar radiation and not for interspecific competition at all.

Questions about the hitherto existing status quo of modeling interspecific competition have still remained open: which data input is necessary? Which species are modeled so far? And which equations and algorithms are typical and often used for modeling competition? Besides, how comprehensive should those models be either to take different competition factors into account or to be easy in handling? This article gives an overview over existing interspecific competition models and their model behaviour, and can also be considered as a starting point for further modeling work. So far, the existing intercropping models are only at their very beginning and lead the way to more intensive and practice-related studies. The various approaches seem to be promising and complementing each other, but there is still a gap between the modeling of case studies and the application of those models and the adjustment of existing cropping systems, especially to extend them to the aspect of field boundary cultivation.

This paper reviews case studies in which various existing intercropping models have been successfully validated. Around 20 different models are considered for modeling interspecific competition in different ways, for example: ALMANAC, APSIM, ERIN, FASSET, GAPS, GROWIT, INTERCOM, KMS, NTRM-MSC, SIRASCA, SODCOM, SOYWEED, STICS, VCROPS and WATERCOMP. Applications range from European organic farming systems to the simulation of maize and legumes growth and development in Africa as well as the prediction of performance of intercropped vegetables (Table 1). Based on the evaluation of existing models, research gaps were identified and a model modification for the simulation of intercropping/field boundary cultivation was developed and introduced in the process-oriented crop growth model DSSAT 4.5 (Decision Support System for Agrotechnology Transfer) (Jones et al., 2003), to extent the view from competition parameters like solar radiation to a whole-species view, e.g., to subdivide not only the canopy layers but also the within species effects and to model one species as the sum of subspecies behaviour under different intercropping related environmental circumstances. Our modified model is more generalized, and offers therefore a more comprehensive and integrative approach.

BACKGROUND

There are different strategies introducing interspecific competition or intercropping into existing crop models:

To supplement, include or link an additional submodel into existing crop growth models, e.g.,

- STICS (Brisson et al., 2004),
- INTERCOM (Baumann et al., 2002; Kropff & van Laar, 1993),
- FASSET (Berntsen et al., 2004),
- ALMANAC (Kiniry et al., 1992).

To incorporate modifications which take account of the competition between intercrops, e.g.,

- APSIM (Carberry et al., 1996; Nelson et al., 1998),
- SODCOM (O'Callaghan et al., 1994).

To evaluate new model approaches based on already existing models, e.g.,

- GAPS (Rossiter & Riha, 1999) based on ALMANAC,
- LTCOMP (Wiles & Wilkerson, 1991) based on SOYWEED respectively SOYGRO,
- NTRM-MSC (Ball & Shaffer, 1993) based on NTRM,
- AUSIM (Adiku et al., 1995) based on APSIM.

To evaluate and validate models which allows the assessment of specific management influences like intercropping, e.g.,

- SUCROS-cotton (Zhang, 2007).

To extend simple equation models, e.g.,

- KMS (Sinoquet et al., 2000) is a simplified Kubelka-Munk equations model which can be extended to multispecies canopies,
- VCROPS (Garcia-Barrios et al., 2001) is a further development of Vandermeer's spatially explicit individual-based mixed crop growth model (Vandermeer, 1989),
- WATERCOMP is a modified form of the Penman-Monteith equation (Ozier-Lafontaine et al., 1998).

Furthermore, there are a few unnamed models concerning competition among different species. They mainly deal with a single phenomenon of competition rather than a whole field system, e.g.,

- Kropff and Spitters (1992),
- Sellami and Sifaoui (1999),
- Tsubo and Walker (2002),
- Tsubo et al. (2005),
- Yokozawa and Hara (1992).

In addition:

- GROWIT (Lowenberg-DeBoer et al., 1991) is some kind of exception, because there are no sub-model modules used, but instead a spreadsheet template for making stochastic dominance comparisons.
- The model EcoSys (Caldwell, 1995; Grant, 1992, 1994) is mainly used for simulating multispecies ecosystems across a landscape and to represent fundamental physical and physiological processes at the scales used especially for plant physiologists and less for agriculture and crop growth purposes.

Table 1. Overview over plant and crop growth models simulating interspecific competition and/or intercropping systems

Model	Cropping System	Model type	Source
ALMANAC	Maize and soybean	Dynamic, process-oriented plant growth, water balance and nutrient balances model	Kiniry and Williams, 1995
APSIM	Maize with leguminous shrub hedge-rows for tropical farming systems in developing countries Rotation of sorghum/maize or crops/ ley pasture or crop with an understorey of volunteer legume in northern Australia	Flexible software system for simulating agricultural production systems, different soil, biological and managerial processes are taken into account arising from interactions between different crops and pasture grown in rotation	Carberry et al., 1996; Nelson et al., 1998
AUSIM	Maize and cowpea	Morphological, physiological and phonological model by linking the respective sole crop models	Adiku et al., 1995
FASSET	Pea and spring barley	Dynamic whole farm model	Berntsen et al., 2004
GAPS	Dynamic simulation of inter-species competition in agricultural systems	Dynamic model of the soil-plant-atmosphere systems where multiple plant species are grown in competition	Rossiter and Riha, 1999
GROWIT	Millet-cowpea	Generic framework using a spread-sheet for making stochastic dominance comparisons, estimates plant growth by integrating over a continuous growth function depending on air temperature	Lowenberg-DeBoer et al., 1991
INTERCOM	Celery and leek	Process-based eco-physiological model, simulates dynamically competition processes based on physiological. morphological and phenological processes	Baumann et al., 2002
SODCOM	Maize and beans in Kenya	Dynamic and mechanistic model taking especially physiological, morphological and phenological as well as soil moisture components into account	O'Callaghan et al., 1994
STICS	Pea and barley in European organic farming *Gliricidia sepium*, natural pasture C_4 grass and maize/canavalia and maize/ sorghum	Whole field soil-plant atmosphere model over one or several crop cycles, simulates a crop situation for which a physical medium and a crop management schedule can be determined	Brisson et al., 2004; Jensen, 2006
VCROPS	Greenhouse diculture with radish and bushbean	A further developed spatially explicit individual-based mixed crop growth model to simulate individual plant growth and to perform statistical analysis of deterministic and stochastic versions of the model	García-Barrios et al., 2001
WATERCOMP	Maize and sorghum in Central-America	Physically based framework including a radiative transfer model associated with a transpiration-partitioning model with special regard to spatial aspects of root competition at the scale of static root systems	Ozier-Lafontaine et al., 1998
Canopy photo-synthesis model in plant popula-tions	Not specified	Dynamic model for growth and mortality of individual plants in a stand assuming an even-aged plant population which grows in a homogenous environment	Yokozawa and Hara, 1992

continued on following page

Table 1.Continued

Extended IBS-NAT models	Beangrow and Ceres-maize models	Hypothetical crop model of simulating a cereal-legume intercrop dealing with only part of the intercropping phenomenon	Thornton et al., 1990
Model for plant and crop growth allowing for competition for light	Cabbage and carrot	Plant growth model applicable to the isolated plant or to even-aged plants, simple mathematical relation to describe the efficiency of light interception	Aikman and Benjamin, 1994
Radiation transmission model and simple model for intercropping	Maize and bean under semi-arid conditions	Instantaneous, radiation transmission model comparison between a geometrical versus a statistical method, simple model to be employed to develop other cereal-legume intercrop models for semi-arid regions	Tsubo and Walker, 2002; Tsubo et al., 2005

Models dealing with interspecific competition get more and more important as the postulation for sustainable agricultural production has become a global political issue. Traditional farming systems like intercropping or mixed cropping are known to be the embryonic form of sustainable production concerning biodiversity, resource use efficiency and yield stability. As field trials are time consuming and expensive, models are the alternatives. They help decision makers by reducing time and human resources as well as researchers to provide a framework for scientific cooperation (Jones et al., 2003).

Intercropping or competition models can be roughly classified: a) those which are able to model plant growth within a field or even farm scale, taking soil, atmosphere and management information into account in a more dynamic and mechanistic way, and b) those which are more specified or simplified to single intercropping phenomenon like partitioning of solar radiation (Tsubo & Walker, 2002) or self thinning (Yokozawa & Hara, 1992) and are more static and empirical. There are examples for both categories in the literature (Table 1):

a.   ALMANAC
       APSIM
       AUSIM

       FASSET
       INTERCOM
       STICS
b.   Canopy photosynthesis model in plant populations
       Radiation transmission model and simple model for intercropping

Competition between (intercropped) species is mainly competition for water, nutrients and light respectively solar radiation. Furthermore, one can distinguish between above- and below-ground interaction and competition, but also beneficial and synergistic effects can occur (Inal et al., 2007; Li et al., 2001ab; Song et al., 2007; Zhang & Li, 2003). But it is striking that almost all models deal solely with competition for light (Baumann et al., 2002; Brisson et al., 2004; Sellami & Sifaoui, 1999; Tsubo & Walker, 2002; Wiles & Wilkerson, 1991), sometimes in combination with competition for water (Lowenberg-DeBoer et al., 1991; O'Callaghan et al., 1994; Ozier-Lafontaine et al., 1998). Concerning multi-species water and nutrient supply most models use similar or even the same basic and common soil properties, which they use for sole crop situations neglecting aspects and characteristics of competing root systems making some species more efficient for water uptake than others. Beneficial interactions especially for nutrient supply like nitrogen (N), phosphorus (P), potassium (K) and iron (Fe) are rarely taken into account. It is known, however, that the structure and distribution characteristics of roots are more important than their own absorption capacity in the competition for water and solutes (Ozier-Lafontaine et al., 1995).

Light partitioning is the most frequently modeled competition resource. Morphological, physiological and also phenological differences between species decide whether a species has an advantage or a disadvantage in intercropping. In most cases, the earlier developing or the taller species becomes to be the dominant one, the other the understorey. Parts of those understorey species are shaded from the dominant one. The shading impact depends on the species height, their development stage and aggressivity, the duration of competition and the distance from the understorey to the dominant species (row effect). The amount of captured solar radiation decreases for the understorey species and has to be taken into account during modeling. Determinants of light partitioning are vertical dominance and differences in foliage inclination, leaf area and plant height. As solar radiation is reduced, also temperature (Zhang, 2007) within the microclimate of the shaded understorey species can decline as a secondary effect of competition for light.

Light capture ability as well as space occupation influence competition impact and crop performance. Accordingly, radiation models for multispecies canopies can be classified into four groups (Sinoquet & Caldwell, 1995):

1. Geometrical models which schematized plants or rows as simple shapes arranged in space according to the planting pattern.
2. Models based on the turbid layer medium analogy where the canopy structure is described by statistical distributions.
3. Hybrid models combine geometrical shapes as subcanopies envelops with statistical description of leaf area distribution within those envelops.
4. 3D plant descriptions.

For process-oriented models, the turbid layer medium analogy has proven to be the most useful. Almost all simulation models devoted to light partitioning between species are based on the classical Beer's law – but modified for a two-species-purpose - and compute light transmission as a negative exponential function of the downward cumulated leaf area index (LAI) (Table 1).

NEW APPROACH FOR MODELING INTERCROPPING WITH SPECIAL REGARD TO FIELD BOUNDARY CULTIVATION

In the current literature, intercropping was considered either as the performance of a secluded cropping system within one field or area and with a specific species combination like maize/legumes or as a spatially explicit occurrence of interspecific competition between different species, especially crops/weeds. Driving forces for modeling were the geometrical shape or the influence of vertical distribution of leaves of a species (Baumann et al., 2002; Berntsen et al., 2004; Wiles & Wilkerson, 1991), the assumption of a reduced leaf area index of the understorey species when shading of the dominant species occurs (O'Callaghan et al., 1994; Rossiter & Riha, 1999), the dividing of the canopies into three different canopy layers (Brisson et al., 2004; Jensen, 2006; Sinoquet et al., 1990) and to calculate – or better estimate – the incoming solar radiation for both species according to a modified Beer's law, taking crop coefficients, leaf area and the height of the neighboring plant into account.

The approach in this study refers in a first step (scenario 1) to the traditional approach of using competition for solar radiation as baseline model. In a second step (scenario 2 and 3) not only competition for solar radiation was taken into account, but also a more general approach to make it possible to transfer the basic assumptions from one intercropping system to an overall intercropping system by evaluating a minimum data set, easily being collected in a field and not restricted to one area. Special regard was taken to the so called unconscious intercropping or field boundary cultivation, because of its importance in African or Asian countries where intercropping plays a major role and field sizes are very small. Three different scenarios were studied to evaluate the model. Scenario 1 takes only competition for solar radiation into account, scenario 2 deals with changes in soil albedo and scenario 3 includes besides competition for solar radiation also changes in soil temperature.

Field trials (for detailed description of field trials: see next subsection), conducted in southwest Germany and in the North China Plain with different species combination, showed that if synergistic or competition effects of intercropping occur, they are mainly based on border row effects (Table 3). Significant differences in grain yield, dry matter accumulation, leaf area etc. from monocropped in comparison to intercropped species were mostly restricted to the first four rows wherefore intercropping could be regarded as borderline or field boundary effect.

Material and Methods

Field trials were conducted in southwest Germany ($48.46°N$ and $8.56°E$) at the University of Hohenheim's experimental station 'Ihinger Hof' during 2007/08. The average rainfall per year is around 690 mm with an average temperature of $7.9°C$. The soils are mainly keuper with loess layers. Alternate plots of winter wheat and maize were arranged within a restricted randomized complete block design and four replications. Randomization was restricted due to the strip intercropping character of the experiment. Each

Table 2. LER[1], RYT[2], RLO[3] and A_{ab}[4] for inter- and monocropped wheat and maize in 2007/08

	Tinsley, 2004 LER[1]	Jolliffe, 1997 RYT[2]	Jolliffe, 1997 RLO[3]	Li et al., 2001a A_{mw}[4]
borderline	1.30	1.16	1.16	-0.819
3./4. row rp. 2-4 m	0.94	0.97	0.97	
5./6. row rp. 2-4 m	0.94	0.97	0.97	
monocropping	1.00	1.00	1.00	

[1] Land equivalent ratio(LER) (Tinsley, 2004) = $[(Y_{1m}-Y_{1i})+(Y_{2m}-Y_{2i})]/100$

Y_m = yield in monoculture

Y_i = yield in intercropping

1, 2 = first and second crop

[2] Relative yield ratio (RYT) (Jolliffe,1997) = $[(Y_i)_m / (Y_i)_p] + [(Y_j)_m / (Y_j)_m]$

Y = yield

i, j = species 1 and 2

m = species mixture

p = pure stand

[3] Relative land output (RLO) (Jolliffe, 1997) = $(Y_i + Y_j + ...)_m / (Y_i + Y_j + ...)_p$

[4] Aggressivity factor (A_{ab}) (Li et al., 2001a) = $[Y_{ia} / (Y_{sa} * F_a)] - [Y_{ib} / (Y_{sb} * F_b)]$

Y = yield

s = sole cropping

i = intercropping

F = proportion of the area occupied by the crops in intercropping

A, B = crop 1 and 2

Table 3. Results of the statistical analysis to detect differences between rows/subplots with different distances from the field border or differences between monocropped and intercropped plots indicated that intercropping was a field border effect. Rows/subplots sharing no letter are significantly different at α = 5%.

Intercropping system	Grain yield differences between different rows/subplots[1] (t ha^{-1})	
Maize (intercropped with wheat)	Row 1+2[a] to row 3+4[a]	0.1
	Row 1+2[a] to row 5+6[a]	0.2
	Row 1+2[a] to row 7+8[a]	0.4
	Row 3+4[a] to row 5+6[a]	0.03
	Row 3+4[a] to row 7+8[a]	0.5
	Row 5+6[a] to row 7+8[a]	0.5
Maize (intercropped with pea)	Row 1+2[a] to row 3+4[b, c, d]	1.5
	Row 1+2[a] to row 5+6[b, c]	2.0
	Row 1+2[a] to row 7+8[d]	1.2
	Row 3+4[b, c, d] to row 5+6[b, c]	0.5
	Row 3+4[b, c, d] to row 7+8[d]	0.3
	Row 5+6[b, c] to row 7+8[d]	0.8
Maize (intercropped with peanut)	Row 1[a] to row 2[a, b]	0.93
	Row 1[a] to row 3[a, b, c]	1.44
	Row 1[a] to row 4[b, c]	2.57
	Row 1[a] to row 5[c]	2.67
	Row 1[a] to row 6[b, c]	2.53
	Row 1[a] to row 7[b, c]	2.24
	Row 2[a, b] to row 3[a, b, c]	0.51
	Row 2[a, b] to row 4[b, c]	1.63
	Row 2[a, b] to row 5[c]	1.74
	Row 2[a, b] to row 6[b, c]	1.60
	Row 2[a, b] to row 7[b, c]	1.31
	Row 3[a, b, c] to row 4[b, c]	1.13
	Row 3[a, b, c] to row 5[c]	1.24
	Row 3[a, b, c] to row 6[b, c]	1.09
	Row 3[a, b, c] to row 7[b, c]	0.80
	Row 4[b, c] to row 5[c]	0.11
	Row 4[b, c] to row 6[b, c]	0.04
	Row 4[b, c] to row 7[b, c]	0.32
	Row 5[c] to row 6[b, c]	0.15
	Row 5[c] to row 7[b, c]	0.43
	Row 6 to row 7	0,29
Wheat (intercropped with maize)	0-2 m[a] to 2-4 m[b]	3.4
	0-2 m[a] to 4-6 m[b]	3.3
	2-4 m[b] to 4-6 m[b]	0.1
Pea (intercropped with maize)	0-2 m[a] to 2-4 m[a]	0.05
	0-2 m[a] to 4-6 m[a]	0.06
	2-4 m[a] to 4-6 m[a]	0.01
Peanut (intercropped with maize)	Row 1[c, d] to row 2[b, c, d]	0.33
	Row 1[c, d] to row 3[c]	0.10
	Row 1[c, d] to rows 4+5[a, d]	0.67
	Row 1[c, d] to rows 6+7[a, b]	0.81
	Row 1[c, d] to rows 8+9[a]	1.22
	Row 2[b, c, d] to row 3[c]	0.42
	Row 2[b, c, d] to rows 4+5[a, d]	0.34
	Row 2[b, c, d] to rows 6+7[a, b]	0.48
	Row 2[b, c, d] to rows 8+9[a]	0.90
	Row 3[c] to rows 4+5[a, d]	0.76
	Row 3[c] to rows 6+7[a, b]	0.91
	Row 3[c] to rows 8+9[a]	1.32
	Rows 4+5[a, d] to rows 6+7[a, b]	0.15
	Rows 4+5[a, d] to rows 8+9[a]	0.56
	Rows 6+7[a, b] to rows 8+9[a]	0.41

plot was 10 x 10 m for wheat and 12 x 10 m for maize respectively and included five subplots (2 x 10 m) for wheat and eight subplots (2 rows x 10 m) for maize. The previous crop for all species was sugar beet and the soil preparation was a reduced tillage system with a chisel plough. Within each subplot data was collected in order to detect differences between the boundaries, different distances from the boundary and the monocropping. The plots were big enough to reflect monocropping within the central subplots. Wheat was sown in October 2007 with a row spacing of 13 cm, a row orientation from north to south and a plant density of 300 plants per m^2. Maize was sown in May 2008 with a row spacing of 75 cm, a row orientation from north to south and a plant density of 10 plants per m^2. During the growing season, neither water nor nitrogen stress occurred so that differences in plant growth and yield performance could be attributed onto intra- and interspecific competition. Wheat was fertilized with 160 kg N ha^{-1}, splitted into three dispensations (60/60/40) of Nitro-chalk. Maize was fertilized once with 160 kg N ha^{-1} (ENTEC). Plant protection was carried out according to 'Good Agricultural Practice'.

During the growing season, three temporal harvests were carried out and dry matter, ratio of stems to leaves and the nitrogen concentration of plants were analysed. Between flowering and maturity, three time harvest were taken to determine grain weight growing rates. In addition, N$_{min}$ content of soil and number of plants per m^2 were determined. LAI was measured destructively according to the DSSAT guide with the LI-3100 Area Meter (LI-COR, Lincoln/Nebraska USA); soil moisture was measured with the Trime-TDR-system (time domain reflectometry) from IMKO GmbH (Ettlingen/Germany) and soil temperature was determined in 2 and 15 cm soil depth with the testo 925 (Testo AG, Lenzkirch/Germany) on a weekly basis as well as solar radiation, growing stages and plant height. Specific DSSAT cultivar coefficients like the phylochron interval in thermal

days, grain filling duration in thermal days, the standard kernel size related to kernel filling rate and the standard dry-weight of a single tiller at maturity for wheat were determined and yield and yield components were measured after the final harvest. Respectively, phylochron interval, kernel filling rate, maximum possible number of kernels per plant and thermal time from seedling emergence to the end of the juvenile phase expressed in degree days were determined for maize (DS-SAT 4.5). Furthermore, the land equivalent ratio (LER) and an aggressivity factor (A$_{ab}$) (Table 2) were calculated for both the intercropping/field boundary and the monocropping. When A$_{ab}$ > 0, the competitive ability of crop A exceeds that of crop B. Concerning maize and wheat, the agressivity factor (A$_{mw}$) was -0.818 indicating that wheat was the more aggressive competitor and was more successful in catching growing factors, e.g., nitrogen, thus being important for further modeling approaches.

Statistical analysis (Table 3) to detect significance between rows/subplots within a plot with different distances from the plot border was done separately for each species and intercropping system in the trial. Analysis was done using the mixed procedure of SAS 9.2 (SAS Institute, 2009) according the model: trait = replicate + position, assuming independent errors of rows within plots. The factor position had levels depending on treatment (see Table 3). Differences of least squares means for positions were subjected to t-tests. Significant differences found were restricted to the first few rows reflecting the intercropping situation and giving evidence of intercropping being a field border effect (Table 3).

Model Evaluation

For the model approach, the DSSAT crop growth model was applied. It is a process-oriented crop model taking soil-plant-atmosphere and -management systems into account. It is designed for

Table 4. Genetic parameters of wheat and maize and their values used in the model evaluation

winter wheat		
parameters	**description**	**value**
P1V	sensitivity to vernalisation	20
P1D	sensitivity to photoperiod	30
P5	grain filling duration	750
G1	kernel number per unit weight at anthesis	25
G2	kernel weight under optimum conditions	40
G3	standard stem and spike dry weight at maturity	0.5
PHINT	phylochron interval	80

helping researchers to adapt and test the cropping system model itself as well as for those operating the DSSAT model to simulate production over time and space for different purposes (Jones et al., 2003). The collected dataset in this case study was used to evaluate a model extension for intercropping including crop management like fertilization, influence of previous crop (sugar beet), soil and genotype characteristics and weather data (© Hohenheimer Klimadaten). Phenology and growth data were used to evaluate the genetic parameters in a first step (Table 4).

Whereas the genotype and soil characteristics as well as the management did not differ between monocropped and intercropped systems and were taken as constants during simulation, the microclimate changed. Especially the influence of shading and the soil temperature (Figure 2) within the boundaries were different between monocropped and intercropped situations and thus being the basic for the model approach. The

Figure 2. Differences in average soil temperature under monocropped and intercropped wheat in June and July 2008

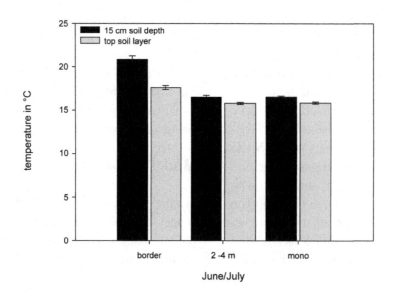

approach was carried out in a stepwise fashion, creating different scenarios. Thus, in a first model run, the identical DSSAT project-oriented programming was used for the intercropping model as well as for the monocropping model except for modified solar radiation. In scenario 2, soil albedo was modified in order to take increased soil temperature into account. In scenario 3, top soil temperature in addition with a higher agressivity factor for wheat was taken furthermore into account including the modification of the initial nitrogen conditions.

The increased ability of intercropped wheat (A_{mw}) to acquire more nitrogen (N) in association with the increased soil temperature coming along with an increased mineralization had to be factored in the modeling. At the field boundary, from sowing date until the sowing of maize in May, wheat faced no interspecific competition and less intraspecific competition. Because of the increased top soil temperature within the first rows – 4°C difference on average - and the higher agressivity of wheat in comparison to maize, our hypothesis was that the mineralization of nitrogen might be favoured and intercropped wheat might get more nitrogen than its monocropped equivalent. The previous crop, sugar beet, had an average N surplus of about 55 kg N ha^{-1} (Reisch & Knecht, 1995) after harvest. As the sugar beet leaves were not removed, they could also be calculated as organic amendment comparable to 140 kg N ha^{-1} (Stammdatenblätter "Nährstoffvergleich Feld-Stall" LEL Schwäbisch (Gmünd et al., 2007). The management system was a reduced tillage system. Lower soil temperature and a reduced mineralization at the beginning of the growing season in comparison to tillage systems are typical for reduced tillage systems (Koeller & Linke, 2001). Collected N$_{min}$-samples after the harvest of wheat showed a similar amount of nitrate in the soil for intercropping (20 kg NO$_3$ ha^{-1}) as well as monocropping (22 kg NO$_3$ ha^{-1}) with only 2 kg NO$_3$ ha^{-1} differences. However, making up the balance between intercropped and monocropped plots

concerning nitrogen proportion and taking N$_{min}$ at the beginning of the growing season, N$_{min}$ after harvest, amount of fertilization and N withdrawal from grain and straw into account, there was a N gap between intercropping and monocropping. Wheat border rows got approximately 130 kg N ha^{-1} more until anthesis. Hence, the changed microclimate within the field boundary might lead to a better N supply of wheat in the first rows (Figure 2).

In comparison to most other modeling approaches, changes in incoming solar radiation were neither calculated according to a modified Beer's law nor by dividing the canopy into different layers nor assuming that LAI was reduced from the time shading occurs. Instead, a linear shading pattern in percentage based on weekly sunlight measurements was determined with regard to the height of neighbouring plants. Solar radiation of monocropped species were set as 0% shading meaning that the monocropping system was driven by the original weather data. Then, the light differences of the border rows in proportion to the monocrops were calculated. The shading pattern was subjected to the plant height of the neighbouring species resulting in a linear function given as:

Shading pattern within wheat: (1a)

$$s = 0.2278h\ 33.417\ (R^2 = 0.6708),$$

with s = shading of wheat border rows (%),

h = plant height of maize.

Shading pattern within maize: (1b)

$$s = -19.724h + 1594.2\ (R^2 = 0.975),$$

with s = shading of maize border rows (%),

h = plant height of wheat.

Logistic models were fitted by nonlinear least squares using the NLIN procedure of the SAS System:

Plant height of wheat: (2a)

$$h = 85.9882/(1 + \exp(4.7888 - 0.059*DAS)),$$
with h = plant height,

DAS = days after sowing.

Plant height of maize: (2b)

$$h = 300.5/(1 + \exp(13.1402 - 0.073*DAS)),$$

with h = plant height,

DAS = days after sowing.

The daily solar radiation (SRAD) expressed in MJ/m²/d was calculated according to (1) and (2) and modified for the weather input as follows:

$$SRADi_{inter/wheat} = SRAD_{mono} -$$
$$((0.2278*(300.5/(1 + EXP(4.7888 + (-0.073)*DAS)))$$
$$-33.417)*SRAD_{mono}/100)$$

$$(3a)$$

$$SRAD_{inter/maize} = SRAD_{mono} -$$
$$((-19.724*(85.9882/(1 + EXP(13.1402 + (-0.059)*DAS)))) + 1594.2)* SRAD_{mono}/100)$$

$$(3b)$$

Summarized, the modeling approach rested not upon introducing a competition sub-model. Instead, the climate and microclimate parameters were modified. Subsequently, the model and the genetic coefficients were evaluated and calibrated for the monocropping system and further used for the intercropping system. The correlation coefficient (R^2) and the root mean square error (RMSE) were used to estimate the variation between simulated and observed values.

Results of Wheat Modeling Experiments

Wheat benefited from being intercropped with maize. Grain yield of intercropped wheat was around 3 t ha⁻¹ higher in comparison to mono-cropped wheat due to a higher number of tillers. The increased tiller number led to an increased dry matter yield of intercropped wheat of about 8 t ha⁻¹ in comparison to monocropped wheat. The thousand kernel weight (TKW) in intercropped wheat was slightly reduced (Table 5).

Scenario 1: Modifying Light Interception

According to most other intercropping models, the DSSAT approach started with modifying the solar radiation as it was expected to be the competition factor with the highest influence on

Table 5. Mean comparisons of grain yield, TKW, tiller number and dry matter of intercropped and monocropped wheat in 2007/08

Treatment	Grain yield (kg [dm] ha⁻¹)	TKW (g)	Tiller number (no./m²)	Dry matter (kg [dm] ha⁻¹)
border rows within a plot	12400[a]	31[b]	864[a]	24506[a]
inner rows within a plot	9054[b]	34[a]	630[b]	16854[b]

[a,b] letters indicate significant differences between borderline (intercropping) and monocropping subplots at $\alpha = 0.05$

crop performance within intercropping systems. A similar approach to the turbid layer medium analogy was used but instead of using a submodel for solar radiation, the weather file in total was changed according to the determined shading pattern algorithms described before (3a) and evaluated throughout measured data.

The monocropping model used the standard weather file and an initial N input of 55 kg N ha^{-1} according to the calculated N surplus due to sugar beet as previous crop. The intercropping model used the modified solar radiation (3a) weather file without changing or modifying any other input parameters like soil, management and cultivar specifics. The results of model evaluation for the monocropped wheat showed a good fit between simulated and observed grain yield as well as dry matter accumulation even though the model did not simulate the slope of the sigmoid curve for grain yield adequately. The R^2 value was 0.96 for grain yield and 0.97 for dry matter yield respectively. Measured grain yield was 9.1 t ha^{-1}, simulated grain yield was 9.0 t ha^{-1}. Measured dry matter yield was 16.9 t ha^{-1}, simulated dry matter yield was 16.7 t ha^{-1}. The RMSE for grain yield at maturity was 49, the RMSE for dry matter accumulation at maturity was 127, indicating a model error of 0.54% and 0.75% respectively.

Running the intercropping model with the modified solar radiation alone only 10.3 t ha^{-1} grain yield was simulated instead of 12.4 t ha^{-1} according to the collected dataset (Table 5). Although the additional solar radiation obtained by the border rows accounted for 1.3 t ha^{-1} additional grain yield, a yield gap of approximately 2 t ha^{-1} remains still unexplained indicating that the increased grain yield could not only be explained by the higher solar radiation wheat border rows obtained until the maize reached a height of 1.4 m and shading occurred up to beginning of July. Similar observations were made for dry matter accumulation. Instead of the measured 24.5 t ha^{-1}, DSSAT simulated only 19.4 t ha^{-1}. The dry matter yield difference between monocropped and intercropped plots was 7.7 t ha^{-1}, but only 2.5 t ha^{-1} additional dry matter could be explained by the higher amount of incoming solar radiation during three-quarters of the growing season. The R^2 value was 0.99 for grain yield and 0.97 for dry matter yield. The RMSE for grain yield at maturity was 2071, the RMSE for dry matter accumulation at maturity was 5083.

Scenario 2: Modifying Light Interception and Soil Albedo

As differences in obtained sunlight could not fully explain the yield gap between monocropped and intercropped subplots, other parameters seemed to have an influence on crop performance. During the growing season there was no water stress so that differences in water availability could be excluded. Between April and August 2008, during co-existence of wheat and maize, there was 450 mm rainfall within 4.5 months. From the end of May until the beginning of July, the average soil moisture (30 cm soil depth) under maize was 48 vol % in both, monocropping and intercropping plots with the minimum value of 36 vol % under monocropped maize in beginning of July and the maximum value of 52 vol % under monocropped maize in beginning of June. In addition, the plots were sown on a relative homogenous field, so that great differences in spatial and temporal yield variability due to soil inhomogeneity dropped, too. However, because of the increased soil temperature and the increase in bare soil placements within the first rows it was assumed that there might have been differences in soil albedo. In the model the reflectance of the solar radiation from the soil surface accounts for potential evaporation from the soil surface. Whereas in the monocropped model the soil albedo value was set to 0.13, in the intercropped version it was reduced to 0.10.

Running the model showed that soil albedo had no great influence on crop performance. Grain yield at maturity increased only 7 kg ha^{-1} and dry matter yield at maturity increased 11 kg ha^{-1}

respectively. Adjusted soil albedo in conjunction with sufficient soil water availability as an indicator for potential evaporation slightly changed performance of plants along field boundaries but could be neglected.

Scenario 3: Modifying Light Interception, Soil Albedo and Initial Conditions

At the field boundary, from sowing date until the sowing of maize in May, wheat faced no inter-specific competition and less intra-specific competition wherefore microclimate changed. Most obvious, incoming solar radiation and top soil temperature increased. In addition wheat had a higher agressivity potential in comparison to maize. Hence, the mineralization of nitrogen was favoured and intercropped wheat got more nitrogen than its monocropped equivalent. Modifying the intercropped model once more, an additional initial N input of 190 kg N ha^{-1} (N_{min} + sugar beet leaves + 40 kg N ha^{-1} surplus) was given, taking the increased mineralization and the competitiveness of wheat into account. The initial condition for intercropped wheat was without limited nitrogen.

As a result, the intercropping model fitted well with R^2 values of 0.98 for dry matter yield and 0.96 for grain yield (Figure 3). The measured dry matter yield was 24.5 t ha^{-1}, the simulated 23.4 t ha^{-1}. The measured as well as the simulated grain yield was 12.4 t ha^{-1}. Wheat border rows used the increased sunlight, but foremost solar radiation in addition to increased N availability could adequately explain the grain yield increase. In comparison to other model approaches, where only solar radiation was taken into account as competition factor, DSSAT showed that other factors have to be regarded when intercropping should be simulated adequately. Otherwise, one competition factor is overestimated. A similar setting was given not only for the grain yield but also for dry matter yield. Running the model without additional N supply and solely with the modified solar radiation input, explained 3.4 t ha^{-1} additional dry matter yield. By contrast, running the model with additional N supply, dry matter yield increased to about 6.5 t ha^{-1}. The RMSE for grain yield at maturity was 2, the RMSE for dry matter accumulation at maturity was 1146, indicating a model error of 0.02% and 4.68% respectively.

Results of Maize Modeling Experiments

Maize intercropped with wheat suffered at the beginning of the growing season because of the competitiveness of wheat and reacted with less plant height ($\sim$ 0.5 m) and less dry matter accumulation (Table 7). But as wheat was harvested around three months earlier than maize, maize showed a recovery-compensation growth, already described by Li et al (2001b), resulting in maize borderline yields (rows at plot borders) at least as high as maize in monocropping (rows in plot centre).

The monocropped model was run taking the measured N_{min} values as well as the N surplus of sugar beet into account. In contrast, the intercropped model was run with N stress at the beginning of the growing season, so starting with less N content in the soil than the monocropped equivalent in order to take into account the increased competitiveness of wheat for N acquisition in comparison to maize. For example, the nitrogen withdrawal from wheat straw from the border rows (76 kg N ha^{-1}) was two times higher than the nitrogen withdrawal from monocropped wheat subplots (35 kg N ha^{-1}). Due to the recovery-compensation growth, the simulation of both monocropped and intercropped maize should be similar to each other (Figure 4), although the intercropping model was run with the modified solar radiation file. The steep slope of grain filling could not be simulated adequately, nevertheless, the simulation of grain yield at maturity showed a good fit between measured and observed grain

Figure 3. Simulated and observed grain yield (A) and dry matter yield (B) of monocropped (♦) and intercropped (∇) wheat in 2007/08 using scenario 3 for intercropped wheat

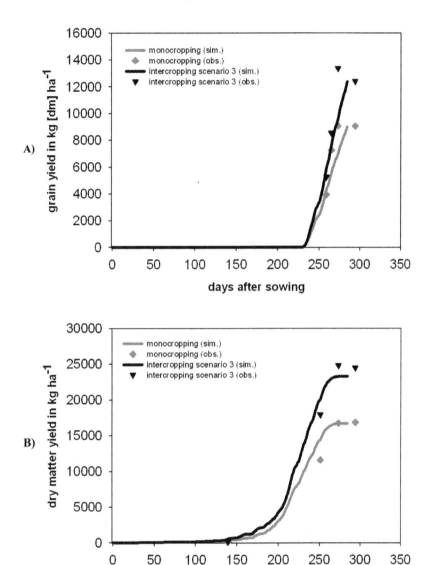

yield. The R^2 value for monocropped maize was 0.83; the R^2 value for intercropped maize was 0.90. Measured grain yield of monocropped maize was 8.9 t ha[-1], simulated grain yield was 8.9 t ha[-1]. The RMSE for grain yield at maturity was 18 for monocropped maize and the RMSE for mean yield was 2017. Measured grain yield of inter-cropped maize was 8.9 t ha[-1], simulated grain yield was overestimated with 9.1 t ha[-1]. The RMSE for grain yield at maturity was 259 for intercropped maize and the RMSE for mean yield was 1353.

The evaluated shading pattern showed a strong shading of intercropped maize until beginning of July and a tanning up to July compared to its

Table 6. R², RMSE, mean observed and simulated values for grain and dry matter yield under different scenarios

Variable	Mean (obs.)	Mean (sim.)	R²	RMSE
Scenario 1: Grain yield (kg ha⁻¹) Dry matter yield (kg ha⁻¹)	9053 14309	6414 12331	0.99 0.97	3351 3192
Scenario 2: Grain yield (kg ha⁻¹) Dry matter yield (kg ha⁻¹)	9053 14309	6419 12338	0.99 0.97	3347 3184
Scenario 3: Grain yield (kg ha⁻¹) Dry matter yield (kg ha⁻¹)	9053 14309	7704 14667	0.96 0.98	2258 1571

monocropped equivalent. Nevertheless, shading at the beginning and tanning at the end of the growing season were restricted to 80 and 20%, respectively, according to measurements. The steep slope of the linear shading pattern might have overestimated those dates. Maize as a C_4 plant could make a much better use of the increased solar radiation than wheat as a C_3 plant. Not the N supply, which was actually even lower for intercropped than for monocropped maize, was responsible for the recovery-compensation growth, but the effective usage of additional solar radiation after wheat harvest.

CONCLUSION

Most intercropping modeling studies were done in the 1990's and at the beginning of 2000. They mark a point where to start from. The various approaches seem to be promising as the validation of the divers models showed. Although a lot of crop growth and weed models have been used to simulate intercropping and interspecific competition, only a few show completely different approaches or ideas how to simulate competition in general. Most often, the turbid layer medium analogy in combination with a modified Beer's law was successfully used, but not applied in succession. Furthermore, the ability to model intercropping is still not introduced in most common process-oriented crop growth models; instead it is often introduced as stand-alone simulation approach. Modeling intercropping should take a step forward from pure modeling to scenario simulation in order to advice crop growers or to improve cropping systems. Park et al. (2003) concluded in a similar way concerning crop-weed models: it is necessary to increase the knowledge of spatial and temporal variability in model parameters if the models' usage should be extended to be more predictive and advisory.

Table 7. Mean comparisons of grain yield, TKW, number of ears/plant, dry matter and LAI of intercropped and monocropped maize in 2007/08

Treatment	Grain yield (kg [dm] ha⁻¹)	TKW (g)	Ear number (no./plant)	Dry matter (kg [dm] ha⁻¹)	LAI
border rows within a plot	8852[a]	261[a]	1.4[a]	14444[b]	2.1[b]
inner rows within a plot	8902[a]	270[a]	1.0[b]	15554[a]	2.9[a]

[a,b] letters indicate significant differences between borderline (intercropping) and monocropping subplots at $\alpha = 0.05$

Figure 4. Simulated and observed grain yield of monocropped (♦) and intercropped (▽) maize in 2007/08

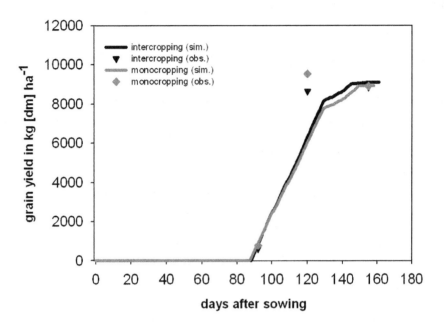

The more statically and empirical models – often no-named – are restricted to model a special effect or phenomenon of intercropping for research use in the main. In contrast, dynamic and mechanistic models which take soil-plant-atmosphere interactions into account like APSIM, INTERCOM and STICS build up an applicative base useful not only for researchers but also for advisers and extension services. Nevertheless, in European, North-American and Australian agriculture, intercropping or smallholder farming is less practiced whereas most models have been evolved in those countries. In addition, modeling the various intercropping systems – and not only maize and legume systems - requires models which include a great number of crops. With 16 integrated species, DSSAT offers a possibility to fulfill those basic requirements. As it is a generic model, other crop models or species can be introduced into DSSAT much easier.

Intercropping is still an up-to-date topic. It is practiced not only in smallholder farming in countries like Africa, India or China, but also in the US. The Alternative Agriculture News titled "Contour strip intercropping can reduce erosion and energy costs" (AANews, March 1994). The American farmer Paul Mugge, who practices strip intercropping with maize and soybean, stated that being profitable, being efficient in the terms of resources, understanding more about ecology and using that understanding (Kendall, 1996, 1997) are his driving forces for doing intercropping. In a comprehensive analysis of our agricultural systems, we should not only examine yields, but also the cost of the inputs used to obtain them. Intercropping may help eliminate unnecessary use of nonrenewable resources in modern agriculture or it may help using these resources more efficiently (Horwith, 1985, p. 289). Models should be extended to more diversified intercropping systems, to a greater variability within countries and to other aspects of intercropping than yield or plant performance, e.g. quality aspects (Andrighetto et al., 1992; Dawo et al., 2007). In addition, the modeling of case studies should be broadened to the modeling and simulating of intercropping scenarios to either study the sustainability potential (e.g., reduced nitrate leaching, reduced fertilizer input) more closely or to adjust and further improve existing cropping systems. That could be done in an inverse way to our model scenario approach: the DSSAT model showed that within an intercropping system of maize and wheat, wheat benefits from its increased nitrogen availability in this system. Hence, less fertilizer may be applied to wheat, reducing leaching and high input costs without reducing yield. Nitrogen scenario simulation could be a possibility to improve the cropping system.

Modeling intercropping with regard to field boundary cultivation broadens the view for unconscious intercropping because of small field size and for patchy agricultural landscapes. There, the amount of field boundaries becomes important and relevant for yield expectance and cultivation practice and hence, for sustainability. In order to model intercropping with special regard to field boundary cultivation, the new model approach with the DSSAT crop growth model showed the possibility to simulate general competition and beneficial effects without introducing a submodel. Instead, shading algorithms were evaluated to modify microclimate and microclimate changes such as incoming solar radiation within field boundaries. In addition, increased soil temperature implicating an increased mineralization and hence a higher N availability for wheat border rows could be taken into account. It is important to consider more than one competition factor like only solar radiation, because species use sunlight more or less efficiently. Different solar radiation amounts could not explain yield differences in all cases. For intercropped maize, solar radiation was an important competition factor. Hence, the recovery-compensation growth could be modeled adequately, because maize could use the increased solar radiation after wheat harvest efficiently even if there was strong shading at the beginning of the maize growing period. In contrast, wheat benefited from the increased solar radiation until flowering

but benefited even more from the increased N availability.

ACKNOWLEDGMENT

The authors' research topic is embedded in the International Research Training Group of the University of Hohenheim and China Agricultural University, entitled "Modeling Material Flows and Production Systems for Sustainable Resource Use in the North China Plain". We thank the German Research Foundation (DFG) and the Ministry of Education (MOE) of the People's Republic of China for financial support.

REFERENCES

Adiku, S. G. K., Carberry, P. S., Rose, C. W., McCown, R. L., & Braddock, R. (1995). A maize (*Zea mays*)-cowpea (*Vigna unguiculata*) intercrop model. In *H. Sinoquet & P. Cruz (Es.), Ecophysiology of Tropical Intercropping* (pp. 397–406). Paris: INRA editions.

Aikman, D. P., & Benjamin, L. R. (1994). A model for plant and crop growth, allowing for competition for light by the use of potential and restricted projected crown zone areas. *Annals of Botany*, *73*, 185–194. doi:10.1006/anbo.1994.1022

Alternative Agriculture News. (1994). Contour strip intercropping can reduce erosion. *AANews*.

Andrighetto, I., Mosca, G., Cozzi, G., & Berzaghi, P. (1992). Maize-soybean intercropping: effect of different variety and sowing density of the legume on forage yield and silage quality. *Journal of Agronomy and Ccrop Science, 168*(5), 354-360.

Ball, D. A., & Shaffer, M. J. (1993). Simulating resource competition in multispecies agricultural plant communities. *Weed Research, 33*, 299–310. doi:10.1111/j.1365-3180.1993.tb01945.x

Baumann, D. T., Bastiaans, L., Goudriaan, J., Van Laar, H. H., & Kropff, M. J. (2002). Analysing crop yield and plant quality in an intercropping system using an eco-physiological model for interplant competition. *Agricultural Systems, 73,* 173–203. doi:10.1016/S0308-521X(01)00084-1

Berntsen, J., Haugaard-Nielsen, H., Olesen, H., Petersen, B. M., Jensen, E. S., & Thomsen, A. (2004). Modelling dry matter production and resource use in intercrops of pea and barley. *Field Crops Research, 88*(1), 59–73. doi:10.1016/j.fcr.2003.11.012

Brisson, N., Bussiére, F., Ozier-Lafontaine, H., Tournebize, R., & Sinoquet, H. (2004). Adaptation of the crop model STICS to intercropping. Theoretical basis and parameterisation. *Agronomie, 24,* 409–421. doi:10.1051/agro:2004031

Caldwell, R. M. (1995). Simulation models for intercropping systems. In *H. Sinoquet & P. Cruz (Es.), Ecophysiology of Tropical Intercropping* (pp. 353–368). Paris: INRA editions.

Carberry, P. S., McCown, R. L., Muchow, R. C., Dimes, J. P., Probert, M. E., Poulton, P. L., & Dalgliesh, N. P. (1996). Simulation of a legume ley farming system in northern Australia using the agricultural production systems simulator. *Australian Journal of Experimental Agriculture, 36,* 1037–1048. doi:10.1071/EA9961037

Dawo, M. I., Wilkinson, J. M., Sanders, F. E. T., & Pilbeam, D. J. (2007). The yield of fresh and ensiled plant material from intercropped maize (*Zea mays*) and beans (*Phaseolus vulgaris*). *Journal of the Science of Food and Agriculture, 87,* 1391–1399. doi:10.1002/jsfa.2879

Federer, W. T. (1993). Statistical design and analysis for intercropping experiments: *Vol. 1. Two crops.* New York: Springer.

García-Barrios, L., Mayer-Foulkes, D., Franco, M., Urquijo-Vásquez, G., & Franco-Pérez, J. (2001). Development and validation of a spatially explicit individual-based mixed crop growth model. *Bulletin of Mathematical Biology, 63,* 507–526. doi:10.1006/bulm.2000.0226

Grant, R. F. (1992). Simulation of competition among plant populations under different managements and climates. *Agron. Abstr, 6.*

Grant, R. F. (1994). Simulation of competition between barley (*Hordeum vulgare L.*) and wild oat (*Avena fatua L.*) under different managements and climates. *Ecological Modelling, 71,* 269–287. doi:10.1016/0304-3800(94)90138-4

Horwith, B. (1985). A role for intercropping in modern agriculture. *Bioscience, 35*(5), 286–290. doi:10.2307/1309927

Inal, A., Gunes, A., Zhang, F., & Cakmak, I. (2007). Peanut/maize intercropping induced changes in rhizosphere and nutrient concentrations in shoots. *Plant Physiology and Biochemistry, 45,* 350–356. doi:10.1016/j.plaphy.2007.03.016

Jensen, E. S. (2006). *Intercrop; Intercropping of cereals and grain legumes for increased production, weed control, improved product quality and prevention of N-losses in European organic farming systems* (Rep. No. QLK5-CT-2002-02352. Risø. Jolliffe, P. A. (1997). Are mixed populations of plant species more productive than pure stands? *Acta Oecologica Scandinavica, 80*(3), 595–602.

Jones, J. W., Hoogenboom, G., Porter, C. H., Boote, K. J., Batchelor, W. D., & Hunt, L. A. (2003). The DSSAT cropping system model. *European Journal of Agronomy, 18,* 235–265. doi:10.1016/S1161-0301(02)00107-7

Kendall, J. (1996/1997). PFI profile: Paul and Karen Mugge. *The practical farmer, 11*(4).

Kiniry, J. R., & Williams, J. R. (1995). Simulating intercropping with the ALMANAC model. In Sinoquet, H., & Cruz, P. (Eds.), *Ecophysiology of Tropical Intercropping* (pp. 387–396). Paris: INRA editions.

Kiniry, J. R., Williams, J. R., Gassman, P. W., & Debaeke, P. (1992). A general process-oriented model for two competing plant species. *Transactions of the ASAE. American Society of Agricultural Engineers, 35*(3), 801–810.

Koeller, K. H., & Linke, C. (2001). *Erfolgreicher Ackerbau ohne Pflug: Wissenschaftliche Ergebnisse – Praktische Erfahrungen*. Frankfurt, Germany: DLG.

Kropff, M. J., & Spitters, C. J. T. (1992). An ecophysiological model for interspecific competition, applied to the influence of *Chenopodium album L.* on sugar beet. I. Model description and parameterization. *Weed Research, 32*, 437–450. doi:10.1111/j.1365-3180.1992.tb01905.x

Kropff, M. J., & van Laar, H. H. (1993). *Modelling crop-weed interactions*. CAB International, in association with the International Rice Research Institute.

Li, L., Sun, J., Zhang, F., Li, X., Rengel, Z., & Yang, S. (2001). Wheat/maize or wheat/soybean strip intercropping II. Recovery or compensation of maize and soybean after wheat harvesting. *Field Crops Research, 71*, 173–181. doi:10.1016/S0378-4290(01)00157-5

Li, L., Sun, J., Zhang, F., Li, X., Yang, S., & Rengel, Z. (2001). Wheat/maize or wheat/soybean strip intercropping I. Yield advantage and interspecific interactions on nutrients. *Field Crops Research, 71*, 123–137. doi:10.1016/S0378-4290(01)00156-3

Lowenberg-De Boer, J., Krause, M., Deuson, R., & Reddy, K. C. (1991). Simulation of yield distributions in millet-cowpea intercropping. *Agricultural Systems, 36*, 471–487. doi:10.1016/0308-521X(91)90072-I

Nelson, R. A., Dimes, J. P., Paningbatan, E. P., & Silburn, D. M. (1998). Erosion/productivity modelling of maize farming in the Philippine uplands part I: Parameterising the agricultural production systems simulator. *Agricultural Systems, 58*(2), 129–146. doi:10.1016/S0308-521X(98)00043-2

O'Callaghan, J. R., Maende, C., & Wyseure, G. L. C. (1994). Modelling the intercropping of maize and beans in Kenya. *Computers and Electronics in Agriculture, 11*, 351–365. doi:10.1016/0168-1699(94)90026-4

Ozier-Lafontaine, H., Bruckler, L., Lafolie, F., & Cabidoche, Y. M. (1995). Modelling root competition for water in mixed crops: a basic approach. In Sinoquet, H., & Cruz, P. (Eds.), *Ecophysiology of Tropical Intercropping* (pp. 189–187). Paris: INRA editions.

Ozier-Lafontaine, H., Lafolie, F., Bruckler, L., Tournebeze, R., & Mollier, A. (1998). Modelling competition for water in intercrops: theory and comparison with field experiments. *Plant and Soil, 204*, 183–201. doi:10.1023/A:1004399508452

Park, S. E., Benjamin, L., & Watkinson, A. R. (2003). The theory and application of plant competition models: an agronomic perspective. *Annals of Botany, 92*, 741–748. doi:10.1093/aob/mcg204

Reisch, E., & Knecht, G. (1995). *Betriebslehre*. Stuttgart, Germany: Ulmer.

Rossiter, D. G., & Riha, S. J. (1999). Modeling plant competition with the GAPS object-oriented dynamic simulation model. *Agronomy Journal, 91*(5), 773–783. doi:10.2134/agronj1999.915773x

SAS Institute. (2009). *The SAS System for Windows (Release 9.2)*. Cary, NC: SAS Institute.

LEL Schwäbisch Gmünd, LTZ Augustenberg, LVVG Aulendorf, LSZ Boxberg, LVG Heidelberg & HuL Marbach. (2007). *Stammdatenblätter Landwirtschaft „Nährstoffvergleich Feld-Stall*. Tabelle 5a.

Sellami, M. H., & Sifaoui, M. S. (1999). Modelling solar radiative transfer inside the oasis; Experimental validation. *Journal of Quantitative Spectroscopy & Radiative Transfer, 63*, 85–96. doi:10.1016/S0022-4073(98)00137-X

Sinoquet, H., & Caldwell, R. M. (1995). Estimation of light capture and partitioning in intercropping systems. In Sinoquet, H., & Cruz, P. (Eds.), *Ecophysiology of Tropical Intercropping* (pp. 79–97). Paris: INRA editions.

Sinoquet, H., Rakocevic, M., & Varlet-Grancher, C. (2000). Comparison of models for daily light partitioning in multispecies canopies. *Agricultural and Forest Meteorology, 101*, 251–263. doi:10.1016/S0168-1923(99)00172-0

Song, Y. N., Marschner, P., Li, L., Bao, X. G., Sun, J. H., & Zhang, F. S. (2007). Community composition of ammonia-oxidizing bacteria in the rhizosphere of intercropped wheat (*Triticum aestivum* L.), maize (*Zea mays* L.) and faba bean (*Vicia faba* L.). *Biology and Fertility of Soils, 44*(2), 307–314. doi:10.1007/s00374-007-0205-y

Thornton, P. K., Dent, J. B., & Caldwell, R. M. (1990). Applications and issues in the modelling of intercropping systems in the tropics. *Agriculture Ecosystems & Environment, 31*(2), 133–146. doi:10.1016/0167-8809(90)90215-Y

Tinsley, R. L. (2004). *Developing smallholder agriculture – a global perspective*. Brussels, Belgium: AgBé Publishing.

Tsubo, M., & Walker, S. (2002). A model of radiation interception and use by maize-bean intercrop canopy. *Agricultural and Forest Meteorology, 110*, 203–215. doi:10.1016/S0168-1923(01)00287-8

Tsubo, M., Walker, S., & Ogindo, H. O. (2005). A simulation of cereal-legume intercropping systems for semi-arid regions. I. Model development. *Field Crops Research, 93*, 10–22. doi:10.1016/j.fcr.2004.09.002

Vandermeer, J. (1989). *The ecology of intercropping*. New York: Cambridge University.

Wiles, L. J., & Wilkerson, G. G. (1991). Modeling competition for light between soybean and broadleaf weeds. *Agricultural Systems, 35*, 37–51. doi:10.1016/0308-521X(91)90145-Z

Yokozawa, M., & Hara, T. (1992). A canopy photosynthesis model for the dynamics of size structure and self-thinning in plant populations. *Annals of Botany, 70*, 305–316.

Zhang, F., & Li, L. (2003). Using competitive and facilitative interactions in intercropping systems enhances crop productivity and nutrient-use efficiency. *Plant and Soil, 248*, 305–312. doi:10.1023/A:1022352229863

Zhang, L. (2007). *Productivity and resource use in cotton and wheat relay intercropping. Chapter 6: Development and validation of SUCROS-Cotton: A mechanistic crop growth simulation model for cotton, applied to Chinese cropping conditions*. Unpublished doctoral dissertation, Wageningen University, The Netherlands.

This work was previously published in International Journal of Information Systems and Social Change, Volume 1, Issue 4, edited by John Wang, pp. 44-65, copyright 2010 by IGI Publishing (an imprint of IGI Global).

Chapter 12

A System Dynamics Approach to Changing Perceptions about Thermal Water Quality Trading Markets

Asmeret Bier
Washington State University, USA

ABSTRACT

Thermal water quality trading markets give point source thermal polluters the option to comply with effluent restrictions by paying nearby landowners to plant shade trees. The shade trees cool the water, offsetting thermal pollution emitted by the point source. Thermal trading has the potential to create greater environmental benefits at a lower cost than traditional regulation, however; only one such program has been implemented to date in the United States. In this regard, a shift in potential stakeholders' perceptions of these markets could be useful in allowing the markets to spread. This paper explains why system dynamics modeling is a useful tool for creating such a shift in perception, and describes a method of teaching participants about thermal trading. The method begins with a classroom simulation exercise, uses lessons from that exercise to create a model of a thermal trading market, and uses that model to conduct policy design and uncertainty analyses.

INTRODUCTION

Thermal water quality trading markets have the potential to create desired water temperature reductions at a much lower cost than conventional policy options. Regardless of this benefit, trading programs have not become widespread. Water quality trading has been used to manage various types of pollution in the United States (Breetz et

al., 2004), but only recently was the first thermal trading program created, on the Tualatin River in Oregon (Clean Water Services, 2004).

One of the major obstacles to the propagation of these markets is landowner participation. Three major barriers to landowner participation have been identified, including perceived complexity of the markets, uncertainty about the cost and effectiveness of the markets, and lack of knowledge

DOI: 10.4018/978-1-4666-0927-3.ch012

about how other market participants and stakeholders might behave (Hosterman, 2008). A change in the overall social perception of these markets may help to reduce these barriers, therefore encouraging the spread of thermal trading as a cost-effective mechanism for decreasing water temperatures.

Models allow low-risk exploration of market dynamics under different scenarios and conditions, and can thus be used to make participants more comfortable with their understanding of potential outcomes of the markets. Models also have the potential to reduce the perceptions of complexity and uncertainty that act as barriers to participation in these markets. This paper explains why system dynamics models can be useful in altering the social perception of thermal water quality trading markets, and also describes an approach that used system dynamics models to teach participants about the potential dynamics of these markets.

This approach began with a classroom simulation, designed to teach participants about thermal water quality trading markets and to allow them to experiment with different trading behaviors and strategies. Debriefing sessions held after the classroom simulations gave insight into how participants made decisions, which informed the creation of a model that simulates trading behavior endogenously. This model was used to explore the dynamics of a thermal water quality trading market under different policy design scenarios. The same model was then used to conduct a simple uncertainty analysis for a thermal water quality trading market. This system dynamics model acted as a system for managing the existing information on these markets, and allowed this information to be used to project the potential dynamics of these complicated systems.

THERMAL WATER QUALITY TRADING

Thermal water quality trading is an emerging policy tool for managing water temperature.

Temperature trading programs give point source thermal polluters the option to comply with effluent restrictions by paying landowners along the same body of water to plant shade trees. The shade trees cool the water, offsetting the thermal pollution emitted by the point source.

Thermal water quality trading programs are likely to use bilateral negotiations market structures, in which the point source and landowner negotiate directly with each other to make trades (Woodward et al., 2002). These markets are also likely to use trading ratios, which weigh different sources of pollution reduction by applying a multiplier to the value of a credit depending on how it was created. To reduce the likelihood of hotspots caused by trading, these policies may also use upstream-only rules, which require each point source to trade only with landowners that are physically located upstream from that source. These markets may allow landowners to sell credits created by other conservation programs, and will generally require landowners to generate some baseline amount of vegetation before they are allowed to sell credits (CTIC, 2006).

Conventionally, water pollution in the United States has been regulated using a command and control approach, in which point sources are issued permits restricting their discharge of specific pollutants. Thermal water quality trading can easily be set up within this system of water quality regulation, by designing pollutant discharge permits so that they allow point sources to comply with regulation through trading.

Trading provides certain benefits over conventional pollution control strategies that make it an attractive means of regulation. First, since planting shade trees is much cheaper than installing refrigeration units onto point sources, trading has the potential to achieve temperature reduction goals in a more cost-effective manner than conventional regulation. A second benefit of trading is the incorporation of nonpoint sources into pollution-reduction policies. A market can create an incentive for landowners, who have not been strictly regulated under conventional water pollution policy, to improve their practices. Finally, shade trees planted through a trading program not only cool the water, but also enhance other ecosystem services by providing riparian habitat, preventing erosion, decreasing nutrient loading, and providing structural fish habitat, among other benefits.

PREVIOUS SIMULATIONS AND EXISTING INFORMATION

Despite the benefits of using trading to control thermal water quality, only one thermal trading program has yet been implemented in the United States. Furthermore, very little information on these markets has been generated (US EPA, 2004; ODEQ, 2005; ODEQ, 2008; CWS, 2004). Information on water quality trading in general, however, is more readily available (US EPA, 2003; US EPA, 2004; US EPA, 2007; Faeth, 2000; CTIC, 2006), and trading has been used to manage many types of water pollution other than thermal pollution (Breetz, 2004).

Two models other than the one described here have been created to simulate thermal water quality trading markets. Rounds (2007) created a spreadsheet model to simulate the spatial variability in water temperature on the Willamette River under various point source-to-point source trading scenarios. Rounds' model also allows different riparian restoration and dam operation scenarios to be included in the analysis. Sandia National Laboratories is currently constructing a model to simulate water temperature in the Willamette River (Tidwell & Lowry, 2008). This model will use a system dynamics platform similar to the one used in the simulation described here to simulate water temperatures under different shading scenarios.

Nguyen and Woodward (2008) created a game called NutrientNet that simulates the economics behind a water quality trading market for nutri-

ents. The game is set up online by an organizer or instructor, and players make trades online to simulate a nutrient trading market. Policy design elements of water quality trading markets have been explored primarily through the use of economic optimization models used to find equations for calculating the trading ratio through which a specified environmental goal can be met at the least cost (Malik et al., 1993; Horan & Shortle, 2005; Horan, 2001; Shortle, 1987; Farrow et al., 2005; Zhang & Wang, 2002).

The simulations described above were meant for scholarly research and teaching. In contrast, the simulations described in this paper were designed to help stakeholders and other participants to better understand thermal water quality trading markets. In addition, unlike the Rounds and Sandia models, this model is not meant to be predictive. Instead, it is meant to help clarify the potential patterns of dynamics that may be involved in a thermal water quality trading market. It focuses not only on water temperature, but also on trading dynamics, hydrology, and tree growth patterns. The Riparian Shading Simulator Exercise is also very different from NutrientNet in that it simulates a temperature, not nutrient, trading market, and focuses on physical as well as economic dynamics. The model described here is also very different from the optimization models that have been used to study policy design, since it is dynamic and not an optimization model.

SYSTEM DYNAMICS MODELING

The tool that was created to inform potential stakeholders about possible outcomes of a thermal water quality trading market is called the Riparian Shading Simulator (RSS). The simulator is a system dynamics model that was created specifically for this analysis using a popular system dynamics software called Vensim (Ventana Systems, Inc., 2005). The model was used for three major purposes, including a classroom simulation, policy design analysis, and uncertainty analysis.

The system dynamics modeling approach was created in the mid-20th century by Jay Forrester (1961), and has since been used in a wide variety of disciplines, including business, economics, education, health care, public policy, energy, and environmental science, among others. Texts by Ford (2009) and Sterman (2000) give overviews of system dynamics modeling.

System dynamics modelers use visual software to create their simulations. The software is used to create stock and flow diagrams that represent the relationships between different components of the system being modeled. The algebraic relationships between variables are also identified and entered into the model. The software uses those relationships to create sets of nonlinear differential equations that represent the structure of the model variables, and then uses numerical integration to simulate the change in each of the model variables over time (Ford et al., 2006). In other words, the software uses the relationships between variables and their initial values to find new values for each model variable after the first time step, repeats this process to find values after the second time step, and so on.

An example of a very simple system dynamics model is shown in Figure 1. This model simulates the hydrology of a reservoir with one river flowing into it and one river flowing out. This is the same structure as that of the river in the RSS, discussed later in the paper. The stock and flow structure of the model, shown in Figure 1a, is a visual representation of the variables that influence the amount of water in the reservoir. Once the stock and flow structure of the system and algebraic relationships between each of the variables are identified, the model creates coupled sets of nonlinear differential equations to represent the system. Figure 1c shows the differential equation that the system dynamics software would create to simulate the reservoir shown in Figure 1a, with

short variable names shown in Figure 1b to make the differential equation clearer.

SYSTEM DYNAMICS MODELS AS TOOLS FOR CHANGING SOCIAL PERCEPTION

The Riparian Shading Simulator (RSS) project required a method of information exchange that would not only address the complex dynamics involved in thermal water quality trading markets, but would also be easily accessible to participants who may not be familiar with modeling. System dynamics modeling has characteristics that make it particularly well suited to a project like this one. First, the stock and flow interface used in system dynamics modeling helps to make these models accessible to anyone familiar with the system being modeled, regardless of the user's familiarity with modeling. For instance, Beall and Zeoli (2008) found that stakeholders taking part in a participatory modeling project were able to easily grasp the structure of a salmon population model based on a stock and flow diagram, without any prior modeling experience.

System dynamics models are also often used in concert with user-friendly interfaces that make interaction with the model intuitive even for a user who is not interested in how the model itself is designed. These interfaces generally allow the user to choose the values of key variables in the model, so that desired scenarios can be simulated. These models run very quickly, usually simulating the entire time horizon within seconds, so many different combinations of variables can be analyzed quickly and relatively easily, even by a novice user. For instance, policy variables can be set up so that the user chooses policy options using the interface to learn how a policy might work under different designs. The RSS makes use of this function, and also allows the user to manipulate uncertain variables like climate change and weather.

Figure 1. a) System dynamics model of a reservoir with one inflow and one outflow; b) Model with short names; c) Model in differential equation form

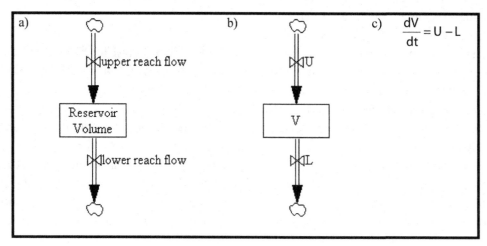

The use of a dynamic modeling paradigm was also beneficial for this project. System dynamics models allow users to see how key variables are likely to change over time. Thermal water quality trading involves major time lags, such as the lag between trees being planted and reaching a size that allows them to substantially cool the water. Trading also takes time to accomplish, and trading behavior is likely to depend on the course of previous events. A non-dynamic modeling paradigm could have been used, but may have neglected these time-dependent factors.

The interdisciplinary capability of system dynamics modeling was also beneficial for this project. The RSS included economic, thermodynamic, hydrologic, and other sectors. Other modeling paradigms might use separate, linked models to simulate these components. System dynamics, however, has the capability of including all of these disciplines in the same model. Since the model simulates stocks and flows, anything that can be represented in this way can be included in a system dynamics model. For example, in the RSS, stocks included a reservoir, bank accounts for landowners and wastewater treatment plants, and heat stored in each river reach. Since the model was able to encompass all of these variables, model

users were able to consider the system as a whole, allowing them to use a systems thinking (Senge, 1990; Kamppinen et al., 2008) perspective.

System dynamics modeling is useful in simulating systems whose behavior is driven by the underlying structures of those systems and feedbacks that exist within those structures. It is particularly useful in modeling systems that are interdisciplinary, involve long time spans, and have distinctive dynamics (Meadows & Robinson, 2007), all of which are characteristics of thermal water quality trading programs. While other modeling paradigms might be useful for analyzing thermal water quality trading policies, system dynamics modeling, for the reasons above, is an ideal tool for creating models intended to teach stakeholders about issues involved with prospective policies.

THE RIPARIAN SHADING SIMULATOR PROJECT

The Riparian Shading Simulator (RSS) Project involved a process of modeling and analysis that led to considerable insight on how the dynamics of a thermal water quality trading market might develop. The project began with a classroom simulation exercise that allowed participants to share their decision-making processes. These processes were then added to a system dynamics model, which was used for policy design and uncertainty analyses.

The RSS Project began with a classroom simulation exercise that was used to teach players about the structure, dynamics, and potential benefits and drawbacks of a thermal water quality trading market, while allowing the model designers to learn how participants might make decisions in one of these markets. System dynamics and other simulation models are often used to create games (Meadows, 2007; Galvão, 2000), which are useful both in creating a common experience between players (Ryan, 2000) and in encouraging participants to think about a market as it works within the larger system.

Participants in the RSS classroom simulation exercise were first taught how a thermal water quality trading market might be designed, and how the exercise would be run. They were given roles, with each player acting as either a landowner or a wastewater treatment plant. The plant and land-owner participants negotiated directly with each other to make trades. This helped the participants to understand the intricacies of a trading policy, and allowed them to experience some of the uncertainties involved with thermal water quality trading markets. Since participant behavior can have a major impact on how the dynamics of the market unfold, this exercise allowed the players to develop contextual trading strategies.

When a buyer and seller agreed upon a trade, the trade decision was entered into a model. An early version of the RSS model, described later in this section, was used to run the classroom simulation exercise. This model simulated the physical dynamics of the river system, including hydrology, heat flows, and the growth of shade trees along the simulated river. The social dynamics of the system, and trading in particular, were simulated by participants in the classroom exercise. This causal

structure of the simulation is shown in Figure 2, with participants' decisions shaded.

The Riparian Shading Simulator Exercise was played three times, with 10 to 25 participants in each exercise. The first was with undergraduate students taking a system dynamics modeling class, the second with a combination of undergraduate and graduate students in a green economics class, and the last with graduate students taking a class on science and public policy. Each simulation ended with a debriefing session, in which participants discussed their thoughts on the exercise, thermal water quality trading, and their particular trading strategies. These discussions were ripe with insight on how people might make decisions in a thermal water quality trading market. By talking with participants in the classroom simulation exercise, the model designers were able to create a new version of the RSS model that simulated not only the physical dynamics of the system, but also trading behavior.

The information about trading behavior that was learned from these debriefing sessions was used to enhance the RSS model by adding trading to the simulation. The new version of the model simulated not only the physical dynamics of a thermal water quality trading market, but also the trading dynamics created by human behavior, and the interactions between the two. Market participants in the updated model make trade decisions based on the current state of the system, and their decisions in turn affect the physical dynamics of the system.

The RSS model was created using Vensim DS software (Ventana Systems, Inc., 2008) on a Windows operating system. The river simulated in the RSS model is hypothetical, with a simple hydrologic structure that includes an upstream and a downstream section with a reservoir between the two (Figure 1). Heat flows are simulated for each section of the river, as well as for the reservoir. These heat flows are affected by weather and hydrology, as well as by the amount of shading provided along the river. This shading is deter-

Figure 2. Causal loop structure of the classroom simulation exercise, with participants' decisions shaded

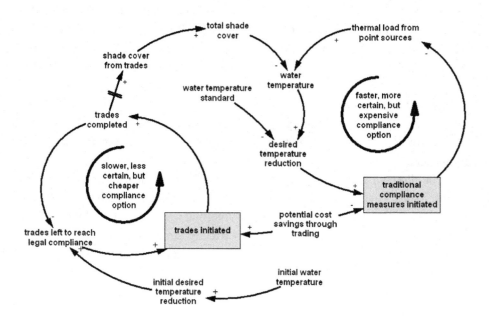

mined by geology, vegetation initially in the area, and vegetation created by the trading program. The trading behavior sector of the model takes into consideration the comments made by participants in the classroom simulation exercises. A sector diagram of the RSS model is shown in Figure 3. A simplified diagram of the credit price sector of the model is shown in Figure 4 as an example of the model structure.

The model was designed so that the user can easily choose policy design and uncertain physical variables depending on the scenario in which they are interested. The user chooses two policy design variables, the trading ratio and upstream-only rule. The user can also choose whether to include climate change and weather-related stochasticity in the model. Finally, the user can decide where the balance of bargaining power falls between buyers and sellers in the market, which determines the price of a trade and therefore influences the way that trading unfolds. By allowing all of these options, the model becomes an adaptable tool, so that the same model can be used for different types of analysis. The model interface

is shown in Figure 5, with shade and water temperature outputs shown for the base case scenario in which no stochasticity is included, a 2:1 trading ratio is implemented, and there is no upstream-only rule.

The updated version of the RSS model was used for two analyses, the first of which studied the design of thermal water quality trading policies. The design of one of these markets can have important repercussions on the outcomes of the policy. If an appropriate number of trades at proper prices do not occur, both the cost-effectiveness and the environmental benefits of a market might be affected. Since these are two of the main benefits of markets over conventional regulation, problems with effectiveness and cost-effectiveness could be detrimental to a market. The RSS was used to learn about how variations in trading ratios and upstream only rules might affect the dynamics of a thermal water quality trading market.

Much of the discussion on the development of water quality trading markets has revolved around how to set trading ratios. When a trading

Figure 3. Sector diagram of the Riparian Shading Simulator (RSS) model

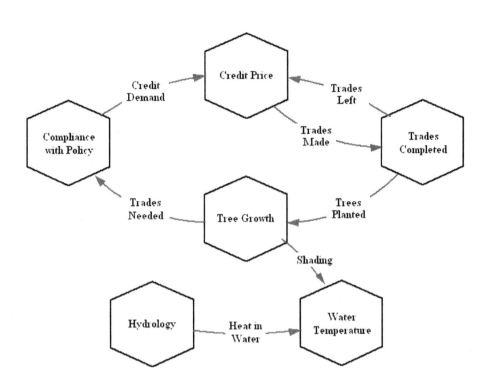

Figure 4. Simplified diagram of the credit price sector of the Riparian Shading Simulator (RSS) model

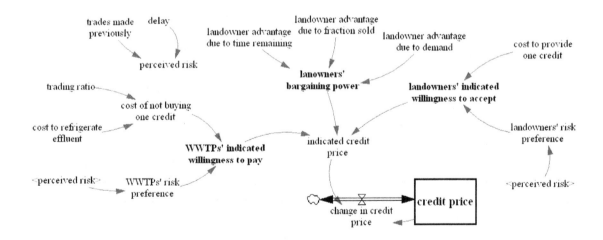

ratio is used in a water quality trading market, the value of a credit is weighted based on how the credit is created. For instance, credits generated by nonpoint sources are often valued less than credits generated by point sources, because of the perception that more uncertainty is involved when pollution reduction comes from nonpoint sources. A higher trading ratio will require point sources

Figure 5. Model interface with base case shade and water temperature outputs

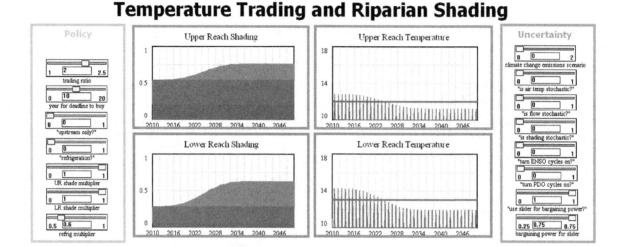

of pollution to make more trades to remain in compliance with pollution regulation, so that the total cost of compliance with the trading policy increases as the trading ratio increases.

Another major policy design issue for thermal water quality trading markets is determining whether there will be geographic limitations on trading. Such limitations are likely to involve rules that require trades to be conducted only upstream from the point source involved in a trade. These upstream-only rules are designed to avoid hotspots created by a water quality trading market, since trades made downstream of the point source might leave an area of uncontrolled pollution in the water body. Upstream-only rules, like trading ratios, have the potential to significantly impact the outcomes of a trading program. They can concentrate trades in specific areas, effectively keeping pollution reduction activities away from other areas. These rules must be carefully implemented so as not to create unintended hotspots.

Uncertainty is another major concern in thermal water quality regulation, regardless of whether conventional pollution control technologies or water quality trading is used to reach thermal pollution reduction goals. Sources of uncertainty include physical factors, such as weather, hydrol-

ogy, and climate change, as well as disturbances like floods and fires. Social factors can also contribute to uncertainty, since participant behavior, trading patterns, and even the continuance of the policy are all unknown. Trading ratios have been the primary method of dealing with uncertainty in water quality trading markets in the United States (US EPA, 2003).

The final use of the RSS model was an uncertainty analysis. Climate change, the first source of uncertainty considered in this analysis, is likely to impact weather-dependent variables in a thermal water quality trading market, including air temperature, inflows of water to the hydrologic system, and tree growth. The second source of uncertainty considered was stochasticity in weather-related variables. Like climate change, this stochasticity affects the modeled air temperature, inflows, and tree growth. The final uncertain variable included in this analysis was the balance of bargaining power between landowners and wastewater treatment plants, which affects the price of a trade and therefore how many trades are made at any given point in time. These sources of uncertainty were included in the model by adding random normal multipliers to the appropriate variables. These multipliers were based on data and projections for the northwestern United States (Mote et al., 2008; Climate Impacts Group, 2009; Climate Impacts Group, 2004). The design of this uncertainty analysis was quite simple. For each source of uncertainty, two or three possible scenarios were chosen. The model was run with all combinations of these scenarios, so that the effects of each source of uncertainty could be analyzed both alone and in combination with the other sources of uncertainty.

BENEFITS OF THIS METHOD OF POLICY ANALYSIS

The combination of system dynamics-based methods used in this project proved to be an interesting way to gain and share understanding about thermal water quality trading markets. The research began with the creation of a classroom simulation. This simulation was run with three different groups of participants, who then shared their decision making strategies with the researchers. The insight gained from this process was used to develop a model that simulated the physical and trading dynamics of a thermal water quality trading market. This model was used to simulate the outcomes of one of these policies under various policy designs, and was also used to run an uncertainty analysis.

This series of methods gave substantial insight into how the dynamics of a thermal water quality trading market might unfold. Only one such market has been implemented so far in the United States, and one of the main obstacles to the propagation of these markets is convincing landowners to participate. The three major barriers to landowner participation are complexity, uncertainty, and lack of knowledge about other participants (Hosterman, 2008).

The classroom simulation was used to teach participants about potential market structures, which helped to reduce the perception that thermal

water quality trading markets must be complex. By simulating a thermal trading market, participants were able to come away with a better understanding of their own motivations for decision making, as well as those of their colleagues. The policy design analysis allowed exploration of potential market outcomes under many different scenarios and policy designs, helping to give insight about the uncertainties involved in one of these markets and their potential impacts on the outcomes of such a policy. Uncertainty was further studied with the uncertainty analysis that was run with the RSS model, and participant behavior was explored using the classroom simulation. This series of methods was therefore able to address all of the major barriers to landowner participation in a thermal water quality trading market.

All of this work was done with one system dynamics model. The model was modified to suit each particular use, but much of the structure of the model remained the same. System dynamics proved to be a very useful modeling paradigm for this work, combining the potential for a user-friendly interface, interdisciplinary capability, and quick simulation of dynamic patterns.

CONCLUSION

The Riparian Shading Simulator has the potential to increase stakeholder familiarity with thermal water quality trading markets, thus reducing barriers to participation in these markets. The combination of simulations available under the Riparian Shading Simulator should be considered as a tool for introducing these and other markets to potential stakeholders. The classroom simulation proved to be a useful tool for giving participants a good understanding of the dynamics of a trading program and its effect on the environmental system that it is meant to protect. A policy design analysis can help to identify institutions that can be put in place to deal with uncertainty. Finally, uncertainty analysis can help users to understand how uncertain input variables might affect the system, and can also help to find the policy design that can best deal with uncertainty. Taken together, this combination of analyses proved to be an interesting method of giving participants the information required to broaden their perspectives, and potentially change their views on thermal water quality trading markets.

FUTURE WORK

This approach to modeling thermal water quality trading markets has so far primarily involved participation by students and researchers. Running the classroom simulation exercise with potential stakeholders in a new thermal water quality trading market would be useful both in teaching those stakeholders about these markets and in gaining new knowledge about decision making strategies. These strategies could then be added to the Riparian Shading Simulator model to strengthen the trading simulation. Sharing the model with potential stakeholders to conduct more project-specific policy design and uncertainty analyses could also be useful, especially in the early stages of program planning. This might also be done with a redesigned model calibrated to a particular river and trading program.

A similar research method could easily be designed for studying other types of market-based policies. For example, carbon markets have been explored using system dynamics models (for example, Ford, 2005) and games (for example, Jones, 2009), and the sequence used for the RSS project could help to link these together. This approach could be used to examine water quality trading policies for other pollutants, such as nutrient trading, as well as other types of pollution markets.

REFERENCES

Beall, A., & Zeoli, L. (2008). Participatory modeling of endangered wildlife systems: simulation the sage-grouse and land use in central Washington. *Ecological Economics*, *68*, 24–33. doi:10.1016/j.ecolecon.2008.08.019

Breetz, H. L., Fisher-Vanden, K., Garzon, L., Jacobs, H., Kroetz, D., & Terry, R. (2004). *Water quality trading offset initiatives in the US: A comprehensive survey*. Hanover, NH: Dartmouth College.

Clean Water Services (CWS). (2004). *Revised temperature management plan*. Retrieved June 7, 2009, from http://www.cleanwaterservices.org/PlansAndProjects/Plans/TempManagementPlan.aspx

Climate Impacts Group. (2004). *Forest growth and climate change*. Seattle, WA: University of Washington.

Climate Impacts Group. (2009). *Climate change streamflow scenario tool*. Seattle, WA: University of Washington. Retrieved June 7, 2009, from http://cses.washington.edu/cig/fpt/ccstreamflowtool/sftscenarios.shtml

Conservation Technology Information Center (CTIC). (2006). *Getting paid for stewardship: An agricultural community water quality trading guide*. West Lafayette, IN: Conservation Technology Information Center.

Faeth, P. (2000). *Fertile ground: Nutrient trading's potential to cost-effectively improve water quality*. Washington, DC: World Resources Institute.

Farrow, R. S., Scheltz, M. T., Celikkol, P., & Van Houtven, G. L. (2005). Pollution trading in water quality limited areas: Use of benefits assessment and cost-effective trading ratios. *Land Economics*, *81*(2), 191–205.

Ford, A. (2005, July). Simulating the impact of a carbon market on the electricity system in the western USA. In *Proceedings of the International Conference of the System Dyamics Society,* Nijmegen, The Netherlands.

Ford, A. (2009). *Modeling the environment: An introduction to system dynamics modeling of environmental systems* (2nd ed.). Covelo, CA: Island Press.

Ford, A., Vogstad, K., & Flynn, H. (2006). Simulating price patterns for tradable green certificates to promote electricity generation from wind. *Energy Policy, 35*(1), 91–111. doi:10.1016/j.enpol.2005.10.014

Forrester, J. W. (1961). *Industrial dynamics.* Waltham, MA: Pegasus Communications.

Galvão, J. R. (2000, December). Modeling reality with simulation games for cooperative learning. In *Proceedings of the 2000 Winter Simulation Conference,* Orlando, FL.

Horan, R. D. (2001). Differences in social and public risk perceptions and conflicting impacts on point/nonpoint trading ratios. *American Journal of Agricultural Economics, 83*(4), 934–941. doi:10.1111/0002-9092.00220

Horan, R. D., & Shortle, J. S. (2005). When two wrongs make a right: Second-best point-nonpoint trading ratios. *American Journal of Agricultural Economics, 87*(2), 340–352. doi:10.1111/j.1467-8276.2005.00726.x

Hosterman, H. (2008). *Incorporating environmental integrity in water quality trading: Lessons from the Willamette. Masters project.* Duke University, Nicholas School of the Environment and Earth Sciences.

Jones, A. (2009). *The Copenhagen Climate Game.* Retrieved June 7, 2009, from http://sustainer.org/climate_change/documents/copenhagen.pdf

Kamppinen, M., Vihervaara, P., & Aarras, N. (2008). Corporate responsibility and systems thinking – Tools for balanced risk management. *International Journal of Sustainable Society, 1*(2), 158–171. doi:10.1504/IJSSOC.2008.022572

Malik, A. S., Letson, D., & Crutchfield, S. R. (1993). Point/nonpoint source trading of pollution abatement: Choosing the right trading ratio. *American Journal of Agricultural Economics, 75,* 959–967. doi:10.2307/1243983

Meadows, D. (2007). A brief and incomplete history of operational gaming in system dynamics. *System Dynamics Review, 23*(2-3), 199–203. doi:10.1002/sdr.372

Meadows, D. H., & Robinson, J. M. (2007). *The electronic oracle: Computer models and social decisions.* Albany, NY: System Dynamics Society.

Mote, P., Salathé, E., Duliére, V., & Jump, E. (2008). *Scenarios of future climate for the Pacific Northwest.* Seattle, WA: University of Washington, Climate Impacts Group.

Nguyen, T. N., & Woodward, R. T. (2008). *NutrientNet: An internet-based approach to teaching market-based policy for environmental management.* Retrieved June 7, 2009, from http://ssrn.com/abstract=1134163

Oregon Department of Environmental Quality (ODEQ). (2005). *Water quality trading: Internal management directive (Version 1.0).* Portland, OR: Oregon Department of Environmental Quality.

Oregon Department of Environmental Quality (ODEQ). (2008). *Water quality trading in Oregon: A case study report.* Retrieved June 7, 2009, from http://www.deq.state.or.us/wq/trading/docs/wqtradingcasestudy.pdf

Rounds, S. A. (2007). *Temperature effects of point sources, riparian shading, and dam operations on the Willamette River, Oregon* (Scientific Investigations Rep. No. 2007-5185). U.S. Geological Survey.

Ryan, T. (2000). The role of simulation gaming in policy-making. *Systems Research and Behavioral Science, 17*, 359–364. doi:10.1002/1099-1743(200007/08)17:4<359::AID-SRES306>3.0.CO;2-S

Senge, P. (1990). *The fifth discipline: The art and practice of the learning organization*. New York: Doubleday.

Shortle, J. S. (1987). Allocative implications of comparisons between the marginal costs of point and nonpoint source pollution abatement. *Northeastern Journal of Agricultural and Resource Economics, 16*(1), 17–23.

Sterman, J. (2000). *Business dynamics: Systems thinking and modeling for a complex world*. Chicago: Irwin/McGraw-Hill.

Tidwell, V., & Lowry, T. (2008). *Personal communication*. Albuquerque, NM: Sandia National Laboratories.

U.S. Environmental Protection Agency (US EPA). (2003). *Water quality trading policy*. Washington, DC: U.S. Environmental Protection Agency, Office of Water.

U.S. Environmental Protection Agency (US EPA). (2004). *Water quality trading assessment handbook: Can water quality trading advance your watershed's goals? (EPA 841-B-04-001)*. Washington, DC: U.S. Environmental Protection Agency.

U.S. Environmental Protection Agency (US EPA). (2007). *Water quality trading toolkit for permit writers (EPA 833-R-07-004)*. Washington, DC: U.S. Environmental Protection Agency, Office of Wastewater Management, Water Permits Division.

Ventana Systems, Inc. (2005). *Vensim DSS*. Version 5.5c.

Woodward, R. T., Kaiser, R. A., & Wicks, A. B. (2002). The structure and practice of water quality trading markets. *Journal of the American Water Resources Association, 38*(4), 967–979. doi:10.1111/j.1752-1688.2002.tb05538.x

Zhang, W., & Wang, X. J. (2002). Modeling for point-non-point source effluent trading: Perspective of non-point sources regulation in China. *The Science of the Total Environment, 292*, 167–176. doi:10.1016/S0048-9697(01)01105-6

This work was previously published in International Journal of Information Systems and Social Change, Volume 1, Issue 3, edited by John Wang, pp. 1-12, copyright 2010 by IGI Publishing (an imprint of IGI Global).

Chapter 13
Reports from the Field:
Assessing the Art and Science of Participatory Environmental Modeling

Allyson M. Beall
Washington State University, USA

Andrew Ford
Washington State University, USA

ABSTRACT

Since the work of Tansley (1935) and others, many have embraced the concept that an ecosystem is a synergy of its parts. Numerous science-centric approaches have been developed to address ecosystem management, while also taking into account the needs of the public. Participatory environmental modeling using system dynamics is an effective process for facilitating the integration of ecosystem science and social concerns. This integration helps break barriers between disciplines while also identifying important feedbacks between traditionally segregated types of data. Using the art of facilitation and the science of model building, the methodology creates a common language that integrates various types of information into simulation models. This paper describes a diversity of case studies, that have used system dynamics to create platforms through which stakeholders can simultaneously explore their system, stressors to that system, potential tipping points, resilience, and prospective policies that address the environment, social concerns, and long-term sustainability.

INTRODUCTION

As the natural world has become dominated by human influences, environmental problems have become increasingly complex. In the United States, many laws (NEPA, CWA, CWA, ESA) endeavor to protect the environment while at the same time consider the economic and social needs of the nation's human population. Yet the diversity of local situations often leaves both agency personnel and the public frustrated with laws and regulations that do not effectively address long term sustainability or the specificities of locale. In addition, since the early work of Tansley (1935) and others we have embraced the concept that an ecosystem is a synergy of its parts and the relationship between those parts. In an effort to support the ecosystem concept and improve

DOI: 10.4018/978-1-4666-0927-3.ch013

or sustain environmental and social quality a number of problem-solving processes have been developed and implemented with varying degrees of success. These include the NEPA assessment process, adaptive management, shared vision planning and state and local planning processes. One critical element that has emerged from these science-centric approaches is that public involvement in the problem-solving process is essential. Furthermore eliminating barriers between science and society is essential if we are to confront the multitude of real world problems that we face (Wang, 2008). Public participation invites a variety of information, knowledge, opinions and worldviews into the decision-making process. Creating a nexus of science and local knowledge through which problems and solutions may be discussed is essential for finding consensus-based solutions to environmental problems.

Participatory environmental modeling that uses system dynamics (SD) is effective for facilitating the integration of natural resource science and social concerns. Using the art of facilitation and the science of model building the methodology creates a common language that integrates various types of information into simulation models. For example information that has been created through Geographic Information Systems (GIS) modeling, hydrologic system modeling (e.g., MODFLOW), population modeling (e.g., Population Viability Analysis, PVA), or economics can be integrated with experiential knowledge and the values of stakeholders into computer models that may be used for exploring potential futures of dynamic systems. Using SD theory for creating this integration adds a powerful means to feedback discovery and analysis between data types. SD allows us to integrate data from various information systems into easy to use, transparent platforms that allow users to investigate potential future scenarios.

Collaboratively built models assist stakeholders with problem definition and evaluation of potential management or policy alternatives. The process of building a model helps stakeholders

clarify their own mental models, better understand those of others, and gain a better understanding of important scientific relationships. The process of evaluating simulation results allows participants to explore "what if" scenarios that depict potential futures. The combination of problem definition, mental model clarification and futures exploration helps participants better understand the scope of a system, potential tipping points and how the system behaves over time. In doing so the barriers between social sciences and natural sciences, between theoretical and applied science and between science and experiential knowledge may be reduced. Furthermore the process requires scientists to interact with decision makers and the lay public. The groups must learn to develop a shared language and understanding of the system in order to create a model. Decision makers and the public become better versed in science; scientists become better versed at the challenges faced by decision makers and the public. And though the results of such processes may be very difficult to measure few would argue "when one part of society offers its services to another, most likely both parties will benefit" (Wang, 2008, p. 2).

This paper recognizes that processes designed for community-based interventions will vary according to the idiosyncrasies of the problem. The availability of quantitative data, types of participation, the timing and length of the intervention, and other variables create challenges for both process design and the comparison of processes. Due to this large degree of variation, the goal of the analysis that follows is to learn about the variety of techniques and a broad range of interventions through an examination of case studies. The diversity of these case studies and the inventiveness of the practitioners to adjust their efforts to the needs of the stakeholders and the environmental problems they are facing illustrates the flexibility of participatory modeling. The art of participatory modeling requires practitioners to develop an understanding of stakeholder values, translate scientific information, and relationships, and well as building model interfaces that are illuminating and educational. The scientific requirements of participatory modeling practitioner include both having an understanding of the scientific issues surrounding the resource of concern and being able to design mathematically correct yet simple and easy to follow parameters and relationships into a transparent and defensible model. Participatory modelers who use SD create customized, transparent information systems through which stakeholders can simultaneously explore their system, stressors to that system, potential tipping points, whether it is fragile or resilient, and any variety of potential policies that address the environment, social concerns, and long-term sustainability.

System Dynamics and Participatory Environmental Modeling

System dynamics (SD) was developed in the early 1960's by Jay Forrester (1961) as a methodology that could be used to gain understanding about the dynamics of any system. "System dynamics can provide that dynamic framework to give meaning to detailed facts, sources of information, and human responses. Such a dynamic provides a common foundation beneath mathematics, physical science, social studies, biology, history and even literature" (Forrester, 1991, p. 27). Meadows (1972, p. 4) maintains that system dynamics training helps "us to see the world as a set of unfolding behavior patterns." System dynamics teaches us to shift our focus from single pieces of a system to the connections between those pieces.

When faced with multi-stakeholder environmental issues, system dynamics has the greatest potential when used in a participatory fashion by scientists and managers working together with others who also have a stake in land management decisions. SD modeling software (e.g., VENSIM, STELLA or POWERSIM) provides modelers and process participants transparent, user friendly, icon based simulation programs.

The models simulate system behavior through the use of stock and flow icons that create a "coupled set of nonlinear differential equations, with a separate differential equation for each stock in the model. The differential equations are "solved" through numerical integration, an approach which is valued in a many disciplines, ranging from ecology to economics" (Ford, 2005, p. 485). The SD paradigm "recognizes all systems as having the same fundamental structure of levels and rates (accumulations and flows) structured into feedback loops that cause all changes through time" (Forrester, 1994, p. 251). While static models advance understanding of systems at rest by providing snapshots of a particular moment, dynamic models provide insight as to how a system changes. Dynamic patterns such as growth, decay and oscillations are the fundamentals of system behavior thus the methodology is useful for exploring system resilience, tipping points, sustainability and for understanding the issues that create limits to growth (Meadows et al., 1972; Ford, 2009).

Participatory environmental modeling is a process that has developed out of the need for public participation, systems thinking and simulation modeling. It is covered under a number of monikers: participatory modeling (Videira, 2003, Langsdale, 2006); Mediated Modeling (van den Belt et al., 1998); cooperative modeling (Cockerill et al., 2006); collaborative modeling; and Computer Assisted Dispute Resolution or CADRe (USACE, 2007).

Modelers in the case studies outlined in this paper have drawn on simulation and group modeling techniques including those of: Forrester (1961, 1969); Meadows et al. (1972); Richardson and Pugh (1981); Roberts et al. (1983); Vennix (1994); Ford (2009); and Sterman (2000, 2002). Cited works include but were not limited to: Morecroft and Sterman (1994); Richardson and Anderson (1995); Vennix (1996, 1999); Anderson and Richardson (1997); Hines (2001); Rouwette et al. (2002); Stave (2002); Rouwette (2003) and van den Belt (2004).

Methodology for Comparison of Case Studies

The number of stocks contained in a model was selected as a proxy for problem complexity and was compared to the need of the process, the time spent, and number of groups involved. This led to questions that inspired an assessment of the following characteristics: 1) Stakeholder involvement in the model building process varies on the "hands on" continuum. 2) Interventions may take place anywhere on the "problem definition to solution producing" continuum. 3) The type of data required varies on the "qualitative to quantitative" continuum. Model and process characteristics often drive one another, creating a need for concurrent evaluation of these characteristics. This paper describes the case studies, participatory model building methodology and the purpose of the models. The impact of the model purpose on the process brings to light two patterns of iterative model building. These patterns are also impacted by problem complexity, the need for and availability of data, and the individual techniques of the modelers.

Case Studies

Nine case studies have been chosen to compare models and group processes to better understand both their homogeneity and diversity. Three of the case studies are specifically concerned with wildlife management, six with water issues. The dominance of water models is indicative of natural resource conflicts. Water resources have long been a source of conflict and are forefront in planning efforts that reach beyond local jurisdictions. Modern communities with finite resources are trying to understand the implications of various types of water use on growth. In addition, the iconic nature of water stocks and flows works well with many types of modeling software. There are fewer examples of species management models. The statistical modeling conventions that are used by biologists, and the localized specificity of species management have perhaps created the perception that icon based modeling software is not useful. However, Beall and Zeoli (2008), and Siemer and Otto (Siemer & Otto, 2005; Siemer et al., 2007) have used traditional life history model conventions in an SD platform then customized the effects of habitat changes to suit the particular attributes of the species and ecosystem.

Table 1 lists the case studies, the general environmental issue of concern and the purpose of the model. Models for management of sage grouse in central Washington (Beall & Zeoli, 2008), and bear management in New York (Siemer & Otto, 2005; Siemer et al., 2007) illustrate how human choices affect wildlife, and in turn how the abundance of wildlife may affect humans. The Gloucester fishery model addressed options to a fishing community that has been greatly affected by the decline of ground-fish stocks (Otto & Struben, 2004). Watershed management models of the Okanagan basin in British Columbia (Langsdale et al., 2006; Langsdale et al., 2007; Langsdale, 2007) and the Rio Grande basin in New Mexico (Tidwell et al., 2004) illustrate the use of SD models for long-term water supply management. The Upper Fox River Basin (van den Belt, 2004) project modeled a watershed with respect to agricultural and urban land use, water quality, natural capital and economics. The model for river basin management in the Baixo Guadiana in Portugal (Videira, 2005; Videira et al., 2009) includes planning for water quality and quantity, agricultural development, nature conservation and tourism. The Ria Formosa Natural Park, also in Portugal (van den Belt, 2000; Videira et al., 2003; van den Belt, 2004; Videira, 2005), modeled land use and estuary management with an emphasis on the development of tourism. The Ria Formosa 2000 and 2003 projects illustrate a modeling process that has progressed over time from an initial scoping model to a management tool.

ENGAGING STAKEHOLDERS AND THEIR SYSTEM

Practitioners use a variety of techniques to engage stakeholders. The choice of technique is determined in part by training or personal preference of the modeler, in part by timing, and in part by the needs of the stakeholder group. In addition, the initial makeup of the group will impact how facilitation must begin.

Stakeholder Groups with a History of Working Together

The sage grouse in Washington study (Beall & Zeoli, 2008) was designed in collaboration with stakeholders. The goal of the modeling process was to produce a decision support tool for the management of a species listed as threatened under the ESA. The participants who had a long history of working together, large amounts of quality GIS and population data, and a need to combine that data into simulation model essentially drove the Foster Creek Conservation District (FCCD) modeling process. Beall and Zeoli introduced the group to systems modeling by using an existing model of a salmon population (Ford, 2009) as an illustration. As residents of the Northwest, stakeholders were familiar with salmon life history so it was easy for them to apply the concepts to their own concerns. We believe that the stakeholders were comfortable with systems thinking because these ranchers, farmers and land managers had been working with their landscape for many years. They are accustomed to integrating a variety of parameters and time frames into their decisions. At the first meeting, the modelers stated they knew little about sage grouse or farming and ranching in shrub steppe ecosystems. Having no preconceived ideas was an asset; it helped build trust. Several hours were spent discussing the concerns and needs of the stakeholders. The modelers returned in two weeks for a presentation that included a simple simulation model of the system. It was based upon stakeholder comments at the first meeting and a great deal of research on life history modeling. The simulation created the reference mode described by the group who then provided a data set that would customize the model to their system. Over the course of the

Table 1. Nine case studies and the general environmental issue of concern and model purpose

Case study	Issue	Purpose of model
Sage grouse in Washington (Beall & Zeoli 2008)	Endangered species	Management tool to assess policy alternatives
Problem Bears in New York (Siemer & Otto, 2005; Siemer et al., 2007)	Human-bear interactions	Group learning tool that developed into an educational support tool
Gloucester Fishery (Otto & Struben, 2004)	Sustainable fishery	Group learning; futures exploration
Middle Rio Grande (Tidwell et al., 2004)	Current water supply management	Management tool
Okanagan Basin (Langsdale et al., 2006 ; 2007 ; Langsdale, 2007)	Future water supply management	Group learning; futures exploration
Upper Fox River (van den Belt, 2004)	Watershed management	Scoping big picture
Baixo Guadiana River Basin (Videira, 2005; Videira et al., 2009)	Watershed management	Group learning; problem scoping
Ria Formosa 2000 (van den Belt, 2000; 2004)	Estuary management	Scoping big picture
Ria Formosa Natural Park 2003 (Videira et al., 2003; Videira 2005)	Estuary management	Management tool

next two months, modelers met two more times with the group and had frequent email and phone discussions with key participants. Total length of the project was three months. The timeline was established in consideration of FCCD's USFWS grants. The modelers had initially planned to spend more time with group on causal loop exercises and building simple models in front of the participants. It became apparent early on that this was not necessary. The group had a clear hypothesis of the cause of their problem. They also had a vision of potential solutions. Spending extra time and effort explaining systems methodology to the group could have been an aggravation to people who had limited time and who intuitively understood systems concepts.

The Gloucester group (Otto & Struben, 2004) needed to evaluate a potential solution for a town struggling with the collapse of the NE bottom fishery. The community was looking for a sustainable substitute such as establishing a surimi factory for pelagic fish and was concerned about the potential impact on both the town's economic situation and on the bottom fish that relied upon this food source. The New York group (Siemer & Otto, 2005; Siemer et al., 2007) was dealing with human-bear interactions. Both projects followed similar protocol; furthermore the NY bear process stakeholders were shown the Gloucester model as an example of system dynamics. The projects were conducted over periods of 18 months with groups that had at least, in part a history of working together. Each had four one half day workshops with the full groups and a series of meetings with subgroups. The modelers acted as facilitators; they were not there to solve a problem but to help with problem solving. Their approach "emphasizes the importance of identifying key variables, which usually involves in-depth discussion with the client, a reference mode to express a "hope" and "fear" scenario, and in-depth analysis of the different loops in the system" (Siemer & Otto, 2005, p. 1). The dynamic hypothesis, in the form of causal loops is built into a models one loop

at a time. Each loop is simulated and analyzed before another is added. The Gloucester models was designed for group learning to investigate a potential new economic future, while NY bears had a definitive problem with human-bear interactions for which stakeholders were trying to evaluate management options.

The three wildlife models began with well-defined stakeholder groups whose participants were self selected by choice or by design (in the case of agency personnel). The stakeholder's interest in system dynamics may be more than a coincidence since natural resource managers and perhaps other stakeholders often have experience with adaptive management theory. Adaptive systems thinking and the need for modeling could easily lead one to system dynamics.

The Middle Rio Grande River (Tidwell et al., 2004) also had a defined set of stakeholders. The group was part of a community-based water planning effort that wanted to use a system dynamics platform to integrate social concerns surrounding water supply with hydrologic data from technical flow models into a technical yet transparent decision support tool. Group members were voluntary to the modeling team but once committed had a stake in participation.

This process (Tidwell et al., 2004) was designed and facilitated to follow five steps that were integrated into the overarching community-based water planning process. The problem and scope of analysis were defined and a system description was developed. Causal loop diagrams were then converted into a system dynamics context with appropriate data. The simulation model is reviewed and then the general public uses the model for education and water planning.

The modelers showed examples of other reservoir models to familiarize the group with system dynamics. They also used an example of a savings account model. Though they often built simple structures with the participants there was limited interactive model building. Modelers and designated representatives from different stakeholder groups met bi-monthly for a year to develop the bulk of the model. For the last six months of the project the "Cooperative Modeling Team" met monthly "to review and update the model and to monitor the use of the model in the planning process" (Tidwell et al., 2004, p. 360).

The Okanagan River in British Columbia project (Langsdale et al., 2006, 2007; Langsdale, 2007) was designed to help stakeholders understand the impacts of climate change and population growth on water resources. The stakeholders were familiar with one another through their work or through previous stakeholder engagement activities; their participation in the project was voluntary (Langsdale, 2007). The first workshop began with visioning to explain systems thinking concepts to the participants. The participants played the "ice cream game" (Durfee-Thompson et al., 2005), which is an offshoot of the beer game, a popular SD training tool developed at the MIT Sloan School of Management. The second workshop included systems mapping, a software introduction, and causal loop exercises of the system. Langsdale began building the model in the office and returned to workshop three for "structure construction and refining" with the first iteration of a simulation model. Between workshops three and four, mini workshops were conducted with small interest-based groups to gather essential quantitative data. Workshop five presented a simulation model and time was used for model calibration. Workshop six presented the calibrated model to the group for exploration. The model integrated information from hydrologic models that had been calibrated into different climate change scenarios, changes in evapo-transpiration due to climate change, different scenarios of crops and their associated hydrologic demand and information from area population growth projections.

Stakeholder Groups with Little History of Working Together

The Upper Fox River (van den Belt, 2004), Ria Formosa, 2000 and 2003 (van den Belt, 2000,

2004; Videira et al., 2003; Videira, 2005), and Baixo Guadiana (Videira, 2005; Videira et al., 2009) processes began with the organization of stakeholder groups who were concerned about water resource management and issues ranging from agriculture and water quality (Upper Fox) to fisheries and tourism (Ria Formosa) to scoping out the plethora of issues that large basins must manage (Baixo Guadiana). Although some of the stakeholders were familiar with one another, or part of a group of people with similar concerns, the practitioner for the purpose of facilitating the group through a new problem-solving methodology brought the modeling group together. This is in contrast to the preceding five case studies whose stakeholder groups had either 1) a history of working together or 2) a defined problem or 3) both a history and a defined problem. This contrast in the dynamics of the group requires an initial added facilitation of interpersonal relationships and problem definition. Van den Belt developed a "mediated modeling" process to address these concerns. Van den Belt divides the process into three steps. (van den Belt, 2004).

Step one, identifies stakeholders, sets the participant group, conducts introductory interviews and prepares a preliminary model. Step two covers a series of workshops in which participants discuss problem identification and build qualitative models of their problem using the mapping layers of modeling software. Van den Belt uses this time to elicit information about non-linear behavior, time lags and feedbacks. She states "qualitative modeling is always a prerequisite for quantitative models, whether performed on a flip chart or on a computer. A quantitative model is a prerequisite for simulation of "what if" scenarios" (van den Belt, 2004, p. 88). Once the qualitative model is complete then participants begin to fill in the parameter equations with quantitative data and then, with behind the scenes work from the modeler, a simulation model is developed. Step three, "typically at the last workshop" (Videira, 2005, p. 112) gives the participants the opportunity to run the model themselves and tutors them so that they may demonstrate the model to others.

Each of the four case studies above followed an individually customized timeline. The Upper Fox River and Ria Formosa 2000 that were both four month projects led by van den Belt, are described in depth in *Mediated Modeling*. Ria Formosa 2003 (Videira, 2005) had four days of workshops spread over eighteen months. The Baixo Guadiana had three days of workshops spread over nine months. The Upper Fox River, Baixo Guadiana and the Ria Formosa 2000 were designed to "scope out the big picture". The Ria Formosa 2003 took the initial model and built upon the process to produce a management model.

MODELING TECHNIQUE AND PROCESS

Emphasis on Model Formulation vs. Simulation

Figure 1 illustrates the eight steps of model formation as described by Ford (2009). Though this is depicted as linear, experienced modelers obtain the best results by iterating through the steps in a trial and error process as models are built and tested.

The case studies indicate two patterns of iteration. The first based on model formulation, the second on simulation evaluation. These patterns may happen in sequence but may also be determined by the preferred technique of the modeler.

Groups of people who come together in response to environmental concerns are problem driven. The collaborative definition of "the problem" is the first hurdle any group must overcome (Step 1 and 2). Qualitative models or system thinking exercises are useful aids for this process. With an emphasis on facilitation, skilled modelers may use the mapping layer of system dynamics software to identify variables of concern and the relationships between variables thus combining individual mental models into a group vision. Learning is driven by iterations of model conceptualization and formulation (Step 3 and 4). Figure 2 illustrates these steps linked together to highlight that this systems thinking exercise is an iterative process.

The group then begins to estimate parameters that help them describe a reference mode (step 5). Parameters are then integrated into a simulation model that produces a graphical representation of their reference mode (step 6). The model is then ready for participants to explore the sensitivity of specific parameters (step 7) and policy alternatives (step 8). Simulation models help the group better understand the dynamics of the problem they have defined with their qualitative model. Figure 2 illustrates these steps as part of an iterative process that produces simulation at the end.

The second pattern of iteration emphasizes the evaluation of simulations to facilitate group learning. Modelers elicit a reference mode of the problem through interviews then integrate scientific and social data provided by the participants into a simulation model (figure 3). Modelers return frequently to the group for discussion and verification of simulation results. A technical yet transparent model is created through a series of iterations that build the model one loop or one reference mode at a time. The participatory development of such a model results in a vetted

Figure 1. The eight steps of model formation (Ford, 2009)

Step 1	Step 2	Step 3	Step 4	Step 5	Step 6	Step 7	Step 8
Problem familiar-ization	Problem definition	Model conceptual-ization	Model formulation	Parameter estimation	Simulate the reference mode	Sensitivity analysis	Policy analysis
Model formation				Necessary for simulation			

Figure 2. Simulate at the end Emphasis of the process is highlighted in black

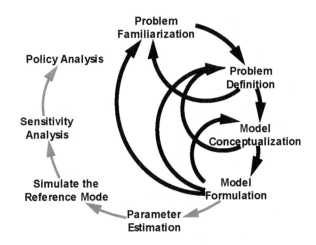

Simulate at the end

simulation tool through which the group can explore policy alternatives.

Simulate Early and Often

Those following the methodology outlined by Forrester (1961, 1969), Meadows et al. (1972), Ford (2009) and others will begin with interviews of participants to elicit a reference mode of their problem. This reference mode is a graphical representation of an important variable and how that variable changes over time. This graphical representation will then drive the model building process. Figure 3 "simulate early and often" illustrates the emphasis that the modelers place on the eight steps of model formation. Practitioners in the sage grouse, Gloucester fishery and NY bears used this procedure, all have training in classic system dynamics that was developed by Forrester and initially taught at the MIT Sloan School of Business.

The Middle Rio Grande and Okanagan modelers came from hydrologic backgrounds. Hydrological studies often require simulation results that rely upon historic water levels or flows to establish historical benchmarks. Benchmarks

differ from reference modes that indicate general trends. They are usually graphical or spreadsheet data of historic stream flow. They typically depict seasonal variations that are of strategic concern. This information is placed in simulation models to establish the flow and volume characteristics upon which other issues may be layered. In processes concerned with the availability of water, a simulation model is typically needed early to help participants decide upon parameters that will aid understanding of potential changes in reservoir levels or stream flows.

Simulate at the End

The Upper Fox River, Baixo Guadiana, Ria Formosa 2000 and 2003 began by using the mapping level of STELLA to build a systems map of the problem. This systems thinking exercise helps participants identify system boundaries and important parameters. When the group begins to quantify parameters, van den Belt lets the situation decide whether to first tackle the "spaghetti" (causal relationships) or the "meatballs" (stocks) (van den Belt, 2004, p. 84). When the group does begin to talk about stocks the reference modes are

Figure 3. Simulate early and often. Emphasis of the process is highlighted in black

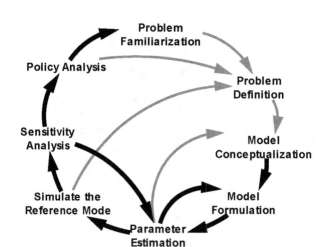

Simulate early and often

elicited. Thus simulations are added at the end of the process (figure 2). This technique is useful for problems that take several workshops to define however it may leave little time for analysis of the simulation results.

Patterns of Iteration and the Benefits of Simulation

Two patterns of iteration emphasis have emerged even though practitioners in the case studies used a variety of techniques. One pattern emphasizes system thinking exercises, model conceptualization and formation as the basis for group learning about problem definition. A model map of the entire problem is produced before simulation exercises are developed and performed. The second pattern emphasizes iterative simulation modeling which builds the model one "loop at a time" or "one reference mode at a time". This helps participants learn about policies or pieces of their problem though simulation results. This approach allows the modeler to build, test and evaluate the assumptions of small sections of the model. In addition it promotes the investigation

of feedback mechanisms early in the process. Feedbacks can over-ride many other issues. It is beneficial to discover these problems early rather than later when they create big surprises.

PROBLEM COMPLEXITY

Natural resource problems are sometimes describes as "wicked" (Rittel & Webber, 1973). Stakeholders have multi-dimensional interests overlaid with often competing values. Distilling these complexities down to a set of negotiable concerns is a common goal of facilitators in natural resource conflicts (Susskind & Field, 1996; Carpenter & Kennedy, 2001). These concerns need to be concise, such as a reference mode, before facilitated processes can begin moving towards finding solutions. The number of stocks that are in the model could be indicative of the number of concerns, and was therefore chosen as a proxy for problem complexity. Though it is arguable that the total number of parameters may also indicate complexity, many parameters help define stocks which are more indicative of the central problems.

If such is the case we would expect to see two reasons for a large number of stocks. The first of these is that the group is in the early stages of problem definition. The second is that a large number of representative groups are at the table bringing with them a diversity of concerns. If one combines these over the hypothetical lifetime of a long-term process, one could expect to see the number of stocks begin high as the group initially expresses all of their interests. The number of stocks would then decline as the group distills their interests to a workable (or model-able) set of issues. Over time, as the group finds cohesiveness and trust in each other and the process, one would expect to see them tackling new issues of concern thus the number of stocks would increase. Figure 4 illustrates general trends that support the effect that time and the number of involved groups has on the complexity of the problem that is modeled. More time, more groups, more stocks.

Though there are few examples of long-term studies with the same core group the Ria Formosa studies do show this trend. Initially a small number of groups came together to build a scoping model to help them clarify their problem. Then as the process developed over time into a management model, more groups were included and with them more complex issues. The number of stocks was initially 24 then progressed to 40 while the number of groups represented grew from 10 to 60.

THE CONTINUUMS

To help further explain the divergence in technique used in the models three continuums will be discussed: 1) the "hands on continuum"; 2) the "problem definition to solution producing continuum"; and 3) the "quantitative to qualitative continuum". The "quantitative to qualitative continuum" in this context refers to the type of data being used in the models, not the models themselves. Although if a qualitative model or system map is being developed rather than an operating simulation model, large amounts of quantitative data will not be of assistance to the model.

Figure 5 illustrates the three continuums together to help elucidate another trend across the case studies. It is helpful to understand in ad-

Figure 4. Sorted by project length, with number of groups represented and number of stocks added to the right of project length

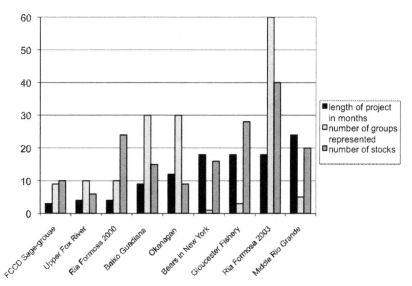

vance that models that fall to one side of a single continuum will tend to fall on the same side of the other two continuums. The continuums will be discussed separately then a compilation of the continuums and modeling technique will follow.

The "Hands On" Continuum

This continuum portrays models built by experts with input from participants at one extreme. The opposite extreme portrays modelers using software to map a problem with the participants during a workshop. Practitioners on both sides of the continuum will educate participants about the basics of model icons. Modelers building structures in front of or with participants tend to teach participants more about the basics of model building.

Teaching stakeholders the basics of model building may accomplish two factors important to the process. First, it helps establish trust in the model and software and an appreciation of model transparency. Established groups who have trust in

one another may have less need for hands on modeling. Second, it helps stakeholders to understand systems thinking. Those who are accustomed to viewing the world in a linear manner may benefit from this exercise.

The sage grouse, Gloucester fisheries, NY bears, Okanagan and Middle Rio Grande performed the bulk of the modeling in the office whereas practitioners in the Upper Fox River, Ria Formosa 2000, 2003 and Baixo Guadiana spend more time involved in actual model building with the participants (though modelers operate the computers). These practitioners built the models from the general to the specific during stakeholder meetings. They began by identifying sectors that are important to the group to establish boundaries of the discussion to follow. Smaller groups then worked on individual sectors and spend time identifying parameters and the relationships of those parameters to one another. Practitioners take time between this step and the last workshop to fill in data and fine tune the equations so that a simula-

Figure 5. The continuums, patterns of model formation and the case studies. 1. Sage grouse in WA; 2. Problem Bears in NY; 3. Gloucester Fishery; 4. Middle Rio Grande; 5. Okanagan Basin; 6. Ria Formosa 2003; 7. Baixo Guadiana River Basin; 8. Upper Fox River; 9.Ria Formosa 2000.

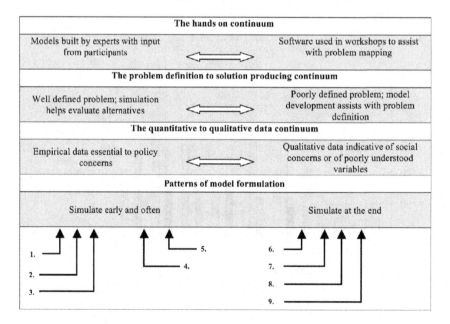

tion model can be operating at the final workshop. The divergence of technique between hands on and hands off (or modeling in the office) is driven in part by the preferences of the modeler-facilitator but it is also driven by the purpose of the model and by the degree of problem definition.

The "Problem Definition to Solution Producing" Continuum

The problem identification to solution producing continuum captures complexity issues and illustrates that modeling may be effective at different points in the problem-solving process. On the right side of the continuum is the Ria Formosa 2000 project that helped participants put boundaries on their problem through discussions that produced sectors and simple stock and flow structures. In the center of the continuum is the Okanagan study that helped concerned stakeholders wrap their minds around a problem they had all considered but had not yet begun to clarify. They worked together as a group to begin to put together all of the issues that may be part of the problem (Langsdale et al., 2006; Langsdale et al., 2007; Langsdale, 2007). On the left side of the continuum is the Washington sage grouse model that will be helping stakeholders identify solutions that will be implemented on the ground (Beall & Zeoli, 2008).

The "Quantitative to Qualitative" Continuum

Quantitative to qualitative in this context is referring to the type of data that is integrated into a model. This is in contrast to previous use of quantitative and qualitative that referred to the model

and whether it was a quantitative simulation tool or a qualitative map of the problem.

This continuum of data may be expressed in many ways: quantitative to qualitative, hard to soft, scientific to social; the divisions may be fuzzy (Table 2). The importance of the concept is in the value of the model to communicate information vital to the process.

Conflict between community members can often erupt due to differences in how people value information. Scientists may be accused of using "black box mumbo-jumbo" or local knowledge referred to as anecdotal stories. Scientific parameters, social parameters and policy choices that may affect both scientific and social concerns may be equally expressed (or representatively expressed according the needs of the group) in a model. Inclusiveness, education and respect can lead to less conflict and more creative problem solving (Carpenter & Kennedy, 2001; van den Belt, 2004). It should also be noted that it is currently not possible to scientifically quantify many environmental parameters. Concepts such as attractiveness can help capture intangibles such as the health of an ecosystem. The complexity of the problem, the number of group represented, and point on the problem definition continuum, will all have an effect on data concerns.

Different problems require different types of data. When dealing with economics, species demographics, habitat, or water flows modelers typically use quantified and often peer reviewed data. When including many human elements, stakeholders request parameters that are qualifications of such things as "tolerance" or "concern" for the NY bears, or "attractiveness" in the Ria Formosa. The demand for quality data whether it is quantified or qualified tends to follow what one

Table 2. The information spectrum (Ford 2009)

Physical laws	Controlled experiments	Uncontrolled experiments	Statistical information	Case studies	Expert judgment	Stakeholder knowledge	Personal intuition

would expect of a non-modeled facilitation. Early in the process stakeholders often talk about their values with respect to potential solutions. These values may be difficult to quantify. As the process progresses the need for specific types of hard data become increasingly important as stakeholders begin to clarify their mental models and begin to focus on viable potential solutions.

The Ria Formosa 2000 model is an example of a simulation model built with a great deal of qualitative data. The following statement is found on the opening page of the model.

This is a "scoping model" meaning that a group of stakeholders interactively scoped out the linkages between ecology and economics. Many of the values incorporated are "estimates", "guesstimates" or assumptions to further the discussion in terms of "what if".... More realistic or complete data and information can be incorporated as the discussion progresses (van den Belt, 2004).

This illustrates how generalities about parameters are useful when placed in a simulation model. When and if more definitive data is needed, it can be added to replace "best guesses".

One of the benefits of using system dynamic platforms for simulation is that "best guesses" based on experiential or anecdotal knowledge can be incorporated when no other data is available. Some argue that this may promote "garbage in garbage out" however the flip side of that argument is that mental models are often based on the same sort of knowledge. At least when placed in a simulation model this information is available to others in a clear and concise manner. Ford (2009) reminds us that a best guess can be very useful. If we exclude an uncertain parameter we are essentially stating that the value of the parameter is zero. Another issue of qualified data includes those parameters for which there is no real value other than a relative value that is understood by the participants. The Ria Formosa models both

had parameters that captured "attractiveness" that were constructs of the participants and their values.

Two of the wildlife case studies illustrate a span of data types. The sage grouse model is primarily concerned with the recovery of an endangered species. It was entirely dependent on quantified, peer reviewed and expert biological data for species viability. As a comparison, the NY bears model is less concerned with species viability. In fact the bears are flourishing which causes concern about human-bear interactions. The model contains both quantified data on life history and habitat but also parameters such as "concern" or "tolerance". In addition, Siemer and Otto stated that "[w]hile exercising the model and providing insights to the team is a means to an end, modeling and its iterative process is a learning opportunity for the team as well as the modelers" (Siemer & Otto, 2005, p. 11). The model has progressed into an education tool for the general public that may be utilized by agency professionals in problem bear areas (Siemer et al., 2007).

In general, the trend across the nine case studies is that management type models required more quantified data that was substantiated with standard scientific protocol. All of the practitioners noted that at some point in the process there was or would be a need for high quality technical data. They also value system dynamics software because it provides a platform to incorporate parameters based on the values of the participants when technical data is unavailable or unable to capture important concepts.

COMPILED ANALYSIS

Figure 5 integrates the continuums, patterns of model formulation, and the nine case studies. The placement of the case studies is not meant to be a specific comparison between the case studies but rather meant to illustrate general trends that reflect their internal issues. Emphasis on any specific continuum could potentially move a case study to either side of another. Models that fall to one side of a single continuum tend to fall on the same side of the other continuums.

On one end of the continuums is the Washington sage grouse model that was developed as a management tool for a group who had consensus on a well-defined problem. They had readily available, quantitative data that had been obtained through peer reviewed or peer reviewable processes. They needed a model to integrate their data into a simulation tool that could be used to explore policy alternatives. When comparing the time length of all of the modeling processes, this process had the shortest time frame. On the other end of the continuums we find the Ria Formosa 2000, Upper Fox and Baixo Guadiana that began as qualitative models that were designed to help stakeholders better define the scope and depth of their problem. The groups were then able to create simulation models of the qualitative problem map that the group developed as part of their problem definition process. These models were able to capture important social information that stakeholders were able to satisfactorily qualify.

The Ria Formosa 2003 built on the 2000 process. The stakeholder group expanded and developed a management tool in a process that still required the modeler to facilitate problem definition and clarification. Time restrictions did not allow these models to develop through a series of iterations driven by simulation results.

The Okanagan model used a combination of model development though group mapping and development though simulation. A large amount of quantitative data was available from the stakeholder group from earlier participatory and scientific efforts. Stakeholders appreciated the model for its ability to integrate these various data types. Model building was somewhat complicated by the large numbers of parameters that stakeholders requested to be included. However, process facilitation was fairly easy at this stage of the participatory effort. The degree of conflict in

future exploration is different than in a situation where conflict over resources is already contentious. This case study exemplifies stakeholders who realize that system thinking is an important skill when planning for the future.

The Rio Grande model was developed as a management tool in a process that required the modelers to facilitate some degree of problem definition and clarification. It is a highly quantitative model requiring data from other water flow models. The quality of this data was essential to the model that was developed as part of a regional planning process. Iterations of simulation and analysis were used during model development. The Gloucester model was developed for a group of stakeholders with a well-defined problem who needed a model to explore a potential future. Stakeholders were trying to understand their potential alternatives so that the decisions of today would be made with the future in mind. Over the seven month modeling period, practitioners incorporated high quality quantitative and qualitative data one loop at a time into the model though iterations of simulation exploration.

The NY bears model also illustrates a model built using a classic SD technique that develops models though a series of iterations of simulation result analysis. Though the model is described as a learning tool it has developed into a model that is part of a public education program and will be used by wildlife managers to explain how humans impact human-bear interactions.

CONCLUSION

These case studies cover a broad spectrum of modeling technique that integrates a variety of data and social values into a single information system. Four began with systems thinking exercises that developed models using the mapping layer of software to link together issues and concerns. Five developed models through iterations of simulation analysis. Problem definition technique varies from the use of causal diagrams to solicitation of reference modes. Process products range from a better understanding of "how we can learn to clarify problems" to management tools which simulate potential policy choices.

The success or long-range usefulness of these techniques is more difficult to tease apart. Case studies that used surveys indicate success in that individuals learned to think in a more holistic fashion and that participants appreciated learning from one another and about their system from a different perspective. The use of models for decision support should also be considered an indication of success; whether the actual model assisted with a decision or if it helped individuals understand the system better and thus made different decisions as a result is a matter for further study. Comparing an SD process to other methods of facilitation is not practical because of the inability to replicate the process with a control that uses another method of facilitation. Comparing case studies to one another has its challenges as well but this should not be a deterrent to using system dynamics in participatory processes but rather an encouragement for more case study assessments. Finally, the diversity of case studies indicates that a broad range of problems can be addressed by varying system dynamics modeling technique. There is no one technique that will always work with every group. Stakeholder groups vary in size, in need, in conflict, and in problem according to their place-based idiosyncrasies. Adaptability and a large repertoire of skills will benefit participatory modeling practitioners and the groups with whom they are working.

The complexity of environmental problems and the desire to find win-win sustainable solutions is driving a paradigm of problem solving that began with the ecosystem concept brought forward by Tansley in the 1930's. When we began to see the natural world as a "system", we recognized that we had to develop an understanding of connections as well as the parts and recognize that systems have inherent behavior. This need to connect "everything" and look at systems holistically is also one of the drivers for the development of Society System Science. Although one of many tools that can help this discipline develop system dynamics is uniquely suited to help us shift our focus from single pieces of a system to the connections between those pieces and to help "us to see the world as a set of unfolding behavior patterns" (Meadows, 1972, p. 4). Modelers using the science of system dynamics and the art of facilitation in a participatory process embrace the value of interdisciplinary communication and create a nexus of science and social concerns. With this understanding we are better equipped to contemplate our place in the system, the implications of our behavior, environmental stressors and the manifestations of tipping points. This in turn will help us understand how a system could be both fragile and resilient and what it means to be sustainable.

ACKNOWLEDGMENT

The authors would like to thank Stacy Langsdale, Peter Otto, Bill Siemer, Vincent Tidwell, Nuno Videira, and Marjan van den Belt and for sharing their modeling and facilitation techniques.

REFERENCES

Anderson, D. F., & Richardson, G. P. (1997). Scripts for group model building. *System Dynamics Review*, *13*(2), 107–130. doi:10.1002/(SICI)1099-1727(199722)13:2<107::AID-SDR120>3.0.CO;2-7

Beall, A., & Zeoli, L. (2008). Participatory modeling of endangered wildlife systems: Simulating sage grouse and land use in Central Washington. *Ecological Economics, 68*(1-2), 24–33. doi:10.1016/j.ecolecon.2008.08.019

Carpenter, S. L., & Kennedy, W. J. D. (2001). *Managing public disputes: A practical guide for government, business and citizens groups.* New York: Jossey-Bass, John Wiley and Sons, Inc.

Cockerill, K., Passell, H., & Tidwell, V. (2006). Cooperative modeling: Building bridges between science and the public. *Journal of the American Water Resources Association, 42*(2), 457–471. doi:10.1111/j.1752-1688.2006.tb03850.x

Durfee-Thompson, J. L., Forster, C. B., Mills, J. I., & Peterson, T. R. (2005, June). The ice cream game: A systems thinking approach to environmental conflict resolution. In *Proceedings of the 8th Biennial Conference on Communication and Environment,* Jekyll Island, Georgia.

Ford, A. (2005). Simulating the impacts of a strategic fuel reserve in California. *Energy Policy, 33,* 483–498. doi:10.1016/j.enpol.2003.08.013

Ford, A. (2009). *Modeling the environment* (2nd ed.). Washington, DC: Island Press.

Forrester, J. (1961). *Industrial dynamics.* Walthan, MA: Pegasus Communications.

Forrester, J. (1969). *Urban dynamics.* Walthan, MA: Pegasus Communications.

Langsdale, S. (2007). *Participatory model building for exploring water management and climate change futures in the Okanagan Basin, British Columbia, Canada.* Unpublished PhD thesis, University of British Columbia, Vancouver, Canada.

Langsdale, S., Beall, A., Carmichael, J., Cohen, S., & Forster, C. (2007). An exploration of water resources futures under climate change using system dynamics modeling. *The Integrated Assessment Journal, 7*(1), 51–79.

Langsdale, S., Beall, A., Carmichael, J., Cohen, S., Forster, C., & Neale, T. (2006). Shared learning through group model building. In Cohen, S., & Neale, T. (Eds.), *Participatory integrated assessment of water management and climate change in the Okanagan Basin, British Columbia.* Vancouver, BC: Environment Canada and University of British Columbia.

Meadows, D., Meadows, D., Randers, J., & Behrens, W. (1972). *The limits to growth.* New York: Universe Books.

Morecroft, J. D. W., & Sterman, J. D. (Eds.). (1994). *Modeling for learning organizations.* Portland, OR: Productivity Press. Waltham, MA: Pegasus Communications.

Otto, P., & Struben, J. (2004). Gloucester fishery: Insights from a group modeling intervention. *System Dynamics Review, 20*(4), 287–312. doi:10.1002/sdr.299

Richardson, G., & Anderson, D. (1995). Teamwork in group model-building. *System Dynamics Review, 11*(2), 131–137. doi:10.1002/sdr.4260110203

Richardson, G. P., & Pugh, A. L. III. (1981). *Introduction to system dynamics modeling with DYNAMO. Cambridge, MA: MIT Press.* Waltham, MA: Pegasus Communications.

Rittel, W. J. R., & Webber, M. M. (1973). Dilemmas in a general theory of planning. *Policy Sciences, 4,* 155–169. doi:10.1007/BF01405730

Roberts, N. H., Andersen, D. F., Deal, R. M., Grant, M. S., & Shaffer, W. A. (1983). *Introduction to computer simulation: The system dynamics modeling approach*. Reading, MA: Addison-Wesley.

Rouwette, E., Vennix, J., & Mullekom, T. (2002). Group model building effectiveness: A review of assessment studies. *System Dynamics Review*, *18*, 5–45. doi:10.1002/sdr.229

Rouwette, E. A. J. (2003). *Group model building as mutual persuasion*. Nijmegen, The Netherlands: Wolf Legal Publishers.

Siemer, W. F., Decker, D. J., Gore, M. L., & Otto, P. (2007). *Working through black bear management issues: A practitioner's guide*. Ithaca, NY: Northeast Wildlife Damage Management Research and Outreach Cooperative.

Siemer, W. F., & Otto, P. (2005, July 17-21). A group model-building intervention to support wildlife management. In *Proceedings of the 23rd International Conference of the System Dynamics Society*, Boston, MA.

Stave, K. (2002). Using system dynamics to improve public participation in environmental decisions. *System Dynamics Review*, *18*(2), 139–167. doi:10.1002/sdr.237

Sterman, J. D. (2000). *Business dynamics – Systems thinking and modeling for a complex world*. Boston: McGraw-Hill.

Sterman, J. D. (Ed.). (2002). The global citizen: Celebrating the life of Dana Meadows. *System Dynamics Review*, *18*(2), 100–310.

Susskind, L., & Field, P. (1996). *Dealing with an angry public*. New York: The Free Press.

Tansley, A. G. (1935). The use and abuse of vegetational terms and concepts. *Ecology*, *16*, 284–307. doi:10.2307/1930070

Tidwell, V. D., Passell, H. D., Conrad, S. H., & Thomas, R. P. (2004). System dynamics modeling for community-based water planning: Application to the Middle Rio Grande. *Aquatic Sciences*, *66*(4), 357–372. doi:10.1007/s00027-004-0722-9

van den Belt, M. (2000). *Mediated modeling: A collaborative approach for the development of shared understanding and evaluation of environmental policy scenarios, with case studies in the Fox, River, Wisconsin and the Ria Formosa, Portugal*. Unpublished PhD thesis, University of Maryland, College Park, MD.

van den Belt, M. (2004). *Mediated modeling*. Washington, DC: Island Press.

Vennix, J. A. M. (1994, July). *Building consensus in strategic decision-making: Insights from the process of group model building*. Paper presented at the 1994 International System Dynamics Conference, Stirling, Scotland.

Vennix, J. A. M. (1996). *Group model building. Facilitating team learning using system dynamics*. New York: John Wiley and Sons.

Vennix, J. A. M. (1999). Group model building: Tackling messy problems. *System Dynamics Review*, *15*(4), 379–401. doi:10.1002/(SICI)1099-1727(199924)15:4<379::AID-SDR179>3.0.CO;2-E

Videira, N. (2005). *Stakeholder participation in environmental decision-making: The role of participatory modeling*. Unpublished PhD thesis, University of New Lisbon, Lisbon, Portugal.

Videira, N., Antunes, P., & Santos, R. (2009). Scoping river basin management issues with participatory modelling: The Baixo Guadiana experience. *Ecological Economics*, *68*(4), 965–978. doi:10.1016/j.ecolecon.2008.11.008

Videira, N., Antunes, P., Santos, R., & Gamete, S. (2003). Participatory modelling in environmental decision-making: The Ria Formosa Natural Park case study. *Journal of Environmental Assessment Policy and Management*, *5*(3), 421–447. doi:10.1142/S1464333203001371

Wang, J. (2008). Society systems science: A brand new discipline. *International Journal of Society Systems Science*, *1*(1), 1–3.

This work was previously published in International Journal of Information Systems and Social Change, Volume 1, Issue 2, edited by John Wang, pp. 72-89, copyright 2010 by IGI Publishing (an imprint of IGI Global).

Chapter 14
The Keys to the White House:
A Preliminary Forecast for 2012

Allan J. Lichtman
American University, USA

ABSTRACT

The Keys to the White House are an index-based prediction system that retrospectively account for the popular-vote winners of every US presidential election from 1860 to 1980 and prospectively forecast the winners of every presidential election from 1984 through 2008. The Keys demonstrate that American presidential elections do not turn on events of the campaign, but rather on the performance of the party controlling the White House. The Keys hold important lessons for politics in the United States and worldwide. A preliminary forecast based on the Keys indicates that President Obama is a likely winner in 2012, but also reveals the specific problems at home and abroad that could thwart his re-election.

THE KEYS TO THE WHITE HOUSE

Every four years the media worldwide spends more than a billion dollars covering the American presidential campaign. In the general election campaign, every gesture, word, and deed of the Republican and Democratic candidates is scrutinized for its purported effect on the outcome of the fall election. As in a horserace, candidates are viewed as spurting ahead or slipping behind day by day, with the superior campaigner ultimately triumphing at the polls. The only problem with this "horserace" model that dominates the coverage of presidential elections is that it is false and misleading.

The historical record of presidential elections shows that a pragmatic electorate chooses a president, not according to events on the campaign trail, but according to the performance of the party holding the White House as measured by the consequential events and episodes of a term - economic boom and bust, foreign policy successes and failures, social unrest, scandal, and policy innovation. This new vision of American politics is based on The Keys to the White House, a prediction system based on the study of every presidential election from 1860 to 2008. I first developed the Keys system in 1981, in collaboration with Vladimir Keilis-Borok, founder of the International Institute of Earthquake Prediction

DOI: 10.4018/978-1-4666-0927-3.ch014

Theory and Mathematical Geophysics. Retrospectively, the keys model accounts for the popular vote winner of every American presidential election since 1860, much longer than any other prediction system. Prospectively, the Keys to the White House has correctly forecast the popular vote winner of all seven presidential elections from 1984 to 2008, usually months or even years prior to Election Day. For example, the keys called Vice President George H. W. Bush's victory in the spring of 1988 when he trailed Mike Dukakis by double-digits in the polls and was being written off by the pollsters and the pundits (Lichtman, 1988, May). The Keys forecast George W. Bush's 2004 re-election in April 2003, nearly a year before any other academic model (Jones, 2007). In February 2006, more than two and a half years ahead of time, the Keys predicted that the Democrats would recapture the White House in the 2008 election (Lichtman, 2006, 5).

As indicated in Table 1, each of the thirteen keys is stated as a threshold condition that always favors the re-election of the party holding the White House. For example, Key 5 is phrased as "The economy is not in recession during the elec-tion campaign." Each key can then be assessed as true or false prior to an upcoming election and the winner predicted according to a simple decision rule. When five or fewer keys are false, the incumbent party wins; when any six or more are false, the challenging party wins.

This system also provides insight into party prospects for the 2012 election at a time when all other forecasting methods are about as reliable as the flipping of coins. The system shows that it is possible to predict well ahead of time the outcomes of presidential elections from indicators that primarily track the performance and strength of the party holding the White House.

LESSONS OF THE KEYS

The Keys have several important implications for our understanding of American history, politics, and public policy. First, the keys demonstrate that American presidential elections have followed a common enduring logic since Republican Abraham Lincoln defeated Democrat Stephen Douglas in 1860. The pragmatic basis by which the Ameri-

Table 1. The 13 keys to the White House

KEY 1 (Party Mandate): After the midterm elections, the incumbent party holds more seats in the U.S. House of Representatives than it did after the previous midterm elections.
KEY 2 (Contest): There is no serious contest for the incumbent-party nomination.
KEY 3 (Incumbency): The incumbent-party candidate is the sitting president.
KEY 4 (Third party): There is no significant third-party or independent campaign.
KEY 5 (Short-term economy): The economy is not in recession during the election campaign.
KEY 6 (Long-term economy): Real per-capita economic growth during the term equals or exceeds mean growth during the previous two terms.
KEY 7 (Policy change): The incumbent administration effects major changes in national policy.
KEY 8 (Social unrest): There is no sustained social unrest during the term.
KEY 9 (Scandal): The incumbent administration is untainted by major scandal.
KEY 10 (Foreign/military failure): The incumbent administration suffers no major failure in foreign or military affairs.
KEY 11 (Foreign/military success): The incumbent administration achieves a major success in foreign or military affairs.
KEY 12 (Incumbent charisma): The incumbent-party candidate is charismatic or a national hero.
KEY 13 (Challenger charisma): The challenging-party candidate is not charismatic or a national hero.

can electorate chooses a president has remained stable in 150 years despite vast changes in the American economy and society, the composition of the electorate, and the technology of campaigns. This insight suggests that successive waves of immigrants to the United States have adapted to the prevailing non-ideological pragmatic culture of American life and politics. It further indicates that current policy could likely regularize the status of undocumented immigrants without undue concern about changing American culture.

Second, the Keys demonstrate that it is governing not campaigning that counts in American presidential elections. If the nation fares well during the term of the incumbent party, that party wins another four years in office; otherwise, the challenging party prevails. Nothing that a candidate has said or done during a campaign, when the public discounts everything as political, has changed his prospects at the polls. Debates, advertising, television appearances, news coverage, and campaign strategies - the usual grist for the punditry mills - count for virtually nothing on Election Day. The public is not duped by the selling of candidates during campaigns. Rather, it heavily discounts as "political," self-promotion and partisan claims made during a campaign. Thus, in choosing presidential nominees, party voters should forget about the so-called "electability" of candidates and choose the candidate that they believe is most qualified to lead the country in accord with their values and policies. In turn, nominees should replace consultant-driven, scripted campaigns and focus instead to establish grassroots support for the bold policy initiatives that will help them govern effectively if elected to the presidency.

Third, the Keys show that elections are not decided by the economy alone as many models of presidential elections would have us believe. The economy does account for two of thirteen keys. However, a wide range of other factors such as foreign policy successes and failures, social unrest, scandal, and general policy change also affect the outcome of elections. This means that incumbent administrations and their congressional allies cannot focus on the economy to the neglect of other issues. It was not primarily the economy, for example, that accounted for the problems faced by incumbent party candidates in 1952, 1968, 1976, or 2000.

Fourth, given that incumbent parties benefit from major policy change another lesson for American presidents is: do not hesitate to advance bold new policies. Conversely, "do not govern from the center." Great presidents don't move to the middle they move the middle to them by fundamentally changing the conversation about government and implementing bold new programs that work. That is what FDR did for liberal governance in the 1930s and Ronald Reagan for conservative governance in the 1980s. No political leader in the history of the government has gained major political success or produced fundamental changes in national policy by attempting to move to the middle. Rather the so-called "center" of American politics is the graveyard of mediocre one-term presidents like William Howard Taft, Herbert Hoover, George H. W. Bush, and Jimmy Carter. The centrist presidents Dwight Eisenhower and Bill Clinton won two terms in office, but they both lost control of Congress in their first term and failed to pass on the presidency to a candidate of their party.

Fifth, although the Keys cannot be mechanically applied to other political systems, the big lessons of the Keys have worldwide implications. As demonstrated in states of the former Soviet Union, Kenya, Afghanistan and Iran people are willing to risk their lives to shape the political destiny of their lands. Electoral experience in the United States, as gauged by the Keys, suggests that leaders who gain power in democratic societies, whether established or developing, should focus on governance, not politics. As democracy inevitably spreads across the globe, world leaders should take heed that those who serve their people well will likely succeed politically in free and fair elections.

THE KEYS MODEL

Social scientists have developed numerous models for predicting the results of American presidential elections. Excellent summaries of leading models can be found in Campbell and Garrand (2000), Jones (2002), and Campbell & Lewis–Beck (2008). Unlike nearly all other models for predicting election outcomes, the Keys to the White House rely on an index rather than a regression-based method of forecasting. This approach to election forecasting differs from the regression models in several ways. First, it forecasts not percentage votes, but wins and losses by the party holding the White House, based upon an index comprised of true or false responses to set of questions, each of which is a "key" to the White House." Second, it uses pattern recognition, not regression, to select relevant keys and develop a decision rule for distinguishing incumbent from challenging party victories. Third, it includes a much wider array of predictor variables than the regression models. Fourth, the model provides for very long forecasts of an upcoming election. Fifth, unlike many regression models, which combine structural parameters with presidential approval or horserace polls, the Keys utilize no polling data. This feature also distinguishes the keys from those predictive systems that rely strictly on the analysis of polling results. See, for example, Gott & Colley (2008) and Erikson and Wlezien (2008).

To develop the predictive model, Keilis-Borok and I applied the simple pattern recognition algorithm known as Hemming's Distance to two binary vectors. First we coded elections from 1860 to 1980 that fell into Class I – the incumbent party prevailed – as 0 and elections that fell into Class C – the challenging party prevailed as 1. In two elections, 1876 and 1888, the tally of electoral

votes reversed the preference set by the popular vote. Given that our model is based on national indicators, we put 1876 in Class C, reflecting the popular vote plurality for the challenging party candidate, Democrat Samuel J. Tilden, rather than the electoral vote victory for incumbent party candidate, Republican Rutherford B. Hayes. We put 1888 in Class I, reflecting the popular vote plurality for incumbent Democratic President Grover Cleveland, rather than the electoral vote victory for the challenger, Republican Benjamin Harrison. In classifying the subsequent elections of 1880 and 1892 the party that actually gained the presidency in the previous election was considered the incumbent party: the Republicans in both years. The incumbent party won in 1880 and lost in 1892 (See Tables 2 and 3).

The second vector consisted true or false answers to a set of questions that can be answered prior to an upcoming election. The questions or "keys" were based upon a version of the theory of retrospective voting – that a pragmatic electorate chooses a president according to the performance of the party holding the White House as gauged by the consequential events and episodes of a term. Our questionnaire initially included twelve questions, but was modified to include thirteen questions prior to its use for advance prediction. As indicated in Table 1 each question is phrased so that an answer of true favors reelection of the party in power and an answer of false favors its defeat. For example, Key 13 is phrased as "The challenging-party candidate is *not* charismatic or a national hero." True answers for any given election are coded as 0 and false answers as 1. When a key is coded as 1, it is in effect, turned against the party holding the White House, whereas a coding of 0 indicates that it is turned in favor of the incumbent party.

Results for the elections of 1860 to 1980 are reported in Tables 2 and 3, partitioned into elections of Class I and Class C. Each election in the Tables is described by the number of keys turned against the incumbent party. Technically,

Table 2. Keys to the White House: Definitions

KEY	DEFINITION
1: Party Mandate	After the midterm elections, the incumbent party holds more seats in the U.S. House of Representatives than it did after the previous midterm elections.
2: Party Contest	The candidate is nominated on the first ballot and wins at least two-thirds of the delegate votes.
3: Incumbency	The sitting president is the party candidate.
4: Third Party	A third-party candidate wins at least 5 percent of the popular vote.
5: Short-term Economy	The National Bureau of Economic Research has declared a recession, which it has declared over prior to the election.
6: Long-term Economy	Real per-capita economic growth during the term equals or exceeds mean growth during the previous two terms.
7: Policy Change	The administration achieves major policy change during the term comparable to the New Deal or the first-term Reagan Revolution.
8: Social Unrest	There is no social unrest during the term comparable to the upheavals of post-civil war Reconstruction or of the 1960s that is sustained or raises deep concerns about the unraveling of society.
9: Scandal	There is no broad recognition of a scandal that directly touches upon the president.
10: Foreign or Military Failure	There is no major failure during the term comparable to Pearl Harbor or the Iran hostage crisis that appears to undermine significantly America's national interests or threaten its standing in the world.
11: Foreign or Military Success	There is a major success during the term comparable to the winning of World War II or the Camp David Accords that significantly advances America's national interest or its standing in the world.
12: Incumbent Charisma/Hero	The incumbent party candidate is a national hero comparable to Ulysses Grant or Dwight Eisenhower or is an inspirational candidate comparable to Franklin Roosevelt or Ronald Reagan.
13: Challenger Charisma/Hero	The incumbent party candidate is not a national hero comparable to Ulysses Grant or Dwight Eisenhower and is not an inspirational candidate comparable to Franklin Roosevelt or Ronald Reagan.

this is represented by the binary vector $Y_i(X_1, X_2 \ldots X_n)$, where $X_i = 0$ or $X_i = 1$, is the answer to the ith question. For each question, statistics are computed that indicate the percentage of negative keys for elections won by incumbent and challenging parties, respectively.

$P(i/I) = n(i/I)/n(I)$ and $P(i/C) = n(i/C)/n(C)$, where

$n(i/I)$ = the number of elections in which $X_i = 1$ for Class I

$n(i/C)$ = the number of elections in which $X_i = 1$ for Class C

$n(I)$ = the number of elections of Class I

$n(C)$ = the number of elections of Class C.

From the results reported in Tables 2 and 3, we computed Hemming's Distance, for each individual election, defined as: $D = \Sigma \, Xi$ which equals to the number of keys turned against the party in power, with no differential weighting. The value of D varies from 0 to 13, with higher numbers indicating the greater likelihood of an incumbent party defeat. As demonstrated in Tables 2 and 3, taken together, the thirteen keys correctly classified all 31 elections from 1860 to 1980 into Class I and Class C according to the decision rule that the incumbent party prevails if D < 6 and the challenging party prevails if D ≥ 6. Thus the party in power is predicted to lose the popular vote if and only if it loses 6 or more of thirteen keys.

No question was included in the analysis unless it distinguished between incumbent and challenger victories according to the criteria that $P(i/C) - P(i/I) > 0.1$. In addition, each question

Table 3. Keys: All results & historical outcomes, 1860-2008

YEAR	K 1	K 2	K 3	K 4	K 5	K 6	K 7	K 8	K 9	K 10	K 11	K 12	K13	SUM	WIN
1860	0	1	1	1	0	0	1	1	0	0	1	1	0	7	N
1864	0	0	0	0	0	1	0	1	0	0	0	1	0	3	Y
1868	0	0	1	0	0	0	0	1	0	0	0	0	0	2	Y
1872	1	0	0	0	0	0	1	1	0	0	0	0	0	3	Y
1876	1	1	1	0	1	1	1	0	1	0	1	1	0	9	N*
1880	0	1	1	0	0	0	0	0	0	0	1	1	0	4	Y
1884	1	1	1	0	1	1	1	0	0	0	1	0	0	7	N
1888	1	0	0	0	0	0	1	1	0	0	1	1	0	5	Y*
1892	1	1	0	1	0	0	0	1	0	0	1	1	0	6	N
1896	1	1	1	0	1	1	1	1	0	0	1	0	0	8	N
1900	1	0	0	0	0	0	0	0	0	0	0	1	1	3	Y
1904	0	0	0	0	0	0	0	0	0	0	0	0	0	0	Y
1908	0	0	1	0	0	1	0	0	0	0	0	1	0	3	Y
1912	1	1	0	1	0	0	1	0	0	0	1	1	0	6	N
1916	1	0	0	0	0	1	0	0	0	0	0	1	0	3	Y
1920	1	1	1	0	1	1	0	1	0	1	0	1	0	8	N
1924	1	0	0	1	0	0	0	0	1	0	0	1	0	4	Y
1928	0	0	1	0	0	0	1	0	0	0	0	1	0	3	Y
1932	1	0	0	0	1	1	1	1	0	0	1	1	1	8	N
1936	0	0	0	0	0	0	0	0	0	0	1	0	0	1	Y
1940	1	0	0	0	0	0	0	0	0	0	1	0	0	2	Y
1944	1	0	0	0	0	0	0	0	0	1	0	0	0	2	Y
1948	1	0	0	1	0	1	0	0	0	1	0	1	0	5	Y
1952	0	1	1	0	0	1	1	0	1	1	0	1	1	8	N
1956	0	0	0	0	0	0	1	0	0	0	0	0	0	1	Y
1960	1	0	1	0	1	1	1	0	0	1	1	1	1	9	N
1964	1	0	0	0	0	0	0	0	0	1	0	1	0	3	Y
1968	1	1	1	1	0	0	0	1	0	1	1	1	0	8	N
1972	1	0	0	0	0	1	1	0	0	0	0	1	0	4	Y
1976	1	1	0	0	0	1	1	0	1	1	1	1	0	8	N
1980	1	1	0	1	1	0	1	0	0	1	0	1	1	8	N
1984	0	0	0	0	0	1	0	0	0	0	1	0	0	2	Y
1988	0	0	1	0	0	0	1	0	0	0	0	1	0	3	Y
1992	1	0	0	1	1	1	1	0	0	0	0	1	0	6	N
1996	1	0	0	1	0	0	1	0	0	0	1	1	0	5	Y
2000	0	0	1	0	0	0	1	0	1	0	1	1	0	5	Y*
2004	0	0	0	0	0	1	1	0	0	1	0	1	0	4	Y
2008	1	0	1	0	0	1	1	1	0	1	1	1	1	9	N**

An entry of 1 favors the party in power and of 0 favors the challenging party. The sum totals the keys against the party in power. Win indicates the popular vote outcome for the party in power.

*The popular vote and the Electoral College vote diverged.

**The 9 key deficit represents a retrospective evaluation. In the final assessment published in August 2008, the Short-Term Economy was not called against the incumbent Republicans and the deficit was 8 keys.

must be part of a set that correctly distinguished incumbent and challenging party victories and must add to the degree of distance between these classifications, as measured by mD(C) – mD(I), where mD(C) is the mean Hemming's Distance for elections classified as challenger victories and mD(I) is the mean Hemming's Distance for elections classified as incumbent victories. These criteria resulted in the exclusion of about 15 initially proposed questions, including whether the economy is in war or peace, whether the incumbent or challenging candidate is more centrist in policies, whether the incumbent party has held office for more than one term, whether the incumbent party gained more than 50 percent of votes cast in the previous election, and whether the incumbent party is Republican or Democratic. For additional elaboration on method see, Lichtman & Keilis-Borok, 1981.

Answers to some of the questions posed in the Keys require the kind of informed evaluations that historians invariably rely on in drawing conclusions about past events. Two constraints distinguish these assessments from the ad hoc judgments of conventional political commentators. First, all judgment calls are made consistently across elections; the threshold standards established in the study of previous elections must be applied impartially to future contests as well. Second, each Key has an explicit definition that is briefly summarized in Table 2. As indicated by these definitions, Keys 1-3 and 5-6, require little or no judgment. Key 4 requires an assessment of prospects for a third party candidate. The rule of thumb is that percentage vote polled by insurgent candidates usually equals about half of their peak standing in the polls. Keys 7-13 require more considerable judgment, but the calls on these keys are not difficult, given their definitions and the history of calls made in the 37 elections from 1860 to 2004. This combination of judgmental and non-judgmental indicators is consistent with recent trends in forecasting methodology (Armstrong &

Cuzon, 2006). For additional details on defining and turning the keys see Lichtman, 2008, 19-48.

It should be noted that because the Keys to the White House diagnose the national political environment, they forecast popular balloting, not the votes of individual states in the Electoral College. However, only once in the last 120 years – in the contested 2000 election -- has the popular vote and the Electoral College vote diverged. In that election, the Keys correctly anticipated that the Democratic candidate Al Gore would win the popular vote tally, although by a margin of only one key. Table 3 provides assessments of the Keys for all elections from 1860 to 2008. Table 4 reports those predictions (1984-2008) made in advance of the election.

In an extension of the Keys model, regression methods were used to convert scores on the keys for the full period from 1860 to 2004 to a numerical prediction of the two party presidential vote. The regression yielded the following result:

$$V = 36.75 + 1.84L$$

V = the percentage of the two-party split going to the incumbent

L = the number of Keys favoring the incumbent party

This approach was suggested in Armstrong & Cuzan, 2006, 12.

For all 38 elections, Table 5 reports the actual two-party percentage for the winning candidate and the predicted percentage based on the equation outlined above. The equation correctly predicts the popular vote winner in each election, with a mean error margin of 3.60 percent for the two-party vote percentage. Table 6 reports the actual and predicted percentage for the seven elections predicted in advance – 1984 to 2008. In these instances the equation correctly predicts the popular vote winner, with a mean error margin of just 1.92 percent. Unlike most other predic-

Table 4. Keys, advance predictions, 1984-2008

YEARrR	K 1	K 2	K 3	K 4	K 5	K 6	K 7	K 8	K 9	K 10	K 11	K 12	K13	SUMmD	WIN
1984	0	0	0	0	0	1	0	0	0	0	1	0	0	2	Y
1988	0	0	1	0	0	0	1	0	0	0	0	1	0	3	Y
1992	1	0	0	1	1	1	1	0	0	0	0	1	0	6	N
1996	1	0	0	1	0	0	1	0	0	0	1	1	0	5	Y
2000	0	0	1	0	0	0	1	0	1	0	1	1	0	5	Y*
2004	0	0	0	0	0	1	1	0	0	1	0	1	0	4	Y
2008	1	0	1	0	0	1	1	0	0	1	1	1	1	8	N**

*The popular vote and the Electoral College vote diverged.

**Prospective assessment. (August 2008). The retrospective assessment turned another key (Short-term Economy Key 5) against the party in power.

***Retrospective assessment.

tions systems that predicted a large Gore margin in the popular vote, the Keys correctly predicted a close election in 2000, missing Gore's popular vote tally by just 1.21 percent (Table 6). In the most recent 2008 election, the advance numerical prediction on the Keys, issued in February 2006, came within .36 percent of the actual two-party percentage achieved by the Republican candidate.

FORECASTING 2012

At the time of this writing, in June 2009, more than three and a half years before the upcoming election, it is not possible to issue a definitive prediction for the 2012 contest. However, the Keys to the White House offer a preliminary forecast and indicate what changes in the political environment could alter that verdict. The preliminary verdict of the Keys is that President Barack Obama will secure re-election in 2012. Currently nine keys are pointing in the direction of the incumbent Democrats, whereas only one key points to the incumbent party's defeat. Three keys are uncertain (Table 7).

The following nine keys preliminarily favor the incumbent Democratic Party:

* The Republicans are unlikely to win the 25 seats in the midterm elections of 2010 needed to topple Mandate Key 1.
* President Obama should not be strongly tested for re-nomination, securing Contest Key 2 for the party in power.
* Obama will be the sitting president in 2012, locking in Incumbency Key 3.
* It is unlikely that any prospective third-party candidate for 2012 would win the 5 percent of the vote needed to turn this Key against the Democrats.
* The economy should have recovered from the recession by 2012, gaining Short-term Economy Key 5 for the incumbent party.
* The absence of social upheavals comparable to the 1960s avoids the loss of Social Unrest Key 8.
* It is unlikely that Obama will suffer a scandal comparable to Teapot Dome in the 1920s or Watergate in the 1970s, thus averting the loss of Scandal Key 9.
* Unless Barack Obama's charisma fades, he should hold Incumbent Charisma/Hero Key 12.
* There is no prospective Republican candidate on the horizon capable of turning Challenger Charisma/Hero Key 13 against the incumbent Democrats.

Table 5. Keys: Historical Outcomes & numerical regression results, 1860-2008

ELECTION	ACTUAL TWO-PARTY % FOR INCUMBENT	PREDICTED TWO-PARTY % FOR INCUMBENT	DIFFERENCE
1860	42.69	47.79	5.10
1864	55.00	55.15	.15
1868	52.70	56.99	4.29
1872	55.94	55.15	-.79
1876	48.48	44.11	-4.37
1880	50.05	53.31	3.26
1884	49.69	47.79	-1.90
1888	50.41	51.47	1.06
1892	48.31	49.63	1.32
1896	47.80	45.95	-1.85
1900	53.14	55.15	2.01
1904	60.00	60.67	.67
1908	54.55	55.15	.60
1912	35.59	49.63	14.04
1916	51.63	55.15	3.52
1920	36.19	45.95	9.76
1924	65.22	53.31	-11.91
1928	58.79	55.15	-3.64
1932	40.89	45.95	5.06
1936	62.49	58.83	-3.66
1940	54.97	56.99	2.02
1944	53.78	56.99	3.21
1948	52.38	51.47	-.91
1952	44.52	45.95	1.43
1956	57.75	58.83	1.08
1960	49.95	44.11	-5.84
1964	61.35	55.15	-6.20
1968	55.38	45.95	-9.43
1972	61.81	53.31	-8.50
1976	48.93	45.95	-2.98
1980	44.66	45.95	1.29
1984	59.15	56.99	-2.16
1988	53.88	55.15	1.27
1992	46.58	49.63	3.05
1996	54.73	51.47	-3.26
2000	50.26	51.47	1.21
2004	51.21	53.31	2.10
2008	44.41	46.31	1.90
ABSOLUTE MEAN DIFF			3.60

Table 6. Keys: Historical outcomes and numerical regression results, advance predictions only, 2004-2008

1984	59.15	56.99	-2.16
1988	53.88	55.15	1.27
1992	46.58	49.63	3.05
1996	54.73	51.47	-3.26
2000	50.26	51.47	1.21
2004	51.21	53.31	2.10
2008	45.95	46.31	0.36
ABSOLUTE MEAN DIFF			1.92

The following single key falls against the incumbent party:

* Given the lingering recession, it is unlikely that real per-capita growth during the term will exceed the growth recorded during the last two presidential terms, forfeiting Long-Term Economy Key 6.

The following three keys are uncertain:

* It remains uncertain whether Obama will secure Policy-Change Key 7 by steering enough of his major domestic policy initiatives through Congress.
* The fate of Foreign/Military Failure Key 10 and Foreign/Military Success Key 11 will obviously depend on the outcome of future events abroad.

Only major setbacks in the economy at home and events abroad can conceivably turn enough keys against the incumbent Democrats to predict their defeat in 2012. The most plausible, if still unlikely scenario, involves two to three currently favorable keys shifting away from the Democrats, the one unfavorable key remaining unchanged, and two to three uncertain keys turning against the party in power. If the recession lingers through 2012 – in essence becoming the first depression since the 1930s -- then Short-term Economy Key 5 would fall against the Democrats and likely Mandate Key 1 could do so as well, given that a sour economy would improve GOP prospects in the 2010 midterm elections. The advent of an economic depression recession would also guarantee the loss of Long-term Economy 6 and perhaps even spark a nomination struggle within the Democratic Party, jeopardizing Contest Key 2. In foreign affairs, major setbacks in Afghanistan and Pakistan could result in the loss of Foreign/Military Failure Key 10 and a failure to achieve a major triumph elsewhere could forfeit Foreign/Military Success Key 11. Thus, unless conditions at home and abroad turn sharply negative for the United States, Obama is a certain winner in 2012.

The regression analysis also provides for a numerical prediction of the 2008 results. Assuming that the incumbent Democrats retain nine keys, their percentage of the two-party presidential vote is an estimated 53.31 percent of the two-party vote. If the Democrats retain ten keys, their percentage is an estimated 55.15 percent. Thus the mean prediction, three and a half years before the 2012 election is that Obama will win with 54.23 percent of the popular vote.

Table 7. Keys: Current standings, June 2009

KEY NUMBER	DESCRIPTION	OUTCOME 2008
KEY 1	PARTY MANDATE	TRUE
KEY 2	CONTEST	TRUE
KEY 3	INCUMBENCY	TRUE
KEY 4	THIRD PARTY	TRUE
KEY 5	SHORT-TERM ECONOMY	TRUE
KEY 6	LONG-TERM ECONOMY	FALSE
KEY 7	POLICY CHANGE	UNCERTAIN
KEY 8	SOCIAL UNREST	TRUE
KEY 9	SCANDAL	TRUE
KEY 10	FOREIGN/MILITARY FAILURE	UNCERTAIN
KEY 11	FOREIGN/MILITARY SUCCESS	UNCERTAIN
KEY 12	INCUMBENT CHARISMA	TRUE
KEY 13	CHALLENGER CHARISMA	TRUE

TRUE: 9 KEYS FALSE: 1 KEY UNCERTAIN 4 KEYS
PRELIMINARY PREDICTION: INCUMBENT DEMOCRATS WIN

GOVERNING AND CAMPAIGNING

The Keys have implications for governing the country and conducting presidential campaigns. The keys do not prove that campaigning is irrelevant to the outcomes of presidential elections. Primary campaigns can influence the turning of Contest Key 2 and general election campaigns could produce charismatic candidates, as measured by Keys 12 and 13, although the threshold for winning these keys is high. However, the keys do suggest that what mainly counts in presidential elections is governing, as measured by the consequential events of a presidential term, not packaging, image-making or campaigning. Effective governing keeps incumbent parties in office and renders futile conventional campaigning by challengers. This relationship between governing and politics has held true across nearly 150 years of American history and vast changes in our economy, society, and politics: suffrage for women and blacks; new immigrants from Eastern Europe, Asia, and Latin America; the rise of the corporation; and the advent of polling, television, and the Internet.

Candidates favored by the Keys do not have an incentive to break historical patterns in their campaign. However, they do have an incentive, within the limits of conventional politics, to run a substantive campaign that builds a foundation for governing and thereby increases their party's chances to retain the White House in the next election. In sum, not just elections, but election forecasts have consequences for politics. The models that we use to predict and understand presidential elections shape the conduct of campaigns, the relationship between candidates and the American people, and ultimately the policies of government.

ACKNOWLEDGMENT

The author acknowledges the Editor-in-Chief of the journal, Professor John Wang, and the anonymous reviewers for their important help with this article.

REFERENCES

Armstrong, J. S., & Cuzan, A. G. (2006, Feb.). Index methods for forecasting: An application to the American presidential elections. *Foresight: The International Journal of Applied Forecasting, 3*, 10–13.

Campbell, J. E., & Garand, J. C. (Eds.). (2000). *Before the Vote: Forecasting American National Elections*. Thousand Oaks, CA: Sage.

Campbell, J. E., & Lewis-Beck, M. (Eds.). (2008, April-June). US presidential election forecasting. *International Journal of Forecasting, 4*.

Erikson, R. S., & Wlezien, C. (2008). Are political markets really superior to polls as election predictions? *Public Opinion Quarterly, 72*, 190–215. doi:10.1093/poq/nfn010

Gott, J. R., & Colley, W. N. (2008, Nov.). Median statistics in polling. *Mathematical and Computer Modelling, 48*, 1396–1408. doi:10.1016/j.mcm.2008.05.038

Gvishiani, A. D., Zelevinsky, A. V., Keilis-Borok, V. I., & Kosobokov, V. I. (1980). Methods and agorithms for interpretation of seismological data. *Computational Semiology, 13*, Nauka, Moscow.

Jones, R. J. (2002). *Who will be in the White House? Predicting Presidential Elections*. New York: Longman.

Jones, R. J. (2007). *The state of presidential election forecasting in 2004*. Paper Presented at the 2007 ISF International Symposium on Forecasting, New York, NY.

Keilis-Borok, V. I., & Lichtman, A. J. (1981). Pattern recognition applied to presidential elections in the United States, 1860-1980: The role of integral social, economic, and political traits. *Proceedings of the National Academy of Sciences of the United States of America, 78*, 7230–7234. doi:10.1073/pnas.78.11.7230

Lichtman, A. J. (1988, May). How to bet in November. *Washingtonian Magazine* (pp. 115-24).

Lichtman, A. J. (2006, Feb.). The keys to the white house: Forecast for 2008. *Foresight: The International Journal of Applied Forecasting, 3*, 5–9.

Lichtman, A. J. (2007). The Keys to the white house: Updated forecast for 2008. *Foresight: The International Journal of Applied Forecasting, 8*, 5–9.

Lichtman, A. J. (2008). *The Keys to the White House, 2008 Edition*. Lanham, MD: Rowman & Littlefield.

Lichtman, A. J. (2008, April-June). The keys to the white house: An index forecast for 2008. *International Journal of Forecasting, 4*, 301–309. doi:10.1016/j.ijforecast.2008.02.004

Lichtman, A. J., & Keilis-Borok, V. I. (July 2004). What Kerry must do to win (but probably won't). *Counterpunch*. http://www.counterpunch.org/lichtman07292004.html

This work was previously published in International Journal of Information Systems and Social Change, Volume 1, Issue 1, edited by John Wang, pp. 31-43, copyright 2010 by IGI Publishing (an imprint of IGI Global).

Section 4
Managing Databases of the Future

Chapter 15
National Game Management Database of Hungary

Sándor Csányi
Szent István University, Hungary

Róbert Lehoczki
Szent István University, Hungary

Krisztina Sonkoly
Szent István University, Hungary

ABSTRACT

Advances in ecological science and increasing public environmental awareness have resulted in changes in the management of renewable natural resources. To achieve sustainable use of wildlife, managers need reliable data on populations, habitats, and the complexities of ecological interactions. The National Game Management Database (NGMD) was first mandated by the Hungarian Game Management and Hunting Law in 1996. In this paper, the authors summarize the origins, characteristics, development, and results leading to the final establishment of and uses for the NGMD. Goals of the NGMD are to store data on game populations and game management, provide input to spatial analyses and mapping, and to facilitate decision-making and planning efforts of game management administration. It contains information on the populations of game species, data from annual game management reports, trophy-scoring data, maximum allowed and minimum huntable population size, and maps and long-term game management plans for each GMU and the 24 game management regions. In Hungary, the NGMD was the first operating database in wildlife management and nature conservation providing full GIS capabilities, supporting geographical analyses.

INTRODUCTION

In the last half century, advances in ecological science and increasing public environmental awareness have resulted in changes in the management of renewable natural resources. Managers are now expected to apply ecological theory, principles, and knowledge to management of wildlife species and their habitats (Brainerd, 2007; Morrison et al., 1998; Sinclair et al., 2006; Walters, 1986). A major goal for today's wildlife biologists and game managers is to conserve natural resources

DOI: 10.4018/978-1-4666-0927-3.ch015

and manage wild populations on ecologically sound bases. Wild animals and their habitats are limited resources that can be renewed and used sustainably if management is based on population demographics and productivity. In the case of game species, sustainable or "wise" use of their populations is the most important objective of management (Damm et al., 2008; Ebner, 2007; Potts et al., 1991).

In order to achieve sustainable use of wildlife resources, game management should be based on intrinsic population attributes, as well as environmental characteristics and processes affecting wildlife populations (Csányi, 2007b). It is important to plan at different temporal and spatial scales for natural resource management (Csányi, 1998, 1999a). To plan effectively, managers need reliable, accessible and well designed data on the managed populations, their habitats, and the complexities of ecological interactions (Braun, 2005).

The National Game Management Database of Hungary was first mandated by the Hungarian Game Management and Hunting Law in 1996. Since then, the database has contributed significantly to several aspects of game management; from plan development to wildlife ecological research and education. This work has been conducted through the Institute for Wildlife Conservation at Szent István University. Management and research conducted utilizing the database have supported the conservation of the famous Hungarian game populations, benefiting both hunters and the public, and has improved understanding and acceptance of ecologically sound wildlife management.

The following paper summarizes the origins, characteristics, development, and results leading to the final establishment of and uses for the National Game Management Database.

ECOLOGICAL AND HISTORICAL BACKGROUND

Sustainable use of wild populations is a priority in international conservation treaties and relevant European Union (EU) legislation (Brainerd, 2007; Ebner, 2007; European Communities, 1979, 1992). However, this is not a new concept; in many countries sustainable use of forests, fish, and game is a century's old tradition. In Hungary, the first elements of modern, "sustainable" game management were established in the late 19th century, along with efforts to integrate forestry, agriculture and game management - three interdependent branches of renewable resources (Csányi, 1994; Tóth, 1991).

An annual harvest (culling) plan is fundamental to game species management. Harvest plans were introduced into Hungarian game management in the 1950s. In the 1970s, the next development was to include a compulsory long-term (10-year) game management plan (Csányi, 1998; Tóth, 1991). Incorporating ecological principles into the management of game populations can be facilitated by identifying relatively homogenous regions in which to base game management planning. Theories supporting regional management first appeared in Hungarian game management literature in the 1960s, summarized as "landscape based game management" (Bencze, 1979; Tóth, 1991). Twenty-four game management regions were established in the 1990s based on available data on game management and environmental variables (Csányi, 1993, 1998, 1999a).

To achieve such far-reaching goals as sustainable use of wildlife populations, balanced management of game and habitats, and conservation objectives, we need comprehensive, organized, and detailed information. For hunted species, this data must include information on population size and structure, data on killed and/or live-caught game, and the quality of the harvested animals, e.g., trophy scoring data, body weight, sex and age composition (e.g., Asferg, 1982; Bergström et al., 1992; Myrberget, 1988; Tapper, 1992). Such databases have been developing in several European countries, e.g. Austria (Forstner et al., 2003), Finland (www.rktl.fi/english/statistics/hunting/), Norway (www.ssb.no/english/subjects/10/04/10/), or France (www.oncfs.gouv.fr/events/point_faune/).

Game bag data was first collected in Hungary in the 1890s by Károly Keleti, the renowned president of the Hungarian Office for Statistics (Csőre, 1996). With some exceptions, game bag records have been available for more than 100 years (Csányi, 1996, 1999b, 2006, 2007a; Tóth, 2005, 2007, 2008). However, data collection and publication of national and/or regional statistics is not enough for detailed analysis; data should be available in a format for analyses using multiple variables or high level details. For example, wildlife population data may need to be correlated with ecological characteristics, public land uses, or spatio-temporal changes of the environment (Csányi, 1993, 1998).

THE NATIONAL GAME MANAGEMENT DATABASE OF HUNGARY

Initial Conditions and Supporting Legislation

Studies had indicated that for further development of game management and consistency of management decisions made by the relevant parties, from hunting area managers to government authorities, better data collection and the development of a national game management database, utilizing technological innovations in computer science, data processing, and statistical methods, was required (Csányi, 1993, 1994). The database needed to include all relevant information for each game management unit and data from regional plans, long-term and annual game management plans of the management units, species populations, game bags, and trophy evaluation.

The initial results indicated that a comprehensive game management database could be developed (Csányi, 1993, 1994). As a result, the *Act on Game Conservation, Management and Hunting* (Act LV, 1996) mandated the formation of the National Game Management Database (NGMD, *Országos Vadgazdálkodási Adattár* in Hungarian). In accordance with the law, the goals of the NGMD are to:

- Store data on game populations and game management in a way that can be used for multiple analytical procedures.
- Provide input to spatial analyses and mapping.
- Facilitate decision-making and planning efforts at various levels of game management administration.

In order to design such a vast database, the Ministry of Agriculture and Rural Development contracted the Department of Wildlife Biology and Management, University of Agricultural Sciences in Gödöllő (currently the Institute for Wildlife Conservation, Szent István University) to evaluate and design a database in 1993. The Institute for Wildlife Conservation was founded in 2007 from the former Department of Wildlife Biology and Management. It is a part of the Faculty of Agriculture and Environmental Sciences and has been a leading institution of wildlife science in Hungary. Thus, the NGMD is housed in the most appropriate scientific and academic environment where results are easily converted to new elements of education (www.vmi.info.hu).

On average, five staff members manage the NGMD, each holding MSc or BSc degrees in Wildlife Management, Computer Science, Agricultural Sciences, or GIS and geography. Students can be involved in NGMD projects and participate in resolving real management issues using high-tech methods- the most talented students may be recruited for future staff.

Design and Data Input for the NGMD

From the start, the NGMD was developed on personal computers using commercial software, including the database format (Paradox 11 Relational Database Program, Corel Corp.) and software used for spatial data management and analysis (ArcInfo and ArcView GIS, ESRI Corp.). Using standard computer resources, the programmers developed the special applications for data input and statistical output (generally descriptive statistics for regions or country level). The NGMD is primarily based on data provided by the 24 game management regions with 1350 game management units (GMUs) (Csányi, 1997; Lehoczki et al., 2008).

The database contains the following information (Figure 1):

- Spring population data for red deer, fallow deer, roe deer, mouflon, wild boar, brown hare, ring-necked pheasant, and grey partridge. This data consists of spring population reports from the GMUs in late February, available from 1987 to the present.

- Game management reports for red deer, fallow deer, roe deer, mouflon, wild boar, brown hare, ring-necked pheasant, grey partridge, wild ducks (5 species), wild geese (2 species), and other hunted species

Figure 1. Graphical representation of the structure of the National Game Management Database

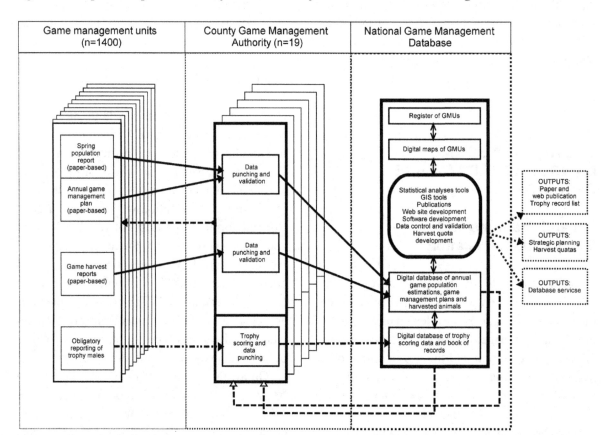

(mainly predators). This data includes the bags, live-catches, available non-hunting mortality, game feeding, and costs of game management activities and incomes from hunting during the hunting season. Game management reports from the GMUs are available since 1986.

- Trophy scoring data for red deer, fallow deer, roe deer, mouflon, and wild boar provided by the National/County Trophy Scoring Committees. Data for each individual animal presented for trophy evaluation since 1990 is stored in the database.
- Maximum allowed population size and minimum huntable population size for red deer, fallow deer, roe deer, mouflon, and wild boar as well as the minimum huntable population size for brown hare, ring-necked pheasant, and grey partridge.
- Address and other data for each GMU. Detailed description of borders and game management maps of each GMU (digitalized, scale 50,000).
- Description and maps of the 24 management regions (based on the GMU maps), long-term (10-year) game management plans of the GMUs (1997-2007, 2007-2017), and regional game management plans of the 24 game management regions (2003).
- Reports and data from the monitoring programs financed by the Ministry of Agriculture and Rural Development (e.g., monitoring hunted and protected carnivores; monitoring birds of prey).

The NGMD is compatible with other data collected in various research and monitoring programs, and thus can be linked with data on forestry, agriculture, and nature conservation. This data includes agricultural land use maps, satellite images, CORINE land-cover maps (Institute of Geodesy, Cartography and Remote Sensing, Hungary [FÖMI], 2009), soil typological maps, forest stand maps from the State Forest Service, and Natura 2000 site maps, among others. In Hungary, the NGMD was the first operating database for wildlife management and nature conservation providing full GIS capabilities and supporting geographical analyses.

Results Achieved and Services Provided

The prime objective of this project has been to bring together database technology and wildlife management requirements and problems for comparative analyses. To achieve this, the technical aspects and inputs to the database were developed in parallel; however, the resulting models have been tested with separate data from the field. The functioning NGMD system was completed in 1996, and has been available for regular use since then.

The database is and has been used for:

- The design of the 24 game management regions based on multivariate analyses of game management and environmental data and input to the plan for the 24 game management regions (2000-2002) (Csányi, 1999a).
- Forming a theoretical framework for the 3-level game management system, introduced in 1996/1997, as well as the development of the annual, long-term and regional management plans, and data input for the long term (10-year) management plans of the GMUs (1996-1998 and 2007) (Csányi, 1993, 1998, 1999a).
- The determination of a maximum sustainable population size for red deer, roe deer, and wild boars in Hungary (1997-1999) (Csányi & Ritter, 1999), and as a follow up, for the design and implementation of the big game harvest quota system launched by the Ministry of Agriculture and Rural Development (2002-present) (Csányi, 2003).

Figure 2. Screenshot of the program used for the input and basic statistical analyses of the game population report and annual game management planning data. In this page the user can see all of the available functions from basic data input to editing, printing, and database integrity checking.

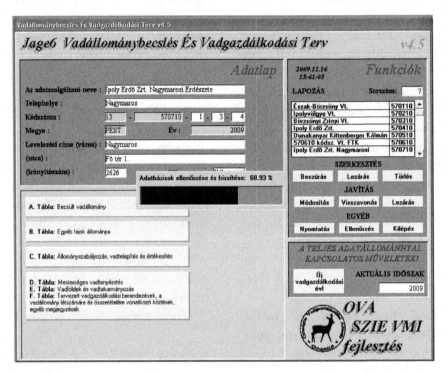

- Data processing of the annual spring population size reports, game harvest plans, and game management reports (1994-present) (e.g., Csányi, 1996, 1999b, 2006, 2007a), and in connection to these, the design and update of the software package used by the hunting authorities (Figure 2 and Figure 3) to collect and statistically analyze reports on spring population size, annual game harvest plans and annual game management reports (1997-present) (Fülemen & Csányi, 2003).

- Designing and updating the software package used by Trophy Scoring Committees for the evaluation process (2002-present).
- The collection, compilation and maintenance of the state and county level databases for game management, starting in 1960 for spring populations and harvest, and in 1970 for trophy scoring/evaluation (e.g., Csányi, 1996, 1999b, 2006, 2007a).

- The annual publication of "Game Management Database," a booklet containing the game population, game harvests, and trophy evaluation data for the previous hunting year (1994-present) (e.g., Csányi, 1996, 1999b, 2006, 2007a).

- Designing and updating a public web site, which makes county, regional and state level game management data freely available for public use. This home page also provides all hunting related legislative information, and documents/guidelines (National Game Management Database [NGMD], 2009; Figure 4) necessary for preparing game management plans (1999-present).

Figure 3. Screenshot of the program used for the input and basic statistical analyses of the game harvest data. In this page the user can input the harvest data of red deer, fallow deer, roe deer, mouflon, wild boar, brown hare, pheasant, and grey partridge.

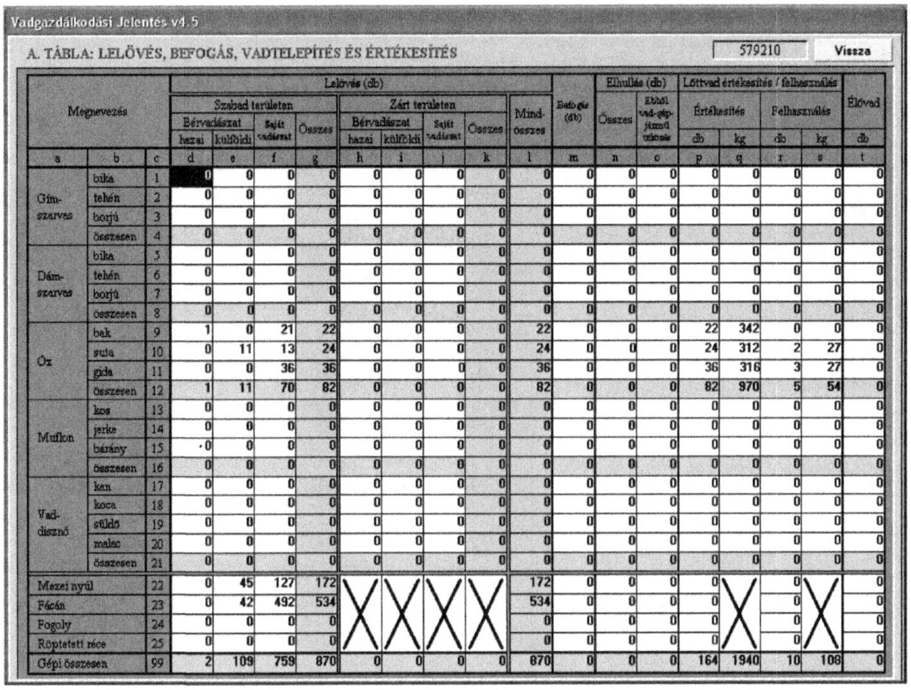

Vadgazdálkodási Jelentés v4.5

A. TÁBLA: LELÖVÉS, BEFOGÁS, VADTELEPÍTÉS ÉS ÉRTÉKESÍTÉS — 579210 — Vissza

Megnevezés			Lelövés (db) Szabad területen Bérvadászat hazai	külföldi	Saját vadászat	Összes	Zárt területen Bérvadászat hazai	külföldi	Saját vadászat	Összes	Mind-összes	Befogás (db)	Elhullás (db) Összes	Ebből vad-gép-ümű ütközés	Löttvad értékesítés / felhasználás Értékesítés db	kg	Felhasználás db	kg	Élővad db
a	b	c	d	e	f	g	h	i	j	k	l	m	n	o	p	q	r	s	t
Gím-szarvas	bika	1	0	0	0	0	0	0	0	0	0	0	0	0	0	0	0	0	0
	tehén	2	0	0	0	0	0	0	0	0	0	0	0	0	0	0	0	0	0
	borjú	3	0	0	0	0	0	0	0	0	0	0	0	0	0	0	0	0	0
	összesen	4	0	0	0	0	0	0	0	0	0	0	0	0	0	0	0	0	0
Dám-szarvas	bika	5	0	0	0	0	0	0	0	0	0	0	0	0	0	0	0	0	0
	tehén	6	0	0	0	0	0	0	0	0	0	0	0	0	0	0	0	0	0
	borjú	7	0	0	0	0	0	0	0	0	0	0	0	0	0	0	0	0	0
	összesen	8	0	0	0	0	0	0	0	0	0	0	0	0	0	0	0	0	0
Őz	bak	9	1	0	21	22	0	0	0	0	22	0	0	0	22	342	0	0	0
	suta	10	0	11	13	24	0	0	0	0	24	0	0	0	24	312	2	27	0
	gida	11	0	0	36	36	0	0	0	0	36	0	0	0	36	316	3	27	0
	összesen	12	1	11	70	82	0	0	0	0	82	0	0	0	82	970	5	54	0
Muflon	kos	13	0	0	0	0	0	0	0	0	0	0	0	0	0	0	0	0	0
	jerke	14	0	0	0	0	0	0	0	0	0	0	0	0	0	0	0	0	0
	bárány	15	0	0	0	0	0	0	0	0	0	0	0	0	0	0	0	0	0
	összesen	16	0	0	0	0	0	0	0	0	0	0	0	0	0	0	0	0	0
Vad-disznó	kan	17	0	0	0	0	0	0	0	0	0	0	0	0	0	0	0	0	0
	koca	18	0	0	0	0	0	0	0	0	0	0	0	0	0	0	0	0	0
	süldő	19	0	0	0	0	0	0	0	0	0	0	0	0	0	0	0	0	0
	malac	20	0	0	0	0	0	0	0	0	0	0	0	0	0	0	0	0	0
	összesen	21	0	0	0	0	0	0	0	0	0	0	0	0	0	0	0	0	0
Mezei nyúl		22	0	45	127	172	╳	╳	╳	╳	172	0	0	0	╳	0	╳	0	0
Fácán		23	0	42	492	534					534	0	0	0		0		0	0
Fogoly		24	0	0	0	0					0	0	0	0		0		0	0
Röptetett réce		25	0	0	0	0					0	0	0	0		0		0	0
Gépi összesen		99	2	109	759	870	0	0	0	0	870	0	0	0	164	1940	10	108	0

- Providing game management data for students preparing thesis at colleges/universities (>150 theses since 1997).
- Professional advisory services to game management units, state foresters, county game management and hunting authorities and NGOs.
- Providing information for expert witnesses in legal cases.
- Advisory input to the Ministry of Agriculture and Rural Development on strategic planning and high level decision-making.

CONCLUSION

Advances in ecological science and increasing public environmental awareness have resulted in changes in the management of renewable natural resources. To achieve sustainable use of wildlife, managers need reliable, accessible and well designed data on populations, habitats, and the complexities of ecological interactions. The information available on game species and their habitats can most efficiently be used if they are organized in well structured databases. In Hungary this need was realized in the early 1990s and it opened the way to start the development of the National Game Management Database. Similar databases are developed in several European countries.

Since 1993, when the initial development of the NGMD started, we managed to build up a comprehensive database of game management and hunting data. This database satisfies the needs of game managers and authorities as it contains the data on game populations and game harvests in a way that can be used for multiple analytical procedures. It provides input to spatial analyses

Figure 4. Opening page of the website of the National Game Management Database (http://www.vmi. szie.hu/adattar/index.html)

and mapping, and it facilitates decision-making and planning at various levels of game management administration.

This information on game populations and management provides sound bases to analyze trends of game populations in relation to harvest and/or environmental changes. The database and the analytical tools are especially useful for understanding local/regional changes in environmental conditions, harvest regimes, management attitudes, etc. Using this organized database as a foundation, temporal and spatial analyses can be set up on much wider scales and understanding of long-term processes can be improved. Regionally stratified data improves modeling capabilities and comparative studies among different game management regions or ecosystems.

In order to increase the usability/functionality of NGMD we kept it as open as possible.

Consequently, it can be connected with another natural resource management, agricultural, or nature conservation databases. It is compatible with data collected from various wildlife research and monitoring programs, and thus can be linked with data on forestry, agriculture, and conservation. In Hungary, the NGMD was the first operating database in wildlife management and nature conservation providing full GIS capabilities, supporting geographical analyses.

During the last 15 years, the NGMD has facilitated the decision-making and planning efforts at various levels of game management administration. Through the implementation of the 3-level game management regions and the partitioning of the 24 game management regions we can solve real world problems. The ability to balance a scientific approach with practical requirements seems to be an essential element for successful conservation of biodiversity and wise use of renewable natural resources like wildlife populations. It is extraordinarily important that the information of the NGMD can be connected to other databases like those pertaining to forestry and nature conservation. This connectivity allows for broadening the applicability of wildlife population and management data.

REFERENCES

Asferg, T. (1982). Sample size in game bag statistics: a preliminary study. In *Proceedings of the 2nd Meeting of the Working Group on Game Statistics of IUGB,* Doorwerth, The Netherlands.

Bencze, L. (1979). *A vadállomány fenntartásának lehetőségei. A vadászati ökológia alapjai.* Budapest, Hungary: Akadémiai Kiadó.

Bergström, R., Huldt, H., & Nilsson, U. (Eds.). (1992). *Swedish game - Biology and management.* Stockholm, Sweden: Svenska Jägareförbundet.

Brainerd, S. (2007). *European charter on hunting and biodiversity (Vol. 2).* Budakeszi, Hungary: CIC - International Council for Game and Wildlife Conservation.

Braun, C. E. (Ed.). (2005). *Techniques for wildlife investigations and management.* Bethesda, Maryland: The Wildlife Society.

Csányi, S. (1993). A basis for sustainable wise use of game in Hungary: defining management regions. *Landscape and Urban Planning, 27,* 199–205. doi:10.1016/0169-2046(93)90050-N

Csányi, S. (1994). Moving toward coordinated management of timber and other resource uses in Hungarian forests. *Forestry Chronicle, 70*(5), 555–561.

Csányi, S. (Ed.). (1996). *Vadgazdálkodási Adattár 1960-1995.* Gödöllő, Hungary: Gödöllői Agrártudományi Egyetem.

Csányi, S. (1997). Országos Vadgazdálkodási Adattár. *Vadgazdálkodás - A Magyar Mezőgazdaság melléklete, 1,* 3.

Csányi, S. (1998). Game management regions and three-level planning in Hungary. *Hungarian Agricultural Research, 7*(2), 12–14.

Csányi, S. (1999a). Regional game management system in Hungary. *Gibier, Faune Sauvage, 15*(3), 929–936.

Csányi, S. (Ed.). (1999b). *Vadgazdálkodási Adattár 1994-1998.* Gödöllő, Hungary: Országos Vadgazdálkodási Adattár, GATE Vadbiológiai és Vadgazdálkodási Tanszék.

Csányi, S. (2003). *A nagyvadállomány körzettervekből adódó szabályozásának megvalósítása (kézirat).* Gödöllő, Hungary: Országos Vadgazdálkodási Adattár.

Csányi, S. (Ed.). (2006). *Útmutató a vadgazdálkodási üzemtervek készítéséhez és vezetéséhez.* Gödöllő, Hungary: Országos Vadgazdálkodási Adattár.

Csányi, S. (2007a). *Országos Vadgazdálkodási Adattár.* Gödöllő, Hungary: Országos Vadgazdálkodási Adattár.

Csányi, S. (2007b). *Vadbiológia.* Budapest: Mezőgazda Kiadó.

Csányi, S., & Ritter, D. (1999). A fenntartható nagyvadlétszám meghatározása az állomány területi eloszlása alapján térinformatikai eszközökkel. *Vadbiológia, 6,* 23–32.

Csőre, P. (1996). *A magyar vadászat története.* Budapest, Hungary: Mezőgazda Kiadó.

Damm, G. R., Baldus, R. D., & Wollscheid, K.-U. (Eds.). (2008). *Best practices in sustainable hunting - A guide to best practices from around the world (Vol. 1).* Budakeszi, Hungary: CIC - International Council for Game and Wildlife Conservation.

Ebner, M. (2007). *Sustainable hunting: 20 years Intergroup "Sustainable hunting, biodiversity and countryside activities" in the European Parliament*. Bozen, Italy: Verlagsanstalt Athesia.

European Communities. (1979). Council directive 79/409/EEC of 2 April 1979 on the conservation of wild birds. *Official Journal of the European Communities, L 103*, 1-15.

European Communities. (1992). Council directive 92/43/EEC of 21 May 1992 on the conservation of natural habitats and wild fauna and flora. *Official Journal of the European Communities, L 206*, 7-49.

Forstner, M., Reimoser, F., Hackl, J., & Heckl, F. (2003). *Criteria and Indicators of Sustainable Hunting* (English Version. Translation of Monograph No. 158 (2001) ed. Vol. 163 (M-163)). Wien, Austria: Federal Ministry for Agriculture, Forestry, Environment and Water Management.

Fülemen, Z., & Csányi, S. (2003). *Programcsomag a vadállománybecslési és a vadgazdálkodási jelentések feldolgozásához (JAGE 1-4)*. Gödöllő, Hungary: Országos Vadgazdálkodási Adattár.

Institute of Geodesy. Cartography and Remote Sensing, Hungary [FÖMI]. (2009). *Hungarian Corine Land Cover 2000 database (CLC2000)*. Retrieved November 17, 2009, from http://www.fomi.hu/corine/

Lehoczki, R., Csányi, S., & Sonkoly, K. (2008, October). Az Országos Vadgazdálkodási Adattár céljai és feladatai. *Nimród Vadászújság*, 13-14.

Morrison, M. L., Marcot, B. G., & Mannan, R. W. (1998). *Wildlife-habitat relationships: consepts and applications*. Madison, WI: University of Wisconsin Press.

Myrberget, S. (1988). Hunting statistics as indicators of game population size and composition. *Statistical Journal of the United Nations ECE, 5*, 289-301.

National Game Management Database [NGMD]. (2009). *NGMD homepage*. Retrieved November 17, 2009, from http://www.vmi.szie.hu/adattar/index.html

Potts, G. R., Lecocq, Y., Swift, J., & Havet, P. (Eds.). (1991). *Proceedings of the International Conference "Wise Use As a Conservation Strategy"*, Brussels, Belgium.

Sinclair, A. R. E., Fryxell, J. M., & Caughley, G. (2006). *Wildlife ecology, conservation, and management*. Boston: Blackwell Publishing.

Tapper, S. (1992). *Game heritage. An ecological review from shooting and gamekeeping records*. Fordingbridge, UK: Game Conservancy Ltd.

Tóth, S. (1991). Game management - hunting. In Keresztesi, B. (Ed.), *Forestry in Hungary 1920 - 1985* (pp. 164–210). Budapest, Hungary: Akadémiai Kiadó.

Tóth, S. (2005). *A hírnév kötelez. Vadászat és vadgazdálkodás Magyarországon 1945-1990* (2nd ed.). Budapest, Hungary: Nimród Alapítvány.

Tóth, S. (2007). *Nyitány a hírnévhez. Vadászat és vadgazdálkodás Magyarországon 1945-1951*. Budapest, Hungary: Nimród Alapítvány.

Tóth, S. (2008). *Szél alatt - hátszélben. Vadászat és vadgazdálkodás Magyarországon 1951-1957*. Budapest, Hungary: Nimród Alapítvány.

Walters, C. (1986). *Adaptive management of renewable resources* (2001 ed.). New York: Macmillan.

This work was previously published in International Journal of Information Systems and Social Change, Volume 1, Issue 4, edited by John Wang, pp. 34-43, copyright 2010 by IGI Publishing (an imprint of IGI Global).

Chapter 16
Managing Demographic Data Inconsistencies in Healthcare Information Systems

Larbi Esmahi
Athabasca University, Canada

Elarbi Badidi
U.A.E. University, UAE

ABSTRACT

Healthcare IT and IS departments have the arduous task of managing the varied information sources into readily accessible, consistent and referential information views. Patient hospital workflows, from admission to discharge, provide a series of data streams for convergences into disparate systems. Protocols such as DICOM and HL7 exist for the purposes of exchanging information within the PACS and RIS information silos in the hospital enterprise. These protocols ensure data confidence for downstream systems, but are not designed to provide referential data cross system in the system-of-systems model. As data crosses the PACS and RIS information domains, data inconsistency is introduced. This paper explores the causes for data disparity and presents a referential data design for disparate systems through the implementation of an XML bus for data exchange and an RDF framework for data semantic.

INTRODUCTION

Healthcare providers typically use technology in a ubiquitous manner. They choose to rely upon the task-specific capabilities of a specific system rather than the integration of all systems in the solution space. A typical example of this would be the advancement of ultrasound technologies for 3-D modeling. Whilst the capabilities of the imaging solutions are highly beneficial to the individual's unique needs for healthcare, the integration of this system into a greater solution or system-of-systems is often overlooked (Maier, 2005; Maier, 1998). As such, the demographic data accompanying the information may be in a format inconsistent with the requirements for the electronic medical record.

DOI: 10.4018/978-1-4666-0927-3.ch016

Workflow Management Systems attempt to simplify and control the primary data entry methods to the data environment (Choennia, 2003; Graeber, 1997). However, the design of these systems focuses on an interpretation layer to gather data from varying input sources, including voice and text. There is no guarantee that this information will propagate throughout the system-of-systems, as required. Common information protocols such as DICOM (Digital Imaging and Communications in Medicine) and HL7 (Health Level Seven) provide a framework by which medical data is communicated. However, these standard protocols are subject to interpretation that allows for a high degree of variance in the presentation of data. This creates problems of data redundancy, and confuses the authoritative provisioning of data with referential copies.

In this paper we present a framework for data exchange and consolidation in the distributed e-health system-of-systems using an XML bus and RDF (Resource Definition Framework). In the next section of this paper, we will discuss the system-of-systems architecture as it is evolving in the health enterprise. We will discuss the Health Level Seven communication protocol and the protocol DICOM. The application of these protocols into solutions for healthcare information repositories is presented with a discussion of both PACS (Picture Archive Communication Systems) and RIS (Radiology Information Systems). The problem of Data Disparity that causes inconsistencies in the intersystem communications will be discussed and the elaborated solution presented. The solution consists of the XML Bus and the RDF extension for DICOM queries. The successes and shortcomings of this design are discussed in the conclusion.

SYSTEM-OF-SYSTEMS ARCHITECTURE FOR E-HEALTH

The electronic healthcare record (EHR) is a merged presentation of the information obtained through various systems in the healthcare enterprise (Hasselbring et al., 2000). Imaging and demographic data contribute to the contents. Additionally, the physician comments, markup and reports also contribute to the record. These individual pieces of the EHR are drawn from many disparate systems throughout the enterprise. The Record Information System (RIS) or alternatively a Health Information System (HIS) will be the primary demographic repository for patient information. As such, this text and contextual information will be used as the primary data source for downstream comparison. The Picture Archive and Communication System (PACS-ADMIN, 2007) will be used as a repository for imaging data (Miltchenko et al., 2003). Figure 1 presents the main components of the electronic health record that need to be integrated and synchronized.

This architecture of system-of-systems describes a large-scale integration of many independent, self-contained systems in order to satisfy the global e-health needs. As the global economy and global business practices increase, individuals tend to be more transient. Their medical histories are an important precursor to successful health care provisioning. Contingent upon this medical history record is the successful integration of data from varied sources (hospitals, clinics, labs, etc.) including the mobile patient's information. This information must be portable, presentable, and independent of the initial data program from which it was obtained. By far the greatest concern relates to data inconsistency and subsequent inaccuracy in an environment of disparate systems.

Figure 1. Main components for the system-of-systems

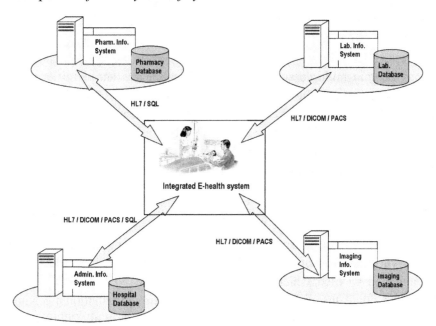

Standard protocols such as DICOM (NEMA, 2008), PACS (Cao, 2000) and HL7 (HL7.org, n.d.) are proposed as a framework by which medical data can be communicated within the system-of-systems. However, many inconsistency problems still exist since the focus of these protocols is on data transfer and not data integration and synchronization. In the next sections we will review these protocols and present different problems

HEALTH LEVEL SEVEN

The HL7 protocol provides an information standard for communicating patients and sites level information into and out of a health information system within the system-of-systems model (HL7.org, n.d.; HL7 Canada, 2002; Neotool, 2007). HL7 allows for a loosely framed communication standard between medical IT systems. Without the provisioning of this ANSI standard, interoperability between systems was performed in an ad hoc manner.

The HL7 standard is based on the concept of events referred to as triggers (HL7, n.d.; Dickinson, 2004). Each of these triggers fires a process that effects some particular communication of information. For example, the relocation of a patient to a new hospital would require the dissemination of information concerning that location throughout the healthcare system-of-systems. This event would be one of such triggers. A trigger may relate to a single record, as in this example, or it may relate to multiple records. A patient may have a name change due to marriage. This would require an update to all existing records in the Information system to ensure data consistency.

Each trigger is composed of segments. The segment is a variable length field separated by a discernable character, such as a comma or pipe. In a manner similar to comma separated values (CSV) files, data can be delineated and also referenced externally though API functions. The content of each segment shall contain ASCII characters. The HL7 committee defines the acceptable character set as "The ASCII displayable character set (hexadecimal values between 20 and 7E, inclusive) is the default character set unless modified in the MSH header segment" (HL7, n.d.). The HL7 trigger can be represented as follow:

Each field may contain multiple subfields, delimited by a caret character. In the case of a name, |DOE^JOHN^^^^| the content between the two pipe symbols is the field of data, where as the data DOE and JOHN are considered subfields. The MSH is the message header segment, providing basic instructions on the contents within the trigger message.

This example also makes reference to three other key items: the PID that is the patient identifier, the EVN identifying that an event is included in this message, and the PV1 filed, which is followed by information about the patient's stay at the hospital. One of the important contents within this message is the event type. As per the example, the message type provided is A04. HL7 defines many different message types, each with unique content. There are 51 defined Admission, Discharge or Transfer (ADT) events for HL7 in the V2.5 standard. The following table describes some of these events.

Without elaborating further on some of the many messages available to the HL7, it becomes clear that many distinct attributes are communicated in this protocol. Static entities such as Patient ID, Accession number, and event dates are provided in the same framework as dynamic information, such as location. The messaging protocol is also intended to communicate changes in state, through the provisioning of state-in-time attributes

that have an expectation of permanence (Evola, 1997). These attributes, such as Patient ID, may have referential integrity for a site perspective. However, in the conglomerate or regional model of healthcare, that identifier now becomes non-referential from a global viewpoint, and as such, introduces disparity at a higher system-of-systems level.

DICOM

The DICOM protocol was developed in a joint effort between the American College of Radiology (ACR) and the National Electrical Manufacturers Association (NEMA, 2008). DICOM exists as an information distribution mechanism for medical devices (Ratib et al., 2000), and can be viewed as a technical protocol for communications and a solution to information exchange. The protocol was introduced as a hardware interface, a minimum set of software commands, and a consistent set of data formats for communication between medical devices. This standard was intended to provide a framework to an emerging technology, medical information technology, allowing the sharing of data amongst Picture Archive Communication Systems (PACS) and compliant sources.

The DICOM protocol is used by a multitude of devices within the hospital enterprise for information transfer, sharing and coordination (Jung, 2005). Some of the systems that rely on the protocol include imaging devices (also known as modalities, such as Ultrasound, X-ray, CR,

Figure 2. Sample HL7 Trigger (Interfaceware, 2009)

```
MSH|^~\&|EPIC|EPICADT|SMS|SMSADT|199912271408|CHARRIS|ADT^A04|1817457|D|2.3|
EVN|A04|199912271408|||CHARRIS
PID||0493575^^^2^ID                1|454721||DOE^JOHN^^^^|DOE^JOHN^^^^|19480203|M||B|254
E238ST^^EUCLID^OH^44123^USA||(216)731-4359|||M|NON|400003403~1129086|999-|
NK1||CONROY^MARI^^^^|SPO||(216)731-4359||EC|||||||||||||||||||||||
PV1||O|168                ~219~C~PMA^^^^^^^^^^||||277^ALLEN        FADZL^BONNIE^^^^||||||||
||2688684||||||||||||||||||||||199912271408||||||002376853
```

Table 1. HL7 message types

Message Type	Definition
Admit/visit notification (event A01)	Assign a bed to an admitted patient
Transfer a patient (event A02)	Patient changes their physical location
Discharge/end visit (event A03)	Patient leaves the facility
Register a patient (event A04)	Patient is brought into the facility, but not given a bed
Pre-admit a patient (event A05)	Patient is not admitted (In the facility), but demographic information is registered in the information system prior to their arrival for procedure.
Change an outpatient to an inpatient (event A06)	If a patients status changes, normally due to severity, they will be given a new location at the facility
Change an inpatient to an outpatient (event A07)	As per A06, defines a state change in the patient location.
Update patient information (event A08)	Represents a change to any of the demographic information related to a patient. This may be name, address, or other field.
Patient departing tracking (event A09)	Patient in transit outbound
Patient arriving - tracking (event A10)	Patient in transit inbound

CT, etc), PACS, Film Printers, and Digitizers (media conversion systems) (Iacucci et al., 2002). Although the implementation of the protocol is proprietary for each manufacturer, the standards as provided by the NEMA organization assist in ensuring general interoperability and definition of expectation for each DICOM function.

The first layer of protocol discussion relates to the negotiation of capabilities between the acquisition device and the subsequent receiver. Two concise roles are defined within DICOM to elucidate the responsibilities of each participant in the information exchange: the Service Class User (SCU) and the Service Class Provider (SCP). The SCU is the requestor of services for the purposes of information storage. In essence, it has information, and solicits a predefined receiver to accept this information. The SCU negotiates the acceptance of the sender's data, typically in one or more ways (Revet, 1997).

The storage transmission starts with a request from the SCU. The SCU identifies itself and asks for a specific function, through a composite request. The request consists of an object and an associated action. For example, a C-STORE message may consist of a request for data storage, and a subsequent object, such as an ultrasound image. The SCP, or storage provider, accepts the association request from the resource, assuming the storage host trusts it.

As illustrated in Figure 3, the bidirectional request-response behavior is typical of the DICOM protocol. The SCP not only accepts the initial request, but also responds with a list of capabilities for that request. The response consists of a list of Service Object-Pair (SOP) classes, reflective of the storage ability of the SCP system. Also included in this request-response exchange is the choice of transfer syntax used for communication. Since there is a multiplicity of available syntaxes in the DICOM standard, some systems require the presence of an explicit value representation in the message. Others rely on an implicit understanding between data dictionary implementations, as provided partly by the DICOM standard, and partly by the SCP developer (McCormick, n.d.).

DICOM data is broken into 6 major groups: File, Study, Acquisition, Image, Object and Presentation. Each of these groups is well defined in terms of permissible content by the DICOM committee, as published in the DICOM standards and Supplements. Seven major groups are used to categorize DICOM Data elements. Group 0002 identifies file level attributes. Group 0008 identify attributes relating to the study. Group 0010 identifies the patient attributes. Group 0018 relates to the acquisition of specific attributes related to the image. Group 0020, contains object level information, including the hierarchal relationship attributes that allow the linking of this image or object to the other objects in the series, study and patient. Group 0028 elements provide display information crucial to the proper visual presentation of the image. Medical software uses this information to apply default settings. Group of Private Data Elements (odd numbered groups), allow vendor to include information that can be used in a proprietary manner (i.e. to display the images, in case that vendor's system is part of the total System-of-Systems solution).

In summary, the DICOM protocol allows not only for the communication of patient, study, series and image level information, it also defines the mechanism by which that information may be exchanged (Kolesnikov et al., 1999; Kolesnikov et al., 1997). This data is the primary source for study information as it related to the patient.

PACS AND RIS

PACS systems (Dwyer, 2000) are built as a central repository for DICOM information (Gell, 2000).

They are typically deployed as a means of replacing typical film based media. Through the implementation of the Storage Class User (SCU) and Storage Class Provider (SCP) mechanisms defined in DICOM, the PACS system receives images for later retrieval. PACS provides an electronic means of long-term storage. This storage serves as the integrated lifecycle management mechanism for a continued inbound stream of data (Miltchenko et al., 2003). The PACS is also the recipient of messages from the RIS. These messages represent unique events such as a patient name change etc. Upon reception of such events, the PACS system is expected to start a process that will eventually update the demographic data using the previous name to the new patient name. The PACS answer to subsequent queries related to the updated patient records is subject to the proper interpretation of the data, as identified through the use of explicit data types, as well as the data dictionary. In fact, the use of DICOM data dictionaries allow for explicit metadata definition of data streams received. In the case of PACS, data dictionaries assist in defining the understanding of data content, both by type and content (Kennedy et al., 2000).

Health Information Systems (HIS) organize demographic records for the purpose of centrally collecting a repository of electronic information. Radiology Information Systems (RIS) build upon

Figure 3. SCU-SCP communications

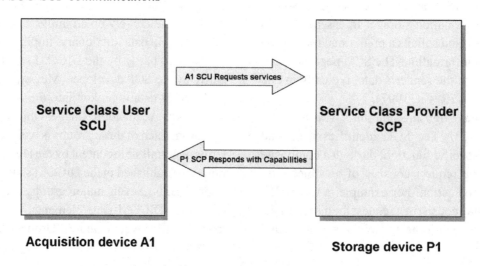

this purpose for the radiology patient by scheduling orders. As information repositories, these systems (HIS and RIS) are constantly updated with both new and changing information. RIS systems can also provide worklists to modalities containing patient names and other demographic information of importance. In order for modalities to communicate outwards to information systems, they rely upon the DICOM protocol (Miltchenko et al., 2003). This may require the HIS system to accept DICOM events. Alternatively, data translation systems occasionally transform DICOM messages to the appropriate HL7 data construct normally understood by the HIS system. The DICOM standard assists PACS implementations in providing a referential target, but only provides DICOM consistency of the data that is independent of the RIS. The RIS always relies on the HL7 protocol and its messaging mechanism for informing the PACS of changes, as well as receiving events from DICOM devices.

The messaging mechanism between different systems, offers the translation medium that serves to both interpret and re-represent the data. However, the interpretation is based on an understanding of the message context inbound. This is a highly subjective interpretation. Resultantly, events and interpretation can result in inconsistency in this messaging based approach.

CAUSES FOR DATA DISPARITY IN THE SYSTEM-OF-SYSTEMS APPROACH

As discussed in the previous sections the event and messaging framework used in the health enterprise system doesn't guarantee the consistency between different instances or parts of the patient records. In this section we will examine some of the events that may end with data disparity in the health enterprise system.

Data Silos in Healthcare Information Systems

Protocols such as DICOM and HL7 exist for the purposes of exchanging information within the PACS and RIS information silos in the hospital enterprise. These protocols ensure data confidence for downstream systems, but are not designed to provide referential data cross system in the system-of-systems model. These protocols provide a framework by which medical data is communicated, but are subject to strict programmatic interpretation. System implementations interpret the protocol standards in unique ways, allowing for a high degree of variance in the presentation of data from multiple independent data sources. This creates problems of data redundancy, inaccuracy and confuses the authoritative provisioning of data with referential copies. By far the greatest concern relates to data inconsistency and subsequent inaccuracy in an environment of disparate systems. Unique data keys used for data alignment or referential integrity may be drawn from human assumptions that are faulty.

Inconsistent Record Identifier for the Patient's Data

Name change: In the system-of-systems, the patient name is always used as a key or part of the key for querying the patient data. Patients sometime change their names, especially after a marriage or divorce. When such an event occurs, demographic references strongly tied to that person's medical history will need to be changed or updated in order to insure the continuous access to relevant historical data.

In order to synchronize a Patients name throughout the system-of-systems enterprise, an HL7 N-event entitled "Patient Update" needs to occur. This type of event will insure that all records containing "patient name" are updated to reference "the new patient name".

Legacy system for scanning film and paper data: Many of the enterprise records for patients in the hospital exist on documents. Admission, Discharge ad transfer records may exist solely on non-electronic medium. These information sources must be manually updated each time an event occurs, such as a patient name change. More information exists in the way of medical film. Not only is the image data present, but often the demographic information for the patient, burnt into the film.

OCR technologies can be helpful in dealing with the shear volume of ADT records for the patients. However, the electronically introduced data will need to be reconciled with the existing HER records.

Data Inconsistency Generated by Automatic Triggers or Cascading Events

Study cancel: On a less frequent basis, patient examinations are not conducted. This could be due to a myriad of causes, including patient absenteeism, acquisition device failure, as well as general infrastructure failure. In any of these events, a decision is made to cancel the acquisition of data relevant to the patient. In these cancellation scenarios, an N-event message is then scheduled. However, when the message is received by the PACS system, the study or appropriate identifier may not be present, as defined in the N-Event. This may be caused if the study acquisition has not yet begun. Also the billing system may not receive the correct event-message. As such, we have an event-ordering problem.

Study split or merges: Data flow allows for the division and recombination in the process of medical diagnosis. A patient may have had a very long CT exam that extends into body parts outside the area of expertise for the radiologist. As such, it may be beneficial, both medically and financially, to split the study into two distinct studies for the patient. The inverse may also occur, resulting in

a study merge. Study or series acquisition may be interrupted for one or more reasons, including equipment failure, resource contention, or multiple system acquisition. In any of these events, two or more distinct studies may need to be merged into a single study record.

A question arises regarding the synchronization of data between these models. It is unclear whether one or more IS records in this environment would exist for each study. As such, we encountered a many-to-one disagreement. Billing systems would need to be correctly informed that only one, albeit larger, procedure was performed. Also, only one read or transcription should have occurred in this model.

Data Exchange and Transfer of Patient Records

In some medical situations, a patient will need to be relocated from one hospital environment to another. In this dataflow scenario, the patient's records may be imported to the new environment. Alternatively, a new record may be created at the newest site. Also the Imaging data is sometime transmitted to the DICOM SCP of the receiving site's PACS. The transmitted and imported data needs then to be reconciled against the new site's information system in order to correlate records to demographic data. So that, any patient movement or other procedures can be referenced to the same patient.

Character Set Translation and Legacy Systems Tagging

ISO_IR Disagreement and Database Character Translation: ISO character sets refer to the specific procedure for mapping a sequence of bytes to a sequence of characters. The DICOM standard includes a specific tag necessary to identify the character set used in the header. This is of extreme importance to the demographic consistency of the data interpretation and action throughout the enterprise.

By way of example, consider a query for all patients whose last name starts with Ł (from ISO 8859-2, decimal 163). If the system were not capable of understanding this character, perhaps through a limited understanding of only ISO_8859-1, then this character would escape the query, possibly with undesirable results. Worst yet, any patient name update including the character Ł would also be problematic.

Private DICOM Tagging: Many imaging devices (also known as Modality) include proprietary information in the DICOM header of the images and objects they transmit. This information is only of use to a system that is programmed to take advantage of it. It allows for a tighter subsystem-of-system model, but at the expense of the greater solution.

Time Synchronization

Time is a critical component to a successful diagnosis. All members of the health enterprise solution normally have their own time keeping facility. However, in the system-of-systems the use of time stamps is critical to insure the coordination of transactions and order of precedence. These time stamps should be synchronized within the whole system-of-systems.

Other Technical Issues

Data Reintroduction for Disaster Recovery Purposes: In the event of system failure, one or more entities within the system-of-systems will need to be repopulated with original data. Upon completion of this, a synchronization effort will need to occur between it and one or more members within the environment. This activity requires coordination of the various information systems within the hospital enterprise.

RIS Feed Interruption: The RIS messaging mechanism is a necessary prerequisite in the system-of-systems for data continuity. Upon failure of any RIS system in this environment, the update events will not properly register for all receiving systems in the enterprise, resulting in an environmental data inconsistency.

AN XML BUS FOR RESOLVING SOME OF THE DATA DISPARITY ISSUES

One of the prevalent issues in message-oriented systems is defining one or more protocols by which messages can be processed. Adherence to standards, bridging between protocols and configurations all raise issues in a multiple systems environment. In the healthcare enterprise, the interdependency of systems for successful patient care only serves to exasperate the situation. XML and semantic web technology presents a great potential for solving some of the disparity issues (Pianykh, 2008; Yu, 2008; Balogh et al., 2003; Pianykh et al., 2003; Heitmann, 2002). In this section we present a solution based on the use of an XML bus for data transfer. Figure 4 presents the XML bus design from a dataflow perspective.

The data bus would allow for a common data conduit. The connection to this conduit would be accomplished through adapters that provide common data typing. Each connection into the data bus would require an adapter that allows for consistent conversion from source protocol to XML.

DICOM to XML Conversion

The adapter, as shown in the arrow in Figure 4, is a translation engine that understands both XML and the healthcare specific protocol, in this case, DICOM. Using open source tools such as DCM4CHE, conversion of DICOM to XML is readily possible.

Figure 4. XML data bus

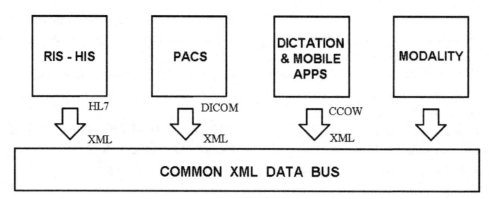

The following code is a truncated output of the dcm2xml.jar transformation performed on a sample DICOM file.

HL7 to XML Conversion

Version 3.0 of the HL7 standard is a pure XML implementation (Heitmann, 2002). As such, the major concern relates not to the transformation of the trigger, but to the interpretation. This is somewhat addressed in the Reference Information Model of HL7 3.0. In versions prior to 3.0, a methodology is necessary to interpret the trigger events as XML. The HL7 organization has devised rules in order to properly encode the HL7 triggers in XML. These rules would enable an adapter framework to implement commonality of meaning across the data bus, as shown in Figure 4.

Modality to XML Data Bus Adapter

There is commonality between the DICOM to XML Adapter and the Modality (imaging device) to XML adapter. Both use DICOM as a protocol for communication, and as such, may rely partially on the implementation details for each other. Modalities also have unique features such as Modality Performed Procedure Steps (MPPS), which must also be taken care of in any successful implementation (Noumeir, 2005). The modality adapter must be able to communicate these specific

events directly to the data bus. Any subsequent queries upon the data bus would then be able to accurately provide procedure start and procedure end dates and times through the Modality to XML adapter shown in Figure 4.

Context to XML

Many applications rely on the Clinical Context Object Workgroup (CCOW) for interoperability notification. This standard and an extension of the HL7 framework, allows singular CCOW-aware applications to interact with other CCOW-aware applications for the purposes of information sharing (Grimson et al., 2001). This standard is extremely beneficial in the system-of-systems approach as it represents a common notification mechanism for changes in status. It also has value in voice dictation systems as a means of coercing dictation information into the patient framework through the identification of common attributes, such as patient name and study instance unique identifiers.

A RESOURCE DEFINITION FRAMEWORK FOR DICOM QUERY

In the previous sections we discussed how protocols such as DICOM and HL7 are used for exchanging information within the PACS and RIS

Figure 5. Excerpt from DCM2XML.jar Output

```
<?xml version="1.0" encoding="UTF-8"?>
<dicomfile>
<filemetainfo>
<attr tag="00020000" vr="UL" pos="132" name="Group Length" vm="1" len="4">196</attr>
<attr tag="00020001" vr="OB" pos="144" name="File Meta Information Version" vm="1" len="2">1\0</attr>
<attr tag="00020013" vr="SH" pos="290" name="Implementation Version Name" vm="1"
len="16">eFilm/efDICOMLib</attr>
<attr tag="00020016" vr="AE" pos="314" name="Source Application Entity Title" vm="1" len="18">
&#19;</attr>
</filemetainfo>
<dataset>
<attr tag="00080005" vr="CS" pos="340" name="Specific Character Set" vm="1" len="10">ISO_IR 100</attr>
<attr tag="00080008" vr="CS" pos="358" name="Image Type" vm="2" len="16">DERIVED\PRIMARY </attr>
<attr tag="00080012" vr="DA" pos="382" name="Instance Creation Date" vm="1" len="8">20010109</attr>
<attr tag="00080013" vr="TM" pos="398" name="Instance Creation Time" vm="1" len="6">095618</attr>
<attr tag="00080016" vr="UI" pos="412" name="SOP Class UID" vm="1"
len="26">1.2.840.10008.5.1.4.1.1.1</attr>
<attr tag="00080018" vr="UI" pos="446" name="SOP Instance UID" vm="1"
len="40">1.3.51.5145.5142.20010109.1105627.1.0.1</attr>
```

information silos in the hospital enterprise. These protocols ensure data confidence for downstream systems, but are not designed to provide referential data cross system in the system-of-systems model. The XML bus discussed in the previous section provide a solution for data exchange preventing many of the inconsistencies and also pave the road for integrating a second layer description for the exchanged data. This second layer (metadata) is a mean for representing relationships between data, in a manner somewhat similar to a database. Using a mesh-like design, information regarding a given data element can be researched further, from both loosely coupled and tightly bound relationships. These relationships, as defined through some descriptive language, may be used to equate metadata concerning these linked data sets. Relating the patient name in a Picture Archive and Communication System (PACS) to the patient name in a Record Information System (RIS) is one simple model of how this mutual meaning is provided. In order to provide descriptions that provide metadata attributes, the Resource Data Framework (RDF) was devised and used to extend the DICOM queries.

The Resource Definition Framework (RDF) provides a technical framework for describing relationships between data, in a systems-friendly format. This model is driven from a minimalist approach, extending the data silos that exist within the system-of-systems environment; RDF extends data from a computer based strict format to a general understood systems data. Through ontology, the metadata may be defined in relation to other metadata.

This example demonstrates a means of defining a patient's name, relative to the context of the hospital Site A domain. Three Attributes are fully described in this context: Name, Title and Accession Number. This data may now be externally shared to other Hospitals, as its meaning is defined as relative to Site A. Site B may now choose to query Site A using the exposed RDF data.

Extending DICOM Query by Relationships

Invariably, the difference between a human parsed statement and a machine parsed statement will result in a difference of understanding or interpretation. By way of example, when looking at the entities in a form, the abbreviation NA is commonly interpreted as Not Available. This can be viewed as a human interpretation. It is most likely based on previous human exposure to similar entries, in a learned environment. In a similar approach, one may begin to abstract the values for a common DICOM attribute, Patient Sex (0010, 0040). This value holds three DICOM compliant enumerated values, M, F and O, representing Male, Female and Other. This is sufficient for a DICOM acquisition methodology, but is not substantive enough to cover non-DICOM integrated systems. For any system that introduced data through non-DICOM compliant means, such as film scanning, the values may also appear as Woman, Unknown or Not Available. These three terms can be well understood from a human perspective, but would not be understood by a data dictionary driven system that only allowed for specific values. The RDF relationships can be used as illustrated in figure 7.

Defining Synonyms

In many instances, importance may be placed on metadata for the purposes of data amalgamation for presentation. In the case of DICOM metadata, certain specific attributes are readily apparent. Occasionally, freeform or non-standard data may be encountered in acronym form. NA, U and W are three such values. Each of these acronyms has an easily understood human meaning (or at least intention of meaning), as defined by relationships, but from a strict compliance method, is outside the realm of the DICOM standard. The following mappings allow for a relationship of meaning to be created for Patient Sex based queries.

W is an abbreviation for Woman

NA is an abbreviation for Not Available

U is an abbreviation for Unknown

From a graph perspective, we may choose to diagram these statements, combined with the original M, F, and O as follows:

Figure 6. Sample RDF reference for a patient

```
<?xml version="1.0"?>
<rdf:RDF xmlns:rdf="http://www.w3.org/1999/02/22-1
xmlns:Patient="http://www.w3.org/medical/SiteA#">
 <Patient:Person rdf:about="http://www.w3.org/Medic:
  <Patient:Name>Jane Smith</Patient:Name>
  <Patient:Title>Mrs.</Patient:Title>
  <Patient:AccessionNumber>1A123</Patient: Acces:
 </Patient:Person>
</rdf:RDF>
```

Thus we may state the following:

W is an abbreviation for Woman, which is equivalent to Female, which is abbreviated as F.

NA is an abbreviation for Not Applicable, which is equivalent to Other, which is abbreviated as O.

U is an abbreviation for Unknown, which most appropriately fits the classification Other, which is abbreviated as O.

The RDF metadata introduced in this section allows us to extend the DICOM C-Find Queries, C-Find Modality Worklist Queries, and Values and wildcards matching. This extended protocol alleviates paper based mechanisms of study orders and simplifies administration by permitting optional filters for query constraint.

Figure 7. Defining RDF relationships

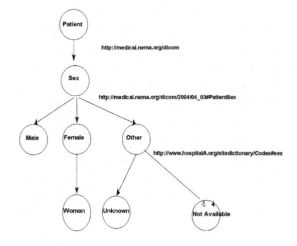

Figure 8. Abbreviation mappings

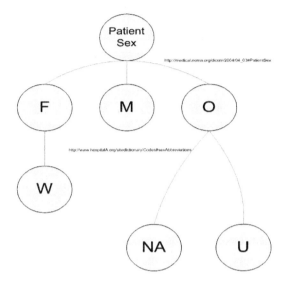

Table 2. Patient study list

Patient	Patient Sex	Study ID
Jane Smith	F	123
Jane Smith	W	124
Jane Smith	O	221
Janet Smith	F	125

C-FIND Results

The results of an extended C-find request using RDF can be reported to be extended above and beyond wildcard matching. Where exact matches are not possible, due to data disparity in the system-of-systems environments presented to IS departments in Hospital environments, Aliasing values is an effective means of gathering appropriate metadata for effective patient care. Using the data in Table 2 as our data repository, a standard DICOM query for Patient Name="Jane^Smith" & Patient Sex ="F" would only produce one result, Study 123. Using our extended query SELECT ?StudyID FROM http://medical.nema.org/dicom/2004/04_03#PatientSex.rdf, we are enabled to see the results of all aliases underneath, which include Study ID 123 and 124. Similarly, through the building of aliases for Jane and Janet, We may be able to extend our query mechanism to provide Study 125.

CONCLUSION

Medical information systems exist as information silos within the global health enterprise, making the task of designing an effective and accurate Enterprise Health Record Viewer very difficult. Each healthcare enterprise system in the system-of-systems acts as a referential entity for the information it contains, but only for the specific domain for which it is specialized. For each system in the enterprise, downstream distributed applications typically rely on the one specific data silo as a means of identifying and enacting decisions within an application framework. Whilst this ensures one to one consistency of data between the application and a centralized data repository, it does not ensure consistency within the enterprise.

In the enterprise health record, two systems were found to be of importance. Radiological clients communicated primarily with a PACS system via DICOM as a means of obtaining study level data for patients. Radiology workstations communicated with RIS systems via HL7 in order to record patient level attributes. Data consistency was often accomplished through the implementation of translation systems converting one protocol to another. In fact, protocols such as DICOM, CCOW and HL7 exist as standards for information sharing, but the exact implementation of message conversion from one standard to another is often an area of information redundancy. Data conversion solutions were also viewed as a possible cause for information loss or inaccuracy due to the incongruity in frameworks between the systems and their protocols. In the translation and representation between systems in the enterprise, data conversion is not always possible. Enterprise inconsistencies also exist as a direct result of data workflow. HIMMS and IHE are leading the way in standardization of data consistency and authority in the healthcare enterprise by defining information pathways and messaging content within the medical information environment.

The development of an Enterprise Record Viewer illuminated the necessity for authority of data. Although protocol translation was seen as a contributing factor to inconsistencies, the production of a solution became reoriented around the creation of a central authority in order to ensure consistency. This hierarchal approach avoided the concern over data consistency in the enterprise by creating another independent silo for data display. Connectivity to the RIS and PACS systems allowed the viewer to query independently of the XML Data Bus in order to allow alternative means of exploring data that may not have been messaged properly.

The production of the framework for the XML data bus is representative of a methodology or approach for an Electronic Healthcare Record. Further effort is necessary to expand upon this singular solution to resolve the data disparity issues driven by the system-of-systems approach in the hospital enterprise. The XML data bus design provides a framework for solving some of the identified causes for data disparity. Patient name changes are addressed through the transmission of this data to the bus. All queries can then be programmed to query via the bus. Similarly, patient moves and study cancellation messages can be communicated into the bus for dissemination and subsequent query. While the bus design alleviates these areas by creating a singular entry point for enterprise systems, other causes for data inconsistency cannot be solely addressed through the XML data bus design. Consistencies in data dictionaries, ISO_IR disagreement and private DICOM tagging practices require future research. These areas may benefit from an assessment of the W3C semantic web design. Another concern remains with data movement and event ordering. Issues such as time synchronization and RIS message repetition may benefit from an asynchronous transactional approach as implemented through the use of a message queuing. Legacy film based scanning practices would benefit from an examination of form based workflow technologies, and would integrate more readily into an XML construct such as the proposed XML data bus.

Future implementations are recommended to focus on the remote user's requirements as a means of both centralizing data, and also on providing a readily accessible, consistent and lightweight viewpoint to data. This latter objective will facilitate a successful adoption through the consistent presentation of patient demographic data. As Scotland, England, Estonia, Canada and others begin the process of providing centralized socialized healthcare through the amalgamation and adoption of country-wide healthcare solutions, Enterprise Healthcare Record Viewers and identification of data authorities inside the system-of-systems healthcare enterprise will become critical to the successful provisioning of healthcare to patients.

ACKNOWLEDGMENT

The author acknowledges the Editor-in-Chief of the journal, Professor John Wang, and the anonymous reviewers for their indispensable input that improved the paper significantly.

REFERENCES

Balogh, N., Kerkovtis, G., Eichelberg, M., Lemoine, D., & Punys, V. (2003). DICOM and XML usage for multimedia teleconsultation and for reimbursement in cardiology. In *Proceedings of the IEEE Conference on Computers in Cardiology* (pp.379-382).

Cao, X., & Huang, H. K. (2000). Current status and future advances of digital radiography and PACS. *IEEE Engineering in Medicine and Biology Magazine, 19*(5), 80–88. doi:10.1109/51.870234

Choennia, S., Bakkera, R., & Baetsa, W. (2003). On the evaluation of workflow systems in business processes. *The Electronic Journal of Information Systems Evaluation, 6*(2).

Dickinson, G., Fischetti, L., & Heard, S. (2004). *HL7 EHR System Functional Model.* Retrieved June 4, 2009, from http://www.telemedicina.buap.mx/PaginaNueva/Archivos/Estandar_7.pdf.

Dwyer, S. J. (2000). A personalized view of the history of PACS in the USA. In G.J. Blaine, & E.L. Siegel (Eds.), *Proceedings of the SPIE: vol. 3980. Medical imaging 2000: PACS design and evaluation: Engineering and clinical issues* (pp. 2-9).

Evola, R. L. (1997). *Patient administration. Health level seven, version 2.3.* Retrieved June 4, 2009, from http://www.dmi.columbia.edu/resources/hl7doc/hl72.3/ch3.pdf.

Gell, G. (2000). PACS-Graz, 1985-2000: from a scientific pilot to a state-wide multimedia radiological information system. In G.J. Blaine, & E.L. Siegel (Eds.), *Proceedings of the SPIE: vol. 3980. Medical imaging 2000: PACS design and evaluation: Engineering and clinical issues* (pp. 19-28).

Graeber, S. (1997). The impact of workflow management systems on the design of hospital information systems. In *Proceedings of the American medical informatics association annual fall symposium* (pp. 856-860).

Grimson, J., Stephens, G., Jung, B., Grimson, W., Berry, D., & Pardon, S. (2001). Sharing health-care records over the internet. *IEEE Internet Computing, 5*(3), 49–58. doi:10.1109/4236.935177

HL7 Canada. (2002). *Guidebook for HL7 development projects in Canada.* Retrieved June 4, 2009, from http://sl.infoway-inforoute.ca/downloads/hl7can_Guidebook_v1_0.pdf.

HL7 (n.d.). *HL7 ANSI-approved standards.* Retrieved June 4, 2009, from http://www.hl7.org/documentcenter/public/faq/ansi_approved.htm.

HL7.org. (n.d.). *What is HL7?* Retrieved June 4, 2009, from http://www.hl7.org/about/hl7about.htm.

Hasselbring, W., Peterson, R., Smits, M., & Spanjers, R. (2000). Strategic information management for a Dutch university hospital. In A. Hasman, B. Blobel (Eds.), *Proceedings of Medical Infobahn for Europe* (pp. 885-889).

Heitmann, K. U. (2002). *XML encoding rules of HL7 v2 messages - v2.xml.* Document number v2.xml Rev. 3.672. Retrieved June 4, 2009, from http://www.hl7.org/Special/committees/xml/drafts/v2xml1mlbb.pdf.

Hollingsworth, D. (1995, January 19). *Workflow management coalition, the workflow reference model.* Document number TC00-1003, Issue 1.1. Retrieved June 4, 2009, from http://www.wfmc.org/standards/docs/tc003v11.pdf.

Iacucci, E., Nielsen, P., & Berge, I. (2002). Bootstrapping the electronic patient record infrastructure. In K. Bødker, P. M. Kühn, J. Nørbjerg, J. Simonsen, & V. M. Thanning (Eds.), *Proceedings of the 25th information systems research seminar in scandinavia* (IRIS 25). *New ways of working in IS*. Retrieved June 4, 2009, from http://heim.ifi.uio.no/~pnielsen/PHD/IaNiBe.doc.

Interfaceware (2009). *HL7 message sample.* Retrieved June 4, 2009, from http://www.interfaceware.com/manual/messages.html.

Jung, B. (2005). DICOM-X - seamless integration of medical images into the EHR. In A. Tsymbal, & P. Cunningham (Eds.), *Proceedings of the 18th IEEE international symposium on computer-based medical systems. Computer based medical systems (CBMS)* (pp. 203-207).

Kennedy, R. L., Seibert, J. A., & Hughes, C. J. (2000). Legacy system integration using web technology. In G.J. Blaine, & E.L. Siegel (Eds.), *Proceedings of the SPIE: vol. 3980. Medical imaging 2000: PACS design and evaluation: Engineering and clinical issues* (pp. 231-234).

Kolesnikov, A., Kauranne, T., & Marsh, A. (1999). Integrating DICOM medical images into Virtual Medical Worlds. In *Proceedings of the IEEE EMBS International Conference on Information Technology Applications in Biomedicine* (pp. 23-24).

Kolesnikov, A., Kelle, O., & Kauranne, T. (1997). Remote medical analysis with web technology. In B. Ramin & P. Karttunen (Eds.), *Proceedings of the finnish symposium on signal processing - FINSIG'97* (pp. 87-96).

Maier, M. W. (1998). Architecting principles for systems-of-systems. *Systems Engineering*, *1*(4), 267–284. doi:10.1002/(SICI)1520-6858(1998)1:4<267::AID-SYS3>3.0.CO;2-D

Maier, M. W. (2005). Research challenges for systems-of-systems. In *Proceedings of the IEEE international conference on systems, man and cybernetics (Vol. 4)* (pp. 3149-3154).

McCormick, P. (n.d). *DICOM and databases.* Retrieved June 4, 2009, from http://icmit.mit.edu/dicomdb.html.

Miltchenko, M. V., Pianykh, O. S., & Tyler, J. M. (2003). Building a Global PACS Network: Choices in Implementing Inter-PACS Connectivity. In *Proceedings of the RSNA 2003 scientific assembly and annual meeting* (pp. 599-605).

National Electrical Manufacturers Association. (2008). *Digital imaging and communications in medicine (DICOM): the DICOM standard (Rep. No. PS 3.x-2008)*. Retrieved June 5, 2009, from ftp://medical.nema.org/medical/dicom/2008/08_01pu.pdf.

NeoTool. (2007). *The HL7 evolution.* Retrieved June 5, 2009, from http://www.neotool.com/pdf/HL7-Version-3-with-HL7-Version-2-History.pdf.

Noumeir, R. (2005). Benefits of the DICOM modality performed procedure step. *Journal of Digital Imaging*, *18*(4), 260–269. doi:10.1007/s10278-005-6702-3

PACS-ADMIN. (2007). *PACS overview.* Retrieved June 5, 2009, from http://www.pacs-admin.com/PACS_Overview.html.

Pianykh, O. S. (2008). Digital Imaging and Communications in Medicine (DICOM): A Practical Introduction and Survival Guide. *DICOM and Teleradiology* (pp. 275-298). Berlin, Heidelberg, Springer-Verlag.

Pianykh, O. S., Miltchenko, M. V., & Tyler, J. M. (2003). Using Online PACS Gateway for Efficient Medical Data Exchange. In *Proceedings of the RSNA 2003 scientific assembly and annual meeting* (pp. 813-819).

Ratib, O. M., Ligier, Y., Rosset, A., Staub, J. C., Logean, M., & Girard, C. (2000). Self-contained off-line media for exchanging medical images using DICOM-compliant standard. In G.J. Blaine, & E.L. Siegel (Eds.), *Proceedings of the SPIE: vol. 3980. Medical imaging 2000: PACS design and evaluation: Engineering and clinical issues* (pp. 30-34).

Revet, B. (1997). *DICOM Cook Book for Implementations in Modalities (Tech. Rep.).* Philips Medical Systems, Eindhoven, The Netherlands.

Yu, D., Xie, S., Wei, X., Zheng, Z., & Wang, K. (2008). A XML-based remote EMI sharing system conformable to Dicom. In *Proceedings of the international conference on technology and applications in biomedicine* (pp. 556-559).

This work was previously published in International Journal of Information Systems and Social Change, Volume 1, Issue 1, edited by John Wang, pp. 56-72, copyright 2010 by IGI Publishing (an imprint of IGI Global).

Section 5
Supporting Critical Decisions

Chapter 17
Multi–Criteria Spatial Decision Support System DECERNS:
Application to Land Use Planning

B. Yatsalo
Obninsk State Technical University (IATE), Russia

V. Slipenkaya
Obninsk State Technical University (IATE), Russia

V. Didenko
Obninsk State Technical University (IATE), Russia

A. Babutski
Obninsk State Technical University (IATE), Russia

A. Tkachuk
Obninsk State Technical University (IATE), Russia

I. Pichugina
Obninsk State Technical University (IATE), Russia

S. Gritsyuk
Obninsk State Technical University (IATE), Russia

T. Sullivan
Brookhaven National Laboratory (BNL), USA

O. Mirzeabasov
Obninsk State Technical University (IATE), Russia

I. Linkov
US Army Engineer Research and Development Center, USA

ABSTRACT

Land-use planning and environmental management often requires an implementation of both geo-spatial information analysis and value-driven criteria within the decision-making process. DECERNS (Decision Evaluation in Complex Risk Network Systems) is a web-based distributed decision support system for multi-criteria analysis of a wide range of spatially-explicit land management alternatives. It integrates mainly basic and some advanced GIS functions and implements several Multi-Criteria Decision Analysis (MCDA) methods and tools. DECERNS can also be integrated with a model server containing generic and site specific models for in-depth analysis of project and environmental risks as well as other decision criteria under consideration. This paper provides an overview of the modeling approaches as well as methods and tools used in DECERNS. Application of the DECERNS WebSDSS (Web-based Spatial Decision Support System) for a housing site selection case study is presented.

DOI: 10.4018/978-1-4666-0927-3.ch017

INTRODUCTION

There exists a need for an integrated land-use management approach supporting economic development and parallel goals. The goals of this approach include the conservation of natural resources, the restoration of habitats in surrounding ecosystems, maintaining and improving biodiversity, all while reducing present and future pollution. These seemingly complicated problems can be effectively addressed by implementing a Geographic Information System (GIS) along with decision analysis tools.

Currently GISs are an indispensable tool for investigating the problems associated with spatial/geographic data, including input of source data, storage and retrieval, manipulation, analysis, and output. The aim of GIS analysis is to help a user or a group of users answer questions related to spatial data, objects and processes. Typically, GIS specialists emphasize using GISs for data analysis and presentation, as well as for decision-making support while solving practical problems.

Decision support can be defined as the assistance for, and substantiation and corroboration of, an act or result of deciding; typically this decision will be a determination of an *"optimal"* or *"trade off"* approach which leads naturally to the use of [multicriteria] decision analysis tools. Decision support integrates specific objective and subjective information about a site and general information such as legislation, guidelines and technical know-how, to produce decision-making knowledge in a way that is transparent, consistent and reproducible.

Land-use planning, searching for the "best" location or a *compromise* location for facilities, and environmental management in a comprehensive manner, which requires implementation of not only (standard) GIS technologies and functions for spatial data representation and processing, but also decision analysis methods and tools to assist the decision-making process for comparison of spatial options/alternatives.

According to Simon (1960), any decision-making process can be structured into three major phases:

- **Intelligence:** Recognition of the decision problem; searching/scanning the decision environment; raw data collection and examination;
- **Design:** Inventing, developing, and analyzing a set of possible solutions;
- **Choice:** Evaluation of alternatives on the basis of a specified decision rule; ranking, sorting alternatives; uncertainty/sensitivity analysis; choice of the "best"/trade-off alternative(s); development of action plans.

A computerized Decision Support System (DSS) is a tool designed specifically for supporting the users in addressing semi-structured problems (Simon, 1960). An extended approach to defining DSS, according to Sprague (1980), suggests that DSSs should meet the following requirements:

- Designed to solve semi-structured problems that upper level managers often face;
- Capable of combining analytical models with traditional data storage and retrieval functions;
- User-friendly and accessible by decision makers with minimal computer experience; and
- Flexible and adaptable to different decision-making approaches.

Spatial DSSs (SDSSs) are essentially DSSs intended to solve semi-structured *spatial* problems. In addition to DSS characteristics, SDSSs provides functions and tools for spatial data processing and representation (Armstrong, 1986; Densham & Goodchild, 1989). Taking into account that most semi-structured spatial problems are multi-criteria by nature, SDSS, in general, may be regarded as some integration of GIS, at least in terms of basic functions, and MCDA tools. Thus, SDSS supports the decision-making process in terms of the analysis of spatial alternatives through providing access to GIS functions and decision analysis tools for the stakeholders (*i.e.*, decision makers, experts, and interested parties) (Armstrong, 1994; Carver, 1991; Jankowski, 1995; Laaribi, 1996).

The general approach to creating an SDSS based on integrating GIS and MCDA functions and decision rules was presented in many publications, e.g. (Armstrong, 1994; Carver, 1991; Chakhar & Martel, 2003; Jankowski, 1995). Along with these publications, a discussion of the Laaribi scheme (Laaribi, 2000) on selecting the appropriate MCDA method(s) within the decision-making process was also produced.

We do not wish to pursue the goal of presenting a detailed review of SDSSs concepts and examples. Instead we refer readers to the profound and comprehensive surveys by *J. Malczewski* (1999, 2004, 2006), where the history and methodology of SDSS development has been presented based on the integration of GIS and MCDA.

The usability of SDSS can lead to problems without proper training and experience. Software and SDSS use integrates skills from a wide range of disciplines and most people are not experts in all of these areas. Software/SDSS users are typically characterized by a variety of backgrounds in terms of types of training, levels of education, degrees of experience, and familiarity with the problems at hand (Balram & Dragievi, 2006). Computerized SDSSs will have the effect of increasing the range of possible users who may be included in the decision-making process. This will potentially lead to more stakeholders, and non-professional software users attempting to perform their own, independent analyses. However, without proper training there is a likely chance that many stakeholders will either misuse the software or find the system difficult to use (Malczewski, 2004).

The development and implementations of the web-based SDSSs, commonly known as WebSDSSs, have also been discussed in a series of publications, e.g., (Balram & Dragievi, 2006; Carver & Peckham, 1999; Malczewski, 1999, 2004, 2006; Rinner, 2003;). Most web-based decision support systems are client-server systems, and their basic functions and system tiers, which include presentation, program logic/application, and database/information are distributed between client and server computers. With regards to the program logic for WebSDSS implementation it is possible to distinguish between:

- Server-side WebSDSS,
- Client-side WebSDSS, and
- Mixed client-and server-side WebSDSS.

The mixed client-and server-side approach allows a user to perform most time and resource intensive operations on the server. Furthermore, the client side is responsible for visualization, the user interface, and, in some cases, realization of some functions, which may be relatively simple.

Distributed computer systems/SDSSs have the following main advantages over stand-alone desktop systems. The advantages include, but are not limited to, platform independency, reductions in costs and maintenance problems, ease of use, sharing of information by the worldwide user community, effective platform for group decision-making support, and an increase in public access and decision-making involvement (*collaborative WebSDSS*) (Balram & Dragievi, 2006; Carver & Peckham, 1999; Malczewski, 1999, 2004, 2006; Rinner, 2003).

SDSSs can be also used as an effective tool for decision-making support when solving a wide range of problems in regards to environmental protection and land-use suitability analysis (Malczewski, 1999, 2004, 2006). Land-use suitability analysis aims to identify the most appropriate spatial pattern for future land uses according to specified requirements, preferences, or predictors of some activity (Malczewski, 2004). Land-use problems typically contain multiple objectives including the maximization of a population's health and safety. Further objectives include minimizing the economic costs while maximizing the benefit to the environment. Maximizing the benefit to the environment implies minimizing pollution while maximizing natural resources. These different objectives have varying measures that include economic costs, reduced exposure to harmful chemicals, reduced deposition of chemicals, etc. However, these measures are not easy to compare. In order to evaluate available management alternatives based on an integration of objective and subjective information, the stakeholders, experts, and/or decision makers can benefit from an SDSS framework that would lead them through a systematic process of priorities elicitation, strategic planning and comprehensive assessments. These in turn would explicitly integrate human health risks, ecological risks, and socio-economic measures (Balram & Dragievi, 2006; Malczewski, 1999, 2004, 2006).

This paper provides a description of the approach used in *DECERNS* (Decision Evaluation in Complex Risk Network Systems) *WebSDSS* followed by a brief overview of methods and tools and an application case study.

DECERNS FRAMEWORK

DECERNS is an SDSS that aims to provide methodology and software tools which will facilitate decision-making support in the field of land-use planning and environmental management.

The strategy followed in *DECERNS*, Figure 1, includes:

1. Development of the *DECERNS WebSDSS* based on integration of basic and some advanced GIS-functions, decision analysis methods, and associated tools (middle part of the Figure 1);

Figure 1. Strategy of the DECERNS SDSS development and implementation

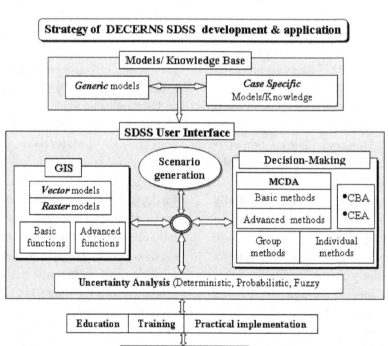

2. Development and/or adjustment of models for generic or case specific application (upper part of the Figure 1); as a rule, model implementation and integration will be carried out within the customization process for investigation of the site-specific problems. The developed models are stored in the model server(s) and the expert or customer can use the available models via the SDSS interface along with other SDSS (GIS and MCDA) functions, methods, and tools. Customized versions of the *DECERNS WebSDSS* and desktop *DECERNS SDSS* may be developed in accordance with customer requests;

3. Implementation, education, and training with *DECERNS* will first include the implementation of *DECERNS* for the solution of practical problems on land-use planning, environmental protection, and many other problems regarding spatial alternatives analysis. Second, education modules within university courses, including information systems, decision analysis, GIS, and ecology

will be developed. Lastly, training courses devoted to *DECERNS* on solving land use management, environmental protection and contaminated land restoration problems using multicriteria decision analysis and GIS tools will be developed. (See bottom of Figure 1).

DECERNS is developed as a distributed web-based SDSS, *WebSDSS,* and as a stand-alone desktop application. Figure 2 presents the framework for the *DECERNS SDSS*.

The Application Programming Interface (API) integrates the three main components onto a single platform. These components are GIS, Decision Support Tools, and Models. The shared graphical user interface provides a uniform, intuitive and friendly method to access all MCDA methods, GIS functions, and models implemented within *DECERNS*. *DECERNS* is developed based on open source java technologies.

Figure 2. The generalized DECERNS SDSS architecture

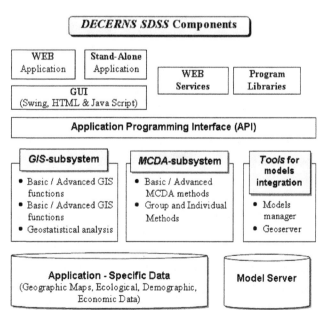

GIS Functions

The GIS subsystem is designed to have all of the basic GIS features, including:

- Multi-layered maps, visualization, and coloring;
- Editing legends;
- Zooming and panning;
- Measurements (distance along line or polylines, polygon area);
- Features selection (single and multi select) and searching;
- Attributes viewing and analysis, including statistical analysis;
- Buffering;
- Overlays, including union, intersection, and subtraction of cartographic layers;
- Rasterization (conversion of vector to raster maps);
- Scalar operations (map math such as addition, subtraction, and multiplication);
- Spatial interpolation (inverse distance weighting), and geostatistics (kriging methods);
- Support of all common GIS map formats;
- Internet access to other GIS functions within the *WebSDSS*.

A realization of the advanced GIS-functions is based on *DECERNS* integration with *R-server*, (www.r-project.org), which provides various statistical methods. In its current form, *DECERNS WebSDSS'* geostatistical analysis tools have been implemented.

As such, *DECERNS* users may use a standard Internet browser to implement all of the main GIS functions and procedures, including vector and raster multi-layered maps visualization, Figure 3, processing, analysis, and data storage.

Figure 3. DECERNS SDSS: visualization of multi-layered maps (landuse, roads and rivers for Novozybkovski and Klintsovski districts, Bryansk region, Russia)

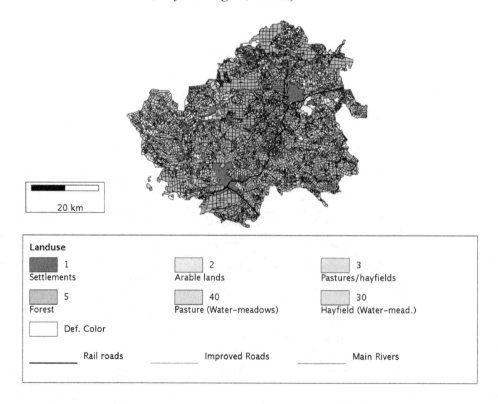

Decision Support Methods and Tools

A key component of the *DECERNS SDSS* is the decision support subsystem, which is based on the implementation of MCDA methods and associated tools.

MCDA methods aim to evaluate alternatives based on multiple criteria using systematic analyses which overcome the limitations of unstructured individual or group decision-making (Belton & Stewart, 2002; von Winterfeldt & Edwards, 1986). The aim of MCDA in a broad sense is to facilitate a decision maker's learning and understanding of the problem. Furthermore, MCDA enhances a decision maker's understanding about their own, other parties' and organizational preferences, values and objectives through exploring these in the context of a structured decision analysis framework. The following are main categories of problems which are considered to be the basis of MCDA (Belton & Stewart, 2002):

- *Sorting* alternatives into classes/categories (*e.g.*, "unacceptable," "possibly acceptable," "definitely acceptable," etc.);
- *Screening* alternatives – a process of eliminating those alternatives that do not appear to warrant further attention, i.e., selecting a smaller set of alternatives that likely contains the "best"/trade-off alternative;
- *Ranking* alternatives (from "best" to "worst" according to a chosen algorithm);
- *Selecting* the "the most preferred alternative" from a given set of alternatives; and
- *Designing* (searching, identifying, creating) a new action/alternative to meet goals.

Some other categories of problems include description or learning problems which involves an analysis of actions to gain greater understanding of what may or may not be achievable. There also exists a portfolio problem where a choice of a subset of alternatives exists. Here it is necessary to take account not only of individual characteristics of each alternative, but also of their positive and negative interrelations. These other problems may also be considered in the implementation and the use of MCDA approaches (Belton & Stewart, 2002).

Three dichotomies within MCDA problems can be distinguished (Malczewski, 1999):

- Multi-attribute decision making (MADM: a finite number of alternatives which are defined explicitly) versus multi-objective decision making (MODM: infinite or large number of alternatives which are defined, as a rule, implicitly);
- Individual versus group decision making; and
- Decisions under certainty versus decisions under uncertainty.

MCDA techniques and software tools are at the center of current decision-making approaches. These techniques offer the possibility of evaluating, analyzing, and comparing alternatives using different objective and subjective, quantitative and qualitative criteria and judgments. MCDA models for addressing all six cases discussed above are provided in *DECERNS*.

The following multi-criteria methods and tools are used in the *DECERNS SDSS* (details of MCDA methods indicated below can be found, *e.g.*, in Belton & Stewart, 2002; Figueira, 2005; Malczewski, 1999; Tervonen & Figueira, 2008):

- Basic MADM methods such as MAVT (Multi-Attribute Value Theory) (Keeney & Raiffa, 1976), AHP (Analytic Hierarchy Process) (Saaty, 1980), TOPSIS (Technique for Order Preference by Similarity to the Ideal Solution) (Hwang & Yoon, 1981), and PROMETHEE (Preference Ranking Organization METHod for Enrichment Evaluations) (Brans & Vincke, 1985);
- Advanced MADM methods such as MAUT (Multi-Attribute Utility Theory)

(Keeney & Raiffa, 1976), and ProMAA (Probabilistic Multi-criteria Acceptability Analysis; developed by authors, not published); ProMAA is an alternative approach to SMAA (Stochastic Multicriteria Acceptability Analysis) realization (Lahdelma, 1998), where distributed or random criteria values and weights are used; and some extensions of MADM methods based on fuzzy set approaches: Fuzzy-MAVT, and Fuzzy-PROMETHEE, developed by authors (not published), where fuzzy criterion values and weights may be used, see, for example, (Carlsson & Fuller, 1996).

Realization of MAUT and ProMAA methods is based on the original library for computation of functions of random variables (without implementation of Monte Carlo methods); and realization the 'fuzzy methods' within the *DECERNS WebSDSS* is based on the original library for computation of functions of fuzzy variables; these two libraries developed as a part of the DECERNS project.

When solving a specific multi-criteria problem, a *DECERNS* user has the opportunity to choose the appropriate MCDA method(s). If desired, the user may compare results after the implementation of several methods, including an analysis of uncertainties associated with the chosen MCDA approaches (Yatsalo, et al., 2007).

Several tools are used while implementing MCDA methods. These include value-tree development and editing for structuring multi-criteria problems, performance table creation and editing, value path and scatter plot analysis, and sensitivity analysis (sensitivity to weights, and to value function changing in MAVT). Uncertainties are addressed through sensitivity analysis (for MAVT, AHP, TOPSIS, PROMETHEE), using random performance (for MAUT), random weights and random performance (ProMAA), and, accordingly, fuzzy weights and fuzzy performance (for Fuzzy-MAVT and Fuzzy-PROMETHEE).

There exists a group decision support application within the *DECERNS*. This tool allows the user to create and process various types of surveys and questionnaires, voting mechanisms, while interacting with MCDA modules within spatial multi-criteria problem structuring (Armstrong, 1994; Balram & Dragievi, 2006; Figueira, Greco & Ehrgott, 2005; Malczewski, 1999, 2004, 2006; Hwang & Lin, 1987).

Spatial Decision Support System

MCDA and GIS subsystems of the *DECERNS SDSS* can work independently as stand-alone web-systems. The *DECERNS SDSS,* (see Figure 1 and Figure 2), contains all of the main functions and tools of MCDA and GIS subsystems, which can be accessed through a set of menu options. Tools are available for:

- Setting alternatives using the basic or created cartographic layers, querying and selecting attributive data, and highlighting the selected map objects;
- Analyzing and processing cartographic maps or attributive data using GIS functions and implementing MCDA tools at each stage of the multi-criteria problem investigation;
- Structuring multi-criteria problems using value trees, and a top-down approach for a small number of alternatives, or bottom-up approach for any number of alternatives;
- Automatically transferring attributes for all the alternatives into the performance table for map-based criteria within the multi-criteria problem under investigation (the values for non map-based criteria are filled manually in the performance table/ value tree by SDSS user);
- Highlighting the specific or selected spatial alternative(s) in the map.

DECERNS SDSS contains all the steps within the decision-making process necessary for the analysis of spatial alternatives. Figure 4 presents a decision process flow chart for typical spatial MCDA/MADM problems. This example highlights the effort of the participants in this process including experts, decision makers, and a wider range of stakeholders and the involved SDSS tools. The process includes input from stakeholders, decision makers, and scientists and involves:

- Problem definition;
- Development of alternatives and criteria specification;
- Generation of a performance table based on the results of the criteria assessments;
- Determination of the preferences and weighting/scaling criteria by the stakeholder community.
- Assessments of the alternatives against the different criteria which are conducted us-

ing models, GIS tools, and expert/stakeholder judgments; the MCDA tools take this information and perform sensitivity/uncertainty analysis;.

- Stakeholder review of the resulting selecting/ranking/screening/sorting of alternatives;
- Recommendations which are made for the decision makers; a process which can be repeated iteratively to refine any of the steps.

Environmental Models

The model block, Figure 2, is the component of the *DECERNS WebSDSS* that provides the model assessments for specific case studies. It can be developed by users or *SDSS* developers in accordance with requirements (the specifications for integration of models and SDSS via model provider/server) that permit the model to be acces-

Figure 4. DECERNS SDSS: Decision process flow chart for multi-attribute decision making (within MADM approach as an example)

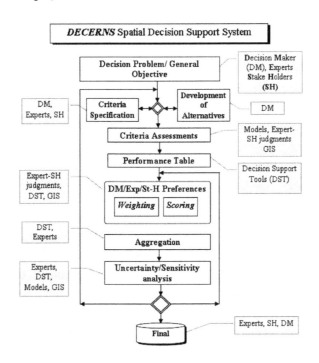

sible through the *SDSS* interface. All of the necessary procedures for preparing input and output information, including interaction of the models with corresponding maps and databases, can be realized by the user-side of the web distributed system. Corresponding model information may be used as cartographic layers, or alternatively, as data to support the multi-criteria decision-making process. This capability to interact between model output and cartographic map layers is an important feature of *DECERNS*.

Several models for human health and ecological risk assessment have been developed and implemented on the *DECERNS* web server. Such models include habitat suitability indices evaluation, and transport models for radionuclides and chemicals in the environment. These models are used within the specific case studies on environmental protection and land use planning (Linkov, 2004, 2006; Yatsalo, 2007).

DECERNS APLICATION CASE STUDY

Various examples of SDSS implementation can be found, *e.g.*, in (Armstrong, 1994; Awasthi, 2008; Balram & Dragievi, 2006; Carver, 1991; Carver & Peckham, 1999; Jankowski, 1995; Malczewski, 1999, 2004, 2006; Rinner, 2003;). SDSSs can effectively be used for:

- Allocation of land to new or different uses, *e.g.* for agriculture, forest, recreational, housing, and other needs;
- Site or land-use-suitability problems including housing development, habitat site selection, location of a facility, etc.;
- Location-allocation problems, including waste disposal, health care resource allocation, reorganizing fire protection services, etc.;

- Restoration of contaminated sites/territory, including population and environmental protection.

In land-use decisions, depending on the size and prominence of the site or territory, there can be a variety of principle stakeholders. Stakeholders would typically include land owners or problem holders, regulatory and planning authorities, site users, workers, visitors, members of financial institutions, site neighbors, environmental organizations, consultants, contractors, and occasionally researchers.

We consider here the case study on *housing development* (HD) in the Bryansk region of Russia. The description of this case study, approaches to its solution, and some results for the specific region and stakeholders' interests and preferences are presented below.

General description: A group of stakeholders has a goal to find an area for HD in a given region. Stakeholders have an interest to find the suitable area for HD in two administrative districts (Novozybkovski and Klintsovski) in the Bryansk region of Russia. These districts (about 60 km from south to north, and about 72 km from east to west) are mainly agricultural with more than one hundred thousand residents. One problem that they may face is that the indicated districts are situated in an area subjected to radioactive contamination as a result of the Chernobyl accident. A map of land-use for these two districts and some additional cartographic layers, including the main towns and villages, hydrological and road systems, are presented in Figure 3. We consider two possible approaches to investigation of the indicated problem:

The first approach (case study 1.1, CS-1.1) is based on implementation of the *DECERNS SDSS* to realize the conjunctive screening process using only GIS functionality in *DECERNS*.

The second approach (case study 1.2, CS-1.2) includes implementation of both GIS and MCDA tools. Suitable lands as a result of the screening process form several alternative sites for land use, which are analyzed using MCDA tools.

CS-1.1: Implementation of GIS Functionality Within Housing Development Problem

The following criteria for *HD* were discussed and agreed by the facilitator with the group of stakeholders:

- C_1 - proximity to the towns;
- C_2 - proximity to major roads;
- C_3 - proximity to major rivers or lakes/ponds;
- C_4 - distance from wetlands; and
- C_5 - distance from rail roads.
- Within this case study the conception of the criteria and constraints were specified:
- (C_1) towns/villages with the population more then 900 people (i.e., not very small settlements) are considered, and (imposed constraint) $1 \leq C_1 \leq 4$ km;
- (C_2) roads with only blacktop are considered, and $0.15 \leq C_2 \leq 1.5$ km;
- (C_3) only large rivers and lakes/ponds are considered (the details of rivers/lakes were discussed with the stakeholders), and $0.1 \leq C_3 \leq 1$ km;
- (C_4, C_5) all types of wetlands, indicated on the land-use map, and rail roads are considered; the following obligatory *constraints* were imposed in accordance with the requirements discussed with the stakeholders: distance from wetlands $C_4 \geq 0.5$ km, and distance from railroads $C_5 \geq 0.3$ km.
- Additional constraints required that houses may not be built:
- On arable lands as well as on water-meadow pastures and hayfields (CN_1);
- On areas of the given villages (CN_2);

Figure 5. CS-1.1: Buffer zones for the selected settlements

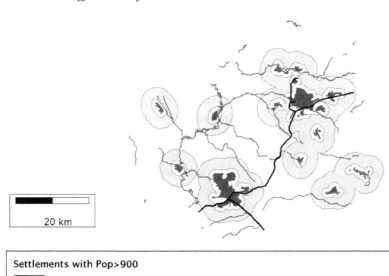

20 km

Settlements with Pop>900

Def. Color

C1 (d(Settl): 1– 4 km)

Def. Color

_____ Rail roads   _ _ _ _ _ _ Main Rivers

- On other unsuitable lands defined at the stage of constraint imposition (ravines, farm lands, sandstones, burial grounds and some other types of land use) (CN_3);
- Suitable lands for housing development with an area less then S_0 (=2500 m²) are not considered (CN_4).

CS-1.1 Solution

Our solution of the CS-1.1 is based on implementation of *vector maps* for the region under consideration, Figure 3. The *conjunctive screening process* within this case study is based on a realization of the following steps (Figure 5):

1. Buffer zones/layer $BL_i = BL(C_i)$ in accordance with the distance constraints for criteria C_i, $i=1,...,5$, are defined as follows: $BL_i = BL(r_i < C_i < R_i)$ for $i=1,2,3$, and $BL_i = BL(0 < C_i < R_i)$ for $i=4,5$, see the constraints for C_i above ($r_1=1$, $R_1=4$; $r_2=0.15$, $R_2=1.5$; $r_3=0.1$, $R_3=1$; $R_4=0.5$, $R_5=0.3$; r and R are indicated in kilometers/km); (the buffer layer for each criterion C_i is automatically created based on aggregating buffer zones for all the objects (or the selected objects) of the corresponding layer)..

2. Conjunctive screening (realization of *all* the requirements) is realized as a two step overlay procedure. The first layer is the result of constraints 1 - 5: $L_1 = L(C(\&; i=1-5)) = (BL_1 \cap BL_2 \cap BL_3) - (BL_4 \cup BL_5)$ (here and below ampersand (&) is used to indicate, that the process of conjunctive (&) screening for indicated criteria is realized; signs $\cap$, $\cup$, and '−' mean, accordingly, intersection, union, and set difference/subtraction). Thus, Layer L_1 is the intersection of the three buffer zone layers that describe proximity to towns, roads, and water bodies minus the intersection of the constraining buffer zone layers for distance from wetlands and railroads.

3. The second layer is generated by taking into account the additional constraints CN_i i=1-3, (see above), subtraction of corresponding layers from layer L_1 is implemented: $L_2 = L_1 - (\cup L(CN_i))$; Thus, layer L_2 is the suitable areas defined in layer L_1 minus the unsuitable areas found in constraints $CN_1 - CN_3$.

4. Taking into account the additional constraint that the size of the plot must be larger than 2500 m², CN_4, layer L_2 is corrected to $L=L_{result}$ through elimination of the vector polygons with the area less then 2500 m².

Thus, layer $L = L(C(\&; i=1-5) - CN(1-4))$ is the resulting layer, which comprises all the lands suitable for HD within the indicated problem, Figure 6.

After a screening process, the next step within the decision making is for the stakeholders to analyze the resulting layer L using additional objective/subjective criteria and preferences. Then those stakeholders will select one or several of the most interesting lands for housing development, Figure 6. The further step within the decision-making process may also include a new request by the stakeholders to continue evaluating the suitable area based on some additional criteria to find the 'optimal' or trade-off suitable land for HD. The last approach was used to form the case study 1.2 (CS-1.2).

CS-1.2: Implementation of GIS and MCDA Tools Within Housing Development Problem

Within the second iteration of the HD problem development, stakeholders extended the list of criteria and working with a facilitator/analytic agreed to use multicriteria methods for ranking alternatives. The approach to CS-1.2 analysis and results are presented below.

A criterion based approach (von Winterfeldt & Edwards, 1986) to structuring the multicriteria

Figure 6. CS-1.1: Suitable area for housing development (polygons) along with other layers (roads, rail roads, and rivers), important for subsequent decision-making

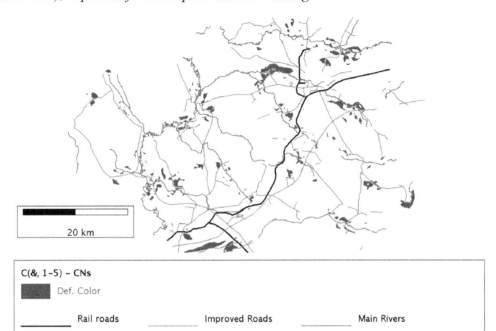

C(&, 1–5) – CNs

▮ Def. Color

_____ Rail roads   _____ Improved Roads   _____ Main Rivers

problem was used. The set of criteria from CS-1.1 was modified.

The following criteria within the CS-1.2 are considered along with corresponding constraints in addition to the indicated ones for CS-1.1:

- C_6 - proximity to forest, $C_6 \leq 1$ km;
- C_7 - distance from stockyards/cattle-breeding farms or manufactures (*maximize*), $C_7 \geq 2$ km (the farther the better, but not less than 2 km);
- C_8 - distance from ecologically adverse objects (*maximize*) $C_8 \geq 3$ km;
- C_9 - level of radioactive contamination (*minimize*) $C_9 \leq 10$ Ci/km²;
- C_{10} - general (qualitative) assessment of the local landscape/site quality (*maximize*);
- C_{11} - cost (*minimize*), (land cost and all the expenses associated with cottage building);

Constraints CN_k, $k=1,\ldots, 4$, are the same as for CS-1.1.

Criteria C_i, $i=1,\ldots, 9$, are considered as the constraints for the conjunctive screening procedure, at that, criteria C_i, $i=7,\ldots,11$, are used within the subsequent multi-criteria decision analysis. Thus, criteria C_7, C_8, and C_9 are used in both the screening procedures and within subsequent multi-criteria analysis.

CS 1.2 Solution

The general approach to implementation of the *DECERNS SDSS* for solving applied spatial multi-criteria problems is indicated in Figure 4. The first step within CS-1.2 solution is the use of the conjunctive screening process for criteria C_i, $i=1,\ldots, 8$, with corresponding constraints and additional constraints CN_k, $k=1,\ldots,4$. This step is similar to one described within the CS-1.1. The second step is elimination of the areas with

Figure 7. CS-1.2: The result of screening process for criteria C_i, i=1,...,9, and additional constraints CN_k, k=1,...,4: polygonal layer L=L(C(&,1-9) − CNs)), and additional vector layers (rail road, rivers, and roads)

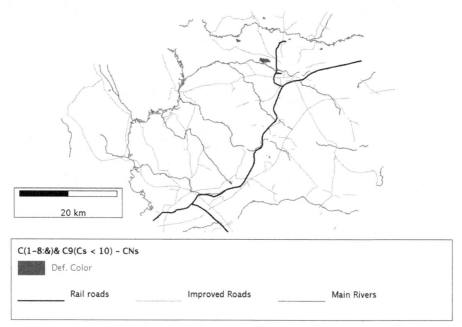

C(1–8:&)& C9(Cs < 10) – CNs

■ Def. Color

___ Rail roads   ----- Improved Roads   ___ Main Rivers

contamination above an indicated constraint for criterion C_9, which will also be in accordance with the approved approach used in formal data on radioactive contamination for all the elementary areas (arable field, pasture, settlement, forest plot, etc.) as determined within the formal monitoring procedures.

The result of screening process for criteria C_i, i=1,...,9, and additional constraints CN_k, k=1,...,4, is the layer L=L(C(&, i=1-9)−CN(1-4)), Figure 7.

MCDA analysis. Four experts and a group of stakeholders took part in the process of multi-criteria decision analysis under the management of a facilitator/analytic in accordance with the scheme in Figure 4. Some details of this process are presented briefly as follows:

- Experts and stakeholders analyze the resulting layer L=L(C(&; i=1-9) − CN(1-4)) as a result of the screening process and, based on the stakeholders' preferences,

select all or several suitable land areas for subsequent multi-criteria analysis. In this case, all five of the resulting areas of the layer L were selected. These regions form the layer/set of *alternatives* $\{A_i, i=1,...,5\}$, Figure 7;

- Jointly with stakeholders the performance table that represents criteria assessments, $a_{ij}=C_j(A_i)$, for criteria C_j, j=7,...,11, and alternatives A_i, i=1,...,5, is formed using SDSS/GIS tools, attributive data for selected areas of the layer L, and expert assessments for criteria C_{10} and C_{11}

- Value functions $V_j(x)$ for all the criteria C_j, j=7,...,11, were determined with the experts; local scales (Belton & Stewart, 2002) ranging from 0 (worst, $V_j(c_{j,worst})=0$) to 1 (best, $V_j(c_{j,best})=1$) for all the criteria were chosen; experts selected linear value functions $V_j(x)$ for all the criteria C_j, j=7,...,11; thus, value functions $V_7(x)$,

$V_8(x)$, and $V_{10}(x)$ have a monotonically increasing value from low score to high score as we are trying to maximize distance from stockyards/cattle-breeding farms or manufactures (criterion C_7), distance from ecologically adverse objects (C_7), and general assessment of the local landscape/site quality (C_{10}), whiles $V_9(x)$ and $V_{11}(x)$ are monotonically decreasing as we are trying to minimize level of radioactive contamination (criterion C_9), and expenses associated with housing development (criterion C_{11});

- Criterion weights were determined with the experts based on the *swing* method to use scaling factors for MAVT implementation (Belton & Stewart, 2002); experts agreed that, taking into account swing from $c_{j,worst}$ to $c_{j,best}$ for each criterion C_j (see performance table, Figure 8), the greatest increase in overall value is for criterion C_9 (level of radioactive contamination), and then, in accordance with experts' judgments, $w_9 > w_{11} > w_{10} = w_8 > w_7$, where w_j is the weight coefficient (scaling factor) for the criterion C_j, j=7,...,11; after ranking criteria weight coefficients were assessed based on comparison of the increase in overall value resulting from an increase from a score of 0 to a score of 1 on the selected criterion as a portion of the increase in overall value resulting in an increase from a score of 0 to 1 on the most highly ranked criterion (with subsequent normalization of weight coefficients, Figure 8);
- Ranking of alternatives was performed using MAVT methods and based on overall value $V(A_i)$, $V(A_i)=\Sigma w_j V_j(A_i)$;
- For all the alternatives A_i, indicated in the performance table, Figure 8, the result of ranking alternatives is indicated in Figure 9/left side;
- Sensitivity analysis was perfomed to evaluate the effects of changing criterion weight w_j, j=7,.., 11, on ranking of alternatives, see Figure 9/right side; in addition, sensitivity analysis to changing partial value function $V_j(x)$ (from the source linear function to close non-linear one) and corresponding changing overall value $V(A_i)$ was performed (this tool was also developed in *DECERNS* and can be effectively used within MAVT);
- The results of ranking and subsequent sensitivity analysis were discussed with stakeholders and experts. Stakeholders agreed with the procedures of weighting and scoring, suggested by experts, and accepted the results of the ranking. Based on sensitivity analysis, and taking into account further

Figure 8. CS-1.2: Performance table for housing development problem: criteria characteristics and weights

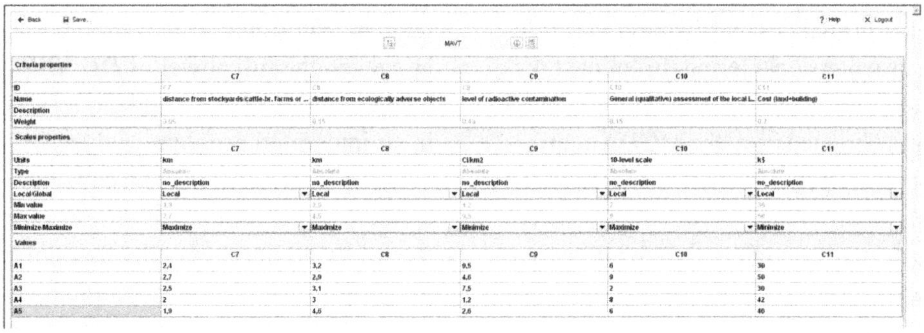

Back | Save... | MAVT | ? Help | X Logout

Criteria properties

	C7	C8	C9	C10	C11
ID	C7	C8	C9	C10	C11
Name	distance from stockyards/cattle-br. farms or ...	distance from ecologically adverse objects	level of radioactive contamination	General (qualitative) assessment of the local L...	Cost (land+building)
Description					
Weight	0.05	0.15	0.45	0.15	0.2

Scales properties

	C7	C8	C9	C10	C11
Units	km	km	Ci/km2	10-level scale	k$
Type	Absolute	Absolute	Absolute	Absolute	Absolute
Description	no_description	no_description	no_description	no_description	no_description
Local/Global	Local	Local	Local	Local	Local
Min value	1,9	2,9	1,2	2	30
Max value	2,7	[illegible]	9,5	9	50
Minimize/Maximize	Maximize	Maximize	Minimize	Maximize	Minimize

Values

	C7	C8	C9	C10	C11
A1	2,4	3,2	9,5	6	30
A2	2,7	2,9	4,6	9	50
A3	2,5	3,1	7,5	2	30
A4	2	3	1,2	8	42
A5	1,9	4,6	2,6	6	40

Figure 9. CS-1.2: ranking alternatives and sensitivity analysis within implementation of MAVT for Housing Development problem

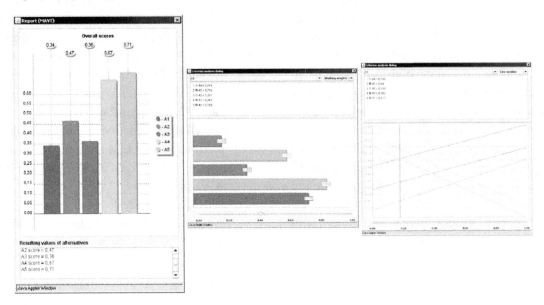

analysis of the criteria for alternatives A_4 and A_5 along with extended GIS analysis of source and developed map layers, stakeholders concurred with the experts that there is no significant difference between alternatives A_5 and A_4. Stakeholders made the decision to choose the area for housing after the field analysis of the areas/alternatives A_4 and A_5.

This two-stage analysis on housing development site selection (i.e., conjunctive screening to find the appropriate areas/alternatives in accordance with the requirements and constraints; and multicriteria analysis of alternatives taking into account objective and subjective values and preferences) yields an analysis that displays the trade-offs that occur when considering different stakeholders interests. Here, while a numerical difference was obtained from the MCDA analysis suggesting a preferred alternative, stakeholders decided that the difference between alternatives A_5 and A_4 was small enough and each alternative was acceptable.

CONCLUSION AND FUTURE DIRECTIONS

The *DECERNS WebSDSS* is an original web-based spatial decision support system. *DECERNS* integrates the basic GIS functions as well as some extended functions, decision analysis tools, based upon several MCDA methods, and a model server. The model server uses the specific models for customized site-specific problems, including ecological and human health risk models, transport and migration models, economic analysis models, etc. All subsystems may be accessed independently as stand-alone software. For example, GIS functions and kriging methods are used for spatial data analysis only. MCDA tools may be implemented for non-spatial multicriteria problem investigation. However, the full power of *DECERNS* is utilized when the GIS, MCDA, and model server are used in an integrated problem analysis.

Each subsystem may be customized in accordance with the users' request. An example of this would be adding new GIS functions or MCDA methods/tools. Complex problems may also be investigated using a single user-friendly *WebSDSS* interface. An example of such a complex problem would be processing cartographical layers along with setting spatial alternatives and subsequent multi-criteria analysis.

DECERNS users have handy tools for uncertainty analysis. These include the choice of several different MCDA models and the ability to address the robustness of the decision to changing the relative importance and value of each decision criteria. For this, the sensitivity of the decision to changes in weights or/and value functions can be used. An alternative approach to uncertainty analysis implemented in *DECERNS* is the use of distributed random or fuzzy weight and/or criterion values.

In addition to existing analytical capabilities, methods for group decision-making support are under development. When fully implemented, the *DECERNS* application will allow supporting surveys, voting, and interacting with MCDA modules for problem structuring, weighting and scoring criteria.

The *DECERNS* features indicated below emphasize key differences of this SDSS from others developed previously:

- *DECERNS* is an MCDA-oriented SDSS which includes the basic and advanced multicriteria/MADM decision analysis methods and tools, and GIS-functions for map layers processing and spatial data analysis; case/site specific models can be integrated with the SDSS through the model provider; thus, *DECERNS* is capable of integrating decision-maker values into a common framework using MCDA and GIS tools (and math models, if necessary) in a user friendly environment (Figure 2);
- Specific tools allow creating and handling a set of spatial alternatives along with transferring map and criteria data to the performance table. This is very effective in

the case of a large number of alternatives for subsequent multicriteria analysis;

- *DECERNS* has been developed as a web-based distributed SDSS (WebSDSS) based on up-to-date Java technologies;
- The architecture of SDSS is easily extendible through adding new MCDA methods and tools, GIS or SDSS functions, and a set of site-specific models;
- *DECERNS WebSDSS* is a working system (software) which can be used and modified by its client.

During development of *DECERNS* we have taken into account the experience of existing GIS/MCDA/DSS software implementation. As a result, the current *WebSDSS* interface has been improved due to users' comments. In addition, we recommend using *DECERNS* under technical/facilitator management, at least in the beginning of SDSS use, which would guide the process of structuring multi-criteria problems and implementing *SDSS* tools.

In this paper the *DECERNS SDSS* is presented along with an actual case study. The case study of housing development, which we analyzed above, demonstrates only some of the basic capabilities of the *DECERNS SDSS* on multi-criteria analysis of spatial alternatives. GIS tools provide all of the key functions for processing and analyzing spatial data, cartographic layers, and attributive information. This includes multi-criteria screening. Furthermore, MCDA tools realize all the steps within discrete multi-criteria decision analysis (Figure 4). All of these steps are interrelated and integrated within one SDSS environment.

New case studies along with demonstration of the *DECERNS* features and unique methods and tools, indicated above, for solving actual multi-criteria (spatial) problems are being undertaken.

ACKNOWLEDGMENT

This work has been carried out within the ISTC/IPP #3549 project. Authors are grateful to all the project participants.

REFERENCES

Armstrong, M. P. (1994). Requirements for the development of GIS-based group decision support systems. *Journal of the American Society for Information Science American Society for Information Science, 45*(9), 669–677. doi:doi:10.1002/(SICI)1097-4571(199410)45:9<669:AID-ASI4>3.0.CO;2-P

Armstrong, M. P., Densham, P. J., & Rushton, G. (1986). Architecture for a microcomputer-based spatial decision support system. In *Proceedings of the Second International Symposium on Spatial Data Handling* (pp. 120-131). Williamsville, NY: IGU Commission on Geographical Data Sensing and Processing.

Awasthi, A., & Chauhan, S. S. (2008). An analytical hierarchical process-based decision-making approach for selecting car-sharing stations in medium size agglomerations. *Int. J. Information and Decision Sciences, 1*(1), 66–96. doi:doi:10.1504/IJIDS.2008.020049

Balram, S., & Dragievi, S. (Eds.). (2006). *Collaborative geographic information systems*. Hershey, PA: IGI Global Publishing.

Belton, V., & Stewart, T. (2002). *Multiple criteria decision analysis: An integrated approach*. Kluwer Academic Publishers.

Brans, J. P., & Vincke, P. (1985). A preference ranking organization method: the PROMETHEE method for multiple criteria decision-making. *Management Science, 31*, 647–656. doi:doi:10.1287/mnsc.31.6.647

Carlsson, C., & Fuller, R. (1996). Fuzzy multiple criteria decision making: Recent developments. *Fuzzy Sets and Systems, 78*, 139–153. doi:doi:10.1016/0165-0114(95)00165-4

Carver, S., & Peckham, R. (1999). Using GIS on the internet for planning. J. C. Stillwell, S. Geertman, & S. Openshaw (Eds.), *Geographical information and planning* (pp. 371–390). New York: Springer.

Carver, S. J. (1991). Integrating multicriteria evaluation with geographical information systems. *International Journal of Geographical Information Systems, 5*(3), 321–339. doi:doi:10.1080/02693799108927858

Chakhar, S., & Martel, J.-M. (2003). Enhancing geographical information systems capabilities with multi-criteria evaluation functions. *Journal of Geographic Information and Decision Analysis, 7*(2), 47–71.

Densham, P. J., & Goodchild, M. F. (1989). Spatial decision support systems: a research agenda. *Proceedings of GIS/LIS'89* (pp. 706-71), Orlando, FL.

Figueira, J., Greco, S., & Ehrgott, M. (Eds.). (2005). *Multiple criteria decision analysis: State of the art surveys*. New York: Springer.

Hwang, C.-L., & Lin, M.-J. (1987). *Group decision making under multiple criteria*. Berlin: Springer-Verlag.

Hwang, C.-L., & Yoon, K. (1981). *Multiple Attribute Decision Making: Methods and Applications*. Berlin: Springer-Verlag.

Jankowski, P. (1995). Integrating geographical information systems and multiple criteria decision making methods. *International Journal of Geographical Information Systems, 9*, 251–273. doi:doi:10.1080/02693799508902036

Keeney, R. L., & Raiffa, H. (1976). *Decision with multiple objectives*. New York: J. Wiley & Sons.

Laaribi, A. (2000). *SIG et analyse multicitere*. Paris: Hermes Sciences Publications.

Laaribi, A., Chevallier, J. J., & Martel, J. M. (1996). A spatial decision aid: A multicriterion evaluation approach. *Computers, Environment and Urban Systems, 20*(6), 351–366. doi:doi:10.1016/S0198-9715(97)00002-1

Lahdelma, R., Hokkanen, J., & Salminen, P. (1998). SMAA - stochastic multiobjective acceptability analysis. *European Journal of Operational Research, 106*, 137–143. doi:doi:10.1016/S0377-2217(97)00163-X

Linkov, I., Grebenkov, A., Andrizhievski, A., Loukashevich, A., Trifonov, A., & Kapustka, L. (2004). Incorporating habitat characterization into risk-trace: software for spatially explicit exposure assessment. In Linkov, I., & Ramadan, A. (Eds.), *Comparative risk assessment and environmental decision making*. Amsterdam: Kluwer.

Linkov, I., Satterstrom, K., Kiker, Batchelor, C.G., & Bridges, T. (2006). From comparative risk assessment to multi-criteria decision analysis and adaptive management: recent developments and applications. *Environment International, 32*, 1072–1093. PubMed doi:10.1016/j.envint.2006.06.013

Malczewski, J. (1999). *GIS and multicriteria decision analysis*. New York: John Wiley & Sons Inc.

Malczewski, J. (2004). GIS-based land-use suitability analysis: a critical overview. *Progress in Planning, 62*, 3–65. doi:doi:10.1016/j.progress.2003.09.002

Malczewski, J. (2006). GIS-based multicriteria decision analysis: a survey of the literature. *International Journal of Geographical Information Science, 20*(7), 703–726. doi:doi:10.1080/13658810600661508

Rinner, C. (2003). Web-based spatial decision support: status and research directions. *Journal of Geographic Information and Decision Analysis, 7*(1), 14–31.

Saaty, T. L. (1980). *The analytic hierarchy process*. New York: McGraw-Hill.

Simon, H. A. (1960). *The new science of management decisions*. New York: Random House.

Sprague, R. H. (1980). A framework for the development of decision support systems. *Management Information Sciences Quarterly, 4*, 1–25.

Tervonen, T., & Figueira, J. R. (2008). A Survey on stochastic multicriteria acceptability analysis methods. *Journal of Multi-Criteria Decision Analysis, 15*, 1–14. doi:doi:10.1002/mcda.407

von Winterfeldt, D., & Edwards, W. (1986). *Decision Analysis and Behavioral Research*. UK: Cambridge University Press.

Yatsalo, B., Kiker, G., Kim, J., Bridges, T., Seager, T., Gardner, K., et al. (2007). Application of multi-Criteria decision analysis tools for management of contaminated sediments. *Integrated Environmental Assessment and Management, 3*(2), 223–233. PubMed doi:10.1897/IEAM_2006-036.1

Yatsalo, B. I. (2007). Decision support system for risk based land management and rehabilitation of radioactively contaminated territories: PRANA approach. *International Journal of Emergency Management, 4*(3), 504–523. doi:doi:10.1504/IJEM.2007.014300

Chapter 18

An Agricultural Decision Support System for Optimal Land Use Regarding Groundwater Vulnerability

Konstantinos Voudouris
Aristotle University, Greece

Nerantzis Kazakis
Aristotle University, Greece

Maurizio Polemio
CNR-IRPI, Italy

Angelo Sifaleras
University of Macedonia, Greece

ABSTRACT

The availability of quality water is a basic condition of socioeconomic development. The agriculture water demand can be damaged by contamination of groundwater resources. This paper proposes a tool to preserve groundwater quality by using groundwater vulnerability assessment methods and a decision support system (DSS). The mapping of intrinsic groundwater vulnerability was based on reliable methods, the DRASTIC and the SINTACS methods. A DSS was developed to assess the groundwater vulnerability and pollution risk due to agricultural activities and land use changes. The proposed DSS software package was designed using the Matlab language and efficiently performs tasks while incorporating new maps to cover new areas. The tool was tested at two study areas located in the Mediterranean that are dominated by different prevalent hydrogeological features, that is, the typical porous features of alluvial deposits in the Greek study area and the typical fissured and karstic features of limestones and dolostones in the Italian study area.

INTRODUCTION

In many countries, including those in the Mediterranean region and numerous coastal areas with worldwide distribution, groundwater is the main source for drinking and irrigation use. The availability of good quality water is a key factor for social and economical development. For this reason, preserving its availability and quality is a crucial issue for the future (EU Council, 1998; UNESCO, 1998). The degradation of groundwa-

DOI: 10.4018/978-1-4666-0927-3.ch018

ter resources can be quantitative if the discharge exceeds the natural recharge and qualitative if the chemical, physical, and biological water quality is threatened. In the former case, if the aquifer is on the coast, overexploitation is also qualitative risk due to possible seawater intrusion, causing salt degradation in the groundwater quality (Polemio et al., 2009a). The definition of a suitable policy for water is important in the context of growing scarcity and competing uses (Bazzani, 2005). For this reason, the importance of integrated water resource management was emphasized in the recent EU Water Framework Directive (2000/60/EC).

If groundwater degradation risks are considered, planning decisions should be reached based on risk assessment procedures in which the effects of anthropogenic activities on natural resources and the environment are considered. Agricultural activities are surely some of the most relevant endeavors. However, massive soil and continuous groundwater exploitation have a relevant negative impact on the environment.

In many farming areas, anthropogenic modifications are mainly caused by the following two types of activity: direct pollution from agricultural activities due to the use of agrochemicals, fertilizers, and pesticides and farming improvements, thereby provoking other negative impacts. Fires and the clearing of forests and stones with the advent of machinery have been widely used to make the land suitable for farming. Over-irrigation and salt-recycling due to overexploitation in the coastal areas also create problems (Voudouris et al., 2004). The effects on groundwater availability and quality are complex and generally negative.

The regional assessment of groundwater vulnerability is a useful tool for water resource management and protection. The results provide important information that can be used by local authorities and decision makers. A groundwater vulnerability assessment could be used to more effectively determine the choice of land use modifications, the location, the type of farming, and use of chemicals and irrigation in the farming endeavor.

The use of computer-based systems to support decision making regarding groundwater resource management has increased significantly over the last decade. In the case of land management, decision support systems (DSSs) are typically used to select an optimal or satisfactory solution from a set of feasible alternatives (Shim et al., 2002; Manos et al., 2004a). DSSs are defined as computerized systems that include models and databases used in decision-making (Uricchio et al., 2004). They are useful tools that help scientists and administrators in the decision-making process and in choosing the economically, socially, or environmentally best alternative solution (Hwang & Yoon, 1981; Manos et al., 2004b; Manos et al., 2007; Leung, 1997; Zhu et al., 1998; Vacik & Lexer, 2001).

The implementation of geographic information systems (GIS) and DSSs in hydrogeology offers effective tools for groundwater resource management. GIS has been widely used to establish a database for collected data (Süzenm & Doyuran, 2003; Gemitzi et al., 2006). In hydrogeology, both GIS and DSS have been developed to support local authorities, decision makers, and stakeholders in terms of groundwater resource management, vulnerability and pollution risk assessment, and protective zoning.

From a theoretical point of view, the paper briefly describes the main methods for groundwater vulnerability assessment while considering typical porous aquifers on the alluvial or coastal plains and the peculiarities of rocky aquifers (i.e., typical karstic aquifers). Additionally, methods to assess groundwater risks and hazards in the case of agricultural activities are described. From an operational point of view, the paper also describes some case studies of relevant farming areas located in southern Italy and northern Greece.

STUDY AREAS

The Florina basin is located in the central part of the Florina prefecture territory in western Greece, and its surface is roughly 319 km2. The average altitude is around 620 m asl, and the average slope is 1.5% (Figure 1). The annual rainfall is 643 mm per year (Kazakis, 2008). Based on results from soil analyses, the predominant soil types are as follows: Clay, Silty-clay, Sandy-clay, Sandy-loam, Silty, Silty-loam, and Loamy. Aquifer systems are developed in alluvial and Neogene deposits in the basin. The depth to groundwater in the alluvial aquifer of the Florina basin ranges from 0 to more than 25 m below ground.

Economic development in the area largely depends on pumped groundwater, which has increased in amount since 1980. The land is predominantly used for agricultural purposes in the lowlands, and irrigated agriculture is predominant in the basin. Groundwater is abstracted for irrigation purposes during the dry season (i.e., May through September). In the wet period, groundwater extraction is limited to domestic use.

The Monopoli area or test site (Figure 2) is located in the low Murgia Plateau (i.e., the Apulia region) and is characterized by Mesozoic limestone and dolostone that is several thousand meters thick. The entire study area is characterized by developed karst landforms, i.e., karst formed in response to several morphogenetic phases that took place in different climatic and structural contexts. As a result, an underground network of cavities, caves, and conduits has been developed; some of these have large dimensions. The landscape is characterized by many dolines, valleys, and drainage lines that are not clearly defined, thereby creating a discontinuous network.

A wide and thick aquifer resides in these carbonate rocks. The aquifer is divided into more permeable strata because of the variable distribution of fractured and karstified strata confined between impermeable levels of various extensions and thickness. This mainly occurred due to tectonic events that fractured the carbonate mass in a poor and discontinuous manner and variation in the base level of groundwater flow. It is generally confined except along a narrow coastal strip; faults govern the major preferential flow paths and seawater intrusion (Polemio, 2005). The groundwater in the study area has undergone a twofold pollution that is all due to human action. Saline pollution has progressively evolved as it affects increasingly large portions of land, and biological and chemical-physical pollution is mainly concentrated around urbanized areas.

Figure 1. Location of the Florina basin in northern Greece

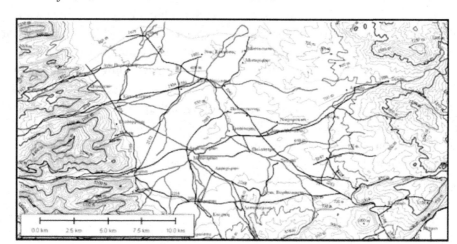

Figure 2. Location and geological map of the Monopoli area in Italy (Polemio et al., 2009b, modified)

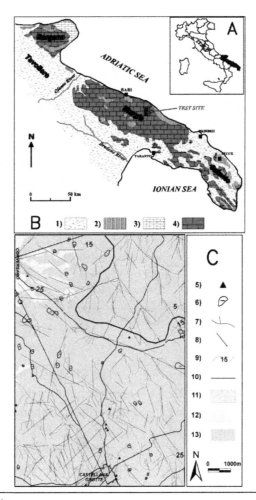

A: Apulian region and Italy.

B: Geological scheme of the Apulian region; 1) Recent clastic cover (Pliocene-Pleistocene), 2) Bioclastic carbonate rocks (Paleogene) and calcarenites (Miocene), 3) Scarp and basin chert-carbonate rocks (Upper Jurassic-Cretaceous), and 4) Carbonate platform rocks (Upper Jurassic-Cretaceous).

C: Schematic geological map of the study area; 5) Cave, 6) Doline/Sinkhole, 7) Drainage pattern, 8) Fault, 9) Piezometric contour line (m asl), 10) Road, 11) Urban area, 12) Alluvial deposits, and 13) Limestone.

GROUNDWATER VULNERABILITY ASSESSMENT

The concept of groundwater vulnerability is based on the assumption that the physical environment may provide some degree of protection for groundwater against human activities. In other words,

vulnerability represents the degree of weakness of one aquifer system to pollution.

In this study, two methods were applied in order to evaluate vulnerability, i.e., DRASTIC and SINTACS. Both the DRASTIC and SINTACS method are representative of rating methods or Point Count System Models (PCSM) for assessing groundwater vulnerability.

Figure 3. SINTACS method (Adapted from Vrba & Zaporozec, 1994)

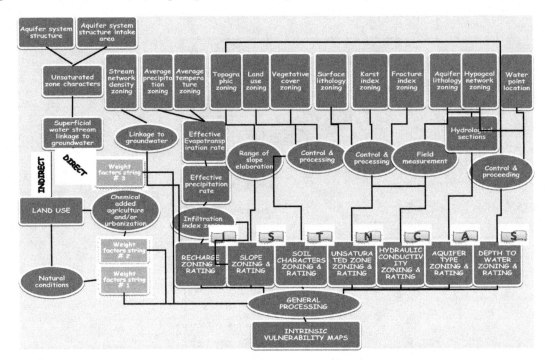

The initials in the acronym DRASTIC (Aller et al., 1987; Secunda et al., 1998; Al-Zabet, 2002; Voudouris, 2009) correspond to the following seven (7) parameters measured in this system: Depth (to water), Recharge, Aquifer media, Soil media, Topography, Impact of the vadose zone media, and hydraulic Conductivity of the aquifer.

Determination of the DRASTIC index involves multiplying each parameter weight by its site rating and summing the total. The equation for the DRASTIC Index (DI) is as follows:

$$DI = \sum_{j=1}^{7} r_j . w_j \qquad (1)$$

or

$$DI = D_r D_w + R_r R_w + A_r A_w + S_r S_w + T_r T_w + I_r I_w + C_r C_w$$

where r is the rating for the study area, and w is the importance weight for the parameter.

The SINTACS method was defined in an attempt to improve the DRASTIC method and uses almost the same parameters (Civita, 1994, 1995), which are as follows: depth to water, recharge or effective infiltration, attenuation capacity of unsaturated (or vadose) zone, soil attenuation capacity, hydrogeological characteristics of the aquifer, aquifer hydraulic conductivity, and slope. The vulnerability index $I_{SINTACS}$ can be computed as follows:

$$I_{SINTACS} = \sum_{J=1}^{7} r_j w_j \qquad (2)$$

where r is the rating of each of the seven parameters, and w is the correlated weight.

The SINTACS point-count system has a complex structure (Gogu & Dassargues, 2000) (Figure 3). The core of the method is the use of five set of weights or strings (i.e., normal impact, relevant impact, drainage, karst, and fissured aquifer) simultaneously in large areas and also if dominated by different prevalent conditions (e.g., in the case of zones that are deeply modified by anthropogenic activities as in urban areas) or due to the intensive use of agricultural chemicals and different types of aquifers, such as porous, fissured, or karstic aquifers (Polemio et al., 2009b).

In both methods, each parameter included in the index must have an assigned numeric value between 1 and 10. A higher index value indicates greater groundwater pollution potential or greater aquifer vulnerability.

Parameters used in the aforementioned method are fundamentally derived from monitoring gauges, hydrogeological field surveys, including water level measurements, pumping tests, soil analyses, and aero-photo and remote sensing studies (Figure 4).

RESULTS

The final vulnerability DRASTIC map of the Florina basin was produced using the values of the DRASTIC index (Figure 5). The highest vulnerability values in the Florina basin are associated with shallow aquifers that do not have great depth in the vadose zone. Low and very low values of vulnerability are observed in the centre of the basin where the aquifer has great depth in the vadose zone with layers of clay and silt and great depth to groundwater level.

The SINTACS intrinsic vulnerability map (Figure 6) reveals the presence of the following four vulnerability classes in the study area: low, medium, high, and very high. Most of the area is classified as medium in terms of vulnerability. High or Very high risk is reported where karst features are present on the ground surface (i.e., dolines) and/or the top soil is negligible. The urban areas are generally classified as medium in terms of vulnerability.

In general, the results of this study describe the relevant vulnerability of the groundwater in the Murgia aquifer. The intrinsic vulnerability map that was produced can provide useful information with sufficient spatial resolution and

Figure 4. Vulnerability assessment: Worksheet of required data in Excel format

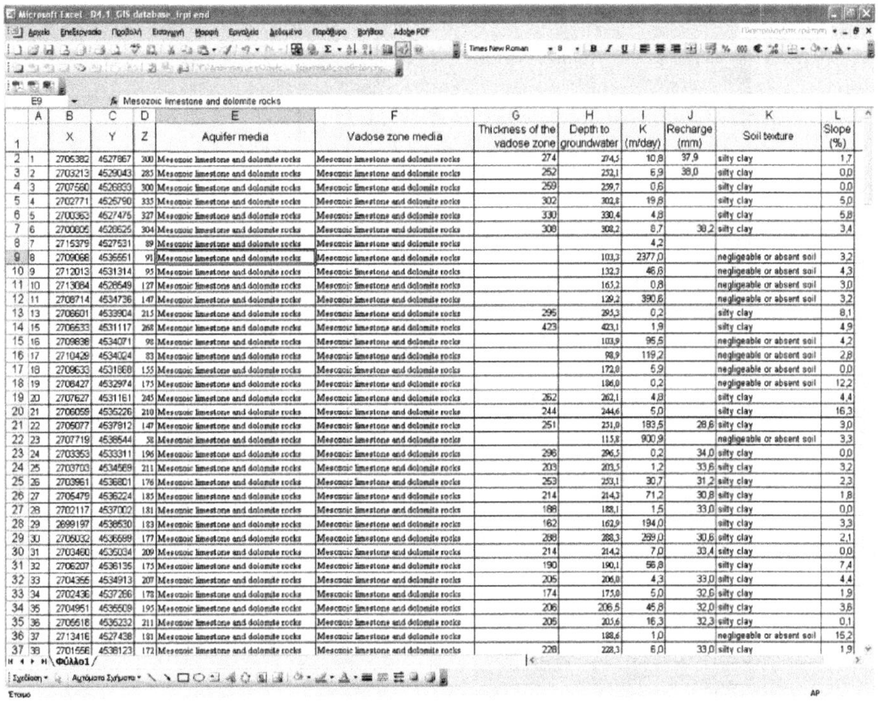

Figure 5. DRASTIC index (DI) worksheet in Excel format

x	y	Dr	Dw	Tr	Tw	Ar	Aw	Sr	Sw	Ir	Iw	Cr	Cw	Rr	Rw	Lr	Lw	DRASTIC
300141	4231756	9	5	10	1	6	2	6	2	3	4	6	3	5	3	8	4	156
300481	4232362	7	5	10	1	6	2	8	2	3	4	7	3	5	3	8	4	153
300466	4232366	7	5	10	1	6	2	8	2	3	4	6	3	5	3	8	4	150
300456	4232138	7	5	10	1	6	2	8	2	3	4	7	3	5	3	8	4	153
300629	4232067	7	5	10	1	6	2	8	2	3	4	7	3	5	3	8	4	153
300782	4232007	7	5	10	1	6	2	8	2	5	4	6	3	5	3	8	4	158
301057	4231496	3	5	10	1	6	2	8	2	7	4	5	3	5	3	8	4	152
301209	4231401	3	5	8	1	6	2	8	2	7	4	5	3	8	3	8	4	150
300914	4232954	7	5	10	1	6	2	8	2	3	4	6	3	5	3	8	4	146
300272	4232155	9	5	10	1	6	2	6	2	3	4	6	3	5	3	8	4	156
300348	4232632	10	5	10	1	6	2	6	2	3	4	6	3	5	3	8	4	161
300326	4231097	7	5	10	1	6	2	4	2	3	4	3	3	5	3	8	4	133
300620	4230781	5	5	10	1	6	2	6	2	5	4	3	3	5	3	8	4	135
300661	4231085	3	5	10	1	6	2	6	2	5	4	3	3	5	3	8	4	125
301265	4230919	2	5	8	1	6	2	6	2	5	4	3	3	5	3	8	4	118
300638	4231240	5	5	10	1	6	2	6	2	5	4	3	3	5	3	8	4	135
300112	4231367	10	5	10	1	6	2	6	2	3	4	6	3	5	3	8	4	161
301449	4230138	2	5	8	1	6	2	6	2	5	4	3	3	5	3	8	4	118
301337	4231672	3	5	8	1	6	2	6	2	5	4	6	3	8	3	8	4	141
302291	4231730	2	5	8	1	8	2	6	2	7	4	6	3	8	3	8	4	148
301667	4231320	2	5	8	1	8	2	8	2	7	4	3	3	8	3	5	4	131
301531	4231175	2	5	8	1	8	2	8	2	7	4	3	3	8	3	5	4	123
301883	4231194	2	5	8	1	8	2	8	2	7	4	3	3	8	3	5	4	143
302214	4230925	2	5	8	1	8	2	8	2	7	4	3	3	8	3	8	4	139
302133	4231325	2	5	8	1	8	2	8	2	7	4	3	3	8	3	5	4	131
302086	4231297	2	5	8	1	8	2	8	2	7	4	5	3	8	3	8	4	137
302759	4231125	1	5	5	1	8	2	8	2	7	4	3	3	8	3	6	4	123
302133	4231325	1	5	5	1	8	2	8	2	7	4	6	3	8	3	8	4	144
303268	4230914	1	5	5	1	8	2	8	2	7	4	3	3	8	3	5	4	123
303007	4232677	2	5	8	1	8	2	8	2	5	4	5	3	5	3	8	4	128
304096	4230634	1	5	5	1	8	2	8	2	7	4	3	3	8	3	5	4	123
302875	4232327	2	5	8	1	8	2	8	2	5	4	6	3	5	3	8	4	131
303936	4231564	1	5	5	1	8	2	6	2	7	4	3	3	8	3	8	4	131
304956	4230734	1	5	5	1	8	2	6	2	7	4	3	3	8	3	5	4	123
302983	4231952	1	5	8	1	8	2	6	2	7	4	6	3	5	3	8	4	134
300061	4229460	3	5	8	1	8	2	8	2	5	4	5	3	5	3	8	4	130
301182	4230998	3	5	8	1	6	2	6	2	5	4	3	3	5	3	8	4	123
301119	4231214	3	5	8	1	6	2	8	2	5	4	5	3	5	3	8	4	133
300212	4230461	6	5	10	1	6	2	4	2	3	4	3	3	5	3	8	4	128
300301	4231588	9	5	10	1	6	2	6	2	3	4	4	3	5	3	8	4	156
300289	4231564	9	5	10	1	6	2	6	2	3	4	4	3	5	3	8	4	156
300636	4230165	9	5	10	1	6	2	4	2	5	4	3	3	5	3	8	4	151
300819	4230013	9	5	8	1	6	2	6	2	5	4	4	3	5	3	8	4	153
301338	4229910	3	5	8	1	6	2	6	2	5	4	3	3	5	3	8	4	123

Figure 6. SINTACS vulnerability map of the Monopoli study area 1) Road, 2) Urban area, 3) low, 4) medium or moderate, 5) high, and 6) very high vulnerability

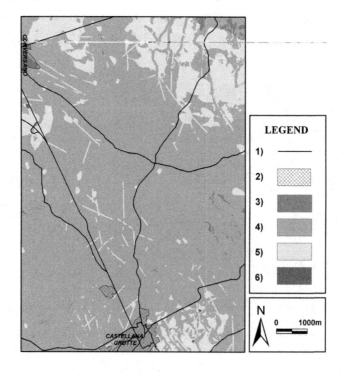

precision for the planning of local anthropogenic activities.

DSS ARCHITECTURE

Implementation and Installation Issues of the DSS Software Package

The proposed DSS software package has been designed using the MATLAB language. More precisely, the proposed DSS software package makes use of all the programming capabilities that are offered from MATLAB version R2009a.

Matlab toolboxes are widely used by many scientists. They are easily deployed while exploiting all the Matlab programming benefits; thus, they are frequently used for diverse types of computational tasks. For example, Dosios et al. (2002) presented the LinPro Matlab toolbox, which is an educational platform for Linear Optimization. Furthermore, Dosios et al. (2003) developed the NetPro Matlab toolbox as an educational tool for the teaching of Network Optimization. Furthermore, Matlab combines animation and graphics (e.g., Marchand & Holland, 2002), thereby enabling the user to deploy complex graphical user interfaces (GUI).

All of the functions in the proposed DSS software package are separate m-files. The installation using Matlab is easy and can be accomplished using similar methods to the installation of any other function or toolbox. The current version of Matlab is quite sophisticated and provides the user with many built-in functions and useful tools (e.g., Hahn & Valentine, 2007).

All the necessary files must be copied to a folder, like Matlab/Work, and the user must consecutively select File → Set Path → Add with subfolders to add the directory of the proposed DSS software package into the current path for Matlab.

The Graphical User Interface (GUI) of the DSS Software Package

The user can start the proposed DSS software package easily by running the function *landuse.m* through the Matlab environment. After the command execution, an introductory screen (Figure 7) is shown to the user for 3 seconds.

The user has two choices depending on whether he has already made a decision on how to utilize the land or not. In the latter case, the user may previously know the ground water vulnerability within his land and wants advice from the DSS software. This user may submit his choice on the screen seen in Figure 8.

The GUI consists of a main menu bar and one toolbar, both of which may contain different buttons depending on the specific figure. In Figure 8, the user may either print this dialogue window or press the "Proceed" button in the menu bar. Assuming that the user already knows the ground water vulnerability of his land, he probably wants direction regarding what types of exploitation for which the land is suitable. In Figure 9, the user

Figure 7. Introductory figure

Figure 8. Possible ways to use the DSS software

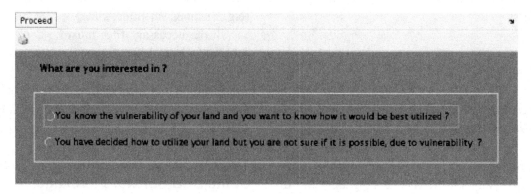

Figure 9. Area identification (Monopoli area left, Florina basin right)

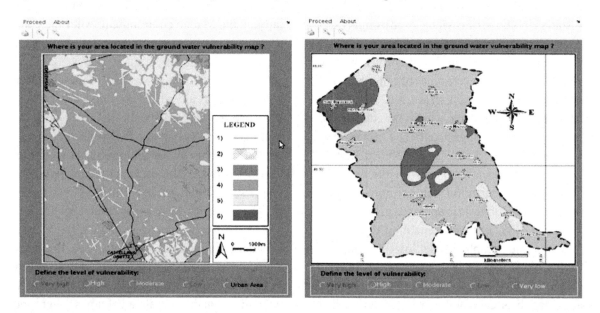

can now submit the vulnerability of his land and press the "Proceed" button again.

Notably, the menu bar and the toolbar now provide some more options. For example, the user is now able to either zoom in or zoom out on the map and even print the map provided in the software. For further explanation, assume again that the user presses the radio button in the lower part of Figure 9, which corresponds to High vulnerability. On the next screen (Figure 10), the DSS software asks the user if he/she has identified a desired use for his/her land. For example, if the user wants to cultivate the area with fertilizers, then he should select the appropriate radio button and press the "Recommendation" button.

The recommendation by the DSS software would then appear in the bottom part of that window. Initially, Figure 10 does not contain any textual recommendation. The recommendation is made visible to the user only after he presses the previously mentioned button in the menu bar. Moreover, if the user wants to make a different decision, he can simply press a different radio

Figure 10. Desired area usage

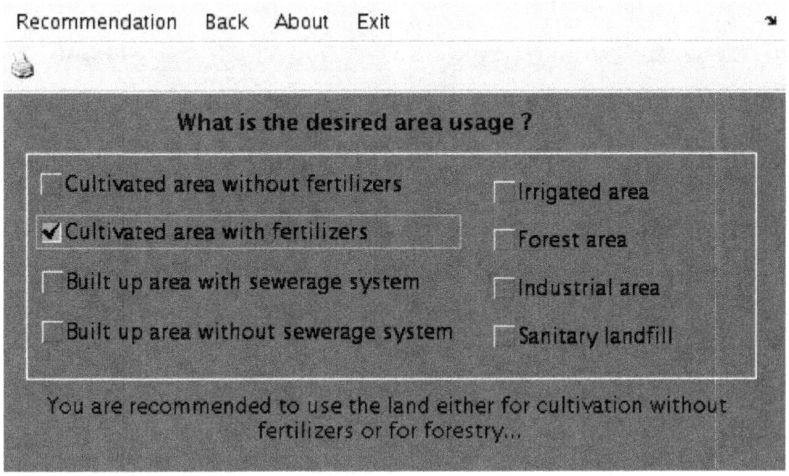

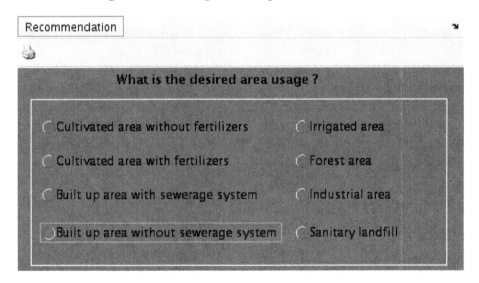

Figure 11. Desired area usage without having decided upon the location

button and then press the "Recommendation" button.

On the other hand, if the user selected the second choice in Figure 8 (i.e., he/she does not know his/her land vulnerability in advance), the screen seen in Figure 11 will appear. For the sake of example, assume that the user wants to build up an area without using a sewerage system.

After pressing the "Recommendation" button, the screen seen in Figure 12 will appear in order to inform the user about the possible acceptable locations for his/her plans. In our example, the DSS software advises the user that he should select an area with very low or low vulnerability on the map. Furthermore, the DSS software visually informs the user that potential, suitable areas are highlighted in blue or green respectively.

The proposed DSS software is a user friendly application for the novice user (e.g., a student) and an operations research scientist alike. It quickly and efficiently performs the task that is scheduled for completion, and it can incorporate

Figure 12. Land utilization (Monopoli area left, Florina basin right)

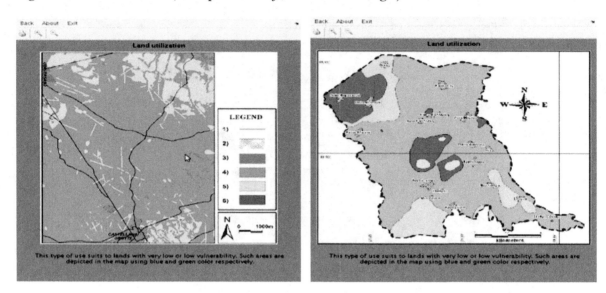

new maps in order to cover new areas. More precisely, a file called "map.jpg" can be found among the files within the DSS application. If the user exchanges this file/map with a new one, then the DSS will advise him about the new areas. In this way, the user does not need to know anything about the groundwater vulnerability or the geological processes in general for the land in question.

CONCLUSION

Methods for groundwater vulnerability were applied to different hydrogeological and socio-economical situations. The assessment results are sufficiently clear and can thus be understood by any kind of stakeholder without specific expertise on hydrogeological or environmental matters. The groundwater vulnerability was relevant in all cases.

The proposed software was demonstrated as a reliable tool for managing the effects of agricultural or anthropogenic activities on groundwater quality while pursuing sustainable growth. In areas with a high degree of hazard, e.g., intensive irrigated areas, a set of measures can be defined in

order to mitigate the groundwater quality impact using the DSS tools.

The proposed DSS could be easily joined to other packages, e.g., irrigation type, crop type, type of fertilizers, water consumption, to create a more comprehensive tool in order to define land allocation and protection zoning.

REFERENCES

Al-Zabet, T. (2002). Evaluation of aquifer vulnerability to contamination potential using the DRASTIC method. *Environmental Geology*, *43*(1-2), 203–208. doi:10.1007/s00254-002-0645-5

Aller, L., Bennett, T., Lehr, J. H., Petty, R. J., & Hackett, G. (1987). *DRASTIC: A standardized system for evaluating ground water pollution potential using hydrogeologic settings*. Washington, DC: US Environmental Protection Agency.

Bazzani, G. M. (2005). An integrated decision support system for irrigation and water policy design: DSIRR. *Environmental Modelling & Software*, *20*(2), 153–163. doi:10.1016/j.envsoft.2003.12.017

Civita, M. (1994). *Le carte della vulnerabilità degli acquiferi all'inquinamento*. Belogna, Italy: Pitarora.

Civita, M., & De Regibus, C. (1995). *Sperimentazione di alcune metodologie per la valutazione della vulnerabilita degli aquiferi*. Bologna, Italy: Pitarora.

E.U. Council. (1998). Council directive 98/83 about water quality intended for human consumption. *Official paper of the European Communities, L330*, 32-54.

Dosios, K., Paparrizos, K., Papatzikos, N., & Sifaleras, A. (2002). LinPro, an educational informational system for linear programming. In *Proceedings of the 15th National Conference of Hellenic Operational Research Society*, Tripoli, Greece (pp. 182-189).

Dosios, K., Paparrizos, K., Samaras, N., & Sifaleras, A. (2003). NetPro, an educational platform for network optimization. In *Proceedings of the 16th National Conference of Hellenic Operational Research Society*, Larissa, Greece (Vol. 1, pp. 287-295).

Gemitzi, A., Petalas, C., Tsihtintzis, V., & Pisinaras, V. (2006). Assessment of groundwater vulnerability to pollution: A combination of GIS, fuzzy logic and decision making techniques. *Environmental Geology, 49*(5), 653–673. doi:10.1007/s00254-005-0104-1

Gogu, R. C., & Dessargues, A. (2000). Current trends and future challenges in groundwater vulnerability assessment using overlay and index methods. *Environmental Geology, 39*(6), 549–559. doi:10.1007/s002540050466

Hahn, B., & Valentine, D. (2007). *Essential MATLAB for engineers and scientists* (3rd ed.). London: Newnes Publications.

Hwang, C. L., & Yoon, K. (1981). *Multiple attribute decision making: methods and applications*. New York: Springer Verlag.

Kazakis, N. (2008). *Groundwater vulnerability assessment using different methods: A case study from the alluvial aquifer of Florina basin*. Unpublished doctoral dissertation, Dept. of Geology, Aristotle University of Thessaloniki, Greece.

Leung, Y. (1997). *Intelligent spatial decision support systems*. Berlin: Springer.

Manos, B., Bournaris, Th., Papathanasiou, J., Moulogianni, Ch., & Voudouris, K. S. (2007). A DSS for agricultural land use, water management and environmental protection. In *Proceedings of the 3rd International Conference on Energy, Environment, Ecosystems and Sustainable Development*, Agios Nikolaos, Crete (pp. 340-345).

Manos, B., Bournaris, Th., Silleos, N., Antonopoulos, V., & Papathanasiou, J. (2004a). A Decision Support System for rivers monitoring and sustainable management. *Environmental Monitoring and Assessment, 96*(1-3), 85–98. doi:10.1023/B:EMAS.0000031717.13972.27

Manos, B., Ciani, A., Bournaris, Th., Vassiliadou, I., & Papathanasiou, J. (2004b). A taxonomy survey of Decision Support Systems in agriculture. *Agricultural Economics Research, 5*(2), 80–94.

Marchand, P., & Holland, O. T. (2002). *Graphics and GUIs with MATLAB* (3rd ed.). London: Chapman & Hall/CRC. doi:10.1201/9781420057393

Polemio, M. (2005). Seawater intrusion and groundwater quality in the southern Italy region of Apulia: a multi-methodological approach to the protection. In *Proceedings of the UNESCO, IHP*, Paris (Vol. 77, pp. 171-178).

Polemio, M., Dragone, V., & Limoni, P. P. (2009a). Monitoring and methods to analyse the groundwater quality degradation risk in coastal karstic aquifers (Apulia, Southern Italy). *Environmental Geology, 58*(2), 299–312. doi:10.1007/s00254-008-1582-8

Polemio, M., Dragone, V., & Limoni, P. P. (2009b). Karstic aquifer vulnerability assessment methods and results at a test site (Apulia, Southern Italy). *Natural Hazards and Earth System Sciences, 9*(4), 1461–1470. doi:10.5194/nhess-9-1461-2009

Secunda, S., Collin, M. L., & Melloul, A. (1998). Groundwater vulnerability assessment using a composite model combining DRASTIC with extensive agricultural land use in Israel's Sharon region. *Journal of Environmental Management, 54*(1), 39–57. doi:10.1006/jema.1998.0221

Shim, J. P., Warkentin, M., Courtney, J. F., Power, D. J., Ramesh, S., & Carlsson, C. (2002). Past, present and future of decision support technology. *Decision Support Systems, 33*(2), 111–126. doi:10.1016/S0167-9236(01)00139-7

UNESCO. *(1998)*. Summary and recommendations of the International Conference on World Water Resources at the beginning of the 21st century 'Water: a looming crisis'. *Paris: France.*

Uricchio, V. F., Giordano, R., & Lopez, N. (2004). A fuzzy knowledge-based decision support system for groundwater pollution risk evaluation. *Journal of Environmental Management, 73*(3), 189–197. doi:10.1016/j.jenvman.2004.06.011

Vacik, H., & Lexer, M. J. (2001). Application of a spatial decision support system in managing the protection forests of Vienna for sustained yield of water resources. *Forest Ecology and Management, 143*(1-3), 65–76. doi:10.1016/S0378-1127(00)00506-5

Voudouris, K. (2009). Assessing groundwater pollution risk in Sarigkiol basin, NW Greece. In Gallo, M., & Herrari, M. (Eds.), *River Pollution Research Progress*. Hauppauge, New York: Nova Science Publishers Inc.

Voudouris, K., Panagopoulos, A., & Koumantakis, I. (2004). Nitrate pollution in the coastal aquifer system of the Korinthos prefecture (Greece). *Global Nest: the International Journal, 6*(1), 31–38.

Vrba, J., & Zaporozec, A. (Eds.). (1994). Guidebook on mapping groundwater vulnerability. In *Proceedings of the International contributions to hydrogeology*. Hanover, Germany: Heise.

Zhu, X., Healey, R. G., & Aspinall, R. J. (1998). A knowledge-based systems approach to design of spatial decision support system for environmental management. *Environmental Management, 22*(1), 35–48. doi:10.1007/s002679900082

This work was previously published in International Journal of Information Systems and Social Change, Volume 1, Issue 4, edited by John Wang, pp. 66-79, copyright 2010 by IGI Publishing (an imprint of IGI Global).

Chapter 19

Verification of a Rational Combination Approach for Agricultural Drought Assessment:
A Case Study Over Indo-Gangetic Plains in India

N. Subash
ICAR Research Complex for Eastern Region, India

H. S. Ram Mohan
Cochin University of Science and Technology, India

ABSTRACT

Agricultural Drought is characterized by a deficient supply of moisture, resulting either from sub-normal rainfall, erratic rainfall distribution, or higher water with respect to a crop. In spite of technological developments in providing improved crop varieties and better management practices, in India, agriculture has been considered a gamble due to higher spatial and temporal variability. The Rice-Wheat (RW) system is the major cropping system of the Indo-Gangetic Plains (IGP) in India and occupies 10 million hectares. In this paper, the authors have examined the possibility of rationally combining the rainfall anomaly index, a weather based index and an agriculture index based on the Crop Growth Simulation Model for a rice-wheat productivity assessment in selected sites of IGP in India. The district average yields of rice varied from 0.9 t/ha at Samastipur to 3.8 t/ha at Ludhiana. Rice yields decreased from the west to east IGP, and farmers in the western IGP harvested more rice-wheat than those in the eastern regions. The productivity gap showed that all the sites were produced only 50% of the potential in RW system productivity during the triennium ending period 2005. This paper may help researchers and planners to take appropriate measures for improving productivity.

DOI: 10.4018/978-1-4666-0927-3.ch019

INTRODUCTION

Drought is one of the most severe and extreme weather events affecting more people than any other form of natural disaster (Wilhite, 2000). Drought which is broadly defined as deficient supply of rainwater to meet the water needs of various forms of life in the ecosystem such as water drinking and other uses for both human and animal population, plants and agricultural crops water needs and decomposition organic matter in the soil etc. The precise quantification of drought is difficult as no universal drought estimation method (e.g., drought indices, hydrological or soil water balance models) can be defined through the complexity of the problem. Common to all types of drought is a lack of precipitation (WMO, 1993). From a meteorological point of view, drought is associated with dry spells of varying lengths and degrees of dryness. The fundamental measure of drought is inadequate precipitation for a particular commotion viz., crop growth, irrigation supply, reservoir/dam level. The American Meteorological Society (1997) suggests that the time and space processes of supply and demand are the two basic processes that should be included in an objective definition of drought, and thus in the derivation of drought estimation methods. There are four types of droughts are commonly differentiated meteorological or climatological, hydrological, agricultural, and socioeconomic (Rasmussen et al., 1993; Wilhite & Glantz, 1985). Among these, agricultural drought relates to a shortage of available water for plant growth, and is assessed as insufficient soil moisture to replace evapotranspirative losses (WMO, 1975). As agriculture is an important economic factor in many countries, drought can have a number of economic and socio-economic consequences (CAgM, 1992, 1993; WMO, 1995, 2001) such as loss of income in agriculture and food industry, significant higher costs for water and production techniques (e.g., irrigation systems). Most places in the world can be affected by agricultural droughts which reduce

the availability of water required in agricultural production, but duration and intensity vary greatly from one climatic zone to another (Wilhite, 1993). Because of climate changes that could change climatic variability including precipitation pattern, extreme weather events such as drought are likely to occur more frequently in different spatial and time scales in future (IPCC, 2007).

The success of drought preparedness and mitigation depends, to a large extent, upon timely information on drought onset, progress, extent and its end. These types of information can be obtained through drought indices which provide decision makers with information on drought severity and can be used to elicit drought contingency plans. Many drought indices such as the Palmer Drought Severity Index (Palmer, 1965), the decile index (Gibbs & Maher, 1967), Bhalme-Mooley Index (Bhalme & Mooley, 1979), the Surface Water Supply Index (Shafer & Dezman, 1982), the China-Z index (CZI) (Wu et al., 2001), Standardized Precipitation Index (SPI) (McKee et al., 1993) are widely used to quantify the drought vulnerability. Most of these indices are normally continuous functions of rainfall and/or temperature. These indices were tested and modified in different parts of the world (Nguyen et al., 1989; Wu et al., 2001; Oza et al., 2002; Ansari, 2003; Ntale & Gan, 2003; Morid et al., 2006; Patel et al., 2007). Generally, meteorological drought in India is defined when rainfall in a month or a season is less than 75% of its long-term mean, if the rainfall is 50-74% of the mean, a moderate drought event is assumed to occur, and when rainfall is less than 50% of its mean a severe drought occurs (Smakhtin & Hughes, 2004).

Agricultural drought occurs when there is inadequate soil moisture to meet the needs of a particular crop at a particular time. Generally refer to situations in which the moisture in the soil is no longer sufficient to meet the demand of the crops. When soil moisture is lacking, this may hinder crops potential development, leading to low growth characters and eventually lower final yield. The production potential of a crop is largely determined by the climatic, edaphic and soil properties and their interactions. Crop Growth Simulation Models (CGSM) deal with interactions of crop growth with climatic factors, soil characteristics, agronomic management, and therefore can be used to estimate climatic limitations to growth and yield (Aggarwal & Kalra, 1994). These are formulated to analyse crop growth using biological and physiological data of the crops and interaction of the plant and the environment (Dorigo et al., 2006). Several studies have been carried out to develop an integrated assessment of climate variability as well as climate change on regional and global supplies and demand (Rosenweig & Parry, 1994; Adams et al., 1995; Alexandrov & Hoogenboom, 2000a) and also used for determining the production potential of a location, for matching agro-technology with the farmers' resources, analyzing yield gaps, forecasting of yields and assessing the impact of climatic variability and climate change on agriculture (Teng & Penning de Vries, 1992; Penning de Vries, 1993; Kropff et al., 1996; Ten Berge et al., 1997; Tsuji et al., 1998; Alexandrov & Hoogenboom, 2000a, 2000b; Matthews & Stephens, 2002; Aggarwal, 2003; Pathak et al., 2003). The Decision Support System for Agrotechnology Transfer (DSSAT) (Tsuji et al., 1994) is a comprehensive decision support system for assessing agricultural management options. It has been widely using in both developed and developing countries for studying the crop growth and development with varying soil, water management aspects as well as climate change and climate variability studies (Singh & Thornton, 1992; Aggarwal & Sinha, 1993; Jagtap et al., 1993; Lal et al., 1993; Porter et al., 1993; Singh et al., 1993; Aggarwal et al., 1996, 1997; Hundal & Kaur, 1996, 1999; Rao & Subash, 1996; Timsina et al., 1996, 1997, 1998; Berge et al., 1997; Chipanshi et al., 1997; Hundal et al., 1998; Saseendran et al., 1998a, 1998b; Sherchand, 1998; Aggarwal et al., 2000a, 2000b;

Matthews et al., 2000a, 2000b; Saseendran et al., 2000; Aggarwal & Mall, 2002; Chander et al., 2002a, 2002b; Gijsman et al., 2002; Aggarwal, 2003; Jones et al., 2003; Pathak et al., 2003, 2004; Timsina & Humphreys, 2006). The crop simulation based analysis of drought is necessary for identification of agricultural drought because it accounts for water losses through percolation (soil effect), run off (slope effect), evapotranspiration (temperature effect) and continuing water deficit (from past drought effect) on the crop, from sowing/transplanting stage to harvest. In this study we have examined the possibility of rationally combining the rainfall anomaly index – which is weather based index and an agriculture index based on Crop Growth Simulation Model for rice-wheat productivity assessment in selected sites of IGP in India.

Characteristics of the Study Site

Rice(*Oryza sativa*)-Wheat(*Triticum aestivum*) (RW) system is the major cropping system of the Indo-Gangetic Plains in India and occupies 10 million hectares, covering the seven administrative States viz., Punjab, Haryana, Uttar Pradesh, Uttaranchal, Bihar, West Bengal and Jharkhand. By 2050, India's population is expected to grow to 1.6 billion people from the current level of 1.0 billion. A large proportion of this increase will be in the Indo-Gangetic Plains. The cereal requirement of India by 2020 will be between 257 to 296 million tons depending on income (Kumar et al., 1998; Aggarwal et al., 2004). The demand for rice and wheat, the predominant staple foods, is expected to increase to 122 and 103 million tons, respectively by 2020, assuming a medium income growth (Kumar et al., 1998). After tremendous increase in productivity during the green evolution era, concerns are being raised over the sustainability of this system (Hobbs & Morris, 1996; Sinha et al., 1998; Aggarwal et al., 2000a, 2000b; Duxbury et al., 2000; Yadav et al., 2000a,

2000b; Timsina & Connor, 2001; Bhandari et al., 2002; Ladha et al., 2003a, 2003b). IPCC (2007) in its fourth assessment indicated with very high confidence (90% probability of being correct) that human activities, since industrialization have caused the planet to warm by about 1°C. Future projections of climate change using global and regional climate models, run by Indian Institute of Tropical Meteorology (IITM) with different IPCC emission scenarios, indicate temperature changes of about 3 – 5°C and increase of about 5-10% in summer monsoon rainfall (NATCOM, 2004). It is also projected that number of rainy days may decrease by 20 to 30%, which would mean that the intensity of rainfall is expected to increase. Extremes in temperature and rainfall also show increase in their frequency and intensity by the end of the year 2100. A more recent study using daily rainfall data for over 50 years shows significant increasing trend in extreme rainfall events over central India (Goswami et al., 2006).

Five sites (Figure 1) covering important agro-ecological sub-regions of the IGP-India were selected for the study based on the availability of soil, weather and crop management data. The sites were distributed from 25.88 to 30.93 °N latitude and 75.73 to 85.80 °E longitude (Table 1). The length of growing period (LGP) varies from 60-90 days at Hisar to 180-210 days at Samastipur. The annual rainfall varies from 745.8 mm at Ludhiana to 1199.5 mm at Samastipur. The general climatology of the selected sites is shown in Figure 2. Normally, in this part of the region, rice season (June-July to October-November) refers to "Kharif" while wheat season (November-December to March) refers to "Rabi". The kharif season rainfall varies from 585.1 mm at Ludhiana and 1069.9 mm at Samastipur, while during rabi, maximum rainfall of 101.9 mm at Ludhiana and least over Faizabad.

DATA AND METHODOLOGY

Data

The daily weather data viz., rainfall, maximum and minimum temperature and sunshine hours recorded in the meteorological observatories located in the selected sites during the period 1970-2007 (except Faizabad (1986-2006) and Kanpur (1971-2006) were collected from CRIDA, Hyderabad. The district rice and wheat yield data were collected from Directorate of Rice and wheat, respectively during the study period.

Rice-Wheat Productivity Index

The production of rice-wheat depends on non-meteorological parameters such as type of seeds used, crop area, availability of irrigation facilities, fertilizers, pesticides and also on the government incentives to the farming sector during the year as well as the previous year and meteorological parameters such as rainfall, temperature, relative humidity and solar energy. The total non-meteorological parameters, i.e., the total technological inputs to the farming sector have been growing steadily and are difficult to quantify. Therefore, to quantify the growth rate of total technological inputs to the rice-wheat productivity the actual productivity was fitted into a linear curve. The actual productivity values were normalized by converting it into indices by the following way.

The Kharif Rice Productivity Index (KRPI) and Wheat Productivity Index (WPI) were taken as the percentage of the technological trend productivity to the actual productivity. The normalized KRPI for the ith year is

$$KRPI_i = \frac{(P_i - TP_i)100}{TP_i}$$

$$WPI_i = \frac{(P_i - TP_i)100}{TP_i}$$

Figure 1. Location map of Indo-Gangetic Plains in India and study sites

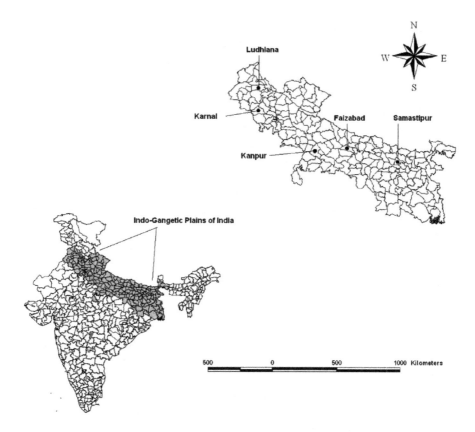

Table 1. Site characterization and agro-ecological characteristics of the study sites

Site	Lati-tude (°N)	Longi-tude (°E)	Altitude (m)	Period	Annual Rainfall (mm)	Agro-ecological characteristics
Ludhiana	30.93	75.87	247	1970-2007	745.8	Hot semi-arid eco-subregion (ESR) with deep loamy alluvium-derived soils, medium available water capacity(AWC) and Length of Growing Period (LGP) 90-120 days
Hisar	29.17	75.73	215	1970-2007	920.6	Hot typic-arid ESR with deep, loamy desert soils, low AWC and LGP 60-90 days
Faizabad	26.78	82.13	133	1986-2006	915.8	Hot dry sub humid ESR with deep loamy alluvium-derived soils, medium to high AWC and LGP 150-180 days
Kanpur	26.43	80.37	126	1971-2006	869.2	Hot moist semi-arid ESR with deep, loamy alluvium-derived soils, medium to high AWC and LGP 120-150 days
Samastipur	25.88	85.80	52	1960-2007	1199.5	Hot dry to moist subhumid transitional EST with deep, loamy alluvium-derived soils, low to medium AWC and LGP 180-210 days

Figure 2. General climatology of the study sites

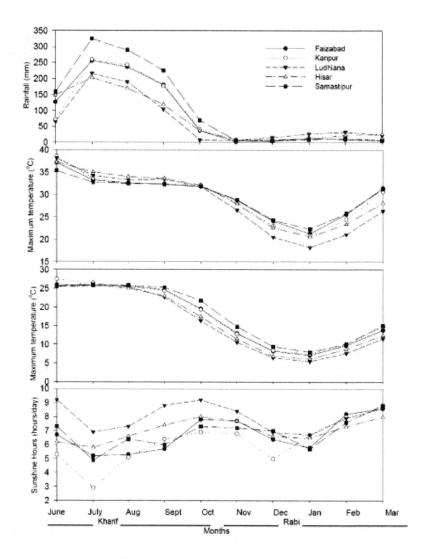

Where *KRPIi and WPIi* are the kharif rice productivity index and wheat productivity indices for the ith year, P_i is the actual productivity for the ith year and TP_i is the technological trend productivity for the ith year, i = 1,2,3, …… representing 1974-75 to 2005-06 for rice and 1966-67 to 2005-06 for wheat.

Crop Growth Simulation Model Based Drought Index (CGSM-DI)

DSSATv4.0 has been used to simulate the rice and wheat yield of five sites during the study period. Rice variety PR 106 and wheat variety HD 2329, which were popularly grown over the region is used in this study and the genotypic coefficients were selected based on past field experiments by repeated iterations until a close match between simulated and observed phenology and yield was obtained (Pathak et al., 2003). The initial soil physical as well as chemical characteristics were collected from various literature and reports (Abrol et al., 2000; Saha et al., 2000; Singh & Swarup, 2000; Bhandari et al., 2002; Pathak et al., 2002, 2003). Normally rice was transplanted on 1st July and wheat sown on 15th November in this region, which may vary due to year-to-year variability of monsoon phenomena. The simulated rice and wheat yields were converted into indices using the gamma distribution function (Nain et al., 2005).

Rainfall Anomaly Based Index

The monthly rainfall during monsoon season was indexed by taking the monthly rainfall in terms of percentage deviation from its mean. The rainfall anomaly index for any month is expressed as

$$RA_i = \frac{(R_i - R) * 100}{R}$$

Where RA_i is the monthly Rainfall Index for the ith year, R_i is the monthly rainfall for the ith year and R is the mean monthly rainfall.

RESULTS AND DISCUSSION

Rice-Wheat Productivity Analysis

The rice and wheat productivity values were fitted into linear technological trend. The district average yields of rice varied from 0.9 t/ha at Samastipur to 3.8 t/ha at Ludhiana. Rice yields decreased from the west to east IGP. As with rice, farmers in the western IGP harvested more wheat than those in the eastern regions. Among other factors, favorable climate is responsible for the greater yields in the western part (Narang & Virmani, 2001).

Simulated and Actual Rice-Wheat Productivity

The technological advancement factor in observed yield of rice and wheat were removed by linearly regressing the yield with the year and removing the contribution of trend from the observed yield. In the case of observed rice yields, the standard deviation was more for Hisar (671 kg/ha) followed by Faizabad (589 kg/ha), but coefficient of variation was higher for Samastipur (37.8%) followed by Faizabad (35%). However, Ludhiana which was showing a decreasing trend of observed rice yield showed less coefficient of variation (10.1%). The same low value of coefficient of variation was also observed in the simulated rice yield of Ludhiana. The results also indicated that the coefficient of variation of simulated rice yields were low compared to observed rice yields in all the sites.

The standard deviation of the observed wheat yield was higher for Hisar (801 kg/ha) followed by Ludhiana (683 kg/ha). A higher coefficient of variation was observed for Hisar (24%) followed by Faizabad (18.5%). The higher standard deviation and coefficient of variation indicated that there were high uncertainties in year-to-year rice yield. The higher coefficient of variation of rice yields over the eastern part of IGP may be due to more rainfed areas in these parts of the region. But in the case of observed wheat yields, higher year-to-year variability was noticed for Ludhiana and Hisar compared to eastern sites.

The observed rice yields ranged from 3000 kg/ha in the year 1974 to 4632 kg/ha in the year 2004 for Ludhiana. However, in the case of simulated rice yields, a higher yield of 5323 kg/ha was observed in the year 2004 and a lowest yield of 3620 kg/ha was observed in the year 1998. In the case of Hisar, the observed rice yields ranged from 1168 kg/ha in the year 1974 to 3782 kg/ha in the year 1994 have been noticed. The same pattern was not followed in the simulated rice yields. The same pattern of observed and simulated rice yield has been noticed for Kanpur and Faizabad sites.

But as far as Samastipur site is concerned, highest observed rice yield of 1271 kg/ha was observed in 1990 and lowest (307 kg/ha) in 2005. However, simulated rice yields ranged from 1890 kg/ha in 1992 to 3100 kg/ha in 1997. In wheat, the same range of pattern of observed as well as simulated yields was noticed for all the sites.

The year-to-year deviation in observed and simulated rice and wheat yields were calculated and compared. The comparison of observed and simulated rice and wheat yield shows that there is very good agreement (Figure 3) between them based on Spearman correlation coefficient (rs),

significant at $P < 0.05$ level for all the sites except Samastipur. In the case of Samastipur, the simulated and observed wheat yields follow the same pattern during lower yield years, but not in agreement during higher yield years.

Yield Gap Analysis

Potential productivity is defined as the maximum productivity of a variety restricted only by the season-specific climatic conditions. This assumes that other inputs (nutrient, water, etc) are not limiting and cultural management is optimal.

Figure 3. Actual (de-trended) and simulated rice and wheat yields at various sites of the IGP

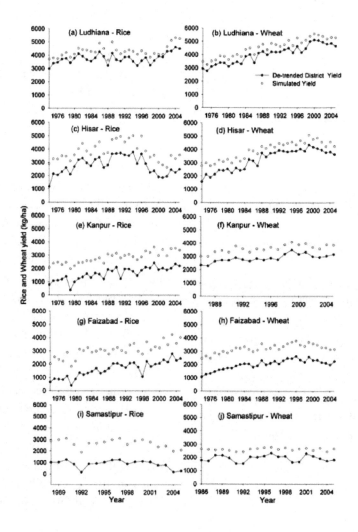

The potential productivity of rice and wheat in the study sites ranged from 8.7 to 10.7 and 6.2 to 8.5 t/ha, respectively. The productivity of both rice and wheat were the highest in Ludhiana and decreased towards the eastern part of the IGP. The productivity declined by 19% for rice and by 29% for wheat from Ludhiana to eastern side of IGP. This is because of the lower solar radiation and higher daily minimum temperature in the eastern part of the IGP, resulting in decreased photosynthesis, and a shortened vegetative and grain-filling period. In all the sites, the per cent of actual to potential productivity is lower for rice compared to wheat (Figure 4). The productivity gap, which is the per cent deviation of actual to potential productivity, showed that all the sites

were produced 50% gap in RW system productivity during the triennium ending period 2005 and there is wide variation between western and eastern part of the IGP. Ludhiana showed a lower gap of 49%; while Samastipur showed a gap of 83% during the triennium ending period 2005.

Crop Growth Simulation Model Based Indices and Productivity

The average site conditions were prescribed in the DSSATv4.0, which were kept constant throughout the study period to observe the variation in rice and wheat yield due to differing inter-annual moisture regime. The simulated rice and wheat yields were converted into indices using the gamma

Figure 4. Per cent of actual to potential productivity during the study period in selected sites of IGP

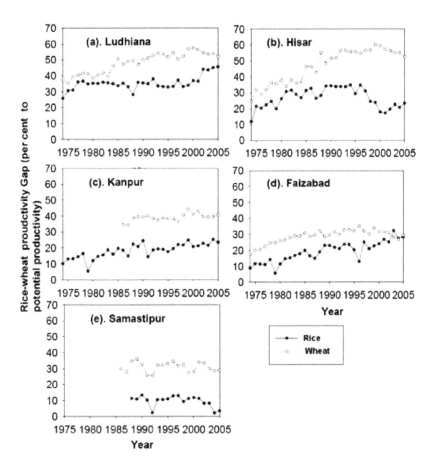

distribution. From Figure 5, it is clear that the Crop Growth Simulation Model based Drought Index (CGSM-DI) and Kharif Rice Productivity Index (KRPI) as well as CGSM-DI and Wheat Productivity Index (WPI) follow the same pattern. Even though, the CGSM-DI could capture all the extreme agricultural drought conditions with respect to rice and wheat for all the sites, its intensity differs. Characterization of drought with crop growth simulation model has advantages that it calculates the water deficiency due to all possible causes including deficient rainfall, runoff, deep

Figure 5. Variability of CGSM-DI and KRPI and WPI for the period 1974- 2005 for Ludhiana, Hisar, Kanpur, Faizabad and 1986-2005 for Samastipur

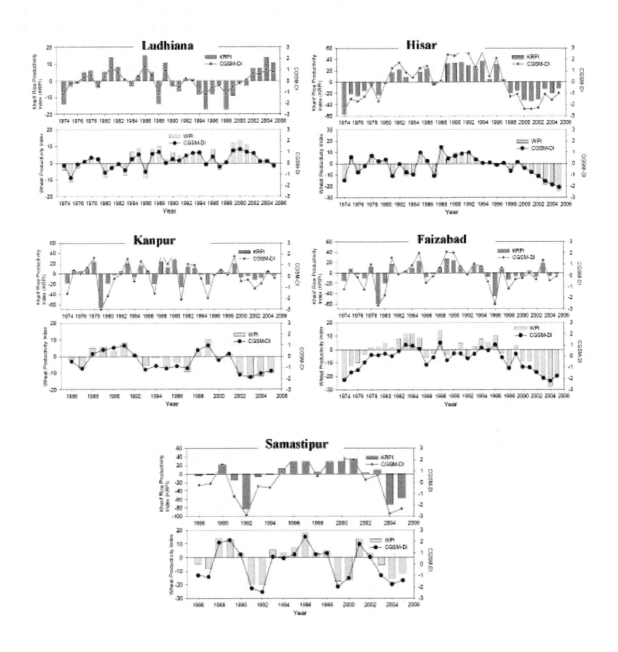

percolation and evapotranspiration. For characterization of agriculture drought water balance approach on weekly or less data set is required because water deficiency for even short duration in sensitive growth stage is more harmful than the long duration water deficiency during insensitive growth stages. Even though, it captures the drought years, but due to variation of intensity indicates that the drought assessment index needs more verification of other parameters also.

Rainfall Anomaly and Productivity

In order to get the influence of monthly distribution of rainfall on yield, the month-wise rainfall anomaly from June to September were regressed to KRPI (Figure 6). Interestingly, the July rainfall anomaly and KRPI showed a negative correlation, though statistically not significant. But combined influence of rainfall anomaly during June to September with KPRI showed 46% contributed

to KRPI. Even though, wheat crop is not directly linked with monsoon season, around 90 per cent of the wheat area over IGP is under irrigated class. Irrigation options such as surface water (i.e., reservoirs and canals) and subsurface water (i.e., ground water), are affected due to variation of rainfall pattern during the monsoon season. Thus, the monthly rainfall anomaly during the monsoon season during June to September was regressed with WPI. Higher rainfall during September may delay the rice harvest and thereby subsequent delay of sowing operations of wheat and this eventually may affect the wheat crop in two ways. The delay of wheat sowing may affect the germination of wheat and it will extend the Crown Root Initiation (CRI) stage and finally expose the milky stage to higher maximum temperature during summer season. This may be the reason for negative correlation of September rainfall anomaly with WPI (Figure 7). The combined effect of rainfall

Figure 6. Correlation between monthly MRI and KRPI

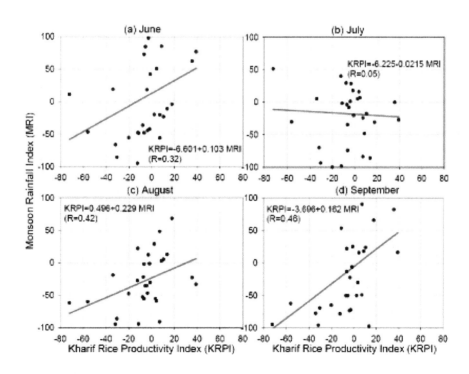

anomaly during June to September explains only 7% variations in wheat productivity.

Rational Combination of CGSM-DI and RA for Rice-Wheat Productivity Assessment

It is found that agriculture drought monitoring with crop simulation models has an edge over other rainfall anomaly based conventional drought monitoring approach. Though simple rainfall based indices can be generated periods ranging from weeks to years, there are also limitations that it cannot account for water deficit caused by evapotranspiration, deep percolation and run off. The CGSM-DI has an additional advantage that it also accounts for the type and stage of crop on evapotranspiration losses. Rainfall anomaly does not consider the intensity factor and temporal distribution of rainfall within the base unit, for

example, month. The intensity factor is necessary to calculate the water losses through runoff, while temporal distribution is necessary to calculate the water stress during the crop growth cycle. A good amount of precipitation in very early stages may be followed by drought like condition in later phase, while similar amount of precipitation well spread over the month may save the crop from moisture stress. Rainfall anomaly cannot differentiate between the two conditions as it considers only the total amount of precipitation during the base unit such as month. Rainfall anomaly index and CGSM-DI are able to explain rice and wheat productivity variability upto different levels. Since all these indices are based on separate variables, the summation or averaging of these indices definitely removes the year-to-year variability. Since CGSM-DI ranged between -3.0 to 3.0 and rainfall anomaly ranged widely, the summation or averaging remove the individual character of the variable

Figure 7. Correlation between monthly MRI and WPI

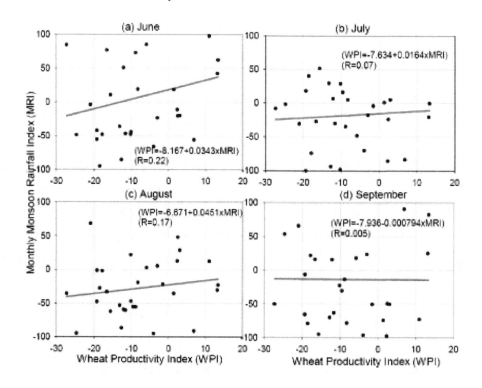

Figure 8. Monthly monsoon rainfall anomaly, kharif rice productivity index and Crop Growth Simulation Model Drought Index during the study period over study sites of IGP

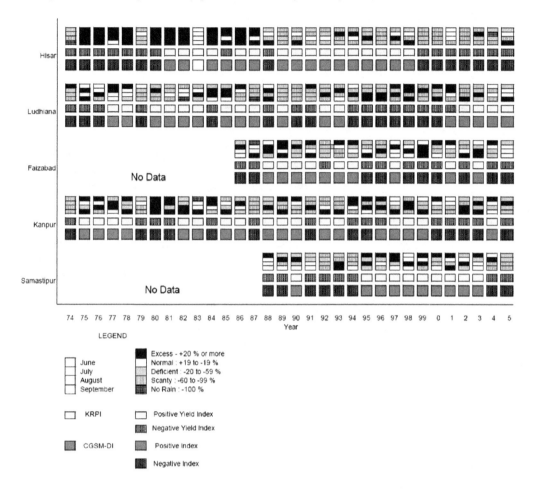

and will not reflect the actual variability of the rice and wheat productivity. The values of rainfall anomaly during June to September and CGSM-DI of rice and wheat and KPRI and WPI during the study period over selected study sites indicated that the year-to-year variability of productivity of rice is more compared to that of wheat in all the stations (Figure 8 and Figure 9). To include both rainfall anomaly as well as dynamic index, we have just rationally integrated rainfall anomaly from June to September and CGSM-DI and carried out multi-regression analysis for rice and wheat productivity. Rational integration of these two indices overcomes most of the limitations of each index and provides a complete picture of crop growth from sowing to harvest. Thus multiple regression equations are suitable for estimating kharif rice productivity and wheat productivity. The actual and estimated KRPI showed that most of the points are centered on 1st and 3rd quadrant (Figure 10). But in the case of wheat, all the points centered on 1st and 3rd quadrant. This implies that this multiple regression equation explains very well to year-to-year variation of weather changes and can be used for assessing the yield variability in wheat due to weather fluctuations.

Figure 9. Monthly monsoon rainfall anomaly, wheat productivity index and Crop Growth Simulation Model Drought Index during the study period over study sites of IGP

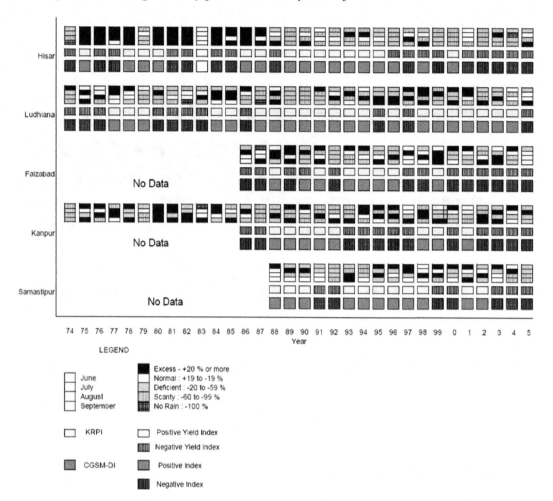

CONCLUSION

The district average yields of rice varied from 0.9 t/ha at Samastipur to 3.8 t/ha at Ludhiana. Rice yields decreased from the west to east IGP. Farmers in the western IGP harvested more rice-wheat than those in the eastern regions. The productivity gap showed that all the sites were produced only 50% of the potential in RW system productivity during the triennium ending period 2005 and there is wide variation between western and eastern part of the IGP. This implies that there is still a scope to increase productivity by adopting integrated approach of bio-technology, resource conservation technology and management practices. It is found that all the study sites the rationally integrated index explains more than 90% variability of rice and wheat productivity and thus this simple multiple regression can be useful for yield assessment in rice and wheat. This drought index tool needs to be used to characterize agricultural droughts of the region with respect to rice and wheat. Even though, there is good agreement of actual and simulated rice and wheat yields, the district yield data represents the average of all the varieties of that district. Hence, sampling methods should be

Figure 10. Estimated and actual Kharif Rice Productivity Index and Wheat productivity Index over study sites of IGP

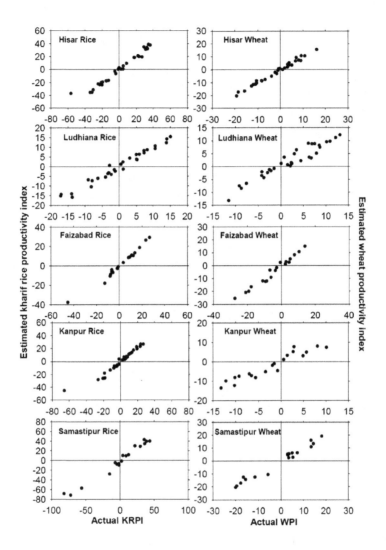

adopted to collect yield data pertaining to popular varieties. Integrated approach of regular monitoring of crops and climatic factors in farmer's fields as well as in research farms would facilitate in assessing agricultural drought in rice-wheat system accurately. This may also help researcher and planners to take appropriate measures to be taken to improve productivity.

ACKNOWLEDGMENT

The authors are gratefully acknowledge the Director, ICAR-RCER, Patna providing sabbatical leave for doing research at Cochin University of Science and Technology as part of the doctoral study. The authors would like to thank the Head, Department of Atmospheric Sciences for providing necessary computing and other facilities to conduct this study. The use of trade, firm, or corporation names in this publication is for the information and convenience of the reader. Such use does not constitute an official endorsement or approval by ICAR or CUSAT.

REFERENCES

Abrol, I. P., Bronson, K. F., Duxbury, J. M., & Gupta, R. K. (2000). *Long-term soil fertility experiments in rice-wheat cropping systems.* Paper presented to the Rice-Wheat Consortium, New Delhi, India.

Adams, R. M., Flemming, R. A., Chang, C. C., Mc Carl, B. A., & Rosenzweig, C. (1995). A reassessment of the economic effects of global climate change on US agriculture. *Climatic Change, 30,* 147–167. doi:10.1007/BF01091839

Aggarwal, P. K. (2003). Impact of climate change on Indian Agriculture. *Journal of Plant Biology, 30,* 189–198.

Aggarwal, P. K., Bandyopadhyay, S. K., Pathak, H., Kalra, N., Chander, S., & Sujith Kumar, S. (2000b). Analyses of yield trends of the rice-wheat system in north-western India. *Outlook on Agriculture, 29,* 259–268.

Aggarwal, P. K., Joshi, P. K., Ingram, J. S., & Gupta, R. K. (2004). Adapting food systems of the Indo-Gangetic Plains to global environmental change: key information needs to improve policy formulation. *Environmental Science & Policy, 7,* 487–498. doi:10.1016/j.envsci.2004.07.006

Aggarwal, P. K., & Kalra, N. (1994). Analysing the limitations set by climatic factors, genotype, wate rand nitrogen availability on productivity of wheat. II. Climatically potential yields and optimal management strategies. *Field Crops Research, 38,* 93–103. doi:10.1016/0378-4290(94)90003-5

Aggarwal, P. K., Kalra, N., Bandyopadhyay, S. K., & Selvarajan, S. (1996). A systems approach to analyze production options for wheat in India. In Bouman, J., (Eds.), *Eco-regional approaches for sustainable land use and food production.* Dordrecht, The Netherlands: Kluwer.

Aggarwal, P. K., Kropff, M. J., Cassman, K. G., & ten Berge, H. F. M. (1997). Simulating genotypic strategies for increasing rice yield potential in irrigated, tropical environments. *Field Crops Research, 51,* 5–18. doi:10.1016/S0378-4290(96)01044-1

Aggarwal, P. K., & Mall, R. K. (2002). Climate change and rice yields in diverse agro-environments of India. II. Effect of uncertainties in scenarios and crop models on impact assessment. *Climatic Change, 52,* 331–343. doi:10.1023/A:1013714506779

Aggarwal, P. K., & Sinha, S. K. (1993). Effect of probable increase in carbon dioxide and temperature on productivity of wheat in India. *Journal of Agricultural Meteorology, 48,* 811–814.

Aggarwal, P. K., Talukdar, K. K., & Mall, R. K. (2000a). Potential yields of the rice-wheat system in the Indo-Gangetic Plains of India. In *Proceedings of the Rice-Wheat Consortium for the Indo-Gangetic Plain*, New Delhi and Indian Agricultural Research Institute, New Delhi, India.

Alexandrov, V. A., & Hoogenboom, G. (2000a). The impact of climatic variability and change on crop yield in Bulgaria. *Agricultural and Forest Meteorology, 104*(4), 315–327. doi:10.1016/S0168-1923(00)00166-0

Alexandrov, V. A., & Hoogenboom, G. (2000b). Vulnerability and adaptation assessments of agricultural crops under climate change in the Southeastern USA. *Theoretical and Applied Climatology, 67,* 45–63. doi:10.1007/s007040070015

American Meteorological Society (AMS). (1997). Meteorological drought - Policy statement. *Bulletin of the American Meteorological Society, 78,* 847–849.

Ansari, H. (2003). *Monitoring and zoning of drought using fuzzy logic and GIS.* Unpublished doctoral dissertation, Tarbiat Modares University, Tehran, Iran.

Bhalme, H. N., & Mooley, D. A. (1979). On the performance of modified Palmer index. In *Proceedings of International Symposium: Hydrological Aspects of Droughts* (pp. 373-383).

Bhandari, A. L., Ladha, J. K., Pathak, H., Padre, A. T., Dawe, D., & Gupta, R. K. (2002). Trends of yield and soil nutrient status in a long-term rice-wheat experiment in the Indo-Gangetic Plains of India. *Soil Science Society of America Journal, 66,* 162–170. doi:10.2136/sssaj2002.0162

Chander, S., Aggarwal, P. K., Kalra, N., Swoop, R., & Parsed, J. S. (2002a). Assessment of yield losses due to stem borer, Scirpophaga incertulas in rice using simulation models. *Journal of Entomological Research, 26*(1), 23–28.

Chander, S., Aggarwal, P. K., & Reddy, P. R. (2002b). Assessment of yield loss in rice due to bacterial leaf blight using simulation models. *Annals Plant Protection Sciences, 10*(2), 277–281.

Chipanshi, A. C., Ripley, E. A., & Lawford, R. G. (1997). Early prediction of spring wheat yields in Saskatchewan from current and historical weather data using the CERES-Wheat model. *Agricultural and Forest Meteorology, 84,* 223–232. doi:10.1016/S0168-1923(96)02363-5

Commission of Agricultural Meteorology (CAgM). (1992). *Monitoring Assessment and Combat of Drought and Desertification.*

Commission of Agricultural Meteorology (CAgM). (1993). Report *of the RA II Working Group on Agricultural Meteorology, Part IV: Drought and Desertification* (Rep. No. 52).

Dorigo, W. A., Zurita-Milla, R., de Wit, A. J. W., Brazile, J., Singh, R., & Schaepman, M. E. (2006). A review on reflective remote sensing and data assimilation techniques for enhanced agro-ecosystem modelling. *International Journal of Applied Earth Observation and Geoinformation, 9*(2), 165–193. doi:10.1016/j.jag.2006.05.003

Duxbury, J. M., Abrol, I. P., Gupta, R. K., & Bronson, K. (2000). Analysis of long-term soil fertility experiments with rice-wheat rotation in South Asia. In Abrol, I. P., Bronson, K., Duxbury, J. M., & Gupta, R. K. (Eds.), *Long-term soil fertility experiments in Rice-Wheat Cropping Systems.* New Delhi, India.

Gibbs, W. J., & Maher, J. V. (1967). *Rainfall Deciles as drought indicators* (Bureau of Meteorology Bulletin No. 48, p. 29). Melbourne, Australia: Commonwealth of Australia.

Gijsman, A. J., Hoogenboom, G., Parton, W. J., & Kerridge, P. C. (2002). Modifying DSSAT for low-input agricultural systems, using a soil organic matter-residue module from CENTURY. *Agronomy Journal, 94*(3), 462–474. doi:10.2134/agronj2002.0462

Goswami, B. N., Venugopal, V., Sengupta, D., Madhusoodanan, M. S., & Xavier, P. K. (2006). Increasing Trend of Extreme Rain Events over India in a warming Environment. *Science, 314,* 1442–1444. doi:10.1126/science.1132027

Hobbs, P. R., & Morris, M. L. (1996). *Meeting South Asia's future food requirements from rice-wheat cropping systems: priority issues facing researchers in the post Green Revolution era* (NRG Paper 96-01). Mexico: CIMMYT.

Hundal, S. S., & Kaur, P. (1996). Climatic change and its impact on crop productivity in Punjab. In Abrol, Y. P., Gadgil, S., & Pant, G. B. (Eds.), *Climatic Variability and Agriculture* (pp. 377–393). India.

Hundal, S. S., & Kaur, P. (1999). Evaluation of agronomic practices for rice using computer model, CERES-Rice. *Oryza, 36.*

Hundal, S. S., Kaur, P., & Dhaliwal, L. K. (1998). Prediction of potential productivity of rice in Punjab, India under synthetic climate change scenarios. In *Proceedings of Modeling for crop-climate-soil-pest system and its applications in sustainable crop production*. Nanjing, China: Jiangsu Academy of Agricultural Sciences Publisher.

IPCC. (2007). Summary for policymakers. In Solomon, S., Qin, D., Manning, M., Chen, Z., Marquis, M., & Averyt, K. B., (Eds.), *Climate change 2007: the physical science basis. Contribution of Working Group I to the Fourth Assessment Report of the Intergovernmental Panel on Climate Change*. New York: Cambridge University Press.

Jagtap, S. S., Mornu, M., & Kang, B. T. (1993). Simulation of growth, development and yield of maize in the transition zone of Nigeria. *Agricultural Systems, 41*, 215–229. doi:10.1016/0308-521X(93)90040-9

Jones, J. W., Hoogenboom, G., Porter, C. H., Boote, K. J., Batchelor, W. D., & Hunt, L. A. (2003). The DSSAT cropping system model. *European Journal of Agronomy, 18*, 235–265. doi:10.1016/S1161-0301(02)00107-7

Kropff, M. J., Teng, P. S., Aggarwal, P. K., Bouman, B. A. M., & van Laar, H. H. (1996). *Applications of Systems Approaches at the Field Level*. Dordrecht, The Netherlands: Kluwer Academic Publishers.

Kumar, P., Joshi, P. K., Johansen, C., & Asokan, M. (1998). Total factor productivity of rice-wheat based cropping system: role of legumes. *Economic Policy Weekly, 26*, A152–A157.

Ladha, J. K., Dawe, D., Pathak, H., Padre, A. T., Yadav, R. L., & Singh, B. (2003a). How extensive are yield declines in long-term rice-wheat experiments in Asia? *Field Crops Research, 81*, 159–180. doi:10.1016/S0378-4290(02)00219-8

Ladha, J. K., Pathak, H., Tirol-Padre, A., Dawe, D., & Gupta, R. K. (2003b). Productivity trends in intensive rice wheat cropping systems in Asia. In Ladha, J. K., Hill, J. E., Duxbury, J. M., Gupta, R. K., & Buresh, R. J. (Eds.), *Improving the Productivity and Sustainability of Rice-Wheat Systems: Issues and Impacts (Vol. 65*, pp. 45–76). ASA.

Lal, H., Hoogenboom, G., Calixte, J. P., Jones, J. W., & Beinroth, F. H. (1993). Using crop simulation models and GIS for regional productivity analysis. *Transactions of the ASAE. American Society of Agricultural Engineers, 36*, 175–184.

Matthews, R. B., & Stephens, W. (2002). *Crop-soil simulation models. Applications in developing countries*. Wallingford, UK: CABI Publishing. doi:10.1079/9780851995632.0000

Matthews, R. B., Wassmann, R., & Arah, J. (2000a). Using a crop/soil simulation model and GIS techniques to assess methane emissions from rice fields in Asia. I. *Model development. Nutrient Cycling in Agroecosystems, 58*, 141–159. doi:10.1023/A:1009894619446

Matthews, R. B., Wassmann, R., Knox, J. W., & Buendia, L. V. (2000b). Using a crop/soil simulation model and GIS techniques to assess methane emissions from rice fields in Asia. IV. Upscaling to national levels. *Nutrient Cycling in Agroecosystems, 58*, 201–217. doi:10.1023/A:1009850804425

McKee, T. B., Doesken, N., & Kleist, J. (1993). The relationship of drought frequency and duration to time scales. In *Proceeding of the 8th Conference on Applied Climatology*. Amer. Meteorol. Soc.

Morid, S., Smakhtin, V., & Moghaddasi, M. (2006). Comparison of seven meteorological indices for drought monitoring in Iran. *International Journal of Climatology, 26*, 971–985. doi:10.1002/joc.1264

Nain, A. S., Kersebaum, K. C., & Mirschel, W. (2005). *Are meteorological parameters based drought indices enough for agricultural drought monitoring: a comparative study of drought monitoring with SPI and Crop Simulation Model.* Paper presented at the ICID 21st European Regional Conference 2005, Frankfurt, Germany.

Narang, R. S., & Virmani, S. M. (2001). *Rice-Wheat cropping systems of the Indo-Gangetic Plains of India.* New Delhi, India: Rice-Wheat Consortium for the Indo-Gangetic Plains.

NATCOM. (2004). *India's Initial National Communication to the United Nations Framework Convention on Climate Change.* India: National Communication Project, Ministry of Environment and Forests, Govt. of India.

Nguyen, V. T. V., In-na, N., & Bobee, B. (1989). New plotting position formula for Pearson type III distribution. *Journal of Hydraulic Engineering, 115*(6), 706–730.

Ntale, H. K., & Gan, T. Y. (2003). Drought indices and their application to East Africa. *International Journal of Climatology, 23,* 1335–1357. doi:10.1002/joc.931

Oza, S. R., Parihar, J. S., & Dadhwal, V. K. (2002). *Proceedings of Evaluating use of Standardized index for drought assessment in the region of North-west India (TROPMET-2002).* India: Bhubaneswar.

Palmer, W. C. (1965). *Meteorological Drought (Paper No. 45).* Washington, DC: U.S. Department of Commerce, Weather Bureau.

Patel, N. R., Chopra, R., & Dadhwal, V. K. (2007). Analysing spatial patterns of meteorological drought using standardized precipitation index. *International Journal of Climatology, 14*(4), 329–336.

Pathak, H., Bhatia, A., Jain, M. C., Kumar, S., Singh, S., & Kumar, U. (2002). Emission of nitrous oxide from soil in rice-wheat systems of Indo-Gangetic Plains of India. *Journal of Environmental Monitoring and Assessment, 77*(2), 163–178. doi:10.1023/A:1015823919405

Pathak, H., Ladha, J. K., Aggarwal, P. K., Peng, S., Das, S., & Singh, Y. (2003). Climatic potential and on-farm yield trends of rice and wheat in the Indo-Gangetic Plains. *Field Crops Research, 80*(3), 223–234. doi:10.1016/S0378-4290(02)00194-6

Pathak, H., Timsina, J., Humphreys, E., Godwin, D. C., Shukla, A. K., Singh, U., & Matthews, R. B. (2004). *Simulation of rice crop performance and water and N dynamics, and methane emissions for rice in northwest India using CERES Rice model* (CSIRO Land and Water Tech. Rep. 23/04). Griffith, Australia: CSIRO Land and Water.

Penning de Vries, F. W. T. (Ed.). (1993). Rice production and climate change. In *Systems Approaches for Agricultural Development.* Dordrecht, The Netherlands: Kluwer Academic Publishers.

Porter, J. R., Jamieson, P. D., & Wilson, D. R. (1993). Comparison of the wheat simulation models AFRCWHEAT2, CERES-Wheat and SWHEAT for non-limiting conditions of crop growth. *Field Crops Research, 33,* 131–157. doi:10.1016/0378-4290(93)90098-8

Rao, G. S. L. H. V., & Subash, N. (1996). Use of CERES-Rice Model to assess potential yield. *International Rice Research Notes, 21*(2-3), 87.

Rasmussen, E. M., Dickinson, R. E., Kutzbach, J. E., & Cleaveland, M. K. (1993). In Maidment, D. R. (Ed.), *Climatology. Handbook of Hydrology* (pp. 5.1–5.51). New York: McGraw-Hill.

Rosenweig, C., & Parry, M. L. (1994). Potential impact of climate change on world food supply. *Nature, 367,* 133–138. doi:10.1038/367133a0

Saha, M. N., Saha, A. R., Mandal, B. C., & Ray, P. K. (2000). Effects of long-term jute-rice-wheat cropping system on crop yields and soil fertility. In Abrol, I. P., Bronson, K. F., Duxbury, J. M., & Gupta, R. K. (Eds.), *Long-term Soil Fertility Experiments in Rice-Wheat Cropping Systems*. New Delhi, India: RWC.

Saseendran, S. A., Hubbard, K. G., Singh, K. K., Rathore, L. S., & Singh, S. V. (1998a). Optimum Transplanting Dates for rice in Kerala, India, Determined Using Both CERESv3.0 and ClimProb. *Agronomy Journal*, *90*, 185–190. doi:10.2134/agronj1998.00021962009000020011x

Saseendran, S. A., Singh, K. K., Rathore, L. S., Rao, G. S. L. H. V., Mendiratta, N., Lakshmi, N., & Singh, S. V. (1998b). Evaluation of the CERES-Ricev3.0 model for the climate conditions of the state of Kerala, India. *Applied Meteorology*, *5*, 385–392. doi:10.1017/S1350482798000954

Saseendran, S. A., Singh, K. K., Rathore, L. S., Singh, S. V., & Sinha, S. K. (2000). Effects of climate change on rice production in the tropical humid climate of Kerala, India. *Climatic Change*, *44*, 495–514. doi:10.1023/A:1005542414134

Shafer, B. A., & Dezman, L. E. (1982). Development of a Surface Water Supply Index (SWSI) to assess the severity of drought conditions in snowpack runoff areas. In *Proceedings of the Western Snow Conference*, Colorado State University, Fort Collins, CO (pp. 164-175).

Sherchand, K. (1998). Use of simulation modelling to assess potential yield in the RW systems in different climatic environments: Progress report. In *Proceedings of the RW research end of project workshop*, Kathmandu, Nepal (pp. 34-38).

Singh, K. N., & Swarup, A. (2000). Effect of long-term rice-wheat cropping sequence on yield and soil properties in reclaimed sodic soils. In Abrol, I. P., Bronson, K. F., Duxbury, J. M., & Gupta, R. K. (Eds.), *Long-term Soil Fertility Experiments in Rice-Wheat Cropping Systems*. New Delhi, India: RWC.

Singh, U., & Thornton, P. K. (1992). Using crop models for sustainability and environmental quality assessment. *Outlook on Agriculture*, *2*, 209–218.

Singh, U., Thornton, P. K., Saka, A. R., & Dent, J. B. (1993). Maize modeling in Malawi: A tool for soil fertility research and development. In Penning de Vries, F. W. T. (Ed.), *Systems approaches for agricultural development*. Dordrecht, The Netherlands: Kluwer Academic.

Sinha, S. K., Singh, G. B., & Rai, M. (1998). *Decline in crop productivity in Haryana and Punjab: myth or reality?* New Delhi, India: Indian Council of Agricultural Research.

Smakhtin, V. U., & Hughes, D. A. (2004). *Review, Automated Estimation and Analysis of Drought Indices in South Asia*. Colombo, Sri Lanka: IWMI.

ten Berge, H. F. M., Aggarwal, P. K., & Kropff, M. J. (1997). *Applications of rice modeling*. Amsterdam: Elsevier Publishers.

Teng, P. S., & Penning de Vries, F. W. T. (1992). *Systems approaches for agricultural development*. New York: Elsevier.

Timsina, J., Adhikari, B., & Ganesh, K. C. (1997). *Modelling and simulation of rice, wheat and maize crops for selected sites and the potential effects of climate change on their productivity in Nepal (Consultancy Rep.)*. Harihar Bhawan, Nepal: Ministry of Agriculture.

Timsina, J., & Connor, D. J. (2001). Productivity and management of rice-wheat cropping systems: issues and challenges. *Field Crops Research, 69*, 93–132. doi:10.1016/S0378-4290(00)00143-X

Timsina, J., & Humphreys, E. (2006). Applications of CERES-Rice and CERES-Wheat in Research, Policy and Climate Change Studies in Asia: A Review. *International Journal of Agricultural Research, 1*(3), 202–225. doi:10.3923/ijar.2006.202.225

Timsina, J., Singh, U., Badaruddin, M., & Meisner, C. (1998). Cultivar, nitrogen and moisture effects on a RW sequence: Experimentation and simulation. *Agronomy Journal, 90*, 119–130. doi:10.2134/agronj1998.00021962009000020001x

Timsina, J., Singh, U., & Singh, Y. (1996). Addressing Sustainability of RW Systems: Analysis of Long-term Experimentation and Simulation. In Kropff, , (Eds.), *Application of systems approaches at the field level* (pp. 383–397). Dordrecht, The Netherlands: Kluwer Academic Publishers.

Tsuji, G. Y., Hoogenboom, G., & Thornton, P. K. (1998). *Understanding options for agricultural production*. Dordrecht, The Netherlands: Kluwer Academic Publishers.

Tsuji, G. Y., Uehara, G., & Balas, S. (1994). *DSSAT v 3*. Honolulu, HI: University of Hawaii.

Wilhite, D. A. (1993). *Drought Assessment, Management and Planning: Theory and Case Studies*. Dordrecht, The Netherlands: Kluwer Academic Publishers.

Wilhite, D. A. (2000). *Drought as a natural hazard: Concepts and definitions. Drought: A Global Assessment*. London: Routledge.

Wilhite, D. A., & Glantz, M. H. (1985). Understanding the drought phenomenon: The role of definitions. *Water International, 10*, 111–120. doi:10.1080/02508068508686328

World Meteorological Organization (WMO). (1975). *Drought and Agriculture*. Tech. Rep. No. 138). Geneva, Switzerland: WMO.

World Meteorological Organization (WMO). (1993). *Drought and Desertification* (Tech. Rep. No. 605). Geneva, Switzerland: WMO.

World Meteorological Organization (WMO). (1995)... *The Global Climate System Review, 819*, 150.

World Meteorological Organization (WMO). (2001). *WMO Statement on the Status of the Global Climate in 2000*. Geneva, Switzerland: WMO.

Wu, H., Hayes, M. J., Welss, A., & Hu, Q. (2001). An evaluation the standardized precipitation index, the China-z index and the statistical z-score. *International Journal of Climatology, 21*, 745–758. doi:10.1002/joc.658

Yadav, R. L., Dwivedi, B. S., & Pandey, P. S. (2000a). Rice-wheat cropping system: assessment of sustainability under green manuring and chemical fertilizer inputs. *Field Crops Research, 65*, 15–30. doi:10.1016/S0378-4290(99)00066-0

Yadav, R. L., Dwivedi, B. S., Prasad, K., Tomar, O. K., Shurpali, N. J., & Panday, P. S. (2000b). Yield trends, and changes in soil organic-C and available NPK in a long-term rice-wheat system under integrated use of manures and fertilizers. *Field Crops Research, 68*, 219–246. doi:10.1016/S0378-4290(00)00126-X

Chapter 20
Irrigation Water Valuation Using Spatial Hedonic Models in GIS Environment

Zisis Mallios
Aristotle University of Thessaloniki, Greece

ABSTRACT

Hedonic pricing is an indirect valuation method that applies to heterogeneous goods investigating the relationship between the prices of tradable goods and their attributes. It can be used to measure the value of irrigation water through the estimation of the model that describes the relation between the market value of the land parcels and its characteristics. Because many of the land parcels included in a hedonic pricing model are spatial in nature, the conventional regression analysis fails to incorporate all the available information. Spatial regression models can achieve more efficient estimates because they are designed to deal with the spatial dependence of the data. In this paper, the authors present the results of an application of the hedonic pricing method on irrigation water valuation obtained using a software tool that is developed for the ArcGIS environment. This tool incorporates, in the GIS application, the estimation of two different spatial regression models, the spatial lag model and the spatial error model. It also has the option for different specifications of the spatial weights matrix, giving the researcher the opportunity to examine how it affects the overall performance of the model.

INTRODUCTION

Water resources are very important for the humans and the natural environment. The availability of adequate water quantities for all uses is also important for the economic development of every country, because water is a necessary input to production in the most of all economic sectors.

Agriculture is the biggest consumer of fresh water among all economic sectors in many regions of the world. The most significant problem in the agriculture sector is the intense use of water, in conjunction with its low efficiency. It is widely accepted in the literature that water must be treated as an economic good and more efficient water prices must be introduced, in order to achieve

DOI: 10.4018/978-1-4666-0927-3.ch020

an efficient water allocation. The establishment of more efficient water prices requires reliable estimation of the economic value of water.

Various valuation techniques have been developed to capture the economic value of environmental resources. These techniques are classified in two major categories, the direct or stated preference methods and the indirect or revealed preference ones. The main methods, which are widely used, and can be used, for the estimation of the economic value of water resources are: hedonic pricing, travel cost, contingent valuation, and choice experiment. The first two of the above belong to the category of indirect methods while the other two to that of direct methods (Birol et al., 2006).

The hedonic pricing method is commonly used in real estate appraisal, real estate economics and consumer price index calculations, but there are also many examples of the use of the method in irrigation water valuation, like the applications of the method presented by Milliman (1959), Hartman and Anderson (1962), Torrel et al. (1990), Faux and Perry (1999). In a hedonic pricing method application a heterogeneous good, usually land property or housing, is treated as a sum of individual goods (characteristics or attributes) that can not be sold separately in the market (Nelson, 1978). Then the individual values of the characteristics of the good under study are estimated (for example the agricultural land value and the individual values of its attributes, such as size, irrigation water etc.) by means of ordinary least squares regression analysis. One of the important assumptions in an OLS regression analysis is that the error must be constant across the sample in order to obtain unbiased parameter estimates, but this is not the case in the most of the hedonic pricing applications. The reason is that the sample, which is used for the estimation of a hedonic pricing model, consists of land property characteristics that are distributed across the study area and, therefore, according to Tobler's "first law of geography": "...everything is related to everything, but closer

things more so,…" (Tobler, 1979). In other words spatial dependence is here not exception but the rule, and is known as "spatial autocorrelation".

There are many statistical techniques that have been developed to deal with the problem of spatial autocorrelation. According to Anselin and Berra (1998), spatial autoregressive models are more appropriate for economic data. These models confront the problem of spatial dependence by means of spatial weights and spatial lag operators. The spatial weights define for each observation (property), the "neighborhood sets", i.e., those locations that interact with it. Therefore, the present research is focused on the estimation of the hedonic pricing function using two well known autoregressive models and, more specifically, the spatial lag and the spatial error model. In a previous work (Mallios et al., 2007b), a specific approach on estimating the value of irrigation water using spatial regression models produced better parameter estimates compared to those obtained by the conventional OLS regression.

In this paper, an important issue on the estimation of the spatial regression models is examined and particularly how the definition of the neighborhood sets of each observation affects the model parameters estimates. The questions arising are how the neighbors of each observation are selected and how each of the neighbors affects the price of it. Here is examined how the specification of the spatial weights matrix affects the overall performance of spatial regression models. More specifically, it is examined if all the neighbors affect in the same way the price of each observation or if this price depends on the distance of each of the neighbors. For this purpose an add-in tool has been developed using ArcObjects and Microsoft Visual Basic technology for the ArcGIS Desktop environment, capable to produce parameter estimates of spatial regression models and providing the user with the option to specify the spatial weights matrix and select the one that improves the overall performance of the model.

METHODOLOGY

The hedonic pricing method is based on the characteristics theory of value developed by Lancaster (1966) and Rosen (1974), which suggests that a good can be described as a bundle of characteristics. These are contained at different levels in the good under study, affecting the price of the good. It is assumed that the commodity under study is described by a vector of m attributes (characteristics), denoted by $\mathbf{x} = (x_1, x_2, ..., x_m)$. More specifically, in the case of irrigation water valuation the value of any land parcel depends on several characteristics like the size, the land use (cultivated crops), the irrigation water availability, the distance from various places of interest or infrastructures, e.g., settlements, urban centers, roads, highways, sea etc. All these characteristics can contribute either positively or negatively to the price (value) of the property; hence each one of them has a separate value, which can be estimated through the hedonic pricing function. In other words, there is a direct relationship between the price of a land parcel, in our case, and the vector of characteristics $\mathbf{x}$ (Young, 2005). In general, the hedonic pricing model that expresses the relation between the price of any land parcel and its characteristics can be written in matrix terms as follows:

$$\mathbf{p} = \alpha + \boldsymbol{\beta}\mathbf{x} + \varepsilon \qquad (1)$$

where $\mathbf{p}$ is the vector of the depended variable (land price), α is the constant term, $\boldsymbol{\beta} = (\beta_1, \beta_2, ..., \beta_m)$ is the vector of coefficients that represent the influence of the attributes on the land parcel's value and ε is the error term.

The model of Equation 1 is estimated by means of multiple linear regression but, in most hedonic pricing applications, the assumption of the normally distributed error term is rejected due to spatial autocorrelation or heteroskedasticity (Anselin, 1988; Anselin, 2005). In this case conventional Ordinary Least Squares estimators

are inconsistent. As mentioned above, spatial autoregressive models are appropriate to deal with the problem of spatial dependence. Ord (1975) introduced a computational scheme for two mixed regressive – autoregressive models, also known as spatial regression models, to deal with the problem of spatial autocorrelation. These models are referred in the literature as spatial lag model and spatial error model (Anselin, 1988; LeSage & Pace, 2009).

The spatial lag model assumes that the price of a property is formed by indirect and direct effects. More specifically, the price of a property is indirectly affected by the spatially weighted average of property prices in the neighborhood. On the other hand the price of a property is directly affected by its individual and neighborhood characteristics. The spatial lag model is an appropriate tool when there is a structural spatial interaction effect that is of interest to be measured. However, the true effect of the explanatory variables can be measured only after removing the spatial autocorrelation. The spatial lag hedonic model is analogous to an autoregressive time-series model. In the spatial lag hedonic model nearby observations of property prices affect, in addition to the standard explanatory variables, the price of each property. A spatial lag hedonic model can be written as follows (Anselin, 2001):

$$\mathbf{p} = \rho\mathbf{W}\mathbf{p} + \boldsymbol{\beta}\mathbf{x} + \varepsilon \qquad (2)$$

where $\mathbf{p}$ is a $n \times 1$ (n is the number of parcels) column vector expressing the value of each parcel and $\mathbf{x}$ is the $n \times m$ matrix of explanatory variables (characteristics of each parcel) with the first column consisting of ones (($m - 1$) is the number of explanatory variables). $\mathbf{W}$ is the ($n \times n$) spatial weight matrix with zero diagonal that assigns the potential spatial correlation and the product $\mathbf{W}\mathbf{p}$ is the spatially lagged dependent variable. ρ is the spatial autocorrelation parameter, $\boldsymbol{\beta}$ is the ($m \times 1$) vector of the coefficients of the independent variables and ε denotes the ($m \times 1$) vector of the independent and identically distributed error term.

Contrary to the spatial lag model, the spatial error model has a different economic interpretation. The spatial error model does not include indirect effects, as spatial lag model does, but it is assumed that there are one or more variables not included in the model specification and these variables vary spatially. Thus, the error term of the hedonic price equation tends to be spatially autocorrelated. This model is particularly appropriate when, although no spatial interaction exists, spatial autocorrelation is present due to the use of spatial data. In brief, the spatial error model is useful when the interest is to obtain efficient parameter estimates of the hedonic model and to arrive at a correct conclusion. When there is a spatial dependence in the error term, a spatial autoregressive specification is assumed to deal with it. The hedonic spatial error model can be written as (Anselin, 2001):

$$\mathbf{p} = \boldsymbol{\beta}\mathbf{x} + \mathbf{u} \qquad (3)$$

$$\mathbf{u} = \lambda\mathbf{W}\mathbf{u} + \varepsilon$$

where, as in spatial lag model, $\mathbf{p}$ is a $n \times 1$ column vector of the depended variable and $\mathbf{x}$ is the $n \times m$ matrix of the independent variables with the first column consisting of ones, $\boldsymbol{\beta}$ is the ($m \times 1$) vector of the coefficients of the independent variables, while λ is the coefficient of the spatially correlated errors and $\mathbf{W}\mathbf{u}$ is the spatially lagged error term.

The spatial weights matrix reflects the structure of the potential spatial interaction. From the specification of the above models it is obvious, that a crucial issue in the estimation of spatial regression models is the formulation of the spatial weights matrix. A spatial weights matrix is an $n \times n$ positive and symmetric matrix which expresses the neighboring observations for each property. More formally $w_{ij} \neq 0$ when observations i and j are neighbours, and $w_{ij} = 0$ otherwise. The elements of the main diagonal are set by convention

to zero. The conventional approach on specifying the neighbours of each observation is to set $w_{ij} = 1$ if the land parcels i and j share a common border or are within a given distance of each other (i.e. $w_{ij} = 1$ for $d_{ij} \leq \delta$, where d_{ij} is the distance between observations i and j and δ is a distance cut off value. The common practice is the row standardization of the weight matrix, such that the elements of a row sum to one (Ord, 1975; Anselin & Bera, 1998).

Many suggestions have been offered in the literature on the specification of which elements of the weights matrix must be non zero and on the value that they must have. Generally the weights may be specified to express any measure of "potential interaction" between two observations (Anselin, 1988). For example, one specification is the one that is directly related to the spatial interaction theory, with w_{ij} equal to a function of the distance between observations i and j, like $w_{ij} = 1/d_{ij}^{a}$ or even more complex specifications. Usually "a", the parameter of the distance function in the specification of w_{ij} is set a priori (e.g., a=2) (Anselin & Bera, 1998).

STUDY AREA

As it is mentioned above, the present work is based on a previous application of the hedonic pricing method (Mallios et al., 2007b). The area selected for the application of the hedonic pricing method belongs to the greater area of the Municipality of Moudania in Chalkidiki, Greece. The interesting issue about the municipality of Moudania is that it is very close to the second biggest city of Greece, Thessaloniki. The distance of the municipality centre from Thessaloniki is about 65 kilometres. This area is mainly a rural region with intense tourist development during the summer period. The resident population is 17,032 according to the census of 2001 while summer visitors (tourists) amount to an annual average of 70,000 according to the local authorities. The demand for irrigation water is significantly high and sums up to 90% of the total local consumption of water. The total cultivated area is about 10,500 hectares, of which 35% are irrigated. The major cultivation of non-irrigated land is wheat, while in the irrigated areas the major cultivation is olive trees (about 70% of the irrigated land) followed by other kinds of trees (about 15%) and vegetables (about 7%). It must be noticed here the importance of olives production for the local economy and the difference of olive trees from all other trees. Olive's production contributes in a very significant way to the farmer's income. On the other hand olive trees must be distinguished from other trees because of their special needs and long lifecycle. Olive trees need many years to be productive but then they can be productive for a very long time.

The municipality, which consists of nine communities, is limited to the south by a coastline along which several tourist resorts have been dynamically developed during the last few decades and continue to develop up to date, due to the proximity of the area to Thessaloniki. Thus, a quite competitive use to the already very high agricultural one is that of domestic water, which reaches its peak also during the summer period. On the other hand, the sole source of water in the whole area is groundwater pumped from the underlying aquifer, while there are no close surface water resources. Especially during the summer months about 800 private and 100 municipal pumping wells operate at an almost continuous pace (Latinopoulos, 2003).

The study area extends in a region that belongs to the main watershed of the total administrative area of municipality of Moudania and comprises seven of the nine municipal communities (N. Moudania, Dionisiou, Flogita, Zografou, Portaria, Simantra and Ag. Panteleimon). Apart from its urban and coastal parts, the region is exclusively an agricultural land in which the prevailing activity is intensive agriculture. This agricultural land consists of about 11,000 parcels, of which a sample

of 1,485 parcels is selected for the application of the hedonic pricing method.

For the 1,485 land parcels in the study area, which have been selected in order to form the sample of data for the case study, relevant data records were created by implementing the well-known GIS application (Figure 1) ArcGIS desktop. In the GIS application a lot of information is stored that can be used for the retrieval of the land parcels characteristics. More specifically the GIS database developed for this study consists of by various maps stored in different layers, like the map of the areas land parcels, the topographic map, the road network, the settlements etc. Specifically to this end, for the quick, ease and accurate retrieval of the data needed for the hedonic pricing application, the add-in toolbar developed for this purpose and presented analytically in our previous works is used (Mallios et al., 2007a; Mallios et al., 2007b). As mentioned previously, the market value of each land parcel depends on its individual characteristics and its neighborhood characteristics. Therefore, this add-in toolbar is utilized to calculate the individual characteristics of each plot, like its area and the elevation and slope of its centroid. The neighborhood characteristics calculated through the ArcMap add-in toolbar is the distances of each land parcel from the sea, the closest settlement, the municipality centre (N. Moudania), as well as from the closest local and the national road. The information for the agricultural land use (crop cultivation) was obtained from the official archives of the Prefecture of Chalkidiki, while the values of the land parcels were assessed by the aid of local experts from the real estate sector. This land value assessment is the only feasible one, as there are no reliable data for the agricultural land transactions, not only in the specific region but in the whole country, due to the particularity of the Greek tax system. All these variables (attributes) are next examined to assess their functional relationship with the land parcels price.

RESULTS

According to Tripplet (2004), two very important issues have to be faced in the hedonic pricing application. The first is the choice of the variables that describe the characteristics of the land parcels and the precision of these data. The variables chosen for the estimation of the hedonic pricing models presented in this paper is a subset of the data contained in the GIS application described in the previous section. As for the precision of the data, this is ensured by the tools that are used for their retrieval, whereas reliability is achieved by the sources that the data are obtained from. The second significant issue in formulating the hedonic pricing function is the choice of an appropriate model that represents the data. Economic theory does not propose a certain model as the most suitable one and, consequently, the researcher can select from several types of functions to formulate the hedonic pricing model. The most popular of the available functional forms are the linear, the log - linear, the semi - log linear, the reciprocal and log - inverse form. It has been shown in a previous work (Mallios et al., 2007b) that the most suitable functional form for the available data in this particular hedonic pricing application is the log – linear form. Using the log – linear form for the estimation of the hedonic pricing function the goodness of fit criterion (i.e., the log likelihood) takes the lowest values. In other words the use the log – linear model achieves a better fit to the data than the other models.

For the estimation of the models of Equations 2 and 3 the specification of the spatial weights matrix is required, which is a two step procedure. First the neighborhood set of each observation must be determined, and second the form of the

Figure 1. The GIS application

313

spatial interaction between each observation and its neighbors must be set. The neighborhood sets are defined here setting a cut off distance, as it is described by Anselin (2005), so that each observation has at least one neighbor, by this way for each observation all the observations that are closer than the cut off distance are selected. On the other hand, the main objective of this study is to examine if the form of the spatial interaction between each observation and its neighbors is important. For this purpose the values w_{ij} of the weights matrix for the neighboring observations are set as $w_{ij} = 1/d_{ij}^{a}$ where d_{ij} is the distance between the neighbor observations and the parameter a takes the values 0 and 2.

By this way two spatial weights matrices are obtained. The first specification (for $a = 0$) leads to a spatial weights matrix that follows the conventional approach where all $w_{ij} \neq 0$ are equal to 1, meaning that all neighbors in the neighborhood set affect the price of the land parcel in the same way. While in the second specification (for $a = 2$) the spatial interaction theory is applied, leading to a spatial weights matrix where it is assumed that the closer to the land parcel neighbors in the neighborhood set affect more its price. Following this procedure the two different spatial weight matrices are then row standardized, which means that the elements of each row sum to one. Then, the

models of equations 2 and 3 are estimated, using as dependent variable p the natural logarithm of the LandPrice variable (Table 1) and as independent variables all other variables shown also in Table 1. The explanatory variables presented in this table are a subset of the total data set that is available for the study area. This set is selected after examining the whole set of data contained in the GIS application, modeling many combinations of the independent variables and evaluating each one of them. Moreover, Table 1 presents the definitions and the descriptive statistics of all the variables that are used for the estimation of the subsequent models.

The estimates of the β_{i} coefficients for the spatial lag model, as well as the model performance statistics for each one of the two spatial weights matrices are presented in Table 2. On the other hand, Table 3 respectively presents the estimates of the β_{i} coefficients of the spatial error model for each one of the two different specifications of the spatial weights matrix. In both Tables 2 and 3 the estimated β_{i} coefficients of all models are similar with the ones used in other similar applications of hedonic pricing and the signs are the presumable ones (Crouter, 1987; Young, 1996, Latinopoulos et al., 2004). It should also be noticed that all estimated coefficients are statistically significant at a level lower than 1%. By comparing the values

Table 1. Definition and statistical summary of variables used for hedonic pricing estimations

Variable	Definition	Mean	Std. Dev.
Ln(LandPrice)	(Natural Logarithm of) parcel value in € (dependent)	9.435	1.161
Irrigation	Irrigated field: 1 if yes, 0 if no	0.304	0.460
Ln(Elevation)	(Natural Logarithm of) parcel elevation in m	3.750	0.753
Ln(Area)	(Natural Logarithm of) parcel area in ha	-0.560	0.763
Ln(DistSea)	(Natural Logarithm of) parcel distance to sea in km	1.106	0.782
Ln(DistSettlement)	(Natural Logarithm of) parcel distance to nearest settlement in km	-0.108	0.875
Ln(DistMoudania)	(Natural Logarithm of) parcel distance to city of N. Moudania in km	1.515	0.600
Ln(DistRoad)	(Natural Logarithm of) parcel distance to nearest main road in km	-0.984	1.143
Ln(DistNatRoad)	(Natural Logarithm of) parcel distance to the national road in km	0.320	1.332
OliveTrees	Olive trees in the plot: 1 if yes, 0 if no	0.227	0.419

Table 2. Estimates for the Spatial Lag Models and performance statistics

	Model 1		Model 2	
Variable	**Coefficient**	**Std. Error**	**Coefficient**	**Std. Error**
W_LnTotalValu	0.38909	0.03251	0.45769	0.02092
Constant	6.24640	0.36370	5.63740	0.24913
Irrigation	0.67287	0.05946	0.64306	0.05406
Ln(Elevation)	0.13607	0.04665	0.07547	0.04238
Ln(Area)	0.96061	0.02410	0.85342	0.02341
Ln(DistSea)	-0.66904	0.04424	-0.50528	0.04118
Ln(DistSettlement)	-0.31675	0.01896	-0.24130	0.01756
Ln(DistMoudania)	-0.15312	0.04235	-0.13831	0.03612
Ln(DistRoad)	-0.19597	0.01526	-0.17676	0.01396
Ln(DistNatRoad)	0.15593	0.02042	0.11820	0.01808
OliveTrees	0.24265	0.06560	0.23400	0.05932
R^2:	0.738016		0.784544	
Log likelihood:	-1336.9100		-1216.6970	
Akaike IC	2695.8200		2455.3930	
Schwarz IC	2754.1470		2513.7210	
σ^2:	0.3530		0.2900	
S.E of regression:	0.5941		0.5388	

of the Log-Likelihood, the Akaike info criterion and the Schwarz criterion, for the models of Tables 2 and 3, it can be seen that for both spatial lag and spatial error models, there is a better fit for the second specification of the spatial weights matrix, i.e., for $a = 2$. A comparison of the goodness of fit statistics of the second model in Tables 2 and 3 leads to the conclusion that the spatial error model fits better to the data. The meaning of this conclusion is that for the region of the Municipality of Moudania the spatial error model describes in a better way the relation between the land parcels price, and their characteristics, so it is more secure to use these parameter estimates for the valuation of irrigation water in this area.

Before getting to the estimation of the value of irrigation water, the relevant importance of all other variables included in the second model of Table 3 is worth discussing. An important remark

is that the value of the constant term is both highly significant and large in magnitude. This means that, to a great extent, there is a base price for agricultural land in the locality that is determined by the – correctly omitted – general and uniform characteristics of the area. The appearance of the dummy variable that represents the olive trees cultivation in the hedonic price function is well explained by the fact that olive production is the dominant profitable agricultural activity in the area. Finally, the proximity of the plots to places of interest and infrastructures, as represented by the variables that expressing the distance of the land parcels from them in Tables 2 and 3, affects in most cases positively the price of the land parcels. More specifically, the coefficients of the variables, that represent the distance of the land parcels from the sea, the inhabited areas and, the local road network, have all negative sign. This indicates that a land parcel that is

Table 3. Estimates for the Spatial Error Model and performance statistics

	Model 1		Model 2	
Variable	Coefficient	Std. Error	Coefficient	Std. Error
Constant	10.15592	0.29796	10.13165	0.28848
Irrigation	0.71535	0.05801	0.73677	0.05122
Ln(Elevation)	0.22049	0.05915	0.14142	0.07241
Ln(Area)	1.00775	0.02396	1.00431	0.02222
Ln(DistSea)	-0.77765	0.07554	-0.57474	0.08234
Ln(DistSettlement)	-0.30478	0.02928	-0.14612	0.03312
Ln(DistMoudania)	-0.44325	0.15591	-0.47189	0.13918
Ln(DistRoad)	-0.31329	0.01731	-0.39340	0.02038
Ln(DistNatRoad)	0.24356	0.02671	0.26319	0.03283
OliveTrees	0.16649	0.06421	0.16377	0.05567
LAMBDA	0.88353	0.02689	0.84367	0.01634
R^2:	0.776078		0.854455	
Log likelihood:	-1242.1050		-1020.5200	
Akaike IC	2506.2110		2063.0410	
Schwarz IC	2564.5460		2121.3760	
σ^2:	0.3020		0.1960	
S.E of regression:	0.5493		0.4428	

close to the sea, a settlement or a local road has a bigger price, because it is more desirable for other uses related probably to tourism which is the other important economic activity in the area. Following this sense the coefficient regarding the distance of a land parcel from the highway is positive, indicating that the price of the land is lower if it is close to the highway. This is explained by the fact that highways produce noise and air pollution. Noise and air pollution make this land less desirable for another use than agriculture.

As for the value of irrigation water, the importance of its availability – in the sense of an immediate access to the underlying aquifer – as a characteristic of the land parcels value is apparent, as expressed by its coefficient in Table 3. In addition, the trend in the real-estate market as it is reported by the local experts, which is that the irrigated land parcels price is about double compared to the price of the non-irrigated ones

with similar all other characteristics, has been confirmed by the model results, as shown in the next paragraph.

The economic theory suggests that the interpretation of β_i coefficients depends on the functional form of the hedonic model (Wooldridge, 2006). For a dummy variable x_k, like the one that describes the availability of irrigation water to a land parcels in the log-linear model that is used in the present study, the estimated coefficient provides the exact percentage difference between the irrigated and non-irrigated land as $\exp(\beta_k) - 1$. Thus, according to the spatial error model for the second spatial weights matrix, where the coefficient of the dummy variable "Irrigation" is 0.73677, the difference between the price of an irrigated land parcel and that of a non-irrigated one, ceteris paribus, is: $\exp(0.73677) - 1 = 1.0892$ or 108.92%. This percentage increase is considered to be quite close to 100%, which is the average reported by the real-estate experts of the region.

The value of irrigated water is estimated via the land value approach in the same way, that it is described by Young (2005) and, presented in previous applications of the hedonic pricing method (Torrell et al., 1990; Faux & Perry, 1999) and is expressed in a total of four different units in Table 4. The values in this table are calculated using the coefficients of the second model of Table 3 by assuming that all other variables, except "Irrigation" dummy variable, take their mean values shown in Table 1. More specifically, the first row of Table 4 shows the corresponding value of an irrigated land parcel, i.e., Irrigation = 1, while the second row shows the value of a non-irrigated one, i.e., Irrigation = 0. The third row is the difference in price of the irrigated and non-irrigated land, in other words is shown the value of a perennial water supply for one hectare. In the forth row is shown the value for one year of water supply, again for one hectare, which is calculated using the appropriate capitalization formula for an infinite time horizon and an assumed 2.5% discount factor. The capitalization formula is:

$$PVP = \frac{pp}{i} \Rightarrow pp = PVP \times i \qquad (4)$$

where *pp* is the annual value of the water supply, *PVP* is the perennial water supply, and *i* is the interest rate. The values of the last two rows are calculated assuming an average annual water consumption of 7,000 m³/ha in the area under study. In this way, in the fifth row is provided the value of irrigation water per cubic meter of a perennial water supply (i.e., the value of a cubic meter of water in perpetuity) and finally the last row of Table 4 shows the marginal value of water for irrigation in the study area, which is estimated to €0.073 per cubic meter, equivalent to €89.7 per acre-foot. This estimation is well comparable to the reported values in other applications of the hedonic pricing (Torrell et al., 1990; Faux & Perry, 1999). But overall, it is indicative of the low value of irrigated water found in numerous applications of alternative techniques (Young, 1996; Johanson, 2000).

In studies like the one presented here is useful to perform a sensitivity analysis because the values of the irrigation water reported here are depended on various assumptions and it is important to know how this values change in respect to the assumed parameters. As mentioned above the estimated value of irrigation water is based on an assumption about the levels of the water consumption per hectare and the interest rates. In Figure 1 it is shown how the annual value of irrigation water changes in respect to a change in the interest rate. So the annual irrigation water value can vary from about €200 to €1200 for an interest rate of 1% to 6% respectively. On the other hand Figure 2 shows the change of the irrigation water value per cubic meter in respect to the water consumption and the interest rate. The irrigation water value per cubic meter can be as low as €0.025 for 1% interest rate and a level of water consumption equal to 8000 m³/ha, to as high as €0.40 for interest rate equal 6% and water consumption of 3000 m³/ha.

Table 4. Value of irrigation water in the are of the Municipality of Moudania in euros

1. Value of irrigated land per hectare	39044.307
2. Value of nonirrigated land per hectare	18688.850
3. Value of water per hectare	20355.457
4. Annual value of water per hectare	508.886
5. Value of water per cubic meter abstracted perennially	2.908
6. Value of water per cubic meter abstracted one time	0.073

Figure 2. Annual Irrigation water value change in respect to the interest rate

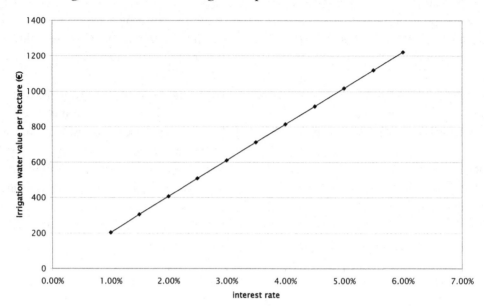

Figure 3. Irrigation water value per cubic meter change in respect to the interest rate

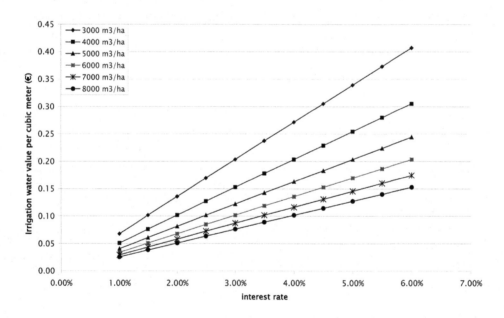

CONCLUSION

The presented application of the hedonic pricing method in the valuation of the irrigation water using spatial regression analysis is considered to be successful. The use of GIS for the formulation of the dataset ensures that the data used for the estimation of the hedonic models are accurate and reliable in conjunction to the quick and easy way that they obtained. The add-in tools for the ArcGIS desktop environment used here for both the formulation of the dataset and the estimation of the spatial regression models, in conjunction to the development of more powerful computers, proves that GIS can be the major tool for the application of the hedonic pricing method, even the datasets used for the estimation of the models are huge. So there is a need to incorporate more econometric tools in the GIS environment.

Two are the main conclusions that arise from the models presented in the previous section, using the different specifications of the spatial weights matrix. The first and most important issue is that the specification of the spatial weights matrix can affect the overall performance of the estimated model. Consequently, it is important for the researcher to test different specifications of the spatial weights matrix, among other tests performed in the modeling procedure, in order to find the suitable specification to the data used in the model estimation. Last but not least is that there is a need to further investigate the specification of the spatial weights matrix and propose different specifications that can lead to more efficient parameter estimates.

All the above lead to an improved performance of the hedonic pricing method application, which is important in order to obtain more efficient estimates of the resources valued in every specific application. Especially, for the valuation of irrigation water, efficient estimates of its value are important to policy makers in order to achieve a more efficient water allocation which is the main objective.

REFERENCES

Anselin, L. (1988). *Spatial econometrics: Methods and models*. Boston: Kluwer Academic Publishers.

Anselin, L. (2001). Spatial econometrics. In Baltagi, B. (Ed.), *A companion to theoretical Econometrics* (pp. 310–330). Oxford, UK: Basil Blackwell.

Anselin, L. (2005). *Exploring spatial data with GeoDA: A workbook*. IL: University of Illinois, Spatial Analysis Laboratory, Department of Geography.

Anselin, L., & Bera, A. K. (1998). Spatial dependence in linear regression models with an introduction to spatial econometrics. In Ullah, A., & Giles, D. E. A. (Eds.), *Handbook of applied economic statistics* (pp. 237–290). New York: Marcel Deker.

Birol, E., Karousakis, K., & Koundouri, P. (2006). Using economic valuation techniques to inform water resources management: A survey and critical appraisal of available techniques and an application. *The Science of the Total Environment, 365*(1-3), 105–122. doi:10.1016/j.scitotenv.2006.02.032

Crouter, J. P. (1987). Hedonic estimation applied to a water rights market. *Land Economics, 63*, 259–271. doi:10.2307/3146835

Faux, J., & Perry, G. M. (1999). Estimating irrigation water value using hedonic price analysis: a case study in Malheur County, Oregon. *Land Economics, 75*, 440–452. doi:10.2307/3147189

Hanley, N., & Spash, C. L. (1993). *Cost benefit analysis and the environment*. London: Edward Elgar.

Hartman, L. M., & Anderson, R. L. (1962). Estimating the value of irrigation water from farm sales in Northeastern Colorado. *Journal of Farm Economics, 44*(1), 207–213. doi:10.2307/1235499

Johansson, R. C. (2000). *Pricing irrigation water: a literature review* (Tech. Rep. No. WPS2449). Washington, DC: The World Bank.

Lancaster, K. J. (1966). A new approach to consumer theory. *The Journal of Political Economy, 74*, 132–157. doi:10.1086/259131

Latinopoulos, P. (2003). *Design of a water potential management plan for public water supply and irrigation in the Municipality of Moudania.* Thessaloniki, Greece: AUTh, Department of Civil Engineering.

Latinopoulos, P., Tziakas, V., & Mallios, Z. (2004). Valuation for irrigation water by the hedonic price method: a case study in Chalkidiki, Greece. *Water Air and Soil Pollution Focus, 4,* 253–262. doi:10.1023/B:WAFO.0000044803.01747.bd

LeSage, J. P., & Pace, R. K. (2009). *Introduction to Spatial Econometrics.* New York: CRC Press/ Taylor & Francis Group.

Mallios, Z., Papageorgiou, A., Latinopoulos, D., & Latinopoulos, P. (2007). Spatial Hedonic Pricing Models for the Valuation of Irrigation Water. In *Proceedings of the 10th International Conference on Environmental Science and Technology,* Kos Island, Greece (pp. A900-907).

Mallios, Z., Papageorgiou, A., & Latinopoulos, P. (2007). The development of a calculation tool and spatial data retrieval in a Geographical Information Systems environment for the estimation of spatial econometric models. In *Proceedings of the 6th National Conference of Greek Committee of water resources management,* Chania, Greece (pp. 223-230).

Milliman, J. W. (1959). Land values as measures of primary irrigation benefits. *Journal of Farm Economics, 41*(2), 234–243. doi:10.2307/1235148

Nelson, J. (1978). Residential choice, hedonic prices, and the demand for urban air quality. *Journal of Urban Economics, 5,* 357–369. doi:10.1016/0094-1190(78)90016-5

Ord, K. (1975). Estimation methods for models of spatial interaction. *Journal of the American Statistical Association, 70,* 120–126. doi:10.2307/2285387

Rosen, S. (1974). Hedonic prices and implicit markets: products differentiation in pure competition. *The Journal of Political Economy, 82,* 34–55. doi:10.1086/260169

Tobler, W. (1979). Cellular Geography. In Gale, S., & Olsson, G. (Eds.), *Philosophy in Geography* (pp. 379–386). Dordrecht, The Netherlands: Reidel.

Torell, A., Libbin, J., & Miller, M. (1990). The market value of water in the Ogallala aquifer. *Land Economics, 66,* 163–175. doi:10.2307/3146366

Triplett, J. (2004). *Handbook on hedonic indexes and quality adjustments in price indexes: Special application to information technology products* (STI Working Paper No. 2004/9). Statistical Analysis of Science, Technology and Industry, OECD.

Wooldridge, J. (2006). *Introductory econometrics: A modern approach* (3rd ed.). Gale, UK: Thomson Learning.

Young, R. (1996). *Measuring economic benefits for water investments and policies* (Tech. Rep. No. 338). Washington, DC: World Bank.

Young, R. A. (2005). *Determining the Economic Value of Water: Concepts and Methods.* Washington, DC: Resources for the Future.

This work was previously published in International Journal of Information Systems and Social Change, Volume 1, Issue 4, edited by John Wang, pp. 1-13, copyright 2010 by IGI Publishing (an imprint of IGI Global).

Compilation of References

Abate, J. (1999). *Inventing the Internet* (chapters 1-2). Cambridge, MA: MIT Press.

Abrol, I. P., Bronson, K. F., Duxbury, J. M., & Gupta, R. K. (2000). *Long-term soil fertility experiments in rice-wheat cropping systems*. Paper presented to the Rice-Wheat Consortium, New Delhi, India.

ABS. (2006). *Australia's environment: Issues and trends 2006*. Cat. no. 4613.0, Australian Bureau of Statistics, Canberra.

Ackoff, R. L. (1999). On learning and the systems that facilitate it. *Reflections, 1*(1), 14–24. doi:10.1162/152417399570250

Adams, J. C., & Brom, T. H. (2008). Microwulf: A Beowulf cluster for every desk. In *SIGCSE '08: Proceedings of the 39th Technical Symposium on Computer Science Education* (pp. 121-125).

Adams, R. M., Flemming, R. A., Chang, C. C., Mc Carl, B. A., & Rosenzweig, C. (1995). A reassessment of the economic effects of global climate change on US agriculture. *Climatic Change, 30*, 147–167. doi:10.1007/BF01091839

Adiku, S. G. K., Carberry, P. S., Rose, C. W., McCown, R. L., & Braddock, R. (1995). A maize (*Zea mays*)-cowpea (*Vigna unguiculata*) intercrop model. In *H. Sinoquet & P. Cruz (Es.), Ecophysiology of Tropical Intercropping* (pp. 397–406). Paris: INRA editions.

Aggarwal, P. K., Talukdar, K. K., & Mall, R. K. (2000a). Potential yields of the rice-wheat system in the Indo-Gangetic Plains of India. In *Proceedings of the Rice-Wheat Consortium for the Indo-Gangetic Plain*, New Delhi and Indian Agricultural Research Institute, New Delhi, India.

Aggarwal, P. K. (2003). Impact of climate change on Indian Agriculture. *Journal of Plant Biology, 30*, 189–198.

Aggarwal, P. K., Bandyopadhyay, S. K., Pathak, H., Kalra, N., Chander, S., & Sujith Kumar, S. (2000b). Analyses of yield trends of the rice-wheat system in north-western India. *Outlook on Agriculture, 29*, 259–268.

Aggarwal, P. K., Joshi, P. K., Ingram, J. S., & Gupta, R. K. (2004). Adapting food systems of the Indo-Gangetic Plains to global environmental change: key information needs to improve policy formulation. *Environmental Science & Policy, 7*, 487–498. doi:10.1016/j.envsci.2004.07.006

Aggarwal, P. K., & Kalra, N. (1994). Analysing the limitations set by climatic factors, genotype, wate rand nitrogen availability on productivity of wheat. II. Climatically potential yields and optimal management strategies. *Field Crops Research, 38*, 93–103. doi:10.1016/0378-4290(94)90003-5

Aggarwal, P. K., Kalra, N., Bandyopadhyay, S. K., & Selvarajan, S. (1996). A systems approach to analyze production options for wheat in India. In Bouman, J., (Eds.), *Eco-regional approaches for sustainable land use and food production*. Dordrecht, The Netherlands: Kluwer.

Aggarwal, P. K., Kropff, M. J., Cassman, K. G., & ten Berge, H. F. M. (1997). Simulating genotypic strategies for increasing rice yield potential in irrigated, tropical environments. *Field Crops Research, 51*, 5–18. doi:10.1016/S0378-4290(96)01044-1

Aggarwal, P. K., & Mall, R. K. (2002). Climate change and rice yields in diverse agro-environments of India. II. Effect of uncertainties in scenarios and crop models on impact assessment. *Climatic Change, 52*, 331–343. doi:10.1023/A:1013714506779

Aggarwal, P. K., & Sinha, S. K. (1993). Effect of probable increase in carbon dioxide and temperature on productivity of wheat in India. *Journal of Agricultural Meteorology, 48*, 811–814.

Aikman, D. P., & Benjamin, L. R. (1994). A model for plant and crop growth, allowing for competition for light by the use of potential and restricted projected crown zone areas. *Annals of Botany, 73*, 185–194. doi:10.1006/anbo.1994.1022

Alavi, M., & Leidner, D. E. (2001). Review: Knowledge management and knowledge management systems: Conceptual foundations and research issues. *Management Information Systems Quarterly, 25*(1), 107–136. doi:10.2307/3250961

Alexandrov, V. A., & Hoogenboom, G. (2000a). The impact of climatic variability and change on crop yield in Bulgaria. *Agricultural and Forest Meteorology, 104*(4), 315–327. doi:10.1016/S0168-1923(00)00166-0

Alexandrov, V. A., & Hoogenboom, G. (2000b). Vulnerability and adaptation assessments of agricultural crops under climate change in the Southeastern USA. *Theoretical and Applied Climatology, 67*, 45–63. doi:10.1007/s007040070015

Al-Gahtani, S. S. (2001). The applicability of the TAM model outside North America: an empirical test in the United Kingdom. *Information Resources Management Journal, 14*(3), 37–46.

Al-Gahtani, S. S. (2004). Computer technology acceptance success factors in Saudi Arabia: an exploratory study. *Journal of Global Information Technology Management, 7*(1), 5–30.

Aller, L., Bennett, T., Lehr, J. H., Petty, R. J., & Hackett, G. (1987). *DRASTIC: A standardized system for evaluating ground water pollution potential using hydrogeologic settings*. Washington, DC: US Environmental Protection Agency.

Al-Mashari, M. (2007). A benchmarking study of experiences with electronic government. *Benchmarking: An International Journal, 14*(2), 172–185. doi:10.1108/14635770710740378

Almutairi, H. (2008). Information system usage and national culture: evidence from the public service sector. *International Journal of Society Systems Science, 1*(2), 151–175. doi:10.1504/IJSSS.2008.021917

Alternative Agriculture News. (1994). Contour strip intercropping can reduce erosion. *AANews*.

Al-Zabet, T. (2002). Evaluation of aquifer vulnerability to contamination potential using the DRASTIC method. *Environmental Geology, 43*(1-2), 203–208. doi:10.1007/s00254-002-0645-5

American Meteorological Society (AMS). (1997). Meteorological drought - Policy statement. *Bulletin of the American Meteorological Society, 78*, 847–849.

Anakwe, U. P., Anandaeajan, M., & Igbaria, M. (1999). Information technology usage in dynamic in Nigeria: An empirical study. *Journal of Global Information Management, 7*(2), 13–21.

Andel, T. (1994). Seal your victory through logistics communication. *Transportation & Distribution*, 88-94.

Anderson, P., Reardon, M., & Sanzogni, L. (2001). Ethical dimensions of knowledge management. *AMCIS2001* (pp. 2058-2062).

Anderson, D. F., & Richardson, G. P. (1997). Scripts for group model building. *System Dynamics Review, 13*(2), 107–130. doi:10.1002/(SICI)1099-1727(199722)13:2<107::AID-SDR120>3.0.CO;2-7

Andrighetto, I., Mosca, G., Cozzi, G., & Berzaghi, P. (1992). Maize-soybean intercropping: effect of different variety and sowing density of the legume on forage yield and silage quality. *Journal of Agronomy and Ccrop Science, 168*(5), 354-360.

Ansari, H. (2003). *Monitoring and zoning of drought using fuzzy logic and GIS*. Unpublished doctoral dissertation, Tarbiat Modares University, Tehran, Iran.

Anselin, L. (1988). *Spatial econometrics: Methods and models*. Boston: Kluwer Academic Publishers.

Anselin, L. (2001). Spatial econometrics. In Baltagi, B. (Ed.), *A companion to theoretical Econometrics* (pp. 310–330). Oxford, UK: Basil Blackwell.

Anselin, L. (2005). *Exploring spatial data with GeoDA: A workbook.* IL: University of Illinois, Spatial Analysis Laboratory, Department of Geography.

Anselin, L., & Bera, A. K. (1998). Spatial dependence in linear regression models with an introduction to spatial econometrics. In Ullah, A., & Giles, D. E. A. (Eds.), *Handbook of applied economic statistics* (pp. 237–290). New York: Marcel Deker.

Apigian, C. H., Ragu-Nathan, B. S., & Ragu-Nathan, T. S. (2006). Strategic profiles and internet performance: an empirical investigation into the development of a strategic internet system. *Information & Management, 43*(4), 455–468. doi:doi:10.1016/j.im.2005.11.003

Armstrong, M. P., Densham, P. J., & Rushton, G. (1986). Architecture for a microcomputer-based spatial decision support system. In *Proceedings of the Second International Symposium on Spatial Data Handling* (pp. 120-131). Williamsville, NY: IGU Commission on Geographical Data Sensing and Processing.

Armstrong, J. S., & Cuzan, A. G. (2006, Feb.). Index methods for forecasting: An application to the American presidential elections. *Foresight: The International Journal of Applied Forecasting, 3*, 10–13.

Armstrong, M. P. (1994). Requirements for the development of GIS-based group decision support systems. *Journal of the American Society for Information Science American Society for Information Science, 45*(9), 669–677. doi:doi:10.1002/(SICI)1097-4571(199410)45:9<669:AID-ASI4>3.0.CO;2-P

Asferg, T. (1982). Sample size in game bag statistics: a preliminary study. In *Proceedings of the 2nd Meeting of the Working Group on Game Statistics of IUGB,* Doorwerth, The Netherlands.

Ashforth, B. E., & Mael, F. (1989). Social identity theory and the organization. *Academy of Management Review, 14*(1), 20–39. doi:10.2307/258189

Awasthi, A., & Chauhan, S. S. (2008). An analytical hierarchical process-based decision-making approach for selecting car-sharing stations in medium size agglomerations. *Int. J. Information and Decision Sciences, 1*(1), 66–96. doi:doi:10.1504/IJIDS.2008.020049

Bagchi, P. K., & Virum, H. (1998). Logistics alliances: trends and prospects in integrated Europe. *Journal of Business Logistics, 19*(1), 191–213.

Baida, Z., Gordijn, J., & Omelayenko, B. (2004). A shared service terminology for online service provisioning. *ACM, 15*(1), 1–10.

Ball, D. A., & Shaffer, M. J. (1993). Simulating resource competition in multispecies agricultural plant communities. *Weed Research, 33*, 299–310. doi:10.1111/j.1365-3180.1993.tb01945.x

Balogh, N., Kerkovtis, G., Eichelberg, M., Lemoine, D., & Punys, V. (2003). DICOM and XML usage for multimedia teleconsultation and for reimbursement in cardiology. In *Proceedings of the IEEE Conference on Computers in Cardiology* (pp.379-382).

Balou, R. (2008). Supply chain/ logistics strategy. *Business Logistics/Supply Chain Management.* Upper Saddle River, NJ: Pearson.

Balram, S., & Dragievi, S. (Eds.). (2006). *Collaborative geographic information systems.* Hershey, PA: IGI Global Publishing.

Bannister, F. (2007). The curse of the benchmark: an assessment of the validity and value of e-government comparisons. *International Review of Administrative Sciences, 74*, 71–188.

Baroudi, J. J., & Igbaria, M. (1994). An examination of gender effects on career success of information systems employees. *Journal of Management Information Systems, 11*(3), 181–201.

Basel (1989). *Basel Convention on the control of transboundary movements of hazardous wastes and their disposal.* United Nations Environment Programme (UNEP). Retrieved May 4, 2008, from www.basel.int/text/con-e-rev.pdf

Basnet, C., Foulds, L., & Igbaria, M. (1996). Fleet manager: A microcomputer-based decision support system for vehicle routing. *Decision Support Systems, 16*, 195–207. doi:10.1016/0167-9236(95)00010-0

Basu, R., & Wright, J. N. (2008). The role of supply chain as a value driver. *Total Supply Chain.* Maryland Heights, MO: Elsevier.

Battelle, J. (2005). *The search: How Google and its rivals rewrote the rules of business and transformed our culture* (pp. 75-76, 152). New York: Portfolio.

Baumann, D. (2008). *Debian live: Live Debian systems*. Retrieved July 19, 2008, from debian-live.alioth.debian. org

Baumann, D. T., Bastiaans, L., Goudriaan, J., Van Laar, H. H., & Kropff, M. J. (2002). Analysing crop yield and plant quality in an intercropping system using an eco-physiological model for interplant competition. *Agricultural Systems, 73*, 173–203. doi:10.1016/S0308-521X(01)00084-1

Baumol, W. J., Panzar, J. C., & Willig, R. D. (1982). *Contestable markets and the theory of industry structure*. New York: Harcourt Brace Jovanovich.

Baxter, P., & Jack, S. (2008). Qualitative case study methodology: Study design and implementation for novice researchers. *Qualitative Report, 13*, 544–559.

Bazzani, G. M. (2005). An integrated decision support system for irrigation and water policy design: DSIRR. *Environmental Modelling & Software, 20*(2), 153–163. doi:10.1016/j.envsoft.2003.12.017

Beachboard, J. C. (2002). Rigor, relevance and research paradigms: A journey from practitioner to neophyte researcher. *AMCIS2002* (pp. 1660-1666).

Beall, A., & Zeoli, L. (2008). Participatory modeling of endangered wildlife systems: simulation the sage-grouse and land use in central Washington. *Ecological Economics, 68*, 24–33. doi:10.1016/j.ecolecon.2008.08.019

Becerra-Fernandez, I., & Sabherval, R. (2001). Organizational knowledge management: A contingency perspective. *Journal of Management Information Systems, 18*(1), 23–55.

Bechek, B., & Brea, C. (2001). Deciphering collaborative commerce. *International Journal of Business Strategy, 3*(4), 36–38. doi:10.1108/eb040157

Bellinger, G., Castro, D., & Mills, A. (2004). *Data, information, knowledge, and wisdom*. available at: www.systems-thinking.org/dikw/dikw.htm, accessed February 14 2009.

Belton, V., & Stewart, T. (2002). *Multiple criteria decision analysis: An integrated approach*. Kluwer Academic Publishers.

Bencze, L. (1979). *A vadállomány fenntartásának lehetőségei. A vadászati ökológia alapjai*. Budapest, Hungary: Akadémiai Kiadó.

Benson, B., & Sage, A. (1993). Emerging technology-evaluation methodology: with application to micro-electromechanical systems. *IEEE Transactions on Engineering Management, 40*(2), 114–123. doi:doi:10.1109/17.277403

Berger, A. N., & Humphrey, D. (1992). Measurement of efficiency issues in commercial banking, in Z. Griliches (Ed.), *Output measurement in the service sector* (pp. 245-278). Chicago: The University of Chicago Press.

Bergström, R., Huldt, H., & Nilsson, U. (Eds.). (1992). *Swedish game - Biology and management*. Stockholm, Sweden: Svenska Jägareförbundet.

Berners-Lee, T. (1999). *Weaving the web*. San Francisco, CA: Harper.

Berntsen, J., Haugaard-Nielsen, H., Olesen, H., Petersen, B. M., Jensen, E. S., & Thomsen, A. (2004). Modelling dry matter production and resource use in intercrops of pea and barley. *Field Crops Research, 88*(1), 59–73. doi:10.1016/j.fcr.2003.11.012

Bhalme, H. N., & Mooley, D. A. (1979). On the performance of modified Palmer index. In *Proceedings of International Symposium: Hydrological Aspects of Droughts* (pp. 373-383).

Bhandari, A. L., Ladha, J. K., Pathak, H., Padre, A. T., Dawe, D., & Gupta, R. K. (2002). Trends of yield and soil nutrient status in a long-term rice-wheat experiment in the Indo-Gangetic Plains of India. *Soil Science Society of America Journal, 66*, 162–170. doi:10.2136/sssaj2002.0162

Billard, M. (1992). Do women make better managers? *Working Woman, 17*(3), 68–71, 106–107.

Birol, E., Karousakis, K., & Koundouri, P. (2006). Using economic valuation techniques to inform water resources management: A survey and critical appraisal of available techniques and an application. *The Science of the Total Environment, 365*(1-3), 105–122. doi:10.1016/j.scitotenv.2006.02.032

Blackler, F. (1995). Knowledge, knowledge work and organizations: An overview and interpretation. In C. W. Choo, N. Bontis (Eds.), *The Strategic Management of Intellectual Capital and Organizational Knowledge*. New York: Oxford University Press.

Boland, R. (1978). The process and product of system design. *Management Science, 28*(9), 887–898. doi:10.1287/mnsc.24.9.887

Bowman, R. J. (1995). A high wire act. *Distribution,* 78-81.

Bradley, P. (1993). Third party logistics: DuPont takes the plunge. *Purchasing,* 33-7.

Braglia, M., & Petroni, A. (1999). Evaluating and selectng investments in industrial robots. *International Journal of Production Research, 37*(18), 4157–4178. do i:doi:10.1080/002075499189718

Brainerd, S. (2007). *European charter on hunting and biodiversity (Vol. 2)*. Budakeszi, Hungary: CIC - International Council for Game and Wildlife Conservation.

Brannen, J. (2005). Mixing methods: The entry of qualitative and quantitative approaches into the research process. *International Journal of Social Research Methodology, 8*(3), 173–184. doi:10.1080/13645570500154642

Brans, J. P., & Vincke, P. (1985). A preference ranking organization method: the PROMETHEE method for multiple criteria decision-making. *Management Science, 31*, 647–656. doi:doi:10.1287/mnsc.31.6.647

Braud, W., & Anderson, J. (1998). *Transpersonal research methods for the Social Sciences: Honoring human experience*. USA: Sage Pub.

Braun, C. E. (Ed.). (2005). *Techniques for wildlife investigations and management*. Bethesda, Maryland: The Wildlife Society.

Breetz, H. L., Fisher-Vanden, K., Garzon, L., Jacobs, H., Kroetz, D., & Terry, R. (2004). *Water quality trading offset initiatives in the US: A comprehensive survey*. Hanover, NH: Dartmouth College.

Brin, S., & Page, L. (1998). The anatomy of a large-scale hypertextual web search engine. *Computer Networks, 30*, 107–117.

Brisson, N., Bussiére, F., Ozier-Lafontaine, H., Tournebize, R., & Sinoquet, H. (2004). Adaptation of the crop model STICS to intercropping. Theoretical basis and parameterisation. *Agronomie, 24*, 409–421. doi:10.1051/agro:2004031

Brown, J., & Langer, E. (1990). Mindfulness and intelligence: A comparison. *Educational Psychologist, 25*(3/4), 305–320. doi:10.1207/s15326985ep2503&4_9

Burn, J., & Robins, G. (2003). Moving towards egovernment: A case study of organizational change processes. *Logistics Information Management, 16*(1), 25–35. doi:10.1108/09576050310453714

Burroughs, S. H., & Lattrell, T. R. (1998). Data compression technology in ASIC cores. *Journal of Research and Development (Srinagar), 42*(6), 725–732.

Burton-Jones, A., & Hubona, G. S. (2005). Individual differences usage behavior: revisiting a technology acceptance model assumption. *The Data Base for Advances in Information Systems, 36*(2), 58–76.

Butler, T. (2001). Making sense of knowledge: A constructivist viewpoint. *AMCIS2001* (pp. 1462 -1466).

Butler, M., Herlihy, P., & Keenan, P. (2005). Integrating information technology and operational research in the management of milk collection. *Journal of Food Engineering, 70*, 341–349. doi:10.1016/j.jfoodeng.2004.02.046

Cairns, C. N. (2005). E-waste and the consumer: Improving options to reduce, reuse and recycle. In *Proceedings of the 2005 IEEE International Symposium on Electronics and the Environment* (pp. 237-242).

Caldwell, R. M. (1995). Simulation models for intercropping systems. In *H. Sinoquet & P. Cruz (Es.), Ecophysiology of Tropical Intercropping* (pp. 353–368). Paris: INRA editions.

Campbell, J. E., & Garand, J. C. (Eds.). (2000). *Before the Vote: Forecasting American National Elections*. Thousand Oaks, CA: Sage.

Campbell, J. E., & Lewis-Beck, M. (Eds.). (2008, April-June). US presidential election forecasting. *International Journal of Forecasting, 4*.

Cao, X., & Huang, H. K. (2000). Current status and future advances of digital radiography and PACS. *IEEE Engineering in Medicine and Biology Magazine, 19*(5), 80–88. doi:10.1109/51.870234

Carberry, P. S., McCown, R. L., Muchow, R. C., Dimes, J. P., Probert, M. E., Poulton, P. L., & Dalgliesh, N. P. (1996). Simulation of a legume ley farming system in northern Australia using the agricultural production systems simulator. *Australian Journal of Experimental Agriculture, 36*, 1037–1048. doi:10.1071/EA9961037

Carlsson, C., & Fuller, R. (1996). Fuzzy multiple criteria decision making: Recent developments. *Fuzzy Sets and Systems, 78*, 139–153. doi:doi:10.1016/0165-0114(95)00165-4

Carpenter, S. L., & Kennedy, W. J. D. (2001). *Managing public disputes: A practical guide for government, business and citizens groups.* New York: Jossey-Bass, John Wiley and Sons, Inc.

Carr, N. (2008). *The big switch: Rewiring the world, from Edison to Google* (p. 219). New York: W.W. Norton & Company.

Carver, S., & Peckham, R. (1999). Using GIS on the internet for planning. J. C. Stillwell, S. Geertman, & S. Openshaw (Eds.), *Geographical information and planning* (pp. 371–390). New York: Springer.

Carver, S. J. (1991). Integrating multicriteria evaluation with geographical information systems. *International Journal of Geographical Information Systems, 5*(3), 321–339. doi:doi:10.1080/02693799108927858

Cater-Steel, A. (2009). IT service departments struggle to adopt a service-oriented philosophy. *International Journal of Information Systems in the Service Sector, 1*(2), 69–77.

Chakhar, S., & Martel, J.-M. (2003). Enhancing geographical information systems capabilities with multi-criteria evaluation functions. *Journal of Geographic Information and Decision Analysis, 7*(2), 47–71.

Chan, C. K., & Lee, H. W. J. (2005). Understanding and managing the intrinsic dynamics of supply chains. In *Successful Strategies in Supply Chain Management* (p. 174). Hershey, PA: IGI Global.

Chander, S., Aggarwal, P. K., Kalra, N., Swoop, R., & Parsed, J. S. (2002a). Assessment of yield losses due to stem borer, Scirpophaga incertulas in rice using simulation models. *Journal of Entomological Research, 26*(1), 23–28.

Chander, S., Aggarwal, P. K., & Reddy, P. R. (2002b). Assessment of yield loss in rice due to bacterial leaf blight using simulation models. *Annals Plant Protection Sciences, 10*(2), 277–281.

Chandra, C., & Grabis, J. (2007). Knowledge management as the basis of crosscutting problem-solving approaches. In *Supply Chain Configuration: Concepts, Solutions, and Applications* (p. 130). New York: Springer.

Charnes, A., Cooper, W. W., & Rhodes, E. (1978). Measuring the efficiency of decision making units'. *European Journal of Operational Research, 2*, 429–444. doi:10.1016/0377-2217(78)90138-8

Checkland, P. (1984). *Systems thinking, systems practice.* Great Britain: John Wiley & Sons Ltd.

Childers, L. (2000). Access grid: immersive group-to-group collaborative visualization. *Argonne National Laboratory.* Retrieved from http://www.fp.mcs.anl.gov/fl/publications-electronic-files/ag-immersive-821.pdf

Chipanshi, A. C., Ripley, E. A., & Lawford, R. G. (1997). Early prediction of spring wheat yields in Saskatchewan from current and historical weather data using the CERES-Wheat model. *Agricultural and Forest Meteorology, 84*, 223–232. doi:10.1016/S0168-1923(96)02363-5

Choennia, S., Bakkera, R., & Baetsa, W. (2003). On the evaluation of workflow systems in business processes. *The Electronic Journal of Information Systems Evaluation, 6*(2).

Choo, C. W. (1998). *The knowing organization: How organizations use information to construct meaning, create knowledge, and make decisions.* New York: Oxford University Press.

Christopher, M. (1999). Logistics and supply chain management: strategies for reducing cost and improving service. *International Journal of Logistics, 2*(1).

Churchman, C. W. (1968). *The systems approach.* New York: Laurel.

Civita, M. (1994). *Le carte della vulnerabilità degli acquiferi all'inquinamento*. Belogna, Italy: Pitarora.

Civita, M., & De Regibus, C. (1995). *Sperimentazione di alcune metodologie per la valutazione della vulnerabilita degli aquiferi*. Bologna, Italy: Pitarora.

Clark, J. (1999). *Netscape time*. New York: St. Martin's Press.

Clayton, D., & Lynch, T. (2002). Ten years of strategies to increase participation of women in computing programs: The central Queensland University experience: 1999-2001. *SIGCSE Bulletin, 34*(2), 89–93. doi:10.1145/543812.543838

Clean Water Services (CWS). (2004). *Revised temperature management plan*. Retrieved June 7, 2009, from http://www.cleanwaterservices.org/PlansAndProjects/Plans/TempManagementPlan.aspx

Climate Impacts Group. (2004). *Forest growth and climate change*. Seattle, WA: University of Washington.

Climate Impacts Group. (2009). *Climate change streamflow scenario tool*. Seattle, WA: University of Washington. Retrieved June 7, 2009, from http://cses.washington.edu/cig/fpt/ccstreamflowtool/sftscenarios.shtml

Cockerill, K., Passell, H., & Tidwell, V. (2006). Cooperative modeling: Building bridges between science and the public. *Journal of the American Water Resources Association, 42*(2), 457–471. doi:10.1111/j.1752-1688.2006.tb03850.x

Cohen, S. L., & Leavengood, S. (1978). The utility of the WAMS: Shouldn't it relate to discriminatory behavior. *Academy of Management Journal, 21*(4), 742–748. doi:10.2307/255716

Commission of Agricultural Meteorology (CAgM). (1992). *Monitoring Assessment and Combat of Drought and Desertification*.

Commission of Agricultural Meteorology (CAgM). (1993). Report *of the RA II Working Group on Agricultural Meteorology, Part IV: Drought and Desertification* (Rep. No. 52).

competitiveness. *International Journal of Society Systems Science, 1*(3), 293-305.

Conger, S. (2009). Information technology service management and opportunities for information systems curricula. *International Journal of Information Systems in the Service Sector, 1*(2), 58–68.

Conservation Technology Information Center (CTIC). (2006). *Getting paid for stewardship: An agricultural community water quality trading guide*. West Lafayette, IN: Conservation Technology Information Center.

Cooper, W. W., Seiford, L., & Tone, K. (2006). *Introduction to data envelopment analysis and its uses with DEA-solver software and references*. New York: Springer Publishers.

Cordano, M., Scherer, R. F., & Owen, C. L. (2002). Attitudes toward women as managers: Sex versus culture. *Women in Management Review, 17*(2), 51–60. doi:10.1108/09649420210421754

Courtney, J. F., Croasdell, D. T., & Paradice, D. B. (1998). Inquiring organizations. *Australian Journal of Information Systems, 6*(1), 75–91.

Crino, M. D., White, M. C., & DeSanctis, G. L. (1981). A comment on the dimensionality and reliability of the women as managers scale (WAMS). *Academy of Management Journal, 24*(4), 866. doi:10.2307/256183

Crossland, M., Wyne, B., & Perkins, W. (1995). Spatial decision support systems: An overview of technology and a test of efficacy. *Decision Support Systems, 14*, 219–235. doi:10.1016/0167-9236(94)00018-N

Crouter, J. P. (1987). Hedonic estimation applied to a water rights market. *Land Economics, 63*, 259–271. doi:10.2307/3146835

Csányi, S. (1997). Országos Vadgazdálkodási Adattár. *Vadgazdálkodás - A Magyar Mezőgazdaság melléklete, 1*, 3.

Csányi, S. (Ed.). (1999b). *Vadgazdálkodási Adattár 1994-1998*. Gödöllő, Hungary: Országos Vadgazdálkodási Adattár, GATE Vadbiológiai és Vadgazdálkodási Tanszék.

Csányi, S. (1993). A basis for sustainable wise use of game in Hungary: defining management regions. *Landscape and Urban Planning, 27*, 199–205. doi:10.1016/0169-2046(93)90050-N

Csányi, S. (1994). Moving toward coordinated management of timber and other resource uses in Hungarian forests. *Forestry Chronicle, 70*(5), 555–561.

Csányi, S. (1998). Game management regions and three-level planning in Hungary. *Hungarian Agricultural Research, 7*(2), 12–14.

Csányi, S. (1999a). Regional game management system in Hungary. *Gibier, Faune Sauvage, 15*(3), 929–936.

Csányi, S. (2003). *A nagyvadállomány körzettervekből adódó szabályozásának megvalósítása (kézirat)*. Gödöllő, Hungary: Országos Vadgazdálkodási Adattár.

Csányi, S. (2007b). *Vadbiológia*. Budapest: Mezőgazda Kiadó.

Csányi, S. (Ed.). (2006). *Útmutató a vadgazdálkodási üzemtervek készítéséhez és vezetéséhez*. Gödöllő, Hungary: Országos Vadgazdálkodási Adattár.

Csányi, S., & Ritter, D. (1999). A fenntartható nagyvadlétszám meghatározása az állomány területi eloszlása alapján térinformatikai eszközökkel. *Vadbiológia, 6*, 23–32.

Csikszentmihalyi, M. (1979). The flow experience. In G. Davidson (Ed.), *Consciousness: Brain and states of awareness and mysticism* (pp. 63-67). Simon & Schuster.

Csőre, P. (1996). *A magyar vadászat története*. Budapest, Hungary: Mezőgazda Kiadó.

Damm, G. R., Baldus, R. D., & Wollscheid, K.-U. (Eds.). (2008). *Best practices in sustainable hunting - A guide to best practices from around the world (Vol. 1)*. Budakeszi, Hungary: CIC - International Council for Game and Wildlife Conservation.

Daugherty, P. J., Atank, T. P., & Rogers, D. S. (1996). Third-party logistics providers: purchasers' perceptions. *International Journal of Purchasing and Materials Managements, 32*(2), 23–29.

Davis, F. D. (1989). Perceived usefulness, perceived ease of use, and user acceptance. *Management Information Systems Quarterly, 13*(3), 319–339. doi:10.2307/249008

Davison, R. M., Wagner, C., & Ma, L. C. K. (2005). From government to e-government. a transition model. *Information Technology & People, 18*(3), 280–299. doi:10.1108/09593840510615888

Dawo, M. I., Wilkinson, J. M., Sanders, F. E. T., & Pilbeam, D. J. (2007). The yield of fresh and ensiled plant material from intercropped maize (*Zea mays*) and beans (*Phaseolus vulgaris*). *Journal of the Science of Food and Agriculture, 87*, 1391–1399. doi:10.1002/jsfa.2879

Day, R. E. (2005). Clearing up "implicit knowledge": implications for knowledge management, information science, psychology, and social epistemology. *Journal of the American Society for Information Science and Technology, 56*(6), 630–635. doi:10.1002/asi.20153

Debian (2007). *Debian – The universal operating system. software in the public interest*. Retrieved May 28, 2007, from www.debian.org

Deering, S., & Hinden, R. (1998). *Internet protocol, version 6 (ipv6) specification*. Retrieved from http://www.ietf.org/rfc/rfc2460.txt

DeLone, W. H., & McLean, E. R. (1992). Information systems success: The quest for the dependent variable. *Information Systems Research, 3*(1), 60–95. doi:10.1287/isre.3.1.60

DeLone, W. H., & McLean, E. R. (2003). The DeLone and McLean model of information systems success: A ten-year update. *Journal of Management Information Systems, 19*(4), 9–30.

DeLone, W. H., & McLean, E. R. (2004). Measuring e-commerce success: applying the DeLone & McLean information systems success model. *International Journal of Electronic Commerce, 9*(4), 9–30.

Densham, P. J., & Goodchild, M. F. (1989). Spatial decision support systems: a research agenda. *Proceedings of GIS/LIS'89* (pp. 706-71), Orlando, FL.

Denzin, N. K., & Lincoln, Y. S. (Eds.). (2000). *The handbook of qualitative research* (2nd ed.). Thousand Oaks, California: Sage Pub.

Denzin, N. K., & Lincoln, Y. S. (Eds.). (2003). *The landscape of qualitative research: Theories and issues* (2nd ed.). Thousand Oaks, California: Sage Pub.

Derekenaris, G., Garofalakis, J., Makris, C., Prentzas, J., Sioutas, S., & Tsakalidis, A. (2001). Integrating GIS, GPS and GSM technologies for the effective management of ambulances. *Computers, Environment and Urban Systems, 25*, 267–278. doi:10.1016/S0198-9715(00)00025-9

Dickinson, G., Fischetti, L., & Heard, S. (2004). *HL7 EHR System Functional Model.* Retrieved June 4, 2009, from http://www.telemedicina.buap.mx/PaginaNueva/Archivos/Estandar_7.pdf.

Diprete, T. A., & Buchman, C. (2006). Gender-specific trends in the value of education and the emerging gender gap in completion. *Demography, 43*(2), 1–24. doi:10.1353/dem.2006.0003

Dobbins, G. H., Cardy, R. L., & Truxillo, D. M. (1988). The effects of purpose of appraisal and individual differences in stereotypes of women on sex differences in performance ratings: A laboratory and field study. *The Journal of Applied Psychology, 73*(3), 551–558. doi:10.1037/0021-9010.73.3.551

Dorigo, W. A., Zurita-Milla, R., de Wit, A. J. W., Brazile, J., Singh, R., & Schaepman, M. E. (2006). A review on reflective remote sensing and data assimilation techniques for enhanced agro-ecosystem modelling. *International Journal of Applied Earth Observation and Geoinformation, 9*(2), 165–193. doi:10.1016/j.jag.2006.05.003

Dosios, K., Paparrizos, K., Papatzikos, N., & Sifaleras, A. (2002). LinPro, an educational informational system for linear programming. In *Proceedings of the 15th National Conference of Hellenic Operational Research Society,* Tripoli, Greece (pp. 182-189).

Dosios, K., Paparrizos, K., Samaras, N., & Sifaleras, A. (2003). NetPro, an educational platform for network optimization. In *Proceedings of the 16th National Conference of Hellenic Operational Research Society,* Larissa, Greece (Vol. 1, pp. 287-295).

Doty, D. H., & Glick, W. H. (1994). Typologies as a unique form of theory building: Toward improved understanding and modeling. *Academy of Management Review, 19*(2), 230–251. doi:10.2307/258704

Douglas, S., Tanin, E., Harwood, A., & Karunasekera, S. (2005). Enabling massively multi-player online gaming applications on a p2p architecture. In *Proceedings of the International Conference on Information and Automation,* Colombo, Sri Lanka (7-12).

Durfee-Thompson, J. L., Forster, C. B., Mills, J. I., & Peterson, T. R. (2005, June). The ice cream game: A systems thinking approach to environmental conflict resolution. In *Proceedings of the 8th Biennial Conference on Communication and Environment,* Jekyll Island, Georgia.

Duxbury, J. M., Abrol, I. P., Gupta, R. K., & Bronson, K. (2000). Analysis of long-term soil fertility experiments with rice-wheat rotation in South Asia. In Abrol, I. P., Bronson, K., Duxbury, J. M., & Gupta, R. K. (Eds.), *Long-term soil fertility experiments in Rice-Wheat Cropping Systems.* New Delhi, India.

Dwyer, S. J. (2000). A personalized view of the history of PACS in the USA. In G.J. Blaine, & E.L. Siegel (Eds.), *Proceedings of the SPIE: vol. 3980. Medical imaging 2000: PACS design and evaluation: Engineering and clinical issues* (pp. 2-9).

E.U. Council. (1998). Council directive 98/83 about water quality intended for human consumption. *Official paper of the European Communities, L330,* 32-54.

Eastham, J. F., Sharples, L., & Ball, S. D. (2001). *The catering and food retails industries: contextual insights. Food Supply Chain Management: Issues for the Hospitality and Retail Sectors* (pp. 3–21). Oxford, UK: Butterworth & Heineman.

Ebner, M. (2007). *Sustainable hunting: 20 years Intergroup "Sustainable hunting, biodiversity and countryside activities" in the European Parliament.* Bozen, Italy: Verlagsanstalt Athesia.

e-commerce practices. *Journal of Technology Research, 1,* 1-19. Retrieved from www.aabri.com

Eicher, C. K., & Staatz, M. J. (1998). *International agricultural development.* Baltimore: Johns Hopkins University Press.

Eisenhardt, K. M. (1989). Building theories from case study research. *Academy of Management Review, 14*(4), 532–550. doi:10.2307/258557

Eisenhardt, K. M., & Graebner, M. E. (2007). Theory building from cases: Opportunities and challenges. *Academy of Management Journal, 50*(1), 25–32.

Erikson, R. S., & Wlezien, C. (2008). Are political markets really superior to polls as election predictions? *Public Opinion Quarterly, 72,* 190–215. doi:10.1093/poq/nfn010

European Communities. (1992). Council directive 92/43/EEC of 21 May 1992 on the conservation of natural habitats and wild fauna and flora. *Official Journal of the European Communities, L 206*, 7-49.

Evola, R. L. (1997). *Patient administration. Health level seven, version 2.3.* Retrieved June 4, 2009, from http://www.dmi.columbia.edu/resources/hl7doc/hl72.3/ch3.pdf.

Faeth, P. (2000). *Fertile ground: Nutrient trading's potential to cost-effectively improve water quality*. Washington, DC: World Resources Institute.

Färe, R., & Grosskopf, S. (1996) *Intertemporal production frontiers: with dynamic DEA*. Norwell, MA: Kluwer Academic Publishers.

Färe, R., & Primont, D. (1988). Efficiency Measures for Multiplant Firms with Limited Data. In W. Eichorn (Ed.), *Measurement in economics: Theory and applications of economic indices*. Heidelberg, Germany: Physica-Verlag.

Färe, R., Grosskopf, S., & Lovell, C. A. K. (1994). *Production frontiers*. Cambridge, UK: Cambridge University Press.

Färe, R. (1988). Addition and Efficiency. *The Quarterly Journal of Economics, 101*(4), 861–866. doi:10.2307/1884181

Farrell, M. J. (1957). The measurement of productive efficiency. *Journal of the Royal Statistical Society* (Series A120), 253-261.

Farrow, R. S., Scheltz, M. T., Celikkol, P., & Van Houtven, G. L. (2005). Pollution trading in water quality limited areas: Use of benefits assessment and cost-effective trading ratios. *Land Economics, 81*(2), 191–205.

Faux, J., & Perry, G. M. (1999). Estimating irrigation water value using hedonic price analysis: a case study in Malheur County, Oregon. *Land Economics, 75*, 440–452. doi:10.2307/3147189

Federer, W. T. (1993). Statistical design and analysis for intercropping experiments: *Vol. 1. Two crops*. New York: Springer.

Fielden, K. (2005). Chapter 11: Mindfulness: An essential quality of integrated wisdom. In J. Courtney, J. D. Haynes & D. Paradice (Eds.), I*nquiring Organizations: Moving from Knowledge Management to Wisdom* (pp. 211-228). Hershey, USA: Idea Group Inc.

Fielden, K., & Joyce, D. (2008). An analysis of published research on academic integrity. *International Journal of Information Integrity, 4*(2), 4–24.

Figueira, J., Greco, S., & Ehrgott, M. (Eds.). (2005). *Multiple criteria decision analysis: State of the art surveys*. New York: Springer.

Flood, R. L. (1990). Liberating systems theory: Toward critical systems thinking. *Human Relations, 43*(1), 49–75. doi:10.1177/001872679004300104

Ford, A. (2005). Simulating the impacts of a strategic fuel reserve in California. *Energy Policy, 33*, 483–498. doi:10.1016/j.enpol.2003.08.013

Ford, A. (2009). *Modeling the environment* (2nd ed.). Washington, DC: Island Press.

Ford, A., Vogstad, K., & Flynn, H. (2006). Simulating price patterns for tradable green certificates to promote electricity generation from wind. *Energy Policy, 35*(1), 91–111. doi:10.1016/j.enpol.2005.10.014

Forrester, J. (1961). *Industrial dynamics*. Walthan, MA: Pegasus Communications.

Forrester, J. (1969). *Urban dynamics*. Walthan, MA: Pegasus Communications.

Forstner, M., Reimoser, F., Hackl, J., & Heckl, F. (2003). *Criteria and Indicators of Sustainable Hunting* (English Version. Translation of Monograph No. 158 (2001) ed. Vol. 163 (M-163)). Wien, Austria: Federal Ministry for Agriculture, Forestry, Environment and Water Management.

Franklin, C. (1992). An introduction to geographic information systems: Linking maps to databases. *Database, 15*, 12–21.

Frank, W., Thill, J., & Batta, R. (2000). Spatial decision support system for hazardous material truck routing. *Transportation Research Part C, Emerging Technologies, 8*, 337–359. doi:10.1016/S0968-090X(00)00007-3

Fukuyama, H. (1996). Returns to scale and efficiency of credit associations in Japan. *Japan and the World Economy*, *8*, 259–277. doi:10.1016/0922-1425(96)00041-2

Fukuyama, H., & Weber, W. L. (2008a). Japanese banking inefficiency and shadow pricing. *Mathematical and Computer Modelling*, *48*, 1854–1867. doi:10.1016/j.mcm.2008.03.004

Fukuyama, H., & Weber, W. L. (2008b). Estimating inefficiency, technological change and shadow prices of problem loans for regional banks and shinkin banks in Japan. *The Open Management Journal*, *1*, 1–11. doi:10.2174/1874948800801010001

Fülemen, Z., & Csányi, S. (2003). *Programcsomag a vadállománybecslési és a vadgazdálkodási jelentések feldolgozásához (JAGE 1-4)*. Gödöllő, Hungary: Országos Vadgazdálkodási Adattár.

Galvão, J. R. (2000, December). Modeling reality with simulation games for cooperative learning. In *Proceedings of the 2000 Winter Simulation Conference*, Orlando, FL.

Gandal, N. (2001). The dynamics of competition in the internet search engine market. *International Journal of Industrial Organization*, *19*, 1103–1117. doi:10.1016/S0167-7187(01)00065-0

Gan, Y., & Zhu, Z. (2007). A learning framework for knowledge building and collective wisdom advancement in virtual learning communities. *Educational Technology & Society*, *10*(1), 206–226.

García-Barrios, L., Mayer-Foulkes, D., Franco, M., Urquijo-Vásquez, G., & Franco-Pérez, J. (2001). Development and validation of a spatially explicit individual-based mixed crop growth model. *Bulletin of Mathematical Biology*, *63*, 507–526. doi:10.1006/bulm.2000.0226

Gell, G. (2000). PACS-Graz, 1985-2000: from a scientific pilot to a state-wide multimedia radiological information system. In G.J. Blaine, & E.L. Siegel (Eds.), *Proceedings of the SPIE: vol. 3980. Medical imaging 2000: PACS design and evaluation: Engineering and clinical issues* (pp. 19-28).

Gemitzi, A., Petalas, C., Tsihtintzis, V., & Pisinaras, V. (2006). Assessment of groundwater vulnerability to pollution: A combination of GIS, fuzzy logic and decision making techniques. *Environmental Geology*, *49*(5), 653–673. doi:10.1007/s00254-005-0104-1

Gibbs, W. J., & Maher, J. V. (1967). *Rainfall Deciles as drought indicators* (Bureau of Meteorology Bulletin No. 48, p. 29). Melbourne, Australia: Commonwealth of Australia.

Gijsman, A. J., Hoogenboom, G., Parton, W. J., & Kerridge, P. C. (2002). Modifying DSSAT for low-input agricultural systems, using a soil organic matter-residue module from CENTURY. *Agronomy Journal*, *94*(3), 462–474. doi:10.2134/agronj2002.0462

Glasser, B., & Strauss, A. (1967). *A discovery of grounded theory*. Chicago: Aldine.

Gogu, R. C., & Dessargues, A. (2000). Current trends and future challenges in groundwater vulnerability assessment using overlay and index methods. *Environmental Geology*, *39*(6), 549–559. doi:10.1007/s002540050466

Goodenough, U., & Woodruff, P. (2001). Mindful virtue, mindful reverence. *Zygon*, *36*(4), 585–595. doi:10.1111/0591-2385.00386

Gooley, T. B. (1994). Partnership can make the customer-service difference. *Traffic Management*, *42*(5).

Gossain, S. (2002). Craking the collaboration code. *The Journal of Business Strategy*, *23*(6), 20–25. doi:10.1108/eb040282

Goswami, B. N., Venugopal, V., Sengupta, D., Madhusoodanan, M. S., & Xavier, P. K. (2006). Increasing Trend of Extreme Rain Events over India in a warming Environment. *Science*, *314*, 1442–1444. doi:10.1126/science.1132027

Gott, J. R., & Colley, W. N. (2008, Nov.). Median statistics in polling. *Mathematical and Computer Modelling*, *48*, 1396–1408. doi:10.1016/j.mcm.2008.05.038

Graafland, I., & Ettedgui, E. (2002). Benchmarking e-government in Europe and the US. *Statistical Indicators Benchmarking the Information Society*. Retrieved September 14, 2008 from http://www.sibis-eu.org/

Graeber, S. (1997). The impact of workflow management systems on the design of hospital information systems. In *Proceedings of the American medical informatics association annual fall symposium* (pp. 856-860).

Grand, G., & Chau, D. (2006). Developing a generic framework for e-government. In H. Gorden & F. Tan (Eds.), *Advance topic in global information management* (Vol. 5 pp. 72-76). Hershey, PA: IGI Global

Grant, R. F. (1992). Simulation of competition among plant populations under different managements and climates. *Agron. Abstr, 6.*

Grant, K., Gilmore, A., Carson, D., Laney, R., & Pickett, B. (2001). "Experiential" research methodology: an integrated academic-practitioner "team" approach. *Qualitative Market Research: An International Journal, 4*(2), 66–74. doi:10.1108/13522750110388563

Grant, R. F. (1994). Simulation of competition between barley (*Hordeum vulgare L.*) and wild oat (*Avena fatua L.*) under different managements and climates. *Ecological Modelling, 71*, 269–287. doi:10.1016/0304-3800(94)90138-4

Greene, J. (2005, September 26). Troubling exits at Microsoft. *Business Week*, 98-108.

Grimson, J., Stephens, G., Jung, B., Grimson, W., Berry, D., & Pardon, S. (2001). Sharing health-care records over the internet. *IEEE Internet Computing, 5*(3), 49–58. doi:10.1109/4236.935177

Grönroos, C. (1984). A service quality model and its marketing implications. *European Journal of Marketing, 18*(4), 36. doi:10.1108/EUM0000000004784

Gulhati, K. (1990). Attitudes toward women managers: Comparison of attitudes of male and female managers in India. *Economic and Political Weekly, 2*(1), 17–24.

Gupta, M. P., & Jana, D. (2003). E-government evaluation: a framework and case study. *Government Information Quarterly, 20*(4), 365–387. doi:10.1016/j.giq.2003.08.002

Gvishiani, A. D., Zelevinsky, A. V., Keilis-Borok, V. I., & Kosobokov, V. I. (1980). Methods and agorithms for interpretation of seismological data. *Computational Semiology, 13*, Nauka, Moscow.

Hafberg, G. (1995). Integration of geographic information systems and navigation systems for moving (dynamic) objects like vehicles and ships. In *Proceedings of ESRI User Conference* (pp. 272-274).

Hahn, B., & Valentine, D. (2007). *Essential MATLAB for engineers and scientists* (3rd ed.). London: Newnes Publications.

Hair, J. F., Tatham, R., Anderson, R., & Black, W. (1998). *Multivariate data analysis.* Upper Saddle River, NJ: Prentice Hall.

Halaris, C., Magoutas, B., Papadomichelaki, X., & Mentzas, G. (2007). Classification and synthesis of quality approaches in E-government services. *Internet Research, 17*(4), 378–401. doi:10.1108/10662240710828058

Hancock, D. (1985). The financial firm: Production with monetary and non-monetary goods. *The Journal of Political Economy, 93*, 859–880. doi:10.1086/261339

Hangrove, W., Hoffman, F., Sterling, T., & Kay, C. (2001). The do-it-yourself supercomputer. *Scientific American, 285*(2), 72–80.

Hanley, N., & Spash, C. L. (1993). *Cost benefit analysis and the environment.* London: Edward Elgar.

Hansell, S. (2001, March 11). Red face for the Internet's blue chip. *New York Times*, Section 3, pp. 1, 14.

Harimaya, K. (2004). Measuring the efficiency in Japanese credit cooperatives. *Review of Monetary and Financial Studies, 21*, 92–111.

Hartman, L. M., & Anderson, R. L. (1962). Estimating the value of irrigation water from farm sales in Northeastern Colorado. *Journal of Farm Economics, 44*(1), 207–213. doi:10.2307/1235499

Hasselbring, W., Peterson, R., Smits, M., & Spanjers, R. (2000). Strategic information management for a Dutch university hospital. In A. Hasman, B. Blobel (Eds.), *Proceedings of Medical Infobahn for Europe* (pp. 885-889).

Haynes, J. (2001). Inquiring organizations and tacit knowledge. *AMCIS2001* (pp. 1544- 1547).

Heeks, R. (2003). *Success and failure rates of e-government in developing/transitional countries: overview* (Tech. Rep.). Manchester, UK: University of Manchester, E-government for development, institute for development policy and management.

Heitmann, K. U. (2002). *XML encoding rules of HL7 v2 messages - v2.xml.* Document number v2.xml Rev. 3.672. Retrieved June 4, 2009, from http://www.hl7.org/Special/committees/xml/drafts/v2xml1mlbb.pdf.

Helft, M., & Sorkin, A. R. (2008, February 2). Eyes on Google, Microsoft bids $44 billion for Yahoo. *New York Times*, A1.

Hellens, L. A. V., Nielsen, S. H., & Trauth, E. M. (2001). *Breaking and entering the male domain: Women in the IT industry.* Paper presented at the 2001 ACM SIGCPR Conference on Computer Personnel Research, San Diego, CA.

Herold, K. (2005). *A Buddhist model for the informational person.* Paper presented at the second Asian Pacific Computing and Philosophy Conference, Bangkok.

Hiraoka, L. S. (2005). *Underwriting the Internet: How technical advances, financial Engineering, and entrepreneurial genius are building the information highway* (pp. 96–97). Armonk, NY: M.E. Sharpe.

HL7 (n.d.). *HL7 ANSI-approved standards.* Retrieved June 4, 2009, from http://www.hl7.org/documentcenter/public/faq/ansi_approved.htm.

HL7 Canada. (2002). *Guidebook for HL7 development projects in Canada.* Retrieved June 4, 2009, from http://sl.infoway-inforoute.ca/downloads/hl7can_Guidebook_v1_0.pdf.

HL7.org. (n.d.). *What is HL7?* Retrieved June 4, 2009, from http://www.hl7.org/about/hl7about.htm.

Hobbs, P. R., & Morris, M. L. (1996). *Meeting South Asia's future food requirements from rice-wheat cropping systems: priority issues facing researchers in the post Green Revolution era* (NRG Paper 96-01). Mexico: CIMMYT.

Holliday, I., & Yep, R. (2005). E-government in China. *Public Administration and Development, 25*, 239–249. doi:10.1002/pad.361

Hollingsworth, D. (1995, January 19). *Workflow management coalition, the workflow reference model.* Document number TC00-1003, Issue 1.1. Retrieved June 4, 2009, from http://www.wfmc.org/standards/docs/tc003v11.pdf.

Holsapple, C. W., & Lee-Post, A. (2006). Defining, assessing, and promoting e-learning success: An information systems perspective. *Decision Sciences Journal of Innovative Education, 4*(1), 67–85.

Horan, R. D. (2001). Differences in social and public risk perceptions and conflicting impacts on point/nonpoint trading ratios. *American Journal of Agricultural Economics, 83*(4), 934–941. doi:10.1111/0002-9092.00220

Horan, R. D., & Shortle, J. S. (2005). When two wrongs make a right: Second-best point-nonpoint trading ratios. *American Journal of Agricultural Economics, 87*(2), 340–352. doi:10.1111/j.1467-8276.2005.00726.x

Horwith, B. (1985). A role for intercropping in modern agriculture. *Bioscience, 35*(5), 286–290. doi:10.2307/1309927

Hosono, K., Sakai, K., & Tsuru, K. (2007). *Consolidation of banks in Japan: Causes and consequences* (Tech. Rep. 07-E-059). Research Institute of Economy, Trade, and Industry, RIETI.

Hossain, M. A., & Tisdell, C. A. (2005). Closing the gender gap in Bangladesh: Inequality in education, employment and earnings. *International Journal of Social Economics, 32*(4), 439–453. doi:10.1108/03068290510591281

Hosterman, H. (2008). *Incorporating environmental integrity in water quality trading: Lessons from the Willamette. Masters project.* Duke University, Nicholas School of the Environment and Earth Sciences.

Hundal, S. S., & Kaur, P. (1999). Evaluation of agronomic practices for rice using computer model, CERES-Rice. *Oryza, 36*.

Hundal, S. S., & Kaur, P. (1996). Climatic change and its impact on crop productivity in Punjab. In Abrol, Y. P., Gadgil, S., & Pant, G. B. (Eds.), *Climatic Variability and Agriculture* (pp. 377–393). India.

Hundal, S. S., Kaur, P., & Dhaliwal, L. K. (1998). Prediction of potential productivity of rice in Punjab, India under synthetic climate change scenarios. In *Proceedings of Modeling for crop-climate-soil-pest system and its applications in sustainable crop production*. Nanjing, China: Jiangsu Academy of Agricultural Sciences Publisher.

Huysman, M. H., Fisher, S. J., & Heng, M. S. (1994). An organizational learning perspective on information systems planning. *The Journal of Strategic Information Systems, 3,* 165–177. doi:10.1016/0963-8687(94)90024-8

Hwang, C. L., & Yoon, K. (1981). *Multiple attribute decision making: methods and applications*. New York: Springer Verlag.

Hwang, C.-L., & Lin, M.-J. (1987). *Group decision making under multiple criteria*. Berlin: Springer-Verlag.

Iacucci, E., Nielsen, P., & Berge, I. (2002). Bootstrapping the electronic patient record infrastructure. In K. Bødker, P. M. Kühn, J. Nørbjerg, J. Simonsen, & V. M. Thanning (Eds.), *Proceedings of the 25th information systems research seminar in scandinavia* (IRIS 25). *New ways of working in IS*. Retrieved June 4, 2009, from http://heim.ifi.uio.no/~pnielsen/PHD/IaNiBe.doc.

Igbaria, M. (1990). End-user computing effectiveness: a structural equation model. *Omega, 18*(6), 637–652. doi:10.1016/0305-0483(90)90055-E

Igbaria, M., & Greenhaus, J. H. (1992). Determinants of MIS employees' turnover intentions: A structural equation model. *Communications of the ACM, 35*(2), 34–49. doi:10.1145/129630.129631

Igbaria, M., Guimaraes, T., & Davis, G. (1995). Testing the determinants of microcomputer usage via a structural equation model. *Journal of Management Information Systems, 11*(4), 87–114.

Igbaria, M., Parasuraman, S., & Greenhaus, J. H. (1997). Status report on women and men in the IT workplace. *Information Systems Management, 14*(3), 44–53. doi:10.1080/10580539708907059

Igbaria, M., Pavri, F. N., & Huff, S. L. (1989). Microcomputer application: an empirical look at usage. *Information & Management, 16*(4), 187–196. doi:10.1016/0378-7206(89)90036-0

Igbaria, M., Zinatelli, N., & Cavaye, A. L. M. (1998). Analysis of information technology success in small firms in New Zealand. *International Journal of Information Management, 18*(2), 103–119. doi:10.1016/S0268-4012(97)00053-4

Ilgen, D. R., & Moore, C. F. (1983). When reason fails: A comment on the reliability and dimensionality of the WAMS. *Academy of Management Journal, 26*(3), 535. doi:10.2307/256265

Imielinski, T., & Navas, J. (1999). GPS based geographic addressing, routing, and resource discovery. *Communications of the ACM, 42,* 86–92. doi:10.1145/299157.299176

Inal, A., Gunes, A., Zhang, F., & Cakmak, I. (2007). Peanut/maize intercropping induced changes in rhizosphere and nutrient concentrations in shoots. *Plant Physiology and Biochemistry, 45,* 350–356. doi:10.1016/j.plaphy.2007.03.016

industry evolution and structure (pp. 24-52). New York: Oxford University Press.

Inouye, L., Moser, L. E., & Melliar-Smith, P. M. (1996). QuickRing ATM switches. In *Proceedings of the Annual Conference on Emerging Technologies and Applications in Communications, (etaCOM)* (32-35).

Institute of Geodesy. Cartography and Remote Sensing, Hungary [FÖMI]. (2009). *Hungarian Corine Land Cover 2000 database (CLC2000)*. Retrieved November 17, 2009, from http://www.fomi.hu/corine/

Interfaceware (2009). *HL7 message sample*. Retrieved June 4, 2009, from http://www.interfaceware.com/manual/messages.html.

IPCC. (2007). Summary for policymakers. In Solomon, S., Qin, D., Manning, M., Chen, Z., Marquis, M., & Averyt, K. B., (Eds.), *Climate change 2007: the physical science basis. Contribution of Working Group I to the Fourth Assessment Report of the Intergovernmental Panel on Climate Change*. New York: Cambridge University Press.

Ivanic, M., & Martin, W. (2008). Implications of higher global food prices for poverty in low-income countries. *World Bank Policy Research Working Paper, 4594.*

Jackson, M. C. (2003). *Systems thinking: creative holism for managers*. Chichester Hoboken, N.J. Wiley.

Jackson, T., Illsley, B., Curry, J., & Rapaport, E. (2008). Amenity migration and sustainable development in remote resource-based communities: Lessons from northern British Columbia. *International Journal of Society Systems Science, 1*(1), 26–46. doi:10.1504/IJSSS.2008.020044

Jagtap, S. S., Mornu, M., & Kang, B. T. (1993). Simulation of growth, development and yield of maize in the transition zone of Nigeria. *Agricultural Systems, 41,* 215–229. doi:10.1016/0308-521X(93)90040-9

Jankowski, P. (1995). Integrating geographical information systems and multiple criteria decision making methods. *International Journal of Geographical Information Systems, 9,* 251–273. doi:doi:10.1080/02693799508902036

Jansen, A. (2005, November 21-23). Assessing E-government progress-why and what. In B. Tessem, J. Iden & G. E. Christensen (Eds.), *Proceedings of the fra norsk konferanse for Organisasjonevs bruk av IT (Nokobit),* Bergen, Norway.

Järvinen, R., & Lehtinen, U. (2004). Services, e-services and e-service innovations – combination of theoretical and practical knowledge. *Frontiers of e-Business Research,* 78-89.

Jashapara, A. (2005). The emerging discourse of knowledge management: a new dawn for information science research. *Journal of Information Science, 31*(2), 136–148. doi:10.1177/0165551505051057

Jennex, M. E., & Olfman, L. (2002). Organizational memory / knowledge effects on productivity, a longitudinal study. In *Proceedings of the 35th Annual Hawaii International Conference on System Sciences, USA* (pp. 1029-1038).

Jensen, E. S. (2006). *Intercrop; Intercropping of cereals and grain legumes for increased production, weed control, improved product quality and prevention of N-losses in European organic farming systems* (Rep. No. QLK5-CT-2002-02352. Risø. Jolliffe, P. A. (1997). Are mixed populations of plant species more productive than pure stands? *Acta Oecologica Scandinavica, 80*(3), 595–602.

Johansson, R. C. (2000). *Pricing irrigation water: a literature review* (Tech. Rep. No. WPS2449). Washington, DC: The World Bank.

Johnson, D., Perkins, C., & Arkko, J. (2003). *Mobility support in IPv6.* Retrieved from http://users.piuha.net/jarkko/publications/mipv6/drafts/mobilev6.html

Joia, L. A. (2007). A heuristic model to implement government-to-government project. *International Journal of Electronic Government, 3*(1), 1–18.

Jones, A. (2009). *The Copenhagen Climate Game.* Retrieved June 7, 2009, from http://sustainer.org/climate_change/documents/copenhagen.pdf

Jones, R. J. (2002). *Who will be in the White House? Predicting Presidential Elections.* New York: Longman.

Jones, R. J. (2007). *The state of presidential election forecasting in 2004.* Paper Presented at the 2007 ISF International Symposium on Forecasting, New York, NY.

Jones, J. W., Hoogenboom, G., Porter, C. H., Boote, K. J., Batchelor, W. D., & Hunt, L. A. (2003). The DSSAT cropping system model. *European Journal of Agronomy, 18,* 235–265. doi:10.1016/S1161-0301(02)00107-7

Jung, B. (2005). DICOM-X - seamless integration of medical images into the EHR. In A. Tsymbal, & P. Cunningham (Eds.), *Proceedings of the 18th IEEE international symposium on computer-based medical systems. Computer based medical systems (CBMS)* (pp. 203-207).

Jung, H., Lee, K., & Chun, W. (2006). Integration of GIS, GPS, and optimization technologies for the effective control of parcel delivery service. *Computers & Industrial Engineering, 51,* 154–162. doi:10.1016/j.cie.2006.07.007

Kaminski, J. A. M., & Reilly, A. H. (2004). Career development of women in information technology. *SAM Advanced Management Journal, 69*(4), 20–30.

Kamppinen, M., Vihervaara, P., & Aarras, N. (2008). Corporate responsibility and systems thinking – Tools for balanced risk management. *International Journal of Sustainable Society, 1*(2), 158–171. doi:10.1504/IJSSOC.2008.022572

Kaplan, B., & Maxwell, J. A. (1994). Qualitative research methods for evaluating Computer Information Systems. In J.G. Anderson, C.E. Aydin, & S.J. Jay (Eds.), *Evaluating Health Care Information Systems: Methods and Applications* (pp. 45-68)., Thousand Oaks, CA: Sage.

Kaplan, B., & Duchon, D. (1988). Combining qualitative and quantitative methods in information systems research: A case study. *Management Information Systems Quarterly*, *12*(4), 571–586. doi:10.2307/249133

Karsak, E. E., & Ahiska, S. S. (2005). Practical common weight multi-criteria decision-making approach with an improved discriminating power for technology selection. *International Journal of Production Research*, *43*(8), 1537–1554. doi:doi:10.1080/13528160412331326478

Kazakis, N. (2008). *Groundwater vulnerability assessment using different methods: A case study from the alluvial aquifer of Florina basin*. Unpublished doctoral dissertation, Dept. of Geology, Aristotle University of Thessaloniki, Greece.

Keenan, P. (1996). *Using a GIS as a DSS generator. Perspectives on DSS*. Mytilene, Greece: University of the Aegean.

Keenan, P. (1998). Spatial decision support systems for vehicle routing. *Decision Support Systems*, *22*, 65–71. doi:10.1016/S0167-9236(97)00054-7

Keeney, R. L., & Raiffa, H. (1976). *Decision with multiple objectives*. New York: J. Wiley & Sons.

Keilis-Borok, V. I., & Lichtman, A. J. (1981). Pattern recognition applied to presidential elections in the United States, 1860-1980: The role of integral social, economic, and political traits. *Proceedings of the National Academy of Sciences of the United States of America*, *78*, 7230–7234. doi:10.1073/pnas.78.11.7230

Kendall, J. (1996/1997). PFI profile: Paul and Karen Mugge. *The practical farmer, 11*(4).

Kennedy, R. L., Seibert, J. A., & Hughes, C. J. (2000). Legacy system integration using web technology. In G.J. Blaine, & E.L. Siegel (Eds.), *Proceedings of the SPIE: vol. 3980. Medical imaging 2000: PACS design and evaluation: Engineering and clinical issues* (pp. 231-234).

Kerr, M. (2008). *Sense of self among mindfulness teachers*. Bangor University, Bangor, UK.

Khor, M. (2008). Global crisis as food price soar: global trend. *Third World Network*. Retrieved from http://www.twnside.org.sg/title2/gtrends/gtrends201.htm

Kim, B., Park, K., & Kim, T. (1999). The perception gap among buyers and suppliers in the semiconductor industry. *Supply Chain Managements: An International Journal*, *4*(5), 231–241. doi:10.1108/13598549910294920

Kiniry, J. R., & Williams, J. R. (1995). Simulating intercropping with the ALMANAC model. In Sinoquet, H., & Cruz, P. (Eds.), *Ecophysiology of Tropical Intercropping* (pp. 387–396). Paris: INRA editions.

Kiniry, J. R., Williams, J. R., Gassman, P. W., & Debaeke, P. (1992). A general process-oriented model for two competing plant species. *Transactions of the ASAE. American Society of Agricultural Engineers*, *35*(3), 801–810.

Koeller, K. H., & Linke, C. (2001). *Erfolgreicher Ackerbau ohne Pflug: Wissenschaftliche Ergebnisse – Praktische Erfahrungen*. Frankfurt, Germany: DLG.

Kolesnikov, A., Kauranne, T., & Marsh, A. (1999). Integrating DICOM medical images into Virtual Medical Worlds. In *Proceedings of the IEEE EMBS International Conference on Information Technology Applications in Biomedicine* (pp. 23-24).

Kolesnikov, A., Kelle, O., & Kauranne, T. (1997). Remote medical analysis with web technology. In B. Ramin & P. Karttunen (Eds.), *Proceedings of the finnish symposium on signal processing - FINSIG '97* (pp. 87-96).

Krikke, J. (2008). Recycling e-waste: the sky is the limit. *IT Professional*, *10*(1), 50–55. doi:10.1109/MITP.2008.16

Krishnamurthy, S. (2009). Case: Mozilla vs. Godzilla – The launch of the Mozilla Firefox browser. *Journal of Interactive Marketing*, *23*(3), 259–271. doi:10.1016/j.intmar.2009.04.008

Kropff, M. J., & van Laar, H. H. (1993). *Modelling crop-weed interactions*. CAB International, in association with the International Rice Research Institute.

Kropff, M. J., & Spitters, C. J. T. (1992). An eco-physiological model for interspecific competition, applied to the influence of *Chenopodium album L.* on sugar beet. I. Model description and parameterization. *Weed Research*, *32*, 437–450. doi:10.1111/j.1365-3180.1992.tb01905.x

Kropff, M. J., Teng, P. S., Aggarwal, P. K., Bouman, B. A. M., & van Laar, H. H. (1996). *Applications of Systems Approaches at the Field Level*. Dordrecht, The Netherlands: Kluwer Academic Publishers.

Kumar, P., Joshi, P. K., Johansen, C., & Asokan, M. (1998). Total factor productivity of rice-wheat based cropping system: role of legumes. *Economic Policy Weekly, 26*, A152–A157.

Kunstelj, M., & Vintar, M. (2004). Evaluating the progress of E-government development: a critical analysis. *Information Polity, 9*, 131–148.

Kurada, H. (2008). Solving Asia's food crisis. *Today's Wall Street Journal Asia.* Retrieved from http://online.wsj.com /public/article print/SB120994263541666093.html

Kurtz, C. F., & Snowden, D. J. (2003). The New dynamics of strategy: sense-making in a complex-complicated world. *IBM Systems Journal*, 1–23.

Laaribi, A. (2000). *SIG et analyse multicitere.* Paris: Hermes Sciences Publications.

Laaribi, A., Chevallier, J. J., & Martel, J. M. (1996). A spatial decision aid: A multicriterion evaluation approach. *Computers, Environment and Urban Systems, 20*(6), 351–366. doi:doi:10.1016/S0198-9715(97)00002-1

Ladha, J. K., Dawe, D., Pathak, H., Padre, A. T., Yadav, R. L., & Singh, B. (2003a). How extensive are yield declines in long-term rice-wheat experiments in Asia? *Field Crops Research, 81*, 159–180. doi:10.1016/S0378-4290(02)00219-8

Ladha, J. K., Pathak, H., Tirol-Padre, A., Dawe, D., & Gupta, R. K. (2003b). Productivity trends in intensive rice wheat cropping systems in Asia. In Ladha, J. K., Hill, J. E., Duxbury, J. M., Gupta, R. K., & Buresh, R. J. (Eds.), *Improving the Productivity and Sustainability of Rice-Wheat Systems: Issues and Impacts* (*Vol. 65*, pp. 45–76). ASA.

Lahdelma, R., Hokkanen, J., & Salminen, P. (1998). SMAA - stochastic multiobjective acceptability analysis. *European Journal of Operational Research, 106*, 137–143. doi:doi:10.1016/S0377-2217(97)00163-X

Lal, H., Hoogenboom, G., Calixte, J. P., Jones, J. W., & Beinroth, F. H. (1993). Using crop simulation models and GIS for regional productivity analysis. *Transactions of the ASAE. American Society of Agricultural Engineers, 36*, 175–184.

Lalonde, B., & Masters, J. (1994). Emerging logistics strategies - blueprints for the next Century. *International Journal of Physical Distribution & Logistics Management, 24*(7), 35–47. doi:10.1108/09600039410070975

Lambert, D. M., Stock, J. R., & Ellram, L. M. (1998). *Fundamentals of Logistics Management* (p. 130). Boston: Irwin.

Lancaster, K. J. (1966). A new approach to consumer theory. *The Journal of Political Economy, 74*, 132–157. doi:10.1086/259131

Langer, E. J. (2000). Mindful learning. *Current Issues in Psychological Science, 9*(6), 220–223. doi:10.1111/1467-8721.00099

Langsdale, S. (2007). *Participatory model building for exploring water management and climate change futures in the Okanagan Basin, British Columbia, Canada.* Unpublished PhD thesis, University of British Columbia, Vancouver, Canada.

Langsdale, S., Beall, A., Carmichael, J., Cohen, S., & Forster, C. (2007). An exploration of water resources futures under climate change using system dynamics modeling. *The Integrated Assessment Journal, 7*(1), 51–79.

Langsdale, S., Beall, A., Carmichael, J., Cohen, S., Forster, C., & Neale, T. (2006). Shared learning through group model building. In Cohen, S., & Neale, T. (Eds.), *Participatory integrated assessment of water management and climate change in the Okanagan Basin, British Columbia.* Vancouver, BC: Environment Canada and University of British Columbia.

Langville, A. N., & Meyer, C. D. (2006). *Google's PageRank and beyond: The science of search engine rankings.* Princeton, NJ: Princeton University Press.

Latinopoulos, P. (2003). *Design of a water potential management plan for public water supply and irrigation in the Municipality of Moudania.* Thessaloniki, Greece: AUTh, Department of Civil Engineering.

Latinopoulos, P., Tziakas, V., & Mallios, Z. (2004). Valuation for irrigation water by the hedonic price method: a case study in Chalkidiki, Greece. *Water Air and Soil Pollution Focus, 4*, 253–262. doi:10.1023/B:WAFO.0000044803.01747.bd

Lau, N. S. E. (2007). *Cultivation of mindfulness: Spirituality in education.* Paper presented at the Conference on Making Sense of Spirituality, United Kingdom.

Laurini, R. (2000). A short introduction to TeleGeo Processing and TeleGeo Monitoring. In *Proceedings of the Second International Symposium on Telegeoprocessing* (pp. 10-12).

Lawrence, S., & Giles, C. L. (1999). Accessibility of information on the web. *Nature, 200*, 107–109. doi:10.1038/21987

Lee-Kelley, L., & Kolsaker, A. (2004). E-government: the 'fit' between supply assumptions and usage drivers. *Electronic Government, 1*(2), 130–140. doi:10.1504/EG.2004.005173

Lehoczki, R., Csányi, S., & Sonkoly, K. (2008, October). Az Országos Vadgazdálkodási Adattár céljai és feladatai. *Nimród Vadászújság,* 13-14.

Lehtinen, U., & Lehtinen, J. R. (1982). *Service quality: a study of quality dimensions.* Finland: Unpublished Research Report, Service of Management Group, OY.

LEL Schwäbisch Gmünd, LTZ Augustenberg, LVVG Aulendorf, LSZ Boxberg, LVG Heidelberg & HuL Marbach. (2007). *Stammdatenblätter Landwirtschaft „Nährstoffvergleich Feld-Stall.* Tabelle 5a.

LeSage, J. P., & Pace, R. K. (2009). *Introduction to Spatial Econometrics.* New York: CRC Press/Taylor & Francis Group.

Leung, Y. (1997). *Intelligent spatial decision support systems.* Berlin: Springer.

Lewis, P. H. (1996, April 13). Yahoo gets big welcome on Wall Street. *New York Times,* 33-34.

Lewis, R. C., & Booms, B. H. (1983). *The marketing aspects of service quality. Emerging Perspectives in Services Marketing* (pp. 99–107). Chicago: American Marketing Association.

Lichtman, A. J. (1988, May). How to bet in November. *Washingtonian Magazine* (pp. 115-24).

Lichtman, A. J. (2008). *The Keys to the White House, 2008 Edition.* Lanham, MD: Rowman & Littlefield.

Lichtman, A. J., & Keilis-Borok, V. I. (July 2004). What Kerry must do to win (but probably won't). *Counterpunch.* http://www.counterpunch.org/lichtman07292004.html.

Lichtman, A. J. (2006, Feb.). The keys to the white house: Forecast for 2008. *Foresight: The International Journal of Applied Forecasting, 3*, 5–9.

Lichtman, A. J. (2007). The Keys to the white house: Updated forecast for 2008. *Foresight: The International Journal of Applied Forecasting, 8*, 5–9.

Lichtman, A. J. (2008, April-June). The keys to the white house: An index forecast for 2008. *International Journal of Forecasting, 4*, 301–309. doi:10.1016/j.ijforecast.2008.02.004

Lieb, R. C., & Randall, H. Y. (1996). A comparison of the use of third–party logistics services by large American manufacturers. *Journal of Business Logistics, 17*(1), 305–320.

Li, H., Kong, C. W., Pang, Y. C., Shi, W. Z., & Yu, L. (2003). Internet-based geographical information systems for e-commerce application in construction and material procurement. *Journal of Construction Engineering and Management, 129*, 689–697. doi:10.1061/(ASCE)0733-9364(2003)129:6(689)

Li, J., Tian, B., Liu, T., Liu, H., Wen, X., & Honda, S. (2006). Status quo of e-waste management in mainland China. *Journal of Material Cycles and Waste Management, 8*(1), 13–20. doi:10.1007/s10163-005-0144-3

Li, L., Sun, J., Zhang, F., Li, X., Yang, S., & Rengel, Z. (2001). Wheat/maize or wheat/soybean strip intercropping I. Yield advantage and interspecific interactions on nutrients. *Field Crops Research, 71*, 123–137. doi:10.1016/S0378-4290(01)00156-3

Ling, L. (2007). Demand management: customer order forecast. In *Supply Chain Management: Concept, Techniques and Practices Enhancing Value Through Collaboration* (p. 117). Hackensack, NJ: World Scientific Publishing.

Lin, H.-F. (2007). Measuring online learning systems success: Applying the updated DeLone and McLean model. *Cyberpsychology & Behavior, 10*(6), 817–820. doi:10.1089/cpb.2007.9948

Linkov, I., Satterstrom, K., Kiker, Batchelor, C.G., & Bridges, T. (2006). From comparative risk assessment to multi-criteria decision analysis and adaptive management: recent developments and applications. *Environment International, 32*, 1072–1093. PubMed doi:10.1016/j.envint.2006.06.013

Linkov, I., Grebenkov, A., Andrizhievski, A., Loukashevich, A., Trifonov, A., & Kapustka, L. (2004). Incorporating habitat characterization into risk-trace: software for spatially explicit exposure assessment. In Linkov, I., & Ramadan, A. (Eds.), *Comparative risk assessment and environmental decision making*. Amsterdam: Kluwer.

Linstone, H. A. (1999). *Decision making for technology executives: Using multiple perspectives to improve performance*. Boston, MA: Artech House.

Loebbecke, C., & Huyskens, C. (2006). What drives netsourcing decisions? An empirical analysis. *European Journal of Information Systems, 15*, 415–423. doi:10.1057/palgrave.ejis.3000621

Lorentz, H. (2006). *Food supply chains in Ukraine and Kazakhstan*. Turku School of Economics, Electronic Publications of Pan European Institute. Retrieved from http://www.tse.fi/pei/pub

Loreto, D., Nordlander, E., & Oliner, A. (2005). *Benchmarking a large-scale heterogeneous cluster*. Retrieved 20 June 2008, from beowulf.lcs.mit.edu/ 18.337-2005/projects/top500writeup.pdf

Lowenberg-De Boer, J., Krause, M., Deuson, R., & Reddy, K. C. (1991). Simulation of yield distributions in millet-cowpea intercropping. *Agricultural Systems, 36*, 471–487. doi:10.1016/0308-521X(91)90072-I

Lozano, S., & Gutierrez, E. (2008). Data envelopment analysis of the human development index. *International Journal of Society Systems Science, 1*(2), 132–150. doi:10.1504/IJSSS.2008.021916

Luna-Reyes, L., Gil-Garcia, J. R., & Estrada-Marropuin, M. (2008). The impact of institutions on interorganizational IT projects in the Mexican federal government. *International Journal of Electronic Government, 4*(2), 27–42.

Lynar, T., Herbert, H., & Chivers, W. (2009). Implementing an agent based auction on a cluster of reused workstations. *International Journal of Computer Applications in Technology, 34*(4), 230–234. doi:10.1504/IJCAT.2009.024071

Maier, M. W. (2005). Research challenges for systems-of-systems. In *Proceedings of the IEEE international conference on systems, man and cybernetics (Vol. 4)* (pp. 3149-3154).

Maier, M. W. (1998). Architecting principles for systems-of-systems. *Systems Engineering, 1*(4), 267–284. doi:10.1002/(SICI)1520-6858(1998)1:4<267::AID-SYS3>3.0.CO;2-D

Malczewski, J. (2004). GIS-based land-use suitability analysis: a critical overview. *Progress in Planning, 62*, 3–65. doi:doi:10.1016/j.progress.2003.09.002

Malczewski, J. (2006). GIS-based multicriteria decision analysis: a survey of the literature. *International Journal of Geographical Information Science, 20*(7), 703–726. doi:doi:10.1080/13658810600661508

Malik, A. S., Letson, D., & Crutchfield, S. R. (1993). Point/nonpoint source trading of pollution abatement: Choosing the right trading ratio. *American Journal of Agricultural Economics, 75*, 959–967. doi:10.2307/1243983

Mallios, Z., Papageorgiou, A., & Latinopoulos, P. (2007). The development of a calculation tool and spatial data retrieval in a Geographical Information Systems environment for the estimation of spatial econometric models. In *Proceedings of the 6th National Conference of Greek Committee of water resources management*, Chania, Greece (pp. 223-230).

Mallios, Z., Papageorgiou, A., Latinopoulos, D., & Latinopoulos, P. (2007). Spatial Hedonic Pricing Models for the Valuation of Irrigation Water. In *Proceedings of the 10th International Conference on Environmental Science and Technology*, Kos Island, Greece (pp. A900-907).

Malone, M. S. (2004, March). Surviving IPO fever. *Wired*, 115.

Manos, B., Bournaris, Th., Papathanasiou, J., Moulogianni, Ch., & Voudouris, K. S. (2007). A DSS for agricultural land use, water management and environmental protection. In *Proceedings of the 3rd International Conference on Energy, Environment, Ecosystems and Sustainable Development*, Agios Nikolaos, Crete (pp. 340-345).

Manos, B., Bournaris, Th., Silleos, N., Antonopoulos, V., & Papathanasiou, J. (2004a). A Decision Support System for rivers monitoring and sustainable management. *Environmental Monitoring and Assessment, 96*(1-3), 85–98. doi:10.1023/B:EMAS.0000031717.13972.27

Manos, B., Ciani, A., Bournaris, Th., Vassiliadou, I., & Papathanasiou, J. (2004b). A taxonomy survey of Decision Support Systems in agriculture. *Agricultural Economics Research, 5*(2), 80–94.

Marchand, P., & Holland, O. T. (2002). *Graphics and GUIs with MATLAB* (3rd ed.). London: Chapman & Hall/CRC. doi:10.1201/9781420057393

Markoff, J. (2004, November 10). Microsoft unveils its Internet search engine, quietly. *New York Times*, C1.

Marsan, C. (2000). Stanford move rekindles 'net address debate. *Network World Fusion*. Retrieved from http://www.nwfusion.com/news/2000/0124ipv4.html

Martha, J., & Krampel, W. (1996). Start relationship on the right foot. *Transportation & Distribution, 73*(3), 75–76.

Matthews, R. B., & Stephens, W. (2002). *Cropsoil simulation models. Applications in developing countries*. Wallingford, UK: CABI Publishing. doi:10.1079/9780851995632.0000

Matthews, R. B., Wassmann, R., Knox, J. W., & Buendia, L. V. (2000b). Using a crop/soil simulation model and GIS techniques to assess methane emissions from rice fields in Asia. IV. Upscaling to national levels. *Nutrient Cycling in Agroecosystems, 58*, 201–217. doi:10.1023/A:1009850804425

McCormick, P. (n.d). *DICOM and databases*. Retrieved June 4, 2009, from http://icmit.mit.edu/dicomdb.html.

McGrath, J., & Cohoon, J. M. (2001). Toward improving female retention in the computer science mMajor. *Communications of the ACM, 44*(5), 109–114.

McKee, T. B., Doesken, N., & Kleist, J. (1993). The relationship of drought frequency and duration to time scales. In *Proceeding of the 8th Conference on Applied Climatology*. Amer. Meteorol. Soc.

McKenna, B., Rooney, D., & Liesch, P. W. (2006). Beyond knowledge to wisdom in international business strategy. *Prometheus, 24*(3), 283–300. doi:10.1080/08109020600877576

McKeon, J. E. (1991). Outsourcing begins in-house. *Transportation & Distribution*, 25-8.

Meadows, D. (2007). A brief and incomplete history of operational gaming in system dynamics. *System Dynamics Review, 23*(2-3), 199–203. doi:10.1002/sdr.372

Meadows, D. H., & Robinson, J. M. (2007). *The electronic oracle: Computer models and social decisions*. Albany, NY: System Dynamics Society.

Meadows, D., Meadows, D., Randers, J., & Behrens, W. (1972). *The limits to growth*. New York: Universe Books.

Mentzer, J. T., DeWitt, W., Keebler, J. S., Min, S., Nix, N. W., Smith, C. D., & Zacharia, Z. G. (2001). Defining supply chain management. *Journal of Business Logistics, 22*(2), 125.

Microsystems (Chapter 1). New York: John Wiley & Sons.

Midgley, G. (2000). *Systemic intervention: Philosophy, methodology, and practice*. New York: Kluwer Academic/Plenum Publishers.

Milliman, J. W. (1959). Land values as measures of primary irrigation benefits. *Journal of Farm Economics, 41*(2), 234–243. doi:10.2307/1235148

Miltchenko, M. V., Pianykh, O. S., & Tyler, J. M. (2003). Building a Global PACS Network: Choices in Implementing Inter-PACS Connectivity. In *Proceedings of the RSNA 2003 scientific assembly and annual meeting* (pp. 599-605).

Mintsis, G., Basbas, S., Papaioannou, P., Taxiltaris, C., & Tziavos, I. (2004). Applications of GPS technology in the land transportation system. *European Journal of Operational Research, 152*, 399–409. doi:10.1016/S0377-2217(03)00032-8

Miras, D. (2002). *A survey of network qos needs of advanced internet applications.* London: University College.

Miyakoshi, T., & Tsukuda, Y. (2004). Regional disparities in Japanese banking performance. *Review of Urban and Regional Development Studies, 16,* 74–89. doi:10.1111/j.1467-940X.2004.00081.x

Morecroft, J. D. W., & Sterman, J. D. (Eds.). (1994). *Modeling for learning organizations. Portland, OR: Productivity Press.* Waltham, MA: Pegasus Communications.

Morid, S., Smakhtin, V., & Moghaddasi, M. (2006). Comparison of seven meteorological indices for drought monitoring in Iran. *International Journal of Climatology, 26,* 971–985. doi:10.1002/joc.1264

Morrison, M. L., Marcot, B. G., & Mannan, R. W. (1998). *Wildlife-habitat relationships: consepts and applications.* Madison, WI: University of Wisconsin Press.

Mossberg, W. S. (1998, March 19). Yahoo! challenges AOL as a portal to World Wide Web. *Wall Street Journal,* B1.

Mostafa, J. (2005). Seeking better web searches. *Scientific American, 292*(2), 67–73. doi:10.1038/scientificamerican0205-66

Mote, P., Salathé, E., Duliére, V., & Jump, E. (2008). *Scenarios of future climate for the Pacific Northwest.* Seattle, WA: University of Washington, Climate Impacts Group.

Mowery (Ed.), *The international computer software industry: A comparative study of*

Myers, M. D. (1994). Quality in qualitative research in Information Systems. In *Proceedings of the 5th Australasian Conference on Information Systems* (pp. 763-766).

Myrberget, S. (1988). Hunting statistics as indicators of game population size and composition. *Statistical Journal of the United Nations ECE, 5,* 289–301.

Nain, A. S., Kersebaum, K. C., & Mirschel, W. (2005). *Are meteorological parameters based drought indices enough for agricultural drought monitoring: a comparative study of drought monitoring with SPI and Crop Simulation Model.* Paper presented at the ICID 21st European Regional Conference 2005, Frankfurt, Germany.

Narang, R. S., & Virmani, S. M. (2001). *Rice-Wheat cropping systems of the Indo-Gangetic Plains of India.* New Delhi, India: Rice-Wheat Consortium for the Indo-Gangetic Plains.

NATCOM. (2004). *India's Initial National Communication to the United Nations Framework Convention on Climate Change.* India: National Communication Project, Ministry of Environment and Forests, Govt. of India.

National Electrical Manufacturers Association. (2008). *Digital imaging and communications in medicine (DICOM): the DICOM standard (Rep. No. PS 3.x-2008).* Retrieved June 5, 2009, from ftp://medical.nema.org/medical/dicom/2008/08_01pu.pdf.

National Game Management Database [NGMD]. (2009). *NGMD homepage.* Retrieved November 17, 2009, from http://www.vmi.szie.hu/adattar/index.html

National Telecommunications and Information Administration. (2004). *Technical and economic assessment of internet protocol version 6 (IPv6).* Retrieved from http://www.ntia.doc.gov/ntiahome/ntiageneral/ipv6/draft/discussiondraftv13_07162004.pdf

Ndubisi, N. O., & Jantan, M. (2003). Evaluating IS usage in Malaysian small and medium-sized firms using the technology acceptance model. *Logistics Information Management, 16*(6), 440–450. doi:10.1108/09576050310503411

Nelson, J. (1978). Residential choice, hedonic prices, and the demand for urban air quality. *Journal of Urban Economics, 5,* 357–369. doi:10.1016/0094-1190(78)90016-5

Nelson, R. A., Dimes, J. P., Paningbatan, E. P., & Silburn, D. M. (1998). Erosion/productivity modelling of maize farming in the Philippine uplands part I: Parameterising the agricultural production systems simulator. *Agricultural Systems, 58*(2), 129–146. doi:10.1016/S0308-521X(98)00043-2

NeoTool. (2007). *The HL7 evolution.* Retrieved June 5, 2009, from http://www.neotool.com/pdf/HL7-Version-3-with-HL7-Version-2-History.pdf.

Nguyen, T. N., & Woodward, R. T. (2008). *NutrientNet: An internet-based approach to teaching market-based policy for environmental management.* Retrieved June 7, 2009, from http://ssrn.com/abstract=1134163

Nguyen, V. T. V., In-na, N., & Bobee, B. (1989). New plotting position formula for Pearson type III distribution. *Journal of Hydraulic Engineering, 115*(6), 706–730.

Nielsen, S. H., Hellens, L. A. v., Beekhuyzen, J., & Trauth, E. M. (2003). *Women talking about IT work: Duality or dualism*? Paper presented at the SIGMIS Conference, Philadelphia, PA.

Nissen, M. E. (2002). An extended model of knowledge-flow dynamics. *Communications of the Association for Information Systems, 8*, 251–266.

Nocera, J. (2008, February 2). A giant bid that shows how tired the giant is. *New York Times*, C1.

Nonaka, I., & Takeuchi, H. (1995). *The knowledge-creating company – How Japanese companies created the dynamics of innovation.* Oxford, UK: Oxford University Press.

Nonaka, I. (1994). A dynamic theory of organizational knowledge creation. *Organization Science, 5*, 14–37. doi:10.1287/orsc.5.1.14

Nonaka, I., & Konno, N. (1998). The concept of "*Ba*": Building foundation for knowledge creation. *California Management Review, 40*, 40–54.

Nonaka, I., & Toyama, R. (2003). The knowledge-creating theory revisited: knowledge creation as a synthesizing process. *Knowledge Management Research & Practice, 1*, 2–10. doi:10.1057/palgrave.kmrp.8500001

Noumeir, R. (2005). Benefits of the DICOM modality performed procedure step. *Journal of Digital Imaging, 18*(4), 260–269. doi:10.1007/s10278-005-6702-3

Ntale, H. K., & Gan, T. Y. (2003). Drought indices and their application to East Africa. *International Journal of Climatology, 23*, 1335–1357. doi:10.1002/joc.931

Nunnally, J. (1967). *Psychometric theory*. New York: McGraw-Hill.

Nunnally, J. C., & Bernstein, I. H. (1994). *Psychometric Theory* (3rd ed.). New York: McGraw-Hill.

O'Callaghan, J. R., Maende, C., & Wyseure, G. L. C. (1994). Modelling the intercropping of maize and beans in Kenya. *Computers and Electronics in Agriculture, 11*, 351–365. doi:10.1016/0168-1699(94)90026-4

Ord, K. (1975). Estimation methods for models of spatial interaction. *Journal of the American Statistical Association, 70*, 120–126. doi:10.2307/2285387

Oregon Department of Environmental Quality (ODEQ). (2008). *Water quality trading in Oregon: A case study report*. Retrieved June 7, 2009, from http://www.deq.state.or.us/wq/trading/docs/wqtradingcasestudy.pdf

Otto, P., & Struben, J. (2004). Gloucester fishery: Insights from a group modeling intervention. *System Dynamics Review, 20*(4), 287–312. doi:10.1002/sdr.299

Owen, B. M., & Portillo, J. E. (2003). *Legal reform, externalities and economic development: measuring the impact of legal aid on poor women in Ecuador*. SSRN Working Paper Series.

Owen, C. L., & Todor, W. D. (1993, March-April). Attitudes toward women as managers: Still the same. *Business Horizons*, 12–16. doi:10.1016/S0007-6813(05)80032-1

Oza, S. R., Parihar, J. S., & Dadhwal, V. K. (2002). *Proceedings of Evaluating use of Standardized index for drought assessment in the region of North-west India (TROPMET-2002)*. India: Bhubaneswar.

Ozier-Lafontaine, H., Bruckler, L., Lafolie, F., & Cabidoche, Y. M. (1995). Modelling root competition for water in mixed crops: a basic approach. In Sinoquet, H., & Cruz, P. (Eds.), *Ecophysiology of Tropical Intercropping* (pp. 189–187). Paris: INRA editions.

Ozier-Lafontaine, H., Lafolie, F., Bruckler, L., Tournebeze, R., & Mollier, A. (1998). Modelling competition for water in intercrops: theory and comparison with field experiments. *Plant and Soil, 204*, 183–201. doi:10.1023/A:1004399508452

PACS-ADMIN. (2007). *PACS overview*. Retrieved June 5, 2009, from http://www.pacs-admin.com/PACS_Overview.html.

Palan, K. M. (2001). Gender identity in consumer behavior research: A literature review and research agenda. *Academy of Marketing Science Review, 10*, 1–24.

Palmer, W. C. (1965). *Meteorological Drought (Paper No. 45)*. Washington, DC: U.S. Department of Commerce, Weather Bureau.

Parasuraman, A., Zeithaml, V. A., & Berry, L. L. (1985). A conceptual model of service quality and its implications for future research. *Journal of Marketing, 49,* 41–50. doi:10.2307/1251430

Parkinson, B. (1996). *Global Positioning System: Theory and applications (Vol. 1).* Washington, DC: American Institute of Aeronautics and Astronautics, Inc.

Park, S. E., Benjamin, L., & Watkinson, A. R. (2003). The theory and application of plant competition models: an agronomic perspective. *Annals of Botany, 92,* 741–748. doi:10.1093/aob/mcg204

Patel, N. R., Chopra, R., & Dadhwal, V. K. (2007). Analysing spatial patterns of meteorological drought using standardized precipitation index. *International Journal of Climatology, 14*(4), 329–336.

Pathak, H., Timsina, J., Humphreys, E., Godwin, D. C., Shukla, A. K., Singh, U., & Matthews, R. B. (2004). *Simulation of rice crop performance and water and N dynamics, and methane emissions for rice in northwest India using CERES Rice model* (CSIRO Land and Water Tech. Rep. 23/04). Griffith, Australia: CSIRO Land and Water.

Pathak, H., Bhatia, A., Jain, M. C., Kumar, S., Singh, S., & Kumar, U. (2002). Emission of nitrous oxide from soil in rice-wheat systems of Indo-Gangetic Plains of India. *Journal of Environmental Monitoring and Assessment, 77*(2), 163–178. doi:10.1023/A:1015823919405

Pathak, H., Ladha, J. K., Aggarwal, P. K., Peng, S., Das, S., & Singh, Y. (2003). Climatic potential and on-farm yield trends of rice and wheat in the Indo-Gangetic Plains. *Field Crops Research, 80*(3), 223–234. doi:10.1016/S0378-4290(02)00194-6

Penning de Vries, F. W. T. (Ed.). (1993). Rice production and climate change. In *Systems Approaches for Agricultural Development.* Dordrecht, The Netherlands: Kluwer Academic Publishers.

Perez, M. P., Carnicer, M. P. L., & Martnez, A. (2002). Differential effects of gender on perceptions of teleworking by human resources managers. *Women in Management Review, 17*(6), 262–275. doi:10.1108/09649420210441914

Peters, L. H., Terborg, J. R., & Taynor, J. (1974). Women as managers scale (WAMS): A measure of attitudes toward women in management positions. *A Catalog of Selected Documents in Psychology, 4*(27).

Petricek, P., Escher, T., & Margetts, H. (n.d.). The web structure of E-government -developing a methodology for quantitative evaluation. In Proceedings of the *The International World Wide Web Conference Committee (IW3C2).* Retrieved on August 29, 2008 from http://www.iw3c2.org/

Petter, S., DeLone, W., & McLean, E. (2008). Measuring information systems success: models, dimensions, measures, and interrelationships. *European Journal of Information Systems, 17,* 236–263. doi:10.1057/ejis.2008.15

Pianykh, O. S. (2008). Digital Imaging and Communications in Medicine (DICOM): A Practical Introduction and Survival Guide. *DICOM and Teleradiology* (pp. 275-298). Berlin, Heidelberg, Springer-Verlag.

Pianykh, O. S., Miltchenko, M. V., & Tyler, J. M. (2003). Using Online PACS Gateway for Efficient Medical Data Exchange. In *Proceedings of the RSNA 2003 scientific assembly and annual meeting* (pp. 813-819).

Piccoli, G., Ahmad, R., & Ives, B. (2001). Web-based virtual learning environments: a research framework and a preliminary assessment of effectiveness in basic IT skills training. *Management Information Systems Quarterly, 25*(4), 401–426. doi:10.2307/3250989

Polemio, M. (2005). Seawater intrusion and groundwater quality in the southern Italy region of Apulia: a multi-methodological approach to the protection. In *Proceedings of the UNESCO, IHP,* Paris (Vol. 77, pp. 171-178).

Polemio, M., Dragone, V., & Limoni, P. P. (2009a). Monitoring and methods to analyse the groundwater quality degradation risk in coastal karstic aquifers (Apulia, Southern Italy). *Environmental Geology, 58*(2), 299–312. doi:10.1007/s00254-008-1582-8

Polemio, M., Dragone, V., & Limoni, P. P. (2009b). Karstic aquifer vulnerability assessment methods and results at a test site (Apulia, Southern Italy). *Natural Hazards and Earth System Sciences, 9*(4), 1461–1470. doi:10.5194/nhess-9-1461-2009

Porterfield, J., & Kleiner, B. H. (2005). A new era: Women and leadership. *Equal Opportunities International, 24*(5-6), 49–56. doi:10.1108/02610150510788150

Porter, J. R., Jamieson, P. D., & Wilson, D. R. (1993). Comparison of the wheat simulation models AFRC-WHEAT2, CERES-Wheat and SWHEAT for non-limiting conditions of crop growth. *Field Crops Research, 33,* 131–157. doi:10.1016/0378-4290(93)90098-8

Potts, G. R., Lecocq, Y., Swift, J., & Havet, P. (Eds.). (1991). *Proceedings of the International Conference "Wise Use As a Conservation Strategy"*, Brussels, Belgium.

Propp, K. M. (1999). Collective information processing in groups. In L. R. Frey, D. S. Gouran, & M. C. Poole (Eds.), *The handbook of group communication theory & research* (pp. 225-250). Thousand Oaks, CA: Sage Publications.

Prospectus. (2004, August 18). *Of initial public offering for Google's common stock filed with Securities Exchange Commission.* Retrieved September 8, 2009, from http://www.sec.gov/Archives/edgar/data/1288776/000119312504073639/ds1.htm

Rao, G. S. L. H. V., & Subash, N. (1996). Use of CERES-Rice Model to assess potential yield. *International Rice Research Notes, 21*(2-3), 87.

Rasmussen, E. M., Dickinson, R. E., Kutzbach, J. E., & Cleaveland, M. K. (1993). In Maidment, D. R. (Ed.), *Climatology. Handbook of Hydrology* (pp. 5.1–5.51). New York: McGraw-Hill.

Ratib, O. M., Ligier, Y., Rosset, A., Staub, J. C., Logean, M., & Girard, C. (2000). Self-contained off-line media for exchanging medical images using DICOM-compliant standard. In G.J. Blaine, & E.L. Siegel (Eds.), *Proceedings of the SPIE: vol. 3980. Medical imaging 2000: PACS design and evaluation: Engineering and clinical issues* (pp. 30-34).

Ray, S., & Mukherjee, A. (2007). Development of a framework towards successful implementation of e-governance initiatives in health sector in India. *International Journal of Health Care Quality Assurance, 20*(6), 464–483. doi:10.1108/09526860710819413

Razzaque, M. A., & Sheng, C. C. (1998). Outsourcing of logistics functions: a literature survey. *International Journal of Physical Distribution & Logistics Management, 28,* 2.

Reading, C. (2002). Synthesizing the strategy. In *Strategic Business Planning: A Dynamic System for Improving Performance & Competitive Advantage*n (2nd ed.). London: Kogan Page Limited.

Reason, P., & Bradbury, H. (Eds.). (2001). *Handbook of action research: Participative inquiry and practice.* Thousand Oaks, CA: Sage.

Reason, P., & Bradbury, H. E. (2005). Living as part of the whole: the implications of participation. *Journal of Curriculum and Pedagogy, 2*(2), 35–41.

Reisch, E., & Knecht, G. (1995). *Betriebslehre.* Stuttgart, Germany: Ulmer.

Reuters. (2009, March 13). Thai rice prices to stay high. *The Rice Problem.* Retrieved from http://www.inquirer.net/specialfeatures/riceproblem/view.php?db=1&article=20090313-193988

Revet, B. (1997). *DICOM Cook Book for Implementations in Modalities (Tech. Rep.).* Philips Medical Systems, Eindhoven, The Netherlands.

Richardson, H. L. (1990). Explore outsourcing. *Transportation & Distribution,* 17-20.

Richardson, G. P., & Pugh, A. L. III. (1981). *Introduction to system dynamics modeling with DYNAMO.* Cambridge, MA: MIT Press. Waltham, MA: Pegasus Communications.

Richardson, G., & Anderson, D. (1995). Teamwork in group model-building. *System Dynamics Review, 11*(2), 131–137. doi:10.1002/sdr.4260110203

Richardson, H. L. (1997). Contract time: switch partners or keep dancing? *Transportation & Distribution, 38*(7), 47–52.

Rinner, C. (2003). Web-based spatial decision support: status and research directions. *Journal of Geographic Information and Decision Analysis, 7*(1), 14–31.

Rittel, W. J. R., & Webber, M. M. (1973). Dilemmas in a general theory of planning. *Policy Sciences, 4,* 155–169. doi:10.1007/BF01405730

Robertazzi, T. G. (1993). *Performance evaluation of high speed switching fabrics and networks: ATM, broadband ISDN, and MAN technology*. New York: IEEE Press.

Roberts, N. H., Andersen, D. F., Deal, R. M., Grant, M. S., & Shaffer, W. A. (1983). *Introduction to computer simulation: The system dynamics modeling approach*. Reading, MA: Addison-Wesley.

Rogers, E. M. (1962). *Diffusion of innovation*. New York: Free Press.

Rosen, S. (1974). Hedonic prices and implicit markets: products differentiation in pure competition. *The Journal of Political Economy*, *82*, 34–55. doi:10.1086/260169

Rosenthal, P. (1995). Gender differences in managers' attributions for successful work performance. *Women in Management Review*, *10*(6), 26. doi:10.1108/09649429510096006

Rosenweig, C., & Parry, M. L. (1994). Potential impact of climate change on world food supply. *Nature*, *367*, 133–138. doi:10.1038/367133a0

Rossiter, D. G., & Riha, S. J. (1999). Modeling plant competition with the GAPS object-oriented dynamic simulation model. *Agronomy Journal*, *91*(5), 773–783. doi:10.2134/agronj1999.915773x

Rounds, S. A. (2007). *Temperature effects of point sources, riparian shading, and dam operations on the Willamette River, Oregon* (Scientific Investigations Rep. No. 2007-5185). U.S. Geological Survey.

Rouwette, E. A. J. (2003). *Group model building as mutual persuasion*. Nijmegen, The Netherlands: Wolf Legal Publishers.

Rouwette, E., Vennix, J., & Mullekom, T. (2002). Group model building effectiveness: A review of assessment studies. *System Dynamics Review*, *18*, 5–45. doi:10.1002/sdr.229

Rowley, J., & Slack, F. (2009). Conceptions of wisdom. *Journal of Information Science*, *35*(1), 110–119. doi:10.1177/0165551508092269

Roy, A. (2003, January). How efficient is your reverse supply chain? *Effective Executive*, 52-55.

Rust, R. T., & Kannan, P. K. (2003). E-service: A new paradigm for business in the electronic environment. *Communications of the ACM*, *46*(6), 36–42. doi:10.1145/777313.777336

Ryan, T. (2000). The role of simulation gaming in policy-making. *Systems Research and Behavioral Science*, *17*, 359–364. doi:10.1002/1099-1743(200007/08)17:4<359::AID-SRES306>3.0.CO;2-S

Saaty, T. L. (1980). *The analytic hierarchy process*. New York: McGraw-Hill.

Saha, M. N., Saha, A. R., Mandal, B. C., & Ray, P. K. (2000). Effects of long-term jute-rice-wheat cropping system on crop yields and soil fertility. In Abrol, I. P., Bronson, K. F., Duxbury, J. M., & Gupta, R. K. (Eds.), *Long-term Soil Fertility Experiments in Rice-Wheat Cropping Systems*. New Delhi, India: RWC.

Sahu, G. P., & Gupta, M. P. (2007). Uses' acceptance of E-government: a study of Indian central excise. *International Journal of Electronic Government Research*, *3*(3), 1–21.

SAS Institute. (2009). *The SAS System for Windows (Release 9.2)*. Cary, NC: SAS Institute.

Saseendran, S. A., Hubbard, K. G., Singh, K. K., Rathore, L. S., & Singh, S. V. (1998a). Optimum Transplanting Dates for rice in Kerala, India, Determined Using Both CERESv3.0 and ClimProb. *Agronomy Journal*, *90*, 185–190. doi:10.2134/agronj1998.00021962009000020011x

Saseendran, S. A., Singh, K. K., Rathore, L. S., Rao, G. S. L. H. V., Mendiratta, N., Lakshmi, N., & Singh, S. V. (1998b). Evaluation of the CERES-Ricev3.0 model for the climate conditions of the state of Kerala, India. *Applied Meteorology*, *5*, 385–392. doi:10.1017/S1350482798000954

Saseendran, S. A., Singh, K. K., Rathore, L. S., Singh, S. V., & Sinha, S. K. (2000). Effects of climate change on rice production in the tropical humid climate of Kerala, India. *Climatic Change*, *44*, 495–514. doi:10.1023/A:1005542414134

Sasser, W. E. Jr, Olsen, P. R., & Wyckoff, D. D. (1978). *Management of Service Operations: Text and Cases*. Boston: Allyn and Bacon.

Satake, M., & Tsutsui, Y. (2002). Why is Kyoto a haven of shinkin banks? Analysis based on the efficient structure hypothesis. In T. Yuno (Ed.), *Regional finance: A case of Kyoto*. Tokyo: Nippon Hyoron Sha.

Saunders, A., & Cornett, M. M. (2008) *Financial institutions management: A risk management approach*. New York: McGraw-Hill/Irwin.

Scharmer, C. O. (2000, May 25-26). Presencing: Learning from the future as it emerges: On the tacit dimension of learning revolutionary change. In *Conference on Knowledge and Intuition*, Helsinki, Finland.

Scharmer, C. O. (2007, May 2). *Theory U: Leading from the future as it emerges* (1st ed.). SoL, the Society for Organizational Learning.

Schmidt, C. W. (2006). Unfair trade e-waste in Africa. *Environmental Health Perspectives, 114*(4), A232–A235.

Schneck, P. B. (1990). Supercomputers. *Annual Review of Computer Science, 4*, 13–36. doi:10.1146/annurev.cs.04.060190.000305

Sealey, C., & Lindley, J. T. (1977). Inputs, outputs and a theory of production and cost at depository financial institutions. *The Journal of Finance, 33*, 1251–1266. doi:10.2307/2326527

Secunda, S., Collin, M. L., & Melloul, A. (1998). Groundwater vulnerability assessment using a composite model combining DRASTIC with extensive agricultural land use in Israel's Sharon region. *Journal of Environmental Management, 54*(1), 39–57. doi:10.1006/jema.1998.0221

Seeley, C., & Reason, P. (2008). Expressions of energy: An epistemology of presentational knowing. In P. Liamputtong & J. Rumbold (Eds.), *Knowing Differently: Arts-based and collaborative research methods*. New York: Nova Science Publishers.

Sellami, M. H., & Sifaoui, M. S. (1999). Modelling solar radiative transfer inside the oasis; Experimental validation. *Journal of Quantitative Spectroscopy & Radiative Transfer, 63*, 85–96. doi:10.1016/S0022-4073(98)00137-X

Senge, P. (1990). *The fifth discipline: The art and practice of the learning organization*. New York: Doubleday.

Sevcik, P. (2006). Application demands outrun internet improvements. *Business Communications Review, 36*(1).

Shafer, B. A., & Dezman, L. E. (1982). Development of a Surface Water Supply Index (SWSI) to assess the severity of drought conditions in snowpack runoff areas. In *Proceedings of the Western Snow Conference*, Colorado State University, Fort Collins, CO (pp. 164-175).

Sheehan, W. G. (1989). Contract warehousing: the evolution of an industry. *Journal of Business Logistics, 10*(1), 31–49.

Shephard, R. W. (1953). *Cost and production functions*. NJ: Princeton University Press.

Shephard, R. W. (1970). *Theory of cost and production functions*. NJ: Princeton University Press.

Sherchand, K. (1998). Use of simulation modelling to assess potential yield in the RW systems in different climatic environments: Progress report. In *Proceedings of the RW research end of project workshop*, Kathmandu, Nepal (pp. 34-38).

Shim, J. P., Warkentin, M., Courtney, J. F., Power, D. J., Ramesh, S., & Carlsson, C. (2002). Past, present and future of decision support technology. *Decision Support Systems, 33*(2), 111–126. doi:10.1016/S0167-9236(01)00139-7

Shipley, C., & Fish, M. (1996). *How the World Wide Web works*. Emeryville, CA: Ziff-Davis.

Shi, W. (2002). The contribution of organizational factors in the success of electronic government commerce. *International Journal of Public Administration, 25*(5), 629–657. doi:10.1081/PAD-120003293

Shortle, J. S. (1987). Allocative implications of comparisons between the marginal costs of point and nonpoint source pollution abatement. *Northeastern Journal of Agricultural and Resource Economics, 16*(1), 17–23.

Siemer, W. F., & Otto, P. (2005, July 17-21). A group model-building intervention to support wildlife management. In *Proceedings of the 23rd International Conference of the System Dynamics Society,* Boston, MA.

Siemer, W. F., Decker, D. J., Gore, M. L., & Otto, P. (2007). *Working through black bear management issues: A practitioner's guide*. Ithaca, NY: Northeast Wildlife Damage Management Research and Outreach Cooperative.

Silverman, D. (2000). Analyzing talk and text. In N. K. Denzin & Y. S. Lincoln (Eds.), *Handbook of qualitative research*. Thousand Oaks, CA: Sage Publications, Inc.

Simon, H. A. (1960). *The new science of management decisions*. New York: Random House.

Sinclair, A. R. E., Fryxell, J. M., & Caughley, G. (2006). *Wildlife ecology, conservation, and management*. Boston: Blackwell Publishing.

Singh, J. (2004). Tackling measurement problems with item response theory: Principles, characteristics, and assessment, with an illustrative example. *Journal of Business Research, 57*, 184–208. doi:10.1016/S0148-2963(01)00302-2

Singh, K. N., & Swarup, A. (2000). Effect of long-term rice-wheat cropping sequence on yield and soil properties in reclaimed sodic soils. In Abrol, I. P., Bronson, K. F., Duxbury, J. M., & Gupta, R. K. (Eds.), *Long-term Soil Fertility Experiments in Rice-Wheat Cropping Systems*. New Delhi, India: RWC.

Singh, U., & Thornton, P. K. (1992). Using crop models for sustainability and environmental quality assessment. *Outlook on Agriculture, 2*, 209–218.

Singh, U., Thornton, P. K., Saka, A. R., & Dent, J. B. (1993). Maize modeling in Malawi: A tool for soil fertility research and development. In Penning de Vries, F. W. T. (Ed.), *Systems approaches for agricultural development*. Dordrecht, The Netherlands: Kluwer Academic.

Sinha, S. K., Singh, G. B., & Rai, M. (1998). *Decline in crop productivity in Haryana and Punjab: myth or reality?* New Delhi, India: Indian Council of Agricultural Research.

Sinoquet, H., & Caldwell, R. M. (1995). Estimation of light capture and partitioning in intercropping systems. In Sinoquet, H., & Cruz, P. (Eds.), *Ecophysiology of Tropical Intercropping* (pp. 79–97). Paris: INRA editions.

Sinoquet, H., Rakocevic, M., & Varlet-Grancher, C. (2000). Comparison of models for daily light partitioning in multispecies canopies. *Agricultural and Forest Meteorology, 101*, 251–263. doi:10.1016/S0168-1923(99)00172-0

Skjott-Larsen, T., Schary, P. B., Mikkola, J. H., & Kotzab, H. (2007). Introduction to the supply chain. In *Managing the Global Supply Chain* (3rd ed.). Frederiksberg, Denmark: Copenhagen Business School Press.

Smakhtin, V. U., & Hughes, D. A. (2004). *Review, Automated Estimation and Analysis of Drought Indices in South Asia*. Colombo, Sri Lanka: IWMI.

Smith, J. E., & Weingarten, F. W. (1997). *Research challenges for the next generation internet*. Wasthington, DC: Computing Research Association.

Snowden, D. J. (2002). Complex acts of knowing: Paradox and descriptive self-awareness. *Special Edition Journal of Knowledge Management, 6*(2), 1–13.

Song, Y. N., Marschner, P., Li, L., Bao, X. G., Sun, J. H., & Zhang, F. S. (2007). Community composition of ammonia-oxidizing bacteria in the rhizosphere of inter-cropped wheat (*Triticum aestivum* L.), maize (*Zea mays* L.) and faba bean (*Vicia faba* L.). *Biology and Fertility of Soils, 44*(2), 307–314. doi:10.1007/s00374-007-0205-y

Southwick, K. (1999). *High noon: The inside story of Scott McNealy and the rise of Sun*

Sprague, R. H. (1980). A framework for the development of decision support systems. *Management Information Sciences Quarterly, 4*, 1–25.

Srivastava, S. C., & Teo, T. H. (2007). E-Government payoffs: evidence from cross-country data. *Journal of Global Information Management, 15*(4), 20–40.

Stake, R. E. (2000). Case studies. In N. K. Denzin & Y. S. Lincoln (Eds.), *Handbook of Qualitative Research* (pp. 435-454). Thousand Oaks, CA: Sage Publications Inc.

Stave, K. (2002). Using system dynamics to improve public participation in environmental decisions. *System Dynamics Review, 18*(2), 139–167. doi:10.1002/sdr.237

Stein, E. W., & Zwass, V. (1995). Actualizing organizational memory with information systems. *Information Systems Research, 6*(2), 85–117. doi:10.1287/isre.6.2.85

Steinmuller, W. (1996). The U.S. software industry: An analysis and interpretive history. In D.

Sterling, T., Salmon, J., Becker, D., & Savarese, D. F. (1999). *How to build a Beowulf*. London, MA: MIT Press

Sterman, J. D. (2000). *Business dynamics – Systems thinking and modeling for a complex world*. Boston: McGraw-Hill.

Sterman, J. D. (Ed.). (2002). The global citizen: Celebrating the life of Dana Meadows. *System Dynamics Review*, *18*(2), 100–310.

Stiglitiz, J., & Weiss, A. (1981). Credit rationing in markets with imperfect information. *The American Economic Review*, *82*(3), 393–410.

Stoneman, P. (2001). *The economics of technological diffusion*. Malden, MA: Blackwell Publishing.

Straub, D., Limayem, M., & Karahanna-Evaristo, E. (1995). Measuring system usage: implication for IS theory testing. *Management Science*, *41*(8), 1328–1342. doi:10.1287/mnsc.41.8.1328

Streicher-Porte, M., Widmer, R., Jain, A., Bader, H.-P., Scheidegger, R., & Kytzia, S. (2005). Key drivers of the e-waste recycling system: assessing and modeling e-waste processing in the informal sector in Delhi. *Environmental Impact Assessment Review*, *25*, 472–291. doi:10.1016/j.eiar.2005.04.004

Sui, D. (1998). GIS-based urban modeling: Practices, problems, and prospects. *International Journal of Geographical Information Science*, *12*, 651–671. doi:10.1080/136588198241581

Susskind, L., & Field, P. (1996). *Dealing with an angry public*. New York: The Free Press.

Tanikawa, M. (2001, March 11). A cautious sibling waits to see what works. *New York Times*, Section 3, p. 14.

Tansley, A. G. (1935). The use and abuse of vegetational terms and concepts. *Ecology*, *16*, 284–307. doi:10.2307/1930070

Tanzi, T. (2000). Principles and practices in TeleGeomatics. In *Proceedings of the Second International Symposium on Telegeoprocessing* (pp. 10-12).

Tapper, S. (1992). *Game heritage. An ecological review from shooting and gamekeeping records*. Fordingbridge, UK: Game Conservancy Ltd.

Tatewaki, K. (1991). *Banking and finance in Japan: An introduction to the Tokyo market*. London: Routledge.

Taylor, S., & Todd, P. (1995). Assessing IT usage: the role of prior experience. *Management Information Systems Quarterly*, *19*(4), 561–571. doi:10.2307/249633

Taynor, J., & Deaux, K. (1973). When women are more deserving than men: Equity, attribution, and perceived sex differences. *Journal of Personality and Social Psychology*, *23*(5), 360–367. doi:10.1037/h0035118

Teague, J. (2002). Women in computing: What brings them to it, what keeps them in it? *SIGCSE Bulletin*, *34*(2), 147–158. doi:10.1145/543812.543849

ten Berge, H. F. M., Aggarwal, P. K., & Kropff, M. J. (1997). *Applications of rice modeling*. Amsterdam: Elsevier Publishers.

Teng, P. S., & Penning de Vries, F. W. T. (1992). *Systems approaches for agricultural development*. New York: Elsevier.

Terazono, A., Murakami, S., Abe, N., Inanc, B., Moriguchi, Y., & Sakai, S.-I. (2006). Current status and research on E-waste issues in Asia. *Journal of Material Cycles and Waste Management*, *8*(1), 1–12. doi:10.1007/s10163-005-0147-0

Terborg, J. R., & Ilgen, D. R. (1975). A theoretical approach to sex discrimination in traditionally masculine occupations. *Organizational Behavior and Human Performance*, *13*, 352–376. doi:10.1016/0030-5073(75)90056-2

Terborg, J. R., Peters, L. H., Ilgen, D. R., & Smith, F. (1977). Organizational and personal correlates of attitudes toward women as mangers. *Academy of Management Journal*, *20*(1), 89–100. doi:10.2307/255464

Tervonen, T., & Figueira, J. R. (2008). A Survey on stochastic multicriteria acceptability analysis methods. *Journal of Multi-Criteria Decision Analysis*, *15*, 1–14. doi:doi:10.1002/mcda.407

The World Bank. (2006). *Reengaging in agricultural water management: challenges and options*. Washington, DC: World Bank. Retrieved from www.worldbank.org

Thornton, P. K., Dent, J. B., & Caldwell, R. M. (1990). Applications and issues in the modelling of intercropping systems in the tropics. *Agriculture Ecosystems & Environment*, *31*(2), 133–146. doi:10.1016/0167-8809(90)90215-Y

Tidwell, V., & Lowry, T. (2008). *Personal communication*. Albuquerque, NM: Sandia National Laboratories.

Tidwell, V. D., Passell, H. D., Conrad, S. H., & Thomas, R. P. (2004). System dynamics modeling for community-based water planning: Application to the Middle Rio Grande. *Aquatic Sciences, 66*(4), 357–372. doi:10.1007/s00027-004-0722-9

Timsina, J., Adhikari, B., & Ganesh, K. C. (1997). *Modelling and simulation of rice, wheat and maize crops for selected sites and the potential effects of climate change on their productivity in Nepal (Consultancy Rep.)*. Harihar Bhawan, Nepal: Ministry of Agriculture.

Timsina, J., & Connor, D. J. (2001). Productivity and management of rice-wheat cropping systems: issues and challenges. *Field Crops Research, 69*, 93–132. doi:10.1016/S0378-4290(00)00143-X

Timsina, J., & Humphreys, E. (2006). Applications of CERES-Rice and CERES-Wheat in Research, Policy and Climate Change Studies in Asia: A Review. *International Journal of Agricultural Research, 1*(3), 202–225. doi:10.3923/ijar.2006.202.225

Timsina, J., Singh, U., Badaruddin, M., & Meisner, C. (1998). Cultivar, nitrogen and moisture effects on a RW sequence: Experimentation and simulation. *Agronomy Journal, 90*, 119–130. doi:10.2134/agronj1998.00021962009000020001x

Timsina, J., Singh, U., & Singh, Y. (1996). Addressing Sustainability of RW Systems: Analysis of Long-term Experimentation and Simulation. In Kropff, , (Eds.), *Application of systems approaches at the field level* (pp. 383–397). Dordrecht, The Netherlands: Kluwer Academic Publishers.

Tinsley, R. L. (2004). *Developing smallholder agriculture – a global perspective*. Brussels, Belgium: AgBé Publishing.

Tiwana, A., & Ramesh, B. (2001). E-services: Problems, opportunities, and digital platforms. In *Proceedings of the 34th Hawaii International Conference on Systems Sciences* (pp. 1-8).

Tobler, W. (1979). Cellular Geography. In Gale, S., & Olsson, G. (Eds.), *Philosophy in Geography* (pp. 379–386). Dordrecht, The Netherlands: Reidel.

Tolbert, C. J., Mossberger, K., & McNeal, R. (2008). Institutions, policy innovation, and e-government in the American states. *Public Administration Review, 68*(3), 549–563. doi:10.1111/j.1540-6210.2008.00890.x

Tompkins, J. A. (2000). *No boundaries*. Raleigh, NC: Tompkins Press.

Tong, X. (2004). Global mandate, national policies, and local responses: scale conflicts in China's management of imported e-waste. In *Proceedings of the 2004 IEEE International Symposium on Electronics and the Environment* (pp. 204-207).

Top500 (2007). *Top500 supercomputing sites*. Retrieved 20 June 2008, from www.top500.org

Torell, A., Libbin, J., & Miller, M. (1990). The market value of water in the Ogallala aquifer. *Land Economics, 66*, 163–175. doi:10.2307/3146366

Tóth, S. (1991). Game management - hunting. In Keresztesi, B. (Ed.), *Forestry in Hungary 1920 - 1985* (pp. 164–210). Budapest, Hungary: Akadémiai Kiadó.

Tóth, S. (2005). *A hírnév kötelez. Vadászat és vadgazdálkodás Magyarországon 1945-1990* (2nd ed.). Budapest, Hungary: Nimród Alapítvány.

Tóth, S. (2007). *Nyitány a hírnévhez. Vadászat és vadgazdálkodás Magyarországon 1945-1951*. Budapest, Hungary: Nimród Alapítvány.

Tóth, S. (2008). *Szél alatt - hátszélben. Vadászat és vadgazdálkodás Magyarországon 1951-1957*. Budapest, Hungary: Nimród Alapítvány.

Trauth, E. M., Quesenberry, J. L., & Morgan, A. J. (2004). *Understanding the under representation of women in IT: Toward a theory of individual differences*. Paper presented at the SIGMIS'04, Tucson, AZ.

Trauth, E. M. (2002). Odd girl out: An individual differences perspective on women in the IT profession. *Information Technology & People, 15*(2), 98–118. doi:10.1108/09593840210430552

Trauth, E. M., Quesenberry, J. L., & Huang, H. (2008). A multicultural analysis of factors influencing career choice for women in the information technology workforce. *Journal of Global Information Management, 16*(4), 1–23.

Triplett, J. (2004). *Handbook on hedonic indexes and quality adjustments in price indexes: Special application to information technology products* (STI Working Paper No. 2004/9). Statistical Analysis of Science, Technology and Industry, OECD.

Trunick, P. A. (1989). Outsourcing: a single source for many talents. *Transportation & Distribution,* 20-23.

Tsubo, M., & Walker, S. (2002). A model of radiation interception and use by maize-bean intercrop canopy. *Agricultural and Forest Meteorology, 110,* 203–215. doi:10.1016/S0168-1923(01)00287-8

Tsubo, M., Walker, S., & Ogindo, H. O. (2005). A simulation of cereal-legume intercropping systems for semi-arid regions. I. Model development. *Field Crops Research, 93,* 10–22. doi:10.1016/j.fcr.2004.09.002

Tsuji, G. Y., Hoogenboom, G., & Thornton, P. K. (1998). *Understanding options for agricultural production.* Dordrecht, The Netherlands: Kluwer Academic Publishers.

Tsuji, G. Y., Uehara, G., & Balas, S. (1994). *DSSAT v 3.* Honolulu, HI: University of Hawaii.

U.S. Congress. (1993). *Advanced network technology background paper* (OTA-BP-TCT-101).

U.S. Environmental Protection Agency (US EPA). (2004). *Water quality trading assessment handbook: Can water quality trading advance your watershed's goals? (EPA 841-B-04-001).* Washington, DC: U.S. Environmental Protection Agency.

U.S. Environmental Protection Agency (US EPA). (2007). *Water quality trading toolkit for permit writers (EPA 833-R-07-004).* Washington, DC: U.S. Environmental Protection Agency, Office of Wastewater Management, Water Permits Division.

UNESCO. *(1998).* Summary and recommendations of the International Conference on World Water Resources at the beginning of the 21st century 'Water: a looming crisis'. *Paris: France.*

Uricchio, V. F., Giordano, R., & Lopez, N. (2004). A fuzzy knowledge-based decision support system for groundwater pollution risk evaluation. *Journal of Environmental Management, 73*(3), 189–197. doi:10.1016/j.jenvman.2004.06.011

Vacik, H., & Lexer, M. J. (2001). Application of a spatial decision support system in managing the protection forests of Vienna for sustained yield of water resources. *Forest Ecology and Management, 143*(1-3), 65–76. doi:10.1016/S0378-1127(00)00506-5

van den Belt, M. (2000). *Mediated modeling: A collaborative approach for the development of shared understanding and evaluation of environmental policy scenarios, with case studies in the Fox, River, Wisconsin and the Ria Formosa, Portugal.* Unpublished PhD thesis, University of Maryland, College Park, MD.

van den Belt, M. (2004). *Mediated modeling.* Washington, DC: Island Press.

Vandermeer, J. (1989). *The ecology of intercropping.* New York: Cambridge University.

Vennix, J. A. M. (1994, July). *Building consensus in strategic decision-making: Insights from the process of group model building.* Paper presented at the 1994 International System Dynamics Conference, Stirling, Scotland.

Vennix, J. A. M. (1996). *Group model building. Facilitating team learning using system dynamics.* New York: John Wiley and Sons.

Vennix, J. A. M. (1999). Group model building: Tackling messy problems. *System Dynamics Review, 15*(4), 379–401. doi:10.1002/(SICI)1099-1727(199924)15:4<379::AID-SDR179>3.0.CO;2-E

Ventana Systems, Inc. (2005). *Vensim DSS.* Version 5.5c.

Videira, N. (2005). *Stakeholder participation in environmental decision-making: The role of participatory modeling.* Unpublished PhD thesis, University of New Lisbon, Lisbon, Portugal.

Videira, N., Antunes, P., & Santos, R. (2009). Scoping river basin management issues with participatory modelling: The Baixo Guadiana experience. *Ecological Economics, 68*(4), 965–978. doi:10.1016/j.ecolecon.2008.11.008

Videira, N., Antunes, P., Santos, R., & Gamete, S. (2003). Participatory modelling in environmental decision-making: The Ria Formosa Natural Park case study. *Journal of Environmental Assessment Policy and Management, 5*(3), 421–447. doi:10.1142/S1464333203001371 von Bertalanffy, L. (1976). *General system theory: Foundations, development, applications.* New York: Braziller.

von Winterfeldt, D., & Edwards, W. (1986). *Decision Analysis and Behavioral Research.* UK: Cambridge University Press.

Vonk, G., Geertman, S., & Schot, P. (2007). New technologies in old hierarchies: the diffusion of geo-information technologies in Dutch public organizations. *Public Administration Review, 67*(4), 745–756. doi:10.1111/j.1540-6210.2007.00757.x

Voudouris, K. (2009). Assessing groundwater pollution risk in Sarigkiol basin, NW Greece. In Gallo, M., & Herrari, M. (Eds.), *River Pollution Research Progress.* Hauppauge, New York: Nova Science Publishers Inc.

Voudouris, K., Panagopoulos, A., & Koumantakis, I. (2004). Nitrate pollution in the coastal aquifer system of the Korinthos prefecture (Greece). *Global Nest: the International Journal, 6*(1), 31–38.

Vrba, J., & Zaporozec, A. (Eds.). (1994). Guidebook on mapping groundwater vulnerability. In *Proceedings of the International contributions to hydrogeology.* Hanover, Germany: Heise.

Waddock, S. (2001). Integrity and mindfulness: Foundations of corporate citizenship. In J. Andriof & M. McIntosh (Eds.), *Perspectives on Corporate Citizenship.* Sheffield, UK: Greenleaf Publishing.

Walsham, G. (1995). Interpretive case studies in IS research: nature and method. *European Journal of Information Systems, 4*, 74–81. doi:10.1057/ejis.1995.9

Walsham, G. (2001). Knowledge management: The benefits and limitations of computer systems. *European Management Journal, 19*(6), 599–608. doi:10.1016/S0263-2373(01)00085-8

Walsham, G. (2006). Doing interpretive research. *European Journal of Information Systems, 15*(3), 320–330. doi:10.1057/palgrave.ejis.3000589

Walsh, J. P., & Ungson, G. R. (1991). Organizational memory. *Academy of Management Review, 16*(1), 57–91. doi:10.2307/258607

Walters, C. (1986). *Adaptive management of renewable resources* (2001 ed.). New York: Macmillan.

Wang, P., Turner, G., Lauer, D., Allen, M., Simms, S., Hart, D., et al. (2004). Linpack performance on a geographically distributed Linux cluster. In *Proceedings of the 18th International Parallel and Distributed Processing Symposium* (pp. 245-250).

Wang, J. (2008). Society systems science: A brand new discipline. *International Journal of Society Systems Science, 1*(1), 1–3.

Wang, J., Xia, J., Hollister, K., & Wang, Y. (2009). Comparative analysis of international education systems. *International Journal of Information Systems in the Service Sector, 1*(1), 1–14.

Wang, Y.-S., Wang, H.-Y., & Shee, D. Y. (2007). Measuring e-learning systems success in an organizational context: Scale development and validation. *Computers in Human Behavior, 23*(4), 1792–1808. doi:10.1016/j.chb.2005.10.006

Weichselbaumer, D. (2004). Is it Sex or Personality? The impact of sex stereotypes on discrimination in applicant selection. *Eastern Economic Journal, 30*(2), 159–186.

Weichselbaumer, D., & Winter-Ebmer, R. (2005). A meta-analysis of the international gender wage gap. *Journal of Economic Surveys, 19*(7), 459–512.

Weick, K., & Sutcliffe, K. (2006). Mindfulness and the quality of organizational attention. *Organization Science, 17*(4), 514–524. doi:10.1287/orsc.1060.0196

Weigel, D., & Cao, B. (1999). Applying GIS and OR techniques to solve Sears technician-dispatching and home-delivery problems. *Interfaces, 29*, 112–130. doi:10.1287/inte.29.1.112

West, D. (2004). E-Government and the transformation of service delivery and citizen Attitudes. *Public Administration Review, 64*(1), 15–27. doi:10.1111/j.1540-6210.2004.00343.x

Westholm, H., & Aichholzer, G. (2003). Prima Strategic Guideline 1: eAdministration. *PRISMA Project and Information Society Technology.* Retrieved on May 25, 2008 from http://www.eivc.org/uni/Uploads/admin/SG1administration.pdf.

Wheatley, M. (2001a). *Listening.* Berkana Institute Writings. Retrieved September 26, 2004, from http://www.berkana.org/resources/listening.hmtl.

Wheatley, M. (2001b). *Partnering with confusion and uncertainty.* Shambala Sun. Retrieved September 22, 2008 from http://www.margaretwheatley.com/articles/partneringwithconfusion.html.

Wheatley, M. (2005). *Leadership and the new science: Discovering order in a chaotic world* (3rd ed.). Berrett-Koehler Publishers, Inc.

Wiles, L. J., & Wilkerson, G. G. (1991). Modeling competition for light between soybean and broadleaf weeds. *Agricultural Systems, 35,* 37–51. doi:10.1016/0308-521X(91)90145-Z

Wilhite, D. A. (1993). *Drought Assessment, Management and Planning: Theory and Case Studies.* Dordrecht, The Netherlands: Kluwer Academic Publishers.

Wilhite, D. A. (2000). *Drought as a natural hazard: Concepts and definitions. Drought: A Global Assessment.* London: Routledge.

Wilhite, D. A., & Glantz, M. H. (1985). Understanding the drought phenomenon: The role of definitions. *Water International, 10,* 111–120. doi:10.1080/02508068508686328

Williams, K. C., Hernandez, E. H., Petrosky, A. R., & Page, R. A. (2008). Fine-Tuning useful

Woodward, R. T., Kaiser, R. A., & Wicks, A. B. (2002). The structure and practice of water quality trading markets. *Journal of the American Water Resources Association, 38*(4), 967–979. doi:10.1111/j.1752-1688.2002.tb05538.x

Wooldridge, J. (2006). *Introductory econometrics: A modern approach* (3rd ed.). Gale, UK: Thomson Learning.

World Bank Online. (2006, March 18). *A global food crisis can be averted.* Washington, DC: World Bank. Retrieved from www.worldbank.org/

World Bank Online. (2008). *Speech of world bank managing director at the US-Arab economic forum.* Washington, DC: World Bank. Retrieved from http://web.worldbank.org/

World Bank Online. (2009). *Food crisis - what the world bank is doing.* Washington, DC: World Bank. Retrieved from http://www.worldbank.org/html/extdr/foodprices

World Meteorological Organization (WMO). (1975). *Drought and Agriculture.* Tech. Rep. No. 138). Geneva, Switzerland: WMO.

World Meteorological Organization (WMO). (1993). *Drought and Desertification* (Tech. Rep. No. 605). Geneva, Switzerland: WMO.

World Meteorological Organization (WMO). (1995)... *The Global Climate System Review, 819,* 150.

World Meteorological Organization (WMO). (2001). *WMO Statement on the Status of the Global Climate in 2000.* Geneva, Switzerland: WMO.

Wu, H., Hayes, M. J., Welss, A., & Hu, Q. (2001). An evaluation the standardized precipitation index, the China-z index and the statistical z-score. *International Journal of Climatology, 21,* 745–758. doi:10.1002/joc.658

Xing, R., Zhang, Y., Wang, Z., & Xia, J. (2009). Broadband challenge facing global

Yadav, R. L., Dwivedi, B. S., & Pandey, P. S. (2000a). Rice-wheat cropping system: assessment of sustainability under green manuring and chemical fertilizer inputs. *Field Crops Research, 65,* 15–30. doi:10.1016/S0378-4290(99)00066-0

Yadav, R. L., Dwivedi, B. S., Prasad, K., Tomar, O. K., Shurpali, N. J., & Panday, P. S. (2000b). Yield trends, and changes in soil organic-C and available NPK in a long-term rice-wheat system under integrated use of manures and fertilizers. *Field Crops Research, 68,* 219–246. doi:10.1016/S0378-4290(00)00126-X

Yang, D., Ghauri, P., & Sonmez, M. (2005). Competitive analysis of the software industry in China. *International Journal of Technology Management, 29*(1-2), 64–91. doi:10.1504/IJTM.2005.006005

Yatsalo, B., Kiker, G., Kim, J., Bridges, T., Seager, T., Gardner, K., et al. (2007). Application of multi-Criteria decision analysis tools for management of contaminated sediments. *Integrated Environmental Assessment and Management, 3*(2), 223–233. PubMed doi:10.1897/IEAM_2006-036.1

Yatsalo, B. I. (2007). Decision support system for risk based land management and rehabilitation of radioactively contaminated territories: PRANA approach. *International Journal of Emergency Management, 4*(3), 504–523. doi:doi:10.1504/IJEM.2007.014300

Yin, R. K. (2003). *Case study research: Design and methods* (3rd ed.). London: Sage Publications.

Yin, R. (2002). *Case study research*. Thousand Oaks, CA: Sage Publications.

Yokozawa, M., & Hara, T. (1992). A canopy photosynthesis model for the dynamics of size structure and self-thinning in plant populations. *Annals of Botany, 70*, 305–316.

Young, R. (1996). *Measuring economic benefits for water investments and policies* (Tech. Rep. No. 338). Washington, DC: World Bank.

Young, R. A. (2005). *Determining the Economic Value of Water: Concepts and Methods*. Washington, DC: Resources for the Future.

Yu, D., Xie, S., Wei, X., Zheng, Z., & Wang, K. (2008). A XML-based remote EMI sharing system conformable to Dicom. In *Proceedings of the international conference on technology and applications in biomedicine* (pp. 556-559).

Zeithaml, V. A., & Bitner, M. J. (1996). Customer expectations of service. In *Services Marketing*. New York: McGraw-Hill.

Zhang, L. (2007). *Productivity and resource use in cotton and wheat relay intercropping. Chapter 6: Development and validation of SUCROS-Cotton: A mechanistic crop growth simulation model for cotton, applied to Chinese cropping conditions*. Unpublished doctoral dissertation, Wageningen University, The Netherlands.

Zhang, F., & Li, L. (2003). Using competitive and facilitative interactions in intercropping systems enhances crop productivity and nutrient-use efficiency. *Plant and Soil, 248*, 305–312. doi:10.1023/A:1022352229863

Zhang, W., & Wang, X. J. (2002). Modeling for point-non-point source effluent trading: Perspective of non-point sources regulation in China. *The Science of the Total Environment, 292*, 167–176. doi:10.1016/S0048-9697(01)01105-6

Zhu, X., Healey, R. G., & Aspinall, R. J. (1998). A knowledge-based systems approach to design of spatial decision support system for environmental management. *Environmental Management, 22*(1), 35–48. doi:10.1007/s002679900082

Zhu, Z., Hsu, K., & Lillie, J. (2001). Outsourcing a strategic move: The process and the ingredients for success. *Management Decision, 39*(5), 373–378. doi:10.1108/EUM0000000005473

Zito, R., D'este, G., & Taylor, M. (1995). Global positioning systems in the time domain: How useful a tool for intelligent vehicle-highway systems? *Transportation Research Part C, Emerging Technologies, 3*, 193–209. doi:10.1016/0968-090X(95)00006-5

Zukav, G. (1989). *The seat of the soul*. New York: Simon and Schuster Inc.

About the Contributors

John Wang is a Professor in the Department of Management and Information Systems at Montclair State University (USA). Having received a scholarship award, he came to the USA and completed his PhD in operations research from Temple University. Due to his extraordinary contributions beyond a tenured full Professor, Dr. Wang has been honored with a special range adjustment in 2006. He has published over 100 refereed papers and six books. He has also developed several computer software programs based on his research findings. He is the Editor-in-Chief of *International Journal of Applied Management Science, International Journal of Information Systems and Supply Chain Management*, and the *International Journal of Information and Decision Sciences*. He is also the EIC for the *Advances in Information Systems and Supply Chain Management Book Series*. He has served as a guest editor and referee for many other highly prestigious journals. He has served as track chair and/or session chairman numerous times on the most prestigious international and national conferences. Also, he is an editorial advisory board member of the following publications: Intelligent Information Technologies: Concepts, Methodologies, Tools, and Applications, End-User Computing: Concepts, Methodologies, Tools, and Applications, Global Information Technologies: Concepts, Methodologies, Tools, and Applications, Information Communication Technologies: Concepts, Methodologies, Tools, and Applications, Multimedia Technologies: Concepts, Methodologies, Tools, and Applications, Information Security and Ethics: Concepts, Methodologies, Tools, and Applications, Electronic Commerce: Concepts, Methodologies, Tools, and Applications, Electronic Government: Concepts, Methodologies, Tools, and Applications, and other IGI Global titles. Furthermore, he is the editor of *Data Warehousing and Mining: Concepts, Methodologies, Tools, and Applications* and the *Encyclopedia of Data Warehousing and Mining* 1st and 2nd editions. His long-term research goal is on the synergy of operations research, data mining, and cybernetics.

* * *

Helaiel Almutairi is Associate Professor of Public Administration and Information Systems at Kuwait University. He holds a BSc from Kuwait University, a MPM from Carnegie Mellon University, and a MSIS and PhD from Pennsylvania State University, U.S. His current research interests include end user computing, the impacts of information systems (IS), IS and leadership, and e-government. He has published several articles in Arabic journals, and the following international journals: International Journal of Public Administration; International Journal of Management; Journal of Global Information Management; and the Journal of Information Systems.

Alexey Babutski graduated from the Department of Cybernetics at IATE in 2009, and started post-graduate work in IS. Main interests: development of distributed applications, GIS, MCDA, group decision-making support, Java

Elarbi Badidi is an Assistant Professor of computer science at the College of Information Technology (CIT) of United Arab Emirates University. Before joining the CIT, he held the position of bioinformatics group leader at the Biochemistry Department, University of Montreal from 2001 to July 2004. He received a Ph.D. in computer science from University of Montreal, Québec (Canada). His research interests include Web services and Service Oriented Computing, Middleware, and Bioinformatics data and tools integration.

Allyson M. Beall is on the faculty at both Washington State University, Pullman WA and University of Idaho, Moscow ID and is the expert to the Education and Outreach lead for the Ecosystem Services Research Program for the USEPA National Center for Environmental Assessment. Her main research and consulting involves the use of participatory system dynamics modeling to facilitate groups through environmental problem definition, potential future scenarios and policy testing. She also designs educational models to help explain the relationships between scientific, social and policy concerns. Dr. Beall earned her Doctorate in Environmental and Natural Resource Science at Washington State University. In addition to her research she teaches environmental science and environmental assessment.

Asmeret Bier is a Postdoctoral Appointee in the Validation and Uncertainty Quantification Department at Sandia National Laboratories in Albuquerque, New Mexico. She recently obtained her PhD in Environmental and Natural Resource Sciences at Washington State University in Pullman, Washington, with a dissertation on System Dynamics Simulation of a Thermal Water Quality Trading Market. Her research interests include market-based environmental policies, system dynamics modeling, model validation, sensitivity analysis, and simulation games.

William J. Chivers completed his Science degree in 1979 and worked in the IT industry and as a teacher of IT in technical colleges before returning to academia as a lecturer in IT. He has a research-based Masters in IT and is completing a PhD in Computer-Based Modelling of Complex Systems.

Brent Chrite is currently the Dean of the School of Business at Montclair State University and Professor of Management and International Business. Prior to arriving to MSU, Dr. Chrite was the Gemelli Faculty Fellow and Associate Dean for graduate programs at the Eller College of Management at the University of Arizona. Dr. Chrite also spent 14 years at the University of Michigan, most recently as the Director of the School's flagship research and outreach institute, the William Davidson Institute, focusing on the transformation of transition and emerging market economies. Dr. Chrite has been actively involved in academic leadership, research, teaching and technical assistance engagements in emerging and transition markets around the world. He has worked extensively with business leaders, policy makers and entrepreneurs in an effort to harness the energy and the dynamism of the private sector toward the alleviation of poverty and the investment in human capital. Dr. Chrite has lead research and development projects in dozens of countries in sub Saharan Africa, the Middle East, Central Asia, Central and Eastern Europe and Russia. Dean Chrite completed his undergraduate work at Michigan State University, his MS at the University of Missouri-Columbia, and his PhD at the University of Michigan.

Wilhelm Claupein is Professor for Plant Production at the Universität Hohenheim, Germany. He did his Ph.D at the Institute for Plant Production and Plant Breeding at the University of Giessen, Germany, and his Habilitation at the University of Göttingen, Germany, was assistant lecturer and lecturer at the Institute for Plant Production and Plant Breeding of the University of Göttingen and Professor for Plant Production at the Institute for Plant Production and Plant Breeding of the Agricultural University Wien, Austria. Between 2002 and 2005, he was executive director of the German Crop Science Society and is since 2005 a member of the board. His major research topics include crop production and cropping systems, soil cultivation systems, concepts for cultivation and traceability of genetically modified organisms, precision agriculture, organic farming, bioenergy, agro-forestry, and sustainable agriculture in the North China Plain.

Sándor Csányi is the Director of the Institute for Wildlife Conservation, Szent István University, Gödöllő, Hungary. He graduated as an agricultural engineer (MSc) at the Gödöllő University of Agricultural Sciences in 1983 and received his Ph.D. degree from the Hungarian Academy of Sciences in 1994. His most important research interests cover the population dynamics of cervids, modeling game population dynamics, and international systems of wildlife conservation and management. He started to work on the National Game Management Database in 1993 and since then is the leader of the program. He was also leading the development of the 24 game management regions of Hungary, and the 3-level planning system of game management introduced in 1997. Sándor Csányi has published >300 papers and wrote several chapters in Hungarian and international books on wildlife management and conservation, including a wildlife biology textbook used in wildlife management programs.

Tugrul Daim is an Associate Professor of Engineering and Technology Management at Portland State University. He is published in many journals including "Technology in Society", "Technology Forecasting and Social Change", "Int'l J of Innovation and Technology Management", "Technology Analysis and Strategic Management", and "Technovation". Dr.Daim received his BS in Mechanical Engineering from Bogazici University in Turkey, MS in Mechanical Engineering from Lehigh University in Pennsylvania, another MS in Engineering Management from Portland State University and a Ph.D. in Systems Science-Engineering Management from Portland State University.

Vladimir Didenko is the head of the Information Technology Lab at IATE. He graduated from Department of Cybernetics at IATE, did post-graduate work there on software development for risk analysis and risk-based landuse management, GIS and MCDA tool development and implementation. Main interests: distributed computer systems, GIS, spatial decision support systems, risks analysis.

Kevin E. Dow is an assistant professor of accounting at the University of Alaska, Anchorage. He received his PhD from the University of South Carolina. His research lies at the intersection of information systems and accounting and focuses on the design and use of accounting information for managing costs and evaluating business value. His papers have appeared in journals including The International Journal of Accounting Information Systems; the European Journal of Information Systems, Information Systems Research, Database for Advances in Information Systems, the International Journal of eCollaboration, the Journal of Emerging Technologies in Accounting, the Journal of Computer Information Systems, Management Accounting Quarterly, and in both national and international conference proceedings.

Larbi Esmahi is an associate professor of the school of computing and information systems at Athabasca University. He was the graduate program coordinator at the same school during 2002-2005. He holds a PhD in electrical engineering from Ecole Polytechnique, University of Montreal. His current research interests are in e-services, e-commerce, multiagent systems, and intelligent systems. He is member of the editorial board of many journals on the field of e-services and intelligent systems (IJISSC, IJISSS, IJAIS, JETWI, IJESMA, JDET, IJWLTT, and TKJSE). He is also member of the editorial advisory board of the Advances in Web-Based Learning Book Series, IGI Global. His articles appeared in the Journal of Electronic Commerce in Organizations, International Journal of Web-Based Learning and Teaching Technologies and the International Journal on Web Services Practices. He also published several book chapters and conference papers.

Rolf Färe is Professor in the Departments of Economics and Agricultural and Resource Economics at Oregon State University, Corvallis, Oregon, USA. He received a Docent in Economics from the University of Lund in 1976. His research interests include efficiency and productivity measurement, production theory, and environmental economics. He has published papers in Econometrica, Journal of Econometrics, Review of Economics and Statistics, and the American Economic Review and is the author and editor of twelve books.

Kay Fielden is Professor of Computing in the Department of Computing at Unitec Institute of Technology. She mentors staff research, supervises postgraduate students and teaches postgraduate research methods. Her research interests are grounded in conceptual modelling, qualitative research and systems thinking in human activity systems and research projects are most commonly conducted in the context of social informatics. Professor Fielden has a multidisciplinary background in mathematics, computer science and social ecology.

Andrew Ford is Professor of Environmental Science at Washington State University. His previous appointments have been in the Systems Management Department at the University of Southern California and the Energy Policy Group at the Los Alamos National Laboratory. His main research and consulting involve the use of computer simulation to support policy formulation on energy and the environmental problems. Dr. Ford earned his Doctorate from the Public Policy and Technology Program at Dartmouth College. He currently teaches modeling with an emphasis on energy and environmental problems in the western USA. He is the author of the Island Press text on *Modeling the Environment.* He uses the system dynamics approach to modeling and is the recipient of the Jay W. Forrester Award for the outstanding contribution to the field of system dynamics.

Hirofumi Fukuyama is Professor of Operations Research at the Faculty of Commerce in Fukuoka University, Japan. He received a Ph.D. in Economics from Southern Illinois University at Carbondale in 1988. Professor Fukuyama's research interest includes efficiency/productivity measurement in financial services industry, theory and applications of data envelopment analysis, Japanese economy and Japanese management. His work has appeared or is forthcoming in refereed journals on operations research, finance and economics. Such journals include European Journal of Operational Research, International Journal of Information Technology and Decision Making, Journal of Productivity Analysis, Journal of the

Operational Research Society, Journal of the Operations Research Society of Japan, Applied Financial Economics, Pacific-basin Finance Journal, Pacific Economic Review, Open Management Journal, Journal of Applied Economics, Managerial and Decision Economics and Socio-Economic Planning Sciences.

Simone Graeff-Hönninger was awarded for her Ph.D. thesis in plant nutrition from the Deutsche Maiskomitee (DMK) and had a fellowship of the Hessische Wissenschaftliche Nachwuchsförderung. After being a scientific coordinator of field trials and field research at Agrostat GmbH and a visiting scientist at the Department of Agricultural and Biological Engineering, Mississippi State University, USA, she completed her Habilitation at Universität Hohenheim, Germany, within her research topic precision agriculture and crop simulation modeling. As apl. Professor at the Institute of Crop Production and Grassland Research at the Universität Hohenheim, her research employs a systems approach to develop, test and improve genetic, physiological, nutrient and pest representation in crop growth simulation models for different spatial scales, and develop decision support systems. She has a research collaboration with the Mississippi State University, USA, on crop model development and improvement and is a member of an international effort to maintain, improve and conduct international validation of the CERES/CROPGRO models. Simone has a Science degree in physics and mathematics, an Arts degree in modern languages, a Computer Science diploma, and a Master of Mathematics degree. He lectures in IT, and his principal research interest is in computing education.

Sergei V. Gritsuik graduated from department of cybernetics at IATE, and is currently doing post-graduate work in Information Systematics (IS). Main interests: distributed applications development, MCDA, MODM, decision support systems, Java.

Gary Hackbarth is an Assistant Professor of Management Information Systems at Northern Kentucky University. He holds a Ph.D. from the University of South Carolina. His teaching, research, and consulting areas of interest include Project Management, Health Informatics, Information System Strategy, and Organizational Memory. He has published in the European Journal of Information Systems, Information & Management, Database for Advances in Information Systems, Information Systems Management, Journal of Web-Based Learning and Teaching Technologies, Journal of Electronic Commerce Research, the Financial Times, and in both national and international conference proceedings.

Raija Halonen currently acts as a Postdoctoral Fellow in the Centre for Innovation & Structural Change, National University of Ireland, Galway, Ireland. She received her Ph.D. in the Department of Information Processing Science, University of Oulu, Finland. Her main research interests are in information systems, and lately she has made research on knowledge management. Her background is in industry where she started her IS career with an IS implementation for factory workers. After that, she has worked both in the public sector and in private IT enterprises with information systems. Later, after entering into academia, due to her versatile working experiences, her interests have focused on social dynamics in information system projects. Despite her short academic career she has participated in several conferences giving presentations and chairing sessions. She has published her research in journals and conferences and gained good results in supervising graduate students.

Ric D. Herbert received his Honours degree in Economics from Macquarie University in 1974 and his Graduate Diploma in Computing Studies from the University of Canberra in 1978. After working in the IT industry, he returned to academia and studied a Master of Science and Computing in 1994, then went on to complete a PhD in Computer Science in 1998. He is currently an academic at the University of Newcastle and his research interests are in economics-based applications of computing.

Leslie S. Hiraoka is a Professor of Management at Kean University and is the author of Underwriting the Internet: How Technical Advances, Financial Engineering, and Entrepreneurial Genius Are Building the Information Highway (2005) and Global Alliances in the Motor Vehicle Industry (2001). He was awarded the Shigeo Shingo Prize for his research on Japanese auto transplants in the USA. He was an AACSB Federal Faculty Fellow at the U.S. Department of Commerce in Washington, D.C. and a contributor to Wiley Interscience's Encyclopedia of Electrical and Electronics Engineering (1999). He has a Doctorate of Engineering Science from Columbia University and an MBA from Rutgers University.

Jeffrey Hsu is an Associate Professor of Information Systems at the Silberman College of Business, Fairleigh Dickinson University. He is the author of numerous papers, chapters, and books, and has previous business experience in the software, telecommunications, and financial industries. His research interests include human-computer interaction, e-commerce, IS education, and mobile/ubiquitous computing. He is Managing Editor of International Journal of Data Analysis and Information Systems (IJDAIS), Associate Editor of the International Journal of Information and Communication Technology Education (IJICTE), and is on the editorial board of several other journals. Dr. Hsu received his Ph.D. in Information Systems from Rutgers University, a M.S. in Computer Science from the New Jersey Institute of Technology, and an M.B.A. from the Rutgers Graduate School of Management.

W. Roy Johnson is currently an Associate Professor of Management at Iowa State University. He received his Ph.D. degree in Industrial/Organizational Psychology from Bowling Green State University. He has published in journals such as Journal of Psychology, Journal of Social Behavior and Personality, Journal of Applied Social Psychology, Journal of Collective Negotiations, and the Journal of Counseling Psychology.

Nerantzis Kazakis received his MSc in Environmental Hydrogeology from Aristotle University of Thessaloniki, Greece in 2007. He is preparing his PhD thesis in Hydrogeology and has participated in many research projects.

Heike Knörzer has a degree in Letters and History at the Technische Universität Darmstadt, Germany, with special regard to agricultural history, and worked as a journalist. After her Master degree at the Universität Hohenheim, Germany, in Crop Production with the topics plant breeding and minimum tillage systems, she got a scholarship from the German Research Foundation (DFG) and the Chinese Ministry of Education. Within the International Research Training Group "Sustainable Resource Use in the North China Plain" she is doing her Ph.D. on design, modeling and evaluation of improved cropping strategies and multi-level interactions in mixed cropping systems.

Witaya Krajaysri is a lecturer and director of Master of Business Administration in Logistics and Supply Chain Management Program at School of Management, Mae Fah Luang University in Chiang Rai, Thailand. He obtained Doctor of Business Administration from University of South Australia. His research interests in logistics and supply chain management. He published his articles such as Strategic Outsourcing of Logistics Services in Chulalongkorn Review. He also taught several subjects at Mae Fah Luang University such as Business Logistics Management, Business Research, Strategic Management, Strategy and Supply Chain Management, Business Finance, Business Management, Business Policy, Business Venture and Entrepreneurship, Post harvest Operation and Marketing, Principles of Business and Finance and Introduction to Logistics and Supply Chain Management etc. He also experienced in working as Logistics and Operations Manager with International Company like APL Logistics, Hoechst and, Clariant etc.

Elisa Laukkanen, M.Sc. currently acts as an Information Systems Designer in the IT Administration Services department, University of Oulu, Oulu, Finland. She has received her master's degree in the Department of Information Processing Science, University of Oulu, Finland. Her main research interests are in information systems, and especially research on knowledge management. She has done IT development, design and maintenance work and acted as a teacher in the public sector. Nowadays she is working as a Technical Line Manager in an IS implementation project. Through her duties, her research interests are focused on social dynamics of transferring knowledge in the work community.

Róbert Lehoczki is a Junior Assistant Professor in the Institute for Wildlife Conservation, Szent István University, Gödöllő, Hungary. He received an MSc in agricultural and environmental management from the Szent István University and two postgraduate degrees, one in wildlife management from Szent István University and another in applied geoinformatics from the Budapest University of Technology and Economics, Hungary. He has been working in the National Game Management Database since 1997. His research interests include geographical information system applications in wildlife management practices and studies on roe deer space use and antler development, focusing on the effects of environmental factors.

Allan J. Lichtman is a Professor of History at American University in Washington, DC, USA. His research interests include American politics, quantitative methods, and political prediction. His seven books include Your Family History, Prejudice and the Old Politics: The Presidential Election of 1928, Ecological Inference, and The Thirteen Keys to the Presidency. The Keys system correctly predicted the popular vote outcome in every presidential election from 1984 to 2008. His latest books are The Keys to the White House, 2008 Edition and White Protestant Nation: The Rise of the American Conservative Movement, which was a finalist for the National Book Critics Circle Award in non-fiction. He has published more than 200 scholarly and op-ed articles that have appeared in such publications as the American Historical Review, the Proceedings of the National Academy of Sciences, the Journal of Law and Politics, the Journal of Legal Studies, the International Journal of Forecasting, the New York Times, the Washington Post, and the Los Angeles Times.

Igor Linkov is the Risk and Decision Science Focus Area lead with the US Army Engineer Research and Development Center, and Adjunct Professor of Engineering and Public Policy at Carnegie Mellon University. The Governor of Massachusetts has appointed Dr. Linkov to serve as a Scientific Advisor to the Toxic Use Reduction Institute. He is the recipient of the 2005 SRA Chauncey Starr Award for exceptional contribution to Risk Analysis. Main interests: ecological and human health risk assessment, risk management.

Timothy M. Lynar received his Honours degree in Information Technology from the University of Newcastle in 2007. He is currently a PhD candidate at the University of Newcastle studying Grid Resource Allocation for E-waste Resources.

Zisis Mallios is a Research Associate at the Department of Civil Engineering, Aristotle University of Thessaloniki, Greece. He obtained his Ph.D degree in Environmental and Resource Economics from Aristotle University of Thessaloniki. His research interests are environmental economics, and water resources management. He presented his research at international conferences, like Protection and Restoration of the Environment and International Conference on Environmental Science and Technology. His articles appeared in the "Water, Air & Soil Pollution: Focus" and "Global Nest Journal".

Oleg A. Mirzeabassov is a senior lecturer in the IS Department at IATE. He graduated from and did post-graduate work at MEPhI. He formerly worked at the Russian Institute of Agricultural Radiology and Argoecology (RIARAE) in the Mathematical modeling and Computer Systems lab, and at the IATE. Main interests: distributed computer systems, math modeling, distributed calculations, GIS, spatial decision support systems.

H.S. Ram Mohan is Professor of Meteorology in the School of Marine Sciences, Cochin University of Science and Technology, Cochin, Kerala, India. He is currently the Director and Dean of the faculty of Marine Sciences. He has 32 years of teaching and research experience. His present research interests include agricultural meteorology, hydrometeorology, and climate change impacts. He has more than 60 research publications and is the Editor in chief of the Journal of Marine and Atmospheric Research. He has guided 12 students for their doctoral degrees.

Bettina U. Müller is a Ph.D. student at the Institute of Crop Production and Grassland, Bioinformatics Unit, at the Universität Hohenheim, Germany. She obtained her Master degree in Agriculture at the University of Göttingen, Germany, and her Diploma degree in Bioinformatics at the University of Applied Sciences Weihenstephan, Germany.

Ramin Neshati is a manager of technology architecture and planning at Intel Corporation with more than 26 years of experience in the development and marketing of innovative technologies. He worked for Xerox Corporation, Dell and S3 before joining Intel in 1998. Ramin has served as director on the PCI-SIG board since 1999. He holds several degrees, including BS in Computer Science from Washington State University, MS in Computer Science from the University of Idaho and MBA from Pepperdine University. Currently he is pursuing a doctoral degree in Engineering and Technology Management at Portland State University.

Jason Papathanasiou holds a Ph.D. in Operational Research and Informatics and a degree in Physics, both from the Aristotle University of Thessaloniki, Greece. He is currently a full time lecturer in the department of Marketing and Operations Management, in the University of Macedonia, Greece. He has worked for a number of years as an external lecturer at the Technical Institute of Technology in Thessaloniki and the University of Western Macedonia and has organised and participated in a number of scientific conferences and workshops. He has conducted research in more than 10 National and EU funded projects such as the "Transactional Environmental Support System (TESS, FP7)", "Governance and Ecosystems Management for Conservation of Biodiversity (GEM-CON-BIO, FP6)", "Assessing the multiple Impacts of the Common Agricultural Policies (CAP) on Rural Economies (CAP-IRE, FP7)". He has a more than 40 papers published in international scientific journals and conferences and speaks Greek and English.

Irina Pichugina is a senior lecturer in the IS Department at IATE. She graduated from MSU under the Mechanics and Mathematics faculty, and completed post-graduate work in Hydrodynamics at MSU. She formerly at the RIARAE and at the IATE. Main interests: GIS, Databases, development and implementation of Spatial Decision Support Systems.

Hans-Peter Piepho is Professor of Bioinformatics at the Universität Hohenheim, Stuttgart Germany. He has a Ph.D. in Plant Breeding from Universität Kiel. His current research revolves around the used of mixed modeling for biological data from the plant sciences, including field trials and genomic data. His articles appeared in applied statistics journals as well as journals related to the plant sciences, mostly plant breeding and agronomy.

Maurizio Polemio is a scientist - CNR researcher - of the Research Institute for the Hydrogeological Protection (IRPI) of the National Research Council (CNR - IRPI) and the person in charge of IRPI-Bari. During his scientific activity, he has tackled water-related phenomena pertaining to Engineering Geology, Hydrogeology and to hydrogeological hazards as groundwater resources degradation and damaging events due to floods and landslides triggered by rainfall. He has maturated editorial experience; at the present he is member of Scientific Committee of the "Acque sotterranee" (Groundwater), and of the Editorial Board of "Quaderni di Geologia Applicata" (Engineer Geology Journal). He has joined a number of research projects, very often as scientific person in charge of the project. He is the person in charge of the scientific-technical Secretary of the International Hydrological Programme (IHP) of UNESCO. He has published more than 120 papers. He was entrusted with University teaching of Engineering Geology and Hydrogeology (Temporary Professor of Calabria University).

Angelo Sifaleras is a researcher at the Department of Technology Management, University of Macedonia, Greece, Naousa. He received his Bachelor of Science degree in Mathematics from the Aristotle University of Thessaloniki, Greece and a PhD degree from the Applied Informatics Department, University of Macedonia, Greece. His primary research interests are in Operations Research, Combinatorial Optimization, Experimental Evaluation of Algorithm Performance and Algorithm Visualization. He is a professional member of INFORMS, EURO/ECCO and SIAM. He has participated as a Guest Co-Editor in a special issue of Operational research. An international Journal, and also as a member of the organizing committee of the 18th Pan-Hellenic Operational Research Conference. He has conducted research in many National and EU funded projects and he also has a number of papers published in international conferences and international scientific journals like the Computers & Operations Research, INFORMS Transactions on Education, Computer Applications in Engineering Education, International Journal of Computers Mathematics, and Yugoslav Journal of Operations Research.

Krisztina Sonkoly is a Junior Assistant Professor in the Institute for Wildlife Conservation, Szent István University, Gödöllő, Hungary. She received an MSc in agricultural management from the Szent István University. She has been working in the National Game Management Database since 2003. Her research interests include game feeding, game field cultivation and studies on roe deer antler development, focusing on the effects of environmental factors.

N. Subash is Scientist of Agricultural Meteorology at the Division of Crop Research, ICAR Research Complex for Eastern Region, Patna, Bihar, India. He obtained his master's degree in Meteorology from Cochin University of Science and Technology. His present research interests include climate change adaptation strategies, crop-weather relationships, crop growth simulation modeling, agro-climatological analysis, remote Sensing and GIS for drought assessment, drought climatology and resource conservation technologies. He presented his research work at several international/national conferences and published 11 research articles in international/ national peer reviewed journals. He has also worked as Database Administrator of the Indo-Gangetic Coordination Unit of the CGIAR Challenge Program on Water and Food. He has undergone training in the field of crop growth simulation modelling. He has developed several computer programs in FORTRAN for meteorological and climatological analysis.

Terry Sullivan is the deputy division head of the Environmental Research Division at Brookhaven National Laboratory where he has worked since receiving his Ph.D. from the University of Illinois in 1983. He is currently the principal investigator on a DOE program, in collaboration with scientists from the former Soviet Union, to develop support tools for remediation decisions to support future land use. Main interests: estimation of the fate and transport of environmental contaminants in the air, subsurface, and sediments, human and ecological risk assessments, environmental remediation decisions.

Heli Thomander, M.Sc. has been working in an organization that offers adult and vocational schooling. She has acted as an educator and a designer for ten years. Prior to that, she used to work both in private and public sector in tasks related to user support and information systems development. She is interested in implementing information processing studies in diverse ways and especially in using virtual learning environment in offering distant learning and services that support studies. In addition, she is interested in challenges connected to educating users in information systems and software. She has experiences in adult learning as she lately finished her master' studies in information processing sciences. She is also a professional teacher.

Alexander Tkachuk is an environmental project engineer in the Department of Civil & Environmental Engineering at Carnegie Mellon University in Pittsburgh PA. He graduated from Department of Cybernetics at IATE, and completed post-graduate work there. His experience includes development of software for risk assessment and decision making, business processes support, and power plant staff training. Main interests: ecological risk assessment and decision analysis concerning new materials and threats.

Slipenkaya Valeriya is an engineer in the IS Department at IATE. He graduated from department of Cybernetics in 2006. Main interests: distributed computer systems, GIS, Java.

Konstantinos Voudouris is an Assistant Professor at the Department of Geology, Laboratory of Engineering Geology & Hydrogeology, Aristotle University of Thessaloniki, Greece. He received his Bachelor of Science degree in Geology and Mathematics from the University of Patras, Greece and a PhD degree from the Department of Geology, University of Patras, Greece. His primary research interests are in Field Hydrogeology, Groundwater Management, Groundwater Quality, Aquifer Vulnerability and Environmental Hydrogeology. He is a professional member of International Association of Hydrogeologists (IAH), Hellenic Committee of Hydrogeology and European Water Resources Association (EWRA). He has conducted research in many national and EU funded projects and he also has a number of papers published in the proceedings of international conferences and international scientific journals.

Yawei Wang is currently an Assistant Professor in the Department of Marketing at Montclair State University, NJ. She holds a Ph.D. in Recreation & Tourism from Clemson University, SC. Her research focuses on travel and tourism - with emphasis on mature tourism and aging issues. Her teaching interests include introduction to marketing, introduction to leisure & tourism, behavioral concepts in leisure & tourism, research methods in leisure & tourism. Prior to joining Montclair State University, Yawei worked with the Gerontology Research Interdisciplinary Team in the College of Health Education & Human Development at Clemson, SC.

Hongmei Wang received her Ph.D. degree in Information Sciences and Technology from the Pennsylvania State University, University Park, USA, in 2007, the M.S. degree in Cartography and Remote Sensing from Chinese Academy of Science, P. R. China, in 1997, and the B. E degree in Geoscience from Changchun College of Geology, P. R. China, in 1994. Since August 2008, she has with Northern Kentucky University as an Assistant Professor in the Department of Computer Science. Her major responsibilities at NKU focus on teaching GIS related courses and conducting GIS related research in three departments, including Geography, Political Science and Criminal Justice, and Computer Science. Her major research interests lie in GIS, Human-Computer Interaction, Artificial Intelligence, and database.

William L. Weber is Professor in the Department of Economics and Finance at Southeast Missouri State University, Cape Girardeau, Missouri, USA. He received a Ph.D. in Economics of Southern Illinois University in 1986. He has published papers in Journal of Econometrics, Review of Economics and Statistics, and Management Science. His research interests include efficiency and productivity measurement with applications in financial institutions, educational institutions, and manufacturing.

Boris Yatsalo is the head of the Information Systems Department at the Obninsk State University (IATE), and a Member of Russian Academy of Natural Sciences. He graduated from Moscow State University (MSU) in Mechanics and Mathematics, and completed post-graduate work in Optimal Control at MSU. He worked at the Russian Institute of Agricultural Radiology and Agroecology, Obninsk before his current position. Main interests: Multi-Criteria Decision Analysis (MCDA), Decision Support Systems, GIS, Math modeling, Risk Analysis, Cost-Benefit Analysis, restoration and sustainable development of contaminated territories.

Bin Zhou is an Assistant Professor in the College of Business and Public Administration, Kean University, USA. He obtained his Ph.D. and MBA degrees in Management Science and Supply Chain Management from Rutgers Business School, Rutgers University. His research interests include theory and application of supply chain management, operations strategy, logistics and transportation, production and inventory systems, and information technology. His research work has appeared in International Journal of Production Economics, European Journal of Operational Research, International Journal of Systems Science, among others. Professor Zhou also serves in the editorial board of International Journal of Information Systems and Social Change.

Index